T0213517

Lecture Notes in Artificial Intelligence 9628

Subseries of Lecture Notes in Computer Science

More information about this series at http://www.springer.com/series/1244

Virginia Dignum · Pablo Noriega
Murat Sensoy · Jaime Simão Sichman (Eds.)

Coordination, Organizations, Institutions, and Norms in Agent Systems XI

COIN 2015 International Workshops
COIN@AAMAS, Istanbul, Turkey, May 4, 2015
COIN@IJCAI, Buenos Aires, Argentina, July 26, 2015
Revised Selected Papers

 Springer

Editors
Virginia Dignum
Delft University of Technology
Delft
The Netherlands

Pablo Noriega
IIIA-CSIC
Barcelona
Spain

Murat Sensoy
Ozyegin University
Istanbul
Turkey

Jaime Simão Sichman
University of Sao Paulo
São Paulo, SP
Brazil

ISSN 0302-9743   ISSN 1611-3349   (electronic)
Lecture Notes in Artificial Intelligence
ISBN 978-3-319-42690-7   ISBN 978-3-319-42691-4   (eBook)
DOI 10.1007/978-3-319-42691-4

Library of Congress Control Number: 2016944911

LNCS Sublibrary: SL7 – Artificial Intelligence

Printed on acid-free paper

This Springer imprint is published by Springer Nature
The registered company is Springer International Publishing AG Switzerland

Preface

The pervasiveness of open systems raises a range of challenges and opportunities for research and technological development in the area of autonomous agents and multi-agent systems. Open systems comprise loosely coupled entities interacting within a social space. These entities join the social space in order to achieve some goals that are unattainable by agents in isolation. However, when those entities are autonomous, they might misbehave and, furthermore, in open systems one may not know what entities will be active beforehand, when they may become active, or when they may leave the system. The key point in the design and construction of open systems is to devise governance mechanisms that foster interactions that are conducive to achieve individual or collective goals.

The COIN (Coordination, Organisations, Institutions and Norms in Agent Systems) Workshop series — that started as the merging of two workshops at AAMAS 2005 — has grown to become the main venue for presenting and discussing work on social and governance aspects of multi-agent systems.

This volume — the 11th in the COIN workshop series — contains revised versions of 23 selected papers presented at COIN workshops in 2015: the first was co-located with AAMAS and took place on May 4 in Istanbul, Turkey, while the second was co-located with IJCAI and was held on July 26 in Buenos Aires, Argentina.

In total, 46 papers were submitted (25 to COIN@AAMAS 2015 and 20 to COIN@IJCAI 2015), of which 25 were accepted for oral presentation (14 at COIN@AAMAS 2015 and 11 at COIN@IJCAI 2015). The 23 papers included in this collection were selected from those accepted and have undergone a substantial process of revision. As in previous editions, for each of the two workshops at least three Program Committee members reviewed each submitted paper, and revised versions of the accepted papers were presented at the workshop sessions. After their presentation, some papers were selected to be part of this volume. The authors of these selected papers were then requested to prepare revised versions that took into account the reviewers' comments and further insights gained from the presentation at the workshops. All these revised versions underwent a second stage of review before producing the final version that appears in this volume.

Together, the papers included in this volume demonstrate the vitality of the community and the quality of the work realized in this area.

We thank the Program Committee and reviewers for the fantastic effort they put in the reviewing process, and the authors for submitting their papers.

May 2016

Virginia Dignum
Pablo Noriega
Murat Sensoy
Jaime S. Sichman

Organization

COIN@AAMAS 2015 Chairs: Pablo Noriega and Murat Sensoy
COIN@IJCAI 2015: Virginia Dignum and Jaime S. Sichman

Program Committee

Mohsen Afsharchi	University of Zanjan, Iran
Huib Aldewereld	TU Delft, The Netherlands
Anarosa Alves Franco Brandão	University of Sao Paulo, Brazil
Estefania Argente	Universidad Politecnica de Valencia, Spain
Alexander Artikis	NCSR Demokritos, Greece
Tina Balke	University of Surrey, UK
Guido Boella	University of Turin, Italy
Olivier Boissier	ENS Mines Saint-Etienne, France
Didac Busquets	Imperial College, UK
Patrice Caire	University of Luxembourg, Luxembourg
Cristiano Castelfranchi	ISTC-CNR, Italy
Amit Chopra	Lancaster University, UK
Rob Christiaanse	TU Delft, The Netherlands
Luciano Coutinho	Universidade Federal do Maranhão (UFMA), Brazil
Stephen Cranefield	University of Otago, New Zealand
Natalia Criado	Liverpool John Moores University, UK
Mehdi Dastani	Utrecht University, The Netherlands
Geeth de Mel	IBM T.J. Watson Research Center, USA
Marina De Vos	University of Bath, UK
Frank Dignum	Utrecht University, The Netherlands
Virginia Dignum	TU Delft, The Netherlands
Nicoletta Fornara	Università della Svizzera Italiana, Switzerland
Amineh Ghorbani	TU Delft, The Netherlands
Aditya Ghose	University of Wollongong, Australia
Davide Grossi	University of Liverpool, UK
Jomi Fred Hubner	Federal University of Santa Catarina, Brazil
Ozgur Kafali	Royal Holloway, University of London, UK
Anup Kalia	North Carolina State University, USA
Martin Kollingbaum	University of Aberdeen, UK
Christian Lemaitre	Universidad Autonoma Metropolitana de Mexico, Mexico
Victor Lesser	University of Massachusetts Amherst, USA
Henrique Lopes Cardoso	University of Porto, Portugal
Maite Lopez Sanchez	University of Barcelona, Spain
Emiliano Lorini	IRIT, France
Samhar Mahmoud	King's College London, UK
Eric Matson	Purdue University, USA

Felipe Meneguzzi	Pontifical Catholic University of Rio Grande do Sul, Brazil
John-Jules Meyer	Utrecht University, The Netherlands
Simon Miles	King's College London, UK
Daniel Moldt	University of Hamburg, Germany
Pablo Noriega	Artificial Intelligence Research Institute (IIIA), Spain
Tim Norman	University of Aberdeen, UK
Eugenio Oliveira	University of Porto, Portugal
Andrea Omicini	Università di Bologna, Italy
Nir Oren	University of Aberdeen, UK
Sascha Ossowski	Rey Juan Carlos University, Spain
Julian Padget	University of Bath, UK
Simon Parsons	University of Liverpool, UK
Jeremy Pitt	Imperial College London, UK
Alessandro Ricci	University of Bologna, Italy
Ana Paula Rocha	LIACC - University of Porto, Portugal
Antonio Carlos Rocha Costa	UCPEL, Brazil
Juan-Antonio Rodriguez-Aguilar	Artificial Intelligence Research Institute, IIIA-CSIC, Spain
Antonino Rotolo	Università di Bologna, Italy
Tony Savarimuthu	Otago University, New Zealand
Silvia Schiaffino	ISISTAN (CONICET - UNCPBA), Italy
Murat Sensoy	Ozyegin University, Turkey
Alexei Sharpanskykh	Delft University of Technology, The Netherlands
Christophe Sibertin-Blanc	University of Toulouse/IRIT, France
Jaime Sichman	University of Sao Paulo, Brazil
Viviane Silva	Universidade Federal Fluminense, Brazil
Liz Sonenberg	Melbourne University, Australia
Charalampos Tampitsikas	University of Lugano, Switzerland
Pankaj Telang	North Carolina State University, USA
John Thangarajah	RMIT, Australia
Luca Tummolini	ISTC-CNR, Italy
Leender van der Torre	University of Luxembourg, Luxembourg
Wamberto Vasconcelos	University of Aberdeen, UK
Harko Verhagen	Stockholm University, Sweden
Dani Villatoro	BBVA Data & Analytics, Spain
George Vouros	University of Piraeus, Greece
Martijn Warnier	Delft University of Technology, The Netherlands

Additional Reviewers

Yoosef Abushark	RMIT, Australia
Graham Billiau	University of Wollongong, Australia
Maiquel De Brito	Federal University of Santa Catarina, Brazil

Chris Haynes   King's College London, UK
Marin Lujak   University Rey Juan Carlos, Madrid, Spain
Ambra Molesini   University of Bologna, Italy

COIN Steering Committee

Huib Aldewereld   Delft University of Technology, The Netherlands
Tina Balke   University of Surrey, UK
Olivier Boissier   ENS Mines Saint-Etienne, France
Stephen Cranefield   Otago University, New Zealand
Frank Dignum   Utrecht University, The Netherlands
Virginia Dignum   Delft University of Technology, The Netherlands
Nicoletta Fornara   University of Lugano, Switzerland
Eric Matson   Purdue University, USA
Pablo Noriega   IIIA-CSIC, Spain
Julian Padget   University of Bath, UK
Birna van Riemsdijk   Delft University of Technology, The Netherlands
Jaime Sichman   University of Sao Paulo, Brazil
Viviane Torres da Silva Universidade Federal Fluminente, Brazil
Wamberto Vasconcelos   University of Aberdeen, UK
Javier Vazquez-Salceda Universitat Politècnica de Catalunya, Spain
Marina de Vos   University of Bath, UK
George Vouros   University of Piraeus, Greece

Contents

Reasoning with Group Norms in Software Agent Organisations

Huib Aldewereld[1], Virginia Dignum[1], and Wamberto Vasconcelos[2(✉)]

[1] Delft University of Technology, Delft, The Netherlands
{H.M.Aldewereld,M.V.Dignum}@tudelft.nl
[2] University of Aberdeen, Aberdeen, UK
w.w.vasconcelos@abdn.ac.uk

Abstract. Norms have been used to represent desirable behaviours that software agents should exhibit in sophisticated multi-agent solutions. An important open research issue refers to group norms, i.e. norms that govern groups of agents. Depending on the interpretation, group norms may be intended to affect the group as a whole, each member of a group, or some members of the group. Moreover, upholding group norms may require coordination among the members of the group. We have identified three sets of agents affected by group norms, namely, (i) the addressees of the norm, (ii) those that will act on it, and (iii) those that are responsible to ensure norm compliance. We present a formalism to represent these, connecting it to a minimalist agent organisation model. We use our formalism to develop a reasoning mechanism which enables agents to identify their position with respect to a group norm, so as to further support agent autonomy and coordination when deciding on possible courses of action.

1 Introduction

Norms have been used to represent, in compact ways, desirable behaviour that autonomous components should have (alternatively, undesirable behaviour they should not have), so as to provide overall guarantees for distributed, open, and heterogeneous computing solutions. Research on norms has tackled important issues, ranging from logic-theoretic aspects (*e.g.*, [28]), to more pragmatic concerns (*e.g.*, [18]).

The study of norms has mostly been limited to abstractions via the use of *roles* from the individual to make norms stable over extended periods of time. However, while addressing multiple agents at once (namely each agent enacting the role), it is important to realise that these norms do not address these agents *together*. A main difference is that when addressing a group of agents, it is necessary to consider aspects as responsibility and fulfilment, that are not typically addressed by most norm representations (since the agent addressed is also responsible, and is also the one to act). To illustrate this difference, we consider an obligation for children under the age of 16 to attend school. While the norm addresses children under the age of 16, who are also the ones who must perform

V. Dignum et al. (Eds.): COIN 2015, LNAI 9628, pp. 1–21, 2016.
DOI: 10.1007/978-3-319-42691-4_1

the task of going to school, the responsibility and blame lays with their parents/guardians. Consequently, by saying that "group G should achieve outcome φ", it is not clear who in the group should actually perform the actions that lead to φ, and who is to blame if the outcome is not achieved. Another example is a removal company obliged by contract to move the contents of someone's house, including a piano. If moving the piano requires specialised qualifications, even though the removal company is the addressee of the obligation, the company will not able to act on the norm by itself and must outsource the task.

Such group norms, explicitly differing groups of agents targeted by the norm, those acting upon it, and those responsible for the outcome, raise coordination issues not typically seen in norms addressing individuals or roles. The agents responsible for the norm will avoid blame, and thus have to ensure that the agents supposed to act upon it are indeed doing what they are supposed to do (or conversely, avoiding forbidden behaviours). The acting agents might need to coordinate whether each of them has to do it, one of them has to do it, or even all of them have to do it together.

In addition to coordination issues, group norms also present challenges in norm reasoning. Reasoning about norms is essential to the regulation of behaviour in multiagent systems [5]. Work on models of norm-governed practical reasoning agents have so far studied the case of norms aimed at one agent (or role) [27]. That is, the cases in which the agent is both addressed and responsible for a norm. In this paper, we present work towards reasoning about group norms. These norms require that the agent is both able to reason about its relation to the norm (*i.e.*, is it addressed, responsible or actor?) and able to coordinate with other agents affected by the norm to determine how to handle the norm.

In the next section we present a formalisation of group norms. In Sect. 3 we present a minimalistic model of agent organisations for the concepts of action, role, and power; we also present an operational semantics for organisations and explain the concepts of individual and collective actions. In Sect. 4 we show how agents can use this model to reason about how to act when they are addressed by, responsible for or actor of a norm. Section 4.4 discusses issues pertaining to the reasoning processes we sketch. We contrast our research with related work in Sect. 5, and in Sect. 6 we draw conclusions, discuss relevant issues, and give avenues for future investigation.

2   Group Norms

Norms are a natural way of constraining behaviours of groups and individuals. However, by simply stating "group G should achieve φ", it is not made explicit who is to act (that is, whether each group member individually, if only one group member, or if all of them together), and who is to blame when violations occur. We can take again the example from the introduction: the obligation for children under the age of 16 to attend school. While the norm *addresses* children under the age of 16, who are also the ones that must *act* upon it, the *responsibility* and blame lie with the parents. In the rest of this section we introduce a language of set definitions to precisely establish the notion of group, present a representation for group norms and provide its semantics using temporal logic.

2.1 Set Definitions

We propose to represent groups as set definitions and operations. We assume the existence of a non-empty and finite universal set $Agents = \{ag_1, \ldots, ag_n\}$ consisting of the unique identifier of each agent in our society.

Definition 1 (Set Definition). *A set definition Σ is*

$$\Sigma :: = \Sigma \cup \Sigma \mid \Sigma \cap \Sigma \mid \Sigma \setminus \Sigma \mid \Sigma^C \mid S$$
$$S :: = \{ag_1, \ldots, ag_m\} \mid \{\alpha : P(\alpha)\}$$

The grammar establishes a language $\mathcal{L}_\Sigma$ of set definitions and it captures some of the common operations of naïve set theory [22], namely, union, intersection, difference, and absolute complement (with respect to the universal set $Agents$). The S stands for an actual set, and it can be represented as an extensive (finite) listing $\{ag_1, \ldots, ag_m\} \subseteq Agents$ of the elements of the set, or an intensional definition $\{\alpha : P(\alpha)\}$, standing for $\forall \alpha \in Agents.P(\alpha)$, that is, all those elements of the universal set that fulfil some property P.

We extend the language of set definitions $\mathcal{L}_\Sigma$ to represent more sophisticated scenarios. It is common for certain norms to address groups with size restrictions, as in "gatherings of more than 5 people are prohibited". We can formalise such requirements as $|\Sigma| \circ n$, where $\circ$ is a comparison operator $>, <, \geq, \leq, =$, or $\neq$ and $n \in \mathbb{N}$ (a natural number). These set definitions can be seen as *constrained sets* and they place restrictions on which sets can be built. For instance, if $Agents = \{a, b, c, d\}$ the definition $|\{\alpha : \top\}| = 3$ (where $\top$ stands for "true", that is a property which is vacuously true for everyone) stands for all subsets of $Agents$ with 3 elements, that is, all groups of 3 agents.

A *set definition* gives rise to different *actual values* of groups, depending on the universal set of agents. Rather than requiring that groups have their individuals listed one by one, our set definitions are more compact and can be re-used for different specific populations of agents. We formally define the value of a set definition Σ with respect to the universal set $Agents$, denoted as $value(\Sigma, Agents) \subseteq Agents$, as follows:

Definition 2 (Set Definition Value).

1. $value(\Sigma' \cup \Sigma'', Agents) \qquad = value(\Sigma', Agents) \cup value(\Sigma'', Agents)$
2. $value(\Sigma' \cap \Sigma'', Agents) \qquad = value(\Sigma', Agents) \cap value(\Sigma'', Agents)$
3. $value(\Sigma' \setminus \Sigma'', Agents) \qquad = value(\Sigma', Agents) \setminus value(\Sigma'', Agents)$
4. $value(\Sigma^C, Agents) \qquad\qquad = Agents \setminus value(\Sigma, Agents)$
5. $value(\{ag_1, \ldots, ag_m\}, Agents) = \{ag_1, \ldots, ag_m\}$
6. $value(\{\alpha : P(\alpha)\}, Agents) \quad = \{ag_0, \ldots, ag_m\}, \forall i, 0 \leq i \leq m, ag_i \in Agents \wedge P(ag_i)$
7. $value(|\Sigma| \circ n, Agents) \qquad = value(\Sigma, Agents) \ s.t. \ |value(\Sigma, Agents)| \circ n$

Cases 1–4 decompose a set definition into its sub-parts, recursively obtaining their values, which then are combined, using the corresponding set operations – this is a straightforward mapping of our notation to the usual semantics of sets. Cases 5 and 6 are the base cases: a set tabulation is itself, and an intensional definition gives rise to every possible sub-set whose elements satisfy property P. Case 7 generically defines the meaning of constrained sets – these are the values of the set definition which satisfy their constraints.

We assume a reference set *Agents* in our discussion, and since we are chiefly interested in what the set definitions actually are, we will simply use the set definitions Σ, meaning $value(\Sigma, Agents)$.

2.2   Group Norms and Their Semantics

We formally capture three different groups as set expressions Σ, as introduced in the previous sub-section, as well as the usual components of norms, namely, the deontic modality and the target of the norm [18,28].

We use a set of propositions $\mathcal{P}$, with which one can construct formulae using the usual operators $\neg, \wedge, \vee, \rightarrow, \leftrightarrow$. We represent generic atomic propositions as p, q, r and we use φ, δ, ψ to indicate propositional formulas. The set of well-formed propositional formulas is denoted as $\mathcal{L}_\mathcal{P}$. We define group norms as follows:

Definition 3 (Group Norms). *Group norms are of the form* $^A\mathbf{O}_G^R\ \varphi < \delta$ *(a group obligation) or* $^A\mathbf{F}_G^R\ \varphi < \delta$ *(a group prohibition), where A, R and G are set definitions (from the language $\mathcal{L}_\Sigma$ of Definition 1), and φ, δ are propositional formulae from $\mathcal{L}_\mathcal{P}$. We refer to group norms in general as* $^A\mathbf{D}_G^R\ \varphi < \delta$ *(where* $\mathbf{D}$ *is either* $\mathbf{O}$ *or* $\mathbf{F}$*).*

Intuitively, the annotations A, R and G of the deontic modalities $\mathbf{O}$ and $\mathbf{F}$ correspond to respectively the *actors* (those agents whose behaviours are affected by the norm), those *responsible* for the norm and the *addressees* of the norm. The construct $\varphi < \delta$ informally states "φ before δ", a temporal constraint which enables us to capture deadlines of obligations and periods of prohibitions. It should be noted that we represent achievement obligations, not maintenance obligations. In future work, we will look at the formalisation of group maintenance norms.

The propositions of formula φ may represent actions or properties of states of affairs. In the case of actions, a norm such as $^A\mathbf{O}_G^R\ paint\_door < \delta$ would place an obligation on groups A, G, R to carry out action $paint\_door$. More flexibility and expressiveness can be achieved though if φ represents *properties of states*; an example norm is $^A\mathbf{O}_G^R\ painted\_door < \delta$ which stipulates an obligation on groups A, G, R to carry out whatever is required in order to achieve a state in which $painted\_door$ holds – that is, they should "see to it that" the door is painted, either by painting it themselves or finding someone to paint it on their behalf [25]. We do not commit ourselves to either of these options – both can be expressed with our formalism, assuming a suitable semantics for actions and a representation of states is available.

We provide the semantics of our group norms via a temporal logic based on CTL* [15]. Our temporal logical language $\mathcal{L}_{\mathcal{TP}}$ extends our propositional logic $\mathcal{L}_{\mathcal{P}}$ by adding path operators A (all paths), E (some paths), and state operators $\bigcirc$ (next), $\square$ (always), $\diamond$ (sometime), and $\mathcal{U}$ (until). The language is further enriched with *stit*, $stit(\alpha, \varphi)$ meaning agent α "sees to it that" φ [4] and expressing individual action, and $stit(G, \varphi)$ meaning that group G together "sees to it that" φ, for collective action[1]. The semantics of this logic is constructed in the typical manner from the semantics of CTL* [15] combined with *stit* [4]. In our semantics the deontic modalities are handled via an Anderson's reduction [3] of the modality to the reserved $viol(G, A, R, \varphi)$ construct indicating that a violation has happened of G's norm on φ by (in)action of A under the responsibility of R. We define the meaning of group obligations as follows:

Definition 4 (Semantics of Obligation).

$$^{A}\mathbf{O}^{R}_{G}\ \varphi < \delta \stackrel{def}{=} \mathsf{A}\left[\diamond\delta \wedge \begin{pmatrix} \neg\delta \wedge \neg stit(A, \varphi)\wedge \\ \neg viol(G, A, R, \varphi) \end{pmatrix} \mathcal{U} \begin{pmatrix} \begin{pmatrix} \neg\delta \wedge stit(A, \varphi)\wedge \\ \bigcirc(\mathsf{A}\square \neg viol(G, A, R, \varphi)) \\ \vee(\delta \wedge viol(G, A, R, \varphi)) \end{pmatrix} \end{pmatrix}\right]$$

Intuitively, this definition expresses that the deadline δ will occur at some point in time and for all paths *either* φ is achieved by the actors ($stit(A, \varphi)$), in which case no violation of the obligation will ever occur ($\bigcirc(\mathsf{A}\square \neg viol(G, A, R, \varphi))$), *or* the state is not achieved, the deadline occurs, and a violation happens ($\delta \wedge viol(G, A, R, \varphi)$). Similarly, we define the meaning of group prohibitions:

Definition 5 (Semantics of Prohibition).

$$^{A}\mathbf{F}^{R}_{G}\ \varphi < \delta \stackrel{def}{=} \mathsf{A}\left[\begin{pmatrix} \neg\delta \wedge \neg stit(A, \varphi)\wedge \\ \neg viol(G, A, R, \varphi) \end{pmatrix} \mathcal{U} \begin{pmatrix} \begin{pmatrix} \neg\delta \wedge stit(A, \varphi)\wedge \\ viol(G, A, R, \varphi) \end{pmatrix} \vee \\ (\delta \wedge \mathsf{A}\square\neg viol(G, A, R, \varphi)) \end{pmatrix}\right]$$

Group prohibitions are similar to group obligations, except that the deadline δ is better seen as a deactivation of the prohibition (and may therefore not actually occur in the future states, meaning that the prohibition is not deactivated). So, no violation happens until *either* a violation is triggered by seeing to it that the prohibited state is achieved before the deactivation ($\neg\delta \wedge stit(A, \varphi) \wedge viol(G, A, R, \varphi)$) *or* the prohibition is deactivated (after which no violation can occur ($\delta \wedge \mathsf{A}\square\neg viol(G, A, R, \varphi)$).

With these definitions of the meaning of group norms, a norm on individual action when $G = A = R$, all referring to a role specification in an organisation, expresses the same as in, for example, [7,13] – all those agents adopting a role (hence belonging to the group) are simultaneously actors, addressees, and responsible parties. For simplification and without loss of generality, in the rest of our discussion we may drop the deadline component of our norms.

To relate the groups and individuals of a norm, we formalise in Sect. 3 a notion of power (Definition 9) – we address *social power* (*viz.*, a relation among

---

[1] We explain in Sect. 3.2 how we differentiate collective and individual actions.

individuals of a society, establishing who has authority or control over others [17]), as opposed to *institutional power* (*viz.*, whereby members of an institution are empowered to perform certain deeds [12,26]). We represent power as a relation $x \preccurlyeq y$ establishing that agent x is under the power of agent y (or conversely, that y has power over x). This relation also applies to groups of agents, as presented later on in the paper.

3   A Minimalist Organisation Model

There are many approaches to modelling organisations (*e.g.*, [13,24,30]), but they possess many features in common. Our organisation model aims at capturing only those aspects necessary to explore the phenomena and mechanisms related to group norms and joint behaviour/coordination. We make use of the agent's identity (*i.e.*, the set *Agents*), and we formalise the following aspects:

- *Roles* – these are useful abstractions for (groups of) individuals, conferring generality on organisation specifications. The organisation remains the same, even though different individuals comprise it.
- *Capabilities* – we associate roles with sets of capabilities, represented as actions. These can be understood in two ways: *(i)* individuals taking up a role should be able to perform what that role entails; *(ii)* they specify what individuals are expected to do in the normal running of the organisation.
- *Power* – within organisations it is necessary to relate roles to one another, so as to facilitate coordination and load-sharing, ultimately enabling objectives (see below) to be achieved. In our proposal, roles exert power (or influence) over other roles, giving rise to power structures such as lines of command, managed teams, hierarchies, and egalitarian teams.

We make use of our propositional language $\mathcal{L}_{\mathcal{P}}$; a set of propositional formulae $\{\varphi_1, \varphi_2, \ldots\}$ represents the *conjunction* $\varphi_1 \wedge \varphi_2 \wedge \cdots$. We use two special propositions $\top$ and $\bot$ to represent, respectively, "true" and "false". We assume that the meaning of propositions are captured with formulae establishing logical relations in a knowledge base (or, to use a more modern terminology, a reference ontology) shared by all stakeholders and components[2] (*e.g.*, engineers, designers, tools, software agents, and so on). We relate our formulae via logical entailment (formally, "$\models$") and deduction (formally, "$\vdash$"): for any formulae φ, ψ, if $\varphi \models \psi$ then $\varphi \vdash \psi$ (completeness) and if $\varphi \vdash \psi$ then $\varphi \models \psi$ (correctness).

We make use of logical implications represented as $(p_1 \wedge \cdots \wedge p_n) \rightarrow q$ to forge relationships among propositions, thus providing a background theory (or axioms). We denote as Ω, a set of formulae from $\mathcal{L}_{\mathcal{P}}$, our background theory and we define the meaning of logical implication in terms of entailment as *if* $((p_1 \wedge \cdots \wedge p_n) \rightarrow q) \in \Omega$ *and* $\Omega \models p_i, 1 \leq i \leq n$, *then* $\Omega \models q$. A similar relation is defined for the "$\vdash$" operator, if we assume its completeness.

---

[2] More realistically, the stakeholders and components have means to relate their knowledge bases (or, to re-phrase this in more modern terms, "align their ontologies"), thus being able to map their knowledge representation on to that of other parties.

We represent a repertoire of actions available during the enactment of an organisation. We propose an idealised representation for actions, and consider these as being *(i)* instantaneous (*i.e.* they take one unit of time to be performed, that is, they do not have a duration or a period for their execution to be completed), *(ii)* they are either executed or not (*i.e.*, we do not capture situations whereby actions are partially performed nor do we address scenarios in which actions are performed with degrees of success/quality). We make use of the set $\mathcal{P}$ of propositions as well as a set of negated propositions $\mathcal{P}^- = \{\neg p \mid p \in \mathcal{P}\}^3$.

Definition 6 (Action). *An action* **ac** *is the triple* $\langle S, ac, S' \rangle$ *where* $S \subseteq \mathcal{P} \cup \mathcal{P}^-$, $S' \subseteq \mathcal{P}$, *and ac is an action label.*

The action labels uniquely identify actions. Our actions model pre-conditions S (a set of possibly negated propositions) which should be satisfied for action ac to be performed, and the result of performing this action (ac's post-conditions) is S', a set of non-negated propositions. We assume a universal, non-empty and finite set of actions $Ac = \{\mathbf{ac}_1, \ldots, \mathbf{ac}_n\}$, such that no two actions have the same label. Since actions have unique labels, we shall use ac and $\mathbf{ac}$ interchangeably.

Importantly, we can model norms addressing *properties of states*, rather than actions. This is without loss of generality since for any action $\langle S, ac, S' \rangle$, where $S' = \{p'_1, \ldots, p'_n\}$, we have ${}^A\mathbf{D}_G^R \ ac \leftrightarrow {}^A\mathbf{D}_G^R \ (p'_1 \wedge \cdots \wedge p'_n)$ that is, a norm on an action is equivalent to a norm on its post-conditions. In the case when $S' = \emptyset$, we have ${}^A\mathbf{D}_G^R \ ac \leftrightarrow {}^A\mathbf{D}_G^R \ \top$ That is, a norm on an action without any effect is equivalent to a norm on the vacuously true proposition "$\top$", as the empty set is a sub-set of any set, $\emptyset \subseteq S$.

We represent roles as labels available to individual agents when they join the organisation during the enactment. We associate with each role a possibly empty set of action labels, depicting what the role requires to be done:

Definition 7 (Role). *A role* **rl** *is the pair* $\langle rl, Ac' \rangle$ *where rl is the role label and* $Ac' \subseteq Ac$ *is a set of action labels (cf. Definition 6).*

When an agent joins an organisation it takes up one or more roles; by taking up a role the agent agrees to perform any of the actions associated with that role, whenever it is required (or whenever the agent is asked to). We assume a universal, non-empty and finite set of roles $Rl = \{\mathbf{rl}_1, \ldots, \mathbf{rl}_m\}$, such that no two roles have the same label. Because roles have unique names, we shall use rl and $\mathbf{rl}$ interchangeably. There are more sophisticated and expressive ways to represent roles, allowing one to define constraints on how many agents can take up the role, the least/highest number of agents for each role, relations among roles (*e.g.*, who takes up roles rl_1, rl_2 should not take up rl_3), and so on, as reported in, for instance, [13,24,30], but as we aim at a minimalist model, we do not include these here.

---

3 It is important to notice that the pre-conditions of an action may contain negated propositions, but not the post-conditions. We present in Sect. 3.1 an operational semantics showing how agents performing actions update a global state of computation.

When individual agents join organisations they take up roles which they will enact during the life-time of the organisation. We thus consider agents associated with a set of roles, $\langle \alpha, Rl' \rangle, \alpha \in Agents, Rl' \subseteq Rl$. We define an agent's *capabilities* – the properties of the states that the agent can bring about based on the roles the agent has adopted and the actions associated with these roles:

Definition 8 (Capabilities). *We define the set of α's capabilities (when enacting roles Rl') as $cap(\alpha, Rl') = \bigcup_{\langle S, ac, S' \rangle \in AllAc} S'$ where $AllAc = \bigcup_{\langle rl, Ac \rangle \in Rl'} Ac$, that is, the capability of an agent α undertaking roles Rl is the union of the post-conditions S' of all actions $AllAc$ of all of α's roles.*

Next, we formally relate roles via *power*, as explored in, for instance, [26,29, 34], and more recently (and closer to our approach) in [14]:

Definition 9 (Power). *Power $\preccurlyeq \subseteq 2^{Rl}$ is a reflexive and transitive relation over the set Rl of roles. If $\mathbf{rl}_1 \preccurlyeq \mathbf{rl}_2$ we say that $\mathbf{rl}_2$ has power over $\mathbf{rl}_1$ or alternatively that $\mathbf{rl}_1$ is under the power of $\mathbf{rl}_2$.*

When an agent enacts a role $\mathbf{rl}_2$ which "has power over" another role $\mathbf{rl}_1$ then that agent may request the help of any agent enacting $\mathbf{rl}_1$ to achieve a particular state of affairs. This request for help is, within a formal organisation, equivalent to *delegation*, since power relations should be followed without question. Power and delegation is best understood via the "see to it" (*stit*) operator [25], $stit(\mathbf{rl}, \varphi)$ standing for "role $\mathbf{rl}$ *sees to it that* φ".

If $stit(\mathbf{rl}, \varphi)$ and $\mathbf{rl} = \langle rl, Ac' \rangle$ hold, then one of the following properties must also hold:

1. Role $\mathbf{rl}$ has associated actions with combined post-conditions logically entailing φ. Formally: $S^* = \left(\bigcup_{\langle S, ac, S' \rangle \in Ac'} S' \right)$ *and* $S^* \models \varphi$
2. Role $\mathbf{rl}$ has power over roles $\mathbf{rl}'_i$ each of which can see to it that φ'_i, and these combined φ'_i logically entail φ. Formally, $\Phi' = \{\varphi'_i : \mathbf{rl}'_i \preccurlyeq \mathbf{rl} \wedge stit(\mathbf{rl}'_i, \varphi'_i)\}$ *and* $\Phi' \models \varphi$.

Since the power relation is reflexive, that is, all roles have power over themselves ($\forall \mathbf{rl} \in Rl.\mathbf{rl} \preccurlyeq \mathbf{rl}$), then property 2 above also addresses scenarios in which agents delegate responsibility over the achievement of some φ'_i but they also retain responsibility for achieving some φ'_i, through their own actions.

The power relation can be extended to relate individual agents: let there be two agents ag_1, ag_2 with associated sets of roles $\langle ag_1, Rl_1 \rangle, \langle ag_2, Rl_2 \rangle$; if there is a role $\mathbf{rl}'' \in Rl_2$ for which there is a role $\mathbf{rl}' \in Rl_1$ such that $\mathbf{rl}' \preccurlyeq \mathbf{rl}''$, then we say $ag_1 \preccurlyeq ag_2$. That is, ag_2 has power over ag_1 if at least one of ag_2's roles has power over one of ag_1's roles. We notice that this is a "weak" definition of power which could, in some situations, lead to loops in delegation – this is an undesirable feature of an organisation specification to which designers should be alerted[4]. A stronger definition would require that, in addition to the requirements above, we also had $\mathbf{rl}'' \not\preccurlyeq \mathbf{rl}'$, for all roles $\mathbf{rl}', \mathbf{rl}''$.

We further extend the power relation to account for groups (sets) of agents, as follows:

Definition 10. *Given sets $Agents_1, Agents_2 \subseteq Agents$, and a power relation $\preccurlyeq \subseteq 2^{Agents}$ we say that $Agents_2$ has power over $Agents_1$, denoted as $Agents_1 \preccurlyeq Agents_2$, if, and only if $\forall \alpha' \in Agents_1, \exists \alpha'' \in Agents_2 : \alpha' \preccurlyeq \alpha''$, that is, every member of $Agents_1$ is under the power of at least one member of $Agents_2$.*

In order to model realistic scenarios, group norms $^{A}\mathbf{D}^{R}_{G}\,\varphi$ (where $\mathbf{D}$ is either $\mathbf{O}$ or $\mathbf{F}$) should fulfil the following properties:

1. $A \preccurlyeq R$ – the group of actors A must be under the power of the responsible group R. This property ensures that those responsible for the norm should be able to delegate to actors.
2. $A \preccurlyeq G$ – the group of actors A must be under the power of the group G addressed by the norm. This property ensures that addressees are also able to delegate to actors.

Both properties above can be checked at run-time, when the groups are instantiated with specific members. Concerning the power relation between Addressees and Responsibles, in most realistic models, it will be the case that $G \cap (A \cup R) \neq \varnothing$, and $G \cap A \neq \varnothing \vee G \cap R \neq \varnothing$, i.e. the Addressee group overlaps in some extent with the Actors or Responsibles group. We consider the specification of these relations for a given application domain to be design decisions, and therefore do not impose $G \preccurlyeq R$ nor $R \preccurlyeq G$. (*E.g.*, a norm aimed at a group of junior engineers G has a senior manager responsible R for it, and operators as actors A) R and G do not directly relate power-wise.

3.1   A Computational Model for Norm-Aware Agent Organisations

We outline a computational model for norm-aware multi-agent organisations, providing a context for Definitions 6–10. Our model is built around an explicit representation of the *global state* $S^* \subseteq \mathcal{P}$ of the computation in which pre-conditions of actions are checked for and their post-conditions (effects) are

---

[4] During the enactment of an organisation (run-time) each agent adopts a sub-set of roles. If the power relation has *any loop* then there is *potential* for loops when agents (acting in different roles) are delegating. By detecting/flagging loops in the power relation at design time we are warning designers about such potential loops in delegation at run-time. More sophisticated representations for roles [10,14,35] addressing features such as "at most one agent should be in this role" (cardinality of a role) and "whomever takes up this role cannot take up this other role" (compatibility of roles), could avoid certain combinations of roles, thus partitioning the graph of roles (vertices) and power relations (edges) into sub-graphs without loops.

recorded: given a state S_i and an action $\langle S, ac, S' \rangle$, if S holds in S_i (see below) then the action can be applied and we obtain a next state[5] $S_{i+1} = S'$.

We follow the architecture for distributed norm management proposed in [19,37], and consider a global state which is updated as a result of individual agent's actions – this is similar to *transition systems* [15]. We represent this as the construct $\boxed{S_0} \Rightarrow \boxed{S_1} \Rightarrow \cdots$, showing a sequence of global states $\langle S_0, S_1, \ldots \rangle$ created from an initial state S_0 with the "$\Rightarrow$" operation indicating the application of a set of actions (from possibly many agents) on S_i, giving rise to S_{i+1}.

Negated propositions in pre-conditions of actions (cf. Definition 6) are interpreted as *negation as failure* [11], that is, they hold if they cannot be proven true. Since we are dealing with single propositions (rather than formulae), to check if a negated proposition $\neg p$ holds in a state S we need to check that p does not appear in S, that is, $S \models \neg p$ if, and only if, $p \notin S$. Given a set $S' \subseteq \mathcal{P} \cup \mathcal{P}^-$ of (possibly negated) propositions, we establish when $S \models S'$:

$$S \models S' \text{ if, and only if, } \begin{cases} \forall (\neg p) \in S', p \notin S \\ \forall p \in S', p \in S \end{cases}$$

Given a set of actions Ac and a global state S^*, individual agents can compute the subset of actions $Ac' \subseteq Ac$ whose pre-conditions hold in S^*:

$$applicableActions(Ac, S^*) = \{\langle S, ac, S' \rangle \in Ac \mid S^* \models S\}$$

An underlying infrastructure controls access to global states, and mediates how and when an update is to take place. Agents decide on the actions they want to perform (chosen from *applicableActions*), and update the global state directly.

We provide means to check which group norms hold, using δ. For simplicity our norms do not have activation conditions, and this is interpreted as a norm being active until δ holds in S^*, that is,

$$active(^A\mathbf{D}_G^R \, \varphi < \delta, S^*) \text{ holds if, and only if, } S^* \not\models \delta$$

Agents are able to find out all those active group norms, and use the group norm reasoning mechanism (Algorithm 1) defined in Sect. 4 to establish how to handle the group norm – as a member of a group of actors, addressees or responsibles.

3.2   Individual and Collective Actions

Our formalisation in Definition 6 caters for both individual and collective actions. We differentiate between these in a pragmatic fashion: collective actions are those whose post-conditions (effects) are achievable via the combination of other (individual or collective) actions. Formally, given a set of actions Ac, $\mathbf{ac} \in Ac$, $\mathbf{ac} = \langle S, ac, S' \rangle$ is a collective action if, and only if, the conditions below hold

---

[5] This means that propositions are not implicitly recorded in (copied onto) the next state; a proposition will only be copied from one state onto the next state if it appears both in the pre- and post-conditions of an action.

1. for some $n \geq 2$, there are $\mathbf{ac}_i \in Ac, \mathbf{ac}_i \neq \mathbf{ac}, \mathbf{ac}_i = \langle S_i, ac_i, S_i' \rangle, 1 \leq i \leq n$, that is, there are (at least two) other actions $\mathbf{ac}_1, \ldots, \mathbf{ac}_n$,
2. $S \models \bigcup_{i=1}^n S_i$, whose pre-conditions are entailed by S
3. $(\bigcup_{i=1}^n S_i') \models S'$, whose post-conditions entail S'
4. Given a set $AssocRl$ of pairs $\langle \alpha, Rl' \rangle, \alpha \in Agents, Rl' \subseteq Rl$, establishing the roles Rl' which individual agents α are enacting, then $S' \not\subseteq cap(\alpha, Rl')$ for all $\langle \alpha, Rl' \rangle \in AssocRl$.

The first condition establishes the "break-down" of a collective action into other actions[6]. The second condition ensures that actions $\mathbf{ac}_i$ are applicable whenever $\mathbf{ac}$ is applicable. The third condition ensures that the combined effect (post-conditions) of actions $\mathbf{ac}_i$ addresses all post-conditions of $\mathbf{ac}$. The fourth condition states that for a particular organisation enactment (that is, agents associated with specific roles), a collective action is not within the capabilities of any one individual agent α however many roles Rl' it has adopted.

When an obliged action cannot be achieved by any one single agent (under its many roles) in an organisation enactment, then the action is deemed collective and it should be "farmed out" to groups of agents so that, by joining their capabilities, the collective action can be achieved and the obligation fulfilled. On the other hand, an individual action is within the capabilities of a single agent in an organisation; formally, $\mathbf{ac} = \langle S, ac, S' \rangle$ is an individual action if, and only if, $S' \subseteq cap(\alpha, Rl')$ for some $\langle \alpha, Rl' \rangle \in AssocRl$.

3.3 Coordination and Group Norms

Agents must coordinate their activities factoring in their roles (with associated capabilities), their membership to groups, and active norms which are applicable to the groups. Our reasoning mechanisms (Algorithms 2 and 3) introduced in the next section make use of two procedures *coordinate* and *coordinate'* to support coordination among agents, which we explain below.

Procedure *coordinate* is invoked by an agent α who is attempting to coordinate with agents $Agents'$ in order to achieve φ, and α is willing to contribute with S': *coordinate*$(\alpha, Agents', contribute, S', \varphi)$. We do not prescribe any solutions to the coordination mechanism itself, that is, the messaging/network topology, actual contents of messages and their order, or any guarantees such mechanism should have – research on distributed coordination [38] and planning [23] provides candidate solutions for this. The coordination process will go through a series of rounds whereby agents $\alpha' \in Agents'$ receive requests from α to help with achieving φ; the request may also include (partial) information on α's contribution S'. Agents will reply to requests offering their own contributions, as part of their deliberation process about what to do next, also factoring in other

---

[6] Collective actions have large sets of post-conditions reflecting the "effort" to be spent in order to achieve them. By breaking apart an action into other (simpler) actions which together achieve the same effects (post-conditions) we capture the delegation process supported by the power relation, and which is explored in our reasoning mechanisms.

group norms – research on how deliberation can be extended with normative considerations is reported in, for instance, [31]. Agent α will select who should contribute with what and consider whether it is necessary to send more requests, in case the responses so far are not sufficient to achieve φ. After a finite number of rounds the coordination process may succeed (and the procedure returns $\top$, that is, the Boolean value *true*) or may fail (and the procedure returns $\bot$, the Boolean value *false*). The same *coordinate* procedure supports agents when they are coordinating about who should *refrain* from carrying out actions.

The other procedure *coordinate'* used in our reasoning mechanisms is invoked by an agent α attempting to coordinate with those agents *Agents'* who belong to the R group of agents responsible for group norm $^A\mathbf{D}_G^R\ \varphi$: *coordinate'*$(\alpha, Agents', {}^A\mathbf{D}_G^R\ \varphi)$. The procedure returns the pair $\langle \alpha', {}^{A'}\mathbf{X}_{G'}^{R'}\ \phi \rangle$ with the outcome of the coordination: $\alpha' \in (Agents' \cup \{\alpha\})$ has agreed (as a member of the group responsible for the norm) to be in charge of $^{A'}\mathbf{X}_{G'}^{R'}\ \phi$. The coordination process may convert the original norm $^A\mathbf{D}_G^R\ \varphi$ into an altogether different norm $^{A'}\mathbf{X}_{G'}^{R'}\ \phi$ (a special case is when $^{A'}\mathbf{X}_{G'}^{R'}\ \phi = {}^A\mathbf{D}_G^R\ \varphi$, that is, the coordination preserves the original norm). This conversion would allow, for instance, group norm $^A\mathbf{O}_G^{\{ag_1, ag_2\}}\ (p \wedge q)$ to become norms $^A\mathbf{O}_G^{\{ag_1\}}\ p$ and $^A\mathbf{O}_G^{\{ag_2\}}\ q$, that is, the group $\{ag_1, ag_2\}$ of agents responsible for the norm have agreed to take responsibility over parts of the original group norm. Another important conversion would make use of domain axioms to work out how a group norm on the effects of a collective action (cf. Sect. 3.2) could be split into distinct group norms (with potentially different groups) over the effects of other (collective) actions.

4   Reasoning About Group Norms

The objectives of an organisation can only be realised when agents take up the roles described in the organisation definition. We assume that agents have their own motivations to decide on which roles they will take on, but once a role enactment is fixed, the agent is able to act on the capabilities described for its role(s). Moreover, agents have access to the organisation specification:

– The set of agents *Agents* enacting/joining the organisation.
– The set of actions Ac (Definition 6), the set of roles Rl (Definition 7) and their associated capabilities (Definition 8).
– A set $AssocRl$ of pairs $\langle \alpha, Rl' \rangle, \alpha \in Agents, Rl' \subseteq Rl$, recording which roles Rl' individual agents α are enacting (hence formally associated with).
– The power relation (Definitions 9–10) among roles and sets of agents (enacting roles).

The organisation specification allows agents to figure out each other's (as well as their own) roles, capabilities, and who has power over whom.

We furthermore assume an open environment in which heterogeneous agents, possibly developed by third parties, may join the organisation. This means that role enactment can take many forms, *i.e.*, depending on the agent's own "personality", its interpretation of what is expected from it as enactor of the role (and how to decide about its role norms) may vary. For instance, an agent with a strong sense of responsibility will first consider the norms for which it belongs to the Responsible group, whereas an agent that has a strong sense of duty may start by considering the norms for which it is an Actor. In the following, we describe, in pseudo-code, reasoning mechanisms for role enacting agents.

Algorithm: *groupNormReasoning*(α, $^A\mathbf{D}_G^R\ \varphi$)

if $\alpha \in value(G, Agents)$ **then** *addressment*(α, $^A\mathbf{D}_G^R\ \varphi$);
if $\alpha \in value(R, Agents)$ **then** *responsibility*(α, $^A\mathbf{D}_G^R\ \varphi$);
if $\alpha \in value(A, Agents)$ **then** *actorship*(α, $^A\mathbf{D}_G^R\ \varphi$);

Algorithm 1. Group norm reasoning

We initially present in Algorithm 1 the general reasoning mechanism, consisting of an assessment of the value of the norm groups and a check whether or not the agent belongs to these. Depending on which group the agent belongs to, separate sub-mechanisms are invoked, and these are explained in the remainder of this section. We assume that the mechanisms have access to a global set *Agents* comprising the organisation, as well as the specific actions, roles, capabilities and (group) power relations (cf. Definitions 6–10).

Input parameters α and $^A\mathbf{D}_G^R\ \varphi$ stand for, respectively, the agent's identity and a group norm under consideration[7]. We order the agent's considerations about group membership: it first checks if it is part of the group of addressees of the norm, then if it is part of the group of agents responsible for the norm, and finally the agent checks if it is an actor of the norm. If none of these situations arise, then the agent does not have to factor in the group norm in its decision. This ordering is due to the relationships among agents belonging to the distinct groups: the addressee analysis may require responsibility and actorship analysis (depending on the circumstances); the responsibility analysis may require actorship analysis, but actorship is self-contained. These mechanisms are described in the rest of this section.

The mechanism above also caters for situations in which agents simultaneously belong to more than one of the groups $A, R,$ or G. As we show below, agents in G that are addressed by the norm will "farm out" the norm among those responsible (in group R) and those acting (in group A); those agents responsible for the norm (in group R) will require the help of acting agents A. When an agent is part of more than one group, then we will have the phenomenon of agents calling upon themselves to handle the norm under a different guise.

---

[7] For simplicity, we omit deadlines/periods of norms in our mechanisms, and the assumption is that the input norm is currently active, that is, its deadline/period has not expired and hence it must be considered. This assumption can be relaxed, but all algorithms should initially check whether or not the norm is still active.

Our group norm representation is used in mechanisms to support agents reasoning about actorship (Algorithm 2), responsibility (Algorithm 3), and addressment (Algorithm 4). We illustrate their interdependence as

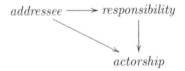

The reasoning invokes individual planning (during actorship reasoning), group coordination (during responsibility reasoning) and individual deliberation (during addressee reasoning). The reasoning is interleaved with message-passing (protocols) to enable coordination, as well as communication regarding who is taking up actorship, and to signal which norm has been violated.

4.1 Reasoning About Actorship

Group norms are ultimately "processed" by actors: these are agents belonging to the group A of norms $^{A}\mathbf{D}_{G}^{R}\ \varphi$ and their behaviours should be affected by these norms. We recall that our group norms consider propositional formulae φ (cf. Definition 3), and we note that these can come about as a result of a coordinated joint action among various agents, each contributing some effort to achieve or avoid φ. We propose the reasoning mechanism depicted in Algorithm 2 to enable norm-aware decision-making and coordination among acting agents. Line 1 computes all those sub-groups of actors whose capabilities (under their respective adopted roles in the organisation) when pooled together logically derive (or entail) φ[8]. Line 2 computes those coalitions to which α, the agent executing the algorithm, belongs. Lines 3–11 describe the provisions for norm-compliant behaviours. Line 12 is a place holder for non-norm-compliant behaviours – these might include, for instance, having α alerting other team-members (that is, all α' such that $\alpha' \preccurlyeq \alpha$ and $\alpha \preccurlyeq \alpha'$) or informing its in-line manager (that is, an α' such that $\alpha \preccurlyeq \alpha'$ and $\alpha' \not\preccurlyeq \alpha$) about its decision to not comply with a norm. We focus on norm-compliant behaviour: line 4 computes agent α's own capabilities $MyCap$ within the organisation, based on its roles.

Lines 5–13 loop through each minimal coalition to which α belongs, checking whether the norm is an obligation (line 6) or a prohibition (line 9). In the case of an obligation, α tries to coordinate with the coalition $Agents'$ to *contribute* with its capabilities $MyCap$ to achieve φ – it is enough for one such coordination attempt to succeed for the actorship algorithm to return $\top$ (line 8). In the case of a prohibition (line 9), α attempts to coordinate with $Agents'$ to agree on who is to refrain from doing what in order to not achieve φ (and hence abide by the prohibition) – it is enough for one coordination attempt to fail (that is,

---

[8] This amounts to finding *all* minimal *coalition* of agents who can achieve φ collectively [1].

Algorithm: $actorship(\alpha, {}^{A}\mathbf{D}_{G}^{R}\; \varphi)$

1   **let** $\mathcal{A} = \{Agents_0', \ldots, Agents_n'\}$, **where each** $Agents_i' \subseteq value(A, Agents)$ **is**
     the smallest set s.t. $\forall \alpha' \in Agents_i'.\langle \alpha', Rl' \rangle \in AssocRl \wedge (\bigcup cap(\alpha', Rl')) \vdash \varphi$

2   $\mathcal{A}^{\alpha} \leftarrow \{Agents_i' \in \mathcal{A} \mid \alpha \in Agents_i'\}$

3   **if** $complyNorm({}^{A}\mathbf{D}_{G}^{R}\; \varphi, \mathcal{A}^{\alpha})$ **then**

4       $MyCap \leftarrow cap(\alpha, Rl)$ **where** $\langle \alpha, Rl \rangle \in AssocRl$

5   **for** $Agents' \in \mathcal{A}^{\alpha}$ **do**

6   **if** $\mathbf{D} = \mathbf{O}$ **then**

7   **if** $coordinate(\alpha, (Agents' \setminus \{\alpha\}), contribute, MyCap, \varphi)$ **then**

8   **return** $\top$

          else

9   **if** $\neg coordinate(\alpha, (Agents' \setminus \{\alpha\}), refrain, MyCap, \varphi)$ **then**

10   **return** $\bot$

11   **if** $\mathbf{D} = \mathbf{O}$ **then**

12   **return** $\bot$

      else

13   **return** $\top$

   else

14   ... *non-norm-compliant behaviour*...

Algorithm 2. Reasoning about actorship

$\neg coordinate$ holds in line 9) for the actorship algorithm to also fail. In both cases, the loop is cut short and a result is returned.

If, however, the loop in lines 5–10 explores all coalitions without returning anything, then the test in lines 11–13 confirms that agent α was unsuccessful in coordinating to fulfill the obligation (line 12) or α was successful in coordinating to abide by a prohibition (line 13), otherwise the commands in line 8 (respectively, line 10) would have been performed and the flow of execution would never have reached line 12 (respectively, line 13).

4.2   Reasoning About Responsibility

Agents belonging to group R of a norm ${}^{A}\mathbf{D}_{G}^{R}\; \varphi$ are responsible for the norm, that is, they are to blame if the norm is violated. Those agents responsible enlist the help of acting agents belonging to the group A of our norms. However, agents responsible for the norm need to agree among themselves who will take the initiative to contact the actors. Moreover, the agents responsible for the norm should only contact actors over whom they have power. This process is represented in Algorithm 3. Line 1 invokes a coordination mechanism whereby α interacts with the other members of R regarding who should be ultimately responsible for the norm. This process should factor in the nature of φ – it might be the case that more than one agent should become involved in procuring actors to fulfill the norm. We note that the result of this coordination exercise could be the re-casting of the original norm into distinct norms whose overall effect, when they are complied with, is the same as the original norm[9] and we indicate this in the algorithm with a (possibly) different norm $^{A'}\mathbf{X}_{G'}^{R'}\,\phi$ being agreed to (line 2) by the group R to have α being in charge.

Algorithm: $responsibility(\alpha,\,^{A}\mathbf{D}_{G}^{R}\,\varphi)$

1   $\langle inCharge,\,^{A'}\mathbf{X}_{G'}^{R'}\,\phi\rangle \leftarrow coordinate'(\alpha,(value(R, Agents)\setminus\{\alpha\}),\,^{A}\mathbf{D}_{G}^{R}\,\varphi)$
2   **if** $inCharge = \alpha$ **then**
3      $ActorsSet \leftarrow \{\alpha'|\,\alpha' \in value(A', Agents) \wedge \alpha' \preccurlyeq \alpha\}$
4   **for** $\alpha' \in ActorsSet$ **do**
5   **if** $actorship(\alpha',\,^{A'}\mathbf{X}_{G'}^{R'}\,\phi)$ **then**
6   **return** $\top$
7   **return** $\bot$

Algorithm 3. Reasoning about Responsibility

Step 3 computes the set of actors α' over which α has power ($\alpha' \preccurlyeq \alpha$). Line 4 establishes a loop over all actors, repeatedly invoking the actorship reasoning mechanism of Algorithm 2, stopping (and returning "$\top$", that is, success) when the first of the acting agents handles the group norm. Otherwise, when we run out of choices for acting agents, the mechanism reports a failure "$\bot$".

4.3   Reasoning About Addressment

We finally consider the case when an agent is a member of the addressed group G of norm $^{A}\mathbf{D}_{G}^{R}\,\varphi$, depicted in Algorithm 4. In this case, the mechanism computes (line 1) the set of agents α' responsible for the norm, and over which α has power ($\alpha' \preccurlyeq \alpha$). Line 2 starts a loop invoking, for each α', the *responsibility* mechanism depicted in Algorithm 3, stopping when the first agent handles the norm. Lines 5–9 explores the exception to the responsibility mechanism, that is, a member α of the addressed group A, directly takes responsibility over finding actors to deal with the norm – this part of the mechanism corresponds to lines 3–7 of the responsibility mechanism.

4.4   Discussion

Our representation of group norms caters for three distinct groups involved. Being able to differentiate among those *addressed* by the norm (*i.e.*, group G), those *responsible* for the norm (*i.e.*, group R), and those *acting* on the norm (*i.e.*, group A), allows us to formally capture interesting and realistic situations. For instance, a norm such as "anyone under the age of 16 is obliged to attend school", can be represented as $^{A}\mathbf{O}_{G}^{R}\,attendSchool$ where

---

[9] We illustrate this with a norm (without the groups) $\mathbf{O}\,liftTable$ and axiom ($liftEndA \wedge liftEndB$) $\leftrightarrow liftTable$, which gives rise to $\mathbf{O}\,LiftEndA \wedge \mathbf{O}\,LiftEndB$.

Algorithm: $addressment(\alpha, {}^{A}\mathbf{D}_{G}^{R} \varphi)$

1 $ResponsibleSet \leftarrow \{\alpha' \in value(R, Agents) \wedge \alpha' \preccurlyeq \alpha\}$
2 **for** $\alpha' \in ResponsibleSet$ **do**
3   **if** $responsibility(\alpha', {}^{A}\mathbf{D}_{G}^{R} \varphi)$ **then**
4   **return** $\top$
5 $ActorSet \leftarrow \{\alpha' \in value(A, Agents) \wedge \alpha' \preccurlyeq \alpha\}$
6 **for** $\alpha' \in ActorSet$ **do**
7   **if** $actorship(\alpha', {}^{A}\mathbf{D}_{G}^{R} \varphi)$ **then**
8   **return** $\top$
9 **return** $\bot$

Algorithm 4. Reasoning about Addressment

– R is $\{x : x \in People \wedge parent(x, y) \wedge under16(y)\}$, that is, the group responsible for the norm consists of anyone who is a parent of an under-16;
– $G = A$ and they are $|\{y : y \in People \wedge under16(y)\}| = 1$, that is, those addressed and the actors are individuals (*i.e.*, sets of size one) under-16.

The norm "groups of more than 3 children are forbidden to be in a shop" is formalised as ${}^{A}\mathbf{F}_{G}^{R} inShop$ where

– G is *Children*, that is, the norm is addressed at all kids;
– R is $|\{x : x \in Children\}| = 1$, that is, each kid is individually responsible for the norm (hence the set has exactly one member);
– A is $|Children'| > 3$, that is, the actors are all groups of 3 or more children.

A third example is the norm "the chairperson of a meeting is obliged to have the secretary circulating the minutes", formalised as ${}^{A}\mathbf{O}_{G}^{R} circulateMinutes$, where

– $G = Meeting$, i.e., the norm is addressed to all those attending the meeting.
– $R = \{chair\}$, i.e., the chairperson (singleton set) is responsible for the norm;
– $A = \{secretary\}$, i.e., the secretary (a singleton set) is the one acting.

Our group norm representation has been put to use in mechanisms to support agents reasoning about actorship (Algorithm 2), responsibility (Algorithm 3), and addressment (Algorithm 4). Completeness is achieved as the net effect of our mechanism is that addresee agents exhaustively try to find someone responsible or someone to act (invoking responsibility and actorship analyses), the responsible agents exhaustively try to find actors, and finally the actors try to plan, factoring in the constraints of the norm (avoiding prohibited states, and aiming at obliged states). Termination of the process is guaranteed if there are no loops in the power relation, as all groups are finite, and so are the agents' individual roles and actions, and the interaction (although not shown) converges with a successful action/plan or a message declining to help. The complexity of the three combined analyses, in the worst case, is the permutation of the elements of all three sets, that is, $2^{|G \times R \times A|}$ – this is increased by the number of actions agents have to comply with norms (different actions may have different but overlapping post-conditions and may thus be used interchangeably) and the different ways in which collective actions can be achieved, as defined by domain axioms.

5 Related Work

Work on collective agency (e.g., [9,10,35]) and collective obligations (*e.g.*, [20]) have addressed similar concerns as ours. These approaches represent norms over actions, establishing groups of agents to whom the norms apply. Some approaches regard group norms as a shorthand for a norm which applies to all/some members of the group (*e.g.*, [10]), whereas other approaches (*e.g.*, [20]) regard group norms (more specifically, collective obligations) as a shared complex action requiring individual contributions (*i.e.*, simpler actions) from those individuals of the group. However, these approaches only deal with the element of shared responsibility, neglecting the element of shared actorship. Research about the concept of shared actorship can be found in work on joint action and coalitions (*e.g.*, [1,6,21]). This line of investigation is relevant as it looks into individual deliberation when coordination is required, whereas work on delegation (*e.g.*, [14,33]) sheds light on how norms can be transferred among individuals and groups. When agents join organisations they will need to consider the implications of taking up roles, since these will determine to which groups agents will ultimately belong, and consequently which norms will be applicable, as well as how power and delegation will impact on the agents' choices. Research has addressed issues of expressiveness and reasoning complexity in various logics of coalition (*e.g.*, [8,36]), establishing that even for simple propositional fragments, complexity is very high (*i.e.*, PSPACE in the size of the formula checked).

The notion of group association and imposing norms on groups of agents is closely related to the concept of *roles*. Roles have been explored in research on electronic institutions [16] and organisations [13,24,30,35]. Roles describe collections of *stereotypical* individuals who, by adopting a role, become subject to any norms associated with that role. We note that norms addressing roles are a useful shorthand for specialised norms addressing individuals, that is, they stand for "any one who has adopted role r is subject to norm ν". For instance, a norm such as "Soldiers are forbidden to enter area (x, y)" and given agents $a_1, \ldots, a_n$ who have taken up the *soldier* role, stands for "Agent a_i is forbidden to enter area (x, y)", for each $i, 1 \leq i \leq n$. Importantly, in existing research role norms typically do not influence the joint behaviour of individuals and do not require coordination.

6 Conclusions and Future Work

In this paper we have proposed a representation for group norms, a topic largely ignored in the literature. Our proposal caters for three distinct types of stakeholders, namely, the addressees of the norm, those responsible for the norm, and those whose behaviours are impacted by the norm (the actors). Our representation has been influenced by a taxonomy of cases for group norms [2], with two dimensions – the individual and the collective – within a group. Certain norms, although addressed at groups, are fulfilled/violated by a single (or some) members; other norms are aimed at the group as a whole. Our reasoning mechanisms are a first attempt at defining how agents can factor in group/individual issues when deciding what to do within an organisation (hence there is a degree of predictability on the agents' part), presenting clear connections with generally agreed organisational concepts.

We are currently extending our mechanisms with the communication layer, using classic, off-the-shelf protocols such as the Contract-Net. We will connect our approach with existing planning techniques (*e.g.*, HTN [32]), to evaluate how our group norms can help agents agree on joint plans with fewer messages and in fewer rounds.

References

1. Ågotnes, T., Alechina, N.: Reasoning about joint action and coalitional ability in K_n with intersection. In: Leite, J., Torroni, P., Ågotnes, T., Boella, G., van der Torre, L. (eds.) CLIMA XII 2011. LNCS, vol. 6814, pp. 139–156. Springer, Heidelberg (2011)
2. Aldewereld, H., Dignum, V., Vasconcelos, W.: We ought to; they do; blame the management!: a conceptualisation of group norms. In: Balke, T., Dignum, F., van Riemsdijk, M.B., Chopra, A.K. (eds.) COIN 2013. LNCS, vol. 8386, pp. 195–210. Springer, Heidelberg (2014)
3. Anderson, A.: A reduction of deontic logic to alethic modal logic. Mind **67**, 100–103 (1958)
4. Belnap, N., Perloff, M.: Seeing to it that: a canonical form for agentives. Theoria **54**(3), 175–199 (1988)
5. Boella, G., van der Torre, L.: Normative multiagent systems. In: Proceedings of Trust in Agent Societies Workshop at AAMAS 2004, New York (2004)
6. Borgo, S.: Coalitions in action logic. In: Proceedings of the 20th International Joint Conference on Artifical Intelligence, IJCAI 2007, San Francisco, CA, USA, pp. 1822–1827. Morgan Kaufmann Publishers Inc. (2007)
7. Broersen, J., Dignum, F.P.M., Dignum, V., Meyer, J.-J.C.: Designing a deontic logic of deadlines. In: Lomuscio, A., Nute, D. (eds.) DEON 2004. LNCS (LNAI), vol. 3065, pp. 43–56. Springer, Heidelberg (2004)
8. Broersen, J., Herzig, A., Troquard, N.: What groups do, can do, know they can do: an analysis in normal modal logics. J. Appl. Non-Class. Logics **19**, 261–290 (2009)
9. Carmo, J.: Collective agency, direct action and dynamic operators. Logic J. IGPL **18**(1), 66–98 (2010)
10. Carmo, J., Pacheco, O.: Deontic and action logics for organized collective agency, modeled through institutionalized agents and roles. Fundam. Inform. **48**(2–3), 129–163 (2001)
11. Clark, K.L.: Negation as failure. In: Gallaire, H., Minker, J. (eds.) Logic and Data Bases, pp. 293–322. Springer, New York (1978)
12. Demolombe, R., Louis, V.: Norms, institutional power and roles: towards a logical framework. In: Esposito, F., Raś, Z.W., Malerba, D., Semeraro, G. (eds.) ISMIS 2006. LNCS (LNAI), vol. 4203, pp. 514–523. Springer, Heidelberg (2006)
13. Dignum, V.: A model for organizational interaction: based on agents, founded in logic. Ph.D. thesis, Universiteit Utrecht, The Netherlands (2004)
14. Dignum, V., Dignum, F.: A logic of agent organizations. Logic J. IGPL **20**(1), 283–316 (2011)

15. Emerson, E.A.: Temporal and modal logic. In: van Leeuwen, J. (ed.) Handbook of Theoretical Computer Science, vol. B, pp. 955–1072. MIT Press, Cambridge (1990)
16. Esteva, M., Rodríguez-Aguilar, J.-A., Sierra, C., Garcia, P., Arcos, J.-L.: On the formal specification of electronic institutions. In: Sierra, C., Dignum, F.P.M. (eds.) AgentLink 2000. LNCS (LNAI), vol. 1991, pp. 126–147. Springer, Heidelberg (2001)
17. Friedkin, N.E.: A formal theory of social power. J. Math. Sociol. **12**(2), 103–126 (1986)
18. García-Camino, A., Noriega, P., Rodríguez-Aguilar, J.-A.: Implementing norms in electronic institutions. In: Proceedings of the 4th International Joint Conference on Autonomous Agents and Multiagent Systems, AAMAS 2005, pp. 667–673. ACM. New York (2005)
19. García-Camino, A., Rodríguez-Aguilar, J.-A., Vasconcelos, W.W.: A distributed architecture for norm management in multi-agent systems. In: Sichman, J.S., Padget, J., Ossowski, S., Noriega, P. (eds.) COIN 2007. LNCS (LNAI), vol. 4870, pp. 275–286. Springer, Heidelberg (2008)
20. Grossi, D., Dignum, F.P.M., Royakkers, L.M.M., Meyer, J.-J.C.: Collective obligations and agents: who gets the blame? In: Lomuscio, A., Nute, D. (eds.) DEON 2004. LNCS (LNAI), vol. 3065, pp. 129–145. Springer, Heidelberg (2004)
21. Grossi, D., Royakkers, L., Dignum, F.: Organizational structure and responsibility. Artif. Intell. Law **15**(3), 223–249 (2007)
22. Halmos, P.: Naïve set theory. Van Nostrand (1960). Reprinted by Springer-Verlag, Undergraduate Texts in Mathematics (1974)
23. Han, X., Mandal, S., Pattipati, K.R., Kleinman, D.L., Mishra, M.: An optimization-based distributed planning algorithm: a blackboard-based collaborative framework. IEEE Trans. Syst. Man, Cybern. **44**(6), 673–686 (2014)
24. Hannoun, M., Boissier, O., Sichman, J.S., Sayettat, C.: MOISE: an organizational model for multi-agent systems. In: Monard, M.C., Sichman, J.S. (eds.) SBIA 2000 and IBERAMIA 2000. LNCS (LNAI), vol. 1952, pp. 156–165. Springer, Heidelberg (2000)
25. Horty, J.F.: Agency and Deontic Logic. Oxford University Press, Oxford (2001)
26. Jones, A.J.I., Sergot, M.J.: A formal characterisation of institutionalised power. Logic J. IGPL **4**(3), 427–443 (1996)
27. Kollingbaum, M., Norman, T.: NoA - a normative agent architecture. In: Proceedings of the 18th International Joint Conference on Artificial Intelligence, IJCAI 2003, pp. 1465–1466. Morgan Kaufmann Publishers Inc., San Francisco (2003)
28. Lomuscio, A., Sergot, M.J.: On multi-agent systems specification via deontic logic. In: Meyer, J.-J.C., Tambe, M. (eds.) ATAL 2001. LNCS (LNAI), vol. 2333, pp. 86–99. Springer, Heidelberg (2002)
29. López y López, F.: Social Power, Norms: Impact on Agent Behaviour. Ph.D. thesis, University of Southampton, UK, June 2003
30. McCallum, M., Vasconcelos, W.W., Norman, T.J.: Organizational change through influence. Auton. Agents Multi-Agent Syst. **17**(2), 157–189 (2008)
31. Meneguzzi, F., Rodrigues, O., Oren, N., Vasconcelos, W.W., Luck, M.: BDI reasoning with normative considerations. Eng. Appl. Artif. Intell. **43**, 127–146 (2015)
32. Nau, D., Ilghami, O., Kuter, U., Murdock, J.W., Wu, D., Yaman, F.: SHOP2: an HTN planning system. J. Artif. Intell. Res. **20**, 379–404 (2003)
33. Norman, T.J., Reed, C.: A logic of delegation. Artif. Intell. **174**, 51–71 (2010)
34. Oren, N., Luck, M., and Miles, S.: A model of normative power. In: Proceedings of the 9th International Conference on Autonomous Agents and Multiagent Systems, AAMAS 2010, IFAAMAS, Richland, SC, pp. 815–822 (2010)

35. Pacheco, O., Carmo, J.: A role based model for the normative specification of organized collective agency and agents interaction. Auton. Agents Multi-Agent Syst. **6**, 145–184 (2003)
36. Troquard, N.: Reasoning about coalitional agency and ability in the logics of "bringing-it-about". Auton. Agents Multi-Agent Syst. **28**(3), 381–407 (2014)
37. Vasconcelos, W.W., García-Camino, A., Gaertner, D., Rodríguez-Aguilar, J.A., Noriega, P.: Distributed norm management for multi-agent systems. Expert Syst. Appl. **39**(5), 5990–5999 (2012)
38. Williams, R.K.: Interaction and Topology in Distributed Multi-Agent Coordination. Ph.D. thesis, Department of Electrical Engineering, University of Southern California (2014)

A Cognitive Framing for Norm Change

Cristiano Castelfranchi[✉]

ISTC-CNR GOAL Lab, Rome, Italy
cristiano.castelfranchi@istc.cnr.it

"Just remove a brick and the wall will sink"
(Arab saying)

Abstract. Norms are within minds and out of minds; they work thanks to their mental implementation but also thanks to their externalized supports, processing, diffusion, and behavioral messages. This is the normal and normative working of Ns. Ns is not simply a behavioral and collective fact, 'normality' or an institution; but they necessarily are mental artifacts. Ns *change* follows the same circuit. In principle there are two (interconnected) *loci* of change with their forces: mental transformations vs. external, interactive ones. Ns change is a circular process based on a loop between 'emergence' and 'immergence'; that is, changes in behaviors presuppose some change in the mind, while behaviors causal efficacy is due to their aggregated macro-result: acts that organize in stable choreographies and regularities build (new) Ns in the minds of the actors. More precisely the problem is: which are the crucial mental representations supporting a N conform (or deviating) behavior? And *which kinds of 'mutations' in those mental representations produce a change in behavior?* I will focus my analysis on Social Norms, in a broad sense.

Keywords: Norm change · Normative mind · Normative agents

1   Premise: Situated Normative Cognition[1]

I will discuss the internalized/externalized nature and working of Norms (Ns) and its impact on N change. What I have in mind is a *hybrid society* (humans and AI-Agents interacting together) with "norm sensible Agents". On the one side the Agent mediating and supporting human interaction, exchange, organization should be able to understand human conduct in terms of Ns and to monitor and support that; on the other side Agents should be themselves regulated by true Ns (not just pre-implemented binds, executive procedures, but real deontic representations with the mission to regulate their decisions and conducts) and be able to violated them in the right situation.

The analysis and typology that I will propose (that will not be complete and fully systematized, but just *in fieri*) is focused on Social Norms (SocNs), in a broad sense,

---

[1] I'm in debt with my colleagues and friends (in particular Rosaria Conte, Luca Tummolini, Giulia Andrighetto) for my work on norms theory.

© Springer International Publishing Switzerland 2016
V. Dignum et al. (Eds.): COIN 2015, LNAI 9628, pp. 22–41, 2016.
DOI: 10.1007/978-3-319-42691-4_2

covering various kinds of.[2] Of course here I will put aside legal Ns (where there are institutional and legal ways for Ns change) although I think that several of the mechanism that I try to enlighten for SocNs also hold for legal ones.

Norms are in minds and out minds; they work thanks to their mental implementation but also thanks to their externalized supports, processing, circulation, and dynamics. This is the normal and normative working of Ns. Also because usually a N is a strange relation between a practical, effective, externalized object (the conduct of X; however mentally/internally regulated) and a cognitive artifact: a written "table of law", a symbolic representation, a (verbal or non-verbal) message that has to pass into minds. This double face of N (cognitive and behavioral, both internal and external) is intrinsic. Ns are not simply a behavioral and collective fact, a "normality" or an institution; but they necessarily are mental artifacts [13, 22]. A N impinges on us and works *thanks to* its mental representation, (partial) understanding, and specific motivations. However, as we just said, they are not just a mental fact: this serves to determine and control the actors' conducts and to build shared practices, scripts, messages and collective effects.

Our claim is that also Ns *change* follows the same circuit. In principle *there are two (interconnected) "loci" of change with their forces: mental transformations vs. external, interactive ones.* Of course, they are interrelated since the mental changes determine behavioral changes, which determine collective new dynamics. vice versa, behavioral changes that we observe will change our mind and our norm conception or repertoire. In other terms it is both a process of 'emergence' [44] and 'self-organization'; and a process of 'immergence' [14, 21] and mentalization: a feedback from behavior and collective structure/phenomenon back to the individual minds layer. Not just a bottom-up and top-down, and an inside-outside and outside-inside process, but a real 'loop': virtuous or vicious *circles* of Ns change or confirmation or instauration. We need the same dynamics in normative Agents, able to learn and evolve SocNs, and to read the behaviors of the others in these terms for monitoring it or adjusting to it.

It would also be relevant to consider that there is no just one and unique normative role for actors with its specific mental attitudes (beliefs, goals, expectations, …). We are not only 'subjects' to the N (prescribing us certain behaviors and mental states), we also have to play the role of 'watchman' and 'punishers' of the others [11, 30]; a fundamental role in N script and for the maintenance of the social order. We have to play the role of 'issuers' too: (either explicitly or implicitly) proclaiming Ns, prescriptively informing about them, explaining and reminding us them (for example parents towards children). I will put aside here these different normative minds and roles[3], although I believe that the role of a normative 'watchman' will be very relevant for Agents.

What we will try to do in this work is to examine: (a) some of the *main mutation 'events'* in particular *internal* to the *subject*'s normative minds; but also (b) as individual

---

[2] From politeness to customs, from moral norms to Ns and rules in organizations, associations, communities of practice with their "rules". For a systematic analysis of social norms and discussion about the general theory see [5, 6, 12, 31, 35].

[3] I will also do not examine the other crucial phenomenon in Ns evolution: the introduction of a completely new N, and its issuing or negotiation. I will mainly focus on adherence or violation (and their reasons) in N changing, adaptation, or extinction.

conducts become signs (cues) and/or messages (signaling), and change the others and the collective emergent conducts, so becoming public phenomena and institutions. Also the other way around; I will give some hints about that: (c) how acts that organize in stable collective conducts build Ns in the minds of the actors [6] but not just as a regularity to conform to, but as expectations and "prescriptions" from the others [19, 23].

2   Roots of Ns into Minds

Real "norms" are based on the possibility to be violated, not obeyed. Otherwise they are not "norms" but physical barriers or ties and chains. Ns are devices for the control of "autonomous" agents that decide what to do on the basis of their beliefs, reasoning, and goals. Ns not only presuppose (accept) but also postulate a freedom in the addressees.
    Our main claims are the following ones:

- A N is not just aimed at regulating our conduct, at inducing us to do or not to do a given action; it is aimed at inducing us to do that action *for specific motives*, with a given mental attitude (belief, goal, expectation). The ideal-typical *Adhesion* (see Sect. 3.2) to a N is for an intrinsic motivation, for a "sense of duty", recognition of the authority, because it is right/correct to respect Ns, etc.; and only sub-ideally one should respect Ns for avoiding external or internal sanctions (see below). Also normative education goes in this direction [18].
- We agree with Bicchieri's theory that an "empirical expectation" and the perception of the existence of a "normal" diffused behavior is not enough for creating a real N in "normative" sense (to use Kahneman' terminology [39]). A merely "descriptive" N is not "injunctive" [42]; a N implies for us a prescriptive character: it is for inducing us to (not) do something. There is a social pressure: expectation and *prescription*.
- As we said, our object is "norms" in the "normative" (prescriptive) meaning/sense, not in the "normality" (descriptive or statistic or standard sense). However there is an important and bidirectional relation between N in *normative* sense and N in *normality* sense:
  (a) Normality-N creates and becomes a Goal for the actors and even a normative-N (a prescription, something "due"), in order to conform, to be like the others. This conformity is either a need of the individual or a need (and request/pressure) of the group, or both.
  (b) Normative-N creates a statistical normality-N, a normal conduct in the community, if it is respected: N conformity is "normal". Moreover:
    - Normative-N has the *goal* and the *function* to be respected and thus to create a normality-N, a normal behavior (at the individual, internal level this helps N also to become an automatic response, just an habit);
    - If normative-N doesn't become/create a normality-N it is weakened and perceived as less credible and less binding [6, 22].
- In order to *perceive* a social practice as a N we have to guess, presume, or understand some "end" in it: the protection of the interest or rights of somebody, of the community; from that a deontic "should", an obligation. Not conforming is an harm, is noxious, not just something irregular, strange. I'm at least frustrating your

prescription to maintain regular practices; you count on that and plan to regulate your behavior on that; so I'm upsetting and betraying you, not just amazing you. I'm harming social order, and the natural 'suspension' of uncertainty, the assumption of normality: a fundamental good [32], a "common".

- Ns have to be "impersonal" and depersonalized (and perceived as such) on both sides: the issuer's and the addressee's side. It is not a conflict between you and me; it is not "my" personal request (for me, for my desires, etc. for my personal will that you have to adopt); and it is not a request to "you". The message is:

   "I do not talk, monitor, sanction, in my name"; "I'm not addressing to you "ad personam", but as an instance of a class, a member, a citizen, ... like any other in the same conditions". Also for that "You have no reasons for rebelling".

   This really is a crucial point in the perception of Ns as Ns; thus it is something that must be signaled in some way (for official Ns: uniform, role symbols, specific documents, etc.; for Social Ns by collective practice or attitude or explicit messages) or at least contextually presupposed and assumed in the script.[4]

- As we said, Ns are social devices controlling behaviors through minds [14] but in a specific way; through a partial understanding. They require (for their existence and effectiveness) their *explicit mental representation*, their (partial) understanding and recognition "as Norms"; specific cognitive representations and motivational processes (*"Cognitive Mediators"*: [22, 24]); differently from other social phenomena like *social functions,* that can be played by social actors even without understanding - and even less intending - them [16]. Not necessarily the agent supporting the N in some role has as his/her mental goals ("intention", "motive") the aims and utility of the N; these are the goals (and functions) of the N not of the individuals.

- Ns have to build in us an "ought", a "duty", "you have to"; with a rather constrictive feeling, a negative "frame", an avoidance orientation (even when it elicits "you have *to do* this action"). And this "ought" is a non-technical "ought", not instrumental to and planned for a given outcome/goal. This entails a process of Adhering *without sharing* the 'instrumental' nature of the N, and without (necessarily) understanding/adopting its 'function' or end. My 'plan' is different from the authority's 'plan'. Citizens are not real "cooperators" but "subjects". They have to "alienate" their own powers and products [18].

3   N Internalization

Anyway, all this requires a specific "translation" of Ns into the minds of the addressees such that they recognize a N as such, and – on the basis of various motives – decide

---

[4] The fact that Ns are always relative to a "class" of subjects, not just to one specific person and it holds "for all the values of X" is one reason why the violation has not an individual meaning. X the violator is just "one of all/many", is a representative, an "example"; that's why his (bad) behavior can be a (bad) "example"; and the impact of the behavior is more that "individual": It is not longer true that "for *any* value of X, X has to, will do, and does action A".

whether to conform or not to it. Let's sketch the basic constituents of Ns internalization in our theory [18, 24]. Ns are based on a *specific* process of *Goal-Adoption* or better *Adhesion*; since they have the nature of an "imperative".

3.1   Goal Adoption and Adhesion

Ns induce new goals through "adoption". *Goal-Adoption* is how an autonomous agent is not an isle but becomes social, or better pro-social[5]; that its s/he does something *for* the others; *puts her/his autonomous goal-pursuing (intentional action), her/his cognitive machinery for that, and her/his powers and resources into the service of the others and of their interests.* What is needed is the architecture of a social Agent able to import goals from outside (and to influence other agents by giving them goals and relying on them) but remaining 'autonomous'. S/he is able to arrive to set up an intention not only from her own endogenous 'desires', but also from imported goals.

Goal-Adoption means that:

> X believes that Y has the goal that p and comes to have (and possibly pursue) the Goal that p just because he believes this.

"I do something 'for' you" (which doesn't mean 'benevolence'!); I want to realize this since and until you wants/ needs this; because it is your goal.

Of course there are different kinds of Goal-adoption, *motivated* by different reasons: merely selfish and instrumental, like in exchange; altruistic; or strictly cooperative, for a common goal. Ns prescribe a specific motive for accepting the injunction: in Bicchieri's view's a "normative expectation", for us also the recognition of the *prescription* by the others and their authority (see below).

A stronger form of G-Adoption is ***Adhesion:*** *when I adhere to your (implicit or explicit) 'request' (of any kind: prey, favor, order, law, etc.). In other words, you (Y) have the goal that I adopt your goal p, that I do something (action a of X) realizing that goal, and I adopt your goal p or of doing a, (also) because I know that you expects and wants so.*

In Adhesion one of the *reasons* for Adopting the goal of the other is that the other wants so:

– She also has the (meta-)goal that we adopt her goal;
– We adopt her goal by adopting the meta-goal.

In a sense, there is a double level of adoption (a meta-adoption): *I know and adopt your goal that I adopt.* Moreover, in case of Adhesion there is a (presupposed) agreement between X and Y about X's adoption, X doing something as desired by Y. Other forms of adoption (like help) can be unilateral, spontaneous, and even against Y's desire. Ns require from us not just adoption but adhesion.

---

[5] Not to be used as synonym of "altruistic", "benevolence", etc.

3.2 Normative Adhesion

Adhesion obviously presupposes specific beliefs into the mind of the agents (and this is the first aim of the N: to be conceived/perceived as such). In particular the recognition of the N as a N, in force on me, and valid in that context.

It is implied a 'generalized' G-Adoption where:

- X believes that there is a goal impinging not directly on a single individual but on a class or group of agents:
  - if X believes to belong to that class,
  - she believes to be concerned by the norm, and
  - she instantiates a Goal impinging on her; adopts it.

Having adopted the 'generalized' goal X doesn't limits her mind and her behavior to this (self-regulation); she will also worry about the others' behavior:

- X is also able to have Goals about the others' behavior: she adopts the Goal not to do but that for any z (DOES z A).
- Given such an Adoption she has *expectations* (predictions + prescriptions) about the others behavior, and is not only surprised, but also 'disappointed' by their non-conformity.

Also because she is paying some cost for respecting the norm and the authority, for maintaining the prescribed social "order", which is supposed to be a "common". She wants the other be fair, reciprocates, contributes.

3.3 Equity and Spreading

Conte and Castelfranchi [23] claim that the decision to conform to what is perceived to be an obligation plays a relevant role in N spreading over a population of cognitive agents. While the conventionalist view derives social norms from the spreading of conformity, in our view *conformity is derived*, so to speak, *from the spreading of obligation-recognition and -adoption*.

"The very act of accepting an obligation implies and turns into enforcing it. The agent respecting the obligation turns into a supporter. Conforming leads to prescribing. The agent undergoing an obligation becomes a legislator. The more an obligatory behavior is believed to be prescribed, the more it will be complied with, and the more, in turn, its prescription will be enforced. Rather than acting only through a behavioral contagion or a passive social impact, the spreading of norms is affected by *cognition* in a variety of ways and attitudes":

(i) *It leads to implementing effective conformity.* When an autonomous agent recognizes a norm as a norm and decides to conform to it, the number of conformers will be increased, and the norm is more effective.

(ii) *Effective conformity contributes to the spreading of normative beliefs.* The larger the number of conforming agents and the more likely the observers will form normative beliefs and the strength/certainty of the belief will increase.

(iii) *The spread of normative beliefs contributes to the spreading of normative actions.*

(iv) *The spread of normative actions contributes to the spreading of normative influ-ence.* The larger the number of agents conforming to one given norm, and the more distributed will be the want that other agents will conform to the same norm. "This is due to:
  – An *equity* rule. People do not want others in the same conditions as their own to sustain lower costs - benefits being equal (this is, indeed, one the most prob-able explanations of the Heckathorn's [36] group sanction control: the more agents respect the norms, and the more likely they will be to urge others to do the same).
  – "*Norm-sharing*". Agents are likely to "share" the respected norms, that is, to believe that those norms are sensible, useful, necessary, etc. This is also a powerful self-defensive mechanism (agents share the norms they happened to respect). Agents will defend the norms they share, implementing the number of agents who want those norms to be respected." [17].
(v) *The spread of normative influence contributes to the spreading of normative beliefs*, and the whole process is started again in a circular way.

The same cognitive mediation holds for an *observed* violation, deviance, and their crucial *interpretations* and meanings by the observer (see also Bicchieri and Mercier [7]).

Also for Agents this might be relevant: do we want/need just agents doing as expected/ordered or agents able to violate but also able to conform to the norm as a decision and for specific deontic motives/reasons (N-Adhesion)? Don't want we to "share" norms (social, moral, legal) with our Agents? To really have a hybrid society regulated by values and norms?

4   *Internal Locus:* Kinds of N Mutation Within Subjects' Mind

Let's identify the various though and 'reasons' of the 'subject' (S) for *abandoning* or *violating* a given N. We will distinguish between:

 (i) 'Unintentional' effects; where changing or weakening that N (or Ns) is not the end or an end of S, and
(ii) 'Intentional' act; where S understands, expects, and intends to jerk the N.

4.1   Norm Decay, a Close Approach

It is useful to cite a recent work on N decay, also in order to underlining some differences with our proposal.

In Hammoud et al. [35] we find a good perception of the role of N decay (not studied enough), and an important formal and simulation study, also with a nice ontology of different forms and reasons for Norm decay.

In their perspective: "***Norms decay*** refers to the case in which *a norm is not practiced or adopted by any of society's members, and eventually deleted and forgotten*." They introduce a framework that contains three cases of norms decay which are: *Norms*

Removal, Norms Disappearance, and *Norms Collapse*. The first case needs an intervention *from a powerful authority*, while the latter two cases happen when society members stop adopting or violate a norm. That is, there is a change starting from the decision of the agents.

- **"Norms disappearance** is the result of abandoning a norm from the majority in a society. Abandoning a norm means not practicing it without being sanctioned from the authority. Norm abandoning happens when it loses its benefit."
- **"Norm collapse** is the case of norm vanishing from a society due to agents' violation of this norm and violation sanction decay. An agent checks the benefit of violating a norm, and the sanction of violation … if the benefit of violation is more than the sanction of violation, the agent violates the norm and gets the benefits he wants".

The main difference with our view is of course our more systematic analysis of the specific changes in the mental aspects of Ns. However, there are also other differences. On the one side, we have a broader view of the 'reasons' why agent respect Ns; not mainly "for" avoiding sanctions, or "for" the social 'utility' of the N.

On the other side, the authors are a bit optimistic on the collective/community 'benefit' of the N. In our approach Ns are not necessarily *well conceived* by the authority or *fair*; and also social norms are *not necessarily good* for the community. They are simply self-maintaining just because they are "social order", reduction of uncertainty, identity, even if on the practical side they can be not so good. In our vocabulary they can be badly 'functional' [16].

So not necessarily a N "is abandoned when it loses its benefit". It can remain there. vice versa, N can be abandoned although it was and would be useful.

We also admit that N can be there even if not respect in practice by any agent, but they know the N′ and are aware of the systematic violation. In a sense a social meta-N is emerging, a shared practice/habits of violating N′. And we admit that not necessarily when "An agent checks the benefit of violating a norm, and the sanction of violation … if the benefit of violation is more than the sanction of violation, the agent violates the norm and gets the benefits he wants" this induces to a "N collapse". This self-interest violation can be there for one or few agents, since agents are in different conditions and with different preferences; what might be convenient for an agent can be not convenient for another one. The mental processing is the crucial device and cannot be so simplified and 'rationalized'.

4.2 Unaware Violations

S does not realize that her behavior is an N violation. Mental conditions for such a conduct:

- Ignorance of the N (*beliefs*); or
- A mistaken interpretation or instantiation (*beliefs*): S does not realize to be a member of the set of the addressees of that N or that it does apply in those circumstances and context; or
- No memory retrieval of the N in those circumstances, lack of attention, absent-mindedness (*beliefs*).

The violation is unintended since it is fully unaware, but - given the observable behavior ("bad example") - it equally injures the N.

There are also extra-mental conditions facilitating or inducing such a "mistake". For example, the N and its local pertinence should have been appropriately and explicitly signaled, not given for obvious: "Please, do not park more than one car in our courtyard; this is our polite convention".[6]

4.3 Aware Violations

A. *Without the goal of injuring/weakening the N*

As we do not intend the supportive 'function' of our conforming to the N, equally we do not necessarily intend the destructive 'function' of out violating it.

There are several *reasons for dropping* a N-goal, do not adhere to it and formulate a conform intention:

(a) *Goal-conflict:* the N-goal contrasts with another goal of the agent;
     Apart from the *belief* that the N is in conflict, what matters are the following parameters:
     – value of the goal based on the value of the meta-goal of respecting Ns;
     – value of the contender goal;
     – value of the negative expected consequences of violation, including feelings associated to N-violation; and in particular the perceived threat: estimated probability and weight of 'punishment' and blame (*beliefs*).[7]
     A sub-case of (a) is a N-conflict: N contrasts with other Ns accepted by the agent (see below).
     The decision to violate if I can a N that is not convenient for me now and here (not necessarily "in general") can just be for my private interests. However, not necessarily the goal in contrast with the N is a private/personal one; it might be a goal formulate for efficiently performing S's role or mission [17]: violating for functional reasons, for an intelligent problem-solving in our work.
(b) *N Application & Instantiation disagreement:* S is aware of N but he contests to be a member of the set of the addressees or that it *does apply* to that circumstances and context.
(c) *Material impossibility:* S forms a N-goal but cannot comply with it (*beliefs*); the intention would be impossible (*beliefs*).
     i. As we said, a remarkable case of (a) – but in a sense close to (c) (in terms of not "material" but of "deontic" impossibility) – is:
(d) *Norm conflict:* the N I should apply and respect is in contrast (*beliefs*) with another N:

---

[6] An interpersonal example may be: X: "You can not go around in underwear!" Y: "But you had to say me that there were guests in our house!".

[7] This expectation should be part of what Bicchieri calls "empirical expectation" ("what we expect the other do"). However, we should distinguish between "to expect that the other conform" and "to expect that the others monitor and sanction". Two different predictions based on different experiences that might also don't be fully correlated.

- Either another social N (social Ns are not so coherent and non contradictory, especially in their application). For ex. the social N about our male group meeting for drinking beer implies the possibility or prescription to burp in public (just for funny and be deviant), while I would desire – due to my "education" – do not burp;
- Or a conflict with legal or organizational N.

In all these cases S will not conform to the N but she is *not* motivated by the aim of weakening it. For sure that violation (given the message to myself and to the stakeholders) weakens the N, however the agent's intention is not necessarily this.

(e) *Expectation of not sanctions:* Either due to some reason in the others of not sanctioning; or just because I expect to not be detected, to hidden: "I will get away with it; they will not see me; nobody will know that"; or "They do not catch any violator, they never punish"[8]. Of course, these beliefs are relevant in particular for agent motivated to respect Ns just by the fear of sanctions.

(f) *Indifference to sanction:* There are cases and individuals where the fact that other people respect N and that there will be a negative judgment by the others (sometime even publically expressed), is not a sufficient reason for not violating: an important sub-kind of conflict. Consider for example a young guy sited in a waiting room where there are quite old waiting people standing up, and not giving up his seat to them, although he knows that he "should do" that, and that he is disapproved. Either there is in this guy (and context) indifference to the judgment and sanction from the others (*goals*), since "I do not care of these guys", "who knows them?" "I will never meet them again ..." (*beliefs*). Or there might even be a provocation attitude (*goals*): "Yes! I'm not like you, I do not care of you", "I'm underbred, so what!". Or the attitude is "motivated" by an opposition specifically to the N, as a meaningless N: a value opposition (like in people violating the rule of giving priority to women).

All these are (more or less sincere and not self-deceptive) beliefs and motives of the violator.

Sometime we (unconsciously) find a new interpretation of framing of our action and circumstance, and of the N, in order to facilitate our violation. Consider the very famous and beautiful case of people "interpreting" the monetary sanction for the violation of the N as a fair, a price, and thus deciding to systematically violating it, and just pay what they have to pay [34]. Let's rewrite in our mind as a tax what in fact would be a fine! But this morally facilitates our decision to violate.

(g) *Violation as epistemic act:* I know and intend (in case) to violate, but my motive is to "see": to see if that N is there or if I correctly understood it; or to see if the violation will be noticed/punished; to see your reaction. Even to see if you know that N, not in order that I know the N, but in order to know if you know it.[9]

Of course, there are other kinds of assumptions and reasoning that induce or facilitate (intentional) N violation; in particular interpretations of observed deviant behaviors,

---

[8] This is a change in our "empirical expectations" in Bicchieri and Xiao terminology [8].

[9] My behavior is like an exam question, where I in fact already know the answer but I want to know if you know it.

changing our mind. We will see some of them below: the effect of external changes (observed deviant behaviors) on our mind and conduct.

B. *Aware violations with the goal of harming, breaking down the N*

Violation is not just intentional but motivating: I violate in order to violate (Ns or that N).

(h) *Violating for changing:* Intentional and public violation of N for rebellion and opposition to that N, for rejecting and breaking it; to send a *message* to the others, to the "authority". Like Gandhi that rips in a central place of Johannesburg in front of the police the special document obligatory for Indian people. The message (and belief) is "This N is discriminatory, unacceptable, unfair; it has to be abolished: rebel to it!"[10] Notice that I can violate an N as unacceptable, not fair even if it does not directly damage me.

(i) *Violation against stigma, for changing values, building our identity:* I violate for provocation and rebellion towards stakeholders' values and attitudes. There are two different cases.

A possible aim is to build our collective identity, to remark that "we" are different, not like you, and we do not want be part of you (like Punk's provocation; or adolescent deviant attitudes). We are not In-group, but Out-group; it is an "exit" or *secession move* from your value and community.

Another possible aim is to change your values, to obtain respect: like in the provocation of the "Gay pride" and exhibition: "Our aim is not splitting from you; on the contrary we want to be accepted, integrated, and respected; you have to change your conservative values and thus your social Ns on that".

A crucial construct in human mind is the "sense of justice" and the related sufferance for iniquitous situations (not only harming us personally but even favoring us, or harming others: we can play the role of the victim, of the privileged guy, or of the stakeholder, but always with some discomfort) ("equity theory"), the *need* for equity (a "value" and a "motivation"[11]). We can consider a given N with this perspective, by evaluating its "equity and justice". This changes very much our disposition in obeying to it, or in supporting/defending it as punisher (Sect. 3.3). I feel "justified" in my violation; not a bad guy but a good guy; I do not feel guilty but proud of me.[12] If I consider a given N unfair I can have a serious conflict between two internal values, intrinsic motivations: the sense of duty/obedience vs. the sense of justice. The conflict is within my own values.[13] Sometimes this mental justification and motivation in terms of "sense

---

[10] This nice example is about a legal N, however similar examples exist also for social ones; like the "provocation" acts of courageous women in Arabic countries.

[11] For a rigorous cognitive notion of "value" and its strict link with evaluations, prescriptions and Ns see [40].

[12] Agents too should have some moral value and should be able at least to interpret our behavior and reasons in these terms, and possibly mediate our interaction caring of moral norms.

[13] This is Antigone tragedy. This also is Socrates' message to us while taking the poison: respecting Ns and authorities (even when their decision is incorrect and harming us) may/ should be a prevalent value.

of injustice" is just a convenient alibi (in front of the others, or in front of myself) for allowing my violation for personal advantages and desires (like the "sense of injustice" sometimes used for covering/hiding our envy).

(j) *Violation to be noticed, to innovate:* Sometime we violate a social Ns or consuetude's just to emerge, to be noticed, and to be original; like women first wearing a bikini or a mini. These provocative guys (actually innovators that may create a new "fashion", but not necessarily with this intention) are aware of and ready to cope with criticism and even insults.

Two examples about previous cases: I violate the N that on the beach one cannot be nude, and (with other people) I use "topless"; so I create or converge a new use, imposing tolerance to the others (they can no longer blame and reproach me). Or I'm completely nude; but this is too disturbing, intolerable for that group, so this creates a scission of groups and places: you nudists must have your own beach (and we will not come there!), but you cannot stay in "our" beach and be nude. If you become part of the new group and go to the nudist beach it become not just tolerate to be nude (the old N doesn't constrains you any longer) but there even is a new N of "being nude".

Similar path for vegans: they want not just be permitted to refuse current food without objection, ridiculous, blame, but they are trying to build new Ns - based on new values - ("Do not eat animals!" etc.) on such a basis to criticize, blame the violator (although they are the majority) and make propaganda. Their aim is not just to build a separate culture and community, but also to change the practices and the Ns of the big community.

Notice that this kind of N change requires (and is grounded on and aimed at) a change of "value" which is first of all a specific mental object.

(k) *Against the authority as such:* It is also possible to violate in order to rebel, but not against a given set of N that we want to reject or change, but against the normative authority A. To impair A, independently from the specific N. What maters is to violate; to show to myself or to my peer or to A that I do not respect A, do not submit: this is the message and motive. Like a "rebel" child that rejects any parents' prescription or restriction to his desires; like some political movement or demonstration where what matters is to broken something, to do something prohibited, not what to broken and why.

The crisis of the authority (see Sect. 6.2) can be due to various assumptions and motives; like the fact that A is no longer credible, trustworthy, correctly and competently playing its role; so I do not want longer depend on and delegate to it. Or a crisis of identity and membership: I do not any longer feel one of "you". Or for a crisis of values grounding that A: I do not any longer feel morally "obliged". And so on.

Again; it is not necessarily a matter of sanctions, power, and fear.

5   *External Locus:* The Others' Observed Behaviors

Which and how many observed changes in normative behavior are necessary for changing our conform conduct? Not necessarily we need diffused and spreading practices. Even a single violation act or meta-violation (for example do not monitoring or punishing) can call into question a given N in my mind (for example, a single resounding act of euthanasia); a single provocation can be enough for discredit authority (see Gandhi's example).

To know that somebody has violated N is an important factor in the crisis of that N. However, this works through our mind and what matters is the *interpretation* we give of that behavior: Accidental? Intentional? And why? And which are the consequences?

Let's first see some examples/kinds of assumptions and reasoning that induce or facilitate (intentional) N violation; in particular interpretations of observed deviant behaviors, changing our mind:

(1) *Interpretations of observed deviant behaviors:*
    - "If he (they) is doing that, me too I can do so! It is not *fair* that he does that and I cannot!"
    - "If he (they) is doing that it *means* (it is a *sign*) that it is permitted/possible: there is not a N or is no longer in force here"
    - "If he (they) is doing that it *means* (it is a *sign*) that this is the right way; what we have to do (he expects that I do so)".[14] Actually this is an intentional action entailing a violation, but not intentional *as* violation.
    - "In fact he is right! He is courageous. It is correct to violate this N!" (Thanks to his violation behavior I change my value-attitude towards N; this goes in the direction of N criticism).

5.1   A Single Bad Example

The impact of an external, observable deviating behavior does not depend only from the *number* of violators: the many the violators the more impaired the N.

A single guy's deviant behavior can be sufficient for a large impact. It depends on the network, on the number of stakeholders and – of course – on his/her role and influence.

It also is important the fact that (a) *not all violations are equivalent, although behaviorally identical*; and (b) that sometimes a single deviating example (not a multitude) be enough for; but of course it depends on its visibility and significance and interpretation. The single violation of a leader is not the same of the one of a follower; the violation a well-known person is not like the violation of an anonymous person, and so on.

The number of violator is of course a relevant factor because one principle for the strength of our persuasion is *the number of converging sources or examples*. But also the single's reliability - as model or authority – and prestige has a precise impact on the degree of our persuasion.

---

[14] This case and the previous one change our "normative expectation" in Bicchieri and Xiao [9] terminology.

5.2 The Others (Deviant) Behaviors as Messages

Since minds are typically read off behavior "it is impossible not to communicate" about our minds even those prescribed by a specific role. Our behaviors or their traces inevitably "signify" our mental attitudes. And we use our everyday behavior or its traces (practical actions not "expressive" ones or conventionalized gestures) on purpose to send this information to others; for *signaling*. This is a special form of communication crucial for human social coordination, and conventions and institutions establishment via "tacit" negotiation and agreement, not to be mixed up with gestural or other forms of non-verbal communication [43].[15]

Also N maintenance or innovation "circles" (observation-interpretation-change-action-observation- and so on) (Sect. 6) works thanks to the fact that a cognitive agent "reads" the others' conducts, and they signify/inform about the existence, respect, or violation of Ns [3]. Thus a violation conduct may acquire either the communicative function or the communicative intention of impairing the N or of explaining my reasons. Demolition or establishment of SocNs is mainly based on such a kind of not explicit communication, negotiation, and tacit agreements.

This factor contributes to the explanation of a crucial issue. As remarked by Christine Cuskley[16] "frequency and stability exhibit an interesting relationship in language: *the more frequent a linguistic construction is, the less it tends to change over time*." In my view this might be generalized to behaviors, and in particular to normatively regulated behaviors. Also linguistic constructions are "norms" and "rules" for people aimed at using that language; just a sub-case (with its specific additional dynamics). "Despite the evident relationship between frequency and stability, it is still unclear what specific social and cognitive factors underlie this relationship." As for social Ns, I would say that part of these factors is rather clear: the more diffused a (normative) behavior, the greater the probability to be observed and imitated/learned (a very strong and repeated "message"!), and thus *not just to spread around but to be "reinforced" in its prescriptive character*. Moreover, the more it is diffused the greater the absolute number of necessary "exceptions" and "violations" for its change or elimination. Thus the more widespread the more stable. And vice versa: the more stable in time and people, the greater the probability to be diffused and repeated (frequency). And so on.

6   Collective Destruction/Construction: Emergence-Immergence Cycles

On the basis of this analysis of internal mutations and their behavioral consequences, let's focus on the description of the internal-external, mental-behavioral, individual-collective loops, and on the description of the phases of Ns change (vicious) 'circles' (Fig. 1).

---

[15] On the relevance of Norm-signaling, and of explicit communication, not just of punishment, see also [2, 3].

[16] Christine Cuskley "Frequency and stability in linguistic rule dynamics", Invited seminar at ISTC October 2014.

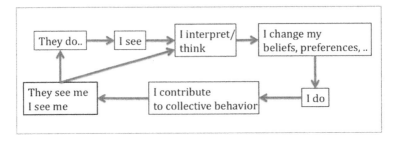

Fig. 1. Internal-external cycle

6.1   External ⇔ Internal Circles

Obviously – as for the "external" observed events (single or regular) – what matters is the Intentional Stance *interpretation*, the ascribed mind and reasons. I observed an individual violation by S or by W (not blame, no sanction); is it by accident, ignorance, or lack of attention? Or was it intentional? And "why"? Was S just egoist and self-maximizing, or is he violating because disagrees about the N or for invalidating the A? As we saw in Sect. 5 there are various possible interpretations and effects. And about norm 'watchman' role: was he indulgent because lazy or corrupted or familiar with S? Or was he thinking that N doesn't apply in that circumstance or is bad and unfair?

The effect on my mind and on my view of the N in the various cases is very different. The external event impact depends on our subjective interpretation of it.

That's why also a very clear collective behavioral regularity is not always and automatically interpreted (and complied) as a N. There are "vicious" and "virtuous" circles, from the point of view of normative behavior. Both, the vicious one (that is, violation, behavioral messages, N impairment, and collapse) and the virtuous one (N emergence, implicit negotiation, establishment, and maintenance) are due to the same internal-external cycle (Fig. 1).

There is also a very interesting self-referential feedback: the violating or conforming subject is observing his/her own behavior, and interpreting it, and confirming or changing his/her beliefs and preferences and feelings (as we saw in Sect. 4), and so on. Our behavior signifies a lot to us, and we send (intentional or unintentional) messages to ourselves. Also because, if I act on the basis of some implicit, presupposed, assumptions or choices, and the action is successful (good results), this automatically reinforces the presupposed mental conditions for that act, and increases the probability to take the same path next time.

6.2 The Crisis of N Authority

A nice example of a multilayer vicious circle between normative behavior and norm-related mental attitudes is the crisis and discredit of the "authority". To work well authority requires not only respect/submission for authoritarian strength, threats, coercive power (credible sanctions), but "prestige" or more precisely "authoritativeness". That is, A's "credibility". An A requires trust for its role; without trust it cannot work. Information authority, source of knowledge must be "credible" in strict sense: it has to be perceived (evaluated and felt) as "competent" in that domain and honest, not cheating for some private interest. Analogously the norm-A must be "credible" and trustworthy, its Ns should be perceived/given as the right one (from a technical and a justice point of view) and not due to private interests. If the A is authoritative, I accept its information or prescription, without need for prices or threats, without conflict, rebellion: I have a *generalized adoption disposition*; in a sense I obey for intrinsic motivations.

However this authoritativeness can collapse, and A can have a crisis of credibility, be discredited and no longer "automatically" respected. Which are changes in individual mind that might start (or reinforce) this process?

(a) I no longer *believe* that A or its behavior is respectable, that A is authoritative, credible; thus
(b) I do not adopt its prescription/N, I start do not conform to (*decision*);
(c) this feedbacks, and reinforce my belief about violability of N and my right to violate, and - since my deviating behavior can be observed
(d) it discredits the A in the others' eyes; diffuses the same evaluation about A (and probably also its perceived capacity or right of sanctioning); it builds a "collective belief"[17]
(e) it infects, diffuses deviating behaviors; but
(f) this spreading of the evaluations and of the deviating behaviors confirms and reinforces my perception of A, of that N, and my behavior; and so on.

The collapse of A's authoritativeness is a mental and behavioral, and internal and external, and individual and collective, fact.[18]

7 Concluding Remarks

Three issues.

• As we said, Ns are *based on* the possibility to be violated, not obeyed. They are devices for the control of "autonomous" agents that decide what to do on the basis of their beliefs, reasoning, and goals. Ns not only presuppose (accept) but also postulate a freedom in the addressees. Is this just a not so good but unavoidable feature? Or violability in this regulating device of social conduct has some advantages? N

---

[17] Not in the sense of a "collective mind" but in the more basic sense of a collective of minds; many minds sharing certain assumptions and infecting each other.

[18] It is clear that such an internal/external dynamics of Ns change might be fully simulated only with cognitive Agents in MAS.

"violation" usually has a negative connotation, since to "violate" is an evil in itself (as harm at a general and meta-level, of order, authority, trust; as we explained). However – actually – not only it can be morally justified and even noble and courageous, but also it plays a key function. It is one of the mechanisms and pressure for N change, adaptation, and evolution[19] [16].[20]

- I'm not sure that the current theory and definitions of social norms (see for example [6, 37]) fully captures some of the aspects we have discussed[21]. For example, there are social norms (not only legal ones) that are still there even if systematically violated by a large part of people. The norm *is still in force since it is perceived as such by that people*, although they violate it. They actually know/decide to "violate" it, thus, in a sense, that N still "regulates" their conduct. For example, in several part of Italy it is very frequent that people throw papers on the street or do not collect the excrements of his dog; however, they know (and even agree) that this is bad, not "correct" (N violation), but since it is tiring do not do so, and since a lot of people does the same … Is that N "in force" in this group? Yes: everybody knows what one "should" do. In our view a social norm to be there doesn't require to be a behavioral norm, a stable practice. It is *sufficient* that the large part of the group knows it, reminds and considers it, although regularly or frequently violating it. It is perceived *as* a N, *taken into account* in the individual cognitive process and mentally shared in the group, although ineffective on the conduct. It is a strange N state: an still in force but ineffective N. We shouldn't forget that first of all a N is into the (shared) mind of the agents; this is its presupposition.

Of course it is fully true – coherently with Bicchieri's theory – that:

(i) On the one side the norm not only is ineffective but is probably in "decadence", close to disappearing also from the mind of people, for example for the learning process of the new guy or for the mental automatization of the bad practice without no longer considering/perceiving that you are violating.

This is reasonably a possible and rather typical *intermediate step in the path of N extinction*: N respect and sanctioning; bad practices but the N is still considered as such; non longer taken into account as a N, no longer impinging on us.

---

[19] This obviously shouldn't be an excuse for the selfish violator just for his own private interests (although – as Adam Smith has explained – even this guy plays his social function, beyond his personal motives).

[20] I worry about the rigorous computational (intelligent) coordination and surveillance on human work and organization. At least in "critical states" we need violations, although not foreseen in the program; but just opportunistic and reactive to a given contingency.

[21] For example, the motto of Bicchieri for synthesizing the spirit and working of social Ns "Do the right thing: But only if others do so" could create some misunderstanding. This might be the mental rule, the prescription that the individual gives to himself in front of a N (it can explain his conformity or violating behavior) but is not the prescription of the N: the N says, prescribes, just "Do the right thing!" Ns want to be obeyed and respected in any case; this is their imperative. I may decide or be leaning to respect this absolute imperative only "if", under certain condition, but the "normative expectation" also by the others doesn't say "only if the others do so".

(ii) On the other side, it is true that the fact that several guy systematically violate that N encourages ignoring it, to consider that it is possible and not so terrible to violate it. We live in a rude world and we adapt/belong to it.[22]

In a sense the norm is still there in the mind of the agents; they know that there is such a norm. However, they are no longer *committed* to respect it [28]; they do not formulate the intention to respect it. One might say that knowledge about the others' conformity to a norm is not only or necessarily the origin and basis of our *believing* that a norm is there (Bicchieri's theory), but is more the basis of our *"commitment"* (and its strength) to that duty.

- Agents are relevant in two ways: for modeling the complexity of such a dynamic and immergent/emergent process, by Agent-based Social Simulation; but also because we need non-passive normative and moral agents in Hybrid Societies where Artificial Intelligences (Agents, robots,) will work and cohabit with humans. In particular *N change* processes (internal and external) should be present in both MAS with cognitive Agents, and in Hybrid Societies. We have even to allow and exploit violations of rules and practices in organization, coordination, and work, but only when it is the case and by understanding "why" (reading behavior and mind) [17]. Actually there is a strong and advanced tradition in AgMAS on Agent architecture for Ns, in N based MAS and organization, in MAS simulation of Ns efficacy[23], however – in my view – we still need some advancements in theoretical modeling of cognitive and collective aspects of Ns dynamics. This work is a partial attempt in this direction.

References

1. Andrighetto, G., Governatori, G., Noriega, P., van der Torre, L.W.: Normative Multi-Agent Systems. Dagstuhl Follow-Ups 4, Schloss Dagstuhl - Leibniz-Zentrum fuer Informatik (2013). http://dblp.uni-trier.de/db/series/dfu/index.html
2. Andrighetto, G., Brandts, J., Conte, R., Sabater-Mir, J., Solaz, H., Villatoro, D.: Punish and voice: punishment enhances cooperation when combined with norm-signalling. PLOS (2013). http://journals.plos.org/plosone/article?id=10.1371/journal.pone.0064941
3. Andrighetto, G., Castelfranchi, C.: Norm compliance: The Prescriptive Power of Normative Actions. Paradigmi **2**, 152–168 (2013)
4. Artikis, A.: Specifying norm-governed computational societies. ACM (2009)
5. Bendor, J., Swistak, P.: The evolution of norms. Am. J. Sociol. **106**(6), 1493–1545 (2001)

---

[22] It is even possible that a meta-norm emerges: the idea that to conform to this N (for example, of politeness) by antiquate, ridiculous, or snob, and this elicits negative attitudes in the others, that I want to avoid. A sort of *meta N of not conforming to the traditional N* is emerged; sometime even justified by new value (for example, "do not give precedence to women" as sign of women discrimination). In this case, for those people the previous N is no longer there, is no longer considered and accepted as a social N. The emergence or formulation of a *meta-N* about the violation (and then abandon) of a previous specific N is one of the processes of N abandoning and N innovation. It requires specific mental changes and contents; including a value-based justification of the "criticism" to the previous impinging N.

[23] See for example: [1], [40], [10], [26] [27], [37], [44], [29] [30].

6. Bicchieri, C.: The Grammar of Society: Nature and Dynamics of Social Norms. Cambridge University Press, New York (2006)

7. Bicchieri, C., Mercier, H.: Norm and beliefs: how change occurs. In: Edmonds, B. (ed.) The Dynamic View of Norms. Cambridge University Press, Cambridge (2009)

8. Bicchieri, C., Xiao, E.: Do the right thing: but only if others do so. J. Behav. Decis. Making **22**, 191–208 (2009)

9. Bicchieri, C., Xiao, E., Muldoon, R.: Trustworthiness is a social norm, but trusting is not. Polit. Philos. Econ. **10**, 170 (2011)

10. Boella, G., Noriega, P., Pigozzi, G.: HarkoVerhagen: introduction to the special issue on NorMAS 2009. J. Log. Comput. **23**(2), 307–308 (2013)

11. Boyd, R., Gintis, H., Bowles, S., Richerson, P.J.: The evolution of altruistic punishment. PNAS **100**(6), 3531–3535 (2003)

12. Brennan, G., Eriksson, L., Goodin, R.E., Southwood, N.: Explaining Norms. Oxford University Press, Oxford (2013)

13. Campennì, M., Andrighetto, G., Cecconi, F., Conte, R.: Normal = Normative? The role of intelligent agents in norm innovation. Mind Soc. **8**, 153–172 (2009)

14. Castelfranchi, C.: Through the minds of the agents. J. Artif. Soc. Soc. Simul. **1**(1) (1998). http://www.soc.surrey.ac.uk/JASSS/1/1/contents.html

15. Castelfranchi, C.: Prescribed mental attitudes in goal-adoption and norm-adoption. AI Law Spec. Issue Norms MAS **7**(1999), 37–50 (1999)

16. Castelfranchi, C.: The theory of social functions. Challenges for multi-agent-based social simulation and multi-agent learning. J. Cogn. Syst. Res. **2**, 5–38 (2001). Elsevier. http://www.cogsci.rpi.edu/~rsun/si-mal/article1.pdf

17. Castelfranchi, C.: Formalising the informal? J. Appl. Log. N° 1 (2004)

18. Castelfranchi, C.: Cognitivizing "Norms". Norm internalization and processing. In: Faro, S., Lettieri, N. (eds.) Informatica e Diritto, Special Issue in "Law and Computational Social Science, vol. XXII, no. 1, pp. 75–98 (2013)

19. Castelfranchi, C., Tummolini, L.: Positive and negative expectations and the deontic nature of social conventions. In: Proceedings of the 9th International Conference of Artificial Intelligence and Law (ICAIL 2003), pp. 119–125. ACM Press (2003)

20. Cialdini, R.: Descriptive social norms as underappreciated sources of social control. Psychometrika **72**(2), 263–268 (2007)

21. Conte, R., Andrighetto, G., Campennì, M., Paolucci, M.: Emergent and immergent effect in complex social systems. In: Proceedings of AAAI Symposium, Social and Organizational Aspects of Intelligence, Washington (2007)

22. Conte, R., Castelfranchi, C.: Cognitive and Social Action. UCL Press, London (1995)

23. Conte, R., Castelfranchi, C.: From conventions to prescriptions. Towards a unified view of norms. Artif. Intell. Law **3**, 323–340 (1999)

24. Conte, R., Castelfranchi, C.: The mental path of norms. Ratio Juris **19**(4), 501–517 (2006)

25. Conte, R., Castelfranchi, C., Dignum, F.: Autonomous norm acceptance. In: Mueller, J. (ed.) Proceedings of the 5th International workshop on Agent Theories Architectures and Languages, Paris, 4–7 July 1999

26. Criado, N., Argente, E., Noriega, P., Botti, V.J.: MaNEA: a distributed architecture for enforcing norms in open MAS. Eng. Appl. AI **26**(1), 76–95 (2013)

27. Criado, N., Argente, E., Noriega, P., Botti, V.J.: Corrigendum to 'Human-inspired model for norm compliance decision making'. Inf. Sci. **245**, 218–239 (2013). Inf. Sci. **258**, 217 (2014)

28. Dastani, M., van der Torre, L., Yorke-Smith, N.: Commitments and interaction norms in organization. In: Autonomous Agents and Multi-Agent Systems, pp. 1–43 (2015)

29. Dignum, F.: Autonomous agents with norms. Artif. Intell. Law **7**(1), 69–79 (1999)

30. Dignum, F., Dignum, V.: Emergence and enforcement of social behavior. In: Anderssen, R.S., Braddock, R.D., Newham, L.T.H. (eds.) 18th World IMACS Congress and MODSIM09 International Congress on Modelling and Simulation, July 2009, pp. 2377–2383. Modelling and Simulation Society of Australia and New Zealand and International Association for Mathematics and Computers in Simulation (2009)

31. Fehr, E., Fischbacher, U., Gächter, S.: Strong reciprocity, human cooperation, and the enforcement of social norms. Hum. Nat. **13**, 1–25 (2002)

32. Galoob, S., Hill, A.: Norms, attitudes, and compliance. Tulsa Law Review (2015, Forthcoming)

33. Garfinkel, H.: A conception of, and experiments with, 'trust' as a condition of stable concerted actions. In: Harvey, O.J. (ed.) Motivation and Social Interaction, pp. 187–238. The Ronald Press, New York (1963)

34. Gneezy, U., Rustichini, A.: A fine is a price. J. Leg. Stud. **29**(1) (2000). http://papers.ssrn.com/sol3/papers.cfm?abstract_id=180117#%23

35. Hammoud, M., Tang, A.Y.C., Ahmad, A.: A norms decay framework in open normative multi-agent systems. Br. J. Appl. Sci. Technol. **12**(4), 1–15 (2016)

36. Heckathorn, D.: Collective sanctions and the compliance norms a formal theory of group-mediated social-control. Am. J. Soc. **94**, 535–562 (1988)

37. Hechter, M., Opp, K.-D. (eds.): Social Norms. Russell Sage Foundation, New York (2001)

38. Hübner, J.F., Matson, E., Boissier, O., Dignum, V. (eds.): COIN@AAMAS 2008. LNCS, vol. 5428. Springer, Heidelberg (2009)

39. Kahneman, D., Miller, D.T.: Norm theory: comparing reality to its alternatives. Psychol. Rev. **80**, 136–153 (1986)

40. Miceli, M., Castelfranchi, C.: A cognitive approach to values. J. Theor. Soc. Behav. **19**(2), 169–193 (1989)

41. Noriega, P., Chopra, A.K., Fornara, N., Cardoso, H.L., Singh, M.P.: Regulated MAS: social perspective. Normative Multi-Agent Syst. **2013**, 93–133 (2013)

42. Schultz, P.W., Nolan, J.M., Cialdini, R.B., Goldstein, N.J., Griskevicius, V.: The constructive, destructive, and reconstructive power of social norms. Psychol. Sci. **18**(5), 429–434 (2007)

43. Tummolini, L., Castelfranchi, C.: Trace signals: the meanings of stigmergy. In: Weyns, D., Van Dyke Parunak, H., Michel, F. (eds.) E4MAS 2006. LNCS (LNAI), vol. 4389, pp. 141–156. Springer, Heidelberg (2007)

44. Ullmann-Margalit, E.: The Emergence of Norms. Oxford University Press, Oxford (1977)

45. Vasconcelos, W., García-Camino, A., Gaertner, D., Rodríguez-Aguilar, J.A., Noriega, P.: Distributed norm management for multi-agent systems. Expert Syst. Appl. **39**(5), 5990–5999 (2012)

Representative Agents and the Cold Start Problem in Contract Negotiation

Federico Cerutti[1]([⊠]), Christopher Burnett[2], and Nir Oren[2]

[1] Cardiff University, Cardiff, UK
CeruttiF@cardiff.ac.uk

[2] Department of Computing Science, University of Aberdeen, Aberdeen, UK

Abstract. Principal Agent Theory (PAT) seeks to identify the incentives and sanctions that a consumer should apply when entering into a contract with a provider in order to maximise their own utility. However, identifying *suitable* contracts—maximising utility while minimising regret— is difficult, particularly when little information is available about provider competencies. In this paper we show that a global contract can be used to govern such interactions, derived from the properties of a representative agent. After describing how such a contract can be obtained, we analyse the contract utility space and its properties. Then, we show how this contract can be used to address the cold start problem and that it significantly outperforms other approaches. Finally, we discuss how our work can be integrated with existing research into multi-agent systems.

1 Introduction

Autonomous agents are often assumed to be rational, self interested entities, interacting with others in order to maximise their own utility. When asked to fulfil a task, they will therefore do so in a way that maximises their expected utility. When acting as a service provider (e.g., in an electronic marketplace), there is thus a risk that the agent will provide a substandard service. Approaches to mitigate this risk include the use of electronic contracts [19,20], which specify the rewards and penalties (or more generally, *incentives*) to be imposed on interacting parties in response to successful or unsuccessful interactions [7]. Principal Agent Theory (PAT) [11,13,18,21] aims to determine the optimal level of incentives—in the form of rewards and penalties—that an agent (the *principal* or *consumer*) must commit to giving others (the *providers*) in order to have the latter act in such a way so as to maximise the principal's utility. To utilise PAT an agent requires beliefs about the behaviour of the provider. However, without previous (potentially negative) experiences, such beliefs cannot be formed. This problem, of lack of experience with others in the system potentially leading to poor experiences when operating within the system, is referred to as the

---

F. Cerutti—The work was performed when the author was affiliated with the University of Aberdeen.

V. Dignum et al. (Eds.): COIN 2015, LNAI 9628, pp. 42–58, 2016.
DOI: 10.1007/978-3-319-42691-4_3

cold start problem [25]. Several approaches have been proposed for addressing the cold start problem, from minimal expectation or random assignment to the capabilities of the providers [23,26], to active learning [16]. In particular, good results have been shown by using samples of the society [24].

Apart from the cold start problem, several other difficulties arise when using PAT. Computing incentives requires solving a highly non-linear optimisation problem. When combined with the need to select between multiple possible providers, the computational costs of creating contracts using PAT, and gathering the information needed to create such contracts, become prohibitive. When dealing with unfamiliar parties humans often resort to general principles to determine incentives, stemming from cultural, psychological or legal foundations. In this paper, we build on this intuition, suggesting that without additional information, an approximate set of incentives can be specified *for all interactions within the system*. We envision that a PAT based system would initially utilise this approximate set of incentives to generate contracts. As more information becomes available through repeated interactions, these approximations become discounted in favour of more accurate incentives to form better contracts. However, in the case of very simple computationally bound agents, our approximations could continue to be used. Our work can therefore be seen to address the cold start problem by allowing an agent to successfully interact with others in the absence of specific information about them.

Our contributions are as follows. We describe a procedure for determining suitable approximate global incentive values. Such incentives aim to be applicable to all agents in the system, and in defining them, we consider their effects on overall system utility, which we refer to as the *social utility*. We define a set of incentives, or a *contract*, as *suitable* if it is the result of a trade-off between the social utility that can be gained, and the regret of paying too much for a given good or task. Informally, the contract is based on an average individual provider computed from the profile of all agents in the system. We experimentally evaluate our contribution, showing how using the global contract significantly outperforms other techniques aimed at addressing the cold start problem.

In the next section, we provide some background on principal agent theory, following which we describe how global contracts are computed in Sect. 3. Section 4 discusses another set of experiments evaluating the performance of using the global contract in solving the cold start problem. Section 5 summarises our results and concludes.

2 Background and Assumptions

2.1 Preliminary Notions

Following [6], we take as given a *society* of agents $\mathcal{A} = \{x, y, \ldots\}$ and a *set of tasks* T. A *consumer* $x \in \mathcal{A}$ desires to see some *task* $\tau \in T$ accomplished and must do so by having a *provider* $y \in \mathcal{A}$ perform the task on its behalf. Given $\tau \in T$, let $\mathcal{O}_\tau = \{o_0, o_1, o_2, \ldots, o_n\}$ denote the set of possible *outcomes* for task τ, where $o_0 \equiv abs$ represents the case where the provider abstained from executing the task. $\succ_o$ induces a total strict order over $\mathcal{O}_\tau$, such that intuitively, if $o_i \succ_o o_j$, o_i is *better* than o_j. $\min_o \mathcal{O}_\tau$ represents the worst possible outcome of task τ, i.e., *complete failure*, while $\max_o \mathcal{O}_\tau$ represents *complete success*. For ease of notation, $o_i \prec_o o_j$ iff $o_j \succ_o o_i$. We assume that all agents share the same task evaluation criteria as well as the same ordering function.[1]

In *delegating* a task to a provider, the consumer asks the provider to execute it. The delegation of a task results in the consumer and provider obtaining some utility (for the consumer, due to the execution of the desired task, and for the provider, due to payment obtained from the consumer). Given this, the utility gained by the consumer is computed by the function $U^x : \mathcal{O}_\tau \mapsto \mathbb{R}$, while the provider gains utility $V^y : \mathcal{O}_\tau \mapsto \mathbb{R}$.

The task provider has autonomy in selecting the method by which a task will be carried out. In particular, let $\mathcal{E}_\tau = \{e_0, e_1, \dots, e_m\}$ denote the set of *effort levels* they can apply when performing τ, where $e_0 \equiv abs$ identifies the case where the provider abstains from performing the task. We define a total ordering $\succ_e$ over $\mathcal{E}_\tau$ such that if $e_i \succ_e e_j$, then e_i requires more effort (or is *higher* than e_j. Similarly as before, $e_i \prec_e e_j$ iff $e_j \succ_e e_i$.

Each effort has an associated cost determined by the function $Cost : \mathcal{A} \times \mathcal{E}_\tau \mapsto \mathbb{R}$. For ease of notation, for agent $y \in \mathcal{A}$, $Cost^y$ denotes its cost function. Different effort levels have an impact on outcomes, which we capture through a probability distribution: $\forall o \in \mathcal{O}_\tau, \forall e \in \mathcal{E}_\tau, p^y(o \mid e)$ represents the probability that agent (provider) y will achieve the outcome o using effort e. It is assumed that $p^y(abs \mid abs) = 1$.

When delegating, the consumer devises a payment function, or *contract*, $\mathcal{C} : \mathcal{A} \times \mathcal{A} \times T \times \mathcal{O} \mapsto \mathbb{R}$. We write $C^x_{y:\tau}(o)$ for a given $o \in \mathcal{O}_\tau$ to represent the contract specifying the compensation consumer x will give to provider y given outcome o of task τ.

Therefore, the *net utility* nV^y for a provider y which achieves an outcome given a specific effort (including abstention) is:

$$nV^y(o, e) = V^y(o) + C^x_{y:\tau}(o) - Cost(e) \tag{1}$$

2.2   A Fair System

In what follows we assume a *fair system* which identifies several desirable and common-sense properties that any system should have. These properties are as follows.

(F_1): $\forall o_i, o_j \in \mathcal{O}_\tau$, if $o_i \succ_o o_j$ then $U^x(o_i) \geq U^x(o_j)$ and $V^y(o_i) \geq V^y(o_j)$;
(F_2): $\exists o_i \in \mathcal{O}_\tau, \exists e \in \mathcal{E}_\tau$ s.t. $nV^y(abs, e) < nV^y(o_i, e)$;
(F_3): $\forall e_i, e_j \in \mathcal{E}_\tau$, if $e_i \succ_e e_j$ then $Cost(e_i) \geq Cost(e_j)$;
(F_4): $\forall o_i, o_j \in \mathcal{O}_\tau$, if $o_i \succ_o o_j$ then $C^x_{y:\tau}(o_i) \geq C^x_{y:\tau}(o_j)$;
(F_5): $C^x_{y:\tau}(abs) = Cost(abs)$.

---

[1] In other words, all agents have the same preference ordering $\succ_o$ over tasks.

(F_1) states that the better the outcome of a task, the greater the utility that both the provider and the consumer independently receive; (F_2) there has to be at least one outcome that gives the provider a better *gross* utility than abstaining (for example by being paid more for this outcome than for abstaining); (F_3) that the higher the effort, the higher the associated cost to the provider; (F_4) that the better the outcome, the higher the compensation to the provider according to the contract (incentive); (F_5) that the contract covers the costs associated with abstaining behaviour, but no more. We note that these constraints are not minimal.

Although in reality some of those properties might fail to be satisfied, they try to capture a minimal set of norms for a free-market society. Far from being unquestionable, we elicit them as postulates on which we base our proposal in the next sections.

2.3   Rationality Assumptions

We assume that each provider rationally decides whether or not to accept a contract, and which effort to use if it does not abstain. In particular, if the provider's expected utility is greater than the utility it would obtain abstaining, then the provider will perform the requested task. Moreover, the provider will utilise the effort on the task which will maximise its own expected utility. EV^y denotes the expected utility for a provider y in performing a task τ with a contract $C^x_{y:\tau}$, and is computed as follows.

$$EV^y = \sum_{e \in \mathcal{E}_\tau} \sum_{o \in \mathcal{O}_\tau} \left(p(o|e) \; (V^y(o) + C^x_{y:\tau}(o) - Cost(e)) \right) \tag{2}$$

Therefore, if $EV^y \leq V^y(abs)$, it is better, or *more convenient* for the provider to abstain from accepting the task. If, instead, $EV^y > V^y(abs)$, then the effort that the provider will expend on performing the task is as follows.

$$\underset{e \in \mathcal{E}_\tau}{\operatorname{argmax}} \sum_{o \in \mathcal{O}_\tau} \left(p^y(o \mid e) \; (V^y(o) + C^x_{y:\tau}(o) - Cost(e)) \right) \tag{3}$$

Let *delegate* denote the non-deterministic function that, given a task τ, a provider y, and a contract $C^x_{y:\tau}$, returns a pair of elements: (1) an element of $\mathcal{O}_\tau \cup \{abs\}$ which depends on the effort resulting from y's decision process (obtained from Eqs. (2) and (3)); and (2) the net utility for y.

As mentioned above, we seek a global approximation for incentives. In order to evaluate the incentives' effectiveness, we must consider how task delegation (i.e., the execution of the task from the consumer by the provider) operates in the presence of these incentives. We therefore consider the total utility of the system over both providers and consumers for a specific contract (i.e., the sum of each provider's and consumer's utility over the whole system). This is measure of *social utility*, with regards to a task τ for a given contract $C^x_{y:\tau}$, is defined as follows.

$$sU(C_{y:\tau}^x) = \sum_{x,y \in \mathcal{A}} U^x(\hat{o}) + n\widehat{V^y} \tag{4}$$

where $\langle \hat{o}, n\widehat{V^y} \rangle = delegate(\tau, y, C_{y:\tau}^x)$.

Finally, following [22, p. 51], we can compute the *regret* of a consumer to have chosen a contract $C_{y:\tau}^x$ from a set of contracts $\mathfrak{C}_{y:\tau}^x$ as follows.

$$Regret(C_{y:\tau}^x, o) = \left(\min_{\overline{C_{y:\tau}^x} \in \mathfrak{C}_{y:\tau}^x} \overline{C_{y:\tau}^x}(o) \right) - C_{y:\tau}^x(o) \tag{5}$$

The regret value is, by definition, negative. However, its value must be interpreted as an absolute value [22, p. 51].

2.4   Traditional Solutions to the Cold Start Problem

Several approaches have been proposed for solving the cold start problem in contract negotiation. For the purpose of this work we will focus on three of them.

The first approach is probably the simplest. It proposes to use, as starting point, the minimum contract possible according to fair systems requests. In this way, by incrementing the value of the contract (in the sense of utility paid to the provider for successful task execution) every time we receive an abstention, we can converge to the minimum contract while guaranteeing providers not abstain. However, this contract is not guaranteed to maximise the consumer's expected utility.

A second approach adopts an exploration strategy, such as Boltzmann selection [7], whereby, given a set of outcomes for a task, contracts are randomly selected initially (i.e., the exploration phase), with the best observed contract being chosen after some time period has elapsed (the exploitation phase). In case the chosen contract does not guarantee participation, we can iterate the interactions and converge sooner to the minimum contract guaranteeing it. However, if the cost of the contract for the consumer is too high, this will result in high regret.

A third approach utilises sampling. This includes widely adopted techniques for solving the cold-start problem via active learning [24]. Given a society of agents $\mathcal{A}$ and the set of contracts $\mathcal{C}$, and given a simple sampling procedure [9], the problem is to determine the number of samples required to achieve some statistical accuracy requirement.

Since our goal is to identify sufficient samples to obtain non-abstaining behaviours, we can divide each unit of the search space $\mathcal{A} \times \mathcal{C}$—assumed to be normally distributed—into one of two classes yielding either abstaining or non-abstaining output. Given the margin of error d that we consider acceptable in the estimated proportion p in the class of non-abstaining output, and given the accepted risk α that we can incur that the actual error is larger than d, then according to [9], we require n samples, computed as follows.

$$n_0 = \frac{t^2 \, p \, (1-p)}{d^2}$$

where t is the abscissa of the normal curve that cuts off an area of α at the tails. If $\frac{n_0}{|\mathcal{A} \times \mathcal{C}|}$ is negligible, n_0 is a satisfactory approximation, and thus $n = n_0$. Otherwise,

$$n = \frac{n_0}{1 + \frac{n_0}{|\mathcal{A} \times \mathcal{C}|}} \tag{6}$$

In the following we identify with $\widehat{\mathcal{C}}_\alpha^d$ the set of sample contracts given the margin of error d and the accepted risk α.

3   Global Contracts

In order to apply PAT, one must be able to compute the provider's expected utility, requiring knowledge about provider costs and success likelihoods for different effort levels. Therefore, in order to assess its own utility, the consumer should know, for each provider and for each effort level, the associated cost, as well as the probability of obtaining each outcome of the task for a given provider's effort level.

To reduce the computational effort for a consumer to explore providers' capabilities, we introduce a *representative agent* w obtained from the providers present in the system. w can be viewed as the simplest stereotype agent [2,5,12] for a given society, which acts as a proxy for the agent's neighbours. Although outside the scope of this work, assessing the quality of the representative agent is an important issue which can impact on other aspects of a multi-agent society, e.g., how much can an agent trust the agents in a society in which it enters for the very first time?

In what follows, without loss of generality and to simplify the presentation, we assume:

- a single task τ;
- a fixed shared cost function $Cost$ for all the providers;
- a fixed shared utility function V for all the providers;[2]
- a fixed shared utility function U for all the consumers;
- contracts $C_{y:\tau}^x$ such that $\forall o \in \mathcal{O}_\tau, C_{y:\tau}^x(o) \in \mathbb{Z}$: moreover, we assume a strong fairness requirement for these contracts, i.e., $C_{y:\tau}^x(o_i) \geqslant C_{y:\tau}^x(o_j)$ if $o_i \succ_o o_j$.

Therefore, the representative agent w is one such that:

$$\forall o \in \mathcal{O}_\tau, \forall e \in \mathcal{E}_\tau, p^w(o \mid e) = \frac{1}{|\mathcal{A}|} \sum_{y \in \mathcal{A}} p^y(o \mid e)$$

3.1   Searching for a Suitable Contract as a Linear Problem

Considering a representative agent as the "average" provider in a given society does not entirely address the problem of identifying a suitable contract. However, by taking into account Eq. (2), we can derive *bounds* for the contracts, such that

---

[2] Shared utility functions are widely employed in cooperative contexts [4], which is also the main focus of our research.

values of contract below the lower bound would have the same effect as the minimum contract itself, and the same for the upper bound.

The lower bound for contracts is:

$$\forall o \in \mathcal{O}_\tau, \ C^x_{\omega:\tau}(o) \geq \left\lfloor \left(\min_{e \in \mathcal{E}_\omega} Cost^\omega(e) \right) - \left(\max_{o \in \mathcal{O}_\tau} V^\omega(o) \right) \right\rfloor \tag{7}$$

Similarly, the upper bound is:

$$\forall o \in \mathcal{O}_\tau, \ C^x_{\omega:\tau}(o) \leq \left\lceil \left(\max_{e \in \mathcal{E}_\omega} Cost^\omega(e) \right) - \left(\min_{o \in \mathcal{O}_\tau} V^\omega(o) \right) \right\rceil \tag{8}$$

Given the bounds of Eqs. (7) and (8), let $\mathfrak{C}^x_{\omega:\tau} \subseteq C^x_{y:\tau}$ be the set of contracts that respect them.

Recall that our aim is to identify a suitable global contract given limited knowledge of the providers, taking into account the trade-off between (i) maximising the social utility, while (ii) minimising the (absolute value of) regret for the consumer.

Concerning (i), from Eq. (2) there is an inverse relationship between the likelihood of abstaining from accepting the task and the utility gained by the provider. This thus limits our search space, as we want to select a contract that is not likely to lead to an *abs* result. Concerning (ii), Eq. (5) suggests that minimising the chosen contract is correlated with minimising the (absolute value of the) regret as well. Let us notice that this requirement does not apply to contracts in general, rather regret minimization is enforced only in searching for a suitable contract given the representative agent. There might be situations where minimising the regret for the consumer is unnecessary: we will investigate them in future work.

Solving the following linear problem thus addresses the above two aims:

$$\min_{C^x_{\omega:\tau}} \sum_{o \in \mathcal{O}_\tau} C^x_{\omega:\tau}(o) \tag{9}$$

subject to

$$\sum_{o \in \mathcal{O}_\tau} C^x_{\omega:\tau}(o) \sum_{e \in \mathcal{E}_\omega} p^\omega(o \mid e) \geq$$
$$V^\omega(abs) - \left(\sum_{o \in \mathcal{O}_\tau} \sum_{e \in \mathcal{E}_\omega} (V^\omega(o) - Cost^\omega(e)) \right) \tag{10}$$

and

$$\forall o \in \mathcal{O}_\tau$$
$$C^x_{\omega:\tau}(o) \geq \left(\min_{e \in \mathcal{E}_\omega} Cost^\omega(e) \right) - \left(\max_{o \in \mathcal{O}_\tau} V^\omega(o) \right), \text{ and} \tag{11}$$
$$C^x_{\omega:\tau}(o) \leq \left(\max_{e \in \mathcal{E}_\omega} Cost^\omega(e) \right) - \left(\min_{o \in \mathcal{O}_\tau} V^\omega(o) \right)$$

and

$$\forall o_i, o_j \in \mathcal{O}_\tau \text{ s.t. } o_i \succ_o o_j, \ C^x_{\omega:\tau}(o_i) > C^x_{\omega:\tau}(o_j) \tag{12}$$

In particular, Eq. (9) seeks to minimise regret, while Eq. (10) constrains the search space to avoid abstentions. Equations (11) and (12) enforce the lower and upper bounds on the contract, as well as the fairness constraint respectively.

In [8] we show how the contract which provides a solution to the linear problem is a suitable—i.e., a trade-off between social utility and regret—approximation to the best solution obtained through exhaustive search.

3.2 Sampling the Society

Deriving a representative agent is a complex task. If there is no *a priori* knowledge to do so, then deriving it is itself an instance of the cold start problem. Therefore, we can adapt the idea of simple sampling discussed in Sect. 2.4 to the case of continuous data [9].

Let us assume the society $\mathcal{A}$ is distributed as a normal distribution $\mathcal{N}(\mu, \sigma)$ with mean μ and standard deviation σ. Given r the acceptable relative error, and α, the risk of being mislead by the sample, the size of the sample n required is as follows.

$$n_0 = \frac{t^2 \ S^2}{r^2 \ \mu^2}$$

Here $S^2 = \frac{\sum_{i=1}^{|\mathcal{A}|}(a_i - a_\mu)}{|\mathcal{A}|-1} \simeq \sigma^2$. If $\frac{n_0}{|\mathcal{A}|}$ is appreciable, $n = \frac{n_0}{1+\frac{n_0}{|\mathcal{A}|}}$ (cf. Eq. 6); otherwise $n = n_0$ [9].

It is worth noticing that we only sample $\mathcal{A}$, while the equations in Sect. 2.4 sample the space $\mathcal{A} \times \mathcal{C}$. In the following, $\mathcal{A}^r_\alpha$ identifies the sampled space of agents with r relative error and α the risk of being mistaken; $\widehat{\omega}^r_\alpha$ identifies the representative agent derived from simple sampling of $\mathcal{A}^r_\alpha$.

4   Global Contract for Cold Start Problem

In the previous section we described how a suitable contract can be found given some knowledge of a society. We now turn our attention to searching for such a contract given no prior information about the society. This is therefore an example of the cold start problem [25], wherein we seek to identify a suitable contract to be used in PAT with minimal information about the providers.

4.1 Searching for Non-abstaining Contracts

According to Eq. (2), given a contract $C^x_{y:\tau}$ a provider will abstain from performing the task τ if doing so will increase its expected utility. In such cases, it is necessary to increment $C^x_{y:\tau}$ towards a "better" (to the provider) fair contract.

Algorithm 1. Increment Contracts

---

contractIncrement$(C_{y:\tau}^x)$

1: **Input:** $C_{y:\tau}^x$ a valid contract
2: **Output:** $\overline{C_{y:\tau}^x}$ an incremented contract
3: $\overline{C_{y:\tau}^x} := C_{\omega:\tau}^x$
4: **for** $o_i \in \langle o_1, \ldots, o_n \rangle$ s.t. $\forall j, k, j > k, o_j \succ_o o_k$ **do**
5:     **if** $o_i = o_1$ **then**
6:         $\overline{C_{y:\tau}^x}(o_i) = \overline{C_{y:\tau}^x}(o_i) + 1$
7:     **else**
8:         **if** $\overline{C_{y:\tau}^x}(o_{i-1}) = \overline{C_{y:\tau}^x}(o_i)$ **then**
9:             $\overline{C_{y:\tau}^x}(o_i) := \overline{C_{y:\tau}^x}(o_i) + 1$
10:         **end if**
11:     **end if**
12: **end for**
13: **return** $\overline{C_{y:\tau}^x}$

To this end, Algorithm 1 defines the **contractIncrement** procedure which returns the closest higher fair contract $\overline{C_{y:\tau}^x}$ of an contract $C_{y:\tau}^x$ given as input.

At line 3 of Algorithm 1, **contractIncrement** copies the value of $C_{y:\tau}^x$ to $\overline{C_{y:\tau}^x}$; at line 6 it increments the value of the contract for the worst outcome $\overline{C_{y:\tau}^x}(o_1)$. Then, for each other outcome o_i in the sequence induced by the ordering function $\succ_o$, **contractIncrement** checks if $\overline{C_{y:\tau}^x}(o_{i-1}) = \overline{C_{y:\tau}^x}(o_i)$ (line 8). If this is the case, $\overline{C_{y:\tau}^x}(o_i)$ is also incremented to ensure fairness.

The following proposition proves that there are no other contracts "smaller" than $\overline{C_{y:\tau}^x} = $ **contractIncrement**$(C_{y:\tau}^x)$ but "greater" than $C_{y:\tau}^x$. Therefore, $\overline{C_{y:\tau}^x}$ is the closest of the contracts (in terms of increments necessary within them) that are more convenient (for the provider) than $C_{y:\tau}^x$.

Proposition 1. *Given a contract $C_{y:\tau}^x$, and $\overline{C_{y:\tau}^x} = $* **contractIncrement**$(C_{y:\tau}^x)$, *it is the case that $\forall o \in \mathcal{O}_\tau \,\, \nexists \widehat{C_{y:\tau}^x} \in \mathfrak{C}_{y:\tau}^x \setminus \{C_{y:\tau}^x, \overline{C_{y:\tau}^x}\}$ s.t. $C_{y:\tau}^x(o) < \widehat{C_{y:\tau}^x}(o) < \overline{C_{y:\tau}^x}(o)$.*

Proof. Let assume that $\exists \widehat{C_{y:\tau}^x}$ s.t. $C_{y:\tau}^x(o) < \widehat{C_{y:\tau}^x}(o) < \overline{C_{y:\tau}^x}(o)$ for some $o \in \mathcal{O}_\tau$.

If $o = o_1$, from line 6 of Algorithm 1 $\widehat{C_{y:\tau}^x} = \overline{C_{y:\tau}^x}$, *quod est absurdum.*

If $o = o_i, i > 1$, without loss of generality let us assume $\overline{C_{y:\tau}^x}(i) = C_{y:\tau}^x(o_i) + 1 = C_{y:\tau}^x(o_i) + 2$. From l. 9 of Algorithm 1, this implies that $C_{y:\tau}^x(o_i) = C_{y:\tau}^x(o_i) + 1$, *quod est absurdum.* □

While Algorithm 1 derives more convenient (for the provider) contracts, Algorithm 2 implements the sound and complete procedure **hillC** for computing the distance of a given contract $C_{y:\tau}^x$ from the closest contract which is more convenient (for the provider) than abstaining from performing the given task.

hillC requires as input the provider y, and a contract $C_{y:\tau}^x$. It returns the number of interactions needed to ensure that y will not abstain. At line 3 it

---

Algorithm 2. Hill-Climbing Contracts

hillC$(y, C^x_{y:\tau})$
  1: **Input:** $y \in \mathcal{A}, C^x_{y:\tau}$ a valid contract
  2: **Output:** S the number of iterations to non-abstain behaviour
  3: $S := 0$
  4: **while** $delegate(\tau, y, C^x_{y:\tau}) = abs$ **do**
  5:     $S := S + 1$
  6:     $C^x_{y:\tau} := \textbf{contractIncrement}(C^x_{y:\tau})$
  7: **end while**
  8: **return** S

---

initialises the variable S which stores the number of interactions with y. Such a variable is incremented (l. 5) every time the delegation process returns abs.[3] In such a case, the contract is incremented (l. 6) using the function **contractIncrement** (Algorithm 1).

The following proposition proves that **hillC** (Algorithm 2) is complete and sound.

Proposition 2. *Algorithm 2 is sound and complete.*

Proof. Immediate from Proposition 1 and Eq. (2).   □

4.2 Experimental Hypotheses

The procedure **hillC** takes a contract as input: determining which contract to use first is the essence of the cold start problem. For the purpose of this work, we compare the following possible initial contracts:

- $C^x_{y:\tau \downarrow \text{global}}$ s.t. $\forall o \in \mathcal{O}_\tau, C^x_{y:\tau \downarrow \text{global}}(o) = C^x_{\omega:\tau}(o)$, where $C^x_{\omega:\tau}$ is a solution to the linear problem of Eqs. (9–12). We denote $C^x_{y:\tau \downarrow \text{global}}$ as GLOBAL. In the following, to show the robustness of our approach, we assume that the capabilities of the representative agents are uniformly perturbed by up to 0.2 from the average.
- $C^x_{y:\tau \downarrow \text{globalS}}$ s.t. $\forall o \in \mathcal{O}_\tau, C^x_{y:\tau \downarrow \text{globalS}}(o) = C^x_{\widetilde{\omega}^r_\alpha:\tau}(o)$, where $C^x_{\omega:\tau}$ is a solution to the linear problem of Eqs. (9–12). We denote $C^x_{y:\tau \downarrow \text{globalS}}$ as GLOBALsample. We considered $\alpha = 0.05$, and $d = 0.20$.

We compare these two contracts to three contracts capturing existing approaches to dealing with the cold start problem.

- $C^x_{y:\tau \downarrow \min}$ s.t. $\forall o \in \mathcal{O}_\tau, C^x_{y:\tau \downarrow \min}(o) = \min_{C^x_{y:\tau}} C^x_{y:\tau}(o)$ according to Eq. (7). We denote $C^x_{y:\tau \downarrow \min}$ as MIN;

---

[3] We admit a small abuse of notation: formally *delegate* returns a tuple of two elements. In this case we silently assume that returns only the first element of such a tuple, namely the outcome of task τ or *abs*.

- $C^x_{y:\tau \downarrow \mathrm{rand}}$ s.t. $\forall o \in \mathcal{O}_\tau, C^x_{y:\tau \downarrow \mathrm{rand}}(o) = \mathrm{rand}$, where rand is a random number between 0 and 1 derived from an uniform distribution. We denote $C^x_{y:\tau \downarrow \mathrm{rand}}$ as RANDOM;

- $C^x_{y:\tau \downarrow \mathrm{S}}$ s.t. $\forall o \in \mathcal{O}_\tau, C^x_{y:\tau \downarrow \mathrm{S}}(o) = \min_{C^x_{y:\tau} \in \hat{\mathcal{C}}} C^x_{y:\tau}(o)$ according to Eq. (7). We denote $C^x_{y:\tau \downarrow \mathrm{S}}$ as CONTRACTsample. We considered $\alpha = 0.05$, and $d = 0.20$.

Our experimental hypotheses are:

I1: on average, the procedure **hillC** invoked on GLOBAL and GLOBALsample (the contracts derived from the representative agent resp. without or with a sampling activity) will require a minor number of interactions to converge to a non-abstaining contract than if it is invoked on, in order, CONTRACTsample, RANDOM, **hillC**(MIN);

I2: GLOBAL and GLOBALsample are more robust with respect to changes of network structure and distribution of competencies in the network.

4.3 Experimental Settings

We ran a set of experiments to evaluate the hypotheses, as detailed below. For all experiments, we used the following base settings. $\mathcal{O}_\tau = \{o_1, o_2\}$ s.t. $o_2 \succ_o o_1$. $V(o_1) = -10$, $V(o_2) = 50$, and $V(abs) = 0$. $\mathcal{E}_\tau = \{e_1, e_2, e_3\}$ s.t. $e_3 \succ_e e_2$, $e_2 \succ_e e_1$, and $Cost(e_1) = 10$, $Cost(e_2) = 15$, $Cost(e_3) = 20$.

Our system consisted of three agent types $(\mathcal{G}_1, \mathcal{G}_2, \mathcal{G}_3)$, described in Table 1. We considered societies of 100 agents. While we evaluated different topologies (namely fully connected; random [10] and scale-free [1], our results were virtually identical, and we therefore discuss and show only the random case.

Finally, we utilised three distributions of agent competencies, aimed at reflecting different types of competences within different societies. These values were picked so as to be sufficiently variable to reflect these differences in societies. Respectively, these are the *poor*, *uniform* and *highly* competent societies. Table 2 describes the three distributions.

Table 1. Agents grouped by competencies

	$\mathcal{G}_1$	$\mathcal{G}_2$	$\mathcal{G}_3$
$p^g(o_1 \mid e_1)$	0.80	0.75	0.70
$p^g(o_1 \mid e_2)$	0.60	0.55	0.50
$p^g(o_1 \mid e_3)$	0.40	0.40	0.20
$p^g(o_2 \mid e_1)$	0.20	0.25	0.30
$p^g(o_2 \mid e_2)$	0.40	0.45	0.50
$p^g(o_2 \mid e_3)$	0.40	0.60	0.80

Table 2. Distribution of competencies in the network

Competence	$p(a \in \mathcal{G}_1)$	$p(a \in \mathcal{G}_2)$	$p(a \in \mathcal{G}_3)$
Poor	0.6	0.3	0.1
Uniform	$\frac{1}{3}$	$\frac{1}{3}$	$\frac{1}{3}$
High	0.1	0.3	0.6

For each configuration (distribution of competencies), we generated 10 different societies (s0–s9) and evaluated each of them 50 times.

Simulations have been programmed using Java 1.6 using parallel computing for reducing the overall execution time.[4] Indeed experiments exploited the Aberdeen Maxwell High Performance Computing Cluster which is composed by 40 nodes, each with two 8 or 12-core Xeon E5 processors and 256 GB of RAM. For each simulation we reserved 512 MBytes of RAM. We used LPSolve[5] as solver for the linear programs which arise during the simulations.

4.4   Experimental Evaluation

Figures 1, 2, and 3 qualitatively depict the results of our experiments: each figure refers to a single distribution of competencies. Figure 1 illustrates our results for poor competence societies, Fig. 2 for uniform competence, and Fig. 3 for high competence. As mentioned above, we observed that the network topology has a little impact on the results and therefore focus on random networks only.

For each configuration, for each society, Figs. 1, 2, and 3 show average and standard deviation—over the 50 explorations for each society, and over the agents in the society—of the number of steps needed to find a contract with no abstaining results when the starting contract is GLOBAL, GLOBALsample, MIN, RANDOM, or CONTRACTsample. Although it is not always the case that these values are normally distributed, we chose to represent average and standard deviation for qualitative purposes.

These results have been proven statistically significant using the Wilcoxon Signed-Rank Test (WSRT) [29] ($p < 0.01$). From Figs. 1, 2, and 3 it is clear that our hypotheses are satisfied. With respect to hypothesis $I1$, the average of **hillC**(MIN) is the highest in any configuration and for any society. On average, values of **hillC**(RANDOM) are always smaller than **hillC**(MIN), and **hillC**(CONTRACTsample) is smaller that both of them. We also perturbed the representative agent by up to 0.2 to evaluate the resilience of the generated contract. In such a situation, **hillC**(GLOBAL) is almost always the smallest, and barely distinguishable from **hillC**(GLOBALsample). This is particularly true when the competencies are distributed uniformly, Fig. 2, or society is highly competent (Fig. 3).

---

[4] The code can be found at the URL https://sourceforge.net/projects/global-approximations-pat/.

[5] https://sourceforge.net/projects/lpsolve/.

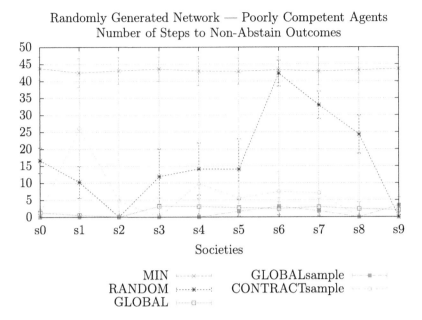

Fig. 1. Average steps and standard deviation necessary to find a contract which avoids abstaining: poorly competent agents

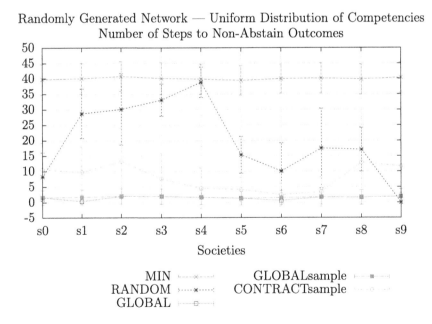

Fig. 2. Average steps and standard deviation necessary to find a contract which avoids abstaining: uniform distribution of competencies

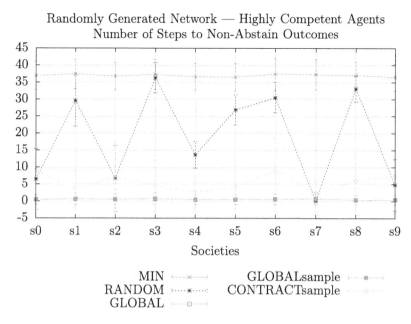

Fig. 3. Average steps and standard deviation necessary to find a contract which avoids abstaining: highly competent agents

Regarding hypothesis $I2$, it is worth noting that the distribution of competencies has an effect on **hillC**(MIN) which varies in the range $[32, 47]$, where 32 is the minimum in the case of highly competent societies, and 47 is the maximum in poorly competent societies: the poorer the agents in terms of competencies, the higher the (average) value of **hillC**(MIN). In contrast, both **hillC**(GLOBAL) and **hillC**(GLOBALsample) returns values that are always in the range $[0, 8]$, independent of the configuration and the societies. This suggests that $I2$ is also verified by this set of experiments.

In order to test the robustness of our approach, we also perturbed the competencies of the representative agent by adding uniform noise in intervals of 0.05 between 0 and 0.25 for each $p^g(o \mid e)$. In 53 % of cases—80 % between uniformly distributed and highly competent agents—they lead to non-significant results ($p > 0.01$) according to the Kruskal-Wallis test [17]. Only in the case of poorly competent agents were these perturbations always significant. This supports our previous analysis regarding the robustness of our approach and the good performance obtained.

5   Conclusions and Future Work

In this paper, we propose techniques to identifying an approximate contract, to be used by consumers before they have obtained sufficient information to craft a specific contract for interactions with providers within the system. This contract provides a trade-off between social utility and regret, and is identified by solving a linear optimisation problem. Our work addresses an instance of the cold-start problem. We evaluated our approach empirically, comparing it to existing cold-start mitigation techniques, and found that our heuristic GLOBAL is robust over different network topologies and provider competencies; furthermore, in its GLOBALsample version, it is also computationally efficient, sampling only a small subset of agents within the system. Finally, it allows agents to converge to contracts which minimise the level of abstention with fewer interactions than heuristics derived from existing cold-start mitigation techniques.

In the empirical evaluation presented in this paper we considered binary task outcomes and discrete domains. Though this covers many situations where an agent is concerned only with the success or failure of the task, there are situations where a more fine-grained set of outcomes should be considered. For instance, in the context of information sharing, an *information consumer* might pay more for higher quality data from *information providers*. To represent these situations we plan to adapt the formalisms presented in [3,27], where the authors discuss a framework for information sharing with different levels of quality within a multi-agent system. Moreover, our approach can be integrated with Carmel and Markovitch [7] to improve the effectiveness of their strategies for explorations.

Moreover, considering (potentially infinite) sets of outcomes and efforts would allow us to integrate our work with trust and reputation systems (e.g., [14,15,28]). We envision that an agent, on entering the system, would use the mechanisms described in the current work, but as it gains experience, would transition to utilising its trust and reputation mechanism to identify optimal contracts (c.f., [6]).

Acknowledgments. We thank the anonymous reviewers for their helpful comments.

Research was sponsored by US Army Research laboratory and the UK Ministry of Defence and was accomplished under Agreement Number W911NF-06-3-0001. The views and conclusions contained in this document are those of the authors and should not be interpreted as representing the official policies, either expressed or implied, of the US Army Research Laboratory, the U.S. Government, the UK Ministry of Defense, or the UK Government. The US and UK Governments are authorized to reproduce and distribute reprints for Government purposes notwithstanding any copyright notation hereon.

This work was performed using the Maxwell High Performance Computing Cluster of the University of Aberdeen IT Service (http://www.abdn.ac.uk/staffnet/research/research-computing), provided by Dell Inc. and supported by Alces Software.

References

1. Barabasi, A.L., Albert, R.: Emergence of scaling in random networks. Science **286**(5439), 11 (1999). http://arxiv.org/abs/cond-mat/9910332
2. Beckett, N.E., Park, B.: Use of category versus individuating information: making base rates salient. Pers. Soc. Psychol. Bull. **21**(1), 21–31 (1995). http://psp.sagepub.com/content/21/1/21.refs

3. Bisdikian, C., Tang, Y., Cerutti, F., Oren, N.: A framework for using trust to assess risk in information sharing. In: Chesñevar, C.I., Onaindia, E., Ossowski, S., Vouros, G. (eds.) AT 2013. LNCS, vol. 8068, pp. 135–149. Springer, Heidelberg (2013). http://link.springer.com/content/pdf/10.10072F978-3-642-39860-5_11.pdf

4. Boella, G., Damiano, R., Lesmo, L.: Cooperation and group utility. In: Jennings, N., Lesprance, Y. (eds.) Intelligent Agents VI. LNCS, vol. 1757, pp. 319–333. Springer, Berlin Heidelberg (2000)

5. Burnett, C., Norman, T.J., Sycara, K.: Bootstrapping trust evaluations through stereotypes. In: Proceedings of the 9th International Conference on Autonomous Agents and Multiagent Systems, pp. 241–248, May 2010. http://dl.acm.org/citation.cfm?id=1838206.1838240

6. Burnett, C., Norman, T.J., Sycara, K.: Trust decision-making in multi-agent systems. In: Proceedings of the Twenty-Second International Joint Conference on Artificial Intelligence —IJCAI 2011, pp. 115–120. AAAI Press (2011). http://dl.acm.org/citation.cfm?id=2283396.2283417

7. Carmel, D., Markovitch, S.: Exploration strategies for model-based learning in multi-agent systems: exploration strategies. Auton. Agents Multi-agent Syst. **2**(2), 141–172 (1999)

8. Cerutti, F., Oren, N., Burnett, C.: Global approximations for principal agent theory. In: Proceedings of the 14th International Conference on Autonomous Agents and Multiagent Systems (AAMAS 2015), pp. 1845–1846 (2015). http://aamas2015.com/en/AAMAS_2015_USB/aamas/p1845.pdf

9. Cochran, W.G.: Sampling Techniques, 3rd edn. Wiley Inc, New York (1977)

10. Erdös, P., Rényi, A.: On random graphs. I. Publ. Math. Debrecen **6**, 290–297 (1959)

11. Grossman, S.J., Hart, O.D.: An analysis of the principal-agent problem. Econometrica: J. Econometric Soc. **51**(1), 7–45 (1983)

12. Hilton, J.L., von Hippel, W.: Stereotypes. Ann. Rev. Psychol. **47**, 237–271 (1996). http://www.annualreviews.org//abs/10.1146/annurev.psych.47.1.237

13. Holmstrom, B.R., Tirole, J.: The theory of the firm. Handb. Ind. Organ. **1**, 61–133 (1989)

14. Jøsang, A., Ismail, R.: The Beta reputation system. In: Proceedings of 15th Bled Electronic Commerce Conference (2002)

15. Kamvar, S.D., Schlosser, M.T., Garcia-Molina, H.: The eigentrust algorithm for reputation management in P2P networks. In: Proceedings of the 12th International Conference on World Wide Web, pp. 640–651. ACM (2003)

16. Karimi, R., Freudenthaler, C., Nanopoulos, A., Schmidt-Thieme, L.: Active learning for aspect model in recommender systems. In: 2011 IEEE Symposium on Computational Intelligence and Data Mining, pp. 162–167 (2011). http://ieeexplore.ieee.org/lpdocs/epic03/wrapper.htm?arnumber=5949431

17. Kruskal, W.H., Wallis, W.A.: Use of ranks in one-criterion variance analysis. J. Am. Stat. Assoc. **47**(260), 583–621 (1952). http://www.jstor.org/stable/2280779

18. Marsa-Maestre, I., Klein, M., Jonker, C.M., Aydoan, R.: From problems to protocols: towards a negotiation handbook. Decis. Support Syst. **60**, 39–54 (2014). http://www.sciencedirect.com/science/article/pii/S016792361300167X

19. Meneguzzi, F., Miles, S., Luck, M., Holt, C., Smith, M.: Electronic contracting in aircraft aftercare: a case study. In: Proceedings of the 7th International Conference on Autonomous Agents and Multiagent Systems – AAMAS 2008, pp. 63–70. International Foundation for Autonomous Agents and Multiagent Systems (2008). http://dl.acm.org/citation.cfm?id=1402795.1402807

20. Miles, S., Groth, P., Oren, N., Luck, M.: Handling mitigating circumstances for electronic contracts. In: Proceedings of the 7th European Workshop on Multi-Agent Systems (2009)
21. Miller, G.J., Whitford, A.B.: Trust and incentives in principal-agent negotiations: the 'Insurance/Incentive Trade-Off'. J. Theor. Politics **14**(2), 231–267 (2002). http://jtp.sagepub.com/content/14/2/231.abstract
22. Peterson, M.: An Introduction to Decision Theory. Cambridge University Press, Cambridge (2009). http://dx.doi.org/10.1017/CBO9780511800917
23. Popescul, A., Pennock, D.M., Lawrence, S.: Probabilistic models for unified collaborative and content-based recommendation in sparse-data environments. In: Proceedings of the Seventeenth Conference on Uncertainty in Artificial Intelligence, pp. 437–444. Morgan Kaufmann Publishers Inc. (2001)
24. Provost, F., Melville, P., Saar-Tsechansky, M.: Data acquisition and cost-effective predictive modeling. In: Proceedings of the Ninth International Conference on Electronic Commerce, p. 389, New York, USA (2007). http://dl.acm.org/citation.cfm?id=1282100.1282172
25. Schein, A.I., Popescul, A., Ungar, L.H., Pennock, D.M.: Methods and metrics for cold-start recommendations. In: Proceedings of the 25th International ACM SIGIR Conference on Research and Development in Information Retrieval, p. 253, New York, USA (2002) http://dl.acm.org/citation.cfm?id=564376.564421
26. Schmidt, S., Steele, R., Dillon, T.S., Chang, E.: Fuzzy trust evaluation and credibility development in multi-agent systems. Appl. Soft Comput. **7**(2), 492–505 (2007). http://www.sciencedirect.com/science/article/pii/S1568494606000755
27. Tang, Y., Cerutti, F., Oren, N., Bisdikian, C.: Reasoning about the impacts of information sharing. Inf. Syst. Front. J. **17**(4), 725–742 (2014). http://link.springer.com/article/10.1007%2Fs10796-014-9521-6
28. Teacy, W.T.L., Patel, J., Jennings, N.R., Luck, M.: TRAVOS: trust and reputation in the context of inaccurate information sources. Auton. Agents Multi-agent Syst. **12**(2), 183–198 (2006). http://link.springer.com/10.1007/s10458-006-5952-x
29. Wilcoxon, F.: Individual comparisons by ranking methods. Biometrics Bull. **1**(6), 80–83 (1945)

Simulating Normative Behaviour in Multi-agent Environments Using Monitoring Artefacts

Stephan Chang and Felipe Meneguzzi[✉]

School of Computer Science, Pontifical Catholic University of Rio Grande do Sul,
Porto Alegre, Brazil
stephan.chang@acad.pucrs.br, felipe.meneguzzi@pucrs.br

Abstract. Norms are an efficient way of controlling the behaviour of agents while still allowing agent autonomy. While there are tools for programming Multi-Agent Systems, few provide an explicit mechanism for simulating norm-based behaviour using a variety of normative representations. In this paper, we develop an artefact-based mechanism for norm processing, monitoring and enforcement and show its implementation as a framework built with CArtAgO. Our framework is then empirically demonstrated using a variety of enforcement settings.

1 Introduction

Multi-Agent Systems are often used as a tool for simulating interactions between intelligent entities within societies, organisations or other communities. This Agent-based Simulation is useful for studying social behaviour in hypothetical situations or situations that may not be easily reproduced in the real world. The entities being simulated, human or otherwise, are represented by programmable intelligent agents, which must present reactive, pro-active and social behaviour [1].

When working with social simulations, we must consider that agents should be free to act in their own best interest, even though their actions might produce negative effects to other agents. For this reason, we establish rules that (1) prohibit actions that harm the society's performance; (2) oblige actions that maintain the society's well being; and (3) permit actions that can be beneficial to society, but never harmful. These rules, referred to as "norms" in multi-agent environments, allow agents to reason and act freely, while still being subject to punishment in the event that a norm is violated [2]. Although the purpose of norms is to mediate the interactions of agents in an environment, sometimes violating a norm can prove advantageous for an agent due to the reward of violation compensating for the penalties of detection. Existing work on normative reasoning [3–10] try to explore the trade-offs between compliance and non-compliance and propose new ways in which agents see and reason about norms. Still, there is no available tool that simulates norm-based behaviour to serve as a common ground for benchmarking implementations of normative behaviour and reasoning. In norm-based behaviour simulations we must define data structures for the various types of norms, including at least one of prohibitions, permissions or

© Springer International Publishing Switzerland 2016
V. Dignum et al. (Eds.): COIN 2015, LNAI 9628, pp. 59–77, 2016.
DOI: 10.1007/978-3-319-42691-4_4

obligations. Once these norms are active, agent interactions shall be observed by a monitoring mechanism and analysed by a norm-enforcing agent, which will then punish agents caught violating norms.

Although there are multiple frameworks that can be used to simulate agent societies, such as the MASSim [11] simulators, or the agent programming languages Jason [12] and JADE [13], relatively less attention has been focused on frameworks for norm-based behaviour simulation [14, Chap. 1]. In this paper, we bridge this gap by developing a scalable norm processing mechanism that performs monitoring and enforcement in multi-agent environments. Our contributions are a mechanism to monitor agents actions in an environment, described in Sect. 4.5 and a mechanism for norm maintenance and enforcement, described in Sect. 4.6. In Sect. 5 we demonstrate the functionality of our mechanism using an empirical experiment applying our mechanism to a Multi-Agent System.

2   Simulating Multi-agent Societies

When self-interested intelligent agents [1] share an environment, competition between them becomes inevitable [15]. This idea becomes clear when we think of multi-agent systems as societies. Each person in a society has their own goals and plans to achieve them, and it is in their best interest to do so by spending as little effort as possible. Take for an example a person interested in eating an apple and another interested in selling one. For the buying person, its goal is to acquire the apple from the seller for the lowest cost possible, preferably with no cost at all. For the seller, the goal is to sell the apple for as high a price as affordable by the buyer, maybe even higher than that. Now, considering that in this hypothetical world no notion of ethics is known yet, the buyer soon realizes that instead of paying for the apple he wants to eat, he could simply grab it and eat it on the spot.

Competition between agents is often intended when working with agent-based simulations, as we desire to see how agents perform under such circumstances. However, to prevent the system as a whole from descending into chaos, we must establish rules in order to control agent interactions while still allowing them to be autonomous. Nevertheless these rules must be limited to directing agents, rather than restraining them, otherwise, much of the benefit from autonomous agents is lost. When rules are set, agents that disregard them are subject to punishment for potentially harming the environment. In our buyer/seller system, we could establish a rule that guarantees items sold at shops must be paid for. If one is caught stealing, it will need to pay for the seller's injury. By doing so, we allow the buyer to reason about the advantages and disadvantages of obeying rules, letting it decide on an appropriate action plan. In multi-agent systems, we refer to these rules as norms.

Usual mechanisms for controlling agent interactions include interaction models, used by simulators such as NetLogo [16], MASON [17] and Repast [18]; strategies, commonly used in Game Theory; and organisation-oriented normative systems, such as $\mathcal{M}$oise [19]. The disadvantage of these methodologies is that agents are constrained to the rules of their environment. They are not allowed to break rules because the system is rule-compliant by design, also known as the regimentation approach [20]. However, unlike environmental constraints, perfect enforcement (regimentation) of social norms is unrealistic and undesirable, because it prevents occasional violations that would bring about a greater good [6,21].

3   Normative Scenario - Immigration Agents

To facilitate explanation and exemplification of our approach, as well as to highlight its capabilities, we present the scenario we use to test our mechanism. This scenario helps understand what norms are and how they control interactions in an environment. First, we present a short story that connects the environment to its agents, then we outline the norms that constrain them.

The government of a fictional emerging nation[1] started an immigration program to accelerate development through the hiring of foreigners. The country welcomes visitors, besides landed immigrants, to the country, since money from tourism greatly boosts the local economy. At the border, immigration officers must inspect immigrant passports. The foreigner acceptance policy is quite straightforward, and immigration agents must immediately accept immigrants with valid passports and no criminal records, and reject John Does and refugees outright. The government believes that the more immigrants it accepts, the better. Each officer's responsibility is to accept as many immigrants as possible, while still following the guidelines that were passed to them. Each accepted able worker nets the officer 5 credits, which eventually turn into a bonus to the officer's salary. There are no rewards for rejecting immigrants. It becomes clear that the bonus each officer accumulates depends entirely on chance, and some officers may accumulate more than others, if at all. As such, some officers might feel inclined to accept immigrants they should not, only to add to their personal gain.

To ensure officers act on the best interests of the nation only, the government introduced an enforcement system to the offices at the borders. Among the officers working in the immigration office, one is responsible for observing and recording the behaviour of those working in booths. This officer is known as the "monitor". His job is to write reports about what the officers do and send these reports to another officer, known as the "enforcer". The enforcer then reads the reports that are passed to him and look for any inconsistencies, such as the approval of an illegal immigrant. As this represents a violation of a rule, or norm, the enforcer then carries out an action to sanction the offending officer. The penalties for approving an illegal immigrant are the immediate loss of 10 credits and suspension of work activities for up to 10 s. Considering that immigrants arrive at a rate of 1 per 2 s, in a 10-s timespan 5 immigrants would have arrived at a given booth, meaning that a violating officer potentially loses 25 credits. Added to the other portion of the sanction, the potential loss rises up to 35 credits.

---

[1] Inspired by the game "Papers, please": http://papersplea.se.

The enforcement system, however, is not cost free. Each monitor and enforcer has an associated cost and it is within the interests of the nation to spend as little as possible with such a system. Therefore, the government wants to know how intensive the system must be to cover enough cases of disobedience so that officers will know violating norms is a disadvantage rather than an advantage.

There are two norms that can be extracted from this scenario, which we define in Examples 1 and 2. Later, in Sect. 4.3, we develop the formal representation of norms in our system and proceed to formally defining these norms. These norms concern the stability of the immigration program by assuring valid immigrants are accepted and discouraging corrupt officers to accept those who should not be.

Example 1. "All immigrants holding valid passports must be accepted. Failure to comply may result in the loss of 5 credits."

Example 2. "All immigrants holding passports that are not valid must not be accepted. Failure to comply may result in the loss of 10 credits and suspension from work activities for up to 10 s."

4   NormMAS Framework

In this section, we develop our monitoring and enforcement framework for normative agents. We start with an outline of the main components in our framework in Sect. 4.1. We them review the agent and environment-based approaches we use in our implementation in Sect. 4.2. Sections 4.3 and 4.4 describe the formalisation of norms and actions we adopt. With these formalisation covered, we explain how monitoring and enforcement work in Subsects. 4.5 and 4.6, respectively.

4.1   Architecture Overview

To allow the reader to better understand this section, we first offer an overview of the architecture envisioned by our work. We illustrate this architecture in Fig. 1, which shows the main elements that compose our framework and their interactions. These elements can be divided into three groups: *agents*, *environment* and *external*.

The *agents* group is self-explanatory, and it is where we put the agents that we are using for simulation and for monitoring/enforcement tasks. The "Simulation Agent Programs" are the agent programs which are simulating the behaviour we wish to study, in this case our immigration officers. "Monitor Agents" are agent programs which observe the actions performed by the simulation agent programs and "Enforcer Agents" make the decision of whether these actions violate some norm or not.

The *environment* group is composed of the elements that define what an environment is like. In our case, our environment is not a centralised entity, but a collection of artefacts through which agents interact. For example, monitor agents use the "Reporting Interface Artefact" to file reports for enforcer agents to analyse, as if they were actually putting reports in a pile over the enforcer agent's desk. As we describe in the next subsection, this approach makes programming the environment easier by separating responsibilities among different artefacts, instead of concentrating actions in a single environment description. The types of artefacts in this group should include all types pertaining to the simulation context, *e.g.* immigration booths for passport reviewing; and three fixed types that are part of our framework: the *reporting artefact*, the *monitoring artefact* and the *normative artefact*. These artefacts are used exclusively by monitoring and enforcement agents to perform tasks of the normative context, the exception being the Normative Artefact, which should be accessible to agents interested in observing normative events. Normative events include the creation, activation, deactivation and destruction of norms and the emission of sanctions to violating agents.

The *external* group is where we keep the elements that are auxiliary to our framework, and although not considered autonomous agents are also not part of the environment. Currently, this group contains the Action History, a structure in which we store actions for normative analysis, and the Normative Base, a database of established norms. In the following subsections we discuss each of these groups in more detail.

4.2   Jason and CArtAgO

In order to show the feasibility of the mechanism proposed in this paper, we use two programming approaches: agent-oriented programming and environment-oriented programming. The former is provided by the Jason interpreter [12], while the latter is achieved with the Common Artifact infrastructure for Agents Open environments (CArtAgO) [22].

Jason provides us with the means to program agents using the *AgentSpeak* language [23] in a Java environment. Agents are built with the BDI [24] architecture, and so their behaviour is directed by beliefs, goals and plans. Beliefs are logical predicates that represent an agent's considerations towards its environment. Predicates such as `valid(Passport)` and `wallet(50,dollars)` indicate that the agent believes the given passport variable is valid and that his wallet currently contains 50 dollars. In *AgentSpeak* variables start with an upper-case letter, while constants start with lower-case.

Goals are states that the agent desires to fulfil, and these can be either *achievement goals* or *test goals*. Achievement goals are objectives or milestones that agents pursue when carrying out their duties. To represent these in *AgentSpeak*, the goal's name is preceded by the '!' character. Test goals are questions an agent may ask about the current state of the environment. These can be identified by a '?' preceding the goal's name.

To achieve these goals, agents need to perform sequences of actions that modify the environment towards the desired states. This sequence of actions is referred to as a *plan* [25]. A plan is not necessarily composed solely of actions, however, it can also contain sub-plans. This allows complex behaviours to be built, creating flows of actions that vary and are influenced by agent beliefs and perceptions.

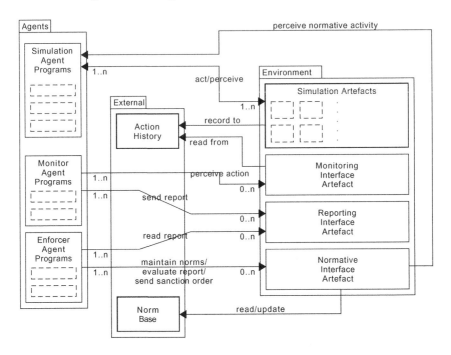

Fig. 1. Components of the NormMAS framework and their interactions.

As with any other programmed system, multi-agent systems must be tested before being effectively deployed to their end environments. To do so, test environments can be programmed for agents to be observed and any faulty behaviour addressed before release. Jason allows the programming of test environments in Java language, by providing an interface between agents and the programmed environment. These environments, however, are centralised, and so they are meant for small systems or specific test scenarios. This hinders scalability, which is an important aspect to consider when working with complex, more realistic scenarios or simply more robust structures. To address this limitation, we use the CArtAgO framework for environment programming.

In CArtAgO, environments are not seen as a centralised domain description, but as a distribution of observable properties and operations among artefacts. These artefacts represent objects in the environment through which agents interact with one another indirectly, *e.g.* a table in an office, on which an agent may stack reports for another agent to pick these reports up and read them. The artefact model is useful because it groups operations according to a context, so it is not only easier to understand the environment model, but also to maintain it. Agents can create and destroy artefacts at their convenience, and should new operations be needed for a new feature in the MAS, it can be done by adding new artefacts, instead of changing existing routines to conform to new protocols. This approach is also more scalable, as one of the basic features of CArtAgO is that it can distribute artefacts among workspaces. Workspaces are artefact containers that can be configured in several nodes in a network, eliminating the need to concentrate the environment on a single machine. In our work, we use artefacts for offering monitoring and enforcement tasks to agents, and we refer to these artefacts as "normative artefacts". These normative artefacts are shared between normative agents so that more monitors and enforcers may be added to the system as it scales up.

4.3 Norms

In order to keep competition between agents manageable a designer creates norms to direct agent behaviour and maintain environment stability. This is achieved by specifying obligations and prohibitions [6]. Here, obligations are behaviours that agents must follow in a given context to comply with the norm, and prohibitions behaviours that jeopardise the environment's stability, and so must be avoided. Violating prohibitions is just as harmful as violating obligations, hence both cases must be addressed when detected. We expect that, when agents are punished for transgression, they are able to learn not to misbehave. Examples 1 and 2, in Sect. 3, correspond to an obligation and a prohibition, respectively.

While norms in the real world are expressed in natural language, they must be translated to a multi-agent environment so that agents are able to reason about them. This requires the extraction of necessary information related to a norm and composition of a mathematical representation. Agents should not have to reason how or why a certain norm came to be, but rather what the norm is about and what are the consequences of violating it. The format can also be extended to include other important information, such as the sanction function associated with a norm's violation, or the conditions for automatic activation and expiration of the norm [6]. In this paper, norms as specified according to the tuple of Definition 1.

Definition 1. *A norm is represented by the tuple* $\mathcal{N} = \langle \mu, \kappa, \chi, \tau, \rho \rangle$, *where:*

- $\mu \in \{obligation, prohibition\}$ *represents the norm's modality.*
- $\kappa \in \{action, state\}$ *represents the type of trigger condition enclosed.*
- χ *represents the set of states (context) to which a norm applies.*
- τ *represents the norm's trigger condition.*
- ρ *represents the sanction to be applied to violating agents.*

Using Definition 1, we can proceed to formalising the norms from our example. We can formalize the first norm of our scenario from Example 1, as shown in Example 3.

Example 3. $\langle obligation, action, valid(Passport), accept(Passport), loss(5) \rangle$

The process can be repeated for Example 2. By identifying the context of a norm, it is possible to define it solely with predicates and atoms, as shown in Example 4, below.

Example 4. $\langle prohibition, action, not\ valid(Passport), accept(Passport), loss(10) \rangle$

4.4 Action Records

Like norms, actions must also be stored as tuples containing essential information. Actions captured by monitors must only be accessed by agents of the enforcer type, and therefore only the pieces of information that can be associated with norms are deemed essential. These are: what was done; who did it; and under what context it was done. Example 5 shows how a monitor reports its observations to an enforcer:

Example 5. "Officer John Doe approved Passport #3225. The passport was known to be valid."

From this report, we can extract the following details:

Example 6. $\langle johndoe, approve(Passport), valid(Passport) \rangle$

In this example, an officer approves the entry of an immigrant holding a valid passport. The next report reads:

Example 7. "Officer John Smith approved Passport #2134. The passport's validity could not be confirmed."

From this report, we can extract the following details:

Example 8. $\langle johnsmith, approve(Passport), notvalid(Passport) \rangle$

As such, we define Action Records:

Definition 2. *An Action Record, stored within the Action History, is represented by the tuple:* $\mathcal{R} = \langle \gamma, \alpha, \beta \rangle$*, where:*

- γ *represents the agent executing the action;*
- α *is the action description in the form "$f(p_0, p_1, \ldots, p_n)$", where f is an action name and $p_0, \ldots, p_n$ are the action's parameter values; and*
- β *represents agent γ's beliefs at the moment of execution.*

4.5 Monitoring System

The monitoring is divided in two parts: a capturing system, which gathers information pertaining to an action's execution context, and a report forwarding system, which provides enforcers with the gathered information for violation detection. To gather relevant information, the capturing system employs two strategies: an action capturing strategy and a belief state capturing strategy. In action capturing, whenever an agent successfully executes an action, the capturing system takes note of that action. In CArtAgO, this means that each successful operation is recorded for further analysis. Should an action fail for any reason, the capturing system ignores it. Yet, recording every successful action is a problem for both scalability and practicality. There is no reason to capture actions that are not enforced by any norm, *e.g* book-keeping actions or CArtAgO's own artefact creation and lookup operations. As such, we include capturing routines only for the operations relevant to the normative context, so as not to waste neither space and time with unimportant actions.

In belief state capturing, we employ a similar strategy to that of action capturing. Much like actions, there may be beliefs which are not related to any norms in the system. Thus, we should apply a filtering procedure when scanning beliefs to avoid wasting space on useless information. We propose a simple filtering technique, which requires monitors to also focus on normative activity:

1. For each new active norm, scan the norm's context for literals to add to a *to be observed* list.
2. If the norm's triggering condition is of the state type, do the same with the condition's literals.
3. For each deactivated norm, remove it from the *to be observed* list only literals that are not seen in any other norms.

We then change our capturing routines to scan the belief bases only for the literals in the *to be observed* list. If any belief *to be observed* cannot be found in the belief base, they can be ignored. Note that this list can contain only predicate names, and not their full list of terms.

Once we capture an action, we store it in the **Action History**, which is a queue-like data structure from which monitors gather information to build the reports that they send to enforcers. Actions are stored in the format discussed in Sect. 4.4 and are removed from the queue as soon as a monitor attempts to read them, regardless of the monitor's success in doing so.

It is the monitors's responsibility to send captured actions to enforcer agents in the form of a report for analysis. To achieve that, we use a producer/consumer model, in which an agent continuously provides information, through a channel, to another agent that consumes this information. With this in mind, we can identify four components that are necessary for this setup: a Producer, a Consumer, a channel for communications and the information itself. In our context, the role of Producer is given to Monitor Agents; the role of Consumer is given to Enforcer Agents; the communication channels are artefacts called "Reporting Interface"; and the information that transits through this channel are reports containing the actions executed by agents. This process is illustrated in Fig. 2.

Since monitoring in the real world is not cost-free, we need to spend resources to have an effective monitoring system in place [26], with the effectiveness of a monitor depending on its intensity. For this reason, we must enable the adjustment of monitoring intensity, so that enforcement can be performed at a cost considered affordable by the society. These adjustments take the form of different monitoring strategies. An example would be a probabilistic strategy, in which each captured action has a probability of being successfully read by a monitor. If the reading is successful, the action is guaranteed to be reported to an enforce, whereas if the reading fails, then the action is lost forever. We can use this to simulate the imperfect monitoring of actions, when some violations may go unpunished. Other strategies that monitors may apply include reading

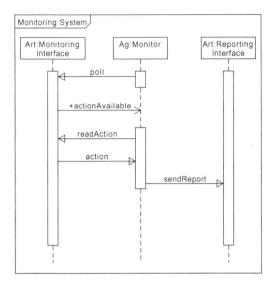

Fig. 2. Monitors poll the monitoring interface for new actions. When a monitor is successful at reading an action, it sends a report containing the action for analysis via the reporting interface.

only actions that they know are being enforced by an active norm. An extension to this strategy would be to add a probability of reading enforced actions with success. In this paper, we use the probabilistic strategy to study the general behaviour of our simulation.

4.6   Enforcement System

The enforcement system represents the Consumer entity in the normative mechanism's Producer/Consumer scheme. An enforcer agent connects to the Reporting Interface and awaits the arrival of new reports to analyse. The arrival of new reports is perceived by the enforcer, and in our implementation this perception is mapped to the +newReport signal. Once the report submission is perceived, the enforcer accesses the Normative Interface in search of currently activated norms and checks for any possible violations by the reported action.

During the violation detection routine, the perception of violations is also mapped to a signal, represented in the sequence diagram of Fig. 3 as the +violation event. When a violation is perceived, it falls to the enforcer to apply associated sanctions. The sanctioning step is the last in this process, and it starts as soon as detection finishes.

In order to sanction violating agents, the normative mechanism must be able to recognise them. It does not make sense to be told "John has approved an invalid passport. He violated a norm". if we do not know who John is in the first place. Therefore agents must be registered to the normative system prior to execution of their designed plans, similar to how people are registered for

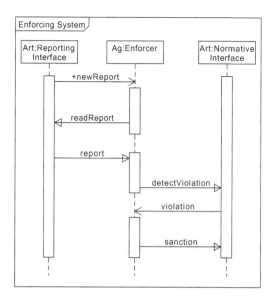

Fig. 3. Enforcers read new reports via the reporting interface. For each report, they use the normative interface to access the normative base and look for violations in agents's actions.

government issued IDs. In CArtAgO, this is accomplished through an operation in the Normative Interface that adds the agent's ID to a list, so that they may be found when needed. The ID they are registered with should be the same that appears in Action Records.

Normative Base. When norms are created, they must be stored within the system so that they may be accessed by an enforcer attempting to detect violations. The Normative Base structure holds all the norms that exist in the system, active or not. Every time a norm is created, it is stored in a list structure with a unique identifier. Norms may be activated or deactivated through the Normative Interface. Every time a norm is created, activated, deactivated or destroyed, agents connected to the Normative Interface perceive the event.

Detecting Violations. The detection operation runs for each action report received by an enforcer agent. Each action read is verified against the normative base, along with the context under which the action was executed. Since it is possible for an action to violate more than one norm, we utilize a list structure to take note of all violations detected so they will be properly addressed at a later time. At first, no norm is seen as violated and thus the list is empty. A norm is only added to the list when all verification steps finish with the variable's *isViolated* value set to *True*. The procedure for detecting violations can be seen in Algorithm 1 and is explained further.

Algorithm 1. Violation detection algorithm.

1: **function** DETECTVIOLATION($\langle \gamma, \alpha, \beta \rangle$)
2:      $V \leftarrow [\,]$
3:      **for each** $n = \langle \mu, \kappa, \chi, \tau, \rho \rangle \in ActiveNorms$ **do**
4:          **if** CONTEXTAPPLIES(χ, β) **then**
5:              **if** CONDITIONAPPLIES($\kappa, \tau, \alpha, \beta$) **then**
6:                  **if** $\mu = prohibition$ **then**
7:                      $V \leftarrow V \cup \{n\}$ ▷ Violation detected! Adds to the list of violated norms.
8:              **else**
9:                  **if** $\mu = obligation$ **then**
10:                      $V \leftarrow V \cup \{n\}$ ▷ Violation detected! Adds to the list of violated norms.
11:      **for each** $n \in V$ **do**
12:          SIGNALVIOLATION(n, γ)

Detection of violations can be achieved in two steps: context analysis and trigger condition analysis. Context analysis is about making sure that the action's execution context is the same as the one predicted by a norm. If it is, then there is a possibility of violation and further analysis is required. Otherwise, violation is considered an impossibility and the routine carries on. Formally, we define the norm's context as χ and the acting agent's belief-base as β. Hence, the context analysis returns $True$ value if $\chi \subseteq \beta$. Algorithm 2 is used for comparing sets of predicates. It checks if all the predicates defined in context χ are present in the agent's belief-base β, one by one. If a predicate in χ is negated (*e.g* not valid(Passport)), then the algorithm checks for its absence in belief-base β instead. This is to reflect how the **not** operator works in Jason. The routine returns $True$ if the trigger condition is satisfied and $False$ otherwise.

A trigger condition of a norm can be either the execution of an action or the achievement of a state by an agent. This is specified by the norm's trigger condition type and directs the way in which the detection algorithm executes. If we are working with an action trigger, then we must compare the action that was executed with the one specified by the norm. However, if we are working with a state trigger, then two contexts must be compared: the agent's belief-base and the norm's state trigger condition. These are compared using the context analysis algorithm of Algorithm 2. We show the pseudo-code for the trigger analysis procedure in Algorithm 3.

When both context and trigger conditions are satisfied, we need only verify whether the norm is an obligation or prohibition to conclude if it was violated or not. A prohibition means that a certain action or state is undesired under the given context. If all the conditions up to now have been met, we conclude that said undesired state has been reached and the norm was violated. On the other hand, an obligation requires the flow specified by the norm to be followed strictly, and if this is the case, we conclude that the norm was complied with. By negating our conditions, we also negate its results: if in a prohibition context the conditions were not met, then we would be home free; if they are not met while in an obligation context, however, we would have just violated it.

Algorithm 2. Context comparison sub-routine.

```
1: function CONTEXTAPPLIES(χ = [l_1, ..., l_n], β = [l_1, ..., l_n])
2:     Require count(χ) ≤ count(β)
3:     for each p ∈ χ do
4:         isPresent ← False
5:         checkAbsence ← False
6:         if p is of the form ¬φ then
7:             p ← φ
8:             checkAbsence ← True
9:         for each l ∈ β do
10:            if l = p then
11:                isPresent ← True
12:                break
13:        if checkAbsence = isPresent then
14:            return False
15:    return True
```

Their modality notwithstanding, every norm that is violated is added to a list that is processed when all norms have been verified. Sanction functions are then executed and agents perceive their punishments. Penalties can be brought directly upon agents through perception or carried out by a third party, while records on agent transgressions can be maintained in a separate structure for greater consistency.

Algorithm 3. Trigger condition analysis sub-routine.

```
1: function CONDITIONAPPLIES(κ, τ, α, β)
2:     if κ = action then
3:         return τ = α
4:     return CONTEXTAPPLIES(τ, β)
```

5   Evaluation

In order to test our solution, we developed agents using Jason and deployed them in a CArtAgO environment following the scenario described in Sect. 3. To visualise the difference between compliant and non-compliant behaviours, two types of agents were used: the *normal* type and the *corrupt* type. The normal type is programmed to approve only those passports that are truly valid, whereas the corrupt one will approve passports indiscriminately for his own personal gain. By making it so, we can more easily tell the effectiveness of the norm enforcing mechanism. Therefore, the following results were expected:

- Corrupt agents attain more credits when under lower monitoring intensity.
- Standard agents maintain an average quantity of credits through all simulations.
- At some point, corrupt agents should start performing poorly due to higher monitoring intensity. This marks the point at which monitoring can change the environment.

We ran 35 experiments for 11 different values of monitoring intensity[2]. Intensity values range from 0 to 100, with a step value of 10. Each simulation was run for 10 min. In this timespan, with our set-up, around 1048 immigrants attempt to cross the border. In what follows, we refer to an agent's obtained credits, or their performance measure, as their utility. We use that measure in the graph of Fig. 4, which illustrates how the environment's monitoring intensity affects the utilities of corrupt agents 1 and 2. The monitoring intensity is the probability as a percentage of a monitor being able to read an agent's action. A value of 100 means that all actions are read, while a value of 0 means no actions are read by the monitor. We notice that, as the intensity of the monitoring mechanism increases, the utility of corrupt agents decreases to the point where performing badly and not performing at all yield the same utility, whereas normal agents maintain their average utility. This allows us to conclude that, for a monitoring intensity value of 40 or more, following norms is a better decision than the contrary.

The data used to plot the graph of Fig. 4 can be seen in Table 1. Values for μ and σ represent the arithmetic mean and standard deviation, respectively. These were calculated to show that utility values for normal agents are near constant. The μ values for corrupt agents show that, at the end of the simulation, their average performance is worse than those of normal agents, due to their constant violation of norms. A high σ value for these agents shows that their performance suffers between simulations. We can then see that through the analysis of recorded agent actions and successful identification of violation occurrences, violating agents are punished by the enforcement system and have their utilities affected.

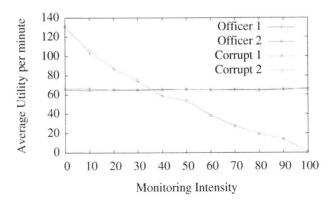

Fig. 4. Utility of corrupt agents is affected by monitoring intensity.

---

[2] Although our experiments correspond in a broad sense to a simulation, we avoid the term for its possibly loaded meaning.

Table 1. Agent utilities × monitoring intensity.

Intensity	Officer1	Officer2	Corrupt officer1	Corrupt officer2
0	65,3285	66,3714	130,6571	130,7000
10	64,5871	66,5714	103,3000	106,2285
20	65,4428	65,0142	86,8000	87,9571
30	65,3142	64,8714	73,7571	75,6571
40	65,7857	65,1857	59,0571	57,8142
50	65,6714	65,7714	54,3285	53,1857
60	65,1571	65,1714	38,7714	38,4571
70	65,0142	65,6571	27,6428	27,3714
80	64,7857	64,9571	19,2285	19,3428
90	65,0714	66,1714	13,7857	13,8142
100	66,7571	65,8000	1,4714	0,0285
μ	65.3559	65.5948	55,3454	55,5051
σ	0.5569	0.5705	38,4836	39,1996

6 Related Work

There are multiple tools available for programming multi-agent environments, few of which provide mechanisms for norm specification. These tools range from programming libraries to model-based simulators. To name a few, NetLogo [16] and its distributed version HubNet [27] are of the model-based type and allow users to work with educational projects and, to some extent, professional ones. Other tools include MASON [17] and Repast [18]. MASON is a simulation library developed in Java that provides functions for modelling agents and visualising simulations as they run. As for Repast, it uses interaction models much like Net-Logo does, although it is meant for professional use and thus offers more alternatives for agent programming. One final example worth mentioning is MASSim [11], which promotes multi-agent research and is used in the MAS Programming Contest[3] [28]. This one, however, provides only the tools related to the contests. Although it is possible to develop custom agents for operation within the simulator, the practice is not encouraged by its developers.

Building a full-fledged norm-based behaviour simulation engine is not a trivial task, and the "Emergence in the Loop" (EMIL) [29] project built a set of tools to accomplish this objective. A toolset which includes an extension of the BDI architecture that is capable of simulating the processes referred to as "immergence" and "emergence" of norms [30]; and an integration with multi-agent modelling tools such as NetLogo [16] and Repast [18]. In this way, agents are modelled in one of these environments and then simulated using the EMIL agent architecture. It is a very powerful tool for studying social behaviour in

---

[3] https://multiagentcontest.org.

autonomous agents, since agents can reason about norms and, together, create conventions of what kinds of behaviours must be avoided or followed. EMIL's approach to normative simulation is more focused on agents and their experience with norms. This contrasts with our approach in that we are more focused on norm monitoring and enforcement tasks, and little is said about these matters in the EMIL literature. We also consider the environmental aspects of Normative Multi-Agent Systems, which is why we employ CArtAgO in our implementation.

Finally, the $\mathcal{M}$oise$^+$ [19] tool (part of the JaCaMo [31] framework) can also be used to specify norms for MAS development. $\mathcal{M}$oise$^+$ allows us to create organisations of agents, and within these organisations agents take up specific roles to act and missions to accomplish. The normative part of $\mathcal{M}$oise$^+$ ties agents to their missions through obligations, prohibitions and permissions. Nevertheless, $\mathcal{M}$oise$^+$ differs from NormMAS in three key aspects. First $\mathcal{M}$oise$^+$ focuses on normative specification for organisations to coordinate agents in performing certain tasks, whereas in NormMAS, we have social norms and regulations that only tell agents what they should or should not do. Consequently, when there is no normative specification in NormMAS, the agents's routines remain intact. Second, while $\mathcal{M}$oise$^+$ norms affect whole plans, NormMAS norms affect only specific actions or states. Third, while $\mathcal{M}$oise$^+$ norms are not regimented, lack of compliance does not incur any penalties for violating agents, which means that they are not enforced either.

7   Conclusions and Future Work

In this paper, we constructed a mechanism of norm processing and enforcement in a multi-agent environment. We show its feasibility with an implementation using Jason [12] and Cartago [22] technologies. By keeping track of agent activities and analysing actions against a normative base, it is possible to detect violations and enforce norms through the sanctioning of violating agents. With this framework, it is possible to evaluate different implementations [6, 32–34] of normative behaviour. Statistics collection can also be customised so that results may be compared between simulations. We provide our example implementation to the public via a GitHub repository [35].

CArtAgO allows us to build environments in a distributed manner, therefore providing scalability for realistic simulation scenarios or complex multi-agent systems. The philosophy behind CArtAgO, which sees the environment as the composition of artefacts through which agents interact, also aided in the framework's construction. Artefacts are modular, they can be attached or detached to a multi-agent system seamlessly. Meaning that artefacts can be created to suit an agent's or group of agents's specific needs, and agents may connect only to those artefacts that are related to their designs. We took advantage of those features to build the interfaces for the monitoring system to access the Action History and Normative Base structures.

As future work, we aim to build improvements and extensions to the framework, such as: a mechanism to be added to the normative system that allows activation and expiration of norms following predefined conditions; agent architectures that can learn from normative environments, and with that avoid penalties by violation or minimising performance loss when violations are inevitable [6]; enable agents to learn about the enforcing intensity and use that information to their advantage [26]; and the introduction of agent hierarchies to control normative power [36].

References

1. Wooldridge, M.: Intelligent agents. In: Weiss, G. (ed.) Multi-Agent Systems, 2nd edn, pp. 3–50. The MIT Press, Cambridge (2013)
2. Jones, A.J.I., Sergot, M.: On the characterisation of law and computer systems: the normative systems perspective. In: Meyer, J.-J.C., Wieringa, R.J. (eds.) Deontic Logic in Computer Science: Normative System Specification, Wiley Professional Computing Series, Chapter 12, pp. 275–307. Wiley, Chichester (1993)
3. Kollingbaum, M.: Norm-governed practical reasoning agents. Ph.D. thesis, University of Aberdeen (2005)
4. Broersen, J., Dastani, M., Hulstijn, J., Huang, Z., van der Torre, L.: The BOID architecture: conflicts between beliefs, obligations, intentions and desires. In: Proceedings of the Fifth International Conference on Autonomous Agents, pp. 9–16 (2001)
5. Governatori, G., Rotolo, A.: BIO logical agents: norms, beliefs, intentions in defeasible logic. Auton. Agent. Multi-Agent Syst. **17**(1), 36–69 (2008)
6. Meneguzzi, F., Luck, M.: Norm-based behaviour modification in BDI agents. In: Proceedings of the Eighth International Conference on Autonomous Agents and Multiagent Systems, pp. 177–184 (2009)
7. Criado, N.: Using norms to control open multi-agent systems. Ph.D. thesis, Universitat Politécnica de València (2012)
8. Alechina, N., Dastani, M., Logan, B.: Programming norm-aware agents. In: van der Hoek, W., Padgham, L., Conitzer, V., Winikoff, M., (eds.) Autonomous Agents and Multi-Agent Systems, IFAAMAS, pp. 1057–1064 (2012)
9. Panagiotidi, S., Vázquez-Salceda, J., Dignum, F.: Reasoning over norm compliance via planning. In: Aldewereld, H., Sichman, J.S. (eds.) COIN 2012. LNCS, vol. 7756, pp. 35–52. Springer, Heidelberg (2013)
10. Meneguzzi, F., Mehrotra, S., Tittle, J., Oh, J., Chakraborty, N., Sycara, K., Lewis, M.: A cognitive architecture for emergency response. In: Proceedings of the Eleventh International Conference on Autonomous Agents and Multiagent Systems, pp. 1161–1162 (2012)
11. Behrens, T.M., Dastani, M., Dix, J., Novák, P.: MASSi: multi-agent systems simulation platform. In: Begehung des Simulationswissenschaftlichen Zentrums. Clausthal University of Technology (2008)
12. Bordini, R.H., Hübner, J.F., Wooldridge, M.: Programming Multi-Agent Systems in AgentSpeak Using Jason (Wiley Series in Agent Technology). Wiley, Chichester (2007)
13. Bellifemine, F.L., Caire, G., Greenwood, D.: Developing Multi-Agent Systems with JADE (Wiley Series in Agent Technology). Wiley, New York (2007)
14. Conte, R., Andrighetto, G., Campennl, M.: Minding Norms: Mechanisms and Dynamics of Social Order in Agent Societies. Oxford Series on Cognitive Models and Architectures. OUP, Oxford (2013)

15. Fagundes, M., Ossowski, S., Meneguzzi, F.: Analyzing the tradeoff between efficiency and cost of norm enforcement in stochastic environments populated with self-interested agents. In: Proceedings of the 21st European Conference on Artificial Intelligence (2014)

16. Wilensky, U.: NetLogo. Center for Connected Learning and Computer-Based Modeling, Northwestern University. Evanston, IL (1999). http://ccl.northwestern.edu/netlogo/

17. Luke, S., Cioffi-Revilla, C., Panait, L., Sullivan, K., Balan, G.: MASON: A multi-agent simulation environment. Simulation **81**, 517–527 (2005)

18. North, M., Collier, N., Ozik, J., Tatara, E., Macal, C., Bragen, M., Sydelko, P.: Complex adaptive systems modeling with repast simphony. Complex Adapt. Syst. Model. **1**(1), 1–26 (2013)

19. Hubner, J.F., Sichman, J.S., Boissier, O.: Developing organised multiagent systems using the MOISE+ model: programming issues at the system and agent levels. Int. J. Agent-Oriented Softw. Eng. **1**, 370–395 (2007)

20. Jones, A.J.I., Sergot, M.: On the characterisation of law, computer systems: the normative systems perspective. In: Deontic Logic in Computer Science: Normative System Specification, pp. 275–307. Wiley (1993)

21. Oren, N., Vasconcelos, W., Meneguzzi, F., Luck, M.: Acting on Norm Constrained Plans. In: Leite, J., Torroni, P., Ågotnes, T., Boella, G., van der Torre, L. (eds.) CLIMA XII 2011. LNCS, vol. 6814, pp. 347–363. Springer, Heidelberg (2011)

22. Ricci, A., Viroli, M., Omicini, A.: CArtAgO: a framework for prototyping artifact-based environments in MAS. In: Weyns, D., Dyke Parunak, H., Michel, F. (eds.) E4MAS 2006. LNCS (LNAI), vol. 4389, pp. 67–86. Springer, Heidelberg (2007)

23. Rao, A.S.: AgentSpeak(L): BDI agents speak out in a logical computable language. In: Perram, J., Van de Velde, W. (eds.) MAAMAW 1996. LNCS, vol. 1038, pp. 42–55. Springer, Heidelberg (1996)

24. Bratman, M.E.: Intention, Plans and Practical Reason. Harvard University Press, Cambridge (1987)

25. Meneguzzi, F., De Silva, L.: Planning in BDI agents: a survey of the integration of planning algorithms and agent reasoning. Knowl. Eng. Rev. **30**, 1–44 (2015)

26. Meneguzzi, F., Logan, B., Fagundes, M.S.: Norm monitoring with asymmetric information. In: Bazzan, A.L.C., Huhns, M.N., Lomuscio, A., Scerri, P. (eds.) International Conference on Autonomous Agents and Multi-Agent Systems, AAMAS 2014, Paris, France, pp. 1523–1524. IFAAMAS/ACM, 5–9 May 2014

27. Wilensky, U., Stroup, W.: HubNet. Center for Connected Learning and Computer-Based Modeling, Northwestern University. Evanston, IL (1999). http://ccl.northwestern.edu/netlogo/hubnet.html

28. Behrens, T.M., Dastani, M., Dix, J., Hübner, J., Köster, M., Novák, P., Schlesinger, F.: The multi-agent programming contest. AI Mag. **33**(4), 111–113 (2012)

29. Andrighetto, G., Conte, R., Turrini, P., Paolucci, M.: Emergence in the loop: simulating the two way dynamics of norm innovation. In: Boella, G., van der Torre, L.W.N., Verhagen, H. (eds.) Normative Multi-agent Systems, vol. 07122, Dagstuhl Seminar Proceedings, Internationales Begegnungs- und Forschungszentrum für Informatik, Schloss Dagstuhl, Germany, 18–23 March 2007

30. Andrighetto, G., Campennì, M., Conte, R., Paolucci, M.: On the immergence of norms: a normative agent architecture. In: Proceedings of the Association for the Advancement of Artificial Intelligence Symposium, Social and Organizational Aspects of Intelligence, Forthcoming (2007)

31. Boissier, O., Bordini, R.H., Hubner, J.F., Ricci, A., Santi, A.: Multi-agent oriented programming with JaCaMo. Sci. Comput. Prog. **78**(6), 747–761 (2013). Special section: The Programming Languages track at the 26th ACM Symposium on Applied Computing (SAC 2011); Special section on Agent-oriented Design Methods and Programming Techniques for Distributed Computing in Dynamic and Complex Environments
32. Lee, J., Padget, J., Logan, B., Dybalova, D., Alechina, N.: Run-time norm compliance in BDI agents. In: International Conference on Autonomous Agents and Multi-Agent Systems, AAMAS 2014, pp. 1581–1582 (2014)
33. Vasconcelos, W.W., Kollingbaum, M.J., Norman, T.J.: Normative conflict resolution in multi-agent systems. Auton. Agents Multi-Agent Syst. **19**(2), 124–152 (2009)
34. Criado, N., Argente, E., Botti, V.J., Noriega, P.: Reasoning about norm compliance. In: Sonenberg, L., Stone, P., Tumer, K., Yolum, P. (eds.) 10th International Conference on Autonomous Agents and Multiagent Systems, Taipei, Taiwan, vol. 1–3, pp. 1191–1192, IFAAMAS, 2–6 May 2011
35. Chang, S.: normmas-sim: NormMAS - paper version. Zenodo, December 2015. doi:10.5281/zenodo.35028
36. Oren, N., Luck, M., Miles, S.: A model of normative power. In: van der Hoek, W., Kaminka, G.A., Lespérance, Y., Luck, M., Sen, S. (eds.) 9th International Conference on Autonomous Agents and Multiagent Systems, Toronto, Canada, vol. 1–3, pp. 815–822, IFAAMAS, 10–14 May 2010

Exploring the Effectiveness of Agent Organizations

Daniel D. Corkill[✉], Daniel Garant, and Victor R. Lesser

University of Massachusetts Amherst, Amherst, MA 01003, USA
corkill@cics.umass.edu

Abstract. Organization is an important mechanism for improving performance in complex multiagent systems. Yet, little consideration has been given to the performance gain that organization can provide across a broad range of conditions. Intuitively, when agents are mostly idle, organization offers little benefit. In such settings, almost any organization—appropriate, inappropriate, or absent—leads to agents accomplishing the needed work. Conversely, when every agent is severely overloaded, no choice of agent activities achieves system objectives. Only as the overall workload approaches the limit of agents' capabilities is effective organization crucial to success.

We explored this organizational "sweet spot" intuition by examining the effectiveness of two previously published implementations of organized software agents when they are operated under a wide range of conditions: (1) call-center agents extinguishing RoboCup Rescue fires and (2) agents learning network task-distribution policies that optimize service time. In both cases, organizational effect diminished significantly outside the sweet spot. Detailed measures taken of coordination and cooperation amounts, lost work opportunities, and exceeded span-of-control limits account for this behavior. Such measures can be used to assess the potential benefit of organization in a specific setting and whether the organization design must be a highly effective one.

1 Introduction

Organization is an important mechanism for improving performance in complex multiagent systems [1–8]. Designed agent organizations provide agents with organizational directives that, when followed, reduce the complexity and uncertainty of each agent's activity decisions, lower the cost of distributed resource allocation and agent coordination, help limit inappropriate agent behavior, and reduce unnecessary communication and agent activities [9–11].

When agents are mostly idle, agents can accomplish needed work whether or not they are well organized. This does not mean that effective organization does not affect how efficiently the agents work together, only that unorganized and even misorganized agents have sufficient time and resources to accomplish system objectives when lightly loaded. Conversely, when every agent is severely overloaded, no choice of agent activities achieves system objectives. In this situation, effective organization can help agents be more efficient while failing to

© Springer International Publishing Switzerland 2016
V. Dignum et al. (Eds.): COIN 2015, LNAI 9628, pp. 78–97, 2016.
DOI: 10.1007/978-3-319-42691-4_5

achieve objectives fully, but whether they are well organized or not, the system is unable to perform acceptably. Only as the overall workload approaches the limit of agents' capabilities does organization play a significant role in system performance.

2   Organizational "Sweet Spot"

We first explored this organizational-impact conjecture empirically using an previously implemented and described system of organizationally adept BDI[1] agents [13–15] operating in a well-instrumented and highly parametrized experimental platform adapted from the fire-extinguishing portion of RoboCup Rescue [16]. Organizationally adept *call center* agents direct *fire brigade* resources under their control to extinguish fires in important buildings as quickly as possible. There are no fire-brigade bases in the adapted RoboCup Rescue environment, and brigades typically move directly from fire to fire, remaining deployed if they become briefly idle. The objective is to minimize the total importance-weighted damage to buildings. A call center can use its fire brigades to execute plans to achieve its own goals of extinguishing building fires, and it can request temporary use of fire brigades from other call centers when necessary.

Our goal was to learn how the relative performance of previously evaluated agent organizations in this multiagent system changed when operating in environments well outside the conditions typically studied. Whether the existing agents and organization designs in this system were the best possible was not a concern, as better candidates would affect only the magnitude of the relative performances and not their qualitative characteristics. Some observations were intuitive, but there were also surprises, and we believe this to be the first systematic study of organizational impact in a multiagent system over such a broad range of conditions. We ran and analyzed thousands of controlled and repeatable simulation experiments involving dynamic environments in which new fires occur at various city locations throughout the entire duration of an experimental scenario. In such settings, call-center agents have an ongoing (but potentially changing) firefighting workload in which following organizational guidance offers potential advantages over unguided, reactive local decision-making.

Observation 1: Sweet-spot behavior ⇒ Figure 1 shows the relative difference in performance (as a percentage increase or decrease) between two organizational configurations, Org and No Org, as the firefighting workload increases. Org is an effective organization design that specifies a responsibility region for each call center, and No Org dictates that call-center agents operate without any responsibility-region directives. Call centers give priority to fighting fires in their responsibility regions when such regions are provided. Each of the four call centers controlled six fire-brigade resources. Performance attained in each of the 320 simulation runs is a raw score of the inverse importance-weighted fire damage in the city. We observed that the performance benefit achieved by organization

---

[1] Belief-desire-intention model of agency [12].

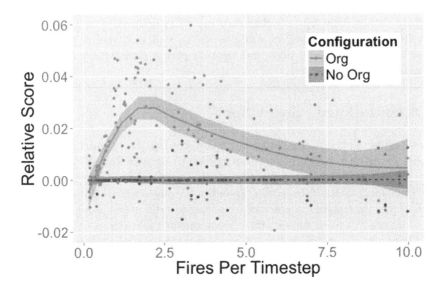

Fig. 1. Relative score achieved by organization (Color figure online)

(the raw score improvement) was greatest when the average firefighting workload on brigades was near their capacity to fight important fires (approximately 2.2 fires per timestep). All figures illustrate trends as workload (e.g., ignition frequency) is varied. Trend lines are fit using a local linear model, with shaded regions representing a 95 % confidence level in the mean of the performance distribution. For example, each trend line in the firefighting experiments fits 320 separate simulation runs (drawn as individual dots).

Attenuation of organization benefit outside the sweet spot is a form of phase transition behavior. The transition occurs as the workload approaches the limit of agents' capabilities. The effect of phase boundaries has proved important in satisfiability problems [17–19] as well as to understanding problem difficulty in constraint satisfaction, number partitioning, and traveling salesmen tasks.[2] With multiagent organizations, it is important to determine where on the control complexity scale a system is operating (how important using an effective organization is to system performance) and more generally, when complex multiagent systems are operating within their organizational sweet spot. One may

---

[2] For example, a typical phase-transition performance plot, such as Fig. 4 in the classic Kirkpatrick and Selman SAT phase-change paper [18] shows the performance cliff that occurs at the phase boundary, which shifts laterally under different conditions. If such a figure is redrawn as relative difference curves from a baseline condition (such as the k = 6/N = 40 values in that figure), it reveals wide "sweet spot" curves similar to the curves shown in this paper. Relative plots highlight the span and magnitude of performance differences near the phase change, and we consider them more informative in highlighting sweet-spot regions than raw performance-value plots.

argue that organizations (multiagent or otherwise) will tend to be inevitably operated within the sweet spot region due to real-world economics that limit capabilities and resources to the minimum required to operate effectively.

Upon observing organizational sweet-spot behavior, we took a more detailed look into what was occurring as workload changed that accounted for the benefit attenuation.

3   Performance Factors

Why do we create agent organizations? One reason is that complex agent behavior becomes more structured and understandable through the definition of roles, behavioral expectations, and authority relationships [20]. Additionally, organizational concepts can be used to help design and build agent based systems (organization-based multiagent system engineering). There is also a line of research that addresses *organizational membership* in open agent societies (incentives for organizational recruitment and retention and for the replacement of agents that leave the organization). Recent work in open and sociotechnical settings [21,22] has this emphasis. Aligning agents' individual goals and objectives with those of the organization are among the issues addressed in that context. Our focus here is on *organizational control*; specifically, the organizational performance of the members ("how they do their jobs"), rather than on attracting participants from an open pool of agents ("obtaining members for the enterprise") or designing the agent system ("defining what the jobs (roles) are"). We assume here that we have acquired the agents we need, that they all share the organizational objectives (e.g., saving the most important buildings in the city), and that they are competent in their ability to perform tasks necessary to attain that objective. For example, there is no need to decide if an agent is able to play some role in the organization [23]. Furthermore, there are no non-cooperative agents trying to burn things down. Nevertheless, the cooperative agents sometimes do work at cross-purposes in attaining those objectives (such as all wanting to fight an important fire). This can occur whether the agents are organized or not, because agents have a limited local view of the situation. If unorganized agents did not have the same shared objective as when organized, then some performance gained through organization could stem from the changed objectives. Our assumptions eliminate such a cooperative-objective bonus.

We distinguish between *operational decision making*, the detailed moment-to-moment behavior decisions made by agents, and *organizational control*, an organization design expressed to agents through directives ("job descriptions") that limit and inform the range of operational decisions made by each agent in the organization. These directives contain general, long-term guidelines, in the form of parametrized role assignments and priorities (e.g., prefer extinguishing fires in region A over fires in region B), that are subject to ongoing elaboration into precise, moment-to-moment activity decisions by the agents [2,4,24]. Ideally, following organizational directives should be beneficial when agent directives can be designed that perform well over a range of potential long-term environment and agent characteristics.

3.1   Operational Challenges

Without organizational directives, a call center must coordinate with other centers to avoid sending redundant fire brigades to the same fire (every call center receives all fire reports) using a highest estimated utility protocol to resolve conflicts. Coordination and *retractions* consume valuable time, delaying extinguishing operations. The designed organization only requires coordination if a call center wants to fight a fire outside its responsibility region. When region responsibilities are inappropriate and do not match workloads, fire-brigade *borrowing* requests from overloaded centers increase, again with a loss in performance. When the design is appropriate, retractions are diminished at the risk of more borrowing (as we will demonstrate when we discuss Fig. 6). Call centers must consider all borrowing and loaning options in the context of estimated opportunity costs that are based on potential new fires and uncertainty in the duration of fighting current fires. These are challenging decisions even when agents are well organized.

The call-center agents are highly competent and can make skillful operational decisions to extinguish fires without organizational guidance. Norms, functions, protocols, etc., are implicitly represented in the plan templates used by these call-center agents. Centers follow these norms (organized or not) and know how to work together to fight fires and share fire-brigade resources.

Appropriately organized call-center agents, when operating in the sweet spot, should function better than unorganized centers, which must consider of all potential activities and explicitly coordinate them. The organizational complexity in the firefighting system is quite simple. Each call center can perform only two roles: (1) extinguishing fires by directing fire brigades to fight them and (2) loaning fire brigades to another call center. Perhaps counter intuitively, organizational design and control of split roles in homogeneous multiagent systems is more challenging than assigning discrete functional roles to specialized agents in heterogeneous multiagent systems because specialization reduces the space of reasonable choices [10]. The organizational "simplicity" in the firefighting setting means that observed organizational performance differences stem from a relatively small set of organizationally-biased behaviors and are not obscured by complex role and agent interactions.

3.2   Factors Affecting Organizational Performance

We analyzed a number of general factors that influence organizational performance. As these factors change, a designed organization may become highly effective or less effective. In the discussion that follows, we provide an intuitive description of each factor, why it is important, and how it can affect organizational performance. We adjusted each factor individually while holding other environmental settings constant in order to observe its effect on organizational performance independent of the other factors. In total, we conducted a broad analysis that included over 5000 simulation runs with over ten terabytes of simulator output to determine how the general factors of coordination requirements, cooperation benefits, lost opportunity, workload imbalance, and span of control impact the effectiveness of organization. We begin with coordination.

Coordination Requirements. Typically, complex tasks performed by multiple agents require coordination, and often a well-coordinated system will perform much better than a system where agents work at cross purposes from only their local, selfish perspectives. In firefighting, coordination is necessary to ensure that call-center agents share responsibility for extinguishing a building only when necessary, and otherwise fight important fires independently (i.e., they do not blindly work on the same fire when more utility could be gained by working on separate fires).

Coordination is not without associated costs, often involving delays while beliefs, desires, and intentions are communicated. The time required for agents to communicate this information and reconcile it with information from other agents can be significant, especially in cases where agents control resources which must be held in reserve while an agent decides whether it wishes to pursue some goal. Even more significantly, when agents take uncoordinated actions that involve operating in the world, they must deal with the consequences of physically moving resources and then withdrawing them (or having wasted them if they are consumables) once they discover their actions are in conflict with those of another agent. In our analyses, this has been the largest contributor to coordination "cost."

The amount of coordination required is not organization-independent. Organizational directives influence agents to assume specific roles and responsibilities pertaining to certain goals, and assume less responsibility for other goals. The best-case organization for a specific situation would be a perfect partitioning of responsibility regions so that agents select the fires for which they are responsible over those that are the responsibility of others. This ideal situation results in minimal *goal conflicts*, where two agents needlessly pursue the same goal (e.g., extinguish the building at 5th and Madison). It is important to note that even this organization is not coordination-free, but when each goal is managed and committed to by the agent with the highest expected utility, the committing agent is best suited for reaching out for assistance if necessary. In the context of firefighting, this assistance comes in the form of lending and borrowing fire brigades, an effective remedy for temporal workload imbalances. However, as we will note shortly, excessive resource borrowing leads to inefficiencies in resource provisioning and is often a sign of a more permanent resource imbalance. The worst-case organization (in terms of coordination complexity) would influence every agent to select the same goals (No Org configuration). We analyzed many organization configurations to explore the full spectrum between these two extremes, where organization sometimes cannot prevent agents from selecting the same goals, and at other times, is effective in preventing a goal conflict (which we will also discuss later in conjunction with Fig. 6).

This coordination phenomena occurs in firefighting because call centers need to negotiate with other call centers about which fires to fight. In order to come to a resolution for a contested goal, call centers need to compute and share their expected utility with peers. The call center with the highest expected utility will then be responsible for managing fighting the fire, and for borrowing fire-brigade resources from peers if necessary. To investigate the effect of adjusting this coordination cost, we adjusted the *resolution period*, during which call centers reserve resources to fight a fire while waiting for and considering bids from other call centers intent on fighting the same fire. Only after the resolution period has elapsed will the call center with the highest utility commit to fighting the fire. By increasing the resolution period, we increase the cost of coordination while simultaneously making centers more "globally aware" of the utility expected by other agents. By lowering the resolution period, we lower the cost of coordination but make call centers more selfish in that they are less open to considering bids from other centers. Figures 2 and 3, to be discussed shortly, show the effects of "Low-Cost" (short) resolution and "High-Cost" (long) resolution times.

Observation 2: The performance separation of effective organization increases with coordination requirements, without shifting the sweet spot laterally ⇒ We analyzed several organizational designs: (1) a specific responsibility region for each call center (Org) and (2) all centers are responsible for the entire city (No Org). It seems reasonable to believe that when fires are uniformly distributed, Org would perform best, minimizing goal conflicts while still providing each agent with sufficient beneficial opportunities in its responsibility region. In practice, this is generally true, however, we have found that in cases where, when the conflict resolution period is very short (corresponding to low coordination cost and more selfish agents), the directives supplied to the organized agents do not improve on the No Org baseline. As coordination cost grows, the performance of the organized agents (which need to coordinate less frequently) improves increasingly on the No Org configuration (see Figs. 2 and 3). Figure 3 shows the total retraction time relative to No-Org, which has the most retractions. In both Figs. 2 and 3, the 0- and 10-time-steps resolution period results are relative to comparable 0- and 10-time-steps resolution No Org baselines.

Note that with low coordination cost (0-timestep resolution), the difference in performance between the Org and the No Org configuration is only statistically significant within a small window, centered at about 2–2.5 fires per timestep. Correspondingly, the scenario with high coordination cost (10-timestep resolution) achieves a prominent global maximum centered at this time window. From this analysis, it can be seen that when coordination does not incur significant costs, organization is not nearly as beneficial as in cases where coordination (or the absence of needed coordination) is costly. At moderate workload levels, the performance gains afforded by organization reach the maximum. When the simplicity of the scenario does not require coordination, the performance of the Org configuration and the No Org configuration are statistically indistinguishable. Extremely overloaded work scenarios are marked by either statistically indistinguishable performance differences or diminished returns.

Observation 3: Increasing call-center capabilities by adding resources results in a lateral shift and widening of the sweet spot ⇒ The width and position of the sweet-spot window is not fixed, as it depends on the agent's capabilities in servicing goals at either end of the workload range. Call centers

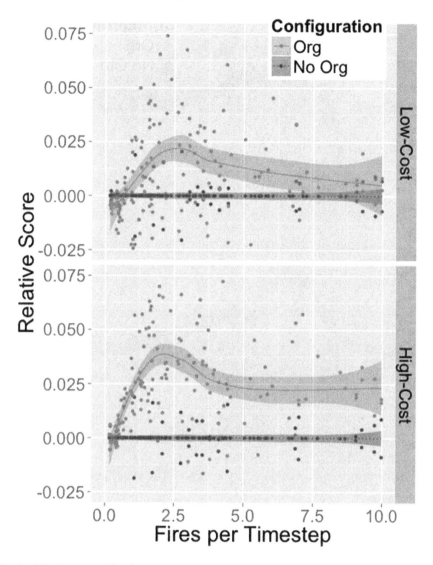

Fig. 2. Varying coordination requirements: score relative to No Org (Color figure online)

become more capable when they have more fire-brigade resources. Figure 4 shows the result of doubling the number of fire brigades controlled by each call center from six to twelve. Now, the organizational sweet spot occurs at a higher workload level: at approximately 2.7 fires per timestep. In addition, the sweet spot is wider as call centers can handle greater task loads before the situation becomes hopeless.

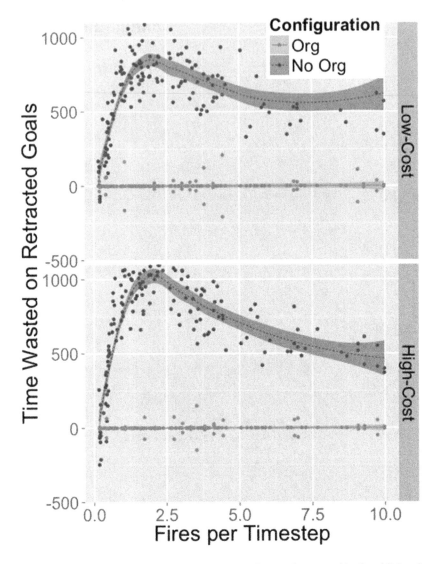

Fig. 3. Varying coordination requirements: cost effects relative to No Org (Color figure online)

By holding the conflict resolution period constant and varying the number of call centers in the system, we see that coordination complexity is also a function of how "well partitioned" the centers' responsibilities are. In experiments with four call centers, we can see that fewer goal conflicts arise in the Org case than the No Org case. However, if we increase the number of call-center agents to twelve, each with two rather than six fire brigades and responsibility regions that overlap with two other centers, the environmental responsibilities are too precisely

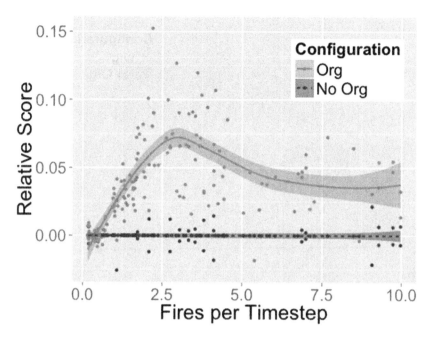

Fig. 4. Relative score with twice as many fire brigades (Color figure online)

partitioned to handle temporal responsibility differences even if, on average over the course of the run, each center's responsibilities are roughly uniform. In Figs. 5 and 6, this behavior is reflected in the fact that the number of goal conflicts in the organized, 12-call-center configuration approach the number of conflicts without organization. Correspondingly, the differences in performance between the two configurations are significant. Any advantages to organization under the 4-call-center scenario are lost with the increase in coordination complexity in the 12-call-center scenario. This observation is consistent with the notion that there is an "ideal" number of call centers given the centers' capabilities and the environmental conditions. We do not know for certain that a 4-center organization is the best choice for the environmental conditions that we simulated, but it is certainly better than a 12-center organization, as the 4-center organization provides a better balance between the partitioning of responsibility regions and coordination complexity [25].

Workload Imbalance. Organizational directives influence agents to assume responsibility over particular goals and tasks. This reduces the amount of coordination involved in meeting these demands, as there is some expectation of which agent will perform or manage a task. In order for this organizational influence to improve performance, the per-agent workload that is suggested by the organizational directives must be consistent with the distribution of tasks in the environment. Otherwise, some agents have too little work and others

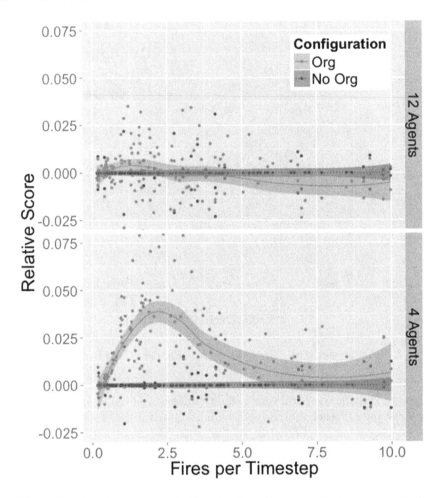

Fig. 5. Varying the number of call centers: relative score (Color figure online)

have too much. As such, highly beneficial tasks may go without consideration by underloaded agents while overloaded agents struggle to complete all of the tasks they are responsible for. Workload imbalance occurs in firefighting when the distribution of fires throughout the city is not consistent with the size of each of the centers' responsibility region. For instance, if 60% of fires occur in the northwest corner of the city, a partitioning of the city into four equally-sized quadrants would result in a significant average workload imbalance, with the call center in the northwest corner of the city having almost six times the workload of other centers. In this setting, an appropriate organization would assign a much smaller responsibility region to the call center responsible for the northwest corner of the city, and expand the responsibilities of other call centers to make up the difference in coverage.

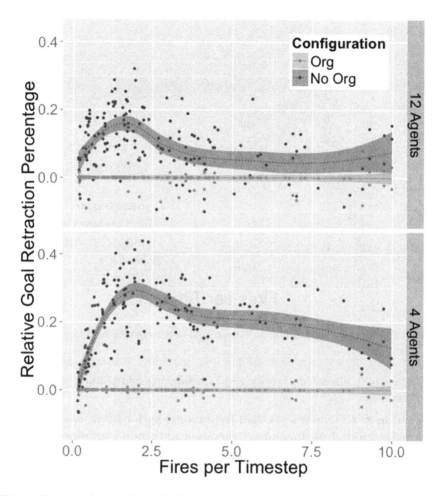

Fig. 6. Varying the number of call centers: relative goal-conflict rate (Color figure online)

Observation 4: The performance separation of effective organization increases with increased workload imbalance ⇒ When workloads are imbalanced in this way, call-center agents are not necessarily idle, but instead they work on less beneficial goals. Thus, the penalty occurred by providing these call centers with an inappropriate organization comes in the form of "lost opportunity," where the agent could have performed much more beneficial tasks if it had not been discouraged from doing so by organizational directives. Correspondingly, Fig. 7 shows that, as the organizational influences becomes less appropriate, the mean benefit of selected goals becomes lower. A surprising observation shown in Fig. 7 is that the No Org case has the highest mean goal benefit of all of the configurations (but not the highest relative score). This is due to No Org agents' preference to selfishly commit to attractive goals which

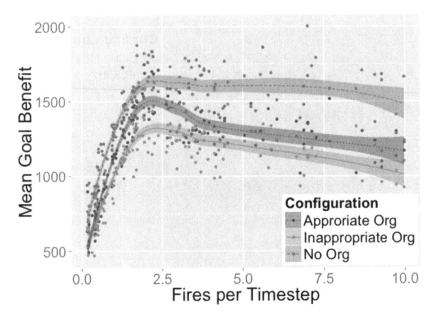

Fig. 7. Varying workload balance: mean goal benefit (Color figure online)

other agents may already be working on, introducing additional goal conflicts and coordination cost.

Observation 5: Extreme workload imbalance, high or low, causes organizationally guided performance to converge to non-organized performance ⇒ On the other end of the spectrum, both Appropriate and Inappropriate Org's less beneficial goals result in a direct lowering of overall score. Figure 8 indicates that this behavior essentially lowers the Appropriate Org curve onto the No Org curve, while still maintaining a window in the workload spectrum where organization is especially advantageous.

Span of Control. An important factor in determining if and how agents should be organized is span of control. Simply adding resources (or performers) to a task does not result in constant gain per added resource, and can even result in a net loss of utility. This phenomena is found in many real-world settings [25] where organizations attempt to scale the number of performers without correspondingly scaling management capacity (e.g., hundreds of construction workers cannot be managed by a single foreman). In the firefighting simulator, per-resource effectiveness is diminished above a parameterized call center span-of-control limit.

Observation 6: Increasing the number of call-center agents beyond what is necessary given their span-of-control capabilities adds coordination requirements (to keep them out of each other's way), decreasing the organizational benefit separation compared to a suitable

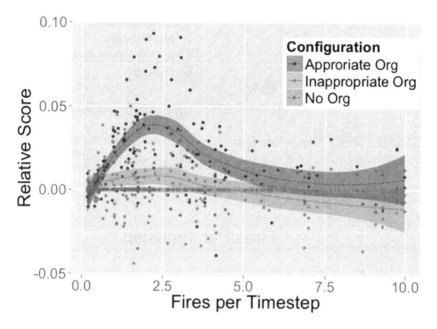

Fig. 8. Varying workload balance: relative score (Color figure online)

number of centers $\Rightarrow$ Span-of-control limits are both important and ubiquitous, since centralization is not generally tractable or realistic. When exceeded in RoboCup Rescue firefighting, performance per brigade is attenuated, counteracting coordination reductions from centralization. Otherwise, one center could handle all brigades.

We explored span of control using a configuration where a single call center agent is responsible for managing all 24 fire-brigade resources in the system, but with a span-of-control limit imposed after 6 utilized brigades. Then, we increased the span-of-control capability of the center to 24 (no span-of-control-limit attenuation) to understand how the single call-center agent would perform with no span-of-control limit. We compared these two cases with the baseline configuration where the fire brigades are distributed evenly across four call centers, each controlling 6 of them. Because no call center coordination is needed when there is a single center, in cases where fewer than 6 brigades are needed to execute all of the tasks in the environment, both of the single-agent configurations outperform the multiagent configuration (Fig. 9).

At a workload level of one fire per timestep, the limited resource effectiveness incurred by the span-of-control penalty becomes more significant than the coordination cost in the multiagent case. Further, since the single-agent case incurs no coordination complexity, there is a noticeable peak in the single-agent configuration without a span-of-control penalty, corresponding to the coordination-cost peak discussed previously.

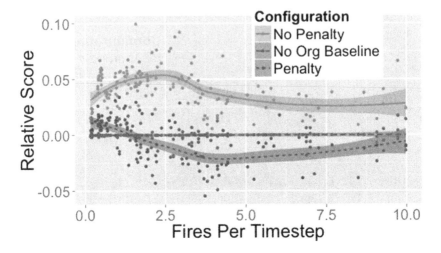

Fig. 9. Span of control analysis (Color figure online)

Observation 7: Coordination requirements that exceed an agent's span-of-control capabilities leads to an inverted performance curve ⇒ Figure 9 shows that the sweet spot obtained when running under the best case scenario of a single call center with no coordination requirements becomes a "sour spot" when span of control is considered. Intuitively, the sweet spot drops below the No Org baseline in the region of the workload spectrum where it is important that fire-brigade resources are managed effectively. With span-of-control limits imposed, fire-brigade effectiveness is diminished.

4   MARL Organizations

We next looked for sweet-spot behavior using a previously described and implemented multiagent reinforcement learning (MARL) system. This second system operates in a very different setting: organizing agents that are learning task-assignment policies that optimize service time for tasks arriving in a network of agents [26,27].

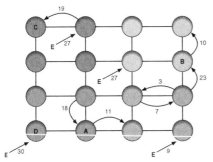

Formally, the structure of this domain can be represented as a graph $G = \langle V, E \rangle$. The vertex set, V, represents the set of agents in the system. The edge set, E, represents connections between pairs of agents through which tasks can be forwarded, illustrated in Fig. 10. Agents maintain a *processing queue* and a *routing queue*. The processing queue contains tasks that an agent is actively working on. The routing queue contains tasks that are

Fig. 10. Illustration of a small MARL domain (Color figure online)

not being actively worked on, and need a decision on the part of the agent to either process or forward to a neighboring agent. Each task is annotated with a duration s, indicating how many time units it takes to complete that task. After a task has been at the head of an agent's processing queue for s steps, that task is dequeued and marked as completed. Three parameters govern the pattern of task generation. First, the task duration, s, is randomly distributed according to an exponential distribution with rate λ, held constant throughout our experiments. Second, a parameter $T \subset V$ controls the potential locations in the network where tasks may originate. In our experiments, T is varied, but $|T|$ is held constant. Third, the rate at which tasks arrive at each vertex in T is Poisson distributed. The rate of this Poisson distribution is used to control task difficulty. Newly created tasks are assigned to a specific agent v and placed in v's routing queue. Agent v may either work on the task itself, by adding the task to its processing queue, or it may forward the task to a neighbor (i.e., those agents j for which $(v, j) \in E$). Forwarding a task to neighbor j places that task in j's routing queue. The reward function in this setting is defined as the reciprocal of the average service time over a time window, where service time is measured as the total time incurred from task creation to task completion. Given this formulation, agents are tasked with learning a forwarding policy given observed behaviors of neighboring agents and their intrinsic queue state. Throughout these experiments, the PGA-APP algorithm [28] and an extension of Q-Learning to the multiagent case with stochastic policies were used to learn those policies.

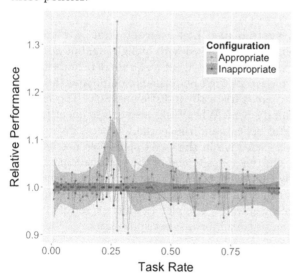

Fig. 11. Relative performance of MARL organizations (Color figure online)

In this domain, each agent is either a subordinate or a supervisor. Supervisors are responsible for transferring experiences between subordinates that are experiencing similar environmental conditions. Appropriate organizations in this task allocation domain are those that arrange supervisors in a way that exploits similarities between agents. If a group of subordinates frequently experience the same environmental conditions, a great deal of transfer learning can take place. If subordinate groups experience vastly different environmental conditions, transfer learning can occur less frequently, thus not taking advantage of the benefits that organization provides. As in firefighting, an organizational arrangement of supervisors that is appropriate given a particular task distribution may be inappropriate under a different task distribution, so the organization is only effective if the actual distribution is consistent with the expectations assumed in the designed supervisor arrangement.

For our experiments, we used a 100-agent lattice network and considered two agent organizations. The first organization arranges 4 supervisors such that agents are assigned to supervisors based on their distance from the border of the lattice. The second organization arranges 4 supervisors according to quadrants of the lattice. Tasks are then distributed on the lattice originating from the boundary. Under this model, the former organization is considered "Appropriate" since it partitions agents in a manner that maximizes the similarity of agents in supervisory groups. The latter organization is considered "Inappropriate" since it arranges agents in a way that prohibits effective experience sharing. Given this setup, we experimentally varied the difficulty of the learning problem by increasing the mean of the Poisson distribution governing task distribution on the range $[0, 1]$, where 1 represents a very heavy task load (averaging one task per time unit). One hundred values of λ were sampled uniformly along this range for each supervisory configuration, resulting in a total of 200 runs. Evaluation was performed in terms of area under a learning curve (AUC), modeled as an exponential moving average of system-wide task service time. When the system converges more quickly to an optimal policy, the area under this curve will be smaller. To characterize relative performance differences across a wide array of problem difficulties, AUC was normalized relative to the Inappropriate Org configuration.

Observation 8: The MARL system also has a sweet spot $\Rightarrow$ Figure 11 shows more performance variability than occurred with firefighting, but a statistically significant sweet spot arises around a per-agent task rate of 0.25 tasks per timestep. At this workload, the Appropriate Org's performance dominates the Inappropriate Org's. Elsewhere, the two are statistically indistinguishable. The results in the MARL domain are particularly clear. When tasks arrive so frequently that agents cannot compute meaningful policies and the learning process diverges, a supervisor structure that is highly effective in the sweet spot does not help in transferring reasonable policies. On the opposite end of the workload spectrum, when tasks arrive so infrequently that agents do not need to act intelligently in order to service the requests in a timely manner, policy transfer is not important. It is clear from this analysis that even with a completely different set of system dynamics and agent behaviors, an organizational sweet spot exists.

5   Closing Thoughts

Although we have measured and analyzed agent-organization performance under widely varying conditions using only two previously implemented and studied systems (each operating in a different problem domain), we believe that the qualitative behaviors we observed are general and apply to multiagent organizations in *any* domain. We hope our observations encourage those working with more complex heterogeneous agent organizations to investigate and report their performance over a wider range of conditions. Recognizing when a multiagent system will be operating in its organizational sweet spot is helpful in deciding how much effort should be spent in designing and using an agent organization as well as for explaining situations where using an agent organization results in little observed benefit (because the system is operating outside the sweet spot). We have observed that coordination and cooperation amounts, lost work opportunities, and span-of-control capabilities all contribute to sweet-spot performance benefits.

Understanding a multiagent system's organizational sweet spot is important, not just for understanding organizational control opportunity and effectiveness, but when considering if organizational adaptation (dynamic agent organizations) might be worthwhile [14, 29–31]. Sweet-spot understanding is also important in open, sociotechnical settings when designing an organization (and sizing that design appropriately) for agent recruitment. Identifying where a multiagent system is operating in relation to its organizational sweet spot is important to any discussion or analysis of organizational suitability, performance, or effectiveness.

Acknowledgment. This material is based in part upon work supported by the National Science Foundation under Awards No. IIS-0964590 and IIS-1116078. Any opinions, findings, conclusions or recommendations expressed in this publication are those of the authors and do not necessarily reflect the views of the National Science Foundation.

References

1. Fox, M.S.: An organizational view of distributed systems. IEEE Trans. Syst. Man Cybern. SMC **11**(1), 70–80 (1981)
2. Corkill, D.D., Lesser, V.R.: The use of meta-level control for coordination in a distributed problem-solving network. In: IJCAI-83, Karlsruhe, Federal Republic of Germany, pp. 748–756, August 1983
3. Gasser, L., Ishida, T.: A dynamic organizational architecture for adaptive problem solving. In: AAAI-91, Anaheim, California, pp. 185–190, July 1991
4. Durfee, E.H., So, Y.P.: The effects of runtime coordination strategies within static organizations. In: IJCAI-97, Nagoya, Japan, pp. 612–618, August 1997
5. Carley, K.M., Gasser, L.: Computational organization theory. In: Weiss, G. (ed.) Multiagent Systems: A Modern Approach to Distributed Artificial Intelligence, Chap. 7, pp. 299–330. MIT Press, Cambridge (1999)
6. Horling, B., Lesser, V.: A survey of multi-agent organizational paradigms. Knowl. Eng. Rev. **19**(4), 281–316 (2004)
7. Dignum, F., Dignum, V., Sonenberg, L.: Exploring congruence between organizational structure and task performance: a simulation approach. In: Boissier, O., Padget, J., Dignum, V., Lindemann, G., Matson, E., Ossowski, S., Sichman, J.S., Vázquez-Salceda, J. (eds.) ANIREM and OOOP 2005. LNCS (LNAI), vol. 3913, pp. 213–230. Springer, Heidelberg (2006)
8. Grossi, D., Dignum, F., Dignum, V., Dastani, M., Royakkers, L.: Structural aspects of the evaluation of agent organizations. In: Noriega, P., Vázquez-Salceda, J.,

Boella, G., Boissier, O., Dignum, V., Fornara, N., Matson, E. (eds.) COIN 2006. LNCS (LNAI), vol. 4386, pp. 3–18. Springer, Heidelberg (2007)

9. Horling, B., Lesser, V.: Using quantitative models to search for appropriate organizational designs. Auton. Agent. Multi-Agent Syst. **16**(2), 95–149 (2008)

10. Sims, M., Corkill, D., Lesser, V.: Automated organization design for multi-agent systems. Auton. Agent. Multi-Agent Syst. **16**(2), 151–185 (2008)

11. Slight, J., Durfee, E.H.: Organizational design principles and techniques for decision-theoretic agents. In: Proceedings of the Twelveth International Joint Conference on Autonomous Agents and Multi-Agent Systems (AAMAS 2013), pp. 463–470, May 2013

12. Rao, A.S., Georgeff, M.P.: BDI agents: from theory to practice. In: Proceedings of the First International Conference on Multi-Agent Systems (ICMAS 1995), San Francisco, California, pp. 312–319, June 1995

13. Corkill, D.D., Durfee, E., Lesser, V.R., Zafar, H., Zhang, C.: Organizationally adept agents. In: Proceedings of the 12th International Workshop on Coordination, Organization, Institutions and Norms in Agent Systems (COIN@AAMAS 2011), pp. 15–30, May 2011

14. Corkill, D., Zhang, C., Silva, B.D., Kim, Y., Zhang, X., Lesser, V.: Using annotated guidelines to influence the behavior of organizationally adept agents. In: Proceedings of the 14th International Workshop on Coordination, Organization, Institutions and Norms in Agent Systems (COIN@AAMAS 2012), pp. 46–60, June 2012

15. Corkill, D., Zhang, C., Silva, B.D., Kim, Y., Garant, D., Lesser, V., Zhang, X.: Biasing the behavior of organizationally adept agents (extended abstract). In: Proceedings of the Twelveth International Joint Conference on Autonomous Agents and Multi-Agent Systems (AAMAS 2013), pp. 1309–1310, May 2013

16. Kitano, H., Tadokoro, S.: RoboCup-Rescue: a grand challenge for multi-agent and intelligent systems. AI Mag. **22**(1), 39–52 (2001)

17. Cheeseman, P., Kanefsky, B., Taylor, W.M.: Where the really hard problems are. In: IJCAI-91, Sydney, Australia, pp. 331–337, August 1991

18. Kirkpatrick, S., Selman, B.: Critical behavior in the satisfiability of random boolean expressions. Science **264**, 1297–1301 (1994)

19. Monasson, R., Zecchina, R., Kirkpatrick, S., Selman, B., Troyansky, L.: Determining computational complexity from characteristic 'phasetransitions'. Nature **400**, 133–137 (1999)

20. Gasser, L.: An overview of DAI. In: Distributed Artificial Intelligence: Theory and Praxis, pp. 9–30. Springer (1993)

21. Sterling, L., Taveter, K.: The Art of Agent-Oriented Modeling. MIT Press, Cambridge (2009)

22. Boissier, O., van Riemsdijk, M.B.: Organizational reasoning agents. In: Ossowski, S. (ed.) Agreement Technolgies, Chap. 19, vol. 8, pp. 309–320. Springer, The Netherlands (2013)

23. van Riemsdijk, M.B., Dignum, V., Jonker, C., Aldewereld, H.: Programming role enactment through reflection. In: Proceedings of the 2011 IEEE/WIC/ACM International Conference on Web Intelligence and Intelligent Agent Technology (WI-IAT 2011), Lyon, France, pp. 133–140, August 2011

24. March, J.G., Simon, H.A.: Organizations. Wiley, New York (1958)

25. Horling, B., Lesser, V.: Analyzing, modeling and predicting organizational effects in a distributed sensor network. J. Braz. Comput. Soc. **11**(1), 9–30 (2005). Special Issue on Agent Organizations

26. Zhang, C., Abdallah, S., Lesser, V.: Integrating organizational control into multi-agent learning. In: Proceedings of the Eighth International Conference on Autonomous Agents and Multiagent Systems (AAMAS 2009), Budapest, Hungary, vol. 2, pp. 757–764 (2009)
27. Garant, D., da Silva, B.C., Lesser, V., Zhang, C.: Accelerating multi-agent reinforcement learning with dynamic co-learning. Technical report UM-CS-2015-004, School of Computer Science, University of Massachusetts Amherst, Amherst, MA 01003, January 2015
28. Zhang, C., Lesser, V.: Multi-agent learning with policy prediction. In: Proceedings of the 24th AAAI Conference on Artificial Intelligence, Atlanta, pp. 927–934 (2010)
29. Hübner, J.F., Sichman, J.S., Boissier, O.: Developing organised multi-agent systems using the MOISE+ model: programming issues at the system and agent levels. Int. J. Agent-Oriented Softw. Eng. 1(3/4), 370–395 (2009)
30. Staikopoulos, A., Saudrais, S., Clarke, S., Padget, J., Cliffe, O., Vos, M.D.: Mutual dynamic adaptation of models and service enactment in ALIVE. In: Proceedings of the Third International Models@Runtime Workshop, Toulouse, France, pp. 26–35, September 2008
31. Quillinan, T.B., Brazier, F., Aldewereld, H., Dignum, F., Dignum, V., Penserini, L., Wijngaards, N.: Developing agent-based organizational models for crisis management. In: Proceedings of the Industry Track of the Eighth International Joint Conference on Autonomous Agents and Multi-Agent Systems (AAMAS 2009), Budapest, Hungary, pp. 45–51, May 2009

SIMPLE: A Language for the Specification of Protocols, Similar to Natural Language

Dave de Jonge[✉] and Carles Sierra

IIIA-CSIC, Bellaterra, Catalonia, Spain
{davedejonge,sierra}@iiia.csic.es

Abstract. Large and open societies of agents require regulation, and therefore many tools have been developed that enable the definition and enforcement of rules on multiagent systems. Unfortunately, most of them have been designed to be used by computer scientists and are not suitable for people with no more than average computer skills. Since more and more tools are nowadays running as cloud services accessible to anyone (e.g. Massive Open Online Courses and social networks) we feel there is a need for a simple tool that allows ordinary people to create rules and protocols for these kinds of environments. In this paper we present ongoing work on the development of a new programming language for the definition of protocols for multiagent systems, which is so simple that anyone should be able to use it. Although its syntax is strict, it looks very similar to natural language so that protocols written in this language can be understood directly by anyone, without having to learn the language beforehand. Moreover, we have implemented an easy-to-use editor that helps users writing sentences that obey the syntax rules, as well as an interpreter that can parse such protocols and verify whether they are violated or not.

1 Introduction

In open multiagent systems (MAS) where any agent can enter and leave at will and the origins of the agents are unknown one needs a mechanism to regulate the behavior of those agents. Just like in human societies, rules need to be imposed in order to prevent the agents from misbehaving and abusing system resources. A good example is that of an auction taking place under a specific protocol. An English auction protocol for example, requires the buyers to make increasing bids and stops when the auctioneer says so, after which the buyer with the highest bid wins the auction. In a Dutch auction on the other hand, bids are decreasing, and the first buyer to accept a bid wins the auction.

Many systems for the implementation of such regulatory systems have been developed, such as ANTE [7], MANET [34], S-MOISE+ [22], and EIDE [15]. They allow users to define a set of rules and then impose those rules on the agents in a MAS (the term 'agents' may here refer to software agents as well as to human beings). This enforcement of rules may happen either by punishing misbehaving agents, or by simply making it impossible to violate them, which is called *regimentation*.

© Springer International Publishing Switzerland 2016
V. Dignum et al. (Eds.): COIN 2015, LNAI 9628, pp. 98–118, 2016.
DOI: 10.1007/978-3-319-42691-4_6

One common characteristic of these systems is that they are mainly designed with computer scientists as their target users. They require knowledge of multi-agent systems, programming languages and/or formal logic. For people with no more than average computer skills they are unfortunately too complicated.

We expect however that agent technologies will become more and more common in the near future, creating a demand for simple tools to maintain and organize such systems and that can be used by ordinary people. We can compare this for example with the evolution of web development. In the early days of the Internet, developing a web page was considered an advanced task that would only be undertaken by computer experts, and hence web development languages such as HTML, PHP and SQL were developed to be used by professional programmers. However, as web pages became more and more abundant and every shop, social club, or sports team wanted to have its own web page, many tools such as DreamWeaver and WordPress were introduced to make the creation of web pages a much simpler task. We strive for a similarly easy tool for the development of multiagent systems.

A good example of where such a tool would be useful is the organization of online classes, because teachers often want to put restrictions on their students. Teachers may for example require that students only take a certain exam after they have passed all previous exams. In this way teachers make sure they do not waste their time correcting exams of students that do not study seriously anyway. Another example could be the process of organizing a conference, where one requires authors to submit before a deadline, or one requires the program chair to appoint at least 3 reviewers to each paper. Also, one can think of a tool that allows users to set up their own social networks, with their own specific rules, as suggested in [23].

Therefore, in this paper we present ongoing work on the development of a new language to define protocols for multiagent systems. This language is so close to natural language that it can be understood directly by anyone without prior knowledge of any other programming language. We call this language SIMPLE, which stands for SIMple Protocol LanguagE. Although it *looks* very similar to natural language, it has in fact a strict syntax. Together with this language we also present two tools: an editor that makes it very easy for users to write well-formed sentences, and an interpreter that parses the source file and makes sure that the rules defined in it are indeed enforced. The fact that the language comes with an editor is very important, because it enables the users to write correct protocols without having to know the rules of the language by heart and makes sure that all sentences are syntactically correct.

We would like to stress that this language is not meant to program the agents themselves. It is only meant to program the organizational structure between the agents. That is: it puts restrictions on the agents in their actions, but does not dictate entirely what they ought to do; the agents still have the freedom to make autonomous decisions, as long as these decisions comply with the protocol. Protocols written in this language do not specify what the agents *must* do, but only what the agents *can* do.

We have developed SIMPLE according to the following guidelines:

- The language should stay as close as possible to natural language.
- The syntax should remain strict: sentences must be well formed, and every well formed sentence can only have one correct interpretation.
- Given a protocol written in this language anyone should immediately be able to understand what it means, even if he or she has never seen our language before.
- Users should be able to write a protocol in this language without having to spend any time learning the language.

The only thing we require from the user is that he or she be familiar with the English language. We still consider the language as presented here (version 0.10) to be in a premature state, and we plan to extend it much more in the future. A working demonstration of the SIMPLE editor and interpreter can be found at http://simple.iiia.csic.es.

The rest of this paper is organized as follows: in Sect. 2 we give a short overview of previous work done in this field. Next, in Sect. 3 we explain the assumptions that we have made about the set-up of any MAS to which our language is applied. In Sect. 4 we describe the syntax rules of our language. Next, in Sect. 5 we explain how our interpreter parses text files written in our language and enforces its rules upon the agents. Then, in Sect. 6 we give two examples of protocols written in SIMPLE, for which we have tested that they are successfully parsed and enforced by our interpreter. In Sect. 7 we make a comparison between the expressivity of SIMPLE and the expressivity of the existing Islander tool. And finally, in Sect. 8 we describe the further extensions that we are planning to add to our language.

2   Related Work

Regulatory systems have been subject of research for a long time and a number of frameworks have been implemented that often consist of tools for implementing, testing, running and visualizing protocols. Examples of such frameworks are ANTE [7], MANET [34], S-MOISE+ [22], and EIDE [15]. A comparative study of some of those systems has been made in [16].

ANTE [7] has been implemented as a JADE-based platform, including a set of agents that provide contracting services. It integrates automatic negotiation, trust & reputation and Normative Environments. Users and agents can specify their needs and indicate the contract types to be created. Norms governing specific contract types are predefined in the normative environment. Although ANTE has been targeting the domain of electronic contracting, it was conceived as a more general framework having in mind a wider range of applications.

The MANET [34] meta-model is based on the assumption that the agent environment is composed of two fundamental building blocks: the physical environment, concerned with agent interaction with physical resources and with the

MAS infrastructure, and the social environment, concerned with the social interactions of the agents. In the MANET meta-model it is assumed that the normative system can be composed of three structural components: agents, objects
and spaces.

In the EIDE framework agents interact with each other in a so called *Electronic Institution*. The agents are grouped in to conversations, which are called
Scenes. The institution has a specification that defines how agents can move from
one scene to another and defines a protocol for each scene. Within a scene the
agents interact by sending messages to one another. Each agent in the system
has a special agent assigned to it, called its Governor, which checks whether the
messages sent by the agent satisfy the protocol, and blocks them when they do
not. The EIDE framework comes with a graphical tool called *Islander* [14] that
allows people to create institution specifications in a visual manner. Protocols
in Islander are represented as finite state machines, drawn as a graph in which
the states are the vertices and the state-transitions are the edges. Every message
sent triggers a state transition.

In order to define rules and norms for multiagent systems, a vast amount of
languages and logics have been proposed. It would be impossible to list all the
relevant work in this field here, so we just mention some of the most important
examples. A logical system to define norms and rules is called a *deontic* logic. The
best known system of deontic logic is called Standard Deontic Logic (SDL) [37].
Important refinements of this logic are Dyadic Deontic Logic (DDL) [26] and
Defeasible Deontic Logic [31]. Furthermore, an extension of this taking temporal
considerations into account was proposed in [20]. In [28] a system to formalize
norms using input/output logic was proposed, while in [21] the authors provide a
model for the formalization of social law by means of Alternating-time Temporal
Logic (ATL). In [25] the author proposes the use of Linear Time Logic (LTL) to
express norms. Other important approaches are based on Propositional Dynamic
Logic (PDL) [29], on See-to-it-that logic (STIT) [4] and on Computational Tree
Logic (CTL) [6]. Models for the verification of expectations in normative systems
are proposed in [1,10], and in [32] the authors introduce the $nC+$ language for
representing normative systems as state transition systems.

The above mentioned systems however mainly focus on the theoretical properties of regulatory systems. Work that is more focused on the actual implementation of such systems is for example [27] which proposes a model to define rules
in the Z language, while in [3] the authors propose the use of Event Calculus
for the specification of protocols. A programming language designed to program
organizations, called 2OPL, was introduced in [11]. Other important examples
of languages and frameworks for the implementation of norms and rules are
described in: [2,9,18,24,35,36].

Although some of the above mentioned languages are more user friendly than
others, it still seems that they all require the user to be a computer scientist or
at least has some knowledge of programming, logic or mathematics.

There do exist a number of programming languages that claim to be similar to natural language such as hyperTalk[1] and PlainEnglish[2], but most of them still aim at real programmers, albeit that they aim for *beginning* programmers. The only exception that we know of, is a language called Inform 7 [30]. This is a language that in many cases truly reads like natural language, but the main difference with SIMPLE is that it is developed for an entirely different domain. Inform 7 is a language to write *Interactive Fiction*: an art form that lies somewhere in between literature and computer games.

We think that one of the main reasons that Inform 7 can stay very close to natural language, is that it is highly adapted to a very specific domain. This restricts the possible things a programmer may want to express and hence keeps the language manageable. We have taken a similar approach: our language is only intended to be used as a language for implementing protocols for multiagent systems, and although it could possibly be useful for other domains too, we restrict our attention to this domain.

Another example of an easy-to-use language is If-This-Then-That[3] (IFTTT). This tool allows users to define if-then rules that trigger some action to occur whenever a certain event takes places. This concept is very similar to SIMPLE, except that in SIMPLE the rules do not trigger events to take place, but rather grant rights to agents.

Controlled natural language has been applied to policy making before in [8,12], which is essentially a mapping between Attempto Controlled English (ACE) [17] and the policy specification language Protune [5]. However, this work seems to focus mainly on the specification of static rules, whereas our work puts emphasis on dynamic rules that may change depending on events that are happening during the execution of the policy. This is reflected by the fact that in their language the conditions of the rules are written in simple present, rather than in present perfect as in our language. A similar tool to write static rules in controlled natural language was presented in [33].

3   Basic Ideas

We assume a multiagent system in which agents exchange messages according to some given protocol. These agents may be autonomous software agents, or may be humans acting through a graphic user interface. The agents are however not in direct contact with one another. Every message any agent sends first passes a central server that verifies whether the message satisfies the protocol. If a message does not satisfy the protocol, then it is blocked by the server and it will not arrive at its intended recipients. Note that this is a form of regimentation. In this paper we will not consider any forms of punishment, and assume protocols are only enforced by means of regimentation. We assume that the life-cycle of the MAS is as follows:

---

[1] http://en.wikipedia.org/wiki/HyperTalk.

[2] http://www.osmosian.com.

[3] https://ifttt.com/.

1. A user (the *protocol designer*) writes a protocol in our language and stores it in a text file.
2. He or she launches a communication server, with the location of the text file as a parameter.
3. The interpreter, which is part of the server application, parses the text file.
4. Agents connect to the server through a TCP/IP connection and send messages to one another.
5. Every such message is checked by the interpreter. If it does not satisfy the protocol, it is blocked. If it does satisfy the protocol it is forwarded to its intended recipients.
6. The agent that intended to send the message is notified by the server whether the message has been delivered correctly or not.

The text file contains the protocol as a set of sentences that follow the SIMPLE syntax, and are therefore human readable. Furthermore, it also stores the protocol in JSON format so that it can be parsed easily by the interpreter.

Protocols written in SIMPLE have a closed-world interpretation: every message is considered illegal by default, unless the protocol specifies that it is legal. In order to determine which messages are legal, we use a system based on the notion of 'rights' and 'events', meaning that an agent obtains the right to send a specific message if a certain event has (or has not) taken place. The assignment of such rights is determined by if-then rules in the protocol.

We currently assume agents can send messages following one of these two patterns:

- ('say', x)
- ('announce', y, z)

in which the sender can replace x, y and z by any character string (we will see later that the 'announce' message has the interpretation that, by uttering this message, the value of z will be assigned to the variable y). The current version of the language does not yet allow users to specify the recipient of a message, so for now we assume that any message is always sent to all the other agents in the MAS. We plan this to change in future versions of SIMPLE. Also, we expect that future versions will support more types of messages.

The interpreter keeps a list of **rights** for each agent in the MAS. A right is a tuple of one of the two following forms:

- ('say', v)
- ('announce', w)

We say that a right ('say', v) **matches** a message ('say', x) if and only if x is equal to v, or v is the keyword 'anything'. A right ('announce', w) matches a message ('announce', y, z) if and only if y equals w. For example: if the agent has the right ('announce', 'price') then it matches the message ('announce', 'price', '$100'). A message is considered legal if the agent sending the message has at least one right that matches the message. Whenever the interpreter determines that a message is legal, it stores a copy of that message, together with the name of its sender, in the interpreter's **event history**.

One concept that we have borrowed from EIDE is the concept of a *role*. The rules in the protocol never refer to specific individuals, because we assume that at design time the designer cannot know which agents are going to join the MAS at run time. Instead, the protocol assigns rights to agents based on the roles they are playing. Every agent that enters the MAS (i.e. connects to the communication server) must choose a specific role to adopt, from a number of roles that are defined in the protocol. An auction protocol for example, could define the roles *buyer* and *auctioneer*. The protocol could then define a rule saying that a buyer can only make a bid after the auctioneer has opened the auction.

4   Description of the Language

A protocol is written as a set of sentences that look like natural language, but follow a strict syntax. Although in this paper we will often start sentences with a capital, this is not necessary, as the language is entirely case-insensitive. Like in natural language, the end of a sentence is marked with a period. Unlike most other programming languages, variable names are allowed to contain spaces. Another important property of this language, as we will see at the end of this section, is that it is impossible to write inconsistent protocols.

4.1   Roles

In order to define a role in the protocol the user must first specify two names for that role: the **singular role name** and the **plural role name**, for example: 'auctioneer' and 'auctioneers'. The user must then specify a role constraint sentence:

Definition 1. *A **role constraint sentence** is a sentence of one of the following forms:*

- *There can be any number of* r.
- *There must be at least* x r.
- *There can be at most* x r
- *There must be at least* y *and at most* x r.
- *There must be exactly* x r.

Where x *and* y *can be any positive integer with* $y < x$ *and* r *is the plural role name, except in the case that* $x = 1$ *in which case* r *it is the singular role name.*

The following sentence is an example of a role constraint sentence:

> *There must be at least 2 buyers.*

For each role in the protocol there must be exactly one such role constraint sentence. The interpreter makes sure that these role constraints are not violated. That is, when an agent tries to connect to the communication server with a role for which there are already too many participants, the connection will be refused. If on the other hand there are not enough participants for every role, then every message is considered illegal. Therefore, the agents cannot start sending messages to one another until there are enough participants for every role.

4.2 Conditions and Consequences

The main idea of the language, as explained above, is that rights are assigned to the agents by means of if-then rules. An example of such a rule could be:

If the auctioneer has said 'open' then any buyer can announce his bid price.

In order to precisely define which sentences are well formed we first need to introduce a number of terms, namely: *quantifiers, identifiers, conditions,* and *consequences.*

Definition 2. *A **quantifier** is any of these keywords: no, any, every, a, an, the, that.*

Definition 3. *An **identifier** is a sequence of characters of one of the following forms:*

– q r
– *no one*
– *anyone*
– *everyone*
– *he*

Where q *can be any quantifier and* r *can be any singular role name. Identifiers of the form no* r *as well as the identifier 'no one' are called **negative identifiers**. All other identifiers are called **positive identifiers**.*

Definition 4. *A **past-event condition** is a string of characters of one of the following forms:*

– id *has said '*x*'*
– id *has announced the* x
– id *has announced his* x
– pid *has not said '*x*'*
– pid *has not announced the* x
– pid *has not announced his* x

where id *can be any identifier,* x *can be any character string, and* pid *can be any positive identifier. A past-event condition is called negative if it contains the keyword 'not' or if it contains a negative identifier. A past-event condition is called positive otherwise.*

A past-event condition is a specific type of condition. We will define other types of condition later on. A positive past-event condition is considered true if and only if there is any message in the event history that matches the condition. For example the condition *any buyer has said 'hello'* is considered true if there exists a message in the event history of the form ('say', 'hello') which was sent by an agent playing the role *buyer*. A negative past-event condition is considered true if and only if there is no message in the event history that matches the condition.

Definition 5. *A **right-update consequence** is a string of characters of one of the following forms:*

– `pid` *can say* 'x'
– `pid` *can announce the* x
– `pid` *can announce his* x

where `pid` *can be any positive identifier and* x *can be any character string.*

A right-update consequence is a specific type of consequence. Other types of consequences are defined later on.

We can now construct sentences ('rules') of the form *If A then B*, where A is a conjunction of conditions and B is a right-update consequence. We say that a rule is **active** if all its conditions are true. Then the idea is that an agent has the right to send a specific message if and only if there is an active rule with right-update consequence that matches that message.

Identifiers are used inside conditions and consequences to determine to which set of agents these conditions and consequences apply. We would like to remark that the quantifiers 'a', 'an', 'any' and 'the' all have exactly the same meaning, so the language contains some redundancy. However, we do consider it very useful to have all of them in the language because they help the protocol designer to write more natural sentences. For example, if an auction protocol contains only one auctioneer it makes much more sense to talk about 'the auctioneer' than about 'any auctioneer'.

Also note that we have included the quantifier 'that'. This quantifier refers to any agent that was also referred to by the last quantifier earlier in the sentence. For example, suppose that a buyer called Alice says 'hello' and then a buyer called Bob says 'hi', then the condition:

   a buyer has said 'hello' and a buyer has said 'hi'

is true. However, the condition:

   a buyer has said 'hello' and that buyer has said 'hi'

is false, because 'that buyer' refers to the same agent as the one that said 'hello' (which is Alice). This second condition would only be true if the messages ('say' 'hello') and ('say', 'hi') had been sent by the same agent. Likewise, we have included the identifier 'he', which refers to the same agent as the last identifier that appeared earlier in the sentence. For example:

   If a buyer has said 'hello' and he has said 'hi'

4.3   Properties

The rights of an agent may not only depend on past events, but may also depend on values of variables. Variables in SIMPLE are called **properties**. A property can be assigned to the protocol (a *global property*), or can be assigned to individual agents (a *role property*). For example, we may specify that every buyer has a property 'age', and that the protocol has a global property 'minimum age', so that we can state conditions such as:

If a buyer has said 'hello' and his age is greater than the minimum age then...

A property can be defined by including a *property initialization sentence* in the protocol.

Definition 6. *A **property initialization sentence** is a sentence of one of the following forms:*

- *This protocol has a* x, *which is initially* v.
- *Every* r *has a* x, *which is initially* v.

where x *can be any character string,* v *can be any character string, number, or identifier and* r *can be any singular role name. The string* x *is called the* **property name**, *and* v *is its* **initial value**.

The first of these sentences is used to define a global property, while the second one defines a role property. If the name of the property x starts with a vowel then the editor will automatically replace the article 'a' in the sentence with 'an'. For example:

Every buyer has an age, which is initially 0.

A property can also be added to a protocol without including a property initialization sentence, but instead by mentioning it in some rule containing the verb 'to announce'. For example, if there is a rule containing the condition

If a buyer has announced his age...

then the interpreter automatically understands that the role 'buyer' has a property named 'age'. Similarly, if the protocol contains a sentence containing the conditions

If the auctioneer has announced the start price...

then the interpreter understands that the protocol has a global property named 'start price'.

The current version of SIMPLE supports three types of properties: strings, numbers and identifiers. The type of a property is determined implicitly. That is: if the parser of the protocol is able to interpret the initial value of a property as a number, then the property is considered to be of type number, and likewise for identifiers. In all other cases the property is considered a string.

Definition 7. *A **property condition** is a clause of one of the following forms:*

- x *is less than* n
- x *is less than or equal to* n
- x *is* v
- x *is not* v
- x *is greater than or equal to* n
- x *is greater than* n

where x *is either the keyword 'the' followed by the name of a global property, or the keyword 'his' followed by the name of a role property.* v *can be any string, number or identifier, and* n *can be any number.*

Definition 8. *A **property-update consequence** is a clause of the form:*

- x *becomes* y
- x *will be* v
- x *is increased by* n
- x *is decreased by* n
- x *is multiplied by* n
- x *is divided by* n

where x *and* y *both are either the keyword 'the' followed by the name of a global property, or the keyword 'his' followed by the name of a role property.* y *can be any character string,* v *can be any string, number of identifier, and* n *can be any number.*

Definition 9. *A **current-event condition** is a string of characters of one of the following forms:*

- pid *says* 'x'
- pid *announces the* x
- pid *announces his* x

where pid *can be any positive identifier and* x *can be any character string.*

In order to change the values of properties we can use property-update rules.

Definition 10. *A **property-update rule** is a sentence of the form:*

- *When* x *then* z.

Where x *is a current-event condition and* z *is a property-update consequence.*

Examples of property-update rules are:

> *When any buyer says 'bid!' then his bid price is increased by 10.*
> *When the auctioneer says 'sold' then the last bidder becomes the winner.*

Note that the clause *x becomes y* means that the value of property y is overwritten with the value of property x. This can be understood as follows: suppose we have a property called *Carol's sister* and a property called *Bob's wife*. Furthermore, suppose that *Carol's sister* is initialized to the value *'Alice'*. Then the clause *Carol's sister becomes bob's wife* means that the value *'Alice'* is copied into the property *Bob's wife*. Note that when a property is assigned to an agent we use the key word 'his' to refer to the agent that owns the property. To be precise: it refers to the last agent that appears earlier in the sentence. So in the above example, 'his bid price' refers to the property named 'bid price' assigned to the agent that said 'bid!'.

Another way that values of properties are updated is when a message of type ('announce', x, y) is sent. In that case the value y is assigned to a property with name x. For example, whenever an agent sends the message ('announce', 'price', 100), the value 100 is automatically assigned to a property with the name 'price'. More specifically, if the property 'price' is global than that unique property is updated, while if it is a role property, for example for the role 'buyer', and the sender of the message indeed plays that role, then it is the property of the sender that is updated. If neither is the case, that is: if the property 'price' is a role property for the role 'buyer', but the sender does not play the 'buyer' role, then the message is illegal.

Definition 11. *A **right-update rule** is a sentence of the form:*

- id *can always say* v.
- id *can always announce the* v.
- id *can always announce his* v.
- *If* x *then* y.
- *If* x *then* y, *as long as* w.

where id *is an identifier,* v *can be any character string,* x *and* w *are conjunctions of past-event conditions and/or property conditions and* y *is a right-update consequence (the conditions in* w *are also referred to as **constraints**).*

Note that we allow such a rule to have no conditions at all, so that it is always active. In that case the protocol designer needs to include the keyword 'always' after the keyword 'can'. Also note that right-update rules have past-event conditions (which are written in present perfect), while property-update rules have current-event conditions (which are written in simple present). This is because they are interpreted in a fundamentally different way, which we will explain in Sect. 5.

4.4   Constraints

We have seen in Definition 11 that right-update rules may contain so-called *constraints*. A constraint is similar to a property condition, but is written at the end of the sentence, and indicated by the keywords *as long as*.

If the auctioneer has said 'open' then any buyer can announce his bid price, as long as his bid price is higher than the current price.

The consequences of a rule only have effect if all conditions and constraints of the rule are satisfied. The difference between constraints and conditions is that constraints refer to property values inside the consequence of the sentence, whereas conditions may only refer to past events or properties that do not appear inside the consequence. This means that when the interpreter verifies the legality of a certain message X, the truth of the constraints of any rule depend on the contents of that message, whereas the truth of the conditions of any rule can already be determined before the interpreter has received message X.

In the example sentence above for instance, the constraint says that the bid price announced by the buyer, must be higher than the current price. This can of course only be checked *when* the buyer is announcing his bid price, and not before.

4.5   Inconsistencies

One very important aspect of our language is that right-update consequences can only have *positive* identifiers. This means that a consequence can only *give* rights to an agent, but not take them away. Nevertheless, we can still make agents lose rights, but we do that by using negative conditions, rather than negative consequences. Take for example the following rule:

If the auctioneer has not said 'sold!' then any buyer can say 'bid!'.

Here, every buyer initially has the right to say 'bid!'. If there is no other rule that gives buyers the right to do that, then buyers will lose this right once the auctioneer says 'sold!', because the condition becomes false. If there is more than one rule that grants the right to say 'bid!' to every buyer then all those rules must become inactive in order for the buyers to lose that rule.

The big advantage of only allowing positive consequences, is that this makes it impossible to write inconsistent rules. Recall from Sect. 3 that for every message submitted the interpreter needs to answer the question: "Does the sender of this message have the right to do so?", with either "yes" or "no". We say that a protocol is *consistent* if for every possible message this question has only one correct answer.

Lemma 1. *A protocol written in SIMPLE is guaranteed to be consistent.*

Proof. The proof is easy: in our language, by definition, an agent has the right to do something if and only if there is at least one active rule that grants this right to the agent. This can never lead to inconsistencies: either such a rule exists or not.

This aspect certainly does not make our language unique, as the same principle applies to several other logical languages, such as GDL [19] and ASP [13] (Fig. 1).

Fig. 1. Two screen shots of the SIMPLE editor. Users write sentences simply by selecting available options, and they can only write free text whenever the syntax rules indeed allow that. Therefore it is impossible to write malformed sentences.

5   The SIMPLE Interpreter

We will now describe the software component that interprets and enforces the protocols.

Whenever an agent tries to send a message, this message is first analyzed by the interpreter. The interpreter verifies if the agent sending the message indeed has the right to send that message and, if so, updates its internal state and forwards the message to the other agents connected to the server. If the sender of the message does not have the right to send that message he or she is notified that the message has failed. The message will in that case not be forwarded to the other agents and the internal state of the interpreter is not updated. In fact, we consider this message as not sent.

The internal state of the interpreter consists of the following data structures:

– a list of all messages that have so far been sent successfully (the *event history*)
– a table that maps the name of each property to the current value of that property
– a table that maps the name of each agent in the MAS to the role it is playing
– a table that maps the name of each agent in the MAS to a list of rights for that agent.

Every time an agent tries to send a message, the interpreter follows the following procedure:[4]

1. The list of rights of that agent is made empty.
2. For each right-update rule in the protocol, the interpreter verifies if its conditions are true:
   – If the condition is a property condition then it checks whether that property currently has the proper value to make the condition true.
   – If the condition is a past-event condition, the interpreter tries to find an event in the event history that matches the condition. If such an event is indeed found, then the condition is considered true.

   A rule for which all conditions are true is labeled as 'active'.

---

[4] This procedure can be implemented in a much more efficient way than presented here, but we think this is not very relevant for this paper, so we prefer to present it in a way that is easier to understand for the reader.

3. For each right-update consequence in each active rule, the interpreter checks whether the identifier matches the sender of the message and, if yes, adds the right corresponding to this consequence to the sender's list of rights. If this consequence has any constraints assigned to it, they are stored together with the right.
4. After all the rights of the sending agent have been determined the interpreter verifies whether any of them matches the message that the agent is trying to send.
5. Next, if the agent indeed has that right the interpreter checks whether its constraints (if any) are satisfied.
6. If the sending agent has the proper right, and all its constraints are satisfied then the interpreter determines if there are any property-update rules in the protocol for which the condition matches the message. If yes, the properties in the rule's consequences are updated accordingly.
7. Finally, if the agent has the right to send the message and its constraints are satisfied, a copy of the message is stored in the event history, together with the name of the sender, and the message is forwarded to all other agents in the MAS.

It is important to note here that property-update rules and right-update rules are treated in a different way. To be precise: to verify whether a past-event condition is true, the interpreter compares the condition with all messages in the event history. Since messages are never removed from the event history this means that whenever a past-event condition becomes true, it remains true forever. For example, when a buyer says 'hello' then the condition *any buyer has said 'hello'* becomes true, and remains true forever. For negative conditions exactly the opposite holds: the condition *no buyer has said 'bye'* is initially true, but as soon as a buyer says 'bye' it becomes false, and will stay false forever. The current-event conditions on the other hand are only considered true at the moment that the corresponding message is under evaluation of the interpreter. That is, the condition *when a buyer says hello* is considered to be true only while the interpreter is evaluating the message ('say', 'hello') sent by some agent playing the role of buyer. As soon as the interpreter handles the next message this condition is considered false again. The reason for this is that we consider that when you obtain a right, you keep that right for an extended period of time, until one of the negative conditions in the rule becomes false. Updating of a property on the other hand, is a one-time event that only takes place at the moment a certain message is sent.

6   Examples

We here provide two examples of protocols. Both have been tested and are correctly executed by the interpreter.

English Auction Protocol:

There must be exactly 1 auctioneer.
There must be at least 2 buyers.

This protocol has a current price, which is initially 0.
Every buyer has a bid price which is initially 0.
This protocol has a highest bidder, which is initially no one.
This protocol has a winner, which is initially no one.

If the auctioneer has not said 'sold!' and the auctioneer has not announced the current price, then the auctioneer can announce the current price.
If the auctioneer has not said 'sold!' and the auctioneer has announced the current price, then any buyer can announce his bid price, as long as bid price is greater than current price.
When a buyer announces his bid price, then his bid price becomes the current price.
When a buyer announces his bid price, then that buyer becomes the highest bidder.
If any buyer has announced his bid price, then the auctioneer can say 'sold!'.
When the auctioneer says 'sold!', then the highest bidder becomes the winner.

Dutch Auction Protocol:

There must be exactly 1 auctioneer.
There must be at least 2 buyers.

This protocol has a current price, which is initially 0.
This protocol has a winner, which is initially no one.

If the auctioneer has not announced the current price, then he can announce the current price.
If the auctioneer has announced the current price and no buyer has said 'mine!', then the auctioneer can say 'next!'.
When the auctioneer says 'next!', then the current price is decreased by 1.
If the auctioneer has announced the current price and no buyer has said 'mine!', then any buyer can say 'mine!'.
When a buyer says 'mine!', then that buyer becomes the winner.

7 Comparison with Islander

Many other tools have been developed for the specification of protocols so it would be impossible to discuss all the advantages and disadvantages of SIMPLE with respect to those existing tools. Therefore, we limit ourselves to a comparison with the Islander tool, which is part of the EIDE framework.

Islander allows users to specify protocols using a graphical model that represents protocols as a directed graph in which the nodes represent states, and edges between nodes represent actions (an agent sending a message to another agent) that lead from one state to the next. This graphical model can be extended by assigning pre-conditions and post-conditions to the edges which are written in a formal language.

The advantage of the graphical model is that is relatively easy to use and understand, but the disadvantage is that it has very limited expressivity. Therefore, it is almost always necessary to use it in combination with the formal language, which however can be very difficult to use, even for computer scientists.

We will now give an example of a protocol that is hard to express using only the graphical representation of Islander. Note that this example uses the verb 'to make' which is currently not yet available in SIMPLE. Therefore, the idea is to show how SIMPLE *will* be more easy to use than Islander in the future, when we have further extended the language.

Suppose we want to implement the following protocol in Islander:

There must be at least 5 students.
Initially, any student can make assignment 1.
If a student has made assignment 1 then he can make assignment 2.
If a student has made assignment 2 then he can make assignment 3.

If there would be only 1 student then this protocol would be very easy to implement in Islander. It would just be a linear graph with 4 nodes and three edges, where each edge corresponds to making an assignment.

With multiple students however, you run into the problem that students may make their assignments at different speeds. For example, one student may quickly deliver assignments 1 and 2, while another is still busy with assignment 1. This means that at any moment each student can be in any of 4 states, and thus the protocol as a whole can be in any of 4^n different states if there are n students. With as little as 5 students drawing the graph would already become practically impossible as it would require the designer to draw $4^5 = 1024$ states plus all their edges. The only realistic way to specify this protocol would be to use the formal language rather than the graph-representation.

Another way to implement this protocol in Islander would be to implement it as a protocol for only 1 student, and then let n of these protocols run in parallel. In this way we again only need to draw a linear graph with 4 nodes and 3 edges. However, this is only possible because in this example there is no interdependency between the students' actions. If we make the example a bit more complicated, for example by adding a final exam that only starts when all students have finished all assignments, this is no longer possible.

Another problem with Islander is that one cannot use universal quantifiers. Even in Islander's formal language one cannot directly state something like *"If all students have finished their assignments..."*. The only way to achieve this is to create a list of names of students, make sure that the name of a student is added to this list when he or she enters the institution, and make sure that the name of a student is removed from this list whenever he or she finishes his or her assignment. Then, whenever you need the precondition that all students must have finished their assignments, you can specify that this list must be empty. In practice, this turns out to be a tedious job to do all this in Islander, making it far from user-friendly.

8   Future Work

We consider that the language as it is, is still too limited to be of real practical use. We here list the shortcoming that we consider most important and that we plan to fix in the near future, as well as other improvements that we are considering.

Firstly, we will add the possibility to specify the recipient of a message. Currently every message is sent to all other agents in the MAS, which makes it impossible to send confidential information. This means we will allow to write sentences such as:

If the auctioneer has said 'welcome' to a buyer then that buyer can say 'hello' to the auctioneer.

Secondly, we would like the protocol designer to be able to express that a certain event must have taken place a certain number of times. For example:

If a buyer has announced his bid price more than 5 times...

Thirdly, we would like to add time-constraints to the language, so that we could define rights that expire after a certain amount of time, such as:

If no one announces his bid during 10 s then the highest bidder becomes the winner.

Furthermore, we would like to add more types of messages and maybe even allow the protocol designer to define message types. That would make it possible to use certain domain-specific verbs. For example:

If a student has finished his assignment...

We could even take this a step further and allow the protocol designer to define new data types, similar to data types in the EIDE framework. For example, one could define a data type "contract" by including a sentences such as:

A contract consists of a date, a price, and a quantity.
A price is a positive number.

One could then define a negotiation protocol with sentences such as

Any negotiator can propose a contract.

If such data types are composed of basic types such as Strings and numbers then during the execution of the protocol the GUI can display the proper input fields for the user to specify the details of the contract to propose. Defining new types of objects is typically something that Inform 7 can handle well, so we may draw some inspiration from that language.

Furthermore, we will add a system that determines at run time, whenever an agent tries to send an illegal message, which conditions first need to be fulfilled before the agent can indeed legally send that message. In this way the system can explain to the user why he or she made a mistake and will help the user to understand new protocols. In order to make the language more flexible and expressive, we will delve into literature about linguistics and apply some of its principles to our language.

Finally, we will perform an empirical study to evaluate how easy-to-use this language really is. We will let random people implement a protocol using our language as well as using some other existing tool such as Islander to compare whether our language indeed makes the task easier.

Acknowledgments. Supported by the Agreement Technologies CONSOLIDER project, contract CSD2007-0022 and INGENIO 2010 and CHIST-ERA project ACE and EU project 318770 PRAISE.

References

1. Alberti, M., Gavanelli, M., Lamma, E., Chesani, F., Mello, P., Torroni, P.: Compliance verification of agent interaction: a logic-based software tool. Appl. Artif. Intell. **20**(2–4), 133–157 (2006)
2. Argente, E., Criado, N., Botti, V., Julian, V.: Norms for agent service controlling. In: EUMAS-08, pp. 1–15 (2008)
3. Artikis, A., Kamara, L., Pitt, J., Sergot, M.: A protocol for resource sharing in norm-governed ad hoc networks. In: Leite, J., Omicini, A., Torroni, P., Yolum, P. (eds.) DALT 2004. LNCS (LNAI), vol. 3476, pp. 221–238. Springer, Heidelberg (2005). http://dx.doi.org/10.1007/11493402_13
4. Belnap, N., Perloff, M.: Seeing to it that: a canonical form for agentives. In: Kyburg Jr., H.E., Loui, R.P., Carlson, G.N. (eds.) Knowledge Representation and Defeasible Reasoning. Studies in Cognitive Systems, vol. 5, pp. 167–190. Springer, Netherlands (1990). http://dx.doi.org/10.1007/978-94-009-0553-5_7
5. Bonatti, P.A., Olmedilla, D.: Driving and monitoring provisional trust negotiation with metapolicies. In: 6th IEEE International Workshop on Policies for Distributed Systems and Networks (POLICY 2005), 6–8 June 2005, Stockholm, Sweden, pp. 14–23 (2005). http://dx.doi.org/10.1109/POLICY.2005.13
6. Broersen, J., Dignum, F., Dignum, V., Meyer, J.-J.C.: Designing a deontic logic of deadlines. In: Lomuscio, A., Nute, D. (eds.) DEON 2004. LNCS (LNAI), vol. 3065, pp. 43–56. Springer, Heidelberg (2004)
7. Cardoso, H.L., Urbano, J., Rocha, A.P., Castro, A.J., Oliveira, E.: Ante: agreement negotiation in normative and trust-enabled environments. In: Ossowski, S. (ed.) Agreement Technologies. Law, Governance and Technology Series, vol. 8, pp. 549–564. Springer, Netherlands (2013). http://dx.doi.org/10.1007/978-94-007-5583-3_32
8. Coi, J.L.D., Kärger, P., Olmedilla, D., Zerr, S.: Using natural language policies for privacy control in social platforms (2009). http://CEUR-WS.org/Vol-447/paper4.pdf

9. Cranefield, S.: A rule language for modelling and monitoring social expectations in multi-agent systems. In: Boissier, O., Padget, J., Dignum, V., Lindemann, G., Matson, E., Ossowski, S., Sichman, J.S., Vázquez-Salceda, J. (eds.) ANIREM and OOOP 2005. LNCS (LNAI), vol. 3913, pp. 246–258. Springer, Heidelberg (2006)
10. Cranefield, S., Winikoff, M.: Verifying social expectations by model checking truncated paths. J. Logic Comput. **21**(6), 1217–1256 (2011). http://logcom.oxfordjournals.org/content/21/6/1217.abstract
11. Dastani, M., Tinnemeier, N.A., Meyer, J.J.C.: A programming language for normative multi-agent systems (2009)
12. De Coi, J.: Notes for a possible ACE → Protune mapping. Technical report, Forschungszentrum L3S, Appelstr. 9a, 30167 Hannover, July 2008
13. Eiter, T., Ianni, G., Krennwallner, T.: Answer set programming: a primer. In: Tessaris, S., Franconi, E., Eiter, T., Gutierrez, C., Handschuh, S., Rousset, M.-C., Schmidt, R.A. (eds.) Reasoning Web. LNCS, vol. 5689, pp. 40–110. Springer, Heidelberg (2009). http://dx.doi.org/10.1007/978-3-642-03754-2_2
14. Esteva, M., de la Cruz, D., Sierra, C.: Islander: en electronic institutions editor. In: Bologna, Italy, vol. 3, pp. 1045–1052. ACM Press, 15–19 July 2002
15. Esteva, M., Rodríguez-Aguilar, J.A., Arcos, J.L., Sierra, C., Noriega, P., Rosell, B., de la Cruz, D.: Electronic institutions development environment. In: AAMAS (Demos), pp. 1657–1658 (2008). http://www.iiia.csic.es/files/pdfs/eide.pdf
16. Fornara, N., Cardoso, H.L., Noriega, P., Oliveira, E., Tampitsikas, C., Schumacher, M.I.: Modelling agent institutions. In: Ossowski, S. (ed.) Agreement Technologies, Chap. 18, vol. 8, pp. 277–307. Springer-Verlag GmdH, Netherlands (2013)
17. Fuchs, N.E., Kaljurand, K., Kuhn, T.: Attempto controlled English for knowledge representation. In: Baroglio, C., Bonatti, P.A., Małuszyński, J., Marchiori, M., Polleres, A., Schaffert, S. (eds.) Reasoning Web. LNCS, vol. 5224, pp. 104–124. Springer, Heidelberg (2008). http://dx.doi.org/10.1007/978-3-540-85658-0_3
18. García-Camino, A.: Ignoring, forcing and expecting simultaneous events in electronic institutions. In: Sichman, J.S., Padget, J., Ossowski, S., Noriega, P. (eds.) COIN 2007. LNCS (LNAI), vol. 4870, pp. 15–26. Springer, Heidelberg (2008). http://dl.acm.org/citation.cfm?id=1791649.1791652
19. Genesereth, M., Love, N., Pell, B.: General game playing: overview of the aaai competition. AI Mag. **26**(2), 62–72 (2005)
20. Governatori, G., Rotolo, A., Sartor, G.: Temporalised normative positions in defeasible logic. In: Procedings of the 10th International Conference on Artificial Intelligence and Law, pp. 25–34. ACM Press (2005)
21. van der Hoek, W., Roberts, M., Wooldridge, M.: Social laws in alternating time: effectiveness, feasibility, and synthesis. Synthese **156**(1), 1–19 (2007). http://dx.doi.org/10.1007/s11229-006-9072-6
22. Hübner, J.F., Sichman, J.S., Boissier, O.: $S - Moise^+$: a middleware for developing organised multi-agent systems. In: Boissier, O., Padget, J., Dignum, V., Lindemann, G., Matson, E., Ossowski, S., Sichman, J.S., Vázquez-Salceda, J. (eds.) ANIREM and OOOP 2005. LNCS (LNAI), vol. 3913, pp. 64–78. Springer, Heidelberg (2006). http://dx.doi.org/10.1007/11775331_5
23. de Jonge, D., Rosell, B., Sierra, C.: Human interactions in electronic institutions. In: Chesñevar, C.I., Onaindia, E., Ossowski, S., Vouros, G. (eds.) AT 2013. LNCS, vol. 8068, pp. 75–89. Springer, Heidelberg (2013)
24. Kollingbaum, M.J.: Norm-governed practical reasoning agents. Ph.D. thesis, University of Aberdeen (2005)
25. Kröger, F.: Temporal Logic of Programs. Springer-Verlag New York, Inc., New York (1987)

26. Lewis, D.: Semantic analyses for dyadic deontic logic. In: Stenlund, S. (ed.) Logical Theory and Semantic Analysis: Essays Dedicated to Stig Kanger on His Fiftieth Birthday, pp. 1–14. Reidel, Dordrecht (1974)

27. López y López, F., Luck, M.: A model of normative multi-agent systems and dynamic relationships. In: Lindemann, G., Moldt, D., Paolucci, M. (eds.) RASTA 2002. LNCS (LNAI), vol. 2934, pp. 259–280. Springer, Heidelberg (2004)

28. Makinson, D., Van Der Torre, L.: Input/output logics. J. Philos. Logic **29**(4), 383–408 (2000)

29. Meyer, J.J.C.: A different approach to deontic logic: deontic logic viewed as a variant of dynamic logic. Notre Dame J. Formal Logic **29**(1), 109–136 (1987). http://dx.doi.org/10.1305/ndjfl/1093637776

30. Nelson, G.: Natural language, semantic analysis and interactive fiction (2014). http://inform7.com/learn/documents/WhitePaper.pdf

31. Nute, D.: Defeasible Deontic Logic. Springer, The Netherlands (1997)

32. Sergot, M.J., Craven, R.: The Deontic Component of Action Language $nC+$. In: Goble, L., Meyer, J.-J.C. (eds.) DEON 2006. LNCS (LNAI), vol. 4048, pp. 222–237. Springer, Heidelberg (2006). http://dx.doi.org/10.1007/11786849_19

33. Shi, L.L., Chadwick, D.W.: A controlled natural language interface for authoring access control policies. In: Proceedings of the 2011 ACM Symposium on Applied Computing (SAC), TaiChung, Taiwan, 21–24 March 2011, pp. 1524–1530 (2011). http://doi.acm.org/10.1145/1982185.1982510

34. Tampitsikas, C., Bromuri, S., Schumacher, M.I.: MANET: a model for first-class electronic institutions. In: Cranefield, S., van Riemsdijk, M.B., Vázquez-Salceda, J., Noriega, P. (eds.) COIN 2011. LNCS, vol. 7254, pp. 75–92. Springer, Heidelberg (2012). http://link.springer.com/chapter/10.1007/978-3-642-35545-5_5

35. Uszok, A., Bradshaw, J.M., Lott, J., Breedy, M., Bunch, L., Feltovich, P., Johnson, M., Jung, H.: New developments in ontology-based policy management: increasing the practicality and comprehensiveness of KAoS. In: IEEE International Workshop on Policies for Distributed Systems and Networks, pp. 145–152 (2008)

36. Vázquez-Salceda, J., Aldewereld, H., Dignum, F.: Implementing norms in multi-agent systems. In: Lindemann, G., Denzinger, J., Timm, I.J., Unland, R. (eds.) MATES 2004. LNCS (LNAI), vol. 3187, pp. 313–327. Springer, Heidelberg (2004)

37. von Wright, G.H.: Deontic logic. Mind **60**, 1–15 (1951)

Mind as a Service: Building Socially Intelligent Agents

Virginia Dignum[(✉)]

Delft University of Technology, Delft, The Netherlands
`M.V.Dignum@tudelft.nl`

Abstract. The ability to exhibit social behaviour is paramount for agents to be able to engage in meaningful interaction with people. In fact, agents are social beings at the core. That is, agent behaviour is the result of more than just rational, goal-oriented deliberation. This requires novel agent architectures that start from and integrate different socio-cognitive elements such as emotions, social norms and personality. Current agent architectures however, do not support the construction of social agents in a structured, modular and computational- and design-efficient manner. Inspired by service-orientation concepts, in this paper we propose MaaS (Mind as a Service) as a modular architecture for agent systems that enables the composition of different socio-cognitive capabilities into a running system. Depending on the characteristics of the domain, agent's deliberation will require different social capabilities. We propose to model these capabilities as services, and define a 'Deliberation Bus' that enables to design deliberation as a composition of services. This approach allows to define deliberation architectures that are situational and dependent on the available components in order to cope with the complexity of social and physical environments in parallel. We furthermore propose a Service Interface Descriptor language to encapsulate service functionalities in a uniform way.

1 Introduction

The potential of artificial intelligent systems to interact and collaborate not only with each other but also with human users is no longer science fiction. Healthcare robots, intelligent vehicles, virtual coaches and serious games are currently being developed that exhibit social behaviour - to facilitate interactions, to enhance decision making, to improve learning and skill training, to facilitate negotiations and to generate insights about a domain. In all these cases, the ability to exhibit social behaviour is paramount for successful functioning of the system.

We informally define social intelligent agents as systems whose behaviour can be interpreted by others as that of perceiving, thinking, moral, intentional, and behaving individuals; i.e. as individuals that can consider the intentional or rational meaning of expressions of others, and that can form expectations about the acts and actions of others [27]. In this light, functionalities required from social intelligent agents include the ability to reason about norms, beliefs and culture-specific

© Springer International Publishing Switzerland 2016
V. Dignum et al. (Eds.): COIN 2015, LNAI 9628, pp. 119–133, 2016.
DOI: 10.1007/978-3-319-42691-4_7

contexts, to display and understand emotions, to balance between goal-directed and reactive behaviour, maintain a sense of identity, to form expectations about the other's acts and actions, etc. An important aspect of social behaviour is the capability to integrate and to choose between different types of behaviour, such as e.g. utility-based, mimicry or altruistic behaviours based on the physical and social context.

In the last years, many systems have been developed which possess some of these characteristics. In particular, work on Intelligent Virtual Agents and on Social Robotics has delivered many promising results. However, we are still lacking theories, tools and methodologies to guide and ground these developments. That is, current approaches often result in ad-hoc, unstructured solutions. Success and applicability are often more due to the expertise and art of the developers, rather than on robust engineering principles. Moreover, in most cases, social aspects are 'added-in' on top of existing architectures, such as BDI, which does not allow to model the rich inter-dependencies between social capabilities needed to generate social behaviour [12].

The necessity to develop working real-world systems capable of exhibiting social behaviour for the purpose of interaction and collaboration with people requires engineering approaches to explore the full potential of social artificial intelligent systems on a larger scale, mandates a new understanding of social intelligent agents. Architectures, tools and methodologies are needed to realize this potential and engineer applications with a high level of robustness and quality. Only then can we reach a level of robustness acceptable by industry and society.

In this paper, we introduce the vision of MaaS (Mind as a Service), a framework to develop the 'minds' of social intelligent systems, based on the composition of different cognitive modules, or services. In the context of this paper, the concept of 'mind' should be understood as an analogy of the human mind rather than as a faithful representation, i.e. representations and processes that enable behaviour that can be interpreted by others as socio-cognitive behaviour. It is important to notice that our aim is to develop synthetic models that exhibit behaviour that can be seen as social, rather to attempt at emulating the human brain with computational capabilities. Furthermore, we use the term 'mind' in order to stress the fact that we are only specifying the deliberation mechanisms. In most applications this mind will be connected to a physical or virtual body of the agent, but the specification of the agent's *body* is outside the scope of this paper.

MaaS combines a service-oriented concepts with formal specification languages to verify behaviour. In this position paper, we outline the MaaS approach, present the grounding theories on which MaaS is based, and discuss its main challenges. The work presented here should be seen as a first proposal towards a comprehensive theory and tools to build and analyse social intelligent agents.

2   Related Work

MaaS is grounded in both the Social Sciences and Artificial Intelligence. Researchers from many different backgrounds, have studied social behaviour and deliberation, resulting in many approaches, of different levels of formalisation, applicability and detail.

Understanding social behaviour is the first step towards building social minds [7]. Social intelligence is defined as an aggregate of different capabilities, including awareness, social beliefs and attitudes, and the ability to change [6,16]. In his book, "The Society of Mind" Minsky explores the notion that the mind consists of a great diversity of mechanisms: every mind is really a rich and multifaceted *society* of structures and processes, different for every individual as result of genetics, millennia of human cultural evolution, and years of personal experience [23]. Societies of Mind are composed of agents with specific functionality that can be combined together to perform functions more complex than any single agent could, and ultimately produce the many abilities we attribute to minds. Despite the great popularity of this work, there have been few attempts to implement the Society of Minds theory, especially due to the fact that Minsky presents his ideas at different level of abstraction and provides few handles for construction of minds. In its main objective, that of providing a modular, compositional and adaptable architecture for intelligent systems, MaaS takes a similar view of mind as that proposed by Minsky and can be seen as providing a principled engineering framework to develop systems similar to the Society of Minds. However, the basic concepts behind MaaS and the Society of Minds are quite different.

Decision-making processes are influenced by individual and social sources [22]. Social influences are often described in terms of social rules that are followed, such as 'obey your parents' or 'mimic the behaviour of your peers'. Individual influences are usually expressed in terms of personal goals or utilities and lead to 'rational' decision rules. The social sciences describe many mechanisms or schemas used by humans to link these capabilities (e.g. salience, priming, motivation and regulation), determine how decisions are made and generate complex social behaviour [1,15]. Similar processes occur in human-agent interaction because social signals (like emotional expressions) produced by computational agents are processed by humans in a similar manner as signals which are produced by humans [32].

Computational cognitive models, such as ACT-R [3] and SOAR [9] produce intelligent behaviour by employing quantitative measures, which means that different factors take the same form in the deliberation process. This makes it difficult to manage, control and vary different socio-cognitive aspects because these cannot easily be isolated in the decision rules. Moreover, once models get larger they lack transparency to link observed behaviour to the implementation. Existing architectures used to construct virtual agents and intelligent game characters, such as FAtiMA [11], GRETA [21] or CIGA [31] can achieve fairly realistic behaviours that are computationally efficient, but are generally developed for a very specific domain of application. Given this domain-oriented focus, their results are not easily reusable in applications that require slightly different social aspects. Sometimes norms play a major role in a training application while in health care applications emotions might take precedence. Moreover, the focus of these approaches is geared to the visualisation of the behaviours by the virtual characters in terms of e.g. gestures, or facial expressions.

Recently, Kaminka and Dignum et al. [12,18] discussed the many challenges of designing the social behaviour of agents. In this paper, we propose an initial architecture to build agents that can meet those challenges. MaaS takes a modular, service-oriented approach to build social intelligent agents, resulting in flexible and adaptable deliberation. Nevertheless, existing cognitive models in AI are often too simplistic, mostly suitable for well-defined problem domains, platform- or domain-specific, or computationally too complex [9,20,29].

Deliberative agent models, such as BDI [33], have formal logic-grounded semantics, but often require extensive computational resources to deal with social contexts, or use game-theoretic rules that are too simple to capture many of the rich interactions that take place in real-world scenarios [5]. BDI does use different modules for beliefs, desires and intentions. However, these are geared towards individual influences on decision making. These models thus lack an explicit representation for social influences. One can represent all these social influences in the beliefs or goals of an agent, but that leads to the same objection as against the cognitive models; the rules become convoluted and different aspects cannot easily be managed separately.

Other decision-theoretic approaches often used are (PO)MDPs - (Partially Observable) Markov Decision Processes, which capture many of the facets of real world problems, but unrealistically assume that whatever system is solving the MDP knows at every point what state it is in. Moreover, (PO)MDPs do not scale well and lack the modularity needed to analyse the results of large models [4].

The Subsumption Architecture [8,30] takes a reactive perspective, through an hierarchy of task-accomplishing behaviours (simple rules) without necessarily a central control. Lower layers correspond to 'primitive' behaviours and have precedence over higher (more abstract) ones. This architecture is simple in computational terms, but is conceptually obscure due to its 'black box' character.

In an attempt to balance different aspects, and improve the separation of concerns, AOSE (Agent-Oriented Software Engineering) addresses adaptation, concurrency, and fault-tolerance issues [13,28] of the development of agent systems. However, most current AOSE approaches see agents as an application layer software component operating on middleware platforms to gain access to standardised infrastructures. Specifically, such approaches provide syntactic constructs to represent domain knowledge and agent functionalities but lack the formal semantics to reason about agent behaviour at higher levels of abstraction, in terms of socio-cognitive concepts. This leads to results that are not generalizable to other frameworks and applications.

3   The MaaS Vision

As discussed in the previous section, many approaches exist to model different aspects of social intelligence. Our proposal is not to develop yet another model, but enables the integration of different models into working software systems, with variable levels of precision and realism. We therefore aim to build social intelligent systems as a modular, service-based architecture which enables formal verification and conceptual clarity while making possible the integration of different reasoning architectures.

The *'Mind as a Service'* (MaaS) architecture proposed in this paper, represents social intelligent agents as a composition of software services, each designed to implement a specific socio-cognitive functionality. MaaS systems behave in human-like fashion by integrating individual considerations and social influences in their decision making process, and taking into account situational differences. This approach follows recent literature suggesting that rational behaviour requires the input from different socio-cognitive abilities [2].

This approach is based on three pillars. Firstly, the development of models for social deliberation and interaction. The models should be grounded in existing proven psycho-sociological theories, but also be computationally sound and sufficiently 'light' to be easily be embeddable into avatars, robots or other intelligent systems. By expressing algorithms in logical terms, explanation and synthesis of socio-cognitive behaviour is possible [24]. This view is orthogonal to current AI research focus on emulating the human brain[1], in such that our aim is to develop synthetic models that exhibit behaviour that can be perceived as social, and not to understand the human brain in order to emulate its computational capabilities.

Secondly, the development of a computational platform to build MaaS as a composition of socio-cognitive services. This platform will allow to build modular socio-cognitive deliberation architectures and to analyse the consistency of different compositions in terms of accuracy of real world behaviour. Given the explicit formal representation of MaaS models this allows for introspection of the drives of an agent's behaviour. We will take inspiration from Service-Oriented Architecture (SOA) principles [14], in order to realise systems that are scalable and flexible, as services can be replaced by other services, and the system includes only those services required for its aims. Note that our use of SOA ideas should be seen in a broad perspective. We are particularly interested in the overall principles of service-orientation design, stressing separation of concerns in software development, and the view of software as partitioned into operational capabilities, the services, each designed to solve an individual concern.

The idea is thus to design agents' minds as a composition of cognitive services, each based on different theories and approaches, and provide the tools to combine and integrate these services into 'minds' fulfilling given requirements in terms of reasoning capabilities, realism and computational efficiency.

---

[1] Such as is advocated e.g. by the Human Brain Project (https://www.humanbrainproject.eu/).

Through composition, new services can be created from a set of existing services. Moreover, each socio-cognitive function can be modelled in many ways, resulting in several services for the same socio-cognitive ability with different levels of complexity and realism, which can be interchanged depending on the requirements of the application. MaaS services can be addressed in a uniform way through a standard Service Description Interface that is platform- and domain-independent.

Thirdly, design of a methodology to develop MaaS to be embedded in artificial interactive systems. This methodology should provide guidelines for domain analysis, evaluate the socio-cognitive functionalities required for interaction and their level of realism, construct and compose the relevant socio-cognitive services, and evaluate results. The use of the methodology and framework will be evaluated in the development of prototypes for three case studies.

Ultimately, we aim to develop a complete framework that integrates formal theory, software development tools, and methodology to build artificial minds in a structured, compositional way. Through this framework, social intelligent agents can be build that are modular, flexible, adjustable and verifiable. This aim leads directly to the following challenges that we face for the realisation of MaaS:

Modular: requires definitions and models to represent different theories (describing socio-cognitive capabilities) and verify the resulting computational models. To address this challenge we propose a meta-modelling approach to specify socio-cognitive capabilities.

Flexible: Each application domain requires different abilities at different levels of precision. Our approach to this challenge is twofold: (1) we provide procedures and guidelines to identify relevant socio-cognitive modules given the requirements of an application domain, and (2) we define uniform interface descriptions that enable the composition and encapsulation of different socio-cognitive models.

Adjustable: Which socio-cognitive capabilities are needed, at which level of realism and computational complexity, and how to integrate the different capabilities into a deliberation mechanism, is dependent on the characteristics of the domain. MaaS should provide an extendible library of socio-cognitive services. We aim at a *plug-and-play* mechanism to combine these services in many ways resulting in different decision-making paradigms (e.g. rational or behavioural models of decision making).

Verifiable: To judge the appropriateness of the behaviour of a MaaS system, computational theories and tools are needed to analyse the composed effects of social capabilities. By specifying formal representations of socio-cognitive theories we will be able to use formal model-checkers to verify whether a MaaS satisfies some desired properties.

3.1 The MaaS Development Process

In order to integrate different models in a structured way we follow a Model-Driven Engineering (MDE) approach [19]. This enables to develop models that make sense from the point of view of a domain expert or a social scientist, and that can serve as a basis for implementing running computational systems. First step, will be to design formal models of socio-cognitive theories as defined in the Social Sciences. The formalisation of these models is needed in order to enable formal verification, or theorem proving, and are the basis for service meta-models. From these meta-models, platform independent models can be generated for specific application domains, realizing the functional requirements and characteristics of those application domain. Finally, these models can be transformed into computational systems to be embedded in specific computational platforms. Without claiming a direct relation, this process can be compared with the MDE ideas of Platform Independent Models (PIM) are used as a blueprint to develop and compose software services, or Platform Specific Models (PSM). We propose a Deliberation Bus (cf. Sect. 4.2) through which these cognitive services are composed into an operational mind (the MaaS) that is embedded in social intelligent systems that interact with people, such as Embodied Virtual Agents (EVAs) or other avatars or cognitive robots. This process is illustrated in Fig. 1.

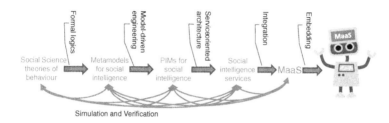

Fig. 1. The MaaS development process

3.2 Development Environment

Our aim is to develop MaaS system that can be embedded in interactive software applications, such as game characters, virtual assistants or robots. To this extent, we are developing MindBuilder, a computational platform to design and implement MaaS. MindBuilder will have the following functionalities:

- design of meta-models for cognitive services, integrating
  - formal languages to specify abstract socio-cognitive capabilities, and
  - theorem provers to verify their formal properties
- tools to specify concrete socio-cognitive services based on the meta-models and define service interfaces using the Service Interface Description language
- tools for composition and adaptation of cognitive services
- a library of cognitive services models and meta-models
- MaaS verification tools, including formal algorithms to model-check behaviour
- a sandbox environment to test and evaluate MaaS

– a methodology to analyse and develop MaaS systems for specific application domains taking into account ethical, social and technical considerations.

MindBuilder platform and methodology will support the specification, integration, simulation and reuse of MaaS as a composition of services, illustrated in Fig. 2. The objective is to generate computational models of socio-cognitive capabilities through a semi-automatic transformation of the formal meta-models with the concrete characteristics and requirements of a specific application domain. For example, a possible normative meta-model will enable the specification and verification of abstract norms as deontic logic expressions. An alternative meta-model for norms, can represent norms as constraint rules. Each of these meta-models will define different models for normative services. Depending on the requirements of the application scenario, one or the other can be chosen resulting in different normative capabilities for the MaaS. For example, in the scenario described in Sect. 3.3, if the deontic meta-model is chosen to represent physical activity norms for children, the norm "children must do 90 min of physical activity per day" can be represented as a deontic expression, enabling rich normative about violated states. If a constraint-based meta-model is chosen, the norm is represented as a constraint and only acceptable behaviours are possible in the system.

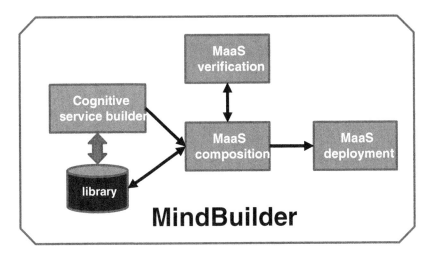

Fig. 2. The MindBuilder architecture

Resulting MaaS systems can be embedded in different interactive software applications, to provide social intelligence capabilities to those applications.

The MindBuilder methodology supports the identification of the socio-cognitive capabilities required for the domain, and their level of realism, guides the development of domain-specific versions of existing models and services, and defines the parameters for analysis of results using simulation.

3.3   Example Scenario

To illustrate the MaaS vision, we describe its possible application to develop a virtual coach for overweight children, JOGG. The socio-cognitive capabilities required by JOGG include the ability to show emotions, and to understand norms and values. For example, the virtual coach should express happiness when the user has successfully performed a task, should be persuading when suggesting a course of action, should monitor norms, such as the obligation to exercise daily, or the prohibition to snack too often, and enforce values such as privacy, but should also be able to decide when to break a norm, for example violate the norm of privacy and notify a doctor if the health of the user is perceived to be very poor.

Different social science theories exist to describe and analyse these socio-cognitive abilities. To name just a few, emotions can be described using e.g. the OCC model [26], or by simple rules that relate happiness to the fulfilment of one's goal, and norms can be modelled using e.g. deontic logics [34], or by the normative theory of Kahnemann [17]. The MaaS methodology will support the analysis of the domain to determine which base sociological theories are the most suitable, and what level of realism is required.

The MindBuilder Library may already contain meta-models or specific services implementing these theories, otherwise new meta-models should be specified using MindBuilder Design. The required services are designed as transformation of the meta-models adapted to the specific characteristics of the JOCCGG domain, e.g. specifying specific norms on physical activity and nutrition, relevant values such as privacy of participants, and suitable emotional expressions in the given cultural context of use. Using MindBuilder Composition component, services are composed into a MaaS. In order to determine the most adequate compositions, and which level of detail and realism of socio-cognitive services is required, MindBuilder Simulation is used to analyse different MaaS configuration options. Different configurations representing different deliberation mechanisms can be checked, e.g. to determine the effect of a norm on the emotion of the MaaS and vice-versa, to check how norm violations affect values, or to determine the effect of e.g. mimicry or goal-orientation as basis for the MaaS deliberation. The resulting MaaS can then be embedded in an app to be used to support the user control their weight and maintain an active lifestyle.

4   MaaS Deliberation

Social deliberation in MaaS results from the integration of different socio-cognitive services. In order to realise the MaaS vision, we need both the means to describe these services in a uniform way (the Service Interface Description), and the ways to combine them into meaningful deliberation (the Deliberation Bus). The aim of the remainder of this section is to provide insight on the vision behind these two functionalities rather than describe existing work. In fact, the development of these functionalities is the aim of further work.

4.1   Service Interface Description

In order to ensure service integration into MaaS systems in a robust, resilient, dependable and scalable manner, we need to develop interfaces between services, and to identify and represent quality of service expectations. A service-oriented approach enables to separate service implementation from service specification. Service Interface Descriptors (SID) will describe the functionality offered by a service, independently from its implementation. As such, services can be seen as black boxes, where operational details are abstracted by the SID. Other services rely on SID to call the service.

As in Situation Calculus, we model the domain world as progressing through a series of states, as a result of various actions being performed within the world. A social state is defined as a set of fluents (properties whose truth changes over time). These fluents represent physical situations (agent is in place X), emotional aspects (agent is happy), relational aspects (agent A is friend of B), and other issues pertinent to the situation. A socio-cognitive service is then a transition from one (social) state to another. I.e., services take a state as input and result in an alteration of that state, that is a change in the value of some of the state fluents. SIDs describe which fluents are modifiable by the service, under which circumstances (i.e. fluents describing the preconditions for using the service).

A service-oriented approach enables to separate service implementation from service specification. We use Service Interface Descriptors (SID) to describe the functionality offered from a service, independently from its implementation. As such services can be seen as black boxes, encapsulated by SID. Other services rely on the SID to call the service. SIDs indicate which fluents are modifiable by the service, under which circumstances (i.e. fluents describing the preconditions for using the service).

Each service acts over a specific set of fluents. Several services may be active at the same time, and can call each other to perform some desired change. For example, in the scenario presented above, for the virtual coach JOGG to propose a possible activity to the user, it will employ services to determine the possible activities, to adapt its emotional expression (which calls a service to determine the user's current emotional state), to decide on the most appropriate way to propose those activities to the user (based on the user's culture, personality, and on holding norms of behaviour), and so on.

Quality of Service. MaaS systems have different requirements concerning the socio-cognitive capabilities needed and the desired level of realism. Although all aspects will play a role in both decisions their relative importance is different. For example, decisions on buying more organic products in the supermarket are mostly based on culture and personality, while decisions on buying cars might be more status driven. This characteristic demands design models that are scalable, and can be flexibly adapted to the varying requirements of quality and scale of different use-cases.

The service-oriented approach taken to build MaaS enables to specify and select services with different levels of precision and computational complexity to execute similar functionality. I.e., depending on the specific demands of an application domain, a socio-cognitive service for normative reasoning can, for example, be based on a temporal-deontic logic [34] or on Ostrom's 'ADICO' model [10]. Given the use of uniform Service Interface Descriptors, a service with a given level of quality can be replaced by another (of lower or higher quality), resulting in different levels of cognitive deliberation, according to the requirements of a given domain.

We conceive an approach to quality of service in MaaS, based on different levels. At the most abstract level, quality is defined as high-level abstractions. For example, can a service handle a specific norm, or a specific emotion. At the level of SID, the quality of a service is described by the service's capability to handle fluents. That is, differences in quality of services are related to which fluents can be handled by the service SID, and how those fluents are interpreted by the service. Assuming an expressive domain representation language, many details can be given about a situation, however not all services are able to handle all the details. This results in different levels of complexity and realism for interchangeable services. Consider for instance, services that analyse the emotion of an user. Rich services can take into account vision, audio and biologic sensor information, while a simple emotion service is only able to take into account input from a dropdown-menu question to the user ("How are you feeling? Choose from the following X options"). Obviously, the result of different emotion-services will be more or less detailed depending on the service option used. However, not all applications require the richer version.

4.2 Deliberation Bus

It is well-known that neither purely reactive nor purely deliberative techniques are capable of producing the range of behaviours required of intelligent agents in dynamic, unpredictable, domains, and specially when interaction with people is needed. I.e. real-time interaction requires both extensive reasoning as well as fast reaction. Therefore, socio-cognitive services have different expectations in terms of time and reaction rate, which demands the integration of goal-based planning and reaction over diverse temporal and functional scopes. At the heart of a MaaS we propose a Deliberation Bus consisting of a central deliberation bus to connect and synchronise different services, and of memory and time management units. Besides socio-cognitive services, the Deliberation Bus also links to sensing and actuator services. These are dependent on the actual system or artefact in which the MaaS is embedded. The Deliberation Synchronisation Bus specifies and implements the communication between services using SID, and takes care of the synchronisation of the different service processes. We use the term 'bus' to stress the fact that we do not assume a fixed deliberation cycle but rather parallel communication between services depending on the situation. In order to allow a uniform quantization of time throughout the model, yet permit different rates of reaction for services, it becomes necessary to interleave sensing and planning. The time management unit allows multiple state updates to occur during deliberation, while keeping in synch with an evolving world. The Deliberation Bus architecture (cf. Fig. 3) integrates deliberation and reaction in flexible and efficient ways. Existing deliberation paradigms such as goal-oriented (BDI) or reactive (Sense-Plan-Act) can be represented in the Bus, which is expressive enough to specify many other deliberation possibilities.

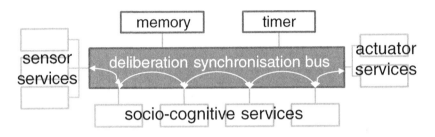

Fig. 3. Abstract deliberation bus architecture

4.3   Service Meta-Models and Verification

Deep theoretical understanding of specific functionalities for social interaction is a pre-requisite to their use in artificial social intelligent systems, yet there is an awareness that current formalisms are not able to deal with the representation of social functionalities and their interrelations in a way that enables verification and proof. Nevertheless, formalisms abound that deal with specific aspects of reasoning, such as decision-making, norms, or emotions. However, such models are quite disparate and integration is not well understood. Our proposal is to start from existing logical formalisms to represent and reason about social-cognitive behaviour and develop formal interpretations of existing social science theories of social behaviour.

There is a long tradition in AI to use logical theories to provide insights into the reasoning problem without directly informing the implementation. The use of logical formalisms as a tool of analysis and knowledge representation, is at the basis of AI research [25]. We will use existing formalisms for different aspects of social behaviour (emotions, norms, culture, personality, ...) as a basis to develop formal theory and algorithms to specify social intelligent systems in a compositional way integrating different theoretical formalisms for socio-cognitive behaviour. To enable the integration and combination of different models we are exploring a meta-modelling approach.

Model checking is a well-known technique to verify properties of a formal model. An attractive feature of model checking is that it can be used to identify behaviours in which the properties do not hold, potentially generating insight in how certain problems can be solved. Well-known limitations of model checking include its inappropriateness to deal with infinite state spaces and branching/alternative time, and it enables only the verification of the model and not validation the process used to transform social science theories into the formal representation. Moreover, the main challenge in model checking is the state explosion problem that can occur if the system being verified has components that make transitions in parallel. However, the scale and complexity of the formalizations that are required for social behaviour are reaching beyond the traditional techniques of philosophical logic. We will explore the combination of logical methods with simulation models to enable the development of a more comprehensive and adequate theory of practical social reasoning than what pure logic can achieve. Simulation results can identify 'interesting' situations that can subsequently be formally checked by model checkers or theorem provers to verify whether the system satisfies certain desired (formal) properties. Simulations produce possible behaviours of the system, which enable to understand the meaning of the abstractions and see whether it corresponds to the system requirements.

5   Conclusions

In this paper, we introduced the *'Mind as a Service'* (MaaS) architecture. Inspired by service models, we propose to build the minds of social intelligent agents as a composition of socio-cognitive services. Each of these services is designed to implement a specific socio-cognitive functionality, based on different theories and providing different levels of deliberation. We are at the initial stages of this research, which we believe has the potential to realise a new paradigm for agents. This paper aims to highlight the main features and challenges of MaaS. We are currently developing a software environment to build and deploy social minds. This platform, MindBuilder, depicted in Fig. 2 enables the specification, composition, simulation and reuse of MaaS, and provides functionalities for (*a*) Design: design services constructed using meta-models based on those formal representations using a uniform interface structure; (*b*) Composition: specify Deliberation Bus models to compose services into MaaS systems with different deliberation models; (*c*) Simulation: simulate and verify the behaviour of those MaaS systems; (*d*) Library: provides library capabilities to store and search for services. The impact of the resulting systems on the people interacting with them is potentially very high. It is therefore crucial to consider the ethical impact of social intelligent systems. We believe that realistic technical solutions are needed before we can fully address the moral and ethical issues inherent to artificial systems that provide care, change behaviour, and interact with vulnerable people across all age-groups. User participation and near-realistic experimentation environments are needed to explore and evaluate technical results and their ethical consequences in a controlled non-evasive way.

Finally, at this stage, we are only considering the development of single agents (as a composition of socio-cognitive services). Future work will focus on the interaction of different MaaS in multi-agent systems, specifically in cooperative teams integrating several agents and people.

References

1. Adolphs, R.: Social cognition and the human brain. Trends Cogn. Sci. **3**(12), 469–479 (1999)
2. Allen, C., Wallach, W., Smit, I.: Why machine ethics? IEEE Intell. Syst. **21**(4), 12–17 (2006)
3. Anderson, J.R., Matessa, M., Lebiere, C.: Act-R: a theory of higher level cognition and its relation to visual attention. Hum.-Comput. Interact. **12**(4), 439–462 (1997)
4. Aras, R., Dutech, A.: An investigation into mathematical programming for finite horizon decentralized pomdps. J. Artif. Int. Res. **37**(1), 329–396 (2010)
5. Beheshti, R.: Normative agents for real-world scenarios. In: Proceedings of the 2014 International Conference on Autonomous Agents and Multi-agent Systems, AAMAS 2014, pp. 1749–1750. International Foundation for Autonomous Agents and Multiagent Systems, Richland, SC (2014)
6. Boyatzis, R.E.: Learning life skills of emotional and social intelligence competencies. In: The Oxford Handbook of Lifelong Learning, p. 91. Oxford University Press (2011)
7. Breazeal, C.: Social interactions in HRI: the robot view. Trans. Sys. Man Cyber. Part C **34**(2), 181–186 (2004)
8. Brooks, R.A.: Cognitive simulators. In: Architectures for Intelligence: The 22nd Carnegie Mellon Symposium on Cognition. Psychology Press (2014)
9. Butt, A.J., Butt, N.A., Mazhar, A., Khattak, Z., Sheikh, J.A.: The soar of cognitive architectures. In: CTIT 2013, pp. 135–142. IEEE (2013)
10. Crawford, S.E., Ostrom, E.: A grammar of institutions. Am. Polit. Sci. Rev. **89**(03), 582–600 (1995)
11. Dias, J., Mascarenhas, S., Paiva, A.: Fatima modular: towards an agent architecture with a genericappraisal framework. In: WS Standards for Emotion Modeling (2011)
12. Dignum, F., Prada, R., Hofstede, G.J.: From autistic to social agents. In: International Conference on Autonomous Agents and Multi-Agent Systems, AAMAS 2014, pp. 1161–1164 (2014)
13. Dragone, M., Jordan, H., Lillis, D., Collier, R.W.: Separation of concerns in hybrid component and agent systems. Int. J. Commun. Netw. Distrib. Syst. **6**(2), 176–201 (2011)
14. Erl, T.: SOA: Principles of Service Design, vol. 1. Prentice Hall, Upper Saddle River (2008)
15. Fiske, S.T., Taylor, S.E.: Social Cognition: From Brains to Culture. Sage, Thousand Oaks (2013)
16. Goleman, D.: Social Intelligence: The New Science of Social Relationships. Bantam, New York (2006)
17. Kahneman, D., Miller, D.T.: Norm theory: comparing reality to its alternatives. Psychol. Rev. **93**(2), 136 (1986)
18. Kaminka, G.A.: Curing robot autism: a challenge. In: International Conference on Autonomous Agents and Multi-Agent Systems, AAMAS 2013. IFAAMAS (2013)
19. Caskurlu, B.: Model driven engineering. In: Butler, M., Petre, L., Sere, K. (eds.) IFM 2002. LNCS, vol. 2335, pp. 286–298. Springer, Heidelberg (2002)
20. Laird, J.: The Soar Cognitive Architecture. MIT Press, Cambridge (2012)
21. Mancini, M., Pelachaud, C.: Dynamic behavior qualifiers for conversational agents. In: Pelachaud, C., Martin, J.-C., André, E., Chollet, G., Karpouzis, K., Pelé, D. (eds.) IVA 2007. LNCS (LNAI), vol. 4722, pp. 112–124. Springer, Heidelberg (2007)

22. March, J.G.: Primer on Decision Making: How Decisions Happen. Simon and Schuster, New York (1994)
23. Minsky, M.: The Society of Mind. Simon & Schuster Inc., New York (1986)
24. Minsky, M.: The emotion machine: Commonsense thinking, artificial intelligence, and the future of the human mind. Simon and Schuster, 2007
25. R. C. Moore. Logic and representation, vol. 39. Center for the Study of Language (CSLI), 1995
26. A. Ortony. The cognitive structure of emotions. Cambridge University Press, 1990
27. A. Schutz. The phenomenology of the social world. Northwestern University Press, 1967
28. Shehory, O.M., Sturm, A.: Agent-Oriented Software Engineering: Reflections on Architectures, Methodologies, Languages, and Frameworks. Springer, Heidelberg (2014)
29. Silverman, B.G., Johns, M., Cornwell, J., O'Brien, K.: Human behavior models for agents in simulators and games: Part I: enabling science with PMFserv. Presence Teleoperators Virtual Environ. **15**(2), 139–162 (2006)
30. Turner, J.T., Givigi, S.N., Beaulieu, A.: Implementation of a subsumption based architecture using model-driven development. In: 2013 IEEE International Systems Conference (SysCon), pp. 331–338. IEEE (2013)
31. van Oijen, J., Vanhée, L., Dignum, F.: CIGA: a middleware for intelligent agents in virtual environments. In: Beer, M., Brom, C., Dignum, F., Soo, V.-W. (eds.) AEGS 2011. LNCS, vol. 7471, pp. 22–37. Springer, Heidelberg (2012)
32. Wagner, J., Lingenfelser, F., Baur, T., Damian, I., Kistler, F., André, E.: The social signal interpretation framework: multimodal signalprocessing and recognition in real-time. In: 21st ACM Conference on Multimedia, pp. 831–834. ACM (2013)
33. Weiss, G.: Multiagent Systems. MIT Press, Cambridge (2013)
34. Wieringa, R., Meyer, J.-J.: Applications of deontic logic in computer science: a concise overview. In: Deontic Logic in Computer Science: Normative System Specification, pp. 17–40. Wiley, New York (1993)

CÒIR: Verifying Normative Specifications of Complex Systems

Luca Gasparini[1(✉)], Timothy J. Norman[1], Martin J. Kollingbaum[1],
Liang Chen[1], and John-Jules C. Meyer[2]

[1] Department of Computing Science, University of Aberdeen, Aberdeen, UK
{l.gasparini,t.j.norman,m.j.kollingbaum}@abdn.ac.uk
[2] Information and Computing Sciences, Utrecht University, Utrecht, The Netherlands
j.j.c.meyer@uu.nl

Abstract. Existing approaches for the verification of normative systems consider limited representations of norms, often neglecting collective imperatives, deadlines and contrary-to-duty obligations. In order to capture the requirements of real-world scenarios, these structures are important. In this paper we propose methods for the specification and formal verification of complex normative systems that include contrary-to-duty, collective and event-driven imperatives with deadlines. We propose an operational syntax and semantics for the specification of such systems. Using Maude and its linear temporal logic model checker, we show how important properties can be verified for such systems, and provide some experimental results for both bounded and unbounded verification.

Keywords: Model checking · Normative systems · Collective imperatives

1 Introduction

The specification and verification of properties of normative systems is an important consideration for the design of complex distributed systems [1,6]. Motivated by the need to capture the requirements of real world scenarios, research on the specification of normative systems has explored conditional [18], event-governed (e.g. activation/expiration condition) norms [16], collective imperatives [9,14], imperatives with deadlines [7], and contrary-to-duty (CTD) norms [18]. A further focus has explored mechanisms for the analysis of systems of norms for the purpose of identifying and resolving conflicts between norms and plans [19]. Although such analyses are of benefit, for safety critical systems it is important to analyse the interactions between normative constraints and agents' actions as a system evolves. For these reasons the use of model checking [3] techniques to analyse liveness and safety properties of norm-governed systems has been explored [1,6,8]. To date, however, this research has focussed on restricted representations of norms such as labelling states or transitions as compliant/non-compliant. Ågotnes et al. [1], for example, study the complexity of this model

© Springer International Publishing Switzerland 2016
V. Dignum et al. (Eds.): COIN 2015, LNAI 9628, pp. 134–153, 2016.
DOI: 10.1007/978-3-319-42691-4_8

checking problem for different robustness-related properties; e.g. whether a certain property is guaranteed in the event of a subset of agents violating a norm.

The focus of this paper is on how to efficiently apply model checking to analyse properties of normative systems specifications with richer representations of norms. In particular, we consider event-governed conditional norms, deadlines for the fulfilment of obligations, and contrary to duty and group imperatives. The contributions we claim are as follows: (i) We propose a norm specification language that is sufficiently expressive to capture all the features discussed above, namely CÒIR [1]; (ii) a Structural Operational Semantics (SOS) [15] for a monitoring component that, given a description of the environment, keeps track of activation, expiration, fulfilment, and violations of norms; and (iii) a realisation of this component using the Maude [4] rewriting logic framework, which allows us to perform formal analysis of normative systems specifications. A particular challenge is that representing time explicitly (in order to reason about temporal deadlines) makes the problem undecidable. For these reasons we explore both the use of bounded model checking and model abstraction to obtain a finite Kripke structure for unbounded model checking. We present some results of both these approaches in an example domain that motivates the requirements for us considering such a rich representation of norms.

2   Motivating Example

Consider a coalition of agents of the sea-guard, consisting of a set of *Unmanned aerial vehicles (UAVs)*, *helicopters*, and *boats*. Their goal is to monitor and intercept unauthorized boats trying to access a restricted area. The norms that guide the behaviour of the coalition are: (1) At any moment at least one member of the coalition must monitor the area. Moreover, we prefer having UAVs monitoring the area over helicopters. We assume that only helicopters and UAVs are capable of monitoring. (2) Whenever an unauthorized boat enters the area, a member of the coalition must intercept it before a certain deadline expires. (3) If no one intercepts the boat, then at least one member of the coalition must send a report to head-quarters before a certain deadline expires. These are all examples of collective imperatives: they require *at least one member* of the coalition to act. Norm 3 is also a CTD obligation that is activated in the event of a violation of the obligation 2. Moreover, norms 2 and 3 require the agents to perform an action *before a certain deadline* (a liveness property), while norm 1 requires that *at any given moment* someone is monitoring the area (a safety property).

3   CÒIR Norm Specification

We now introduce a formalism for representing norms that satisfies our requirements, which we call CÒIR. We allow for the definition of *obligations with deadlines* and *prohibitions* and we assume that everything that is not prohibited is

---

[1] CÒIR is Scottish Gaelic for obligation.

permitted. Compliance with norms is evaluated against a knowledge base KB that is dynamically updated to represent the environment and the observable properties of the agents acting within it. We rely on the closed-world assumption, which we believe to be reasonable in a verification setting. We include the description of previous violations in the knowledge base. These can then be used to activate CTD norms. An issue that has been discussed, for example, by Dignum et al. [7] is whether an obligation with a deadline should persist or be deactivated after a violation; i.e. after the deadline has expired without the obligation being fulfilled. CÒIR supports the specification of either of these alternatives. By default obligations do not expire when violated, but, thanks to the fact that violations are represented in KB, it is always possible to specify the expiration condition as being triggered by a violation of the current instance.

3.1 Syntax

A norm **nd i** is defined as a tuple $\langle id_i, mod_i, act_i, exp_i, goal_i, ddl_i \rangle$ where: id_i is a unique identifier; $mod_i \in \{O, F\}$ specifies whether the norm is an obligation with deadline or a prohibition; act_i (activation condition) describes a pattern that, when matched in KB, causes a norm instance to be detached; $goal_i$ represents the situation that needs to be brought about (for an obligation) or avoided (for a prohibition); exp_i (expiration condition) is a condition that, when met, causes the expiration of the instance; and the deadline for the fulfilment of the norm (ddl_i) can be temporal or symbolic and is defined only for obligations.

Figure 1 shows the EBNF grammar of the operational language used to represent the components of a norm specification. `functor` and `strTerm` are identified by strings that start with a letter, `numTerm` by numbers and `varTerm` by strings that start with a ? character. `?actTime`, `?violTime`, `?tick`, `?this-id`, `?violated` and `?flag` are reserved terms. The description of the environment, KB, consists of a set of ground predicates; i.e. predicates with no `varTerm`. Intuitively, a `boolExpr` represents a condition that is evaluated against KB returning a boolean result, while a `formula` is a pattern with a set of variables that is evaluated by returning the set of substitutions that make the pattern match a subset of KB. In a norm description, act_i is represented by a `formula`, while exp_i, $goal_i$, and ddl_i are `boolExprs`.

The formula `VIOLATION-OF`(n, s) is matched when there is a violation of norm n and is used for the activation of CTD obligations. The meaning of the parameter s will be explained in Sect. 4. The meanings of `EQUALS`, `EXISTS` and the usual boolean operators are intuitive. `TEMPORAL`(n) is evaluated to `true` if a temporal deadline has expired, while `VIOLATED` can be used in exp_i and returns `true` if the instance being evaluated has been violated. `COUNT` (v `IN` $\{f\}$) `>n` evaluates to `true` if the number of different assignments of the variable v that matches the pattern f is higher than the number n.

```
⟨constTerm⟩      = ⟨strTerm⟩ | ⟨numTerm⟩ ;
⟨term⟩           = ⟨constTerm⟩ | ⟨varTerm⟩ | ⟨predicate⟩ ;
⟨predicate⟩      = ⟨functor⟩ "(" ⟨term⟩ { "," ⟨term⟩ } ")" ;
⟨binding⟩        = "BIND( " ⟨varTerm⟩ "," ⟨term⟩ ")" ;
⟨violationCond⟩  = "VIOLATION-OF(" ⟨numTerm⟩ "," ⟨strTerm⟩ ")" ;
⟨formula⟩        = ⟨predicate⟩ | ⟨binding⟩ | ⟨violationCond⟩ | ⟨formula⟩ "/\" ⟨formula⟩
                 | ⟨formula⟩ "\/" ⟨formula⟩  | "IN {" ⟨formula⟩ "} FILTER" ⟨boolExpr⟩ ;
⟨constant⟩       = "false" | "true" ;
⟨existsPattern⟩  = "EXISTS {" ⟨formula⟩ "}" ;
⟨equalsCond⟩     = "EQUALS (" ⟨term⟩ "," ⟨term⟩ ")" ;
⟨temporal⟩       = "TEMPORAL (" ⟨numTerm⟩ ")" ;
⟨violated⟩       = "VIOLATED" ;
⟨compareOp⟩      = "=" | ">" | "<" | "<=" | ">=" ;
⟨count⟩          = "COUNT(" ⟨varTerm⟩ "IN{" ⟨formula⟩ "})" ⟨compareOp⟩⟨numTerm⟩ ;
⟨boolExpr⟩       = "NOT" ⟨boolExpr⟩ | ⟨violated⟩ | ⟨count⟩ | ⟨boolExpr⟩ "/\" ⟨boolExpr⟩
                 | ⟨boolExpr⟩ "\/" ⟨boolExpr⟩ | ⟨existsPattern⟩ | ⟨equalsCond⟩ | ⟨constant⟩ ;
```

Fig. 1. EBNF grammar for the COIR language.

3.2   Representing Collective Obligations

We now discuss how our formalism allows us to represent different types of collective obligations [14]. In contrast to Tinnemeier et al. [17], we allow $goal_i$, exp_i, and ddl_i to include variables that have not been bound at activation time. Through the use of the patterns $\text{EXISTS}\{f_i\}$ and $\text{NOT EXISTS}\{f_i\}$ we are able to express existential and universal quantification on these variables. Inspired by Norman and Reed [14] we discuss some common patterns of collective obligations and show how they can be expressed in our language (See [9,14] for discussions of responsibility in collective obligations). In order to ease the presentation, we assume that agents are organized in groups, group membership is represented by predicates of the type $\texttt{memberOf(agent,group)}$, and an agent's performance of an action by $\texttt{perform(agent,action)}$.

Joint distributive obligations are obligations where all the members of group **g** are responsible for all the members of the group performing the action **a**. This can be expressed by an obligation where:

$$act_i = \texttt{memberOf(?add,g)}$$
$$goal_i = \text{NOT EXISTS } \{\text{IN } \{\texttt{memberOf(?ag,g)}\}$$
$$\text{FILTER NOT EXISTS } \{\texttt{perform(?ag,a)}\}\}$$

$goal_i$ is met when there is no member of **g** that has not performed **a**; i.e. when all the members of **g** have performed **a**. As a result, if any of the members of the group do not perform the task, all the members will be responsible for the violation. Alternatively we could consider the group as an entity to be responsible for the fulfilment of the obligation by specifying the activation condition as:

$$act_i = \texttt{BIND(?add,g)}$$

and referring to the group as ?add in the goal. Note that if a group has no members, such an obligation would be trivially fulfilled. It might be appropriate to add the constraint EXISTS{memberOf(?add,g)} in act_i or in $goal_i$.

Joint collective obligations specify that all the members of a group g are responsible for at least one member of the group performing the action a.

$$act_i = \texttt{memberOf(?add,g)}$$

$$goal_i = \texttt{EXISTS\{ memberOf(?ag,g) /\textbackslash perform(?ag,a)\}}$$

4   CÒIR Semantics

We define the semantics of CÒIR through a Structural Operational Semantics (SOS) [15], a framework for the description of the semantics of programming and specification languages. SOS consists of a set of transition rules that generate a transition system whose states are called configurations. Transition rules are of the form $\frac{P}{C \to C'}$ meaning that, whenever P holds, a transition from the configuration C to C' is applicable. We use SOS to describe how the active norm instances and violations are updated every time we detect a change in KB.

In formalising these semantics we assume two functions that evaluate formula and boolExpr; these will be summarised below. We define a substitution $\theta_j \in \Theta$ as a set of assignments $[v/c]$ where c is a constTerm and v a varTerm. Formulae are evaluated by means of a function $match : 2^P \times Q \to 2^\Theta$, where P is the set of all predicates, Q the set of all formulae, and Θ the set of all substitutions. Intuitively, $match(KB, f)$ returns all the substitutions θ_i such that $f \cdot \theta_i$ is entailed by KB. Boolean expressions (boolExpr) are evaluated by means of a function $eval : 2^P \times E \times \Theta \to bool$ where E is the set of all boolExpr and $bool \in \{$ true, false $\}$. A norm instance $[id_i, \theta_j, at]$ is detached at time at for each substitution $\theta_j \in match(KB, act_i)$. Then $eval(KB, e, \theta_j)$ is used to evaluate exp_i, $goal_i$, and ddl_i. The addressee of the norm, identified by the value assigned to ?add in θ_j, is responsible for complying with the obligation (reaching a state where $eval(KB, goal_i, \theta_j) = $ true before the deadline) or with the prohibition (avoiding states where $eval(KB, goal_i, \theta_j) = $ true until the prohibition expires).

A further issue to address prior to detailing the transition rules of our operational semantics is that of "duplicate activations". Consider a simplified version of norm 3 from Sect. 2. We specify its activation condition as follows:

```
type(?add,coalition) /\ type(?boat,unBoat)
   /\ type(?area,rArea) /\ inArea(?boat,?area)
```

In other words, an instance of the obligation to send a report should be detached when an unauthorized boat is in the restricted area. Intuitively, if the same boat remains in the restricted area for more than one consecutive instant of time, we do not want the coalition members to send more than one report. However, if the boat exits and then re-enters the area, we would expect the coalition to be obliged to send another report. Formally, if we denote by KB_t the state of the knowledge base at time t, we capture this distinction by activating an instance of a norm ndi, associated with a substitution θ_j, at an instant of time t whenever $\theta_j \in match(KB_t, act_i)$ and $\theta_j \notin match(KB_{t-1}, act_i)$; i.e. when we find a substitution such that act_i goes from "unmatched" to "matched" in two subsequent instants of time. To do that we keep record of the instances $[id_i, \theta_j, at]$ such that the act_i was matched in the previous instant of time.

Following Dennis et al. [6], in order to enforce an order of execution among the transitions of the operational semantics, we organize the reasoning cycle in three stages: (**A**) Deactivate instances for which the expiration condition holds or the obligation has been fulfilled; (**B**) Check for violations of active obligations (if the deadline has passed, but the goal has not been achieved) and prohibitions (if the state to avoid is achieved). (**C**) Check for the activation of new norms and update the list of previously matched instances.

In the following we denote by $a_1 : a_2 : \ldots$ a list of elements and we use ϵ to indicate the end of a list. Moreover, we assume that KB contains a predicate cT(n), where n is a numTerm that represents the current time of the system and we denote by $time(KB)$ the value n such that cT(n) $\in KB$. A configuration $Conf$ is defined as $\langle KB, \Delta, I, \Pi, \Phi, \Sigma, r \rangle$ where KB is the current state of the knowledge base, Δ is a list of norm descriptions, I is the list of active norm instances and Π the list of previously matched instances, which, as discussed above, is needed to avoid the problem of multiple activations. Φ is the set of violations detected in the current reasoning cycle[2], and a violation is represented as $v = [id_i, \theta, t]$, where t corresponds to the violation time. Σ is the stage of the computation and r is a flag that is set initially to false, and changed to true if we need to loop again through the reasoning cycle. This is necessary because, whenever we activate a new instance (stage **C**), we need to check whether this is instantly fulfilled or violated (**A** and **B**). Moreover, detecting a violation (**B**) could trigger an expiration or an activation (**A** and **C**).

The initial configuration is $\langle KB_0, \Delta, \epsilon, \epsilon, \epsilon, \mathbf{A}, \texttt{false} \rangle$, where KB_0 describes the initial state and Δ the normative specification. We now illustrate the key rules of the operational semantics. For each rule we include only the components of the configuration that are involved in it.

Rule R1 applies when the first instance in I is such that its expiration condition holds. In this case we simply remove the instance from the list. Similarly another rule (not included) is defined for the case of a fulfilled obligation. Rule R2 accounts for the case where the first instance in the list is a prohibition and the expiration condition is not met. In this case we move the instance to the end of the list, after the ϵ symbol. We write a similar rule (not included) for an obligation instance that it is neither fulfilled nor expired. Rule R3 represents the end of stage A, which occurs when the first instance is ϵ.

---

[2] We refer to the whole updating procedure as a reasoning cycle, while **A**, **B** and **C** are the stages of a cycle.

$$\frac{\langle KB, \Delta, [id_i, \theta_j, at] : I, \mathbf{A}\rangle, \ nd_i \in \Delta,}{\langle KB, \Delta, [id_i, \theta_j, at] : I, \mathbf{A}\rangle \to \langle KB, \Delta, I, \mathbf{A}\rangle} \tag{R1}$$

$$\frac{nd_i \in \Delta, \ mod_i = F, \ eval(KB, exp_i, \theta_j) = \texttt{false}}{\langle KB, \Delta, [id_i, \theta_j, at] : I, \mathbf{A}\rangle \to \langle KB, \Delta, I : [id_i, \theta_j, at], \mathbf{A}\rangle} \tag{R2}$$

$$\frac{\texttt{true}}{\langle \epsilon : I, \mathbf{A}\rangle \to \langle I : \epsilon, \mathbf{B}\rangle} \tag{R3}$$

Rule R4 detects violated obligations; i.e. obligations whose deadline has expired before the goal is satisfied. Since fulfilled obligations have been deleted in stage **A**, we just need to check whether the deadline has expired. When we detect a violation we update the violations list, add the violation description (denoted by $d([id_i, \theta_j, \tau])$) to KB and we set the flag r to $\texttt{true}$ since the violation predicate might trigger the expiration condition of that instance. $d([id_i, \theta_j, \tau])$ consists of a predicate $\texttt{v}(id_i, \texttt{p}(\theta_j), \tau)$ where $\texttt{p}(\theta_j)$ is a representation of the substitution in the form of a predicate. In rule R5 if the first obligation in the list is not violated we move it at the end of the list. Similarly we add two rules (not included) for prohibitions, where we consider a prohibition to be violated if its goal condition evaluates to $\texttt{true}$. Φ is included to avoid infinite loops. In fact, since rule R4 sets r to $\texttt{true}$, detecting the same violation in each loop would cause infinite iteration. Rule R6, together with the condition $[id_i, \theta_j, \tau] \not\in \Phi$ of rule R4 ensures that each violation is detected only once for each reasoning cycle. Another rule similar to rule R3 (not included) is defined for the end of stage **B**.

$$\frac{mod_i = O, \ [id_i, \theta_j, \tau] \not\in \Phi,}{eval(KB, ddl_i, \theta_j) = \texttt{true}, \ KB^* = KB \cup d([id_i, \theta_j, \tau])}{\langle KB, \Delta, [id_i, \theta_j, at] : I, \Phi, \mathbf{B}, r\rangle \to}{\langle KB^*, \Delta, I : [id_i, \theta_j, at], [id_i, \theta_j, \tau] : \Phi, \mathbf{B}, \texttt{true}\rangle} \tag{R4}$$

$$\frac{nd.mod = O, eval(KB, ddl_i, \theta_j) = \texttt{false}}{\langle KB, \Delta, [id_i, \theta_j, at] : I, \mathbf{B}\rangle \to \langle KB, \Delta, I : [id_i, \theta_j, at], \mathbf{B}\rangle} \tag{R5}$$

$$\frac{[id_i, \theta_j, \tau] \in \Phi}{\langle [id_i, \theta_j, at] : I, \Phi, \mathbf{B}\rangle \to \langle I : [id_i, \theta_j, at], \Phi, \mathbf{B}\rangle} \tag{R6}$$

Rule R7 checks for the activation of new instances of the first norm nd_i in Δ. Let $\tau = time(KB)$, for each $\theta_j \in match(KB, act_i)$, we add a new instance $[id_i, \theta_j, \tau]$ at the end of Π (list Π_2), while we add to I only those instances that are not in Π (list I_2). The substitutions of the instances added to I_2 are integrated with the assignment of the variables $\texttt{?actTime}$ and $\texttt{?this-id}$ which are needed to evaluate the $\texttt{TEMPORAL}$ and the $\texttt{VIOLATED}$ conditions as we will show below. If we activate at least one new instance we set $r = \texttt{true}$. By adding new instances at the end of Π, we ensure that, at the end of the reasoning process, the instances added to Π during the current reasoning cycle will be those after ϵ. Formally the pattern $\Pi_3 : \epsilon : \Pi_4$ identifies with Π_4 all the instances added in the current step and with Π_3 all the instances added during the previous reasoning cycle. This is exploited in rule R8, where, at the end of stage **C**, if r is equal to `false`, we end the reasoning cycle (stage **end**) and discard Π_3 and Φ. We define another rule (not included) for the case where r is equal to `true`. In this case we move ϵ at the end of Δ and go back to stage **A**. In rule R7, when we check if a new instance is not in Π, we consider also instances added in previous loops of the current reasoning cycle. In this way it is guaranteed that we do not reactivate the same instances in each loop.

$$
\frac{
\begin{array}{c}
\theta_k = [\text{?actTime}/\tau] \cup [\text{?this-id}/id_i] \text{ and} \\
I_2 = \langle [id_i, (\theta_j \cup \theta_k), \tau] : \ldots \rangle \text{ s.t. } \theta_j \in match(KB, act_i) \text{ and} \\
eval(KB, exp_i, \theta_j) = \textbf{false} \text{ and } [id_i, \theta_j, \tau - 1] \notin \Pi, \\
\Pi_2 = \langle [id_i, \theta_j, \tau] : \ldots \rangle \text{ s.t. } \theta_j \in match(KB, act_i), \\
r* = \textbf{true} \text{ iff } (I_2 \neq \emptyset) \text{ or } (r = \textbf{true})
\end{array}
}{
\begin{array}{c}
\langle KB, nd_i : \Delta, I, \Pi, \mathbf{C}, r \rangle \to \\
\langle KB, \Delta : nd_i, I_2 : I, \Pi : \Pi_2, \mathbf{C}, r* \rangle
\end{array}
} \tag{R7}
$$

$$
\frac{\textbf{true}}{\langle \epsilon : \Delta, \Pi_3 : \epsilon : \Pi_4, \Phi, \mathbf{C}, \textbf{false} \rangle \to \langle \Delta : \epsilon, \Pi_4 : \epsilon, \epsilon, \textbf{end}, \textbf{false} \rangle} \tag{R8}
$$

With these transition rules in place, we now provide further details of the *match* and *eval* functions for querying KB. We denote by $\theta_i[v]$ the value c assigned by θ_i to the variable v. Given a formula f, $f \cdot \theta_i$ denotes the `formula` obtained by substituting, for each `varTerm` v with an assignment in θ_i, each occurrence of v in f with $\theta_i[v]$. Moreover we say that two substitutions θ_1 and θ_2 are compatible if and only if there is no variable v that is bound in both the substitutions such that its assigned values are different. Formally:

$$
compatible(\theta_1, \theta_2) = \textbf{true} \text{ iff } \nexists\, v, ([v/c_1] \in \theta_1 \text{ and } [v/c_2] \in \theta_2 \text{ and } c_2 \neq c_1)
$$

Let p denote a `predicate`, e a `boolExpr`, f_i a `formula`, v_i a `varTerm`, n and a `numTerm`, s_i a `strTerm` and t a `constTerm`. We denote by $s_1.\theta_k$ the substitution obtained by adding the string s_1 as a prefix to all `varTerms` in θ_k. Figure 2 summarizes the semantics of *match* and *eval*.

The construct `TEMPORAL(n)`, where `n` is a `numTerm`, will be used to evaluate a temporal deadline of `n` steps relative to the activation time of a norm instance. In defining its semantics we assume that the variable `?actTime` is bound in θ_j to the activation time (see Rule R7 of above). The construct `VIOLATION-OF(n, s)` presented in Sect. 3.1, can be used in the activation condition of a CTD norm to return the description of a detected violation of a norm with id n. For a violation $[id_j, \theta_j]$, with $n = id_j$, it returns the substitution obtained by adding the prefix s to all the variable names of θ_j. The prefix is added in order to allow the norm designer to distinguish between variables bound by the substitution of the violation and variables bound by the activation condition, even when they have

$match(KB, p) = \{\theta_i : p \cdot \theta_i \in KB\}$

$match(KB, \texttt{BIND} \ (\ v_1 \ , \ t \ ) \ ) = \{[v_1/t]\}$

$match(KB, f_1 \bigwedge f_2) = \{(\theta_1 \cup \theta_2) : \theta_1 \in match(KB, f_1)$
    and $\theta_2 \in match(KB, f_2)$ and $compatible(\theta_1, \theta_2)\}$

$match(KB, f_1 \bigvee \ f_2) = match(KB, f_1) \ \cup \ match(KB, f_2)$

$match(KB, \texttt{VIOLATION-OF}(t_1, s_1)) = \{s_1.(\theta_j \cup \ [\texttt{?violTime}/vt]) : d([t_1, \theta_j, vt]) \in KB\}$

$eval(KB, \texttt{EXISTS} \ \{ \ f_1 \ \}, \theta_i) = \texttt{false}$ if $match(KB, f_1 \cdot \theta_i) = \emptyset$; $\texttt{true}$ otherwise.

$eval(KB, \texttt{EQUALS} \ (\ t_1 \ , \ t_2 \ ), \theta_i) = \texttt{true}$ iff $t_1 = t_2$. If t_1 or t_2 are $\texttt{varTerm}$, θ_i is used
    to replace them with their assigned constant terms.

$eval(KB, \texttt{VIOLATED}, \theta_i) = \texttt{true}$ iff there exists a vt such
    that $d([t_1, \theta_i, vt]) \in KB$ and $\theta_i[\texttt{?thisId}] = t_1$

$eval(KB, \texttt{TEMPORAL}(n), \theta_i) = \texttt{true}$ iff $\theta_i[\texttt{?actTime}] + n <= time(KB)$

$eval(KB, \texttt{COUNT}(v_1 \ \texttt{IN}\{f_1\}) > n, \theta_i) = \texttt{true}$ iff $|\{\theta_j[v_1] : \theta_j \in match(KB, f_1 \cdot \theta_i)\}| > n$.
    same for the other $\texttt{compareOp}$.

$\texttt{NOT}, \backslash/,$ and $/\backslash$ have the usual meaning when applied to $\texttt{boolExpr}$

$match(KB, \texttt{IN} \ \{ \ f_1\} \ \texttt{FILTER} \ e) = \{\theta_i : \theta_i \in match(KB, f_1)$ and $eval(KB, e, \theta_i) = \texttt{true}\}$.

Fig. 2. Semantics of $match$ and $eval$

the same variable name. The construct VIOLATED is used when we want to ask whether the current instance has been violated (e.g. for the expiration condition of an obligation). It is evaluated to true if KB contains the description of a violation of the instance being evaluated. Note that, since, for each instance, we bind the activation time in the substitution, VIOLATED is able to distinguish between violations of different instances associated with the same pair $(\texttt{nd}j, \theta_j)$.

Figure 3 illustrates the life-cycle of an obligation (left) and a prohibition (right) instance in CÒIR. Circles represent states and arrows represent transitions and are labeled with the condition that triggers the transition. A norm instance is activated when the activation condition (act) holds and an equivalent instance (an instance of the same norm associated with the same substitution) is not in the previous matches (Π) list. An active obligation becomes fulfilled when the goal (goal) condition holds, it expires if the expiration condition (exp) but not the goal holds, and it becomes violated if the deadline (ddl) condition holds true before the expiration or the goal condition. Once an obligation instance is violated, it remains so until the expiration condition holds (in which case it becomes expired) or the goal condition holds (in which case it becomes fulfilled). Once an obligation is fulfilled or expired it will remain so for the remainder of the execution. An active prohibition expires when the expiration condition holds, and becomes violated if the goal holds, but the expiration condition does not. A violated prohibition becomes expired if the expiration condition holds. It is important to notice that, when a previously violated norm becomes expired it will not be detected as a current violation. A norm designer, however, can specify the clause NOT VIOLATED in the expiration condition in order to avoid this. The same applies to violated obligations that becomes fulfilled.

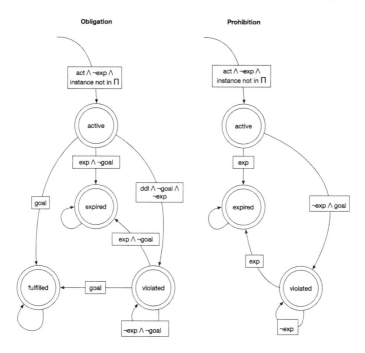

Fig. 3. Norm instance life-cycle

5   The *Seaguard* Example

We now show how we can capture the norms described in our motivating example (Sect. 2) using the CÒIR formalism. Norm 1 states that at any instant of time, at least one agent must monitor the area. This may be captured by a prohibition from achieving a state where no agent is monitoring the area (a safety property). The fact that a UAV monitoring the area is preferred to a helicopter can be represented by separating the norm in two as shown in Fig. 4 (**nd1** and **nd4**). Norm **nd1** is a prohibition that is violated if no UAV is monitoring the area. Norm **nd4** is violated if neither a UAV nor a helicopter is monitoring the area. Therefore, a situation where a UAV is monitoring the area would comply with both the norms, while having a helicopter monitoring would violate only **nd1**.

Norms **nd2** and **nd3** capture the specification of norms 2 and 3 from our motivating example respectively. An instance of the obligation **nd2** is activated, for a coalition, every time an unauthorized boat **?ag1** enters the restricted area **?ar**. The obligation is fulfilled if one member of the coalition **?ag2** intercepts **?ag1** before a deadline of three time steps, while it expires if **?ag1** exits **?ar** or the obligation is violated. Obligation **nd3** is activated by a violation of norm **nd2**, and is addressed to the same coalition. It requires at least one member of the coalition to report the unauthorized access.

```
nd1 = ⟨1, F, act1, false, goal1, false ⟩
    act1 = type(?add,coalition) /\ type(?ar,rArea)
    goal1 = NOT EXISTS{ memberOf(?ag1,?add) /\ type(?ag1,uav) /\ monitoring(?ag1,?ar) }
nd4 = ⟨4, F, act1, false, goal4, false ⟩
    goal4 = NOT EXISTS{ memberOf(?ag1,?add) /\ monitoring(?ag1,?ar) /\
            ( type(?ag1,uav) \/ type(?ag1,heli) ) }
nd2 = ⟨2, O, act2, exp2, goal2, ddl2⟩
    act2 = IN{ type(?add,coalition) /\ type(?ar,rArea) /\ inArea(?ag1,?ar) } FILTER
        NOT EXISTS{ type(?ag1,?type) /\ subType(?type,authAgent) }
    exp2 = VIOLATED \/ NOT EXISTS { inArea(?ag1,?ar) }
    goal2 = EXISTS{ intercepting(?ag2,?ag1) /\ memberOf(?ag2,?add) }
    ddl2  = TEMPORAL(3)
nd3 = ⟨3, O, act3, exp3, goal3, TEMPORAL(3) ⟩
    act3 = IN { type(?add,coalition) /\ VIOLATION-OF(2,v) } FILTER EQUALS(?add,?v:add)
    exp3 = NOT EXISTS{ inArea(?v:ag1,?v:ar) } \/ EXISTS { intercepting(?ag2,?v:ag1) }
    goal3 = EXISTS{ reporting(?ag2,?v:ag1) /\ memberOf(?ag2,?add) }
```

Fig. 4. Specification of norms nd1, nd2 and nd3.

6   Formal Verification

In this section we explore the problem of verifying properties of multi-agent systems specified using CÒIR. Firstly we discuss our implementation of the operational semantics in Maude [4], a rewriting logic framework that allows us to specify the semantics of a system by means of rewriting rules. We chose Maude because its syntax for specifying rewriting rules is very close to that for SOS. Moreover, by implementing our system in Maude, we obtain a specification which is executable and on which we can perform formal verification using the Maude Linear Temporal Logic (LTL) model checker. In this way we can: (i) Validate our normative specification; for example by verifying that a specified non compliant behaviour always results in a detected violation; and (ii) Verify how robust a multi-agent system is to violations; for example by verifying if a certain property is guaranteed under certain compliance assumptions [1,8].

We discuss the reasons why, by representing our model as explained in Sect. 4, we obtain an infinite state model. We show how we can use the LTL model checker to perform bounded model checking of the infinite state system, and then show how we can modify our model in order to make the state space finite and apply unbounded model checking.

6.1   Maude Implementation

Maude modules can contain *conditional equations*: simplification rules used to define data-types and language constructs and to specify how they are evaluated by the system. Modules may also contain *conditional rewriting rules*: transition rules that describe how the state of a system can evolve over time. We defined the CÒIR language (Fig. 1) and we implemented the *match* and *eval* functions. We then implemented our operational semantics by means of an operator **reason** that takes as arguments a configuration and returns the configuration resulting from the application of the reasoning cycle. The reasoning process is described by a set of conditional equations, which are a direct (syntactical) translation of the rules of Sect. 4 into the Maude syntax. The dynamics of the system is specified by a set of rules that follow the pattern:

```
crl C => reason( tick(C', n) ) if condition.
```

where `C` and `C'` are two configurations and the only component that can change from `C` to `C'` is the knowledge base. `tick` is a function that takes a configuration `C` and an integer `n` as parameters and increases the time in `C` by `n` units. The meaning of this rule pattern is that, at each step, after applying the changes in the description of the environment, we invoke the `reason` operator to update the list of active instances, previous matches and violations accordingly. The Maude model checker, given one initial state i, and a set of transition rules T, generates a Kripke structure containing all the states that are reachable from i.

6.2 Bounded Model Checking

Properties of a norm-governed multi-agent system can be verified using the Maude LTL model checker. In order to do so we need to define a labelling function λ, specifying the set of atomic propositions $q \in Q$ that hold in some state $s \in S$ [4, Chap. 13]. We denote by $((s \models_\lambda q) = \texttt{true})$ the fact q holds in s and by $((s \models_\lambda q) = \texttt{false})$ the fact that q does not hold in s. The state of a multi-agent system is represented by the configuration $Conf$ of the monitoring component. Let Q be the set of all **predicates** as defined in Fig. 1. Equations 1–4 defines λ.

$$\langle KB, \Delta, I, \Pi, \Phi, \Sigma, r \rangle \models_\lambda p = \texttt{true} \text{ if } p \in KB. \tag{1}$$

$$\langle KB, \Delta, I, \Pi, \Phi, \Sigma, r \rangle \models_\lambda violated(n) = \texttt{true}$$
$$\text{if } \exists\, \theta_j, \tau \text{ s.t. : } d([n, \theta_j, \tau]) \in KB \tag{2}$$

$$\langle KB, \Delta, I, \Pi, \Phi, \Sigma, r \rangle \models_\lambda violated(n, t) = \texttt{true} \text{ if}$$
$$\exists\, \theta_j, \tau \text{ s.t. : } d([n, \theta_j \cup [\texttt{?add/t}], \tau]) \in KB \tag{3}$$

$$\langle KB, \Delta, I, \Pi, \Phi, \Sigma, r \rangle \models_\lambda p = \texttt{false} \text{ otherwise.} \tag{4}$$

Equation 1 makes it possible to use the predicates of KB as atoms of LTL properties. Equations 2 and 3 define properties about the normative state of a configuration, allowing us to query the model checker for states where a certain norm has been violated (optionally specifying an addressee).

The principal requirement to make the LTL model-checking decidable is for the transition system to have a finite number of reachable states. However, the fact that we represent time explicitly in KB means that the state space is infinite. One way of dealing with this is to limit the state space to the states reachable in a fixed number of transitions, l. We can do this, for example, by modifying the specification of the system so that all the conditional rewriting rules that increase the time by n are applicable only to states where $time(KB) < l - n$. Ideally, however, we want to be able to verify system properties in the unbounded case.

6.3   Unbounded Model Checking

In order to make the unbounded model checking problem decidable, we need to remove any explicit reference to the current time from the semantics. We remove the predicate `cT(n)` from KB and the references to activation and violation time from instances and violations respectively (now represented as $[id_j, \theta_k]$). In order to represent temporal deadlines, we take an approach similar to the one proposed by Lamport [12]. When we activate an instance (Rule R7), instead of binding `?actTime`, we add the assignment $[\text{?tick}/n]$ in the substitution of instances of norms that include a statement of type `TEMPORAL(n)`. Rule R7 is substituted with:

$$\frac{\begin{array}{c} I_2 = \langle [id_i, (\theta_j \cup \theta_k)] : \ldots \rangle \text{ s.t. } \theta_j \in match(KB, act_i) \text{ and} \\ eval(KB, exp_i, \theta_j) = \texttt{false} \text{ and } \theta_k = isTemp(ddl_i) \text{ and} \\ [id_i, \theta_j] \notin \Pi, \Pi_2 = \langle [id_i, \theta_j] : \ldots \rangle \text{ s.t. } \theta_j \in match(KB, act_i), \\ r* = \texttt{true} \text{ iff } (I_2 \neq \emptyset) \text{ or } (r = \texttt{true}) \end{array}}{\langle KB, nd_i : \Delta, I, \Pi, \mathbf{C}, r \rangle \rightarrow \langle KB, \Delta : nd_i, I_2 : I, \Pi : \Pi_2, \mathbf{C}, r* \rangle} \quad (R7^*)$$

where $isTemp(ddl_i)$ checks whether a deadline is temporal and, in that case, returns the initialisation for the `?tick` variable.

$$isTemp(ddl_i) = \begin{cases} [\text{?tick}/t] & \begin{array}{l} \text{if } ddl_i \text{ contains one and only one statement} \\ \text{of the type } \texttt{TEMPORAL(t)} \end{array} \\ \\ \emptyset & \text{otherwise.} \end{cases}$$

We then modify the `tick(C, m)` operator so that, for each instance $[id_j, \theta_k]$, it will decrease all the values t such that $[\text{?tick}/t] \in \theta_k$ by a value equal to the minimum of t and m. The semantics of $eval(KB, \texttt{TEMPORAL(n)}, \theta_j)$ is then changed to return `true` if and only if the `?tick` variable reaches value zero:

$$eval(KB, \texttt{TEMPORAL(n)}, \theta_j) = \texttt{true} \text{ iff } [\text{?tick}/0] \in \theta_j.$$

In other words, for every instance of a norm with a temporal deadline, we activate a timer that is decremented by a call to the function `tick`. The deadline is considered expired when the timer reaches 0. Another consequence of removing the explicit reference to the current time is that, without a reference to the activation time, multiple instances or violations associated with the same pair (nd_i, θ_j) become indistinguishable. This leads to a number of problems at the implementation level. Consider the example in Sect. 5. When the coalition fails to intercept an unauthorized boat **ub** (violation of **nd2**), an instance of **nd3** that binds to **ub** will be activated and included in the list Π. Subsequent violations will bind to the same substitution in the activation condition of **nd3**, preventing any new activation. In order to solve this problem we need to make sure that every new violation of **nd2** will match, for the activation condition of **nd3**, to a substitution that is not currently in Π. We do this by adding a boolean flag in the representation of the violation in the knowledge base. When the first violation of **nd2** associated with θ_j is detected, its description is added to KB with the flag set to **false**. At every subsequent violation associated with the same pair $(\text{nd2}, \theta_j)$ we change the value of the flag. We update the semantics of *match* for the construct $\text{VIOLATION-OF}(t_1, s_1)$ to include the variable ?flag bound to the flag value instead of the variable ?violTime. When, for example, the flag values goes from **false** to **true**, the previous match for the activation of **nd3** is deleted while the instance with ?flag set to **true** gets activated. This mechanism guarantees that we can activate at least one CTD instance per step for each pair $(\text{nd3}, \theta_j)$. Further, to correctly interpret the VIOLATED expression, we need to check for a violation of the current instance. Again, without relying on the activation time, we are not able to distinguish between different violations associated to the same pair $(\text{nd}i, \theta_j)$. We solve this by adding to the substitution θ_j of each instance $[id_i, \theta_j]$ a variable ?violated which is initially unbound. We modify Rule R4 (and the equivalent for violated prohibitions) to set ?violated to **true** when a violation is detected, and update the semantics of *eval* for VIOLATED as follows:

$$eval(KB, \text{VIOLATED}, \theta_j) = \textbf{true} \text{ iff } [\text{?violated}/\textbf{true}] \in \theta_j \tag{5}$$

As a result of these modifications, Rule R4 becomes as follows:

$$\frac{\begin{array}{c} mod_i = O, \ \theta_k = \theta_j \cup [\text{?violated}/\textbf{true}] \\ [id_i, \theta_j] \notin \Phi, \ eval(KB, ddl_i, \theta_j) = \textbf{true}, \\ KB^* = addV(KB, [id_i, \theta_j]) \end{array}}{\begin{array}{c} \langle KB, \Delta, [id_i, \theta_j] : I, \Phi, \mathbf{B}, r \rangle \rightarrow \\ \langle KB^*, \Delta, I : [id_i, \theta_k], [id_i, \theta_k] : \Phi, \mathbf{B}, \textbf{true} \rangle \end{array}} \tag{R4*}$$

where θ_k is the substitution obtained by setting the value of the ?violated flag and $addV$ updates the content of KB as discussed above:

$$addV(KB, [id_i, \theta_j]) = \begin{cases} KB \cup \text{v}(id_i, \text{p}(\theta_j), \textbf{false}) & \begin{array}{l} \text{if } \forall f \in \{\textbf{true}, \textbf{false}\} \\ \text{v}(id_i, \text{p}(\theta_j), f) \notin KB \end{array} \\ \\ \begin{array}{l} KB \setminus \text{v}(id_i, \text{p}(\theta_j), f) \\ \cup \text{v}(id_i, \text{p}(\theta_j), \neg f) \end{array} & \text{if } \text{v}(id_i, \text{p}(\theta_j), f) \in KB \end{cases}$$

6.4   Model Checking Results

We implemented our scenario in Maude and ran the LTL model checker to verify properties of the system for both bounded and unbounded cases.

Table 1 shows the results for bounded model checking[3]. The scenario implemented includes a single UAV a Helicopter and two unauthorized boats and is regulated by norms nd1, nd2 and nd4. In all these scenarios agents can perform, according to their capabilities, at most seven actions: start and stop monitoring, start and stop intercepting, start and stop reporting, and move to a different area. We checked the following property, which asks whether a state where uav does not monitor the restricted area area2 always results in a violation of nd1:

$$\Box((\neg monitoring(uav1, area2)) \rightarrow violated(1))$$

To prove that this property is always true the model checker has to observe the whole state space, giving us a worst-case scenario in terms of execution time. We can see that both the execution time and the number of states increase exponentially with the number of steps.

Table 2 shows the results for unbounded model checking in different scenarios. cA is the number of coalition agents, uB the number of unauthorized boats, while for each ndi, a ✓ indicates that the norm was included in the scenario.

Table 1. Model checking results: bounded steps

	Step limit				
	7	8	9	10	11
States	4647	12352	32336	81504	202007
Execution time	10 s	29 s	78 s	3 m 8 s	8 m

The scenario in row 2 (Table 2.a) is equivalent to that used to produce the results in Table 1. Note that the execution time for bounded model checking at 10 steps is higher than the unbounded case. This is due to the fact that, since we include the time value in *KB*, conceptually equivalent states are not recognized because their time values differ, making it impossible for the model checker to take advantage of optimizations that rely on state matching.

As we can see from Table 2.a, the scenarios where both nd2 and nd3 are enforced are those with higher execution times. We believe this is due to an interaction between temporal deadlines and CTD obligations: In fact nd3 is a CTD of nd2 and each of them has a temporal deadline of 3 steps. Values for the ?tick variable range from 3 to 0 in instances of nd2 and, whenever nd2 is violated, the timer for nd3 is initialized. Our intuition is confirmed by Table 2.b: by decreasing the deadline to 1, we obtain significantly smaller state spaces and execution times.

We now show how model checking can be used to verify that our normative specification is correct, by checking that non compliant behaviours are detected

---

[3] All tests ran on a Intel Core i5 2.7Ghz, 16 GB RAM.

Table 2. Model checking result: unbounded

Part a: ddl2 = ddl3 = TEMPORAL (3)

cA	uB	nd1	nd2	nd3	nd4	States	Time
2	2	✓	✓			5250	20s
2	2	✓	✓		✓	20012	2m
2	2	✓	✓	✓	✓	243994	1h,16m
3	2	✓	✓			19032	2m
3	2	✓	✓		✓	72327	15m
3	2	✓	✓	✓	✓	870165	25h

Part b: ddl2 = ddl3 = TEMPORAL (1)

cA	uB	nd1	nd2	nd3	nd4	States	Time
1	2	✓	✓	✓	✓	5717	40s
2	2	✓	✓	✓	✓	17653	5m
3	2	✓	✓	✓	✓	75245	16m

as violations. Let's consider a variation of nd2 stating that, in order to optimize the allocation of resources, we want one and only one member of the coalition to intercept the unauthorized boat detected in the restricted area. Intuitively we would be tempted to express the norm with the following goal:

$$goal2 \; = \; \text{COUNT (?ag2 IN \{ memberOf(?ag2,?add)}$$
$$\text{/\textbackslash\ intercepting(?ag2,?ag1) \}) = 1}$$

which holds true if the number of agents (?ag2) that are members of the coalition and are intercepting ?ag1 is equal to 1. We can now use model checking to verify whether this specification captures the meaning we intend. For example, we might ask whether it is true that having two agents intercepting the same boat results in a violation. We refer to area2 to be the restricted area, ub the unauthorized boat, and uav and heli the UAV and the helicopter respectively. We check the following property, which says that having both uav and heli intercepting ub always results in a violation of nd2.

$$\Box((\text{intercepting(uav,ub)} \land \text{intercepting(heli,ub)}$$
$$\land \text{ inArea(ub,area2))} \rightarrow \text{violated(2))}$$

The model checker returns an execution trace that violates the property as a counter example. In fact, if the uav and heli start intercepting at two different instants of time, the obligation is fulfilled (and thus deleted) when the first agent starts intercepting. We can capture the intended meaning with an obligation to have at least one agent intercepting before the deadline and a prohibition from having multiple agents intercepting the same boat.

We now show, with an example, how model checking can be used to verify robustness-related properties. We want to verify whether compliance with nd2 and nd3 guarantees that an unauthorized boat cannot enter and exit the restricted area without being reported or intercepted. We denote by area1 and area2 an unrestricted and a restricted area respectively. The following property says that there is no path such that ub goes from area2 to area1 being neither intercepted nor reported and without triggering a violation of nd2 or nd3.

$$\neg\Diamond(\texttt{inArea(ub,area2)} \land \Diamond\texttt{inArea(ub,area1)} \land$$
$$\Box(\neg\texttt{violated(2)} \land \neg\texttt{violated(3)} \land$$
$$\neg\texttt{intercepting(uav,ub)} \land \neg\texttt{reporting(uav,ub)} \land$$
$$\neg\texttt{intercepting(heli,ub)} \land \neg\texttt{reporting(heli,ub)}))$$

The model checker shows as a counterexample a path where ub moves from area2 to area1 before the deadline for it being intercepted, causing the expiration of nd2. We thus verified that our normative system does not guarantee that the specified critical situation will never occur, even if we consider only compliant paths. If we want to make sure that, in a situation of compliance, a boat that exits the area is at least reported, we can modify *exp2*, *ddl2* and *exp3* as:

$exp2$ = VIOLATED   ; $exp3$ = false
$ddl2$ = TEMPORAL(3) \/ NOT EXISTS{inArea(?ag1,?ar)}

In this way, both the expiration of the temporal deadline or ub exiting area2 before being intercepted trigger a violation of nd2, thus activating an instance of nd3. By applying model checking we can see that compliance with revised norms nd2 and nd3 guarantees that the boat is intercepted or reported.

7   Discussion

The formalism we use to represent norms builds upon a number of approaches to formalise norms for practical applications. For example Tinnemeirer et al. [17] describe the operational semantics of a normative language with support for norms with deadlines and CTD obligations. Hüber et al. [11] adopt an SOS-approach to formalise the norm lifecycle (activation, fulfilment, violation, etc.) and for monitoring the execution of norm-governed systems, which provides the underpinning for a language (NOPL) for programming such systems. Alvarez-Napagao et al. [2] propose a semantics based on production systems for a norm monitoring component that supports norms with deadlines. Similarly, Hindriks and Van Riemsdijk [10] propose a semantics based on *timed transition systems* to keep track of activation, fulfilment and violation of obligation with real time relative deadlines. This semantics could be used for verification purposes, for example with tools such as *Real-Time Maude* [13]. This issue, however, is only discussed briefly by the authors and no details are offered. We complement this existing research by addressing the issue of verifying temporal logic properties of such systems. CÒIR also permits the representation of collective imperatives, which are not considered in existing models defined using semantics at the operational level.

Existing research on the verification of properties of normative systems has focussedon restricted representations of norms, considering only variations of conditional deontic logic, without considering deadlines, event-driven norms, or collective imperatives. Dennis et al. [6], for example, integrate the ORWELL normative language in the MCAPL verification framework in order to verify properties of agents' organisations. In ORWELL norms are represented through *counts as* rules, which label states as compliant or non-compliant by saying that a *brute fact* counts as an *institutional fact* (e.g. a violation) in a certain context. Our results (Table 2), show that, despite using a more expressive representation, verification times are comparable to those reported by Dennis et al. [6].

In research that shares some similarities with ours, Cliffe et al. [5] describe a formalism for specifying obligations with deadlines, permissions and contrary to duty norms. They use answer set programming to verify properties of systems. Their approach is, however, only able to analyse execution traces up to a certain length, and in this regard, is equivalent to bounded model checking.

Ågotnes et al. [1] consider transitions of a Kripke structure that are labelled as compliant or non compliant. It is then possible to use model checking to verify properties of the system under different compliance assumptions. While such a labelling might be expressive enough to represent the kind of norms captured by our formalism, it is not clear how to compute it from a declarative normative specification.

We believe that this mismatch between formalisms used to specify and monitor norms and those used to verify and analyse normative systems makes it difficult to ensure that norms satisfy certain desired properties. Our work attempts to bridge the gap between norm specification, monitoring and verification by providing an executable specification that is verifiable through model checking.

For future research we plan to explore techniques to exploit domain symmetries in order to improve performance and to extend our model to allow agents to issue imperatives at run-time.

8   Conclusion

In this paper we proposed CÒIR, a language for the specification of obligations and prohibitions with support for common features of real world norms, including deadlines, contrary to duty and event-based activation/deactivation. We showed how, thanks to the fact that we allow existential and universal quantification over variables, our formalism can be used to specify common patterns of collective obligations. We then formalized how norms are to be interpreted by means of an operational semantics which we then implemented in Maude. We discussed how the fact that we explicitly represent time in our model leads to an infinite state space, and hence proposed an abstraction that preserves the semantics and makes unbounded model checking decidable. We then used the Maude LTL model checker to validate our normative specification and to verify its robustness to violations.

Acknowledgments. This research was sponsored by Selex ES.

References

1. Ågotnes, T., Van der Hoek, W., Wooldridge, M.: Robust normative systems and a logic of norm compliance. Logic J. IGPL **18**(1), 4–30 (2010)
2. Alvarez-Napagao, S., Aldewereld, H., Vázquez-Salceda, J., Dignum, F.: Normative monitoring: semantics and implementation. In: De Vos, M., Fornara, N., Pitt, J.V., Vouros, G. (eds.) COIN 2010. LNCS, vol. 6541, pp. 321–336. Springer, Heidelberg (2011)
3. Clarke, E.M., Grumberg, O., Peled, D.: Model Checking. The MIT Press, Cambridge (1999)
4. Clavel, M., Durán, F., Eker, S., Lincoln, P., et al.: All About Maude - A High-Performance Logical Framework. Springer, Heidelberg (2007)
5. Cliffe, O., De Vos, M., Padget, J.: Modelling normative frameworks using answer set programing. In: Erdem, E., Lin, F., Schaub, T. (eds.) LPNMR 2009. LNCS, vol. 5753, pp. 548–553. Springer, Heidelberg (2009)
6. Dennis, L., Tinnemeier, N., Meyer, J.-J.: Model checking normative agent organisations. In: Dix, J., Fisher, M., Novák, P. (eds.) CLIMA X. LNCS, vol. 6214, pp. 64–82. Springer, Heidelberg (2010)
7. Dignum, F.P.M., Broersen, J., Dignum, V., Meyer, J.-J.: Meeting the deadline: why, when and how. In: Hinchey, M.G., Rash, J.L., Truszkowski, W.F., Rouff, C.A. (eds.) FAABS 2004. LNCS (LNAI), vol. 3228, pp. 30–40. Springer, Heidelberg (2004)
8. Gasparini, L., Norman, T.J., Kollingbaum, M.J., Chen, L.: Severity-sensitive robustness analysis in normative systems. In: Ghose, A., et al. (eds.) COIN 2014. LNCS, vol. 9372, pp. 72–88. Springer, Heidelberg (2015). doi:10.1007/978-3-319-25420-3_5
9. Grossi, D., Dignum, F.P.M., Royakkers, L.M.M., Meyer, J.-J.C.: Collective obligations and agents: who gets the blame? In: Lomuscio, A., Nute, D. (eds.) DEON 2004. LNCS (LNAI), vol. 3065, pp. 129–145. Springer, Heidelberg (2004)
10. Hindriks, K.V., Van Riemsdijk, M.B.: A real-time semantics for norms with deadlines. In: Proceedings of the 2013 International Conference on Autonomous Agents and Multi-agent Systems, AAMAS 2013, pp. 507–514. International Foundation for Autonomous Agents and Multiagent Systems, Richland (2013)
11. Hübner, J.F., Boissier, O., Bordini, R.H.: A normative organisation programming language for organisation management infrastructures. In: Padget, J., Artikis, A., Vasconcelos, W., Stathis, K., da Silva, V.T., Matson, E., Polleres, A. (eds.) COIN@AAMAS 2009. LNCS, vol. 6069, pp. 114–129. Springer, Heidelberg (2010)
12. Lamport, L.: Real-time model checking is really simple. In: Borrione, D., Paul, W. (eds.) CHARME 2005. LNCS, vol. 3725, pp. 162–175. Springer, Heidelberg (2005)
13. Lepri, D., Ábrahám, E., Ölveczky, P.C.: Timed CTL model checking in real-time maude. In: Durán, F. (ed.) WRLA 2012. LNCS, vol. 7571, pp. 182–200. Springer, Heidelberg (2012)
14. Norman, T.J., Reed, C.: A logic of delegation. Artif. Intell. **174**(1), 51–71 (2010)
15. Plotkin, G.D.: A structural approach to operational semantics. Technical report, DAIMI FN-19, University of Århus (1981)
16. Şensoy, M., Norman, T.J., Vasconcelos, W.W., Sycara, K.: OWL-POLAR: a framework for semantic policy representation and reasoning. Web Semant.: Sci. Serv. Agents World Wide Web **12–13**, 148–160 (2012)

17. Tinnemeier, N., Dastani, M., Meyer, J.J.C., van der Torre, L.: Programming normative artifacts with declarative obligations and prohibitions. In: International Joint Conference on Web Intelligence and Intelligent Agent Technologies, pp. 145–152 (2009)
18. van der Torre, L.: Contextual deontic logic: normative agents, violations and independence. Ann. Math. Artif. Intell. **37**(1–2), 33–63 (2003)
19. Vasconcelos, W.W., Kollingbaum, M.J., Norman, T.J.: Normative conflict resolution in multi-agent systems. Auton. Agents Multi-agent Syst. **19**(2), 124–152 (2009)

The Role of Knowledge Keepers in an Artificial Primitive Human Society: An Agent-Based Approach

Marzieh Jahanbazi[✉], Christopher Frantz, Maryam Purvis,
and Martin Purvis

Department of Information Science, University of Otago,
Dunedin, New Zealand
marzieh.jahanbazi@postgrad.otago.ac.nz,
{christopher.frantz,maryam.purvis,
martin.purvis}@otago.ac.nz

Abstract. This paper discusses knowledge accumulation and diffusion mechanisms and their effect on social and institutional change in an artificial society. The focus of this paper is to model the role of *knowledge keepers* in the context of social control in the CKSW institutional meta-role framework. In literature this role has been associated with helping to maintain social order by spreading social awareness and resolving disputes. In addition to outlining the model of a complex, adaptive, and self-sustaining artificial society, we examine in this context the societal mechanism of violence control.

Keywords: Artificial social systems · Social simulation · Institutions · Complex social systems · Agent-based modelling

1 Introduction

An increasingly popular approach for understanding complex social interactions in the social sciences is agent-based modelling and simulation [1–5]. Most of the works in this area take a specific perspective on the complex world of human societies and model phenomena related to that perspective in isolation from any other aspects of the society. However, agent-based modelling affords the opportunity to see how multiple interconnected factors may interact and affect an overall outcome.

This paper exemplifies this using a model of primitive human communities with thousands of agents across multiple generations. Apart from representing an archetypical primitive society, the model affords measuring changes of social relationships over time and their effects on societal functioning. Furthermore, it demonstrates how these modelled individuals dynamically adapt to different levels of resource availability or different demographic compositions. The model introduces a set of specific social interactions, such as mutual sharing, maintaining personal relationships, and keeping up with social reputation changes. We deem those to be applicable to primitive societies in particular in order to measure their long-term effect on the society's structural makeup and socio-economic development.

© Springer International Publishing Switzerland 2016
V. Dignum et al. (Eds.): COIN 2015, LNAI 9628, pp. 154–172, 2016.
DOI: 10.1007/978-3-319-42691-4_9

A notable feature of our model is its representation of generic roles that characterize some of the fundamental social activities in the society and how they are coordinated. In particular the generic role of the knowledge keeper will be shown below to be a key element in the coordination of the society's activities. It is our belief that such generic agent roles, such as that of the knowledge keeper, shape a society's social interactions and are as fundamental to social sustainability as the coordination by norms and institutions.

2 Background

As discussed in [6], primitive communities can be considered a good starting point for modelling human interactions and societies' structures. Agent-based models of such societies typically have agents operate according to simple rules that are derived from ethnographic field studies. We built our model based on the earlier extensive studies of primitive cultures that were initiated by Younger [6–10]. Younger's work was based on his observations of pre-contact Pacific Island societies, and serve as an archetype for pre-modern societies without advanced and explicit institutional structures. In order to define both the society's and agents' internal structure we apply the CKSW approach of Purvis and Purvis [11, 12] that identifies four fundamental meta roles of social interaction that are believed to be found in every society. The CKSW Meta-Role Model consists of four basic meta roles:

- **C** – the Commander role. It characterizes leaders and those who are in charge of decision-making and have access to coercive authority to control others.
- **K** – the Knowledge role. The Knowledge role has the responsibility to create, maintain, control, and transmit institutional knowledge. Since its central feature lies in the management of knowledge, we refer to it as *knowledge keeper* in the remainder of the text.
- **S** – the Skill role characterizes know-how intelligence. Skilled people develop tools to enhance their operations, and they have historically engaged in trade to exchange these tools with other groups.
- **W** – the Worker role represents the general working population which can use tools to engage in productive activities.

The reflection of the CKSW meta-role model in real human societies suggests that it can provide a natural structural scaffolding for agent-based models in artificial societies. Its application to our model of an evolving primitive society is particularly suitable, since it allows us to model and retrace structural developments of a society both on an individual-centred micro level, an intermediate level (classes of agents that are primarily dedicated to a particular role), and a macro level (the overall structural outcome). The internal (individual level) CKSW element defines different types of agents with varying preferences in the light of similar opportunities. For example an individual with a relatively high K (knowledge)-value would be more able to use and exploit knowledge that becomes available. In earlier work by

Jahanbazi et al. [13], covering social interaction in primitive societies, only the C and W meta roles were included in the social model. In general, when societies become more organized, it is natural for them to start keeping track of and managing knowledge of general value, thereby shaping their value system and culture. For example, a K-specific aspect is the interpretation of the natural environment and phenomena. Thus special social roles with a focus on K-management have arisen in early societies, such as the "medicine man" or priest that managed and interpreted knowledge. Thus we believe that societies first emerged with C and W meta-role sectors (the most primitive societies) and then developed into societies with C, W, and K meta-role sectors. Only later were all four C, K, W, and S meta-role sectors present in more developed societies. The work presented here describes a model for early C-K-W societies that have agents that activate the C, K, and W meta roles.

Work on the part of other social scientists and agent-based modelers has investigated building artificial societies, but without the CKSW scaffolding. Each uses a different approach and different angle to define the complex world in their model. The models developed in [3, 14] share our objective for developing a model which allows endogenous progression of institutional development. There are many works which only focus on singular aspects captured in our model, for instance population dynamics [15–17], mate selection [18–20], kinship [21], leadership and governance [3, 6], institutions [3, 14], economic development [2, 5, 22] or modelling the society's history [23, 24].

Due to the multifaceted nature of our model and limited space, in the upcoming section we can only briefly introduce the various elements of the model as well as features relevant to the knowledge keeper role.

3   Model Description

Our model consists of one or more villages of people, each with a leader. All agents have a finite lifetime (they can die of "old age") and need to eat food resources in order to sustain themselves. If an agent doesn't eat enough food, it can die of hunger. For this reason agents may sometimes be motivated to steal food from others. But agents may be killed for either stealing food or for reasons of revenge due to negative opinions of each other or previous negative experience. During their fertility ages, agents find mates (based on the matching of their mutual relationship values) and reproduce offspring that inherits (with a small possibility of mutation) their parents' characteristics.

Model Overview. In summary, our core model follows the idea that ordinary worker agents live in a village that is ruled by a leader agent and undergo a regular daily life cycle. They gather food from the environment and bring it to storage locations controlled by the leader. In our model an agent's time schedule is based on its own characteristics. For example, while the length of day is a universal parameter and is the same for all agents, an agent's "productive time" depends on its loyalty and defines how many time units during the day they must work for the village leader. During their productive time period, the follower (i.e. non-leader) agents are under the command of the leader and gather food from the surrounding area which they then deposit into a central storage controlled by the leader.

After an agent's productive time period has elapsed, it is free from obligations to the leader. At this point agents can keep the collected food. Agents can carry this food around, or can store it in their home. The stored food at home is accessible by all members of a household and is secure from theft, while the food that agents carry might be subject to theft. Beyond these activities, agents engage in other activities, such as sharing food (in order to increase their reputation and hence increase their chance of finding a mate), stealing, socializing (sharing what they know about other agents' reputations with third parties), and taking revenge if they hold a negative relationship value towards another agent. An agent could have a negative relationship value towards another agent if it were to witness that agent's stealing and/or killing acts, or witness an out-group agent (an agent from another village) collecting food from the observer's village's food sources. Apart from these actions, agents also perform automated activities that do not require deliberation. Those include growing older, experiencing increase in the hunger level due to energy consumption, eating (if they carry food and their hunger level is high), observing other nearby agents, and mating (under the condition that they had already found a mate).

Leaders maintain order in the village, but they do not gather food. They have control over the village's storage, however. They issue orders to collect food. Furthermore, they might share food with hungry follower agents based on their own loyalty and altruism level. They also have the power based on their aggression level to arrest agents who commit crimes in their vicinity. The overall social climate is affected by the leader's behavior. For example, leaders with high personal altruism levels tend to share more food with their followers, which can lead to social welfare without starvation (but also possibly to overexploitation with deleterious results). On the other hand, leaders with high personal aggression levels prevent more crimes and therefore decrease overall deaths due to crime. A schematic and high-level overview of the simulation is shown in Algorithm 1.

Schematic overview of the simulation run
1:    **Initialize** global parameters and physical environment
2:    **Instantiate** agents
3:    Assign Leader to each village
4:    **for** *simulation duration* **do**
5:            **if** *clock < (Loyalty * LengthOfDay)* **and** *Is Follower* **and**
6:                    *Leader's order = collect food* **do**
7:            Move toward food sources
8:            Collect food
9:            Move back to individual's village
10:            Deposit food into central storage
11:            **else if** *Leader's order = share food* **do**
12:                    Get a share of food
13:            **end if**
14:            Eat food at food source
15:            Share food
16:            Move back to individual's home
17:            Deposit food into home storage
18:   Steal
19:   Take revenge
20:            Share normative reputation
21:            Observe others
22:            Eat food from home storage
23:            Procreate
24:            **while** *Death Condition = False* **do**
25:                    Grow older
26:                    Consume energy
27:                    Forget old or unimportant relationships
28:                    Find mate
29:            **end while**
30:    Update food resources
31:    Update statistics
32:    Update leaders
33:    **end for**

Algorithm 1. High-level schematic overview of the simulation.

Functional Aspects of the Model. Our agent-based model is implemented in Netlogo [25], in which locations are referred to as "patches", and relationships between agents are represented as "links". In the following we will give insight into the functional aspects of the model.

The individual agents in our model have the following feature categories:

- **Simulation-related variables.** These track an individual's states, such as its needed food resource level, the amount of food resources it may be carrying, its current chosen goal, or the location of its home (its "patch"). This also includes a list of known resource locations.
- **Demographic variables.** Age, sex, and fertility rate are part of this group.
- **Kinship-related variables.** These include references to parents, children, mate, lineage, siblings, and their village.

- **Personal variables.** These include Altruism, Aggression, Loyalty, Physical Ability, and they are represented by a value between 0 and 1.0. These variables are adopted from [6].
- **Role-related variables.** Agents can be Leaders or Followers (corresponding to Commanders (C) and Workers (W)). In addition we consider a notion of Leader Class in the form of agents with family ties to the current leader (they are still follower agents but they may have special privileges). In this connection with this there is a loyalty-level parameter. For the leader of a village, it determines the extent to which his ruling is coercive. But for followers, this parameter determines how likely they are to obey orders.
- **Agents' internal CKSW variables.** Each agent has C, K, S, and W attributes, and for each such attribute there are two values – a capability value and an achievement value. The capability variable reflects how an agent will react to various opportunities available in the environment. For example, if an agent must choose between (1) exploring ways to be able to collect more food resources, and (2) exchanging information with other agents about known resources, then its choice will be determined by the dominance of either its knowledge (K) capability or skill (S) capability. If its knowledge capability is dominant, then the agent will choose to exchange information. This achievement level can be enhanced over time according to defined individual learning rates.

Agents' Interactions. Agents keep track of their relationships with other agents. The relationships of agents are maintained using an internal interaction matrix maintained by each agent that holds information about other agents it has encountered. The matrix is modified based on the observation of 'good deeds', such as sharing, and likewise adjusted based on negative experiences with an agent, such as observing or being the victim of stealing. Associated with this is the essential action of socialization. Similar to the notion of gossiping, whenever agents socialize they align their interaction matrix values in congruence with shared common acquaintances.

Relationships are represented by Netlogo "links". Each agent has a set of incoming links which are carrying another agent's opinion of the agent. Additionally each agent has a set of outgoing links that hold its opinion about other agents. The reputation of one agent is the sum of all the observational values on incoming links.

Links have the following attributes:

- **Age:** the creation time of the link.
- **Frequency:** the number of interactions so far with the agent at the end of this link.
- **Material exchange value:** the amount of resources exchanged with this agent by sharing or stealing.
- **Observational Values:** the "strength" of the relationship based on *observing* the other agent's actions or by *being informed* about that agent from other sources (for example by gossiping about a known third agent's reputation).

Agents' Decision-Making. Agents choose actions based on their internal state, which can include their hunger level, levels of altruism or aggression, as well as external state, which can be changed by the presence of a leader or enforcer agent in their vicinity.

In general, we aim to use a minimum of fixed behaviour parameters to determine an agent's actions, and instead make use of social comparison in most decision-making activities. For example, aggressive agents are not necessarily just those with aggression levels higher than 0.5 (or any other hard-wired parameter); instead, they define a personal threshold based on self-comparison with other people that they know in their village. This implies that an agent with an aggression level of 0.6 who lives near another agent whose aggression level is 0.4 might act more aggressively compared to a similar 0.6 aggression level agent who lives next to an agent with a 0.8 aggression level. (If an agent's aggression level is higher than those in its vicinity, then it is more likely to act aggressively.)

Another example of how an agent's activities can vary according to the social context concerns the conditions under which an agent might be motivated to steal. Ordinarily the conditions determining when an agent might commit a crime are dependent on whether a composite set of threshold conditions is met (the *MaxHunger* value is the level of hunger at which the agent will die of starvation):

(1) There is no law enforcer (e.g. a leader) nearby.
(2) The perpetrating agent is not carrying food.
(3) Another agent is nearby who carries food.
(4) *HungerLevel/(MaxHunger) > AltruismLevel*
(5) *HungerLevel/(MaxHunger) > (1- AggressionLevel).*

In addition to such situations, however, there are other conditions that could prevail. A potential crime perpetrator could evaluate the risk of getting caught and decide that it is worth committing the crime, for example, when condition (1) is not met. In that case the perpetrator agent might temporarily elevate its aggression level and commit the crime anyway.

3.1   The Incorporation of Knowledge into the Model

Having discussed the fundamental features of this model, we proceed with introducing new features added to the model. In order to make the model more comprehensible, we have classified its main features based on their related structural components, which we use as a rough guide for the introduction of the model additions. Figure 1 shows the defined model components. The *Physical Environment* covers infrastructural aspects related to the simulation environment, such as the locations of resources, growth rates, defining distances between different locations, the distances between villages, village settings, and the locations of distributed village storages. The *Institutional Structure* is the social structure we impose upon the agents; it defines the structure of the society in which agents live, including the norms and the rules they must consider in their decision-making. The *Individual Agent* covers anything related to features and capabilities of individual agents.

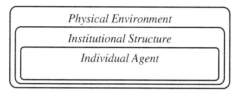

Fig. 1. Model components.

Physical Environment. As shown in Fig. 2 at the center of each village is a central storage area that the leader controls. In addition, each village has four distributed storage locations, which are also controlled by the leader and which make it easier for villages to deposit food so that there is less time spent commuting from and to food sources. There is also a common food source area between the villages, for which each village claims ownership. Collecting food from this area may lead to revenge attacks or negative reciprocity relationships (since villagers look negatively on any other agent from another village who collects food from the common area that they claim as theirs). We generalized this model to permit a varying number of villages.

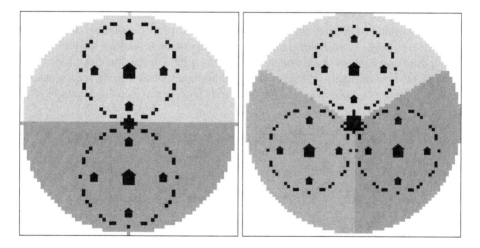

Fig. 2. Multi-Village Configurations. Each village has a central storage in the center that is surrounded by four distributed storage locations (small houses). Food sources, shown by black squares, are organized in a circle around the center. A common food source area is located between villages with the same distance to the center of each village.

Institutional Structure. As a society grows in size, it becomes increasingly difficult for a leader to maintain a monopoly on coercive control. For social scalability we have thus introduced a class of people appointed by the leader who monitor and prevent crimes. Those agents are recruited from the "Worker Class" (i.e. regular villagers) and selected based on the strength of their kinship relationships to the leader. This is associated with the leader selection strategy that builds on heredity. That is, when a leader dies, either his son, or his next closest kin will step up to become the new leader. And the new leader class will be selected based on the new leader's kinship relationships; members of the old "Leader class" will be 'converted' back to regular workers.

The daily course of action of people in the "Leader class" group is similar to that of the normal worker class. They have all basic responsibilities, but in addition they have the authority to secure locations identified by the leader to prevent crimes. This is governed by a probability related to their *aggression* and *loyalty* levels. The *aggression* level determines the successful prevention of crimes, while the *loyalty* level determines how long (how many time units) these agents are under orders to maintain security at a location. They have the power to arrest agents who dare to commit a crime in their presence. Resulting prisoner agents are required to work full time for the public good and collect food and deposit it into village storage. This strategy is in accordance with Boehm [26], who argues that in Pacific Island societies, instead of elimination of the offender, a sort of temporary punishment had been applied, which motivated the offender to regain group acceptance again and be able to return to life in the society. Whenever agents do get arrested, their reputation values will decrease significantly based on their current reputation level and the type of the crime they were caught committing. The secondary form of punishment is in accordance with [27], which discusses the effectiveness of combining material punishment (having to collect certain amounts of food for the leader) with normative punishment (lowering one's reputation), which is a form of group punishment [28] in that it decreases the chance of the offending agent in finding a mate or receiving shared food (since an agent's reputation is publicly visible).

But this system of law enforcement only works if knowledge about notable events is shared widely. Ordinarily whenever any notable event such as a crime occurs, nearby agents who have a high *Knowledge Capability* may observe this event and record it. But

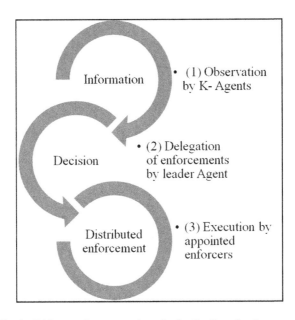

Fig. 3. Different elements and parties in distributed enforcement.

ordinary agents have only information about the areas that they visited and they don't have a big picture of the whole village. However, a group of agents with high loyalty have the opportunity to share their observations with the leader. This is in line with the notion of having a group of people who care more for their society's wellbeing and see themselves responsible to report crimes whenever they see them and take action in order to make their society safer [29]. Then the leader can decide on locations which need more control of violence. Since agents with a high *Knowledge Capability* have the motivation to share and distribute their knowledge, if they collocate with another agent with a similar *Knowledge Capability,* they can share information about their observations of events and agents they know.

Thus the distributed enforcement relies on three essential elements (see Fig. 3): (1) distributed knowledge accumulation of K-agents, (2) transmission of this information by a loyal subset of K-agents to the leader who will accumulate a global overview of what's happening in his territory, and (3) the leader's decisions on whether to send enforcers to a certain area.

Conflict Mediation. Historians have observed that people living in small groups often go to an elder to resolve their disputes [26, 30]. An elder with good reputation can resolve the intra-group conflicts, whereas inter-group conflicts should be resolved by the leader himself. Different cultures qualify different individuals as the ones who can resolve disputes – sometimes a person with high verbal skills, a good warrior reputation or a warm personality can be considered a good candidate. In some other groups, wealth (or the ability to offer a material gift), generosity, aggression, self-assertion, and reputation are considered to be important. We employ the most often mentioned property, which is reputation. In our model, reputation is also a signal of kindness, since it improves by sharing, and as kind agents grow old, they have more opportunities to share. If they have high *Knowledge Capability*, they have a higher chance of getting to know other agents and thereby have more knowledge to make judgment about contesting agents inasmuch as they know all parties involved in a dispute. Therefore high-reputation agents who have a high *Knowledge Capability* are good candidates for resolving intra-group disputes.

A significant aspect of dispute mediation is the procedure itself. In some cultures a material gift from the offending person will work, while in some other situations a duel, physical harm, or ostracism is needed to resolve the dispute [30, 31]. In our model, we used a practice of gift exchange. The amount required for this material exchange is the quantity of food units needed to make the relationship between two agents reach a neutral value.

In simulation runs which have this feature enabled, whenever an agent is collocated with another agent with whom he has a negative relationship and his aggression level is not sufficiently high to trigger revenge, a dispute resolution mechanism will be sought. In this case the offended agent will identify another agent in the vicinity with a high reputation. Then both parties will move toward the identified mediator, and the "neutral" mediator will prescribe a penalty based on the relationship values. The target agent must pay the penalty amount to the other party to restore his reputation. The cost involved in this procedure is mostly the time both agents spend finding the mediator agent and moving towards him. The mediator agent increases its own reputation in return, which makes him more likely to be chosen in connection with future disputes. Thus, over time, agents with higher reputation are expected to become experienced dispute mediators [13].

The combination of these two new features empowers our artificial society with a simplified version of both legal and civil justice. Legal justice aims to prevent crimes, and if enforcers catch someone committing a crime, there is a penalty of imprisonment and loss of reputation. On the other hand, civil justice attempts to resolve issues between agents by a reputable mediator agent without any actual penalty. Figure 4 shows different parties in both mechanisms.

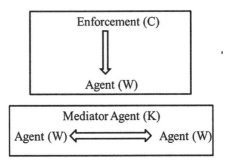

Fig. 4. Crime prevention and mediation mechanisms.

At this stage we have introduced the essential aspects of our relatively feature-rich agent model. Below, we present the results of our sensitivity analysis which we used to test the system for plausibility, but also to inform further parameter choices for selected scenarios.

4 Sensitivity Analysis

By using multi-agent modelling as a research tool, a repetitive process of defining and re-defining model requirements based on extensive literature in different disciplines can be followed in order to validate the model based on observational studies and reports from related literature. Thereafter simulations of different scenarios can help to gain deeper understanding of the causes of deviations or optimal ways to trigger the desired outcomes [11]. We have followed a systematic approach in this fashion by tuning each model parameter to find the most reasonable value (or range of values). As defined in [32], 'reasonable parameters' are those which help the model to reproduce patterns observed in reality. We tested hundreds of configurations for single parameters, even for the most trivial ones, such as the degree in which agents change their direction when exploring, or the hunger level at which they start eating.

We began our simulation study by starting with similar parameters used as reported in previous work [7, 13, 33]. In our attempts to extend those models with new features, whenever we needed a new parameter, we have tested wide ranges of values for each one of them. Nevertheless, the selection of the range of possible values in itself is not straightforward. In order to illustrate how we went about it, we provide an example showing the steps we went through to define one of the parameters used. Although in this example we ended up with a different tactic (using social comparison instead of using a parameter), we basically followed similar steps for most of the used parameters.

Initially, by adopting a perspective similar to [7, 13, 33], we decided to use the *revenge threshold* parameter, which could be set at any negative value. We tested a range from 0 to −1000 (in decrements of 20) to see how it affected the simulation outcomes. Each value was tested with 20 different random number generator seeds which led to 1000 rounds for a single-village setting. The outcomes revealed that having high-magnitude values led to the collapse of the simulation (values higher than −100), due to high numbers of revenge killings (since revenge killing could start a vicious cycle of revenge attacks and thereby lead to a population collapse). On the other hand, by using very low-magnitude values, revenge attacks never happen (−600 and lower). However, since our overall approach was to employ a minimal number of parameters and by considering that not all the people have the same threshold, we took a step back and considered other factors which helped us to facilitate parameter estimation. We observed the minimum and maximum relationship values for each agent and used this range for each individual agent in the following way:

$$RevengeThreshold = Max - ((Max-Min) * AggressionLevel)$$

Accordingly, an agent will take revenge if (a) the agent has a negative revenge threshold (indicating negative reciprocity) and (b) is collocated with an agent who has a lower-than-threshold relationship value toward him. In summary, we tested every single parameter with hundreds of experiments and used those which seemed more plausible and led to results closest to [33]. Of course the issue of "plausibility" can be subjective and is not objectively measurable, which is a framing consideration for all agent-based models.

In summary, as we stated earlier we avoided hard-wired thresholds to introduce new institutional activities that keep the social order intact. Instead we have used notions of social comparison among the agents to define their own views towards welfare at the societal level and at the individual level. This is also in accordance with theories of the social self and the idea that we are influenced by people around us, and have a tendency to adopt the characteristics of those who are close to us [34]. We believe that this is missing in many agent-based models, inasmuch as they mostly define arbitrary global parameters for such thresholds set at low, medium, or high values. We argue that it is preferable to look from a situated perspective and ask whether the effects of a particular parameter can be shown to emerge from the social and environmental context.

5   Experimental Design

We used 30 different random seeds for each pair of experiments in 2-village configurations with 100 agents as initial populations for each village. Agents can live up to 4,000 time units, and we used 40,000 time units as the total duration of the each simulation run. There were three major scenario categories that we examined:

(1) Scenarios without distributed control of violence (or distributed enforcement).
(2) Scenarios with distributed control of violence but **without** the use of observation of events by agents with high *Knowledge Capability*. Instead we simulated global knowledge of criminal occurrences by storing the criminal events locally in the patch and making them globally visible to the enforcers.
(3) Scenarios with distributed control of violence and with the use of observation of events by agents with high *Knowledge Capability*.

For each scenario we tested it with and without conflict resolution, which made a total of 6 experiments per random seed (180 in total). We considered Scenario (2) and (3) in order to compare the relative efficiency difference between global knowledge about crime and knowledge about crime that is passed through knowledge-aware agents. For simulation efficiency it can be useful to store the criminal results in the patches, but it is less realistic. We found that Scenario (3), which employed criminal event observation and communication by high Knowledge-Capability agents to be almost as efficient as Scenario (2) and a more realistic representation.

6 Results and Discussion

In this section we summarize our experimental results with regard to specific features.

Effectiveness of Distributed Information Gathering. Before moving to our main features and their effects, the scenarios that test the accuracy of information will be discussed. The results show that the correlation between decline in death due to revenge and enabling enforcers who use crime information stored in the patches is −0.80, while the correlation between decline in death due to revenge and enabling enforcers who use the information collected by distributed knowledge gathering is −0.78. The results indicate that distributed information gathering is almost as effective as using accurate information stored in the history of patches.

Enabling Distributed Control of Violence. Other than a leader's control of the distribution of food based on his altruism level, there is only one institutional element that prevents agents from stealing and violence: this is provided by the authorized members of the Leader class engaged in distributed violence control. The correlations between enabling this distributed form of crime control and different causes of death are significant. Correlation with the death rate due to (a) revenge is −0.78, (b) thefts is −0.54, and (c) hunger is +0.8. The correlation of distributed violence control and the total number of thefts is −0.77. In general, theft and killings are reduced considerably by implementing distributed control of violence, while death due to hunger rises. This could suggest that even in this artificial society, mere prevention of violence is not enough. There should be further institutions beyond stopping crime, such as providing the deprived agents with assistance for food acquisition. Additionally, since agents who are enforcing the rules are not productive anymore, they do not contribute to central storage sites any longer, leaving the society has fewer contributors and more consumers. This result raises the question concerning to what degree can distributed law enforcement be tailored to achieve a balance between crime and starvation. Figure 5 shows the average percentages of different causes of death for all scenarios with activated observation of events for configurations with and without distributed enforcement. As shown in Fig. 5, death due to old age is hardly affected by this feature.

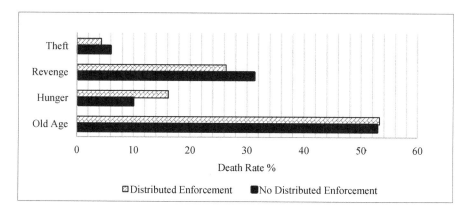

Fig. 5. Effect of distributed enforcement on different causes of death.

Conflict Mediation. Introducing conflict mediation made much more of a difference in the absence of other types of crime prevention (see Figs. 6 and 7). Unsurprisingly, it has a correlation of +0.8 with the *Reputation Gini,* which defines the inequality in agent reputations[1]. The reason behind this effect is due to the role of the mediator who gains in reputation as he resolves the disputes. In addition, those with negative reciprocity towards each other have the chance to remedy their relationship and thus improve it. However, this indicates the emergence of class stratification based on reputation. While we expected that conflict mediation improves the overall welfare of the society, it has the unforeseen effect in population rise which leads resource scarcity and more conflict over resources. This is schematically illustrated in Fig. 8.

---

[1] The reputation Gini index shows the relative reputation inequality in a group. In particular, it reveals the gap between agents with very high reputation and agents with low reputation. In order to calculate the Gini index, we implement formula used by [35]. *Agent*$_i$'s reputation represented by y_i. Then we sort y_i, $i = 1\ to\ n$ in ascending order $(y_i <= y_{i+1})$. Finally, Gini is calculated as $G = \frac{1}{n}\left(n + 1 - 2\left(\frac{\sum_{i=1}^{n}(n + 1 - i)y^1}{\sum_{i=1}^{n}y_i}\right)\right)$.

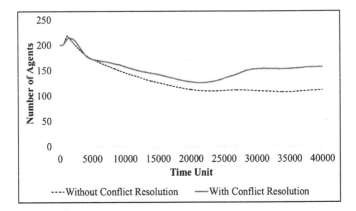

Fig. 6. Population change over 10 generations for scenarios with and without conflict resolution.

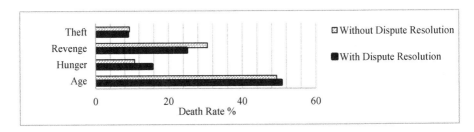

Fig. 7. Average rates of different causes of death with and without dispute resolution.

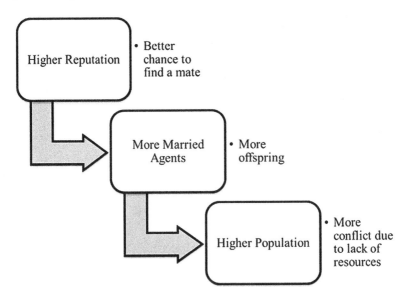

Fig. 8. Effect of higher reputation results from conflict resolution.

The correlations between population increase and different causes of death are significant (see Figs. 6 and 7). The correlation between the number of agents and: (a) death due to hunger is +0.51, (b) death due to thefts is +0.63, and (c) death due to old age −0.8. Moreover, it decreases the life expectancy of agents in such a way that the average age at death decreases considerably when population size increases (correlation is −0.8). Figure 6 shows the average population change for scenarios with and without dispute resolution, and Fig. 7 shows the average rates of different causes of death in scenarios with and without dispute resolution.

In addition to calculating the correlations between each feature and different outputs, we have used regression analysis to confirm the results. Table 1 summarizes the regression analysis of 180 experiments which shows the p-values and coefficients of regression test with a confidence level of 95 %.

Table 1. Regression results.

	Revenge		Hunger		Thefts	
	P-value	Coefficients	P-value	Coefficients	P-value	Coefficients
Intercept	0.79	661.29	0.46	−2196.00	0.69	317.62
Distributed enforcement	4E−40	−8.53	5E−50	12.47	5E−20	−1.70
Event observation	0.020	1.27	0.00	−2.14	0.11	0.28
Conflict resolution	0.000	−1.59	8E−07	2.52	7E−13	1.03
Adjusted R square	0.685		0.73		0.48	

Distributed enforcement has significant p-values for all three output variables. It is worth mentioning that the reason behind less significant p-values for event observation compared to distributed enforcement lies in its comparison with scenarios in which enforcers had actual knowledge of crime areas. As shown in the results, distributed enforcement comes with the cost of higher death due to hunger. As mentioned earlier, this can be due to more consumers and less contributors. In the same way, in the real world, enforcement comes at a cost too, and this brings up the challenge of balancing enforcement and the cost of enforcement.

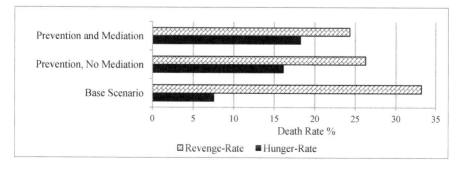

Fig. 9. Death rates due to revenge and hunger for different scenarios.

Figure 9 compares the average values for three main scenarios at once. It can be seen that as crime prevention features are added, deaths due to revenge decrease, but deaths due to starvation increase which shows the cost of resolving conflicts or its prevention.

7 Conclusion and Future Work

As supported by the claim made in [36] that agent-based modelling is "a new standard of explanation", there has been a growing interest in agent-based modelling of complex social phenomena. However, perhaps partly due to computational limitations, the complexity and interactive scope of the modelled agents is often limited. In the work presented in this paper and by expanding the model developed by [33], we have included a wider range of aspects found in real societies and studied their interaction in different simulation settings. In this work we have explored the impact of compliance and dispute resolution mechanisms on the functioning of a society, along with the structural change of the society's configuration based on the different social roles.

However, our path toward building more realistic artificial human societies has much ahead of it. We believe that continued development of CKSW-based meta-role models can offer new opportunities in the area of social modelling. The CKSW perspective takes into account social ordering activities that have been observed across the history of human societies. Building models using agents with these meta-role capabilities will enable us to reproduce some of the observed higher-level social structures in an organic fashion. These general role scenarios offer a more realistic representation of how primitive societies of autonomous agents achieve a measure of societal coordination.

Considerably more work will need to be done to achieve our main objective of modelling a human society with the internal ability to construct essential institutions to sustain and enhance the overall social prosperity. A number of important limitations need to be considered in order to refine and improve the current model. Some immediate extensions we will be pursuing include improving the current simplistic view of mate selection (the selected mate cannot reject the proposal) by considering real mate selection criteria in different cultures. Furthermore, we will be introducing more variation in food resource fertility rates and transportation channels. The next major extension of the model will be implementing the skill (S) class and introducing concepts such as agricultural technology for different societies.

References

1. Huang, H.Q., Macmillan, W.: A generative bottom-up approach to the understanding of the development of rural societies. Agrifood Res. Rep. **68**, 296–312 (2005)
2. Macmillan, W., Huang, H.Q.: An agent-based simulation model of a primitive agricultural society. Geoforum **39**, 643–658 (2008)
3. Makowsky, M.D., Smaldino, P.E.: The evolution of power and the divergence of cooperative norms. J. Econ. Behav. Org. **126**, 75–88 (2016)

4. Gilbert, N., den Besten, M., Bontovics, A., Craenen, B.G.W., Divina, F., Eiben, A.E., Griffioen, R., Hévízi, G., Lörincz, A., Paechter, B., Schuster, S., Schut M.C., Tzolov, C., Vogt, P., Yang, L.: Emerging artificial societies through learning. J. Artif. Soc. Soc. Simul. **9** (2006)

5. Tesfatsion, L.: Agent-based computational economics: growing economies from the bottom up. Artif. Life **8**, 55–82 (2002)

6. Younger, S.: Leadership, violence, and warfare in small societies. J. Artif. Soc. Soc. Simul. **14**, 8 (2011)

7. Younger, S.: Leadership in small societies. J. Artif. Soc. Soc. Simul. **13**, 5 (2010)

8. Younger, S.: Reciprocity, sanctions, and the development of mutual obligation in egalitarian societies. J. Artif. Soc. Soc. Simul. **8**, 9 (2005)

9. Younger, S.M.: Discrete agent simulations of the effect of simple social structures on the benefits of resource sharing. J. Artif. Soc. Soc. Simul. **6** (2003)

10. Younger, S.: Reciprocity, normative reputation, and the development of mutual obligation in gift-giving societies. JASSS-THE J. Artif. Soc. Soc. Simul. **7** (2004)

11. Purvis, M.K., Purvis, M.A.: Institutional expertise in the service-dominant logic: knowing how and knowing what. J. Mark. Manag. **28**, 1626–1641 (2012). doi:10.1080/0267257X.2012.742454

12. Purvis, M., Purvis, M., Frantz, C.: CKSW: a folk-sociological meta-model for agent-based modelling. Social Path Workshop (2014)

13. Jahanbazi, M., Frantz, C., Purvis, M., Purvis, M.: Building an artificial primitive human society: an agent-based approach. In: Ghose, A., et al. (eds.) COIN 2014. LNCS, vol. 9372, pp. 89–96. Springer, Heidelberg (2015). doi:10.1007/978-3-319-25420-3_6

14. Makowsky, M.D., Rubin, J.: An agent-based model of centralized institutions, social network technology, and revolution. PLOS ONE **8** (2013)

15. Cervellati, M., Sunde, U.: Life expectancy and economic growth: the role of the demographic transition. J. Econ. Growth **16**, 99–133 (2011). doi:10.2307/41486924

16. Read, D.W.: Emergent properties in small-scale societies. Artif. Life **9**, 419–434 (2003). doi:10.1162/106454603322694852

17. Axtell, R.L., Epstein, J.M., Dean, J.S., Gumerman, G.J., Swedlund, A.C., Harburger, J., Chakravarty, S., Hammond, R., Parker, J., Parker, M.: Population growth and collapse in a multiagent model of the Kayenta Anasazi in Long House Valley. Proc. Natl. Acad. Sci. U.S.A. **99**(Suppl 3), 7275–7279 (2002)

18. Diaz, B.A., Fent, T.: An agent-based simulation model of age-at-marriage norms, pp. 85–116 (2006)

19. Billari, F.C., Prskawetz, A., Diaz, B.A., Fent, T.: The "Wedding-Ring": an agent-based marriage model based on social interaction. Demogr. Res. **17**, 59–82 (2008)

20. Bentley, G.R.: Hunter-gatherer energetics and fertility: a reassessment of the! Kung San. Hum. Ecol. **13**, 79–109 (1985)

21. Read, D.: Kinship based demographic simulation of societal processes. J. Artif. Soc. Soc. Simul. **1** (1998)

22. Ewert, U.C., Roehl, M., Uhrmacher, A.M.: Hunger and market dynamics in pre-modern communities: insights into the effects of market intervention from a multi-agent model. Hist. Soc. Res. Sozialforsch, 122–150 (2007)

23. Lake, M.: Explaining the Past with ABM: On Modelling Philosophy (2015). doi:10.1007/978-3-319-00008-4_1

24. Barceló, J., Del Castillo, F., Del Olmo, R., Mameli, L., Quesada, F.M., Poza, D., Vilà, X.: Simulating Patagonian territoriality in prehistory: space. Front. Netw. Among Hunter-Gatherers (2015). doi:10.1007/978-3-319-00008-4_10

25. Tisue, S., Wilensky, U.: Netlogo: a simple environment for modeling complexity. Int. Conf. Complex Syst., pp 16–21 (2004)
26. Boehm, C.: Hierarchy in the Forest: The Evolution of Egalitarian Behavior. Harvard University Press, Cambridge (2009)
27. Villatoro, D., Andrighetto, G., Brandts, J., Nardin, L.G., Sabater-Mir, J., Conte, R.: The norm-signaling effects of group punishment combining agent-based simulation and laboratory experiments. Soc. Sci. Comput. Rev. **32**, 334–353 (2014)
28. Boyd, R., Gintis, H., Bowles, S.: Coordinated punishment of defectors sustains cooperation and can proliferate when rare. Science **328**, 617–620 (2010)
29. Fry, D.P., Bjrkqvist, K., Bjorkqvist, K.: Cultural Variation in Conflict Resolution Alternatives to Violence. Taylor & Francis, New York (2013)
30. Wagner, G. The political organization of the Bantu of Kavirondo. Afr. Polit. Syst., 197 (1940)
31. Wolff, P.M., Braman, O.R.: Traditional dispute resolution in Micronesia. South Pac. J. Psychol. **11**, 44–53 (1999)
32. Thiele, J.C., Kurth, W., Grimm, V.: Facilitating parameter estimation and sensitivity analysis of agent-based models: a cookbook using NetLogo. R. J. Artif. Soc. Soc. Simul. **17**(3), 11 (2014)
33. Jahanbazi, M., Frantz, C., Purvis, M., Purvis, M., Nowostawski, M.: Agent-based modelling of primitive human communities. In: Intelligent Advanced Technology, vol. 3, pp. 64–71 (2014)
34. Gould, M.: Culture, personality, and emotion in George Herbert mead: a critique of empiricism in cultural sociology. Sociol. Theor. **27**, 435–448 (2009). doi:10.2307/40376122
35. Gastwirth, J.L.: The estimation of the Lorenz curve and Gini index. Rev. Econ. Stat. **54**(3), 306–316 (1972)
36. Epstein, J.M.: Why model? J. Artif. Soc. Soc. Simul. **11**(4), 12 (2008)

Modeling and Detecting Norm Conflicts in Regulated Organizations

Jie Jiang and Huib Aldewereld[(✉)]

Delft University of Technology, Delft, The Netherlands
{jie.jiang,h.m.aldewereld}@tudelft.nl

Abstract. In regulated organizations, norms may come from various regulation sources imposed by different institutions. With possibly conflicting values and interests, inconsistencies are likely to occur among these norms, e.g., one norm obliges some actions to be done while another norm prohibits the same actions. In this paper, we propose a formalization of norm conflicts based on the normative states of interrelated norms. Then via operationalizing the normative structure based on Colored Petri Nets, we propose a method for detecting such conflicts.

Keywords: Regulated organizations · Normative systems · Norm conflicts · Agent organizations

1 Introduction

A common problem for organizations is the increasing amount and complexity of norms that they have to consider in the design of their business processes. For example, when dairy products are exported, besides the internal process control of the dairy exporter, many other sources of norms are imposed by different institutions [4]. For instance, customs regulates the activities concerning export declaration, and transportation. An health agency regulates the activity of health certification. An agriculture agency puts information requirements on export declaration. A tax agency regulates the activities of Value-Added Tax settlement and invoicing. Given the diversity of regulation sources and possibly conflicting interests, it is likely that the norms imposed by these institutions are not consistent. In such cases, it is impossible to reach an agreement on whether the organizations comply with the regulations, which may cause misunderstanding and decrease the effectiveness of laws and regulations. To this end, mechanisms are needed to detect the norm conflicts.

Such a problem has been extensively investigated by researchers in the domain of normative systems. An early work is presented by [14], in which the concept of normative conflict is formally analyzed and two approaches of reasoning with normative conflicts are discussed. [16,17] applied first-order unification to discover overlapping substitutions to the variables of laws/norms in which legal/norm conflicts may occur. Targeting distributed management of norms, [2] proposed a normative model based on the propagation of normative positions

© Springer International Publishing Switzerland 2016
V. Dignum et al. (Eds.): COIN 2015, LNAI 9628, pp. 173–190, 2016.
DOI: 10.1007/978-3-319-42691-4_10

as consequences of agents' actions, and realized conflict detection by providing a mapping of the normative model into Colored Petri Nets. Focused on normative conflicts in electronic contracts, [3] presented a set of primitive conflict patterns and proposed the representation of e-contracts in default logic to facilitate conflict detection. [10,11] proposed a computational model for detecting norm conflicts given traces of agent actions by means of Answer Set Programming. Focused on identifying conflicts between obligations in dynamic settings, [15] introduced a new semantics for the obligations to identify the necessary and sufficient conditions to detect conflicting obligations. Though these approaches provide useful formalisms and detection techniques, there are two issues that have not been discussed. One is the analysis of how the interrelations between norms might influence the existence of norm conflicts. The other one is how compliance status of norms is linked to the existence of norm conflicts.

Targeting these two issues, this paper investigates the concept of norm conflicts in the setting of interrelated norms. To formalize the specification of norms, we adopt the normative language Norm Nets (NNs) [8] which provide formalisms for representing the interrelations between norms. Based on NNs, we present an analysis of norm conflicts in terms of the compliance status of norms and show how interrelations between norms may influence the formation of norm conflicts. Moreover, we distinguish between two types of norm conflicts, i.e., weak conflicts and strong conflicts. To detect the conflicts, a computational model is developed by using Colored Petri Nets [5].

The rest of the paper is organized as follows. Section 2 introduces the formalisms that are used to model norms. Section 3.2 gives the definition of norm conflicts and presents the mechanism of detecting such conflicts. Section 4 provides a case study. Finally, Sect. 5 concludes this paper and identifies the directions for future work.

2   Normative Structure

In this paper, we consider an institution as a set of norms used to regulate the behavior of participating agents in organizations [12], which is formalized by Norm Nets (NNs) [8].

2.1   Conceptual Model

(i) **Preliminaries.** *Events* are defined to represent the actions available to the roles in organizations.

Definition 1 (Event). *Let R be a finite set of roles and $\mathcal{A}$ be a finite set of actions. The set of events $E \subseteq R \times \mathcal{A}$ where an element from E is denoted as $\varepsilon = (r, \alpha), r \in R, \alpha \in \mathcal{A}$.*

An event $\varepsilon = (r, \alpha)$ describes an action α available to a role r. For example, we can express an institutional observation "a student enters the library" by defining an event *(Student, enter_library)*. Using the notion of events, a propositional language L_E is defined over the set of events.

Definition 2 (Event Language). *Given an event $e \in E$, let the event language L_E be the set of expressions generated by the following grammar:*

$$\varphi ::= e|(\varphi \wedge \varphi)|(\varphi \vee \varphi)|(\varphi < \varphi)|\lambda$$

$\varphi_1 \wedge \varphi_2$ indicates both φ_1 and φ_2 occur (conjunction), $\varphi_1 \vee \varphi_2$ indicates either φ_1 or φ_2 occurs (disjunction), $\varphi_1 < \varphi_2$ indicates φ_1 occurs before φ_2 (sequence), and λ represents a null event. E_φ is used to indicate all the events contained in φ. The event expressions can be evaluated to *true* or *false* based on the occurrence of prescribed events and their relations.

For example, given $\varphi_1 = (Student, enter\_library)$ and $\varphi_2 = (Librarian, check\_identity)$, $\varphi_1 \wedge \varphi_2$ means that the student enters the library and the librarian checks the identity; $\varphi_1 \vee \varphi_2$ means that either the student enters the library or the librarian checks the identity; $\varphi_1 < \varphi_2$ means that the student enters the library and then the librarian checks the identity.

(ii) Norms. *Norms* are defined to prescribe how agents ideally should (not) behave in terms of the roles they enact. In NNs, two types of norms are defined, i.e., obligations and prohibitions, as formalized in Definition 3.

Definition 3 (Norm). *A norm $n = (D, \rho, \delta, \sigma)$ where (1) $D \in \{O, F\}$ indicates the deontic type of the norm, i.e., $\underline{O}$bliged, $\underline{F}$orbidden, (2) $\rho \in E$, describing a non-empty target to which the deontic modality is assigned, (3) $\delta \in L_E$, describing the deadline of the norm, and (4) $\sigma \in L_E$, describing the precondition of the norm.*

The target is indicated by a role-action pair in which the role specifies to whom the norm applies and the action specifies the behavior that is constrained by the norm. Both the precondition and the deadline are event formulas. The precondition determines when the norm is activated and enforced, and the deadline determines when an obligation has to be ensured or a prohibition ceases.

For example, we can model a regulation that "If a student borrows a book from the library, the student should return the book within 1 month" by defining a norm $n = (O, (Student, return\_book), (Timeline, pass\_1month), (Student, borrow\_book))$. In this norm, we have defined two roles *Student* and *Timeline*, in which *Timeline* is a reserved role used to indicate the elapsing of time.

(iii) State Transitions of Norms. A norm is *instantiated* when it is created. As soon as the precondition holds, the norm is *activated*. An obligation is considered *satisfied* when both its precondition and target are true while its deadline is false, and considered *violated* when both its precondition and deadline are true while the target is false. A prohibition is considered *satisfied* when both its precondition and deadline are true while its target is false, and considered *violated* when both its precondition and target are true while its deadline is false.

(iv) Norm Nets. To capture the interrelations between norms, the concept of *Norm Net* is introduced.

Definition 4 (Norm Net). *A norm net NN is defined by the following BNF:*

$$NN ::= n|\mathrm{AND}(NN, \ NN)|\mathrm{OR}(NN, \ NN)|\mathrm{OE}(NN, \ NN)$$

where n is a norm; S_{NN} is used to denote the set of component norm nets contained in NN and E_{NN} is used to denote the set of events contained in NN.

A norm net can be a single norm or a nested structure composed of norms with three different relations. **AND** indicates that both component norm nets should be satisfied and the violation of either component will result in a violation to the combination. **OR** indicates a choice between the two component norm nets and only when both are violated the combination is considered as violated. **OE** indicates that the two component norm nets are conditional and exclusive, i.e., (1) only when the first component is violated can the second component be activated, (2) the violation of the first component can be repaired by the second component being satisfied. Based on the state transitions of single norms, the state transitions of NNs can be derived according to the interrelations between its component norms.

For example, consider the following normative constraint "students should return the book within 1 month after they borrow the book, otherwise they have to pay a fine within 1 week." This piece of constraint indicates a reparation/sanction relation between two norms, which can be represented by a norm net $OE(n_1, n_2)$ where $n_1 = (O, (Student, return\_book), (Timeline, pass\_1month), (Student, borrow\_book))$ and $n_2 = (O, (Student, pay\_fine), (Timeline, pass\_1week), \lambda)$.

Note that while n_2 has an empty activation condition λ, the norm is still only triggered *after* n_1 is violated, due to the semantics of the OE operator. The activation condition of the second norm in an OE-construction (the sanction norm) can thus be used to further specify conditions that should hold to activate the sanction (or, create exceptions when not to activate the sanction norm).

2.2 Operational Semantics

The operational semantics of NNs are obtained by a mapping to Colored Petri Nets (CPNs) following the approach presented by [8].

(i) Colored Petri Nets. A CPN [5] is a directed graph consisting of two types of nodes, called *places* and *transitions*, where *arcs* are either from a place to a transition or from a transition to a place. Tokens in CPNs may have different colors or data types and carry data attributes that characterize the entities the tokens represent.

A place serves as a placeholder for the entities in the system being modeled. Each place is associated with a type or a color set that determines the kind of tokens the place may contain. Besides a type, each place has a *marking* (denoted as M)

to indicate its state, which is defined as a multiset of values over the type of the place. A *multiset* is similar to an ordinary set except that the same element can occur multiple times. A *token* is an element of such a marking, i.e., it has a value and resides in a place. If a marking consists of tokens with different values, we separate them with two pluses $(++)$. The subtraction of tokens with different values is expressed as two minuses $(--)$.

An arc has an *inscription* which may contain one or more free variables. Transitions represent the events that can occur in the system being modeled. A transition has a set of variables, i.e., the ones occurring on all the arcs connecting to it. Each of these variables can be assigned a value from the set represented of its type. A transition along with an assignment of each of its variables is referred to as a *binding* (denoted as b). Given a CPN with a marking and a binding, the binding is considered to be enabled if all input places contain at least the tokens specified by the evaluation of the expression on the corresponding input arcs in the binding. A transition is enabled in a marking if there exists at least one binding which is enabled in the marking. If a binding or a transition is enabled, it can occur or be fired. This results in consuming all the tokens from input places corresponding to the evaluations of the expressions on input arcs and producing new tokens on output places corresponding to the evaluations of the expressions on output arcs. The marking of a model before we start simulation is called the *initial marking*.

Based on the description above, the formalization of a CPN is shown in Definition 5.

Definition 5 (CPN). *A CPN is a tuple $(P, T, A, \Sigma, V, C, E, I)$ where (1) P is a finite set of places, (2) T is a finite set of transitions such that $P \cap T = \emptyset$, (3) $A \subseteq P \times T \cup T \times P$ is a set of directed arcs, (4) Σ is a finite set of non-empty color sets (data types), (5) V is a finite set of typed variables such that $Type[v] \in \Sigma$ for all variables $v \in V$, (6) $C : P \to \Sigma$ is a color set function that assigns a color set to each place, (7) $E : A \to EXPR_V$ is an arc expression function that assigns an arc expression to each arc $a \in A$ such that $Type[E(a)] = C(p)_{MS}$, where p is the place connected to the arc a and MS indicates $C(p)_{MS}$ is a multiset, (8) $I : P \to EXPR_\emptyset$ is an initialization function that assigns a closed expression to each place p such that $Type[I(p)] = C(p)_{MS}$.*

(ii) Mapping from NNs to CPNs. In organizations, roles are enacted by agents, and the agents' behavior is constrained by the norms regulating the roles they enact. In this paper, we assume a set of agents Ag participating in a regulated organization and an explicit enactment relation REA between the agents and the roles specified in the norms. Based on the definition of NNs and their state transitions, correspondences between a norm net and a Colored Petri net can be generalized as follows.

- $R \to \Sigma$: each role corresponds to a color set which can be assigned to the places,
- $\mathcal{A} \to T$: actions are represented by the transitions,

- $E \to P \times T$: events are indicated by the connections from places to transitions,
- $(REA \subseteq Ag \times R) \to I$: role-enacting agents are indicated by the initial distribution of tokens in the places (i.e., initial marking),
- $Satisfied \subseteq P$, $Violated \subseteq P$, $Satisfied \cap Violated = \emptyset$: the satisfied and violated states of norms are indicated by two disjoint subsets of the places.

Agents are represented by the tokens which can only reside in the places with the matching colors according to the roles the agents are enacting.

Based on the correspondences between the elements in NNs and that in CPNs, we follow the approach presented by [8] and the CPN patterns in [13] to construct the CPN model of NNs. The resulting CPN model of a norm net is given as follows.

Definition 6 (CPN Model of NNs). *The CPN model of a norm net NN with an enactment relation REA is denoted as $\Theta(NN, REA) = (\mathcal{N}, Satisfied, Violated, p_s, p_v)$ where (1) $\mathcal{N}$ is a CPN according to Definition 5, (2) $Satisfied \in P_{\mathcal{N}}$ is a subset of the places of $\mathcal{N}$, indicating the satisfied states of all the component norm nets in NN, (3) $Violated \in P_{\mathcal{N}}$ is a subset of the places of $\mathcal{N}$, indicating the violated states of all the component norm nets in NN, (4) $p_s \in Satisfied$ is a place of $\mathcal{N}$ such that $\nexists t \in T_{\mathcal{N}} : (p_s, t) \in A_{\mathcal{N}}$, indicating the overall satisfied state of NN, (5) $p_v \in Violated$ is a place of $\mathcal{N}$ such that $\nexists t \in T_{\mathcal{N}} : (p_v, t) \in A_{\mathcal{N}}$, indicating the overall violated state of NN.*

(iii) Visual Mapping of Norms to CPN. Following the approach presented in [8], we briefly present a visual guidance how norms are translated to CPN models. Given a regulative norm $n^r = (D, \rho, \delta, \sigma)$, the construction of its CPN model follows three steps:

1. constructing CPN snippets for each event in the construction of the target ρ, the deadline δ and the precondition σ (see top-left of Fig. 1);
2. combining the CPN snippets obtained from the first step according to the relations ($\wedge, \vee, <$) between the corresponding institutional events in the precondition σ and deadline δ (see bottom of Fig. 1); and
3. connecting the combined CPN snippets obtained from the second step to obtain the CPN model of a regulative norm according to the deontic type of the norm (see Fig. 2).

An event (r, α) is replaced by a two places (input and output) connected by a transition. Both places are associated with a color set r_{ag} indicating that agents represented by the residing tokens are enacting the role r. Note that the "color" of a token is only a data-type/label, not per se an actual color (black, green, red, etc.). The transition refers to action α, thus indicating that the firing of that transition represents that an agent playing role r has performed α.

The combination of events (bottom part of Fig. 1) is realized through the three operators in L_E: $\wedge$ (and), $\vee$ (or), $<$ (before). Based on the workflow patterns presented in [13], the CPN patterns for the three types of combination are described as follows.

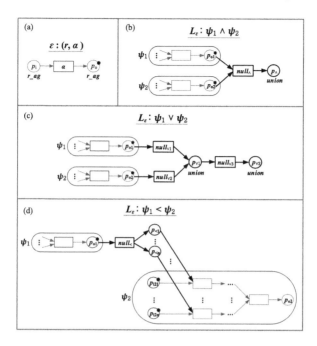

Fig. 1. CPN patterns for events, conjunction, disjunction, and before.

$\wedge$ **relation:** top-right of Fig. 1 shows the CPN pattern for two event formulas ψ_1 and ψ_2 combined with a $\wedge$ relation which indicates that only when both ψ_1 and ψ_2 occur, the combination of these two occurs. Accordingly, the output places of both branches are connected to a single transition, thus converging the thread of control only when both output places contain a token.

$\vee$ **relation:** the middle of Fig. 1 shows the CPN pattern for two event formulas ψ_1 and ψ_2 combined with a $\vee$ relation which indicates that as long as one of ψ_1 or ψ_2 occurs the combination of the two occurs. Accordingly, the output places of both branches are connected to the same place in such a way that the thread of control is converged when either branch has a token in its output place.

For both the $\wedge$ and $\vee$ relation, the places in the succeeding branch are assigned a new color set, being the union of the color sets of the input branches. This is to enable the conjunction/disjunction of events with different roles, allowing either role from the input branches to proceed to the output place.

$<$ **relation:** the bottom of Fig. 1 shows the CPN pattern for two event formulas ψ_1 and ψ_2 combined with a $<$ relation, which indicates that only when ψ_1 occurs first and then ψ_2 occurs the combination occurs. To achieve this, the output places of the pattern representing ψ_1 are connected to the first transitions occuring in ψ_2. This ensures that those transitions (of ψ_2) can only fire when ψ_1 has finished (i.e., ψ_1 has tokens in its output places).

Notice that there is a set of transitions labelled *null*, which are necessary in order to apply the synchronization mechanism of CPNs. These transition will fire as soon as their input places have sufficient tokens.

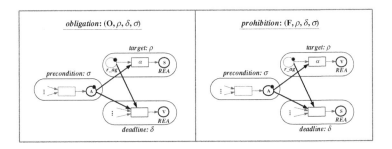

Fig. 2. CPN patterns for obligation (left) and prohibition (right).

The combination of the target, precondition, and deadline of a regulative norm should follow the logic that after the occurrence of the precondition, the target should (not) occur, before the occurrence of the deadline (otherwise a violation is generated). The precondition determines when the regulative norm is activated, while the deadline determines when the norm can be evaluated to be satisfied or violated (depending on the deontic type of the norm). To represent these correlations in a norm, the construction of its CPN model follows these two steps (see Fig. 2):

(1) activation: connecting the output place of the precondition to the transition of the target, and to the last transition of the deadline, such that only when the precondition is fulfilled, the target and the deadline are enabled to fire.

(2) evaluation: connecting the first place of the target to the last transition of the deadline, such that (a) when the target occurs first (the deadline has not finished), the token in the source place of the target, representing the agent, moves to the last place of the target, or (b) when the deadline finished first (and the target has not occurred), the token moves to the output place of the deadline instead. The label of these output places depends on the deontic type of the norm; for an obligation the output of the target is labelled 'Satisfied' and the one of the deadline 'Violated', in the case of a prohibition, the labels are reversed.

The places in Fig. 2 labelled A, S, V represent the state of the norm, being respectively 'Activated', 'Satisfied', or 'Violated'.

For more details on the mapping from norms to CPN, and the combination of the CPN models using the NN operators **AND**, **OR** and **OE**, we refer interested readers to [7,8].

3   Norm Conflicts

Based on the formalism of NNs, in this section, we propose a definition of norm conflicts in terms of the compliance status of norms. Taking into account the interrelations between norms, the definition gives a comprehensive representation of norm conflicts. Furthermore, a computational model is developed to detect the conflicts.

3.1   Definition

A conflict occurs between an obligation and a prohibition when they constrain on the same behavior and have an overlapped activation period (cf. [17]). That is, if some behavior of the same role is obliged and forbidden at the same time, a conflict arises. From this definition, we differentiate between two types of norm conflicts. First, *weak conflicts*: the activation period of the prohibition does not cover the whole activation period of the obligation. In this sense, a weak conflict can be avoided when the event constrained by the two norms, occurs during the time period when the obligation is activated while the prohibition is not. In this way, both norms can be satisfied. Second, *strong conflicts*: the activation period of the prohibition covers the whole activation period of the obligation. That is, whenever the event constrained by the two norms occurs, or whether or not it occurs, one of the norms will be violated. In essence, a conflict occurs between an obligation and a prohibition when the two norms cannot be satisfied at the same time, i.e., the compliance status of the two norms is evaluated to be contradictory with respect to the occurrence of an event.

Furthermore, to determine whether a norm conflict exists, there is another criterion that has to be considered, i.e., the compliance relation between norms. In Sect. 2, we have introduced three compliance relations between norms, i.e., AND, OR and OE. Therefore, with an event occurring, if two (or more) norm nets with contradictory compliance evaluations are combined, the conflicting status of the combined norm net depends on the compliance relations of the component norm nets. If the compliance relation is AND, a conflict occurs since the combined norm net cannot reach an agreement on the compliance of the event. If the compliance relation is OR, there is no conflict since the combined norm net only picks up the positive evaluation result, i.e., satisfied. As for the compliance relation of OE, there is never a conflict since the activation period of the two component norm nets will never overlap, i.e., only when the origin is violated can the reparation be activated. Therefore, a norm conflict between two norm nets may occur only when the two norm nets are connected by an AND compliance relation.

Based on the description above, we give the definition of a *norm conflict* as follows.

Definition 7 (Norm Conflict). *Given the occurrence of an event e, a norm conflict arises in a norm net NN iff $\exists\ NN_x,\ NN_y \in S_{NN}(NN)$ such that (1) NN_x and NN_y have an AND compliance relation, and (2) NN_x is evaluated to be satisfied and NN_y is evaluated to be violated.*

Given the occurrence of an event, a conflict occurs in a norm net when there are two AND-related component norm nets in the norm net whose normative states are respectively evaluated to be satisfied and violated. While for the conflicting component norm nets themselves, they may have a nested structure of norms connected by other compliance relations such as OR and OE.

It can be seen that our definition of norm conflicts is from the perspective of norm compliance, which is different from other definitions provided in the literature (e.g., [11,17]). The advantage of our definition is that it can be easily extended to other types of norms or normative structures since it captures the root cause of norm conflicts. For example, it is possible that a role-enacting agent is regulated by both an obligation to sit and another obligation to stand whose activation period have an overlap. In this case, a conflict occurs since the two actions "sit" and "stand" are physically exclusive to each other, which can be reflected from the compliance evaluation results of the two norms. While, if defining a norm conflict at the level of norm specification between an obligation and prohibition, such conflicts may not be covered. The differentiation between weak and strong conflicts is based on whether there are possible event sequences that can avoid introducing conflicting normative states (i.e., satisfied and violated), which will be detailed in Sect. 3.3. Moreover, we take into account the impact of the compliance relations between norms.

3.2　Detection

Given the definition above, we now illustrate how to make use of the CPN models of NNs to computationally detect the norm conflicts. To do this, there are three steps. The *first* step is to construct the CPN model of the norm net NN, following the procedure presented in [8]. The *second* step is to obtain the new marking of the CPN model with respect to the occurrence of the enabled transitions given the event e. Comparing the new marking with the previous marking, we can derive the changes of the normative state of all the component norm nets in NN by looking at the satisfied places and the violated places. The *third* step, including two sub-steps, is to determine whether there is any norm conflict in NN with respect to the occurrence of the event e. The first sub-step checks whether NN is evaluated to be violated. If so, the second sub-step is to further check whether there are any two component norm nets in NN that are respectively evaluated to be satisfied and violated, by looking at the token distribution in the places representing the satisfied and violated states. Algorithm 1 gives the procedure of detecting norm conflicts in a norm net with respect to the occurrence of an event.

The problem of detecting whether a sequence of events will cause any conflicts in a norm net can be transformed into the problem of pattern matching of CPN markings/states, the complexity of which is shown to be $O(L \cdot W^2)$ where L is the size of the event sequence and W is the size of the CPN model (i.e., the number of nodes in the CPN model).

Algorithm 1. Conflict Detection

Require: (NN, REA, e) ▷ A norm net with an enactment relation and an event
Ensure: CFS ▷ Conflicting status

 1:      ▷ Obtain the enabled bindings of the CPN model $\mathcal{N}$ given the occurrence of event e and
      the current marking M
 2: **function** ENABLEDSTEP$(e, M, \mathcal{N})$
 3:      $Y \leftarrow \emptyset$
 4:      $(r, \alpha) \leftarrow e$
 5:      **for all** $(p, t) \in A_{\mathcal{N}}$ **do**
 6:          **if** $C(p) = r$ and $t = \alpha$ and $E(p, t)\langle b\rangle \leq M(p)$ **then**
 7:              $Y \leftarrow Y \cup (t, b)$
 8:          **end if**
 9:      **end for**
10: **return** Y
11: **end function**

12:      ▷ Obtain the new marking of the CPN model $\mathcal{N}$ given the occurrence of event e and
      the current marking M
13: **function** UPDATESTATE$(Y, M, \mathcal{N})$
14:      **for all** $p \in P_{\mathcal{N}}$ **do**
15:          $M'(p) \leftarrow M(p) -- \left(\begin{smallmatrix}++\\MS\end{smallmatrix}\right) \sum_{(t,b)\in Y} E(p, t)\langle b\rangle ++ \left(\begin{smallmatrix}++\\MS\end{smallmatrix}\right) \sum_{(t,b)\in Y} E(t, p)\langle b\rangle$
16:      **end for**
17:      $Y \leftarrow$ EnabledStep$((*, null), \mathcal{N}, M')$
18:      **if** $Y \neq \emptyset$ **then**
19:          $M' \leftarrow$ UpdateState$(Y, M', \mathcal{N})$
20:      **end if**
21: **return** M'
22: **end function**

23:      ▷ (**Step 1**) Obtain the CPN model of the norm net NN with the role enactment REA
24: $(\mathcal{N}, Satisfied, Violated, p_s, p_v) \leftarrow \Theta(NN, REA)$

25:      ▷ (**Step 2**) Obtain the new normative state of NN given the occurrence of the event e
26: $M \leftarrow I_{\mathcal{N}}$
27: $Y \leftarrow$ EnabledStep$(e, M, \mathcal{N})$
28: $M' \leftarrow$ UpdateState$(Y, M, \mathcal{N})$

29:      ▷ (**Step 3**) Check the normative state changes of all the component norm nets in NN
30:          ▷ (**Step 3.1**) Check whether the normative state of NN is evaluated to be violated
31: $CFS \leftarrow false$
32: **if** $M'(p_v) -- M(p_v) > 0$ **then**
33:      **for all** $(p, p') \in Satisfied \times Violated$ **do**
34:          ▷ (**Step 3.2**) Check whether there are two component norm nets in NN such that
      one is evaluated to be satisfied and the other is evaluated to be violated
35:          **if** $(M'(p) -- M(p)) > 0$ and $(M'(p') -- M(p')) > 0$ **then**
36:              $CFS \leftarrow true$
37:          **end if**
38:      **end for**
39: **end if**

3.3 Weak and Strong Conflicts

We have shown the mechanism of detecting norm conflicts using the CPN models of NNs. Now we continue with the question of whether a norm conflict found in a norm net is a weak or strong conflict. To this end, we assume the set $\aleph$ of all the possible instances of a norm net (i.e., all the possible states of the real system) and give the following definition.

Definition 8 (Weak Conflict). *A weak conflict is detected in a norm net NN with respect to an event e iff*

1. *there exists an instance of NN from the set of all possible instances $\aleph$ such that a norm conflict exists in the instance, and*
2. *there exists an instance of NN from the set of all possible instances $\aleph$ such that no norm conflict exists in the instance.*

The first condition indicates that there exists a norm net instance of NN in which a conflict is found with respect to the occurrence of the event e. The second condition indicates that there exists a norm net instance of NN in which no conflict is found with respect to the occurrence of the event e.

    In a similar way, a strong conflict is defined as follows.

Definition 9 (Strong Conflict). *A strong conflict is detected in a norm net NN with respect to an event e iff for every instance of NN from the set of all possible instances $\aleph$, there is always a norm conflict existing in the instance according to Definition 7.*

The condition of a strong conflict indicates that for every possible instance of the norm net NN there is always a conflict found with respect to the occurrence of the event e. Given the definition of a weak conflict and strong conflict, we define a consistent norm net as follows.

Definition 10 (Consistent Norm Net). *A norm net NN is consistent iff $\forall e \in E_{NN}$, neither a weak conflict nor a strong conflict is detected in NN.*

A norm net is consistent if and only if the occurrence of any event specified in the norm net does not lead to a norm conflict (weak and strong).

    The complexity of determining whether the occurrence of an event causes a weak conflict or a strong conflict in a norm net is $O(W^2 \cdot V)$ where W is the size of the CPN model of the norm net and V is the number of nodes in the state space of the CPN model. That is, in the worst case, we have to search over the complete state space of the CPN model.

3.4 Design-Time vs. Run-Time Verification

The approach mentioned above was initially meant as a design-time verification of the consistency of the norms (as part of the Consistency and Compliance Checker Toolkit (CCCT) [9]). As the detection of weak and strong conflicts requires a search over all the states of the system (state space search), the verification of the existance of such conflicts can only be done during the design of a system.

However, during run-time the consistency of the Norm Net can also be verified, because conflicts are identified by the occurrence of both a 'Satisfied' as well as a 'Violated' with respect to a single event. One can monitor the evaluation of the different (parts of) the Norm Net and fire the enabled transitions based on the events that are occuring (in real-time). Monitoring and comparing the evaluation states of the (parts of the) Norm Net gives you not only information about the compliance of the system (as presented in [9]), but also about possible conflicts.

However, it has to be noted, that such an evaluation during the run-time of a system cannot detect whether a conflict is a strong conflict or a weak conflict, as the amount of information (i.e., a single trace/run of the system) is not enough to make that distinction.

4   Case Study

4.1   Case Description

The World Customs Organization has defined a framework called the Authorized Economic Operator (AEO) program [1] in order to address the tensions created by the simultaneous growth in international trade and requirements for increased security. The European Communities' implementation of AEO permits various customs administrations to grant AEO certificates to qualified companies under which they enjoy special privileges. Taking the scenario of importing food from a country outside the EU to the Netherlands, a number of governmental authorities and companies are involved, which are governed by different sets of regulations concerning different aspects of the food importation process. For example, the EU has a set of general regulations, one of which specifies that the food authority is *obliged* to carry out a food quality inspection. With the introduction of the AEO programme, the Dutch government introduced new regulations for the specific domain of AEO-certified goods in order to improve trading efficiency. For example, one regulation specifies that a food authority is *forbidden* to carry out a food quality inspection, if the customs has already done so. Additionally, companies such as *container terminals* play an important role and bring their own regulations, e.g., a regulation at one container terminal is that carriers are *obliged* to transport their goods thence within two days of unloading. With different values and interests, the regulations from these institutions are likely to be inconsistent.

4.2   Modeling Norms

In this case study, we consider three institutions $\mathcal{I}_1$, $\mathcal{I}_2$ and $\mathcal{I}_3$ respectively corresponding to the regulation of EU, Dutch government and a Container terminal, captured by three norm nets NN_1, NN_2, and NN_3 described as follows.

- $NN_1 = \text{AND}(\text{AND}(n_{11}, n_{12}), n_{13})$ where
  n_{11} = (O, (*Food_authority*, *inspect_quality*), (*Carrier*, *transport_goods*), (*Carrier*, *arrive*)); n_{12} = (F, (*Carrier*, *unload_food*), (*Food_authority*, *inspect_quality*), λ); n_{13} = (F, (*Carrier*, *choose_inspectLocation*), λ, λ))

- $NN_2 = \text{AND}(n_{21}, n_{22})$ where
  n_{21} = (F, (*Food_authority*, *inspect_quality*), λ, (*Customs*, *inspect_quality*)); n_{22} = (F, (*Carrier*, *unload_food*), (*Food_authority*, *inspect_quality*), λ)

- $NN_3 = \text{OE}(n_{31}, n_{32})$ where
  n_{31} = (O, (*Carrier*, *transport_goods*), (*Timeline*, *pass_2days*), (*Carrier*, *arrive*)); n_{32} = (O, (*Carrier*, *pay_fine*), (*Timeline*, *pass_1month*), λ)

Four roles are defined in the three norm nets, i.e., *Carrier*, *Food_authority*, *Customs* and *Timeline*. In particular, *Timeline* is a reserved field for representing the pass of time. At the moment, we assume an equal status of regulation between different institutions, i.e., the norm nets representing the three institutions are combined with an AND relation, represented as $\text{AND}(\text{AND}(NN_1, NN_2), NN_3)$. We will explore more advanced relations between institutions such as priority relation in future work.

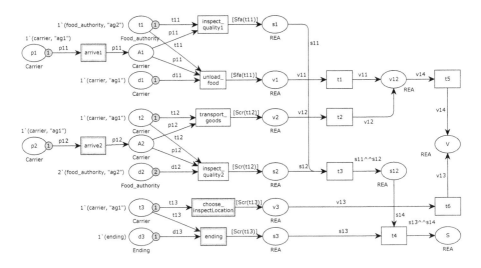

Fig. 3. The CPN model of NN_1.

In this case study, we assume three agents ag_1, ag_2, ag_3 respectively enacting the roles *Carrier*, *Food_authority*, *Customs*. To operationalize the regulation of the three institutions, we build for each norm net a CPN model following the approach presented by [8]. As an example, we show the CPN model of NN_1 in Fig. 3. Places are drawn as ellipses and transitions are drawn as rectangles. Enabled transitions are indicated by bold outlines. The color assigned to each place is indicated by the label below the ellipses. The action each transition represents is indicated by the label inside the rectangles. Role-enacting agents are represented by the dots with a number inside. For example, there is a token valued $1'(carrier, "ag1")$ in place $p1$, representing an agent named $ag1$ enacting the role $carrier$. The satisfied and violated states of all the component norm nets are indicated by the places whose labels start with s and v. Specifically, a color set REA is assigned to all these satisfied and violated places/states in the CPN model, which is defined as a union of the set of all the roles specified in the corresponding norm net, indicating that any role-enacting agents may satisfy or violate the norms. The color set $Ending$ together with the transition $ending$ is defined specifically to signal the ending of an event sequence such that norms whose deadline is null can be evaluated accordingly, e.g., the prohibition n_{13}.

4.3   Detecting Conflicts

Figure 4 shows a part of institutional evolutions with respect to three sequences of events in this case study. In general, when an event occurs (shown above/below the arrows), the system will identify which norms in the relevant institutions are triggered/activated. Each circle represents a normative state of the three institutions. With more than one norm from different institutions being triggered simultaneously, conflicts might occur. For example, three norms from the three institutions are triggered simultaneously at M_3, between which two conflicts occur. In this case study, there are in total three pairs of conflicts (indicated by a line with a cross).

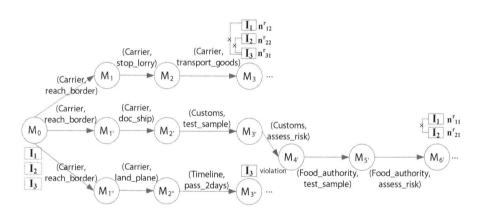

Fig. 4. Institution evolution and norm conflicts.

As an example, we show how the normative states of the three institutions change along with the first event sequence in terms of the markings of the corresponding CPN models implemented in CPN tools [6], as shown in Fig. 5. There are three markings, denoted as nodes 1, 2 and 3, each of which is indicated by

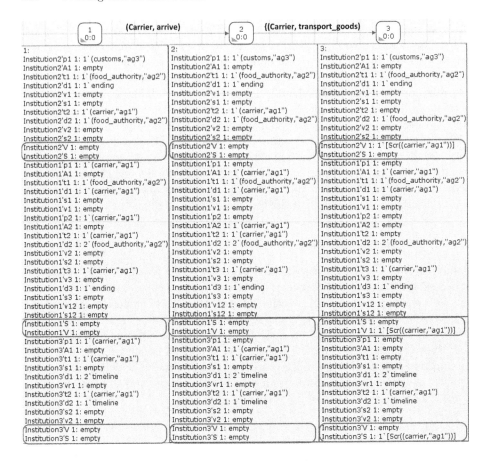

Fig. 5. Normative state transition of the three institutions.

the number of tokens each place of the CPN models contains, as listed in the box under each node. It can be seen that initially at the marking represented by node 1, all the overall satisfied and violated states (places labeled with S and V) of the three institutions are empty, highlighted by the red rectangles. From node 1, an event (*Carrier, arrive*) occurs. As a result, another marking represented by node 2 is generated, in which the states of the three pairs of satisfied and violated places remain the same as that at node 1. From node 2, an event (*Carrier, transport_goods*) occurs. As a result, we obtain a new marking represented by node 3, in which the overall violated places of the first and second institutions $Institution1'V$ and $Institution2'V$ both get a token (*carrier, "ag1"*) while the overall satisfied places $Institution1'S$ and $Institution2'S$ remain empty, indicating that the agent $ag1$ enacting the role $Carrier$ produces a violation in both $\mathcal{I}_1$ and $\mathcal{I}_2$. However, the overall violated place of the third institution $Institution3'V$ remains empty but the overall satisfied place $Institution3'S$ gets a token (*carrier, "ag1"*), indicating that $\mathcal{I}_3$ is satisfied with respect to the agent behavior. These imply that the three institutions give contradictory compliance evaluation results with respect to the same event. Therefore, we can derive two norm conflicts, respectively between $\mathcal{I}_1$ and $\mathcal{I}_3$, and between $\mathcal{I}_2$ and $\mathcal{I}_3$.

5 Conclusions

In this paper, we provide an analysis of norm conflicts in the setting of interrelated norms. From the perspective of compliance, we show how norm conflicts can be modeled and analyzed. Moreover, we consider the influence of compliance relations between norms with respect to norm conflicts, which provides an integrated view on the analysis of sets of norms. To operationalize conflict detection, we make use of the CPN models of NNs and show the application of the state space analyzing tools from CPNs in detecting (potential) conflicts. Our definition of norm conflicts is not bound to a specific computational mechanism but can also be combined with other detection techniques, e.g., the model based on Answer Set Programming proposed by [11]. However, the choice of CPNs is supported by its capability of modeling concurrent systems, graphical expressions, tool support and advanced state space analyzing techniques. Moreover, variants of CPNs such as hierarchical CPNs, timed CPNs and stochastic CPNs, provide extended support for the analysis of norm conflicts when aspects such as levels, time and probability are considered.

There are several directions for future work. Firstly, we will further investigate the interrelations between norms and their impact on norm conflicts. For example, norms may have different priority in the regulation of organizational behavior, and the fulfillment of a norm may cancel the enforcement of some other norms. In practice, norms are not always specified at a single level of abstraction, which necessitates research on norm conflicts between norms at multiple abstraction levels. Given the results of norm conflicts, an important question is how to resolve such conflicts. To this end, we are going to investigate approaches that can learn from agents' past behavior and find optimal solutions for norm revision in terms of, e.g., the number of norms to be changed, the number of roles involved, the overall social risk and welfare, etc.

References

1. European Commission. Authorised economic operator (2013). http://ec.europa. eu/taxation_customs/customs/policy_issues/customs_security/aeo/
2. Gaertner, D., Garcia-Camino, A., Rodriguez-Aguilar, J.A., Vasconcelos, W.: Distributed norm management in regulated multi-agent systems. In: Proceedings of the International Conference on Autonomous Agents and Multiagent Systems, pp. 624–631 (2007)
3. Giannikis, G.K., Daskalopulu, A.: Normative conflicts in electronic contracts. Electron. Commer. Res. Appl. **10**(2), 247–267 (2011)
4. Henningsson, S., Bjørn-Andersen, N., Schmidt, A., Flügge, B., Henriksen, Z.: Food living lab - complexity of export trade. In: Tan, Y.H., Bjorn-Andersen, N., Klein, S., Rukanova, B. (eds.) Accelerating Global Supply Chains with IT-Innovation. Springer-Verlag, Berlin (2011)

5. Jensen, K.: Coloured Petri Nets: Basic Concepts, Analysis Methods and Practical Uses. Springer, Heidelberg (1997)

6. Jensen, K., Kristensen, L.M., Wells, L.: Coloured petri nets and CPN tools for modelling and validation of concurrent systems. Int. J. Softw. Tools Technol. Transf. **9**(3–4), 213–254 (2007)

7. Jiang, J.: Organizational compliance: an agent-based model for designing and evaluating organizational interactions. Ph.D. thesis, Delft University of Technology (2015)

8. Jiang, J., Aldewereld, H., Dignum, V., Tan, Y.H.: Compliance checking of organizational interactions. ACM Trans. Manage. Inf. Syst. **5**(4), 1–24 (2015)

9. Jiang, J., Aldewereld, H., Dignum, V., Wang, S., Baida, Z.: Regulatory compliance of business processes. AI Soc. **30**(3), 393–402 (2015)

10. Li, T., Jiang, J., Aldewereld, H., De Vos, M., Dignum, V., Padget, J.: Contextualized institutions in virtual organizations. In: Balke, T., Dignum, F., Riemsdijk, M.B., Chopra, A.K. (eds.) COIN 2013. LNCS, vol. 8386, pp. 136–154. Springer, Heidelberg (2014)

11. Li, T., Balke, T., De Vos, M., Satoh, K., Padget, J.: Detecting conflicts in legal systems. In: Motomura, Y., Butler, A., Bekki, D. (eds.) JSAI-isAI 2012. LNCS, vol. 7856, pp. 174–189. Springer, Heidelberg (2013)

12. Ostrom, E.: Understanding Institutional Diversity. Princeton University Press, Princeton (2005)

13. Russell, N., ter Hofstede, A.H.M., van der Aalst, W.M.P., Mulyar, N.: Workflow control-flow patterns: a revised view. Technical report BPM-06-22, BPM Center (2006)

14. Sartor, G.: Normative conflict in legal reasoning. Artif. Intell. Law **1**, 209–235 (1992)

15. Colombo Tosatto, S., Governatori, G., Kelsen, P.: Detecting deontic conflicts in dynamic settings. In: Cariani, F., Grossi, D., Meheus, J., Parent, X. (eds.) DEON 2014. LNCS, vol. 8554, pp. 65–80. Springer, Heidelberg (2014)

16. Vasconcelos, W., Kollingbaum, M., Norman, T.: Normative conflict resolution in multiagent systems. Auton. Agents Multi-Agent Syst. **19**(2), 124–152 (2009)

17. Vasconcelos, W., Kollingbaum, M.J., Norman, T.J.: Resolving conflict and inconsistency in norm-regulated virtual organizations. In: Proceedings of 6th International Joint Conference on Autonomous Agents and Multiagent Systems, pp. 644–651 (2007)

Revising Institutions Governed by Institutions for Compliant Regulations

Thomas C. King[1]([✉]), Tingting Li[2], Marina De Vos[3], Catholijn M. Jonker[1], Julian Padget[3], and M. Birna van Riemsdijk[1]

[1] Delft University of Technology, Delft, The Netherlands
{t.c.king-1,c.m.jonker,m.b.vanriemsdijk}@tudelft.nl
[2] Imperial College London, London, UK
tingting.li@imperial.ac.uk
[3] University of Bath, Bath, UK
{mdv,jap}@cs.bath.ac.uk

Abstract. Institutions governing multi-agent systems (MASs) are a pervasive means to guide agents towards the aims of the MAS (e.g. collecting data) with regulations on the outcomes of agents' behaviour. Yet, wider organisations/governments often intend to guide the design of institutions governing MAS in meeting different aims (e.g. preserving the rights of agents). A pervasive means to guide the design of MAS-governing institutions (or any institution, for that matter) is to use institutions at higher tiers of governance (e.g. directives, constitutions) to regulate the regulations of institutions at lower tiers of governance (e.g. national legislation, software policies). A recent innovation has been an automated means to determine the compliance of a lower-tier institution's regulations with a higher-tier's. However, for a designer of a non-compliant institution there remains a dilemma: be punished for non-compliant regulations or arduously determine and rectify the underlying causes of non-compliance. In this paper we propose a way to automatically determine how to revise an institution to be compliant that also minimises the change in the regulations' outcomes thus keeping as closely as possible to the institution designers' original intentions.

Keywords: Multi-tier institutions · Norm revision · Institution revision · Institutional compliance

1 Introduction

Legal institutions have long been used to govern Multi-Agent Systems (MAS) away from anarchic and uncoordinated behaviour towards a collaborative society through regulations that impose norms (obligations and prohibitions) on agents, leading to many frameworks for automated institutional reasoning (see [1] for a review). However, an institution governing an MAS is typically designed with only the global aim of the MAS (according to its stakeholders) in mind (e.g. collecting and aggregating data). Yet, institutions governing MASs can operate

© Springer International Publishing Switzerland 2016
V. Dignum et al. (Eds.): COIN 2015, LNAI 9628, pp. 191–208, 2016.
DOI: 10.1007/978-3-319-42691-4_11

in the realm of governments and organisations with different aims to the MAS being governed, such as maintaining the rights of agents (e.g. ensuring children's personal data is not collected and aggregated). Inevitably, tensions arise between the aims of institutions guiding MAS with the aims of the wider organisations and governments they reside in.

The social-world resolves such tensions by using institutions to govern other institutions, guiding institutional design towards wider aims with regulations on the outcomes of other institutions' regulations. Known variously as multi-tier/multi-level/vertical governance [15], these governance structures comprise a tiering of institutions: a tier-1 institution governing an MAS by imposing obligations/prohibitions on agent behaviour, a tier-2 institution governing through regulating the outcomes of tier-1 regulation by obliging/prohibiting the imposition of specific obligations/prohibitions (i.e. imposing higher-order norms), and so on. In [10] we addressed the apparent lack of frameworks for institutions governing institutions with a formal and computational framework for the representation and reasoning of vertical governance structures which we call *multi-tier institutions*. By formalising multi-tier institutions, where institutions govern other institutions, lower-tier institutions can automatically be checked for compliance.

However, once non-compliance has been automatically determined, the problem remains for the designer of a non-compliant institution – determining how to revise the institution to be compliant and thus avoid any potential punishments for non-compliance (e.g. fines in the case of EU Directives). The difficulty is that there can be many causes of non-compliance due to the complexity of an institution and its multiple interacting rules. Thus, in this paper we use the framework in [10] for multi-tier institution representation and reasoning and propose an automated means to *revise* lower-tier institutions to comply with higher-tier institutions. To do so, we view revising an institution to be compliant as an Inductive Logic Programming problem where hypotheses (explanations for non-compliance) are sought. In order to solve the problem, we use abductive search implemented in Answer-Set Programming to abduce inductive explanations for non-compliance (ways to revise for compliance).

In the rest of this paper, we first introduce a running example of a two-tier institution in the domain of collecting audio data in Sect. 2. Then, we give some background in Sect. 3 on the formal multi-tier institution representation and reasoning, the computational multi-tier framework in Answer-Set Programming (ASP), and a brief re-introduction of Inductive Logic Programming (ILP) theory revision. In Sect. 4 we show how revising an institution to be compliant is an instance of an ILP problem, and show how we can resolve it by transforming a program representing an institution in ASP to a program for abducing revisions for compliance in ASP. The revision process is based on [12] for revising conflicting institutions adapted for revising non-compliant lower-tier institutions in multi-tier institutions with the following extensions: (i) creating or modifying existing rules for imposing higher-order norms, (ii) deleting existing rules and (iii) minimising the changes in the *consequences* of a revised institution compared to before revision. We further discuss differences with related work in Sect. 5 and conclude the paper in Sect. 6.

2 Running Example

Our running example is in the context of a system for crowdsourcing audio data from users using specialised cellphone apps, called a soundsensing system [16]. A tier-1 soundsensing institution is designed to guide the cellphone app users (i.e. an MAS) in collecting audio data. The soundsensing institution is described as follows:

Soundsensing Tier-1 Institution

- Users are forbidden from turning their microphone off to ensure data is collected continuously.
- Users are obliged to provide their location on request to give the collected data location context.
- If a user violates a norm they are obliged to pay a fine.

In turn, the soundsensing institution is governed by a tier-2 governmental institution designed to meet different aims (e.g. maintaining agents' rights), partly inspired by real-world regulations [19]:

Governmental Tier-2 Institution

- It is obliged that fines are only imposed on users after they violate a norm.
- When a user is in an area that forbids audio recording, it is forbidden to forbid them from turning their microphone off.
- It is forbidden to oblige children (users under the age of 14) to share their location (similar regulations can be found in the United States Government's Child Privacy and Protection Act [19])

Putting these two institutions together, the tier-1 institution can be non-compliant for many reasons. Due to institution designer error, users might be obliged to pay a fine even when not violating a norm, and/or the tier-1 institution might not take into account areas where recording is forbidden or the possibility that users are children. Even if the tier-1 institution has, on the face of it, taken into account these factors, the interaction between different rules can mean all things considered it does not.

3 Background

To provide context for this paper, we re-introduce the conceptualisation and operationalisation of individual and multi-tier institutions from [10]. Then, we give an overview of ILP theory revision which we later use to formulate the problem of institution revision for compliance.

3.1   Formal Framework: Individual and Multi-tier Institutions

An individual legal institution acts as a mechanism to guide the behaviour of the system it governs. Institutions define a set of constitutive and regulative rules which respectively establish an institutional description and prescription of reality (see Searle's counts-as relation [18]). Constitutive rules *describe* the system governed through creating institutional facts that can represent events caused by other events (e.g. entering a location which is private counts-as entering a private location), or they can represent changes to the institutional state (e.g. entering a private location causes an agent to be at a private location). Regulative rules *prescribe* what properties should hold/events should occur in a system by creating obligations and prohibitions in states (e.g. when requested an agent is obliged to share their location). An institution's regulative rules regulate over a social interpretation of reality constructed from brute facts by constitutive rules.

Conceptually, a multi-tier institution extends the notion of an individual institution governing an MAS to institutions governing institutions in a tiered structure. Each institutional tier governs the tier below. The first-tier imposes norms on what occurs and holds in an MAS (first-order norms), the second-tier norms on the norms imposed by the first (norms about first-order norms, i.e. second-order norms), and so on.

Formally, individual and multi-tier institutions are specified and reasoned about accordingly. The obligations/prohibitions which hold in states are represented as normative fluents describing an obligation/prohibition for an aim to occur before a deadline. Formally the grammar is $n := obl(a, d) \mid pro(a, d)$ where a is the aim and d the deadline defined over a set of propositions Pr s.t. $a, d \in Pr$. The set of all expressible elements n is $\mathcal{N}|_{Pr}$. When Pr contains propositions denoting events (e.g. Bertrand sharing his location *share_location(betrand)*,) and *non-normative* fluents, normative fluents about descriptive propositions are expressible allowing *first-order* norms to be expressed (e.g. Bertrand is obliged to share his location before leaving it:
obl(share_location(betrand), leave(betrand, street_d))). When Pr contains normative fluents, normative fluents about other normative fluents are expressible, allowing *higher-order* norms to be expressed (e.g. it is prohibited to oblige Bertrand to share his location until he turns 14: *pro(obl(share_location(betrand), leave(betrand, street_d)), birthday(betrand, 14))*).

An individual institution specification, based on the InstAL framework [4] is a tuple $\mathcal{I}|_{Pr} = \langle \mathcal{E}, \mathcal{F}, \mathcal{G}, \mathcal{C}, \Delta \rangle$ (defined over a set of propositions Pr which in places we omit). The elements are: (i) The set of events $\mathcal{E}$ that occur in the institution and bring about state change. These comprise observable events $\mathcal{E}_{obs}$, events that have an institutional meaning $\mathcal{E}_{instact}$ (e.g. an agent enters a *private* area) and events denoting a norm is discharged/violated $\mathcal{E}_{norm}$. (ii) The set of fluents $\mathcal{F}$ that can hold in states. These comprise fluents used to describe the domain $\mathcal{F}_{dom}$ and normative fluents $\mathcal{F}_{norm} \subseteq \mathcal{N}|_{Pr}$. (iii) An institutional event generation function $\mathcal{G} : \mathcal{X} \times \mathcal{E} \rightarrow 2^{\mathcal{E}_{instact}}$. The function is conditional on the fluents that hold in a state (called a state condition represented with $\mathcal{X} = 2^{\mathcal{F} \cup \neg \mathcal{F}}$ as a set of positive fluents that hold and negative fluents that do not hold in a state) and an event. (iv) An institutional state change function describing the fluents initiated and terminated from one state to the next conditional on the previous state and an event $C : \mathcal{X} \times \mathcal{E} \to 2^{\mathcal{F}} \times 2^{\mathcal{F}}$. The codomain is a pair of sets $\langle C^{\uparrow}(\mathcal{X}, \mathcal{E}), C^{\downarrow}(\mathcal{X}, \mathcal{E}) \rangle$ of initiated and terminated fluents. (v) The institution's initial state $\Delta \subseteq \mathcal{F}$.

Table 1. Formalisation of the tier-1 soundsensing institution and tier-2 governmental institution.

Soundsensing System Tier-1 Institution	Governmental Tier-2 Institution
$\mathcal{G}^1(\mathcal{X}, \mathcal{E})$:	$\mathcal{G}^2(\mathcal{X}, \mathcal{E})$:
1.1 $\langle \{at(Loc0, Ag0)\}, enter(Loc1, Ag0) \rangle \to$ $\{leave(Loc0, Ag0)\}$	2.1 $\langle \{at(Loc0, Ag0)\}, enter(Loc1, Ag0) \rangle \to$ $\{leave(Loc0, Ag0)\}$
1.2 $\langle \emptyset, viol(obl(share\_location(Ag0),$ $leave(Ag0, Loc0)))\rangle \to \{norm\_violation(Ag0)\}$	2.2 $\langle \emptyset, viol(obl(share\_location(Ag0),$ $leave(Ag0, Loc0)))\rangle \to$ $\{norm\_violation(Ag0)\}$
1.3 $\langle \emptyset, viol(pro(microphone\_off(Ag0),$ $leave\_soundsensing(Ag0)))\rangle$ $\to \{norm\_violation(Ag0)\}$	2.3 $\langle \emptyset, viol(pro(microphone\_off(Ag0),$ $leave\_soundsensing(Ag0)))\rangle$ $\to \{norm\_violation(Ag0)\}$
1.4 $\langle \emptyset, enter(Ag0, Loc0) \rangle \to \{norm\_violation(Ag0)\}$	$C^{2\uparrow}(\mathcal{X}, \mathcal{E})$:
1.5 $\langle \{private(Loc0)\}, enter(Ag0, Loc0) \rangle \to$ $\{enter\_private(Ag0)\}$	2.4 $\langle \emptyset, enter(Loc0, Ag0) \rangle \to \{at(Ag0, Loc0)\}$
1.6 $\langle \{private(Loc0)\}, leave(Ag0, Loc0) \rangle \to$ $\{leave\_private(Ag0)\}$	2.5 $\langle \emptyset, disch(obl(pay\_fine(Ag0),$ $leave\_soundsensing(Ag0)))\rangle \to$ $\{obl(norm\_violation(Ag0), obl(pay\_fine(Ag0),$
$C^{1\uparrow}(\mathcal{X}, \mathcal{E})$:	$leave\_soundsensing(Ag0)))\}$
1.7 $\langle \emptyset, enter(Loc0, Ag0) \rangle \to \{at(Ag0, Loc0)\}$	2.6 $\langle \{private(Loc0)\}, enter(Loc0) \rangle \to$
1.8 $\langle \emptyset, \{request\_location(Ag0)\} \rangle \to$ $\{obl(share\_location(Ag0), leave(Ag0, Loc0)\}$	$\{pro(pro(microphone\_off(Ag0),$ $leave\_soundsensing(Ag0)), leave(Loc0))\}$
1.9 $\langle \emptyset, \{norm\_violation(Ag0)\} \rangle \to$ $\{obl(pay\_fine(Ag0), leave\_soundsensing(Ag0))\}$	$C^{2\downarrow}(\mathcal{X}, \mathcal{E})$:
$C^{1\downarrow}(\mathcal{X}, \mathcal{E})$:	2.7 $\langle \emptyset, \{leave(Loc0, Ag0)\} \rangle \to \{at(Loc0, Ag0)\}$
1.10 $\langle \emptyset, \{leave(Loc0, Ag0)\} \rangle \to \{at(Loc0, Ag0)\}$	$\langle \{child(Ag0)\}, \{birthday(Ag0, 14)\} \rangle \to$ $\{child(Ag0)\}$
1.11 $\langle \{child(Ag0)\}, \{birthday(Ag0, 14)\} \rangle \to$ $\{child(Ag0)\}$	$\Delta^2 = \{obl(norm\_violation(Ag0),$
$\Delta^1 = \{private(street\_b), at(ada, street\_b),$	$obl(pay\_fine(Ag0),$
$at(bertrand, street\_c), child(bertrand)$	$leave\_soundsensing(Ag0)),$
$pro(microphone\_off(ag0),$	$pro(obl(share\_location(bertrand),$
$leave\_soundsensing(ag0))\}$	$leave(Ag0, Loc0)),$
	$birthday(bertrand, 14))\} \cup \Delta^1$

Formally, a multi-tier institution is specified as a tuple $\mathcal{M} = \langle \mathcal{T}, \mathcal{GX}^i, \mathcal{CX}^i \rangle$. The components are: (i) A tiering of individual institutions $\mathcal{T} = \langle \mathcal{I}^1|_{Pr^1}, ..., \mathcal{I}^n|_{Pr^n} \rangle$ where we say an institution $\mathcal{I}$ is in $\mathcal{M}$ iff $\exists i \in \mathbb{N} : \mathcal{I}^i = \mathcal{I}$. (ii) A function $\mathcal{GX}^i$ for providing the normative events occurring during a state transition in one tier to the tier above for monitoring. (iii) A function $\mathcal{CX}^i$ for providing the normative fluents that hold in a state to the tier above for monitoring. The tiering of institutions restricts each institution in only imposing ith-order norms over the behaviour of the system it governs such that the normative fluents are defined over Pr^i which contains everything expressible in the

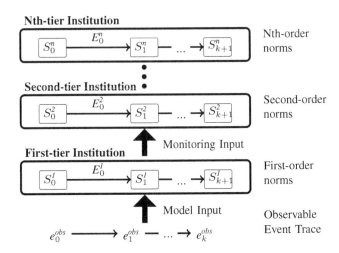

Fig. 1. Schematic view of a multi-tier institution model

tier below (i.e. Pr^2 contains first-order norms and thus $\mathcal{I}|^2_{Pr^2}$ imposes second-order normative fluents over Pr^2. For formal details see: [10]).

Table 1 formalises the running example as a multi-tier institution consisting of the soundsensing system's tier-1 institution and a governmental tier-2 institution (upper-case symbols stand for variables and for brevity we leave out the set of events and fluents for each institution). Both institutions consist of rules describing the domain (e.g. an agent entering a new location causes the agent to be at that location) and consider the location 'street b' to be private and the agent 'Bertrand' to be a child (see the initial states). The formalised example has three issues of non-compliance between the two institutions. Firstly, when an agent enters a new location this causes a generic norm violation event in the soundsensing institution (1.3) due to designer error and which in turn initiates an obligation to pay a fine (1.9). However, the governmental institution only recognises actual norm violation events as causing a generic norm violation event (2.2 and 2.3) and obliges an actual norm is violated before an obligation to pay a fine is imposed (2.5 and Δ^2). Secondly, in the soundsensing institution agents are unconditionally prohibited from turning their microphone off (Δ^1), however the governmental institution prohibits such a prohibition when an agent enters a private location (2.6). Thirdly, when an agent is requested to provide their location the soundsensing institution obliges them to do so (1.8), but this is forbidden by the governmental institution if the agent is a child (Δ^2), such as Bertrand.

The operational semantics of a multi-tier institution, first presented in [10], allow such non-compliance to be determined by checking a multi-tier institution model for norm violations. Depicted in Fig. 1, the model describes how each ith-tier institution evolves over time, as an event-state sequence, in response to the evolution of the tier below. The first-tier evolves in response to a trace of observable events that *could* occur in an MAS (i.e. produced for a pre-runtime check). Each tier above the first evolves in response to the event-state sequence of the institution they govern (i.e. the tier below). States contain domain fluents describing the MAS and normative fluents prescribing the events that should occur and fluents that should hold in the tier below (including other normative fluents). Each state transition is caused by events occurring in the institution from the previous state, which are in turn driven by the events and states from the tier below. If a normative fluent in a state is violated by an event or fluent in the tier below (including another normative fluent) a norm violation event occurs in the transition to the next state. Thus, model-checking can be used to compliance-monitor one institution with another by checking for higher-order norm violation events.

3.2 Computational Framework for Multi-Tier Institutions in ASP

The formal framework described is complemented by a corresponding computational framework in ASP (see [10]) for automatic compliance checking of lower-tier institutions with higher-tier institutions. ASP [2] is a non-monotonic logic programming language for representing problems where solutions to those problems, known as answer-sets, are computed according to the stable model semantics [8] using an answer-set solver (e.g. [7,11]). An ASP program is built from first-order atoms which can be weakly negated with not. In an ASP program facts are of the form p_0. Rules are horn clauses of the form $p_0 : -p_1, ..., p_n.$, which states the head p_0 is true when $p_1, ..., p_n$ are true. Constraints on answer-sets produced can be represented as $: -p_1, ..., p_n.$ meaning falsity is in the head of the rule and thus $p_1, ..., p_n$ is not true in any answer-set. Finally, choice constructs of the form $l\{p_1, ..., p_n\}u$ where l and u are positive integers state that at least l and at most u members of the set can arbitrarily be included in an answer-set (when omitted, l is 0 and u is infinity).

   The computational framework consists of several components which we refer to later in this paper (i) an implementation of the operational semantics, the reasoning program $\mathcal{P}_{reas}$ (ii) a program representing the trace of observable events used as input for producing multi-tier models, the timeline program $\mathcal{P}_{time}$ and (iii) a representation in ASP of a multi-tier institution $M = \langle \mathcal{T}, \mathcal{GX}^i, \mathcal{CX}^i \rangle$ according to the translation given in Table 2, which produces an ASP program $\mathcal{P}_{\mathcal{I}^i}$ for each individual institution $\mathcal{I}^i$ in the multi-tier institution $\mathcal{M}$. For brevity we leave out the details of the translation, but note that (i) In is a unique name for the institution $\mathcal{I}^i$, (ii) initiated(p, In, I) and terminated(p, In, I) means the fluent p is initiated/terminated at time I in institution In, (iii) occurred(e, In, I) means the event e occurs at time I in institution In, (iv) holdsat(f, In, I) means a fluent f holds at time I in institution In, (v) $start(I)$ means I is the initial time interval according to the timeline program, and finally, (vi) $EX(X, In, I)$ is shorthand for translating a state condition $X \in \mathcal{X}^i$ into a corresponding set of ASP body literals holdsat(f, In, I) for all positive elements of X and not holdsat(f, In, I) for all negative elements of X.

Table 2. Multi-tier institution translation to ASP.

$$\mathcal{M} = \langle \mathcal{T}, \mathcal{GX}^i, \mathcal{CX}^i \rangle, \mathcal{T} = \langle \mathcal{I}^1, ..., \mathcal{I}^n \rangle, \forall i \in [n], \ (\mathcal{I}^i = \langle \mathcal{E}^i, \mathcal{F}^i, \mathcal{C}^i, \mathcal{G}^i, \Delta^i \rangle) :$$

$$\mathcal{I}^i \Leftrightarrow \texttt{tier}(\textit{In,i}). \ \texttt{inst}(\textit{In}). \in \mathsf{P}_{\mathcal{I}^i}$$
$$e \in \mathcal{E}^i_{obs} \Leftrightarrow \texttt{evtype}(\texttt{e},\textit{In}, \texttt{ex}). \in \mathsf{P}_{\mathcal{I}^i}$$
$$f \in \mathcal{F}^i \Leftrightarrow \texttt{ifluent}(\texttt{f},\textit{In}). \in \mathsf{P}_{\mathcal{I}^i}$$
$$e \in \mathcal{E}^i_{instact} \Leftrightarrow \texttt{evtype}(\texttt{e},\textit{In}, \texttt{in}). \in \mathsf{P}_{\mathcal{I}^i}$$
$$f \in \mathcal{F}^i \Leftrightarrow \texttt{ifluent}(\texttt{f},\textit{In}). \in \mathsf{P}_{\mathcal{I}^i}$$
$$\mathcal{C}^{i\uparrow}(X,e) = P \Leftrightarrow \forall p \in P : \texttt{initiated}(p,\textit{In}, \texttt{I}) : - \texttt{occurred}(e,\textit{In}, \texttt{I}), \textit{EX(X, In, I)}. \in \mathsf{P}_{\mathcal{I}^i}$$
$$\mathcal{C}^{i\downarrow}(X,e) = P \Leftrightarrow \forall p \in P : \texttt{terminated}(p,\textit{In}, \texttt{I}) : - \texttt{occurred}(e,\textit{In},I), \textit{EX(X, In, I)}. \in \mathsf{P}_{\mathcal{I}^i}$$
$$\mathcal{G}^i(X,e) = E \Leftrightarrow \forall e' \in E : \texttt{occurred}(e',\textit{In}, \texttt{I}) : - \texttt{occurred}(e,\textit{In}, \texttt{I}), \textit{EX(X, In, I)}. \in \mathsf{P}_{\mathcal{I}^i}$$
$$f \in \Delta^i \Leftrightarrow \texttt{holdsat}(f,\textit{In}, \texttt{I}) : -\texttt{start}(\texttt{I}). \in \mathsf{P}_{\mathcal{I}^i}$$

3.3 Inductive Logic Programming: A Brief Overview

We view the problem of revising lower-tier institutions to be compliant with higher-tier institutions as a theory revision (TR) problem that can be solved using Inductive Logic Programming (ILP). ILP [17] is a machine learning technique concerned with the induction of logic theories that generalise (positive and negative) examples with respect to a prior background knowledge. In non-trivial problems it is crucial to define the search space accurately. This is done by a *language bias*, that can be expressed using the notion of mode declarations [17], describing the structure of the elements in the target theory. In the case presented here, we want to find ASP rules that contain certain elements in the head and body. So we will have head and body mode declarations.

An *ILP theory revision task* is a tuple $\langle P, B, M \rangle$ where P is a set of conjunctions of literals, called *properties*, B is a normal program, called the *background theory*, M is a set of mode declarations describing the form that rules in the revised theory can take and $s(M)$ is the set of rules adhering to M. A theory H, called a *hypothesis*, is an inductive solution for the task $\langle P, B, M \rangle$, if (i) $H \subseteq s(M)$, and (ii) P is true in all the answer sets of $B \cup H$.

Our approach to making a lower-tier institution in a multi-tier institution compliant is based on the introduction of new rules, and deleting and revising existing ones. As discussed in [5], non-monotonic inductive logic programming can be used to revise an existing theory. The key concept is that of *minimal revision*. In general, a TR system is biased towards the computation of theories that are similar to a given revisable theory. The difference between two programs T and T' is denoted as $c(T, T')$.

The theory T', called a *revised theory*, is a *TR solution* for the task $\langle P, B, T, M \rangle$ with distance $c(T, T')$, iff (i) $T' \subseteq s(M)$, (ii) P is true in all the answer sets of $B \cup T'$, (iii) if a theory S exists that satisfies conditions (i) and (ii) then $c(T, S) \geq c(T, T')$, (i.e. minimal revision).

4   Revising Institutions for Compliance

In this section we give the details of the paper's main contribution: a system for revising a lower-tier institution to be compliant with a higher-tier institution in a multi-tier institution. In particular, we are interested in revising the institution which the system user (an institutional designer) has the power to effect change. We call this institution to be revised a *mutable* institution. We are interested in revising a mutable institution to meet two properties:

- **Success** meaning that a formerly non-compliant institution for an event-trace is compliant for the same event trace after being revised. This means when normative fluents are obliged to be imposed they are, and conversely any prohibited normative fluents are not imposed.
- **Minimality** is a requirement for any revision to minimise the change in *consequences* of the new institution compared to the old one. That is, following changes to the institution the institution's states are as close as possible to the states prior to the change(s) for a trace of events. To give an example, the soundsensing institution prohibits agents to turn their cellphone microphone off, whilst the governmental institution prohibits such a prohibition in areas deemed 'private'. In this case, an institution revision can be successful by removing the soundsensing institution's prohibition altogether, but only successful *and* minimal by removing the prohibition in just those cases where an agent is at a private location.

We instantiate the problem of revising a mutable institution as an ILP theory revision task in Sect. 4.1. Then, we take a computational approach to solving the ILP theory revision task by performing *abductive* search in ASP [6]. Abductive search is achieved by transforming the mutable institution represented in ASP to an ASP representation encoding the space of ILP theory revisions and enabling different revisions to be tried. We describe our computational approach using ASP in Sect. 4.2, and the implementation and revision results for our running example in Sect. 4.3.

4.1   Revising Institutions to be Compliant is an ILP Theory Revision Task Instance

In this section, we define the revision for compliance task as an ILP revision task according to the revision for compliance requirements outlined previously. We begin by formally defining the search space of possible revisions with *mode declarations*. Mode declarations define the literals that can appear in the head and body of rules. In the case of revising a mutable institution in a multi-tier institution, the mode declarations describe the valid rules for: generating non-normative institutional events, initiating and terminating domain fluents, and given the mutable institution is the ith-tier, initiating and terminating ith-order normative fluents (i.e. restricted to only initiating/terminating a normative fluent f if it is not in the language of norms $\mathcal{N}|_{Pr^{i-1}}$ of the tier $i-1$ below).

Definition 1. Mode Declarations. *Let $\mathcal{I}^i = \langle \mathcal{E}^i, \mathcal{F}^i, \mathcal{G}^i, \mathcal{C}^i, \Delta^i \rangle$ be a mutable institution for which In is a unique label. The mode declarations for $\mathcal{I}^i$ are a pair $M = \langle M^h, M^b \rangle$ where M^h is the set of head mode declarations and M^b the set of body mode declarations, defined as:*

$$M^h = \{\texttt{initiated}(f, In, \texttt{I}), \texttt{terminated}(f, In, \texttt{I}) : f \in \mathcal{F} \setminus \mathcal{N}|_{Pr^{i-1}}\} \cup$$
$$\{\texttt{occurred}(e, In, \texttt{I}) : e \in \mathcal{E}^i_{instact}\}$$
$$M^b = \{\texttt{holdsat}(f, In, \texttt{I}), \neg\texttt{holdsat}(f, In, \texttt{I}) : f \in \mathcal{F}^i\} \cup$$
$$\{\texttt{occurred}(e, In, \texttt{I}) : e \in \mathcal{E}^i\}$$

The set of *compatible rules* with the head and body mode declarations are also required to contain one event in the body and are defined as:

Definition 2. Compatible Rules. *Let $M = \langle M^h, M^b \rangle$ be the mode declarations for a mutable institution $\mathcal{I}^i = \langle \mathcal{E}^i, \mathcal{F}^i, \mathcal{G}^i, \mathcal{C}^i, \Delta^i \rangle$. An ASP rule $\texttt{l}_0 : - \texttt{l}_1, ..., \texttt{l}_n.$ where $n \in \mathbb{N}$ is compatible with M iff $l_0 \in M^h$, $\forall i \in [1, n] : l_i \in M^b$ and $|\{l_1, ..., l_n\} \cap \{\texttt{occurred}(e, In, \texttt{I}) : e \in \mathcal{E}^i\}| = 1$. The set of all compatible rules with M is $s(M)$.*

Having described the search space of revisions, a theory revision task TR needs to be instantiated with the properties P that a solution must meet. These properties are typically positive examples (formulae that are true following a revision) and negative examples (formulae that are false following a revision). In our case we are only interested in supplying negative examples, stating that non-compliance is eradicated in a solution to TR. The negative examples in P are represented as ASP integrity constraints requiring a revised mutable institution is compliant with all higher-order norms it can violate – including those it does not violate before revision – ensuring revision does not cause further non-compliance.

Definition 3. Compliance Properties. *Let $\mathcal{I}^i$ be a mutable institution and $\mathcal{I}^{i+1} = \langle \mathcal{E}^{i+1}, \mathcal{F}^{i+1}, \mathcal{C}^{i+1}, \mathcal{G}^{i+1}, \Delta^{i+1} \rangle$ be the institution with unique name In^{i+1} governing $\mathcal{I}^i$ where $i \in \mathbb{N}$. The compliance properties for $\mathcal{I}^i$ is the set of constraints:*

$$P = \{: - \texttt{occurred}(\texttt{viol}(n), In^{i+1}, \texttt{I}), \texttt{instant}(\texttt{I}). : n \in \mathcal{F}^{i+1}_{norm}\}$$

We can now instantiate an ILP theory revision task, as a *compliance* theory revision task in a multi-tier institution according to the previous definitions:

Definition 4. Compliance Theory Revision Task. *Let $\mathcal{I}^i$ be a mutable institution in the multi-tier institution $\mathcal{M}$. An ILP theory revision task $TR = \langle P, B, T, M \rangle$ is a compliance theory revision task for $\mathcal{I}^i$ iff: (i) P is a set of compliance properties for $\mathcal{I}^i$, (ii) B is the normal program comprising (a) a multi-tier reasoning program $\mathcal{P}_{reas}$, (b) the timeline program $\mathcal{P}_{time}$ and (c) the institution representation program $\mathcal{P}_{\mathcal{I}^j}$ for each institution $\mathcal{I}^j$ in $\mathcal{M}$ apart from the mutable institution $\mathcal{I}^i$, (iii) T is the institution representation program $\mathcal{P}_{\mathcal{I}^i}$ for the mutable institution $\mathcal{I}^i$, and (iv) M is the set of mode declarations for $\mathcal{I}^i$.*

As outlined previously, we require solutions to theory revision to minimise the revision cost in order to remain as close to an institution designer's original intentions as possible. More precisely, the requirement is that the changed, mutable, institution's model for a composite trace contains as many similarities between states compared to before the changes were made (i.e. minimising the changes to consequences). We derive the cost of revision from the changes in consequences rather than the number of rule changes – as used in [12] – since due to non-monotonicity, as the changes in consequences between two versions of a mutable institution increases, the number of rule changes does *not* necessarily monotonically increase. The changes in consequences are the number of added and deleted fluents in the answer set for $B \cup T$ compared to the answer-set $B \cup T'$ for some revised institution T' (i.e. the symmetric set difference between the answer-sets for $B \cup T$ and for $B \cup T'$).

Definition 5. Theory Revision Cost. *Let $TR = \langle P, B, T, M \rangle$ be a compliance theory revision task for a mutable institution $\mathcal{I}$ with unique label In, T' be a solution to TR, ans be the answer-set for $B \cup T$ and ans' be the answer-set for $B \cup T'$ and $\oplus$ be the set symmetric difference operation. The cost $c(T, T')$ is defined as:*

$$c(T, T') = \left| \left\{ f = \texttt{holdsat}(p, In, i) : i \in \mathbb{N}, \ f \in ans \oplus ans' \right\} \right|$$

4.2 Solving ILP Institution Revision in ASP

Based on [12] we use abductive search in ASP to solve an ILP theory revision task $TR = \langle P, B, T, M \rangle$ instantiated as institutional revision for compliance. The approach we take is to transform the theory to be revised T (a mutable institution) into an ASP program where different changes to the theory can be tried/abduced (body literal and rule addition and deletion) that fit into the space of possibilities $s(M)$. We call this program the *revision* program $\mathcal{P}_{rev}$. The background theory B remains unchanged and provides both the unchangeable parts of the multi-tier institution and multi-tier reasoning. The background theory allows the effects of different revisions to be determined. The properties to be met, P, constrain any revisions found by the ASP program $\mathcal{P}_{rev}$ to result in a compliant institution. The cost measure between a revisable T and revised theory T', $c(T, T')$ is encoded as an ASP optimisation statement. Computing the answer-sets for these components as a single ASP program explores the search space, with each answer-set representing an outcome (revised theory) that meets the properties P and with those that minimise the difference (changes in consequences) ranked highest and presented to the user for selection. The advantage of this approach is that the representation and reasoning for the non-revisable portions of the multi-tier institution are encoded as the same ASP programs for the computational and revision framework requiring no re-implementation.

In order to go from a revisable theory T representing a mutable institution to a revision program $\mathcal{P}_{rev}$, we need to alter T in some way such that adding new rules and changing existing rules can be tried by the new program with

Table 3. Explanation of how abducible revision predicates can (re-)define institutional rules for finding revisions of the institution In

Rules Describing Institution Changes	Explanation
$l_0: - l_1, ..., l_n, \texttt{rev}(In, i, \texttt{details}(\texttt{rDel}))$. $\{\texttt{rev}(In, i, \texttt{details}(\texttt{rDel}))\}$.	*Rule deletion:* Existing rules are extended with an abducible $\texttt{rev}(In, i, \texttt{details}(\texttt{rDel}))$, which when included in an answer-set has the effect of deleting the rule with index i.
$l_0: - l_1, ..., l_{j-1}, \texttt{try}(i, j, B_-^+(l_j), l_j),$ $l_{j+1}, ..., l_n.$ $\texttt{try}(i, j, B_-^+(l_j), l_j): - l_j,$ $\quad \texttt{not rev}(In, i, \texttt{details}(\texttt{bDel}, j)).$ $\texttt{try}(i, j, B_-^+(l_j), l_j): -$ $\quad \texttt{rev}(In, i, \texttt{details}(\texttt{bDel}, j)).$ $\{\texttt{rev}(In, i, \texttt{details}(\texttt{bDel}, j))\}$.	*Body literal deletion:* Each body literal l_j of an existing rule is replaced with the literal $\texttt{try}/4$ for trying to delete the body literal l_j. When the abducible $\texttt{rev}(In, i, \texttt{details}(\texttt{bDel}, j))$ is included in an answer-set the effect is to make the try literal true and thus effectively delete the literal l_j, otherwise the try literal is only true when l_j is true (effectively keeping l_j).
$l_0: - \texttt{rev}(In, i, \texttt{details}(\texttt{rAdd})), l_1, ..., l_n.$ $\{\texttt{rev}(In, i, \texttt{details}(\texttt{rAdd}))\}$.	*Rule addition:* Including the abducible $\texttt{rev}(In, i, \texttt{details}(\texttt{rAdd}))$ has the effect of including the rule with index i in the program.
$l_0: -l_1, l_2, ..., l_n,$ $\quad \texttt{extension}(i, l_0, l_{n+1}, B_-^+(l_{n+1})).$ $\texttt{extension}(i, l_0, l_{n+1}, B_-^+(l_{n+1})): -$ $\quad \texttt{not rev}(In, i, \texttt{details}(\texttt{bAdd},$ $\qquad B_-^+(l_{n+1}), l_{n+1})).$ $\texttt{extension}(i, l_0, l_{n+1}, B_-^+(l_{n+1})): -$ $\quad \texttt{rev}(In, i, \texttt{details}(\texttt{bAdd},$ $\qquad B_-^+(l_{n+1}), l_1), l_1.$ $\{\texttt{rev}(In, i, \texttt{details}(\texttt{bAdd},$ $\qquad B_-^+(l_{n+1}), l_{n+1}))\}$.	*Body literal addition:* Existing rules are appended with $\texttt{extension}/4$ predicates for each body mode literal a rule can be extended with. Including the abducible $\texttt{rev}(In, i, \texttt{details}(\texttt{bAdd}, pos, l_1)$ in an answer-set has the effect of extending the rule with index i with the body literal l_1 (constraining the rule). That is, adding the revision predicate to an answer set makes the extension predicate true only when the literal with the specified variable bindings are true, effectively adding a constraint/body-literal to the rule. Otherwise, the extension predicate is always true (no constraint is tried for addition).

each answer-set corresponding to different revised theories. The approach we take, as in [6,12], is to introduce *abducible* predicates which represent the different revision operations. Abducible predicates are selected by the program for inclusion in answer-sets. If an abducible is selected for inclusion in an answer-set then the effect is to perform the revision operation the abducible represents. The abducibles have the form $\texttt{rev}(In, i, \texttt{details}(...))$ conveying to the user the revision operation described in $\texttt{details}(...)$ (e.g. a rule deletion operation) is carried out on a rule with label i in institution In. To give a simple example the rule $l_0 : - l_1$. cannot be selected for deletion by an ASP program, but we can modify it to become $l_0 : -l_1, \texttt{not rev}(In, i, \texttt{details}(\texttt{rDel}))$. meaning if the abducible $\texttt{rev}(In, i, \texttt{details}(\texttt{rDel}))$ is included by the program in an answer-set the effect is to delete the rule i by ensuring the body is never true. The selection of revision tuples for inclusion in an answer-set is encoded in the ASP revision program using the ASP *choice* construct of the form $\{\texttt{rev}(In, i, \texttt{details}(...))\}$.

Each type of revision operation (rule and body literal addition and deletion) requires a different abducible and set of rules in the ASP revision program $\mathcal{P}_{rev}$. In Table 3 we describe the details of the different rules for trying revisions and the transformation from a revisable theory T to a revision program $\mathcal{P}_{rev}$ using In to represent an institution's name, i to represent a rule identifier (e.g. an integer) and $B_-^+(l)$ to represent whether a literal l is positive or negative.

Finally, the cost $c(T, T')$ between two theories is encoded as an ASP optimisation constraint causing the ASP program to only present answer-sets that are minimal in the changes to consequences between $T \cup B$ and $T' \cup B$, which we also extend with a secondary preference for revisions that *generalise* the institution (deleting body literals and rules) rather than specialising (adding new body literals and rules). The optimisation statement is given below where $X@n$ represents the priority n of minimising the numerical value X, `difference/1` measures the difference between the states in the answer-set for the institution before and after revision (in terms of added and removed fluents for each state), `rAdd/1` counts the rule additions, `bAdd/1` the body additions, `bDel/1` the body deletions and `rDel/1` the rule deletions.

```
#minimize {D@5: difference(D); RA@4: rAdd(RA); BA@3: bAdd(BA); BD@2: bDel(BD);
           RD@1: rDel(RD)}.
```

4.3   Implementation and Results

A prototype system for revising a lower-tier institution to be compliant with a higher-tier is implemented according to the description in the preceding sections[1]. The implementation is a compiler written in Java which, as depicted in Fig. 2, takes as input the mutable institution the institution designer has the power to effect change represented in ASP (the mutable institution program $\mathcal{P}_{\mathcal{I}^i}$) and outputs a revision program $\mathcal{P}_{rev}$. The revision program is then put together with compliance properties to be met by revisions, revision cost minimisation optimisations and the background theory to remain unchanged (the non-mutable institutions, the timeline program and the multi-tier institution reasoning). An answer-set solver applied to the composition of these programs then produces minimal revision suggestions for compliance (answer sets). The suggestions are passed to a user who selects and applies a set of revisions, resulting in a compliant institution represented as an ASP program.

In addition to the system presented in this paper, the ASP compiler also addresses an apparent lack of re-usability of institutions (e.g. using the same institution for different sets of agents) due to their propositional nature. Rather than taking just propositional institutions as input, the compiler also takes *first-order* institution theories containing variables in the head and body of rules, together with bindings and monadic predicates to denote types. To give an example, `agent(ada)` denotes `ada` is of type agent and `agent(X)` denotes the

---

[1] The prototype, multi-tier reasoning in ASP and the examples used in this paper can be found at https://sourceforge.net/projects/multitierinstitutionlearning/files/.

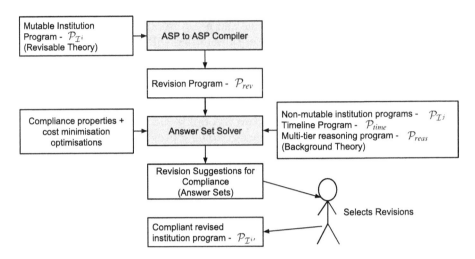

Fig. 2. Overview of using the implemented compiler and the multi-tier institution framework to resolve non-compliance.

variable X is any ground term of type agent. Thus, a designer does not need to write a new propositional institution for the case where a new agent, Charles, joins the institutionalised society with all the norms and domain fluents that are about Charles. Instead, a fact `agent(charles)` can be added stating Charles is of type agent. In turn, the compiler takes these more re-usable first-order institution theories as input and outputs a first-order institution revision program that tries different variable bindings between head and body literals' variables of the same type.

For our running example, we have used our prototype compiler to produce a revision program for sub-sets of the compliance problem. That is, dividing the program up into smaller parts and resolving one case of non-compliance at a time for tractability, and testing all revision suggestions together at the end to confirm they are consistent. Some of the minimal and successful revisions found are given below (we keep to those we find most intuitive).

The first change suggested addresses the issue of non-compliance due to an obligation to pay a fine being imposed by the tier-1 institution when an agent enters a new area. Non-compliance occurs, because an agent entering a new area triggers a norm violation event in the first tier institution regardless of whether a norm has been violated, whilst the second tier obliges that a norm is genuinely violated before a fine is imposed. The revision suggestion is to delete the rule in the first-tier institution causing a norm violation event to occur when an agent enters an area:

```
occurred(norm_violation(Agent0), soundsensing, I) :- agent(Agent0), instant(I),
    occurred(enter(Agent0, Location0), soundsensing, I), location(Location0).
```

The second issue is that children (people under the age of 14) are obliged to share their location when requested, but this is prohibited by the tier-2 institution. The following suggestion is one of several minimal changes found to ensure the non-compliant obligation is not imposed on children. An additional constraint is placed that an agent, `Agent2`, is not a child and the variable `Agent2` is bound to the variable `Agent0` denoting the agent who would be obliged to share their location. This means that the obligation can not be imposed on a child. The new variable `Agent2` is introduced since the implementation relies on using unique variables for all literals and then systematically trying different optional bindings between the variables (or no bindings). The new rule is:

```
initiated(obl(share_location(Agent0), leave(Agent0, Location0)), soundsensing, I)
   :- occurred(request_location(Agent1), soundsensing, I),
      holdsat(at(Agent1, Location0), soundsensing, I),
                                         , Agent0 = Agent1,
                    , agent(Agent0), agent(Agent1),                    ,
      location(Location0), instant(I).
```

Finally, the tier-2 institution prohibits a prohibition on an agent to turn their microphone off when they are in a private area. Yet, the tier-1 institution always prohibits turning a microphone off until the agent leaves the system (the prohibition exists in the initial state). The revisions found are not to delete the rule initiating a prohibition in the tier-1 institution's initial state, but instead, to terminate the prohibition when an agent enters a private area and then initiate it again when they leave. Although the revision adds two rules, it is minimal in the outcome of the tier-1 institution since there is still a prohibition on turning the microphone off in all other cases where it is allowed by the tier-2 institution:

5   Related Work

There has been much work on norm change in normative systems, however, as far as we are aware we are the first to propose a way to revise institutions to be *compliant* with other institutions in a multi-tier institution.

The most closely related work is by Li et al. [12,13] who also uses abductive search in ASP to resolve an ILP *theory revision* task. Unlike us, their focus is on resolving norm conflicts between multiple institutions governing a group of agents (e.g. when an agent is prohibited to perform an action by one institution and obliged by another) and later the general case of debugging ASP programs [14]. In comparison, we focus on revising *non-compliance* between lower-tier and higher-tier institutions in a *multi-tier* institution. Our proposal is based on Li et al. and extended to revising an ith-tier institution by adding new rules or modifying/deleting pre-existing rules to impose *ith-order* norms. We also extend the work to revising with minimal changes in the *consequences* of a revised institution (as opposed to changed rules), finally we look at the creation and deletion of existing rules which in our running example provides more minimal changes in the consequences compared to rule modification.

Vasconcelos et al. [20] have proposed a technique for revising conflicting norms based on first-order unification. Their proposal provides a fine-grained way to revise obligation/permission/prohibition predicates' terms. For example, an obligation to be in an area that overlaps with a prohibited area is revised by changing the obliged/prohibited areas for an agent to be in. In contrast to our work, their focus is on modifying the obligation/permission/prohibition predicates and not with adding/removing/modifying *rules* to meet a particular property (compliance between institutions in our case).

Governatori and Rotolo [9] propose a way to use a defeasible logic to modify legal systems by introducing new norms which derogate, abrogate and annul norms using defeasible rules. Central to their proposal is the idea of a legal system being *versioned* and having two timelines: the versioning timeline and the timeline of the legal system's evolution (i.e. which norms are imposed and when). We only consider the latter timeline, the evolution of an institution (in our case during pre-runtime model checking) and focus on diagnosing *causes* of non-compliance between institutions rather than assuming it is known what the new information (rules) is.

Finally, on the more conceptual and theoretical side, Boella et al. [3] look at how to classify different systems of norm change by investigating a set of rational norm change postulates. Specifically, they look at normative system change to incorporate new *conditional* norms in input/output logics and they investigate the set of consistent postulates for different input/output logics. Again, this work also presupposes which conditional norms should be added to the normative system/institution, thus any system meeting these postulates is quite different from our proposal.

6   Conclusions

In this paper we proposed an implemented automated system for revising a lower-tier institution's regulations to be compliant with the regulations of a higher-tier institution it is governed by. The proposal addressed a problem created by pervasive legal artefacts in the social world, where on the one hand institutions are used to govern other institutions in a vertical governance structure we call multi-tier institutions, creating the potential for non-compliant regulations. On the other hand, revising institutions' regulations to be compliant is non-trivial due to their inherent complexity.

Our proposal takes our previous formal and computational framework [10] for determining the compliance of institutions in multi-tier institutions. Then, viewing the problem of revising an institution to be compliant as an instance of an ILP (Inductive Logic Programming) theory revision task, we use abductive search in ASP based on [12] to solve the ILP theory revision task for compliance.

Abductive search in ASP is performed by translating, using an implemented compiler, from an ASP representation of an institution that needs to be revised to be complaint where revisions cannot be tried and searched for, to an ASP representation where all possible revisions can be tried and thus revisions for compliance determined. Then, our system goes about finding revisions that are successful in resolving non-compliance and minimal in the changes to the institution's consequences thus keeping the regulations as close as possible to the institution designer's original intentions.

The system for revising institutions, for tractability, considers a fragment of the search space of revisions: modifying and deleting existing rules and extending a single mutable institution with a limited number of rules. The successful and minimal revisions that do exist (if any) within the space explored are guaranteed to be found. However, there may be more minimal revisions that result in a well-formed institution (according to our representation of institutions) outside of this space, but this space is bigger and takes longer to explore.

We consider this a problem that is important to address. Firstly with formal analysis of the complexity of the full problem. Secondly, by studying the applicability of various heuristics to the full search problem (e.g. genetic algorithms) which cannot guarantee a minimal solution is found (i.e. in the case of genetic algorithms instead converging on local optima) but can help resolve tractability issues. As yet, it is unclear which heuristics are appropriate and how they can be incorporated into ILP revision as abducible search in ASP, presenting an interesting challenge for future work.

Another avenue for future work is to go beyond the problem of revising a single non-compliant mutable institution in a multi-tier institution. There remains the question of how to revise for compliance when multiple institutions are non-compliant. One approach is to simply extend the work presented in the paper from searching rule changes for a single institution to all non-compliant institutions. Yet due to combinatorial explosion this is a more complex task for non-trivial multi-tier institutions. Another option is to revise institutions in a specific order, searching a fragment of possible changes to multi-tier institutions. However, it remains to be seen if there is procedural order in which to search for revisions that offers the same guarantees of minimality and success, with the additional guarantee of the procedure terminating. This makes revising multiple institutions for compliance an interesting avenue for formal analysis in future work, in particular when looking at more general governance structures rather than multi-tier institutions, such as arbitrary graphs.

Acknowledgements. Thomas C. King is supported by TU Delft's SHINE (http:// shine.tudelft.nl) project. Authors would like to thank the anonymous reviewers of COIN@IJCAI 2015 for their helpful comments and Brian Logan for the discussion following the workshop.

References

1. Andrighetto, G., Governatori, G., Noriega, P., van der Torre, L.: Normative Multi-Agent Systems, vol. 4. Schloss Dagstuhl-Leibniz-Zentrum fuer Informatik (2013)
2. Baral, C.: Knowledge Representation, Reasoning and Declarative Problem Solving. Cambridge University Press, Cambridge (2003)
3. Boella, G., Pigozzi, G., van der Torre, L.: Normative framework for normative system change. In: Proceedings of The 8th International Conference on Autonomous Agents and Multiagent Systems, vol. 1, pp. 169–176 (2009)
4. Cliffe, O., De Vos, M., Padget, J.: Answer set programming for representing and reasoning about virtual institutions. In: Inoue, K., Satoh, K., Toni, F. (eds.) CLIMA 2006. LNCS (LNAI), vol. 4371, pp. 60–79. Springer, Heidelberg (2007)
5. Corapi, D., Ray, O., Russo, A., Bandara, A., Lupu, E.: Learning rules from user behaviour. Artif. Intell. Appl. Innov. **III**(296), 459–468 (2009)
6. Corapi, D., Russo, A., Lupu, E.: Inductive logic programming as abductive search. In: ICLP (Technical Communications), pp. 54–63 (2010)
7. Gebser, M., Kaufmann, B., Kaminski, R.: Potassco: the Potsdam answer set solving collection. AI Commun. **24**(2), 107–124 (2011)
8. Gelfond, M., Lifschitz, V.: The stable model semantics for logic programming. In: ICLP/SLP, pp. 1070–1080 (1988)
9. Governatori, G., Rotolo, A.: Changing legal systems: legal abrogations and annulments in defeasible logic. Logic J. IGPL **18**(1), 157–194 (2010)
10. King, T.C., Li, T., De Vos, M., Dignum, V., Jonker, C.M., Padget, J., Riemsdijk, M.B.V.: A framework for institutions governing institutions. In: Proceedings of the 14th International Conference on Autonomous Agents and Multiagent Systems (AAMAS 2015) (2015)
11. Leone, N., Pfeifer, G., Faber, W., Eiter, T., Gottlob, G., Perri, S., Scarcello, F.: The DLV system for knowledge representation and reasoning. ACM Trans. Comput. Logic (TOCL) **7**(3), 499–562 (2006)
12. Li, T.: Normative conflict detection and resolution in cooperating institutions. Ph.D. thesis, University of Bath (2014)
13. Li, T., Balke, T., De Vos, M., Padget, J., Satoh, K.: Legal Conflict Detection in Interacting Legal Systems. In: DoCoPe@ JURIX (2013)
14. Li, T., Vos, M.D., Padget, J., Satoh, K., Balke, T.: Debugging ASP using ILP. In: Technical Communcations of ICLP 2015 (2015)
15. Liesbet, H., Gary, M.: Unraveling the central state, but how? Types of multi-level governance. Am. Polit. Sci. Rev. **97**(2), 233–243 (2003)
16. Lu, H., Pan, W., Lane, N., Choudhury, T., Campbell, A.: SoundSense: scalable sound sensing for people-centric applications on mobile phones. In: Proceedings of the 7th International Conference on Mobile Systems, Applications, and Services, pp. 165–178 (2009)
17. Muggleton, S.: Inverse entailment and Progol. New Gener. Comput. **13**(3–4), 245–286 (1995)
18. Searle, J.R.: What is an institution? J. Inst. Econ. **1**, 1–22 (2005)
19. United States Federal Law. Children's Online Privacy Protection Act (1998)
20. Vasconcelos, W., Kollingbaum, M.J., Norman, T.J.: Resolving conflict and inconsistency in norm-regulated virtual organizations. In: Proceedings of the 6th International Joint Conference on Autonomous Agents and Multiagent Systems, vol. 5, pp. 632–639. ACM Press, New York (2007)

Reinforcement Learning of Normative Monitoring Intensities

Jiaqi Li[1], Felipe Meneguzzi[2]($\boxtimes$), Moser Fagundes[2], and Brian Logan[3]

[1] Department of Computer Science, University of Oxford, Oxford, UK
jiaqi.li@cs.ox.ac.uk
[2] School of Computer Science, Pontifical Catholic University of Rio Grande do Sul,
Porto Alegre, Brazil
{felipe.meneguzzi,moser.fagundes}@pucrs.br
[3] School of Computer Science, University of Nottingham, Nottingham, UK
bsl@cs.nott.ac.uk

Abstract. Choosing actions within norm-regulated environments involves balancing achieving one's goals and coping with any penalties for non-compliant behaviour. This choice becomes more complicated in environments where there is uncertainty. In this paper, we address the question of choosing actions in environments where there is uncertainty regarding both the outcomes of agent actions and the intensity of monitoring for norm violations. Our technique assumes no prior knowledge of probabilities over action outcomes or the likelihood of norm violations being detected by employing reinforcement learning to discover both the dynamics of the environment and the effectiveness of the enforcer. Results indicate agents become aware of greater rewards for violations when enforcement is lax, which gradually become less attractive as the enforcement is increased.

1 Introduction

Norm-driven behaviour and monitoring have traditionally make four assumptions about the enforcement mechanism and the environment in which agents act, namely:

- the environment is fully deterministic (e.g. [10,12,20]);
- enforcement is either perfect or limited in known ways (e.g. "coverage" is limited [1]);
- agents are perfectly aware of all information regarding the environment and monitoring;
- agents do not change their behaviour due to changes in enforcement capability [7].

While settings based on these assumptions are a useful abstraction for theoretical work on norm-driven behaviour, when norm-driven agents are meant to either model or mimic rational decision-making behaviour in realistic environments, such as in agent-based simulation [2], they must either be relaxed or dropped

© Springer International Publishing Switzerland 2016
V. Dignum et al. (Eds.): COIN 2015, LNAI 9628, pp. 209–223, 2016.
DOI: 10.1007/978-3-319-42691-4_12

entirely [11]. Consider the following example. An agent driving a car enters a city in a foreign city,[1] which has streets and traffic dynamics that are known to the agent, and the agent has a goal to drop off a passenger as close as possible to the passenger's desired destination. The agent is unaware of the meaning of the signs in this city and of the frequency with which traffic wardens patrol the streets, and must make a decision as to where to drop off the passenger, knowing that traffic may force it to stop at undesirable locations. In this kind of situation, existing approaches to norm reasoning fail to provide the agent with the means to make a decision due to a number of factors. First, although the agent is aware of the optimal way of dropping off the passenger from a movement point of view, it is unaware of exactly which spots are forbidden, and, if so, whether a sanction will be immediately applied. Second, the environment is stochastic, and some movements of the agent may be sanctioned because the environment forced the agent (by chance) to be at a certain spot. Third, if the agent makes a decision and is not sanctioned, nothing guarantees that sanctions may not be applied in the future.

In this paper, we use a reinforcement learning-based mechanism to learn normative rewards, and investigate norm enforcement mechanisms to regulate such reinforcement learning agents. Our mechanism assumes no prior knowledge of the normative state or enforcement intensity, and yields policies that are close to optimal using multiple reinforcement-learning techniques. We show the effectiveness of our approach empirically via simulations and identify key learning algorithm and parameter combinations for our scenario. The ultimate aim of our work is to allow enforcement agents to improve enforcement over time.

The remainder of the paper is organised as follows. We formalise the problem we aim to solve with our approach in Sect. 2 and proceed to describe our approach in Sect. 3, which we validate empirically using the experiments in Sect. 4. Finally, we compare our approach to related work in Sect. 5 and conclude the paper with a discussion of our contributions and directions for future work in Sect. 6.

2   Problem Formalisation

Norms have been widely advocated as a means of coordinating multi-agent systems and several approaches have been proposed in the literature, including state-based norms (where norms are defined in terms of states that should or should not occur), e.g., [9], and event-based norms (where norms are defined in terms of what agents should or should not do), e.g., [3,5]. Similarly, various approaches to the implementation of norms have been proposed, including *enforcement* (where sanctions are imposed on norm-violating states and behaviours) and *regimentation* (where norm-violating states and behaviours are eliminated).

2.1   Norms and Enforcement

In this paper, we adopt essentially a state-based approach to norms and assume norms are regulated using enforcement. Each state of the environment

---

[1] A city foreign to the agent's designer.

is described in terms of a set of features $\{\varphi_1, \ldots, \varphi_n\}$, where each feature corresponds to a binary variable that must be either true or false (i.e. each feature is a propositional variable). Thus, the combination of all features (i.e. the enumeration of all possible models of $\varphi_1, \ldots, \varphi_n$) induces a state-space $\mathcal{S}$. Using such features, we define an entailment relation $\models$ over states and formulas using the standard logic connectives ($\wedge, \vee, \neg, \rightarrow$), so that $(s \in \mathcal{S}) \models \varphi$ means that the set of features present in s is a model of φ.

Norms specify conditions (sets of states) that either must hold (obligation) or should not hold (prohibition) when a triggering or activation condition is true. For example, parking in a no-parking zone may be prohibited between 8am and 6pm. If a norm is violated, a penalty or sanction is applied in the violation state, e.g., parking illegally may result in a fine of \$100. This has some similarities to the use of 'counts as' rules in normative multi-agent programming, e.g., [4]. However we feel our approach is more intuitive in allowing the direct representation of obligation deontic modalities, rather than simply violations as in [4].

Definition 1. *A norm is a tuple* $\langle \delta, \mathcal{G}, \phi, \psi, \rho \rangle$ *where:*

- $\delta \in \{obligation, prohibition\}$ *is the deontic modality;*
- $\mathcal{G}$ *is a set of agent roles to which the norm applies;*
- ϕ *is the activation condition, which induces a set of states* $\mathcal{S}_\phi$ *such that* $\mathcal{S}_\phi = \{s \mid s \in \mathcal{S} \wedge s \models \phi\}$;
- ψ *is the normative condition, which induces a set of states* $\mathcal{S}_\psi$ *such that* $\mathcal{S}_\psi = \{s \mid s \in \mathcal{S}_\phi \wedge s \models \psi\}$;
- $\rho : \mathcal{S} \rightarrow \mathbb{R}$ *is a function that specifies the penalty for violating the norm in a given state (* $\rho(s)$ *returns the penalty to be paid in* s*).*

A norm $n = \langle \delta, \mathcal{G}, \phi, \psi, \rho \rangle$ is activated in a state $s \in \mathcal{S}_\phi$, i.e., a state in which the activation condition ϕ of the norm holds for an agent a if the role of the agent $role(a)$ is a role to which the norm applies, $role(a) \in \mathcal{G}$. The norm is *obeyed* if the normative condition ψ holds in s (in the case of obligations) or does not hold in s (in the case of prohibitions). Otherwise the norm is *violated* in s, and the agent must pay a penalty $\rho(s)$ in s. We assume that agents are self interested, and only comply with norms if the expected penalties for non-compliance outweigh the benefits of violating a norm from the agent's perspective.

2.2   Monitoring Compliance

Norms are monitored and enforced by a normative organisation. The normative organisation is responsible for: determining when a norm is activated in a state, whether an activated norm is obeyed or violated, and (in the case of violations), for applying the appropriate penalty.

A normative organisation monitors a set of norms $\mathcal{N}$, and (c.f. Definition 1) a state $s \in \mathcal{S}$ violates a norm $n = \langle \delta, \mathcal{G}, \phi, \psi, \rho \rangle \in \mathcal{N}$ if $\delta = prohibition$ and $s \models \psi$, or $\delta = obligation$ and $s \not\models \psi$. The set $\mathcal{N}_s^-$ of norms violated in state s is defined as

$$\mathcal{N}_s^- = \{\langle \delta, \mathcal{G}, \phi, \psi, \rho \rangle \in \mathcal{N} \mid \delta = prohibition \wedge s \models \psi\} \cup$$
$$\{\langle \delta, \mathcal{G}, \phi, \psi, \rho \rangle \in \mathcal{N} \mid \delta = obligation \wedge s \not\models \psi\}$$

We assume that the probability that violations of a norm will be detected is under the control of the normative organisation. The *enforcement intensity* of the norm is a measure of the 'effort' the normative organisation is prepared to invest in detecting violations of the norm. An enforcement intensity of 1 indicates violations will be detected with probability 1, while an enforcement intensity of 0 indicates that the norm is not enforced (no violations are detected).

The enforcement intensity is modelled as a detection function $\mathcal{D}(n, t)$, which gives the detection probability of the violation of the norm $n \in \mathcal{N}$ at time step t.[2] In Fagundes [6], the detection function takes into account the current state, that is, $\mathcal{D}(n, s)$ where $n \in \mathcal{N}$ and $s \in \mathcal{S}$, but ignores the fact that in some systems the detection probabilities are not constant since they can be changed over time as part of a norm enforcement strategy.

Note that, as part of its norm enforcement strategy, a normative organisation may choose not to disclose the current enforcement intensity to the agents. This disparity in information regarding the enforcement intensity was termed *information asymmetry* in [11]. In this case, agents must determine the likelihood of norm violations being detected either by assuming the enforcement intensity to be some constant, or by trying to learn it. Critically, given that agents cannot learn the enforcement intensity perfectly or even approximate the actual intensity without a temporal delay to observe sufficient instances of norm enforcement, it becomes possible for the normative organisation to optimise the effort spent monitoring to achieve a given level of compliance.

In the remainder of the paper we investigate norm enforcement mechanisms to regulate the behaviour of self-interested rational agents in a fully-observable stochastic environment. The mechanisms take into account not only the immediate costs and benefits of enforcing the norms with a given intensity, but also information asymmetry, and the adaptive capabilities of the agents which can change their behaviour in response to perceived changes in the norm enforcement intensity.

2.3   Example

In this section we introduce a simple Parking World scenario to illustrate the idea of variable enforcement of a norm. In the scenario, an agent drives from a start location to a destination location (e.g., from work to home). The agent can

---

[2] In a slight abuse of notation, we shall denote by $\mathcal{D}(n)$ the detection probability of the violation of the norm $n \in \mathcal{N}$ where n is constant at all time points t.

stop on the way (e.g., to buy groceries on the way home). There are two places the agent can park: a legal parking zone, which has lower utility, but does not violate a parking norm, and an illegal parking zone, which violates the parking norm, but may have higher utility. If the violation is undetected (the parking norm is not enforced), the utility of parking illegally is higher than of parking legally; however if the norm if enforced the agent incurs a large sanction.

The Parking World is shown in Fig. 1, and consists of a 5×5 grid of cells. The environment contains four distinguished cells: the $START$ cell $(1, 1)$, the END cell $(5, 5)$, a "legal parking cell" $(2, 4)$ and an "illegal parking cell" $(4, 2)$. The agent enters the environment at the $START$ cell and can move from cell to cell orthogonally and may revisit each cell apart from the END cell an arbitrary number of times. When the agent reaches the END cell the simulation stops. Visiting a parking cell counts as parking, and we assume that the agent parks at most once (legally or illegally) en route. The reward structure if the agent has not already parked is shown in Fig. 1a. When visiting all cells except the END cell and the parking cells, the agent receives a small negative reward (penalty) of -4 (i.e., short routes between $START$ and END have higher utility). Visiting the legal parking cell $(2, 4)$ has a positive utility of $+20$. The reward for visiting the illegal parking cell $(4, 2)$ depends on whether the normative organisation enforces the parking norm. If the norm is not enforced, the agent receives a positive reward of $+50$; if the norm is enforced, the agent receives a large negative reward -100 (i.e., a sanction). Visiting the END results in a reward of $+100$. The reward structure after the agent has parked at least once is shown in Fig. 1b. In this case, visiting all cells except the END cell results in a small negative reward (penalty) of -4, and visiting the END results in a reward of $+100$. After the agent has parked once, the parking cells effectively become 'normal' cells and the parking norm is no longer enforced on the illegal parking cell $(4, 2)$.

The scenario is designed such that the agent has to make a single decision about where to park on its way home (parking repeatedly does not increase the agent's utility). Parking legally gives a positive reward. The reward for visiting the illegal parking cell is controlled by the normative organisation. Specifically, the probability that the agent will receive a negative rather than a positive reward for parking illegally is determined by the enforcement intensity. Critically, the agent has limited information about the enforcement intensity of the parking norm. However the agent can attempt to learn the enforcement intensity over multiple trials, and we discuss this in the next section.

3   Reinforcement Learning in Normative Organisations

The process of reinforcement learning (RL) can be described as follows: an RL agent first obtains the initial state of the environment and then selects and executes an action. The environment then responds with a numerical reward and a new state. The agent makes its second move based on the reward it received in the first step and the new state. This process repeats until the agent reaches the end state or it cannot proceed any further. For example,

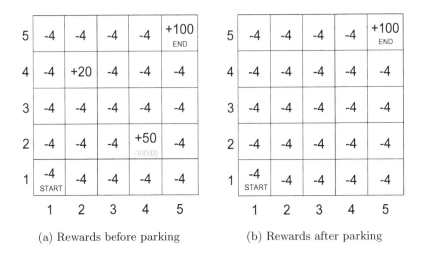

(a) Rewards before parking   (b) Rewards after parking

Fig. 1. Two layer parking world

$$s_0 \xrightarrow[\;\;\;]{a_0 \quad r_1} s_1 \xrightarrow[\;\;\;]{a_1 \quad r_2} s_2 \ldots s_{n-1} \xrightarrow[\;\;\;]{a_{n-1} \quad r_n} s_n$$

where s_n is state n, a_n is an action made by agent at state n, $r_{n+1} = R(s_{n+1})$ is the reward given by the environment for reaching state $n + 1$.

RL can be formulated as Markov Decision Process (MDP). An MDP is a five-tuple, $MDP =< S, A, P(s'|s,a), R >$, where

- S is a set of possible states. For all states in discrete time steps, $s_t \in S$.
- A is a set of possible actions, where for all actions a possible in a given state, $a \in A$.
- $P(s'|s,a)$ is the probability of moving from state s to s' when executing action a, such that $\sum_{s'} P(s'|s,a) = 1$ and $P(s'|s,a) \geq 0$.
- R is the reward function, mapping from states to reward values. $R : S \mapsto \mathbb{R}$.
- γ is the discount factor, $0 \leq \gamma \leq 1$. The discount factor determines the importance of future rewards.

The goal of agent is to maximise its total reward, $\Sigma_{i=0}^n R(s_i)$, by computing a control policy. The policy is a function, π, that maps from each possible state of the environment to an action.

$$\pi : S \to A$$

The optimal policy is obtained by learning a value function, V, that maps each state (or state-action pair for Q-learning) to a numeric value, indicating expected total reward following that state. The optimal value function, V^*, is defined as

$$V^*(s) = R(s) + \max_{a \in A} \gamma \sum_{s' \in S} P(s'|s,a) V^*(s')$$

Therefore, the optimal policy, π^*, can be defined as the best action a such that future expected total reward is maximised in state s.

$$\pi^*(s) = \arg\max_{a \in A} \sum_{s' \in S} P(s'|s, a)V^*(s')$$

We assume that the agents do not know exactly what the rewards are for states where norms apply, nor exactly which states are affected by norms (and thus, the probability of being sanctioned). We have therefore developed an approach that can use any model-free reinforcement learning mechanism, and have implemented the two most common reinforcement learning algorithms, namely SARSA [14] and Q-Learning [19].

A key problem in RL, is balancing exploration and exploitation. For each step, the agent needs to decide whether to follow the best action given by its learned policy (exploitation) or randomly pick an action (exploration). It's obvious that we cannot do exploration all the time, which means that agent makes no use of the learned knowledge about the environment. On the other hand, exploitation fails to discover potential better actions. In our approach, we use an epsilon-greedy strategy, which chooses an exploitation action in most cases; however with probability ϵ, the agent chooses a random action. This guarantees that eventually all states are visited after an infinite number of runs. If a^* is the optimal action given by agent's policy, the probability of choosing an action $a \in A$ using an epsilon-greedy strategy is:

$$P(a) \leftarrow \begin{cases} 1 - \epsilon + \frac{\epsilon}{|A|}, & \text{if } a = a^* \\ \frac{\epsilon}{|A|}, & \text{if } a \neq a^* \end{cases}$$

In practice, ϵ should be large enough to help the agent interact with the environment and learn quickly, and small enough to maximise the total rewards. A value of 0.1 is often used in the literature.

The basic reinforcement learning algorithm is shown in Algorithm 1. Each trial t represents a full execution of the agent starting from the initial state to the end state. The current state s and the next state s' are initialised to the initial state s_0. For each step in a trial, if the agent is not already in the end state, we calculate all applicable states of the agent given its current state. The exploration-exploitation strategy then decides whether the agent chooses exploration (selects a random action), or exploitation (an action given by agent's policy). The next state s' is given by executing the action in a non-deterministic environment. The optimal next state s^* is the state followed by agent's policy without consideration of environment (Algorithm 3). The mechanism of assigning the reward of each step r is given Sect. 2.3 and in detail in Algorithm 2. Finally, we update the utilities of states (or state-action pairs) using either SARSA or Q-learning algorithms (Algorithms 4 and 5) (depending on the experimental setup, see Sect. 4).

SARSA and Q-Learning are temporal difference approaches to learning the optimal policy. The core of the two algorithms are update equations for the

---

Algorithm 1. Reinforcement learning for the Parking World

```
1  foreach t ∈ totalTrials do
2  |    s ← s' ← s₀
3  |    while ¬isTerminal(s) do
4  |    |    A ← applicableActions(s)
5  |    |    if isExploration(t) then
6  |    |    |    a ← random a ∈ A
7  |    |    else
8  |    |    |    a ← π(s)
9  |    |    s' ← execute(a)
10 |    |    s* ← getOptimalState(s)
11 |    |    r ← getReward(s)
12 |    |    V(s) ← Update(s, s', s*, α, γ)
13 |    |    s ← s'
       |    /* Update final state                                    */
14 |    r ← getReward(s)
15 |    err ← r + 0 − V(s)
16 |    V(s) ← V(s) + α ∗ err
17 |    reset
```

Algorithm 2. getReward(state)

```
1  if s = illegalState then
2  |    if isDetected(s) then
3  |    |    r ← penaltyOfIllegalParking;
4  else
5  |    r ← R(s);
   /* Once the illegal cell or the legal cell is visited, they become
      'normal' cells and norms are not enforced                       */
6  if s = illegalState or s = legalState then
7  |    illegalState.reward ← defaultReward;
8  |    legalState.reward ← defaultReward;
9  |    enforcementIntensity ← 0
10 return r
```

Algorithm 3. getOptimalState(state)

```
1  foreach a ∈ applicableAction(s) do
2  |    s' ← execute(a);
3  |    if V(s') > V(s*) then
4  |    |    s* ← s'
5  return s*
```

---

value function, which are given in Algorithm 4 (for SARSA) and Algorithm 5 for (Q-learning). α is the learning rate that controls the amount of difference that contributes to the update of the value of state s.

Algorithm 4. SARSA: Update(s, s', s^*, α, γ)

---
1 **return** $V(s) + \alpha \cdot [r + \gamma \cdot V(s') - V(s)]$

Algorithm 5. Q-learning: Update(s, s', s^*, α, γ)

---
1 **return** $V(s) + \alpha \cdot [r + \gamma \cdot V(s^*) - V(s)]$

The SARSA and Q-learning algorithms have distinct characteristics [15, p. 844] when exploration takes place. In this context, Q-learning is more flexible in the sense that it is able to converge towards an optimal policy even if the initial policy is random or very low quality, since its update rule always takes the best Q-value backed up so far. Conversely, SARSA is more realistic in that its update rule always uses the actual values obtained in each learning episode (and thus has less bias towards optimistic assessments). This has important implications for the results we might expect from these algorithms in our approach. Namely, we expect Q-learning to perform better when the penalties for violation are high, resulting in a norm-compliant policy substantially different than a norm-ignoring policy, whereas we expect SARSA to perform better when the enforcer agent changes enforcement more often.

4 Experiments

We carried out two experiments using the scenario described in Sect. 2 to study the behaviour of the SARSA and Q-learning agents:

1. under different fixed enforcement intensities; and
2. under variable enforcement intensities.

In both experiments, we used the following parameter values (the meanings are explained Sect. 3):

- the ϵ-greedy strategy has $\epsilon = 0.1$;
- the discount factor, γ, is set to 0.9; and
- the learning rate, α, is set to 0.01 for the first 100,100 trials to help the agents learn efficiently in the earlier trials.

$$\alpha \leftarrow \begin{cases} \frac{1}{c - 100000}, & \text{if } c \geq 100,100 \\ 0.01, & \text{if } c < 100,100 \end{cases} \tag{1}$$

where c is the number of times that a cell has been visited.

4.1   Fixed Enforcement Intensities

We know that if the enforcement intensity is high, choosing a path that goes through the legal parking cell gives a higher total reward. On the other hand, choosing a path through the illegal cell is better if the enforcement intensity is low. Therefore, there exists a critical value of enforcement intensity where the agent switches its preference from a path through the legal cell to a path through the illegal cell or vice versa. The purpose of the first experiment is to find this critical value.

In the first experiment, we varied the enforcement intensity from 0 to 1 in steps of 0.1. Having identified the critical range of values, we performed a further set of experiments using a step size of 0.01. For each experiment the agent was run 10 times with 1 million episodes per run to obtain an average utility.

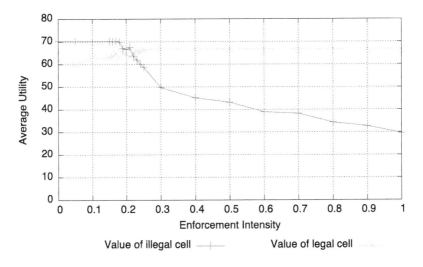

Fig. 2. Learned utilities for differing enforcement intensity (SARSA)

The results for the SARSA agent are shown in Fig. 2. As can be seen, the critical enforcement intensity is around 0.22. Moreover, Fig. 2 shows that when the enforcement intensity is greater than 0.3, further increases in enforcement intensity have no significant effect on the utility of the legal cell. Similarly, when the intensity is below 0.18, decreasing the enforcement intensity has very little effect on the utility of illegal cell.

The results for the Q-learning agent are shown in Fig. 3. In this case, the utilities of the legal and illegal cells are very close when the enforcement intensity is lower than 0.15. While the utility of the legal cell is stable when the enforcement intensity increases, the utility of the illegal cell decreases.

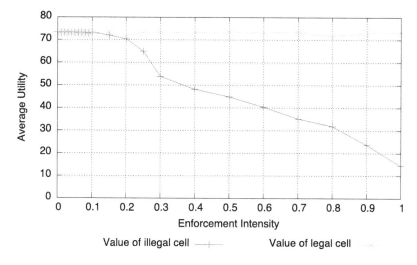

Fig. 3. Learned utilities for differing enforcement intensity (Q-learning)

4.2 Variable Enforcement Intensities

The second experiment was designed to show how the SARSA and Q-learning agents behave when the enforcement intensity changes during a single run. This experiment was divided into two phases. In the first phase, the agent was trained with an enforcement intensity of 0 until its learned utilities for the legal and illegal cells converged. The agent was then evaluated 1,000 times using this learned policy (the policy was kept fixed during the evaluation period). The agent then entered the second phase with the policy it learned in the first phase. In this phase, the enforcement intensity was changed to 1 and the agent was trained 1,000 times followed by 1,000 runs for evaluation (again the policy learned in the second phase was kept fixed during the evaluation period). We ran this experiment 10 times and took the average total reward of each episode. Since the length of the training period in the first phase varied from run to run, we do not report the data collected in this period in our results.

The total rewards for the first 1,000 runs collected during the evaluation of the SARSA agent trained under an enforcement intensity 0 are shown in Fig. 4. In this period, the agent chooses the illegal path as no sanctions are applied, resulting very high total rewards (about 110 on average). At the 1,001st episode, the intensity changes to 1, resulting in all illegal parking being punished. As a consequence, the total reward drops immediately, because the agent continues to follow a policy that believes an illegal path is better, which is no longer correct. However, the SARSA agent is able to adapt to this change very quickly. After a few episodes with very low total rewards, its policy is updated to a legal path. As we can see from the figure, the average total rewards after the change in enforcement intensity is about 80. In addition to this main result, we also observe that the average total reward of an illegal path is 30 units higher than

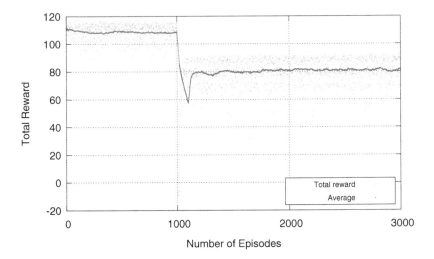

Fig. 4. Total rewards received by the SARSA agent for enforcement intensities 0 and 1. The green dots are the average total reward of 10 runs and the red dots are the averages of 100 recent green dots. (Color figure online)

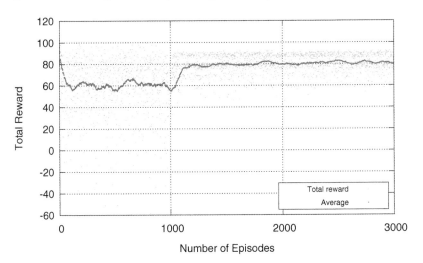

Fig. 5. Total rewards received by Q agent under different enforcement intensity. The green dots are the average total reward of 10 runs and the red dots are the averages of 100 recent green dots. (Color figure online)

an legal one. This is expected and is exactly what we defined in the scenario, where the rewards of the legal cell and illegal cell are 20 and 50 respectively.

However, the results of the first evaluation period for the Q-learning agent (first 1,000 episodes in Fig. 5) fluctuate, as it has difficulty deciding between a legal path or an illegal one, i.e., the utilities of legal and illegal parking cells are very close when the enforcement intensity is 0. When the intensity is increased to 1 after the first 1,000 episodes, the agent also quickly learned a new policy which gives similar total rewards as the SARSA agent. At the moment we are investigating the causes of this behaviour, and our future work aims to use different scenarios to replicate it and hopefully explain under what conditions this shift in utility happens.

5   Related Work

Our work builds upon the basic model of Fagundes et al. [8]. While the NMDPs in that work are slightly more expressive in allowing penalties in the form of enforced transitions, the basic assumption of constant enforcement intensity throughout an agent's lifetime in [8] precludes the kind of learning mechanism and normative organisation adaptation we define in this paper.

Our work is also related to work on norm identification. Norm identification techniques have mostly been developed in deterministic environments, with a focus on identifying the actual norms present in a normative MAS rather than in detecting the enforcement intensity of the norms [16]. Savarimuthu et al. [17,18] propose learning-based norm identification mechanisms to identify conditional norms. This work differs from ours in two fundamental respects: first, it assumes the norms are not known (and the task is discovering them and their conditions), and second, the environment is deterministic. In addition, their use of learning techniques focuses on data-mining techniques to be used in environment interaction histories, whereas our work is based on the use of reinforcement learning by an agent acting in the environment. Thus, whereas Savarimuthu's agents learn norms by observation, ours learn the enforcement intensity of (known) norms by acting on the environment.

Morales et al. [13] have proposed a mechanism for the automated synthesis of norms that ensures norms are conflict free and achieve certain coordination properties. In contrast, we assume the set of norms is static, and the synthesis approach proposed by Morales et al. does not consider the possibility of imperfect or variable enforcement. We believe the combination of norm synthesis approaches and a variable enforcement mechanism are a promising avenue of future work.

6   Conclusion

Our experiments show that reinforcement learning agents can: (1) learn different policies to maximise their total rewards under different unknown norm enforcement intensities in a non-deterministic environment; and (2) adapt to a change of enforcement intensity very quickly so as to obtain maximum total reward under the new enforcement intensity.

There are several directions for future work. The behaviour of the Q-learning agent under low enforcement intensities requires further investigation to explain why the agent is unable to choose between the legal and illegal parking cells.

In addition, we would like to include enforced transitions in our learning framework, e.g., instead of a penalty after violation, the agent is returned to the initial state. Finally, we plan to explore the behaviour of the normative organisation, i.e., how the normative organisation can maximise its utility by changing enforcement intensities given the agent's policies.

References

1. Alechina, N., Dastani, M., Logan, B.: Norm approximation for imperfect monitors. In: Proceedings of the International Conference on Autonomous Agents and Multi-Agent Systems, AAMAS, pp. 117–124 (2014)
2. Beheshti, R., Sukthankar, G.: A normative agent-based model for predicting smoking cessation trends. In: Proceedings of the International Conference on Autonomous Agents and Multi-Agent Systems, pp. 557–564 (2014)
3. Cliffe, O., De Vos, M., Padget, J.: Specifying and reasoning about multiple institutions. In: Noriega, P., Vázquez-Salceda, J., Boella, G., Boissier, O., Dignum, V., Fornara, N., Matson, E. (eds.) COIN 2006. LNCS (LNAI), vol. 4386, pp. 67–85. Springer, Heidelberg (2007)
4. Dastani, M., Meyer, J.-J.C., Grossi, D.: A logic for normative multi-agent programs. J. Log. Comput. $23(2)$, 335–354 (2013)
5. Esteva, M., de la Cruz, D., Sierra, C.: ISLANDER: an electronic institutions editor. In: Proceedings of the First International Joint Conference on Autonomous Agents and Multiagent Systems, AAMAS 2002, pp. 1045–1052. ACM, New York (2002)
6. Fagundes, M.S.: Sequential Decision Making in Normative Environments. Ph.D. thesis, Universidad Rey Juan Carlos (2012)
7. Fagundes, M.S., Billhardt, H., Ossowski, S.: Reasoning about norm compliance with rational agents. In: Coelho, H., Studer, R., Wooldridge, M. (eds.) ECAI. Frontiers in Artificial Intelligence and Applications, vol. 215, pp. 1027–1028. IOS Press (2010)
8. Fagundes, M.S., Ossowski, S., Luck, M., Miles, S.: Using normative markov decision processes for evaluating electronic contracts. AI Commun. $25(1)$, 1–17 (2012)
9. Hübner, J.F., Sichman, J.S., Boissier, O.: Developing organised multiagent systems using the $\mathcal{M}OISE^+$ model: programming issues at the system and agent levels. Int. J. Agent-Oriented Softw. Eng. $1(3/4)$, 370–395 (2007)
10. Kollingbaum, M.J., Norman, T.J.: Norm adoption and consistency in the NoA agent architecture. In: Dastani, M., Dix, J., El Fallah-Seghrouchni, A. (eds.) PRO-MAS 2003. LNCS (LNAI), vol. 3067, pp. 169–186. Springer, Heidelberg (2004)
11. Meneguzzi, F., Logan, B., Fagundes, M.S.: Norm monitoring with asymmetric information. In: Proceedings of the Thirteenth International Conference on Autonomous Agents and Multiagent Systems, pp. 1523–1524 (2014)
12. Meneguzzi, F., Luck, M.: Norm-based behaviour modification in BDI agents. In: Proceedings of the International Conference on Autonomous Agents and Multiagent Systems, pp. 177–184 (2009)
13. Morales, J., Lopez-Sanchez, M., Rodriguez-Aguilar, J.A., Wooldridge, M., Vasconcelos, W.: Automated synthesis of normative systems. In: Proceedings of the International Conference on Autonomous agents and Multi-agent systems, pp. 483–490 (2013)
14. Rummery, G.A., Niranjan, M.: On-line q-learning using connectionist systems. Technical report TR 166, Cambridge University Engineering Department (1994)

15. Russell, S.J., Norvig, P.: Artificial Intelligence - A Modern Approach, 3rd edn. Pearson Education, Upper Saddle River (2010)
16. Savarimuthu, B.T.R., Cranefield, S.: Norm creation, spreading and emergence: a survey of simulation models of norms in multi-agent systems. Multiagent Grid Syst. **7**(1), 21–54 (2011)
17. Savarimuthu, B.T.R., Cranefield, S., Purvis, M.A., Purvis, M.K.: Obligation norm identification in agent societies. J. Artif. Soc. Soc. Simul. **13**, 4 (2010)
18. Savarimuthu, B.T.R., Cranefield, S., Purvis, M.A., Purvis, M.K.: Identifying conditional norms in multi-agent societies. In: De Vos, M., Fornara, N., Pitt, J.V., Vouros, G. (eds.) COIN 2010. LNCS, vol. 6541, pp. 285–302. Springer, Heidelberg (2011)
19. Watkins, C.: Learning from Delayed Rewards. Ph.D. thesis, King's College Cambridge (1989)
20. Yan-bin, P., Gao, J., Ai, J.-Q., Wang, C.-H., Hang, G.: An extended agent BDI model with norms, policies and contracts. In: 4th International Conference on Wireless Communications, Networking and Mobile Computing, pp. 1–4, October 2008

Communication in Human-Agent Teams for Tasks with Joint Action

Sirui Li, Weixing Sun, and Tim Miller[✉]

Department of Computing and Information Systems,
University of Melbourne, Melbourne, Australia
{siruil1,w.sun}@student.unimelb.edu.au, tmiller@unimelb.edu.au

Abstract. In many scenarios, humans must team with agents to achieve joint aims. When working collectively in a team of human and artificial agents, communication is important to establish a shared situation of the task at hand. With no human in the loop and little cost for communication, information about the task can be easily exchanged. However, when communication becomes expensive, or when there are humans in the loop, the strategy for sharing information must be carefully designed: too little information leads to lack of shared situation awareness, while too much overloads the human team members, decreasing performance overall. This paper investigates the effects of sharing beliefs and goals in agent teams and in human-agent teams. We performed a set of experiments using the BlocksWorlds for Teams (BW4T) testbed to assess different strategies for information sharing. In previous experimental studies using BW4T, explanations about agent behaviour were shown to have no effect on team performance. One possible reason for this is because the existing scenarios in BW4T contained joint tasks, but not *joint actions*. That is, atomic actions that required interdependent and simultaneous action between more than one agent. We implemented new scenarios in BW4T in which some actions required two agents to complete. Our results showed an improvement in artificial-agent team performance when communicating goals and sharing beliefs, but with goals contributing more to team performance, and that in human-agent teams, communicating only goals was more effective than communicating both goals and beliefs.

Keywords: Human-agent collaboration · BlocksWorld for Teams · Joint action · Interdependence

1 Introduction

Over the past decade or so, there has been a realisation that "autonomous" intelligent agents will offer more value if they work semi-autonomously as part of a team with humans [4]. Semi-autonomous agents must therefore be designed to explicitly consider the human in the loop to work effectively as part of a team.

In a joint task, a team has a joint aim to achieve a goal, and they must work together to do achieve this goal. While in some simple scenarios, team

© Springer International Publishing Switzerland 2016
V. Dignum et al. (Eds.): COIN 2015, LNAI 9628, pp. 224–241, 2016.
DOI: 10.1007/978-3-319-42691-4_13

members may be able to operate individually to achieve the joint goal, in most scenarios, the individual actions within a task are *interdependent* [17]. However, to successfully operate on an interdependent task, team members must have a shared situation awareness of at least part of the task, and must coordinate the actions that comprise the task. As such, communication between team members is important to efficiently complete a task.

This is the case in human-human teams, but also in human-agent teams. For example, Stubbs et al. [18] observed over 800 h of human-robot interaction and noted that as the level of autonomy in the robot increased, the efficiency of the mission decreased as operators started increasingly questioned the robot's decision making. Stubb et al. concluded that having an agent explain relevant parts of the behaviour to maintain a *common ground* on the task is important for effective collaboration. The process to achieve common ground requires communication, taking into account what is necessary and important, and what the other team members already know.

The aim of our work is to identify the types of and amount of information that are relevant for interdependent tasks. We use the BlocksWorlds for Teams (BW4T) [11] test bed for this. BW4T is a simulation tool that allows experimentation of scenarios involving humans and agents. The joint goal of the human-agent team is to locate and retrieve a sequence of coloured blocks in a given order. Harbers et al. [5,6] have experimented with the same concept in BW4T, however, they found that communication did not have a significant impact on team efficiency in completing the task. They hypothesise that one reason may be the simple nature of the task, and that more complex scenarios show results similar to those seen in field experiments such as the ones by Stubbs discussed above.

In this paper, we develop a new scenario for BW4T that contains *joint actions*, rather than just joint *tasks*. By "action", we mean the atomic actions that make up a task. Our simple extension is to introduce a type of heavy block that requires one agent to hold the door to a room for another agent, meaning that moving the block out of the room is a joint action. That is, no individual agent can move the block out of a room. In terms of the model proposed by Saavedra et al.[15], this extension moves the task from one of a team merely working in parallel towards a common goal, called *pooled interdependence*, to one of *team task interdependence*, where team members must execute actions jointly.

We performed initial experiments to assess different communication strategies teams of artificial agents, demonstrating that sharing goals improves task efficiency better than sharing beliefs. Then, we used this to determine experimental parameters for human-agent experiments on similar scenarios, and showed sharing goals in the scenarios does indeed increase the efficiency of the team in completing the task. Further, we observed that sharing too much information resulted in decreased performance due to information overload.

This paper is outlined as follows. Section 2 presents the most closely related work, and Sect. 3 presents relevant background on the BW4T simulator.

Section 4 outlines the agent communication models used in our experiments, including how agents handle communication for joint tasks. Section 5 presents the experimental evaluation, including results, for both sets of experiments (agent teams and human-agent teams), while Sect. 6 concludes.

2   Related Work

In this section, we discuss the most closely related work to the work in this paper. While there is a large body of work investigating how human teams work together on interdependent tasks [14,15] and how the process of *grounding* a common ground [3,12], and their relation to shared cognition of a team [2,16], this section will focus on related work on interdependence in human-agent teams.

The primary questions of work in this domain are: (1) "how much" autonomy should we grant a semi-autonomous agent, and; (2) given this, what information needs to be communicated between the agent and the human for efficient task completion. In this paper, we look mostly at the second question.

In recent years, the realisation that human-agent teams offer more than agent-only teams has lead to many empirical studies of human-agent teams [1,4,13] that address the issue of what and when to communicate to team members. For example, Stubbs et al. [18] discuss their experience observing over 800 h of human-agent teamwork in a scientific setting. Their team remotely deployed a robot in the in Chile's Atacama Desert to investigate microorganisms that grow there, with the view that such a deployment would be similar to deploying a semi-autonomous robot on other planets. The team changed the level of autonomy of the deployed robot, giving it more responsibility on some tasks in certain cases, and observed the scientific teams' response. Stubbs et al. found that as the level of autonomy increased, the effectiveness of the team reduced. This was mostly caused by a lack of transparency in the robot's decision-making, resulting in cases where the scientific team spent more time discussing and trying to understand why the robot had made certain decisions, rather than on the scientific aims related to microorganisms. Stubbs et al. hypothesis that establishing a *common ground* between the relevant parties on tasks is essential.

Bradshaw et al. [1] hypothesise that human-agent teams will become more effective if agents are considered peers and team members, rather than just tools to which to delegate tasks. They later discuss the concept of *coactive design* [9], and argue that the consideration of interdependence between agents in performing joint tasks is key to effective human-agent teams. They define interdependence as the relationships between members of a team, and argue that these relationship determine what information is relevant for the team to complete a task, and in that sense, the interdependent relationships define the common ground that is necessary. In more recent work [10], they present the Coactive Design Method for designing intelligent agents that must interact with humans. In this model, interdependence is the organising principle. Human and artificial agents worked together through an interface that is designed around the concepts of Observability, Predictability and Directability (OPD). The model was applied to the design of a simulated teleoperated robot for the DARPA Virtual Robotics Challenge, and obtained an excellent score due to the advantages the coactive system model. They describe scenarios in which the identification of interdependent tasks improved their agent design, such as the robot having to attach a hose to a spigot. The robot is unable to identify the hose — a task done by the human —, but attaching the hose itself was a joint task, in which the robot positioned the hose and the human directed the arm to the spigot.

Other recent work looks at how to simulate such scenarios in a laboratory setting to allow for more controlled experimentation. In particular, the BlocksWorld for Teams (BW4T) testbed [11], used in our work, was developed to support experimentation of human-agent teaming in joint activities.

Harbers et al. [5,6] use the BW4T testbed to experiment with explanation in human-agent teams. In particular, they looked at the effect of sharing beliefs and intention within teams, providing the humans with the ability to exploit information about intentions to improve their understanding of the situation. Their results showed that, while participants reported increased awareness of what the agents were doing, there was no improvement in team effectiveness measured by completion time. Thus, their explanation model did indeed explain the situation, but this information was not useful for the human players to coordinate their actions. Harbers et al. hypothesise that this may be because the team tasks are so straightforward that the human player can easily predict what behaviour it requires, and thus processing the explanations has a cost that is similar to what the explanation is worth. We agree with this analysis. Our experiments are similar in spirit to these experiments, however, the introduction of joint action helps to provide a more complex scenario without increasing the complexity to a point that confuses the human players or requires extensive training.

In other work, Harbers et al. [7] used BW4T to investigate communication in agent-only teams, and found that sharing intentions and taking advantage of this knowledge increased the team efficiency, while sharing beliefs had minimal impact — a finding consistent with the work in this paper.

Wei et al. [19] study the construction and effectiveness of shared mental models between artificial agents using BW4T. They designed four scenarios with different numbers of artificial agents and environment sizes, and measured completion time as a proxy for the effectiveness of different communication strategies. Their results showed that communicating between team members improved efficiency, especially in the case in which there were sequential interdependencies between tasks; that is, the tasks had an explicit order in which they must have been completed. Further, they also found that communicating more information lead to more interference between agents, indicating that even in agent teams where processing is not a large issue, it is important to communicate only the most relevant and important information. Our work goes further than the experiments by Wei, Hindriks, and Jonker by looking at joint actions and including humans in the loop.

3   BlocksWorld for Teams

BlocksWorld For Team (BW4T) is a simulator that extends the classic blocks world domain, written specifically for experimenting with human-agent teams. The overall goal of the agent team is to search for the required blocks in a given set of rooms. The task can be performed by a single agent or a group of agents. Agents can be either artificial or human. The role of the agents can be distinguished based on how it is programmed.

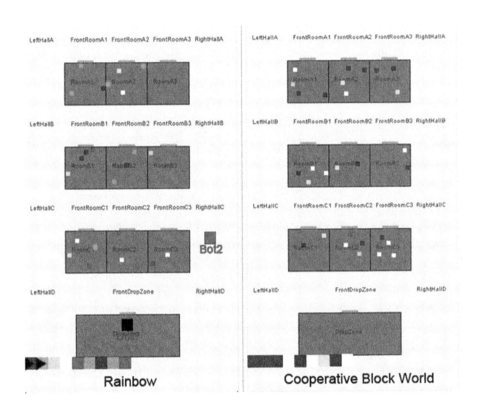

Fig. 1. The BW4T environment (Color figure online)

Figure 1 displays the three different BW4T maps we used in our experiments. The environment of BW4T consists of rooms and coloured blocks scattered in different rooms. Each room has one door, which is represented by the small green bold line. The dark area on the bottom is the drop zone, where blocks are dropped once collected. The small black squares with red labels represent agents. At the bottom, the sequence of colours specifies the blocks that the team is tasked with collecting. The team must put down the block with the right colour into the drop zone, otherwise, the block will disappear. The sequence is represented by the colourful bar on the bottom of the environment. The small triangles on the colourful bar means the completed tasks.

The agents within BW4T are programmed using the GOAL programming language [8], and the BW4T simulator provides specific constructs for interacting with GOAL agents. Agents can perceive the environment using an environmental sensor, including information such as the next target block, or the blocks in the room they are in.

Agents communicate to each other using messaging, and the contents can be arbitrary. On receiving a message, it is stored in a "mailbox" for reading. When an agent representing a human (which we call the *supervisor* agent) receives a message, it translates the message into a human-readable format, and displays this on the GUI that is viewable by the human. The human player can inform and direct the supervisor agent using a drop-down menu of commands; e.g. telling the agent which room a particular-coloured block is in.

4   Agents and Joint Actions in BW4T

In this section, we present the scenario and models of agents that we used to experiment with human-agent teams in joint activity. We model how an artificial agent communicates with artificial team members, and then with humans.

4.1   The Scenario

From the perspective of the rules of the BW4T game, we alter only one aspect: we introduce *types* of block. In the BW4T simulator, blocks have colours, and the sequence of target blocks must be returned according to a specific colour in each slot. In our model, blue blocks are given a special status, in that they are considered *heavier* than other blocks, and they require two agents to get the block from its location to the drop zone. As part of our experiments, we implemented a simple scenario in which, when an agent wanted to take a blue block from a room, a second agent was required to hold the door open for them (because the block is too heavy to hold in one arm, and the carrying agent therefore has no hand to open the door). As soon as the carrying agent exited the room, the second agent holding the door was free to return to another task.

This represents an *interdependent action* [17]: an agent can only take a blue block from a room if another agent opens the door, and the agent opening the door receives no value from this unless the block is taken from the room and back to the drop zone. One can imagine different implementations; e.g. two or more agents must carry blocks together, but this simple variation is enough to test out joint actions in BW4T.

4.2   Agent Models

In this section, we outline our model for dealing with the joint activity of collecting a blue block. We adopt a basic model of searching and retrieving blocks, and extend this with the ability for agents to *request* and *offer* assistance for heavy blocks. In our basic model, all agents know the sequence of blocks to be found. They search rooms in a semi-random fashion, not revisiting rooms known to have been visited by themselves or a team member, and maintain a belief set of the locations of blocks (which colours and in which rooms) that they have perceived. An agent's "default" goal is to find and retrieve the next block in the sequence, until they receive a request for assistance, or until another agent finds the block and broadcasts this fact, in which case they adopt the goal of finding the next block.

4.2.1 Requesting and Offering Assistance

Requesting help and offering assistance are required for the particular joint activity of heavy blocks. As mentioned before, blue blocks represent heavy blocks. This process for request and offering assistance for a blue block is shown in Fig. 2.

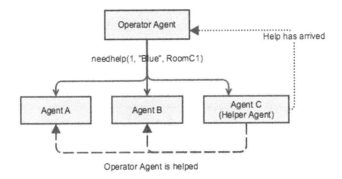

Fig. 2. Request help and offer assistance

All available agents will search for the blue block. The first agent to find one, who we call the *operator agent* will broadcast the `needhelp` message to all other agents. Any artificial agent ready to assist will move towards the room, and send a message ("Help has arrived") indicating they are at the help position (e.g. holding the door at `Room1`). The first agent to arrive will inform all others, who adopt their default goal of searching for the next block in the sequence. All agents attempting to help may not be an efficient use of their time, but we opt for a simple policy here to avoid any possibility of this policy influencing results about communication. As this policy is consistent across all experiments, we do not consider that this meaningfully affects the results.

4.2.2 Supervisor Agent

Recall that humans are represented by a *supervisor* agent, who can direct other agents to perform tasks. This agent acts as an interface between the human and artificial agents, but is also a player capable of finding and retrieving blocks.

Human players direct their representative agents using high-level commands, such as which block to search for; in sense, simulating a basic remote teleoperation of a robot. Human players can request and offer assistance like artificial agents, however, the decision making about whether to offer assistance is left up to the human, rather than coded in GOAL.

Figure 3 shows the models used for a supervisor agent. The first model is used when taking on a new task (Fig. 3a), and the second is used when the player intends to provide assistance to another agent trying to retrieve a blue block (Fig. 3b).

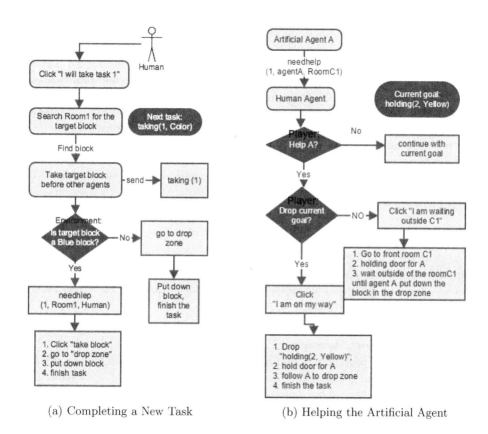

(a) Completing a New Task   (b) Helping the Artificial Agent

Fig. 3. Supervisor agent (Color figure online)

From Fig. 3a, one can see that a supervisor agent is idle unless directed by the human player to take a task; that is, to starting searching for a particular colour block. The supervisor agent then searches autonomously for the block. If it finds the block and the block is non-blue, it will update the other agents to inform them that the block has been located and is being taken back to the drop zone, allowing other agents to drop this task[1]. If the block is blue, it will request help and wait. After getting help from other agent, the *"take block"* option is made available on the human player's GUI, and clicking this directs the supervisor agent to take the block to the drop zone autonomously.

The other artificial agents adapt the player's changing actions. For example, if the supervisor agent drops its goal while carrying a block (e.g. yellow) to the drop zone, the other agents will drop their current task of searching for the next block in the sequence, and will adopt the goal of finding a yellow block.

The model outlined in this section is put in place to provide human decision support into the system. In a team with only artificial agents, if all agents have a current goal and one agent finds a blue block, it will be required to wait for one of its team members to complete its tasks.

However, in our model, we offer the human player the possibility to drop its own goal to help complete the tasks. We opted not to have the human player directing other artificial agents to drop goals when other agents find blue blocks, as we believed that the extra decision of *which* agent to direct could increase the cognitive load of the human player to the point where decisions became arbitrary. By allowing the human player to direct only their own agent, this model provides a complex-enough scenario to introduce an interdependent action into BW4T, without the complexity of the scenario overwhelming participants.

Ultimately, we believe that the results from our experiments (see Sect. 5) demonstrate that our decision is justified.

4.3   Information Exchange Between Agents

It is clear that sharing information can improve team efficiency. However, the information shared, and how much of it, is crucial, especially in human-agent teams, where the humans' capacities to process information is reduced compared to its artificial team members.

4.3.1   Information Messaging

In this section, we present the communication protocols between agents, which consist of individual messages. Several types of message can be sent, enabling agents to inform others about part of the environment, or its own goals.

Beliefs are the information about the environment, which are perceived via agents, such as the location of different coloured blocks. *Goals* are mental states that motivate action. To complete a single task, an agent must complete a sequence of goals. We enabled agents to share their beliefs and goals.

Five messages can be transferred amongst agents:

1. `block(BlockID, ColourID, PlaceID)`: block `BlockID` with colour `Colour ID` has been found by the message sender at room `PlaceID`. When in a room, an agent broadcasts information about any block colours that are in the goal sequence.

---

[1] Artificial agents are also programmed with this capability in our model.

2. `visited(PlaceID)`: room `PlaceID` has been visited by the message sender. While this can be inferred when a `block` message (above) is sent, the `visited` message is sent when the room does not contain any blocks that are in the target sequence.
3. `hold(BlockID, ColourID)`: block `BlockID` with `ColourID` is held by the message sender.
4. `will_deliver(Index, ColourID)`: a block of colour `ColourID`, which is also the $Index^{th}$ block in the sequence of the main goal, is being delivered to the drop zone.
5. `dropped(Index, ColourID)`: the $Index^{th}$ block in the task sequence, with colour `ColourID`, previously held by the message sender, has been dropped.

While all messages are sharing information about the task, the intention of the first three is to share belief about the environment, while the intention of the last two is to share goals; e.g. when an agent delivered the task, it will drop this goal.

Agents use the information about where they have visited and what colour blocks are in the rooms to inform their search strategy. We model the artificial agents to used the shared information about block locations and room searching to improve the completion of the task. For example, when the agents share their belief about the location of blocks, others can update their own beliefs with this information, preventing unnecessary searching of rooms.

Our models use shared information about blocks being retrieved and dropped to further improve this. That is, when an agent broadcasts that they have located the next block, others will stop searching for that colour, and when a block in the main sequence is dropped, others will starting searching for this again.

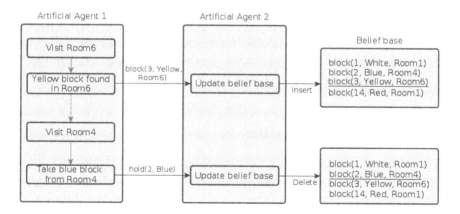

Fig. 4. The effect of sharing belief

Figure 4 shows how information about block location and holding blocks. Suppose artificial agent 2 is stationary, while artificial agent 1 is exploring for a blue target. Agent 1 visits room 6, there is no blue block, but a yellow block is inside of the room. If the agents share beliefs, agent 1 will send a message block(3, Yellow, Room6) to all the other agents, and all other agents will update their belief base with this information.

Next, suppose agent 1 goes to room 4, which contains a blue block. The agent will pick up the block and broadcast the message hold(2, Blue). The others agents will then update their belief base to remove the belief block(2, Blue, Room4), if they had this belief in their belief base.

4.4   Filtering for Human Players

The hypothesis in human-agent collaboration research is that explanation from the later can improve team performance in the joint activities. However, it is clear that humans do not have sufficient processing capabilities to use all information shared in the previous section. Despite this, the human player also needs to know some of the critical information such as the environment states and other artificial agents' message.

In our model, the supervisor agent takes on the role of an information broker who is responsible to deliver and translate information for the human player, and to filter the "explanation" from artificial agents. From the artificial agents' perspective, a supervisor agent is another artificial agent that receives and sends messages, and supervisor agents are the bridge between the environment, artificial agents, and human players.

Figure 5 shows two examples of translating information between the artificial agents and human agents — one for each direction. In Fig. 5a, the supervisor agent accepts two parts of input: (1) from the environment, including information such as the room occupancy and current team target; and (2) from another agent, including the requesting assistance and sharing the goals. The supervisor agent selects some of the incoming information and "explains" this to the human agent.

The key part of any design is what information should be filtered out, and what should be filtered in and explained. In the next section, we describe an experiment design that looks at three levels of filtering, and their effect on the performance of the overall system.

5   Experimental Evaluation

In this section, we outline two sets of experiments to provide evidence towards our hypothesis that communication can improve the team performance in joint activities, and report the results. The first set of experiments runs three BW4T scenarios using a team made entirely of artificial agents, while the second set includes a human player in the loop, along with its supervisor agent. Within each experiment, the information that is shared between team members is changed to measure the effect of information exchange.

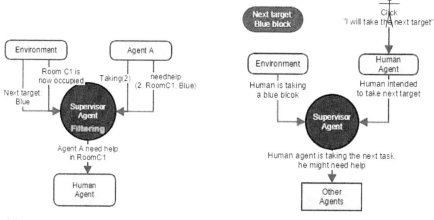

(a) Supervisor transfers artificial agent intentions to human player

(b) Supervisor transfers human intentions to artificial agents

Fig. 5. Filtering by the supervisor agent

5.1 Artificial Agent Team Experiment

5.1.1 Experiment Design

The aim of this experiment is to study which type of information sharing between artificial agents effects the team performance: sharing beliefs, goals, or both.

Independent Variable. We modify two independent variables: (1) communication strategy; and (2) the environment type.

For the communication strategy, we use four values: (a) minimal information shared: the only communication is to ask for help moving a blue block; (b) belief only: minimal plus belief about the environment (items 1–3 in Sect. 4.3.1); (c) goals only: minimal plus agent goals (items 4–5 in Sect. 4.3.1); and (d) belief and goals.

For the environment, we use three different maps: (a) cooperative block world; (b) rainbow; and (c) simple. The first two are shown in Fig. 1 (page 5). Cooperative block world contains seven block colours, but only three occur in the main goal, and these are randomly allocated to the main goal in a uniform manner. Rainbow contains seven coloured blocks, and all seven colours can appear in the main goal. Simple contains randomly allocated blocks, but with no blue blocks; and therefore, no joint action.

Measures. We measure completion time of the entire scenario as a proxy for the effectiveness of each communication strategy.

Setup. For each map, we run all four communication strategies giving us 12 combinations. Each combination is run 30 times, with different random seeds to generate different block locations, resulting in 360 experiments run in total.

All experiments were run with two artificial agents, nine rooms, and nine blocks in the main goal.

5.1.2 Results

Figure 6 shows the average completion time for all combinations of scenarios and communication strategies. This figure demonstrates several interesting findings from our experiments.

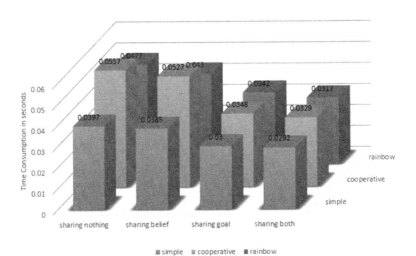

Fig. 6. Average task completion time for the artificial agents team (Color figure online)

With regards to the three scenarios maps, cooperative blocks world consumes more time than other two, and the simple map, with no strictly joint action, took the least time to finish on average. This supports our hypothesis that having joint actions in a scenario increasing the complexity more than simply joint tasks. The largest gap (40 %) between the cooperative block world and simple world results is in the scenario where "nothing" is shared (recall that agents still request help once they pick up a heavy blue block), indicating that sharing beliefs and goals is useful in this environment. Further, for the cooperative blocks world scenario, there is a large step between sharing belief and sharing goals, indicating that sharing goals is far more valuable that sharing just belief. This is further backed up by the small decrement from sharing goals to sharing both belief and goals. In all three maps, sharing belief had only a small impact. This finding is interesting, because while agents share their knowledge of the environment, meaning that searching for the right coloured block can be reduced, it is in fact coordinating the joint action early that increases efficiency the most in this scenario.

Table 1 shows the outcomes of a two-way factorial ANOVA to examine the influence of the two different independent variables. The p-values for the rows (maps), columns (communication strategy), and the interaction, are all < 0.001,

Table 1. The two-way factorial ANOVA results for the artificial agents team

Source of variance	SS	F	P-value
Communication strategy	6669.31	110.39	9.20E-33
Map	1948.40	48.38	9.97E-16
Interaction	585.17	4.84	2.04E-04

indicating that the results are statistically significant to this level. Comparing the sum of square errors (SS), we see that communication has more impact than the scenarios, but both factors have a significant influence on the results.

The results show that communication is beneficial for improving cooperative team work, and sharing goals has the largest impact. We drilled down into the experiment data and found that the primary reason for this was labour redundancy. An agent will update its team members once a block is placed in the drop zone, limiting the team members' knowledge of task progress. By sharing the goal that they have collected a block suitable to fulfil the current team sub-goal, the other team members can start on a new task.

5.2 Human-Agent Teams

The results from the artificial agent teams helped to inform the design of the human-agent team experiments. In this section, we outline the experimental design and results for the human-agent team scenarios.

5.2.1 Experiment Design

The aim of this experiment is to study how the type of information shared between the human player and other agents effects the team performance. Due to the introduction of a human into the loop, the experiment is much simplified compared to the experiments in the previous section, as we aimed to keep total completion time to under 30 min for each participant.

Independent Variable. The independent variable in the experiments is filtering strategy used by the supervisor agent to exchange information with the human player: (1) *full info*: everything is shared as in the artificial team; (2) *partial info*: only information that will change the goals of the human player are shared; and (3) *silence*: only information that a block has been delivered to the drop zone. Table 2 outlines what information is shared in each of the three cases.

Measures. As in the artificial team experiment, we use completion time of the entire scenario as a proxy for the effectiveness of each communication strategy.

Setup. We recruited 12 participants to perform three runs of the experiment — one with each communication strategy. No participant had used or heard of the BW4T simulator previously. To avoid bias, the order in which the participants used the various communication strategies were systematically varied.

Table 2. The information shared in the three scenarios

Information	Full info	Partial info	Silence
Next target	✔	✔	✔
Other agent's current task	✔	✔	
Request assistance	✔	✔	
Offer assistance	✔	✔	
Task completion	✔	✔	
Block location	✔		
Room occupancy	✔		
Other agents' state	✔		

Due to the relative difficult of recruiting participants and running the experiments, we used only one map in all three scenarios: the cooperative block world map (Fig. 1). We chose this map because the results of the agent-team experiments demonstrate that this best simulates a reasonably complex scenario with joint action. The speed of the BW4T simulation is adjusted to be slow to provide the human player with sufficient time to make decisions. Each experiment consisted of two artificial agents, one supervisor agent, and one human players. There was no time out for completion of the experiment, and none of the participants failed to complete the scenario.

5.2.2 Results

Figure 7 shows the results for the human-agent team experiments. Due to the relatively smaller number of data points, results for each participant is shown. The x-axis is the communication strategy, the y-axis are the individual participants, and the z-axis is completion time. Results are sorted roughly by completion time. The overall average completion time for the three scenarios are: full info = 4.92 min, partial info = 4.36 min, and silence = 4.72 min.

From the figure, it is clear that results differ among people, but that the difference between the strategies per person establishes a trend. From the average scores, having full information took the longest time, followed by silence, and finally, the partial information. These results support the hypothesis that explanation can improve the team performance in scenarios with joint action, and further, that too much explanation can hinder a human players ability for decision making.

To test the effect of different communication scenarios, we performed a repeated measures two-way ANOVA between groups, and a pairwise Tukey HSD comparison between all pairs of groups. Relevant values for the ANOVA are shown in Table 3. For the pairwise Tukey HSD test, the full information vs. partial information results are significant at the 0.05 level, while the other two pairs are not. These tests demonstrate that the results between groups is significant (Table 3).

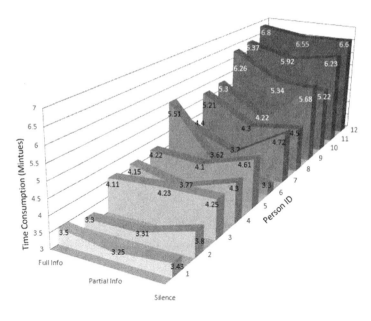

Fig. 7. The results of human-artificial agents' team

Table 3. ANOVA analysis of human-artificial agents' team results

Source	SS	df	MS	F	P-value
Treatment (between groups)	1.985	2	0.9925	5.07	0.0154
Error (within groups)	4.305	22	0.1957		

6   Conclusions and Future Work

In this paper, we studied the effectiveness of communication in artificial agent teams and human-agent teams using the BW4T testbed. Extending previous studies using BW4T, we added the concept of a *joint action* — a single atomic action that requires more than one agent to complete.

For the artificial agents team, we performed extensive simulation experiments to assess the value of sharing beliefs, sharing goals, and sharing both belief and goals. The results showed that sharing goals, namely, agents exchanging their immediate goals, increase team efficiency significantly more than sharing beliefs.

Using these results, we designed an experiment using the same joint action scenario, but with a human player in the loop. We recruited 12 people to each play in three scenarios using three different communication strategies: (1) update only when a block sub-task has been completed; (2) share goals; and (3) share goals and beliefs. We observed that sharing goals and beliefs lead to information overload of the human, resulting in a less efficient team than just sharing goals, and that sharing almost nothing is more efficient than sharing all goals and beliefs, most likely because the scenario is still straightforward enough to guess the optimal next movement.

We identify two areas of future work: (1) a more fine-grained study on the types of goals that are shared; and (2) study of tasks in which communication is necessary to complete a task.

Acknowledgements. The authors thank Christian Muise for his valuable feedback on drafts of this paper. This research is partially funded by Australian Research Council Discovery Grant DP130102825: *Foundations of Human-Agent Collaboration: Situation-Relevant Information Sharing.*

References

1. Bradshaw, J.M., Feltovich, P., Johnson, M., Breedy, M., Bunch, L., Eskridge, T., Jung, H., Lott, J., Uszok, A., van Diggelen, J.: From tools to teammates: joint activity in human-agent-robot teams. In: Kurosu, M. (ed.) HCD 2009. LNCS, vol. 5619, pp. 935–944. Springer, Heidelberg (2009)
2. Cannon-Bowers, J.A., Salas, E.: Reflections on shared cognition. J. Organ. Behav. **22**(2), 195–202 (2001)
3. Clark, H.: Using Language. Cambridge University Press, Cambridge (1996)
4. Cummings, M.M.: Man versus machine or man + machine? IEEE Intell. Syst. **29**(5), 62–69 (2014)
5. Harbers, M., Bradshaw, J.M., Johnson, M., Feltovich, P., van den Bosch, K., Meyer, J.-J.: Explanation and coordination in human-agent teams: a study in the BW4T testbed. In: Proceedings of the 2011 IEEE International Conferences on Web Intelligence and Intelligent Agent Technology, pp. 17–20. IEEE Computer Society (2011)
6. Harbers, M., Bradshaw, J.M., Johnson, M., Feltovich, P., van den Bosch, K., Meyer, J.-J.: Explanation in human-agent teamwork. In: Cranefield, S., van Riemsdijk, M.B., Vázquez-Salceda, J., Noriega, P. (eds.) COIN 2011. LNCS, vol. 7254, pp. 21–37. Springer, Heidelberg (2012)
7. Harbers, M., Jonker, C., Van Riemsdijk, B.: Enhancing team performance through effective communication. In: Proceedings of the 4th Annual Human-Agent-Robot Teamwork Workshop, pp. 1–2 (2012)
8. Hindriks, K.V.: Programming rational agents in GOAL. In: El Fallah Seghrouchni, A., Dix, J., Dastani, M., Bordini, R.H. (eds.) Multi-Agent Programming, pp. 119–157. Springer, New York (2009)
9. Johnson, M., Bradshaw, J.M., Feltovich, P.J., Jonker, C.M., van Riemsdijk, B., Sierhuis, M.: The fundamental principle of coactive design: interdependence must shape autonomy. In: De Vos, M., Fornara, N., Pitt, J.V., Vouros, G. (eds.) COIN 2010. LNCS, vol. 6541, pp. 172–191. Springer, Heidelberg (2011)
10. Johnson, M., Bradshaw, J.M., Feltovich, P.J., Jonker, C.M., Van Riemsdijk, M.B.: Coactive design: designing support for interdependence in joint activity. J. Hum.-Robot Interact. **3**, 43–69 (2014)
11. Johnson, M., Jonker, C., van Riemsdijk, B., Feltovich, P.J., Bradshaw, J.M.: Joint activity testbed: blocks world for teams (BW4T). In: Aldewereld, H., Dignum, V., Picard, G. (eds.) ESAW 2009. LNCS, vol. 5881, pp. 254–256. Springer, Heidelberg (2009)

12. Kashima, Y., Klein, O., Clark, A.E.: Grounding: sharing information in social interaction. In: Fiedler, K. (ed.) Social Communication, pp. 27–77. Psychology Press, New York (2007)

13. Langan-Fox, J., Canty, J.M., Sankey, M.J.: Human-automation teams and adaptable control for future air traffic management. Int. J. Ind. Ergon. **39**(5), 894–903 (2009)

14. Puranam, P., Raveendran, M., Knudsen, T.: Organization design: the epistemic interdependence perspective. Acad. Manag. Rev. **37**(3), 419–440 (2012)

15. Saavedra, R., Earley, P.C., Van Dyne, L.: Complex interdependence in task-performing groups. J. Appl. Psychol. **78**(1), 61–72 (1993)

16. Salas, E., Prince, C., Baker, D.P., Shrestha, L.: Situation awareness in team performance: implications for measurement and training. Hum. Factors: J. Hum. Factors Ergon. Soc. **37**(1), 123–136 (1995)

17. Singh, R., Miller, T., Sonenberg, L.: A preliminary analysis of interdependence in multiagent systems. In: Dam, H.K., Pitt, J., Xu, Y., Governatori, G., Ito, T. (eds.) PRIMA 2014. LNCS, vol. 8861, pp. 381–389. Springer, Heidelberg (2014)

18. Stubbs, K., Wettergreen, D., Hinds, P.J.: Autonomy and common ground in human-robot interaction: a field study. IEEE Intell. Syst. **22**(2), 42–50 (2007)

19. Wei, C., Hindriks, K., Jonker, C.M.: The role of communication in coordination protocols for cooperative robot teams. In: International Conference on Agents and Artificial Intelligence, pp. 28–39 (2014)

Manipulating Conventions in a Particle-Based Topology

James Marchant[(✉)] and Nathan Griffiths

Department of Computer Science, University of Warwick, Coventry CV4 7AL, UK
{james,nathan}@dcs.warwick.ac.uk

Abstract. Coordination is essential to the effective operation of multi-agent systems. Convention emergence offers a low-cost and decentralised method of ensuring compatible actions and behaviour, without requiring the imposition of global rules. This is of particular importance in environments with no centralised control or where agents belong to different, possibly conflicting, parties. The timely emergence of robust conventions can be facilitated and manipulated via the use of fixed strategy agents, who attempt to influence others into adopting a particular strategy. Although fixed strategy agents have previously been investigated, they have not been considered in dynamic networks. In this paper, we explore the emergence of conventions within a dynamic network, and examine the effectiveness of fixed strategy agents in this context. Using established placement heuristics we show how such agents can encourage convention emergence, and we examine the impact of the dynamic nature of the network. We introduce a new heuristic, LIFE-DEGREE, to enable this investigation. Finally, we consider the ability of fixed strategy agents to manipulate already established conventions, and investigate the effectiveness of placement heuristics in this domain.

Keywords: Dynamic networks · Conventions · Social norms · Influence

1 Introduction

Within multi-agent systems (MAS) cooperation and coordination of individuals' actions and goals are required for efficient interaction. Incompatible actions result in clashes that often incur a resource cost, such as time, to the participating agents. The predetermination of which actions clash is not always possible, particularly for large action spaces and dynamic populations.

The emergence of *conventions* is often used to solve these problems. Conventions represent socially-adopted expected behaviour amongst agents and thus facilitate coordinated action choice without the dictation of rules. Convention emergence has been shown to be possible in static networks with minimal requirements, namely agent rationality and the ability to learn from previous interactions [5,25]. This adds little design overhead, and is of particular importance in open MAS where agent modification is likely to be impractical or impossible.

© Springer International Publishing Switzerland 2016
V. Dignum et al. (Eds.): COIN 2015, LNAI 9628, pp. 242–261, 2016.
DOI: 10.1007/978-3-319-42691-4_14

Fixed strategy (FS) agents continue to choose the same action regardless of its efficacy or the choices of others in the system. Their presence has been shown to affect the direction and speed of convention emergence in static networks. Small numbers of these agents are able to influence much larger populations [21], especially when placed using appropriate heuristics [7,10]. Fixed strategy agents can also be used to cause a system to abandon an already established convention in favour of an alternative [13,15].

In many domains, the nature of the relationships between agents is not static. Agents may leave the system, new agents can enter, and the links between agents may change over time. These dynamic interaction topologies induce different system characteristics than those found in static networks. Relatively little work has studied the nature of convention emergence in these types of network.

This paper considers the emergence and manipulation of conventions within dynamic topologies. We introduce a new heuristic, LIFE-DEGREE, to support this investigation, which considers aspects of the dynamic nature of the system when placing fixed strategy agents. We examine the importance of dynamic topology characteristics by comparing the performance of LIFE-DEGREE against previously used heuristics based on network metrics. We then consider the efficacy of the various heuristics when fixed strategy agents are used to destabilise or remove an established convention.

The remainder of this paper is organised as follows: Sect. 2 discusses the related work on convention emergence, fixed strategy agents and dynamic topologies. Section 3 describes the model of convention emergence being used, as well as the simulation model used to generate the topologies. Additionally this section introduces the heuristics used to place fixed strategy agents. Our results are shown in Sect. 4 and, finally, we present our conclusions in Sect. 5.

2   Related Work

A *convention* is a form of socially-accepted rule regarding agent behaviour and choices. Conventions can be viewed as "an equilibrium everyone expects in interactions that have more than one equilibrium" [26]. No explicit punishment exists for going against a convention, nor is there any implicit benefit in the action represented by the convention over other possible actions. Members of a convention expect others to behave a certain way, and acting against the convention increases the likelihood of incompatible action choices and the costs associated with these. Conventions have been shown to emerge naturally from local agent interactions [5,12,23,25] and enhance agent coordination by placing *social constraints* on agents' action choices [22].

Although the terms are often used interchangeably in the literature [17,21], in this paper we differentiate between conventions and *norms*. Norms typically imply an obligation or prohibition on agents with regards to a specific action. Failure to adhere to norms and exhibit the expected behaviour is often associated with punishments or sanctions [1,3,11,19]. Alternatively, agents may be explicitly rewarded for adherence to norms. Thus, norms generally require additional system or agent capabilities as well as incurring a system-level overhead for punishment/reward. In this paper, we assume that agents do not have the capability to punish one another, nor can they observe defection in others. Instead, we use conventions as a lightweight method of increasing coordination.

We make only minimal assumptions about agent architecture and behaviour; we assume that agents are rational and that they have access to a (limited) memory of previous interactions. Numerous studies have focused on convention emergence with these assumptions [5,10,21,25] and have shown that they allow rapid and robust convention emergence. Walker and Wooldridge [25] investigated convention emergence whilst making few assumptions about agent capabilities. In their model, agents select actions based on the observed choices of others, and global convention emergence is shown to be possible.

Expanding on this, Sen and Airiau [21] investigated social learning for convention emergence, where agents receive a payoff from their interactions which informs their learning (via Q-Learning). They showed convention emergence can occur when agents have no memory of interactions and only observe their own rewards. However, their model is limited in that agents are able to interact with any other member of the population rather than being situated in a network topology. Additionally, the convention space considered is restricted to only two possible actions. In more realistic settings larger convention spaces and more restrictive connecting network topologies are likely. The network topology agents are situated in has been shown to have a significant effect on convention emergence [4,5,12,24], affecting the speed with which emergence occurs. Recent work has shown that a larger number of actions typically slows convergence [7,10,18].

The use of fixed strategy agents, who always choose the same action regardless of others' choices, to influence convention emergence has also been explored. Sen and Airiau [21] show that a small number of such agents can cause a population to adopt the fixed strategy as a convention over other equally valid choices. This indicates that small numbers of agents can affect much larger populations.

In Sen and Airiau's model, due to the lack of connecting topology, all agents are identical in terms of their ability to interact with others. However, in many domains, agent interactions may be limited to neighbours in the network. As such, some agents will have larger sets of potential interactions than others. In the context of static topologies, Griffiths and Anand [10] establish that which agents are selected and *where* they are in the topology is a key factor in their effectiveness as fixed strategy agents. They show that placement by simple metrics such as degree offers better performance than random placement.

Franks *et al.* [6,7] investigated fixed strategy agents where interactions are constrained by a static network topology and agents are exposed to a large convention space. They found that topology affects the number of fixed strategy agents required to increase convergence speed. This also expanded on the work of Griffiths and Anand [10] by investigating the effectiveness of placing by more advanced metrics such as eigenvector centrality.

Few studies have focused on convention emergence in dynamic topologies, with most work focusing on static networks. Savarimuthu et al. [20] consider the related phenomenon of norm emergence in a dynamic topology. They show that norms are able to emerge under a number of conditions, but their work differs from ours due to the requirements placed on agents. The interaction model used requires agents to maintain an internal norm as well as being able to query other agents. We make minimal assumptions about agent internals or the information available. Additionally, our work investigates the manipulation of convention emergence, something not considered by Savarimuthu et al.

Mihaylov et al. [16] briefly consider convention emergence in dynamic topologies using the coordination game. However, their work focuses on a new proposed method of learning, rather than on the emergence itself. In particular, they do not consider fixed strategy agents, or the action that emerges as a convention. In this paper, we consider both convention emergence in dynamic topologies and the use of fixed strategy agents to understand the impact of network dynamics.

Relatively little work has considered destabilising established conventions, with previous investigations of fixed strategy agents typically inserting them at the beginning of interactions. We have previously [13,15] investigated using fixed strategy agents in static topologies to cause members of the dominant convention to change their adopted convention and hence *destabilise* it. We found that this required substantially more fixed strategy agents than is needed to influence conventions before emergence. This paper expands on this work to examine aspects of dynamic networks when selecting fixed strategy agents for destabilisation. We also expand on [14] and consider the general nature of convention emergence in dynamic topologies, particularly without the use of fixed strategy agents, and the effect of topology features on convention emergence time. Finally, we explore the relationship between placement heuristics, number of fixed strategy agents and the speed of convention emergence.

3   Convention Emergence Model

Our experimental setup consists of three main components, introduced below: the network topology, the interaction regime used by agents and the heuristics used for placing fixed strategy agents.

3.1   Dynamic Topology Generator

Similar to Savarimuthu et al. [20] we utilise a particle-based simulation, developed by González et al. [8,9], to model dynamic network topologies with characteristics comparable to those observed in real-world networks. Agents are represented as colliding particles and the topology is modified by collisions creating links between the agents. A population of N agents, represented as a set of particles with radius r, is placed within a 2D box with sides of length L. Initially, all agents are distributed uniformly at random within the space and are assigned a velocity of constant magnitude v_0 and random direction.

Each timestep, agents move according to their velocity and detect collisions with other agents. When two agents collide, an edge is added between them in the network topology if one does not already exist. Both agents then move away in a random direction with a speed proportional to their degree. Thus, higher degree nodes have an increased probability of further collisions, which in turn further increases their degree. In this way, the model exhibits preferential attachment, a characteristic found in static scale-free networks [2]. Such networks are often studied in the field of convention emergence [5,7,10,18] due to characteristics that are representative of real-world networks.

Additionally, all agents are assigned a Time-To-Live (TTL) when created. This is drawn uniformly at random between zero and the maximum TTL, T_l. After each timestep agents' TTLs are decremented by one. When an agent's TTL $= 0$ the agent and all its edges are removed. A new agent is placed at the same location within the simulation with the randomised initial properties discussed above. In this manner, the topology is constantly changing.

Different topologies can be characterised by the value of T_l/T_0 where T_0 is the characteristic time between collisions. This can be expressed as:

$$\frac{T_l}{T_0} = \frac{2\sqrt{2\pi}rNv_0T_l}{L^2} \tag{1}$$

González et al. show that this value dictates key characteristics of the generated topology, primarily the average degree and degree distribution.

The concept of a quasi-stationary state (QSS) is discussed by González et al., such that a QSS emerges after a number of timesteps and is characterised by macro-scale stability of network characteristics. Micro-scale characteristics, for individual agents, remain in flux. In [8] it is shown that the QSS can be described as any timestep, t, where $t \gtrsim 2T_l$. Our approach here differs from Savarimuthu et al. [20] as we consider agent interactions starting from $t = 0$ rather than waiting for the QSS. This allows us to mimic scenarios where agents have been placed in a new environment rather than only considering already established networks.

3.2   Interaction Regime

Agents within the system interact with one another and, learning from these interactions, converge to a shared behaviour in the form of a convention. Agent interactions occur during each timestep of the regime. In each timestep, every agent chooses one of its neighbours in the network at random. These agents play a round of the n-action pure coordination game. In this game, both agents are given a choice from a set of n-actions, A. Agents do not know what their opponent has chosen. The payoff that each agent receives depends on the combination of the chosen actions: if both chose the same action they receive a positive payoff, otherwise a negative payoff. Alternative payoff matrices and their effect on the effectiveness of the intervention strategies are discussed in Sect. 4.4.

Each agent monitors their expected payoff for each action, based on the previous payoffs they have received when choosing that action. We adopt the approach of Villatoro et al. [24] in this regard by using a simplified form of

Q-Learning. For each action, $a \in A$, the agent maintains a Q-Value which is updated by $Q^i(a) = (1 - \alpha) \times Q^{i-1}(a) + \alpha \times payoff$ where α is a parameter known as the learning rate and i represents the number of times a has been chosen. All agents start with $Q^0(a) = 0, \forall a \in A$. To combat the issue of local optima, we allow each agent, with probability $p_{explore}$ to randomly select an action. Otherwise, as each agent is rational, they will always select the action with the highest Q-Value, selecting randomly between ties.

In the formulation proposed by Kittock [12], a convention is considered to have emerged when a high proportion (90 %) of non-fixed strategy agents, when not exploring, would choose the same action. We adopt this definition of a convention but modify it to better fit the dynamic nature of the network topology. Instead of considering the entire population, we monitor adoption within the largest connected component. This follows from the findings of Gonzalez et al. [8] that in most simulations a giant cluster consisting of nearly all agents will emerge. Agents not within this cluster are likely to be recently created agents and, as such, should not be included in the adoption rate calculation as they have not interacted. This is reinforced by our simulations which showed that most agents not within the largest connected component had degree zero. Similarly, 100 % adoption is unlikely due to new agents joining.

The Kittock criteria sets a high threshold and measures nearly pervasive conventions. If a convention does not emerge at this threshold there is often still a highly dominant strategy in the system. By considering a different threshold and defining these as conventions, we can examine the effectiveness of the heuristics in situations not normally considered. This approach can be seen in Sect. 4.4.

Fixed strategy agents will be placed within the network to study the effect on convention emergence. These agents will replace selected agents upon insertion, keeping all of that agent's edges. This can be justified in real-world scenarios as persuading the agents to act in a desired manner via some reward mechanism. Such agents will be assigned the same fixed strategy and their placement will be determined heuristically as discussed below. If a fixed strategy agent's TTL should reach zero, a new agent will be selected using the same heuristic.

We consider two different scenarios: placing fixed strategy agents at the beginning of a system's life, to encourage and direct initial convention emergence, and inserting fixed strategy agents once a convention has emerged to attempt to change it. In the former case, the fixed strategy will be randomly chosen from the available actions. In the latter, it will be randomly chosen from the available actions excluding the already established convention. Initial insertion will occur once a connected component of size greater than $N/2$ has emerged. This prevents convention emergence being declared prematurely for a non-giant cluster. Additionally, placement heuristics which rely on network metrics (such as degree) may select sub-optimal agents if used before a main cluster has emerged.

3.3   Placement Heuristics

Previous work has utilised placement heuristics to enhance the effect of fixed strategy agents. Metrics such as degree, eigenvector centrality and betweenness centrality have been used with greater efficacy than random placement [6,10]. In this paper, we focus on degree-based placement. However, the dynamic nature of the topology introduces a number of ways to apply it. All heuristics are calculated with respect to the largest connected component.

Our initial heuristic, Static Degree, corresponds to the equivalent heuristic for static networks. At the time of insertion, agents are chosen to be fixed strategy agents in descending order of degree. This selection is static once chosen, only being modified upon agent expiration as detailed above. This simplistic approach is computationally cheap, a factor of importance in settings where gathering or computing this information is expensive. However, this risks selected agents potentially becoming sub-optimal choices as the simulation progresses. The static nature of this heuristic means that if another agent acquires a larger degree it will not be selected until one of the current agents expires. Depending on the TTL of the current fixed strategy agents, this could be a substantial period.

To address this issue we propose another degree-based heuristic: Updating Degree. This approach is sensitive to the dynamic nature of the topology and reselects the fixed strategy agents each timestep, based on highest current degree. Whilst this offers a solution to the potential sub-optimality of Static Degree it suffers from two problems. Firstly, the ability to acquire this information each timestep in a timely manner may be infeasible in many domains. Secondly, there is the potential that the fixed strategy agents will not remain in a given location long enough to influence the local area before being replaced.

The Static and Updating Degree heuristics do not fully consider the dynamic network context. Whilst high degree agents are likely to be influential due to their ability to interact with many others, additional dimensions may affect their applicability. Agents close to expiring may be less desirable than younger agents as their expected number of interactions before replacement is lower. However, the youngest agents, those newly created, cannot be guaranteed to become influential later on. Hence, the age of an agent adds an additional consideration. We propose a new heuristic, LIFE-DEGREE, that allows exploration of the effect of age in addition to degree on a fixed strategy agent's efficacy.

In many settings it may be impossible to *know* an agent's TTL. However, we can estimate an agent's remaining life. Given the upper bound, T_l, and the uniformly distributed nature of TTL, the normalised expected remaining TTL, E_{rTTL}, for an agent $n \in N$ is:

$$E_{rTTL}(n) = 1 - \frac{age(n) \times 2}{T_l} \tag{2}$$

We can also calculate the normalised degree of a node within the largest connected component as:

$$deg_{norm}(n) = \frac{deg(n)}{\max_{n' \in LCC} deg(n')} \tag{3}$$

The LIFE-DEGREE heuristic is then defined as:

$$\text{LIFE-DEGREE}(n) = \omega \times deg_{norm}(n) + (1 - \omega) \times E_{rTTL}(n) \tag{4}$$

In this, $0 \leq \omega \leq 1$ is a weight, determining the relative contributions of degree and expected TTL.

LIFE-DEGREE allows combination of the relevant information, normalised against theoretical maximums, in a manner that allows exploration of the importance of both. Two variations of LIFE-DEGREE will be used, Static and Updating, to compare against the heuristics discussed above.

4   Results and Discussion

In this section we present our findings on convention emergence in dynamic topologies and consider the effect of agent age via our proposed heuristic, LIFE-DEGREE. Unless otherwise mentioned, all experiments used 1000 agents, the 10-action coordination game and an exploration and Q-Learning rate of 0.25. Results were averaged over 100 runs. A payoff of +4 for coordinated actions and -1 for conflicting actions was used. This was found to rapidly emerge thorough and robust conventions. Additional payoff schemes are considered in Sect. 4.4.

4.1   Characterising Topology

We initially consider convention emergence without external manipulation in dynamic topologies. This gives insight into the impact of network dynamics on convention emergence and provides a baseline. Additionally, it allows us to quantify the point at which a stable convention will have emerged for later experiments that focus on destabilisation.

The features of the dynamic topology can be manipulated by varying the parameters of the network model, and are encapsulated in different values of T_l/T_0. González et al. [9] show that the features of the topology thus only depend on the ratio T_l/T_0 and the density, $\rho \equiv N/L^2$. Additionally, they show that the average degree is a non-linear function of T_l/T_0 that depends on the chosen ρ. As such, for all experiments we use a constant $\rho = 0.625$ (i.e. $N = 1000$, $L = 40$) to allow meaningful comparisons of the T_l/T_0 values.

Parameter settings were chosen that generated values of T_l/T_0 between 0 and 20. These were rounded to the nearest integer to combine similar T_l/T_0 values, with each bucket containing 10 values. The average time taken, over 30 rounds, for convention emergence to occur was measured on the generated topologies and the average time over the bucketed values was then calculated. Values which did not result in convention emergence after 20,000 timesteps were discounted from the second average as they were unlikely to result in conventions emerging. Only runs with $T_l/T_0 \lesssim 4$ are affected by this. Simulations with a higher T_l/T_0 exhibited convention emergence for all runs. With $T_l/T_0 \lesssim 4$ as much as 80 % of the runs for a given simulation did not result in convergence. The transition is notable and is discussed below.

It is clear that convention emergence is successful in the dynamic topology, and for most values of T_l/T_0 there is little variation in the average time for convention emergence as shown in Fig. 1. Values of $T_l/T_0 \gtrsim 5$ all have a convention

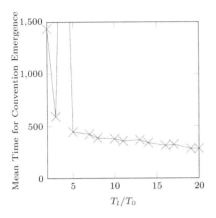

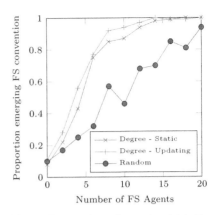

Fig. 1. Average convention emergence time for different values of T_l/T_0 with no fixed strategy agents.

Fig. 2. Proportion of runs in which the fixed strategy emerged as a convention after initial intervention using standard heuristics

emergence time of around $t = 500$ with little variation between runs. However, values of $T_l/T_0 \lesssim 4$ displayed significant variation and, in general, much more time was required for convention emergence to occur if it occurred at all. Higher values of T_l/T_0 did not exhibit this.

At low T_l/T_0 values the topology either did not generate a giant cluster or agents were found to expire before meaningful convention emergence could occur. This follows from the parameter settings required to give a small T_l/T_0 and means that there is a lower threshold for the topology to experience convention emergence. In particular, there is a minimum level of connectedness and lifespan that must be present. Below this threshold the network will be partially disconnected and not representative of real-world topologies. However, once this is achieved the time required for convention emergence is mostly independent of T_l/T_0. As such, we select parameter settings that are used for all following simulations that give $T_l/T_0 = 4.7$ which was found to provide stable convention emergence times. For completeness, additional T_l/T_0 values in the range 20 to 200 were also examined. There was a slight decrease in the average time at higher values, although the low variation remained. As the real-world networks examined by González et al. had T_l/T_0 values around 5–6 these results were purely to determine the impact of high T_l/T_0 values, and have not been included.

4.2 Initial Intervention

Having established that convention emergence occurs in dynamic topologies, we now examine the effect of fixed strategy agents. We start by considering the scenario where fixed strategy agents are introduced early in a system's lifespan to manipulate convention emergence. As discussed in Sect. 3, this initial insertion is delayed until a cluster of size greater than $N/2$ has emerged. This was found empirically to always have occurred by $t = 200$. Fixed strategy agents are inserted after this "burn-in" period has elapsed.

We begin by considering the initial heuristics discussed in Sect. 3: Static Degree and Updating Degree. We also consider random placement of the fixed strategy agents as a baseline. The fixed strategy agents were inserted into the system at $t = 200$ and the simulation allowed to run for 5000 timesteps. Prior simulations showed that conventions always emerged well before this time even without the presence of fixed strategy agents. The number of fixed strategy agents inserted into the system was varied from zero to twenty and the proportion of simulations in which the fixed strategy emerged as the convention was monitored. The results of this setting are shown in Fig. 2.

As expected, given the size of the action space (10), when no fixed strategy agents were inserted, the proportion of times the fixed strategy emerged as the convention is approximately 0.1. With the introduction of only a few fixed strategy agents placed at targeted locations we are able to readily manipulate the emerged convention more than 50 % of the time. The results also show that even randomly placed fixed strategy agents are able make a large difference in convention emergence. This corroborates the findings in previous work on static networks [10,21], although larger numbers of fixed strategy agents are needed comparatively. As the number of inserted agents increases, the difference between the targeted heuristics and random placement becomes more pronounced. The targeted heuristics are able to cause convention emergence in nearly 100 % of cases with only 12 agents whilst random placement requires 20.

Importantly, there is little difference between the two targeted heuristics. Updating Degree slightly outperforms Static Degree although in most cases this is not statistically significant (only 4 and 10 FS agents exhibited differences at a 10 % significance level with most showing a Z-Score less than 1.0). Given this, and the additional complexity and resource requirements for calculating the Updating Degree heuristic, Static Degree is likely sufficient in most cases.

Having established the efficacy of the traditional heuristics, we now examine the effect of considering agent age using our new heuristic, LIFE-DEGREE. We begin by examining Static LIFE-DEGREE, contrasting this to Static Degree. Various weightings of LIFE-DEGREE were considered and the results are presented in Fig. 3. The results of Static Degree have also been included for comparison.

When given equal weighting between expected life and degree ($\omega = 0.5$), LIFE-DEGREE performs markedly worse than Static Degree for nearly all numbers of fixed strategy agents. This is due to the fact that such a weighting is heavily biased to much younger agents. The range of possible ages is larger than that of degree and as such, even when normalised, age was found to be the primary selector. A weighting of 0.7 in favour of degree exhibits the same performance as Static Degree (within a 90 % confidence interval). Further increasing the weighting offers no further improvement in performance, with $\omega = 0.9$ also performing the same as Static Degree. Additional weightings of 0.95 and 0.99 were also considered and similarly offered no improvements.

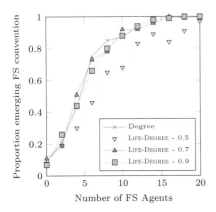
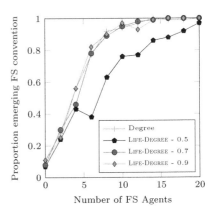

Fig. 3. Proportion of runs in which the fixed strategy emerged as a convention after initial intervention using Static Degree and Life-Degree

Fig. 4. Proportion of runs in which the fixed strategy emerged as a convention after initial intervention using Updating Degree and Life-Degree

These results show that an agent's connectivity, indicated by its degree, is a much larger contributor to its ability to influence others than how long that agent will remain in the system. The fact that considering age can only decrease the effectiveness of the chosen agents indicates that agents' short-term influence is a larger factor in convention emergence than choosing long-term targets.

Life-Degree was also used in an updating manner, such that the set of fixed strategy agents was recalculated each iteration. The results from this and, for comparison, Updating Degree are shown in Fig. 4. Similar to the Static Life-Degree experiments, the performance of Updating Life-Degree depends heavily on the value of ω being used. As before, giving equal weighting to each factor results in poor performance, far below that of pure degree. Increasing the weighting again enhances performance but only to that of Updating Degree. This mirrors the results of Static Life-Degree and shows that, regardless of the ability to continuously assess an agent's remaining lifespan, choosing agents with numerous connections is the most important factor. This indicates that, even in the extreme case where an agent is expected to expire in a few timesteps, on average equal performance can be achieved when selecting them compared to selecting an agent who remains in the system much longer.

Static Life-Degree and Updating Life-Degree, like their pure degree counterparts, have only slight differences in performance, with Updating Life-Degree performing slightly better. At each weight, Updating Life-Degree outperforms Static Life-Degree at a 10 % significance level for several numbers of FS agents. This is most pronounced when $\omega = 0.9$ where Updating Life-Degree performs significantly better between 4–8 FS agents. However, the constant information updates may make Updating Life-Degree untenable in many domains. In domains where this information is readily available, we have

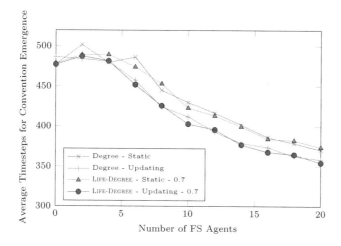

Fig. 5. Effect of fixed strategy agents on convention emergence speed

shown that using up-to-date estimates of degree is sufficient to offer improved outcomes from fixed strategy agent selection.

The results presented above show that it is possible to influence the direction of convention emergence in dynamic topologies. Another commonly used metric of the efficiency of fixed strategy agents is the effect they have on the *speed* of convention emergence [7,10]. Figure 5 shows how time for convention emergence varies for different numbers of fixed strategy agents using the heuristics. As is to be expected, given the asymptotic behaviour exhibited above, consideration of age, depending on weighting, causes either an increase in the average time required or results in similar times to the equivalent pure degree heuristics. Omitted from the graph for clarity, a value of $\omega = 0.5$ requires more time for convention emergence to occur for any number of fixed strategy agents. Values higher than 0.7 perform similarly to 0.7 and hence have also been omitted.

The standard deviation of the convention emergence time also decreases rapidly as the number of fixed strategy agents rises, from up to 100 with zero agents to around 20 with 20 agents. The standard deviation of the results from the Life-Degree simulations are equivalent to those of the pure degree heuristics except for $\omega = 0.5$ which exhibits much larger variance. Thus, consideration of age has a negative effect both in establishing conventions as well as the time it takes to do this. This indicates that, in all aspects, degree is the factor that contributes most to how influential a given agent will be.

4.3   Late Intervention

We now look to the related use of fixed strategy agents in *destabilising* and replacing an already established convention [13,15]. This requires a convention to already have emerged within the system. So that the results are representative of the general case, we allow a convention to naturally emerge without the use

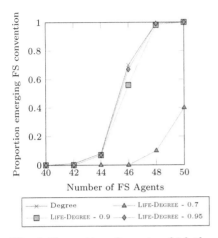
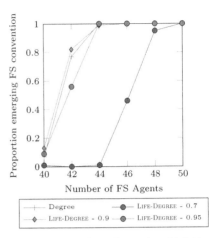

Fig. 6. Proportion of runs in which the fixed strategy emerged as a convention after late intervention using Static Degree and LIFE-DEGREE

Fig. 7. Proportion of runs in which the fixed strategy emerged as a convention after late intervention using Updating Degree and LIFE-DEGREE

of fixed strategy agents to encourage it. It was found that conventions always emerged before timestep $t = 1500$ and, as such, insertion of fixed strategy agents occurs at this time. This also means that the system will have entered the QSS. The action of the fixed strategy is chosen uniformly at random from the actions that exclude the established convention.

In common with the findings of Marchant et al. [13,15] for static networks, our initial experiments showed a much larger number of fixed strategy agents was required to affect the established convention compared to the number needed when inserted into a system earlier. However, a relatively small set of fixed strategy agents are still able to effect a change. In contrast to static networks, the transition between no effect and guaranteed change occurs over a much smaller range of fixed strategy agents. For nearly all heuristics (excluding random) there is little or no effect at 40 fixed strategy agents (4% of the population), whilst 50 fixed strategy agents (5% of the population) results in the targeted convention supplanting the established convention in almost 100% of cases. This narrow window indicates that there is a critical number of fixed strategy agents that is required to guarantee replacement of a convention in dynamic topologies.

Figure 6 shows the proportion of runs in which the convention represented by the fixed strategy became established when using the static heuristics: Static LIFE-DEGREE and Static Degree. In common with initial intervention, consideration of age induces poorer performance here. With $\omega = 0.7$, LIFE-DEGREE is substantially outperformed by Static Degree for any non-trivial proportion, in contrast to the case in initial intervention when such a weighting produced similar performances. Even when increasing the weighting to 0.9, previously equivalent to the performance of pure degree, Static LIFE-DEGREE is still slightly outperformed by Static Degree though this is within the margin of error (only

46 FS agents produce significant differences at a 10 % level). The performance of higher weights asymptotically approached that of Static Degree.

Similar results are presented in Fig. 7 for updating heuristics. The difference between Updating LIFE-DEGREE and Updating Degree in this scenario is even more pronounced. A weighting of 0.7 is again substantially worse than the pure degree heuristic with the higher weightings, 0.9 and 0.95, being of similar quality to Updating Degree.

Of note, the difference in performance between static heuristics and updating heuristics is more pronounced here than in initial interventions; the updating heuristics consistently require significantly fewer fixed strategy agents to effect a change. This indicates that inclusion of up-to-date information of agent state is more important when combating an existing convention and makes a larger contribution compared to establishing a convention from a state of neutral agents.

These findings indicate that destabilisation of an existing convention is even more sensitive to the consideration of agent longevity than initial convention emergence. Indeed, the age or expected lifespan of an agent can be safely ignored with no detrimental effects to the performance of the fixed strategy agents. This strongly implies that the major factor in destabilising conventions is instead choosing agents with high degree, regardless of how long that agent will last. High degree is more effective at spreading influence than choosing a lower degree agent with longer life. The difference between Static and Updating Degree, not present in initial intervention, also supports this view; the importance of choosing the current highest degree agents is far more pronounced.

4.4   Alternative Payoffs

We now turn our attention to the effect the payoff matrix has on intervention effectiveness. In particular, we examine whether the positive and negative rewards the agents receive (and the symmetry or asymmetry of these) changes the relationship or relative performance of the various placement heuristics.

This exploration uses 3 different payoff matrices: *4v-1* (positive reinforcement), *1v-1* (neutral reinforcement) and *1v-4* (negative reinforcement) where the first number represents the payoff for coordinated strategy choice, the second the payoff for conflicting strategy choice. *4v-1* is the payoff structure that has been used in all previous experiments and represents situations where coordination is more beneficial than conflict is harmful, or where coordination is more encouraged. For example, attempting to find a mutual radio channel over which to communicate; whilst there is an expenditure of time for each failure, it is not necessarily very harmful whilst correctly communicating is very beneficial. This structure has been used in previous work [21] and has been shown to allow rapid and thorough convention emergence. *1v-1* can instead represent situations where there is symmetry between the benefit and harm, such as choosing which side of a corridor to walk on; there are both minor inconveniences and minor benefits but neither of a larger scale than the other. Finally, *1v-4* represents situations where conflicting action choices could be very detrimental and should be discouraged rapidly. An example of this is which side of the road to drive on

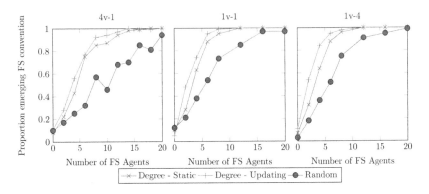

Fig. 8. A comparison of the effect of game payoff on the effectiveness of the standard heuristics in encouraging initial convention emergence.

(although this is often described using a symmetric payoff); the negative effects of a crash are substantial.

As this paper is concerned with the effectiveness of strategies to either direct or replace convention emergence, we primarily concern ourselves with the payoff matrix that best enables conventions to emerge rapidly and thoroughly, so the strategies can be studied. The *4v-1* payoff matrix performs best in this regard. Indeed, the other payoff matrices nearly always fail to reach the Kittock criteria of 90 % for convention emergence, even when the simulation is run for 50000 timesteps. This is related to both the number of strategies available and the payoff matrix. As the number of strategies increases, the average percentage of agents adhering to the primary convention decreases and, with the alternative payoff structures, falls below the 90 % Kittock threshold for our strategy space of 10. Whilst the positive reinforcement system teaches agents which choice is best, the other payoff structures instead teach agents which choices are worst. Due to the asymmetry of this, and the fact that coordination is not as heavily rewarded, the level of coordination is lower.

However, although the 90 % threshold of the Kittock criteria is not met, there is in general still a singular strategy that dominates agent choice and if we reduce the threshold to 80 % we can view this as convention emergence. Lowering the threshold of convention emergence enables us to compare the effectiveness of the strategies under different payoff matrices whilst still considering situations where the system is heavily dominated by a single strategy. All the results in this subsection use the 80 % threshold, with all other parameters kept as defined at the beginning of this section.

Initial Intervention. We begin by considering the payoff matrices as applied to initial intervention. Using the same heuristics and weightings as before the simulations were run with the three different payoff matrices and, using a threshold of 80 %, the proportion of runs in which the fixed strategy emerged above this threshold was compared. Figure 8 shows the comparison when using the

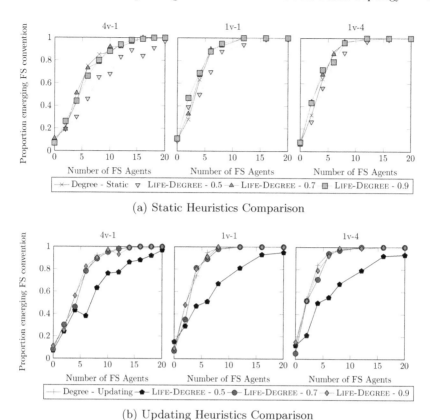

(a) Static Heuristics Comparison

(b) Updating Heuristics Comparison

Fig. 9. A comparison of the effect of game payoff on the effectiveness of the advanced heuristics in encouraging initial convention emergence.

standard heuristics. As this figure shows, the relative performance between the random, static degree and updating degree placement strategies never changes. However, the *absolute* performance of each of the heuristics increases in both *1v-1* and *1v-4* with fewer FS agents needed to enact the same change. This is likely due to it being easier for the system to overcome any partial convention that has started to emerge by the time the FS agents are inserted ($t = 200$) as the reward for perpetuating this emerging convention is lower and, in the case of *1v-4*, the negative payoff for conflicting with the FS agents is higher. Additionally, whilst the other payoff structures may provide easier to manipulate systems, *4v-1* is the only one of those examined that reached the Kittock criteria.

Figure 9 shows the comparison for both static and updating placement heuristics. The findings in Fig. 8 are also present here: the relative performance between the heuristics does not change as the payoff is altered but performance for all heuristics increases. Additionally, the poor performance of the 0.5 weighting of LIFE-DEGREE has a reduced penalty compared to the other weightings.

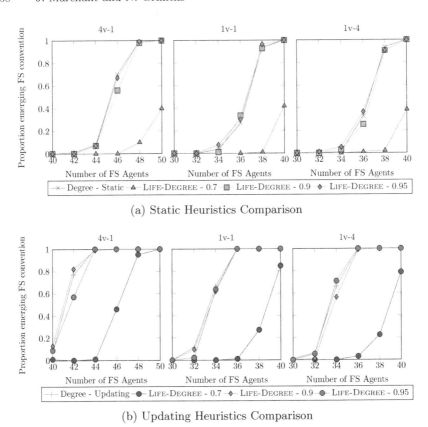

(a) Static Heuristics Comparison

(b) Updating Heuristics Comparison

Fig. 10. A comparison of the effect of game payoff on the effectiveness of the advanced heuristics in encouraging replacement of an already established convention via late intervention. Note the different x-axes between the original payoff structure and the others.

Late Intervention. Having examined the effect of the payoff matrix on initial interventions we now investigate the effect on late interventions and destabilisation. For these experiments the threshold for both destabilisation and considering a new convention to have replaced the old are both 80 %. Figure 10 shows the results for both static and updating heuristics. Of particular note is the difference in x-axis range between *4v-1* and the other payoffs: the former ranges from 40 to 50, the latter from 30 to 40.

Similar to the findings for initial intervention, the relative performances amongst the heuristics are the same across the different payoff matrices. However the absolute performance, in the number of agents needed, is substantially smaller for the latter payoff matrices. This provides additional evidence for the hypothesis discussed above, that it is easier to get agents to switch away from the established convention as the reward for continuing to use it is less compared to switching to the introduced strategy. As with other aspects discussed in this paper the effect is amplified in late interventions compared to similar effects present in initial intervention.

Overall, changing the payoff matrix, either from positive asymmetry to neutral symmetry or negative asymmetry caused no change on the relative effectiveness of the various interventions. Degree placement still performs best in both initial and late interventions and, depending on weighting, can offer large improvements over the consideration of agent age. However, the absolute performance change is interesting and future work will further explore this difference.

5   Discussion and Conclusions

Convention emergence is often used in multi-agent systems to encourage efficient and coordinated action choice. It provides a mechanism through which such behaviour can naturally occur without requiring changes to, or assumptions about, underlying agent capabilities. How best to facilitate robust convention emergence in a timely manner is an area of ongoing research. Fixed strategy agents can be used to speed up and direct emergence. In particular, placing small numbers of fixed strategy agents at targeted locations within the network topology connecting agents has been shown to better facilitate convention emergence than untargeted placement. The heuristics used to choose these locations often make use of metrics derived from an agent's location within the topology.

In this paper, we initially considered uninfluenced convention emergence in a dynamic network, using the topology model proposed by González et al. [8,9]. We showed that conventions emerge in a dynamic environment and that the average time taken for this is largely independent of the parameter settings used in the network model provided the value of T_l/T_0 is above a threshold of approximately 4. Below this, the topology or agent lifespans are not conducive to any convention emergence occurring at all. This indicates that there is a minimum connectedness required in dynamic topologies for conventions to emerge.

We proposed a new placement heuristic, LIFE-DEGREE, that utilises information unique to dynamic topologies in its decision making process, allowing us to test the importance of that information. We contrasted this to the performance of the traditionally used placement heuristics. We examined the scenario where fixed strategy agents are introduced early in the life of the system to direct and encourage faster convention emergence. We showed that, as in static networks, targeted placement offers better performance than untargeted. A small number of agents are able to influence a population much larger than themselves. We established that, in domains where it is possible to change the fixed strategy agents after selection, doing so offers small improvements in performance. In both settings, the most important aspect of selected agents was found to be their degree, ignoring their longevity. This both increased the probability of a specific convention emerging as well as increasing the speed of that emergence.

Additionally, we considered the destabilisation of already established conventions in dynamic networks. We found that destabilisation is more sensitive to the inclusion of agent lifespan than when using fixed strategy agents to establish a convention at the beginning of simulation. Choosing locations that will maximise an agent's influence, regardless of how long they will remain, is the most important aspect to consider when destabilising conventions in dynamic networks. Future work will investigate this further and examine if other features of dynamic networks offer beneficial information when selecting fixed strategy agents. We showed that the updating heuristics cause more destabilisation than the static heuristics and that this effect was much larger than the equivalent difference when encouraging initial convention emergence.

Finally we explored the effect that different payoff schemes had on the effectiveness of the heuristics. We showed that the ordering of performance was not affected by the payoff scheme but that the overall effectiveness of all heuristics is sensitive to the rewards the agents receive.

Overall, we have shown that convention emergence is possible in dynamic topologies and that many characteristics have direct parallels in static networks. We have shown that the degree of an agent is a major factor when choosing them and can be used to cause rapid convention emergence and destabilisation.

References

1. Axelrod, R.: An evolutionary approach to norms. Am. Polit. Sci. Rev. **80**, 1095–1111 (1986)
2. Barabási, A.L., Albert, R.: Emergence of scaling in random networks. Science **286**(5439), 509–512 (1999)
3. Bicchieri, C., Jeffrey, R.C., Skyrms, B.: The Dynamics of Norms. Cambridge Studies in American Literature and Culture. Cambridge University Press, Cambridge (1997)
4. Delgado, J.: Emergence of social conventions in complex networks. Artif. Intell. **141**(1–2), 171–185 (2002)
5. Delgado, J., Pujol, J.M., Sangüesa, R.: Emergence of coordination in scale-free networks. Web Intell. Agent Syst. **1**(2), 131–138 (2003)
6. Franks, H., Griffiths, N., Anand, S.: Learning agent influence in MAS with complex social networks. Auton. Agents Multi-agent Syst. **28**(5), 836–866 (2014)
7. Franks, H., Griffiths, N., Jhumka, A.: Manipulating convention emergence using influencer agents. Auton. Agents Multi-agent Syst. **26**(3), 315–353 (2013)
8. González, M.C., Lind, P.G., Herrmann, H.J.: Networks based on collisions among mobile agents. Physica D **224**(1–2), 137–148 (2006)
9. González, M.C., Lind, P.G., Herrmann, H.J.: System of mobile agents to model social networks. Phy. Rev. Lett. **96**, 088702 (2006)
10. Griffiths, N., Anand, S.S.: The impact of social placement of non-learning agents on convention emergence. In: 11th International Conference on Autonomous Agents and Multiagent Systems, vol. 3, pp. 1367–1368. International Foundation for Autonomous Agents and Multiagent Systems, Richland (2012)
11. Kandori, M.: Social norms and community enforcement. Rev. Econ. Stud. **59**(1), 63–80 (1992)
12. Kittock, J.: Emergent conventions and the structure of multi-agent systems. In: Lectures in Complex Systems: The Proceedings of the 1993 Complex Systems Summer School, pp. 507–521. Addison-Wesley, Reading (1995)
13. Marchant, J., Griffiths, N., Leeke, M.: Destabilising conventions: characterising the cost. In: 8th IEEE International Conference on Self-Adaptive and Self-Organising Systems (2014)

14. Marchant, J., Griffiths, N., Leeke, M.: Convention emergence and influence in dynamic topologies. In: 14th International Conference on Autonomous Agents and Multi-Agent Systems (2015)
15. Marchant, J., Griffiths, N., Leeke, M., Franks, H.: Destabilising conventions using temporary interventions. In: Ghose, A., Oren, N., Telang, P., Thangarajah, J. (eds.) Coordination, Organizations, Institutions, and Norms in Agent Systems X. LNCS, vol. 9372, pp. 148–163. Springer, Heidelberg (2014)
16. Mihaylov, M., Tuyls, K., Nowé, A.: A decentralized approach for convention emergence in multi-agent systems. Auton. Agents Multi-agent Syst. **28**(5), 749–778 (2014)
17. Mukherjee, P., Sen, S., Airiau, S.: Norm emergence with biased agents. Int. J. Agent Technol. Syst. **1**(2), 71–84 (2009)
18. Salazar, N., Rodriguez-Aguilar, J.A., Arcos, J.L.: Robust coordination in large convention spaces. AI Commun. **23**(4), 357–372 (2010)
19. Savarimuthu, B.T.R., Arulanandam, R., Purvis, M.: Aspects of active norm learning and the effect of lying on norm emergence in agent societies. In: Kinny, D., Hsu, J.Y., Governatori, G., Ghose, A.K. (eds.) PRIMA 2011. LNCS, vol. 7047, pp. 36–50. Springer, Heidelberg (2011)
20. Savarimuthu, B.T.R., Cranefield, S., Purvis, M., Purvis, M.: Norm emergence in agent societies formed by dynamically changing networks. In: 2007 IEEE/WIC/ACM International Conference on Intelligent Agent Technology, pp. 464–470 (2007)
21. Sen, S., Airiau, S.: Emergence of norms through social learning. In: 20th International Joint Conference on Artifical Intelligence, pp. 1507–1512. Morgan Kaufmann, San Francisco (2007)
22. Shoham, Y., Tennenholtz, M.: On the emergence of social conventions: modeling, analysis, and simulations. Artif. Intell. **94**(1–2), 139–166 (1997)
23. Villatoro, D., Sabater-Mir, J., Sen, S.: Social instruments for robust convention emergence. In: 22th International Joint Conference on Artificial Intelligence, pp. 420–425. AAAI Press (2011)
24. Villatoro, D., Sen, S., Sabater-Mir, J.: Topology and memory effect on convention emergence. In: 2009 IEEE/WIC/ACM International Joint Conference on Web Intelligence and Intelligent Agent Technology, pp. 233–240. IEEE Computer Society, Washington, DC (2009)
25. Walker, A., Wooldridge, M.: Understanding the emergence of conventions in multi-agent systems. In: International Conference on Multi-agent Systems, pp. 384–389 (1995)
26. Young, H.P.: The economics of convention. J. Econ. Perspect. **10**(2), 105–122 (1996)

Formation of Association Structures Based on Reciprocity and Their Performance in Allocation Problems

Yuki Miyashita, Masashi Hayano, and Toshiharu Sugawara[✉]

Department of Computer Science and Communications Engineering,
Waseda University, Tokyo 1698555, Japan
{y.miyashita,m.hayano}@isl.cs.waseda.ac.jp, sugawara@waseda.jp

Abstract. We describe the reciprocal agents that build virtual associations in accordance with past cooperative work in a bottom-up manner and that allocate tasks or resources preferentially to agents in the same associations in busy large-scale distributed environments. Models of multi-agent systems (MAS) are often used to express tasks that are done by teams of cooperative agents, so how each subtask is allocated to appropriate agents is a central issue. Particularly in busy environments where multiple tasks are requested simultaneously and continuously, simple allocation methods in self-interested agents result in conflicts, meaning that these methods attempt to allocate multiple tasks to one or a few capable agents. Thus, the system's performance degrades. To avoid such conflicts, we introduce reciprocal agents that cooperate with specific agents that have excellent mutual experience of cooperation. They then autonomously build associations in which they try to form teams for new incoming tasks. We introduce the N-agent team formation (TF) game, an abstract expression of allocating problems in MAS by eliminating unnecessary and complicated task and agent specifications, thereby identifying the fundamental mechanism to facilitate and maintain associations. We experimentally show that reciprocal agents can considerably improve performance by reducing the number of conflicts in N-agent TF games with different N values by establishing association structures. We also investigate how learning parameters to decide reciprocity affect association structures and which structure can achieve efficient allocations.

1 Introduction

Many computational tasks are completed by not just a single agent but by teams or groups of cooperative agents. For example, a task in service computing is often dynamically composed of a number of service elements and can be achieved by allocating the elements to appropriate agents. These agents are usually software entities on the Internet created by different developers. We can find such applications not only in computer science-related areas such as ad hoc networks, e-commerce, and sensor networks but also in other areas such as coalition formation for tackling pollution control problems (economics and social science) [22]

© Springer International Publishing Switzerland 2016
V. Dignum et al. (Eds.): COIN 2015, LNAI 9628, pp. 262–281, 2016.
DOI: 10.1007/978-3-319-42691-4_15

and group work in education (e.g., [24,29]). In these applications, the efficient and effective formation of teams for doing tasks is vital for providing qualitative service in a timely manner. However, forming a team in large-scale multi-agent systems (MAS) is costly because agents have to select team members from a large pool of agents. In addition, if tasks are numerous and appear simultaneously in distributed environments, many allocation conflicts occur because multiple self-interested agents attempt to allocate tasks to a single or to a few capable agents simultaneously. This hinders team formation and degrades the entire performance.

Much of literature in the multi-agent systems context has discussed methods for forming coalitions and teams for group-based tasks. For example, a number of studies on coalition formation (e.g., [7,13,23]) have proposed methods to find the combinatorial formation that provides the maximum social utility under the assumption that characteristic functions for all possible groups are given. However, real-world applications often cannot assume characteristic functions in advance. Therefore, a few studies have focused on identifying characteristic functions [18,30]. However, they assume that their environments are static and not busy. Another approach to team formation is market-based methods, such as the conventional contract net protocol and its extensions. However, these also assume that the system is not large or busy; when it does become busy and large, the efficiency for forming teams, i.e., allocating the elements of the given tasks to agents, is severely degraded. More importantly, most of these studies do not take into account the conflicts in allocations in busy environments.

We often form groups for doing tasks in the real world, and if conflicts in group formation occur and if no prior communications for pre-negotiation are possible, we first find reliable and dependable persons with whom to work. Such people are usually identified according to past reciprocity and an agreement for benefit distribution within the groups (e.g., [9]). Furthermore, if the opportunities for group work are frequent, we try to form collaborative relationships with these mutually reliable people. In an extreme case when group work with unreliable people is offered, we can refuse the offers for the sake of finding possible future proposals with reliable people and for punishing the proposing agents because of their past unreliable behavior [9,10]. Although such behavior is irrational because of its self-interest, it can stabilize collaborative relationships and avoid the possibility of conflicts in team formations. Thus, we expect stable benefits in the future through working with reliable and dependable agents. We previously proposed a reciprocal agent that builds associations in accordance with past cooperative work in a bottom-up manner and that allocate tasks or resources preferentially to agents in the same associations [19]. We then experimentally showed that the society of the reciprocal agents could reduce the number of conflicts by associating with dependable agents, thus enabling tasks to be executed efficiently. However, the method in [19] was limited and the experiments were not enough because we assumed that all tasks had a certain identical structure. Thus, in this paper, we have extended the method in [19] for use in more complex environments where different types of tasks are requested.

This paper describes the first attempt to create a computational method for team formations that have fewer conflicts (thereby ensuring stability) and more acceptable benefit distributions among teams. This is done by introducing non-rational behavior—much like that in humans. Initially, agents form teams randomly, so many trials may fail due to conflicts or may result in unacceptable benefit distributions. However, through these trials, the agents mutually memorize the reciprocal and non-reciprocal behaviors by agents encountered in teams and also learn the appropriate behaviors for other reciprocal agents. Then, agents with enough experience in group work will identify which agents are dependable when necessary and virtually build collaboration relationships, called *associations* of agents, in a bottom-up manner. Agents also learn how the benefits should be shared with collaborators in the associations. At the same time, agents that are found to be dependable by certain agents will try to behave as expected. Agents often behave irrationally (like humans) in this learning process because they may decline group work offers from undependable or first-time agents. However, from a long-term viewpoint, these behaviors and learning will help agents build associations consisting of mutually dependable and trusted agents and will enable teams to be formed stably within the associations to which they belong. Such teams within an association may not be the best from the viewpoint of optimality, but if they can complete tasks with the required quality, the effectiveness and reduced conflicts are more important in a large-scale and busy MAS.

This paper is organized as follows. Section 2 discusses related work and Sect. 3 describes the model of agents and the game of team formation by detailing an abstract resource allocation problem in a multi-agent system context. In Sect. 4, we describe several types of agents, including reciprocal agents, and explain how they perform the games by building associations consisting of dependable agents. Section 5 shows how the performance of the game improved by learning payoff distributions and by building associations based on the behavior in games. We also investigate how learning parameters to decide reciprocity affected association structures and which structure could achieve efficient allocations. Section 6 briefly discusses the experimental results. We conclude the paper in Sect. 7.

2   Related Work

Many studies on resource or task allocation have been conducted in multi-agent systems contexts. Resource and task allocation problems are usually formulated by using integer or linear programming techniques (e.g., [25]). These techniques are centralized methods and thus are applicable only when all information is available at a single point. However, this assumption is often impractical in distributed environments. An important approach in such environments is coalitional formation based on cooperative game theory and teamwork [7,23,26,27]. Although this approach has numerous applications, such as disaster control [2], sensor networks [13], and unmanned air vehicles [1], it assumes coalitions for one-shot situations, making it applicable only to static and unbusy environments. Furthermore, it assumes that characteristic functions for coalitions are shared among agents in advance. However, this assumption is often implausible in real-world applications.

Research more related to ours in this respect is coalitional formation in dynamic environments [6,16,18,30]. For example, Chalkiadakis and Boutilier [6] proposed stable coalitional formation within the framework of cooperative game theory using Bayesian reinforcement learning, but this method is not sufficiently scalable. Kluschand and Gerber [18] proposed a dynamic coalition formation mechanism using rational agents, called DCF-A, in which fixed leader agents learn how coalitions should be formed. The leaders are the central points and DCF-A assumes that all agents are constantly available. Ye et al. [30] proposed a dynamic method in environments where agents are connected with a certain network structure. However, we focus on autonomous and bottom-up generation of a stable coalitional (or association) structure formation in busy environments where tasks continuously arrive at the MAS. Jones and Barber [16] proposed a bottom-up method that uses heuristics combining team formation strategies and task selection strategies to adapt to dynamic environments. Faye et al. [8] proposed coalitional formation in environments where the availability of agents is unpredictable, although the focus theme was network applications. Our study is different in that we address how dependable agents are mutually recognized and make associations for stable task executions.

Of course, a lot of research on groups and reciprocity in human societies has been conducted in sociobiology and economics (e.g., [28]), and we wanted to utilize the findings in these research areas. Numerous studies have attempted to explain non-self-interested behavior using reciprocity. The simplified meaning for this is that people do not engage in selfish actions towards and do not betray others who are reciprocal and cooperative, even if such selfish actions could result in higher payoffs for themselves [11,12,21]. Panchanathan and Boyd [21] stated that cooperation can be established from indirect reciprocity, meaning that people work together with certain persons and expect future rewards through cooperating with others [9]. The authors of [11,12] insisted that fairness in cooperation produces non-self-interested behavior; agents do not betray relevant reciprocal agents because such a betrayal would be unfair. One important study related to our work is the results of a repeated ultimatum game [14] done by Fehr and Fischbacher [9] that showed how payoffs shared among collaborators affected the strategies in subsequent games. The same authors also found that punishment towards those who distribute unfair payoffs is frequently observed, although the punishment can be costly [10]; fairness and punishment are key points in continuing cooperation in an ultimatum game.

Group formation and selection are also related work. For example, Bowels et al. [5] argued that people form groups because those belonging to groups have high probabilities to win races occurring in their societies (we believe the notion of *race* in [5] corresponds to *conflict* in our work). Bowles et al. [4] also investigated using agent-based simulations and found that groups and group-adapted behavior that may be individually costly evolved because group institutions can limit the fitness cost of for the behavior.

Bornstein and Yaniv [3] experimentally found that in the ultimatum game, people in a group can receive lower payoffs than in individual-based games but are nonetheless likely to accept the proposals in the group. The situations we address in this paper are quite similar to those of the repeated ultimatum game—more specifically, the dictator game [17], which is a variant of the ultimatum game—but we focus on algorithmic methods to understand how agents can autonomously form groups and how they become likely to accept group proposals; in our context, this means that conflict situations can be avoided by choosing group-based behavior.

We already introduced two models in our previous studies [19,20]. First, we proposed reciprocal agents that build virtual associations though an association invitation protocol with punishment according to past cooperative work in a bottom-up manner [19]. We also proposed a self-organizing mechanism based only on cooperative relationships for task allocation without using association protocols or punishment [20]. We then showed that many agents (but not all) form implicit associations based on the reciprocity while a few agents continued to act as self-interested agents. Interestingly, this mixed structure improved the entire performance. This paper extends the method in [19] for application to more general cases by partly introducing the method proposed in [20].

3   Model and Problem

3.1   Overview of Allocation Problem

Our source of motivation in this paper is a continuous task or resource allocation problem in which a task consisting of a number of subtasks is executed by a number of agents that have sufficient resources to process the allocated subtasks [15]. Briefly, the problem is formulated as follows: Let $A = \{1, \ldots, n\}$ be the set of agents and let agent $i \in A$ have its resources expressed by $R_i = \{r_i^1, \ldots, r_i^p\}$, where r_i^k is a non-negative number and p is the number of types of resources. Task $T = \{s_1, \ldots, s_k\}$ consists of a number of subtasks s_k. Some amounts of various resources are required to execute subtask s, so we identify it as $s = \{u_s^1, \ldots, u_s^p\}$, where u_s^k is a non-negative number expressing and the k-th resource required for s. Agent i can process s when its resources satisfy

$$r_i^k \geq u_s^k \quad (1 \leq \forall k \leq p). \tag{1}$$

T is executed by a team of agents, but any agent can belong to only one team at a time. When the agents in the team satisfy Condition (1) for the given subtasks, the team can successfully execute T.

For a positive integer v_o, called the *task load*, v_o tasks on average are given to the systems every tick, where 'tick' is the time unit in our model. Let $Q = \{T_1, \ldots, T_l\}$ be the set of given tasks. For task $T \in Q$, one agent works as a leader and is an initiator to form the team. The leader selects one agent (or a few) for each subtask in T and then sends it (them) a solicitation message with a subtask to join the team. The agents that receive the messages select one of them and send back an acceptance message. If agents accepting the solicitation message satisfy Condition (1) for all subtasks, the team can execute T with a certain game duration. Then, the leader receives the payoffs for T and distributes them to members with a certain policy. In this process, a number of (capable) agents may receive multiple solicitation messages simultaneously or during execution. Because agents can belong to only one team simultaneously, they have to decline the rest of the solicitations. Thus, team formation may fail. This sort of conflict frequently occurs when the system is busy, so the performance is degraded.

We previously proposed the aforementioned task allocation method based on past successful cooperation in forming teams and achieved efficient team formation [15], on the basis of agent's rational decision. However, the success rate was insufficient for use in actual applications. One major reason for the low success rate was the allocation conflicts. This kind of request for group work is often observed in human society; even so, we attempted to improve the success rate. For example, we typically invite to work with only dependable people we believe will probably accept them if they are inactive. Conversely, when we receive multiple solicitations, we tend to select the solicitation from the most reliable leader, meaning that that leader selects us over others. To stabilize such team formations, we often build a group, called an *association*, whose members consider each other to be dependable. Our purpose is to reduce these conflicts in task allocation by using the associations of computer systems from which leaders select the candidates for team members.

3.2   Abstract Model of Allocation Problem

We referenced the findings in other disciplines in an attempt to identify what information affects the building of virtual associations in a society of agents and how that information should be used. For this purpose, we created an abstract of a model of an allocation problem with team formation in Sect. 3.1 by eliminating unnecessary specifications of tasks and agents and then identified the fundamental mechanisms in building associations in a bottom-up manner.

The abstract version of the allocation problem with team formation is called the *team formation game* (TF game). It is similar to the repeated N-person ultimatum game ($N \geq 2$ is an integer) in that we focus more on how teams should be formed by distributing the received payoffs. More precisely, this is more similar to the N-person dictator game because member agents cannot refuse the payoffs proposed by the leader but can refuse the solicitation to join the TF game next time.

The N-agent Team Formation Game proceeds as follows. Leader $l \in A$ selects $N-1$ agents from $A \setminus \{l\}$ and solicits them to form a team. The solicited agents then select zero or one solicitation (on the basis of their own policy). If no solicited agents accept them, the game is deemed a failure and ends. Otherwise (if all agents accept), the game succeeds, and the formed team is retained for d ticks. After that, l receives the pre-defined payoffs $P > 0$. l picks up some payoffs from P in return for playing the leader and the remaining payoffs are distributed to all other members equally. Then, the game ends. We assume that agents cannot accept and attend multiple games simultaneously. An agent currently engaged in a TF game is called *active*; otherwise, it is called *inactive*. Every tick, v_o inactive agents are randomly selected and initiate the TF games as leaders. This process is then reiterated. We propose a method to increase the success rates of TF games. The number of TF games succeeding during a certain period is called the *game performance*, after this. The number of agents N is called the *game size*. Integer d corresponds to the processing time for the allocated task.

The findings in (socio-)biology and experimental economy discussed in Sect. 2 suggest that although humans are usually motivated by self-interest, fairness is a key feature for group-based activities; that is, people tend to behave fairly within a group. Often, they give punishments for unfair behaviors, though punishments incur some costs to themselves and, in this sense, do not represent rational behavior [9]. Therefore, we attempted to find a control method for agents to build associations. We herein show that these associations can improve game performance by reducing conflicts.

4   Proposed Method: Reciprocal Agents and Associations

4.1   Reciprocal Agents

We introduce a *reciprocal* agent that is concerned with who is dependable, i.e., who is likely to accept forming teams in TF games and to distribute payoffs fairly on the basis of the past reciprocal activities of other agents. Then, the agent tries to build associations of mutually dependable agents. A reciprocal agent is different from a cooperative agent in the sense that a reciprocal agent demonstrates cooperative attitudes to those that were cooperative in the past and may ignore or understate messages from non-reciprocal and unfair agents as punishment.

We introduce three learning parameters in reciprocal agents for N-agent TF games: *greediness*, the *threshold rate for dissatisfaction* (TRD), and *confidence degree*. The definition of confidence degree is described in the next section. The parameter of greediness of i, $0 \leq g_i \leq g_{max}$, determines that when i has worked as the leader of a successful team, i picks up $P \cdot g_i \cdot 1/N$ and so $(P - P \cdot g_i \cdot 1/N) \cdot 1/(N-1)$ is distributed equally to other members. For example, when the rate of $g_i = 1$, rewards are distributed equally to the leader and members. As leader agents want to earn more payoffs, the higher g_i is better. However, other members may become dissatisfied.

Parameter TRD, $0 \leq Trd_i$, denotes the threshold for i's (dis)satisfaction toward leader j with the received payoffs from j and is defined by the relative value of their own greediness parameter. It is calculated by

$$Trd_i = g_i + \beta_i^{Trd}, \tag{2}$$

where β_i^{Trd} is the margin to express dissatisfaction. We assume that the values of β_i^{Trd} represent the fixed character of individual agents. Thus, they are initially defined inherently as constant values. When the parameters of greediness is updated, TRD is updated simultaneously. How the parameters of greediness are learned on the basis of the game results and the received payoffs is described in Sect. 4.4. After i joins a successful team whose leader is j, if j's greediness holds

$$g_j > Trd_i, \tag{3}$$

i expresses dissatisfaction to leader j. Note that i is able to calculate g_j from the received reward.

4.2 Association and Its Formation

Agent i can belong to a number of *associations*, which are the sets of agents including i. Agent i knows L_i, the collection of the associations it belongs to. We also assume that agents know the current state, either active (attending another TF game) or inactive, for those in the same associations. We feel this assumption is reasonable if the number of agents in each association is low; actually, we experimentally show that it is quite low. Initially, i has a singleton association, so $L_i = \{\{i\}\}$. We also define

$$\mathcal{L} = \cup_{i \in A} L_i, \tag{4}$$

which is the collection of all associations. Note that if $L_2 \subset L_1$ for L_1, $L_2 \in \boldsymbol{L}$, L_2 is redundant and so is eliminated from $\boldsymbol{L}_i$. Agents working as a leader first select one of their associations and try to find team member candidates from within it.

Reciprocal agent i has a set of parameters called a *confidence degree* (CD), $\{c_{ij} \mid j \in A \setminus \{i\}, 0 \le c_{ij} \le 1\}$, to extend or reduce the member of associations. Intuitively, the CD denotes how much agent i wants to form teams with $j \in A \setminus \{i\}$ again, and it is learned through j's past behavior to i using

$$c_{ij} = (1 - \alpha_c) \cdot c_{ij} + \alpha_c \cdot \lambda_{ij}, \tag{5}$$

where $0 < \alpha_c \ll 1$ is the learning rate and λ_{ij} is defined in accordance with the process of TF games as follows:

Case 1: If i worked as a leader and j accepted the solicitation from i, then $\lambda_{ij} = 1$, and if it refused the solicitation, $\lambda_{ij} = 0$.

Next, suppose that i worked as a member of a team whose leader is j.

Case 2: If the TF game succeeded and i did not complain about the rewards from j, $\lambda_{ij} = 1$; otherwise, $\lambda_{ij} = 0$.

Case 3: Furthermore, if the game succeeded, i raises the CD values to other members by $\lambda_{ik} = 1$ for any $k(\neq i, j)$ in the team. Conversely, i lowers the CD for agent k by $\lambda_{ik} = 0$ if k refused the solicitation from j because this is a reason for the failure of the TF game. However, for agent k' who accepted the invitation, $c_{ik'}$ remains unchanged.

The association is extended or reduced as follows in accordance with the CD values. Agent i starts the process to invite non-associating agent j when $c_{ij} > F_c$, where F_c is the threshold value for invitation to i's associations after team formation. Such j is called i's *dependable* agent. For $\forall L \in L_i$ s.t. $j \notin L$, if $c_{i'j} > F_c$ for more than half agent $i' \in L$, j is accepted to join L so $L = L \cup \{j\}$. Then, redundant associations are eliminated. Conversely, if $\exists j \in L$ s.t. the number of agents $i \in L$ whose confidence satisfies $c_{ij} < F_{exp}$ is more than half, j is expelled from L. Note that i may have low confidence for agent $j \in L_i$ ($c_{ij} < F_{exp}$) in the shared association if other members in L_i have high CD values for j. Agent j is called an *undependable* agent for i when $c_{ij} < F_{exp}$. Agent i can also withdraw from association $L_i \in L_i$ when the average of the CDs of other members is lower than F_{exp}, i.e.,

$$\sum_{j \in L_i \setminus \{i\}} c_{ij}/(|L_i| - 1) < F_{exp} \tag{6}$$

is held.

4.3   Forming Teams Based on Associations and Confidence Degree

A reciprocal agent plays N-agent TF games using an ε-greedy strategy as follows. Agent i working as a leader first selects one association, L_i, that has the most dependable inactive agents; this is possible because agents know the states of other agents in the common associations. If the number of dependable inactive agents in L_i is greater than or equal to $N - 1$, i selects the $N - 1$ agents from it according to a descending order of the CD values of i. If the number is smaller than $N - 1$, the rest of the members are selected according to i's CD values, so some members may not belong to i's association. However, with probability ε, one of the selected members is replaced by another agent that is selected randomly.

Next, suppose that i is currently not a leader and has received a number of solicitation messages. Agent i first ignores the message from undependable agent j who is deemed based on $c_{ij} < F_{exp}$, even if it has received only such messages. This ignorance may be irrational behavior because accepting one solicitation may produce some payoffs, but we can think of it as a kind of punishment to the sender because the low CD value is the result of past unfair and betrayal behavior. Agent i then selects one of the messages in accordance with the CD values for senders with probability $1 - \varepsilon$; otherwise i selects one randomly.

4.4   Response and Payoff Distribution Strategies in Reciprocal Agents

The CD values are updated using the new value of λ_{ij} in Sect. 4.2 after the TF game with the team members. These values are determined in accordance with (not only the CD values of other agents but also) the responses to the specifications and the rates of the received payoffs. These responses and payoffs are decided in accordance with the parameters of greediness and TRD. We already mentioned update function for Trd_i as Formula (2). The greediness parameter g_i in agent i also learns to find the appropriate values by using the update function

$$g_i = (1 - \alpha_g) \cdot g_i + \alpha_g \cdot \delta_g, \tag{7}$$

where α_g is the learning rate. We will describe when reciprocal agents update them and how δ_g is decided.

The basic concept behind reciprocal agents for greediness is that when the game succeeds, they want to obtain larger rewards only if no members of the TF game complain. However, when the game fails (at least one agent declined the solicitation), or when one member of the TF game complains, the leader's greediness should decrease. The details are as follows. If leader i succeeds in the TF game with the members of M_i and no agents in M_i complain, i updates g_i with $\delta_g = g_{max}$ using Formula (7). If one member of the TF game complains or the game failed, i decreases g_i with $\delta_g = 0$.

4.5   Comparative Agents

We introduce two types of agents, a self-interested agent and an *associating self-interested* (AS) agent, for comparison in the following experiments because self-interestedness is a basic concept not only in multi-agent systems literature but also in economics and computational biology. Self-interested agents in this article behave so that they get more payoffs based on past game interactions and do not intend to build new associations. AS agents try to build associations by estimating which ones are more beneficial in accordance with past interactions, in addition to behaving to get more payoffs, the same as self-interested agents.

We introduce two learning parameters for self-interested agent i. The *expected value of distributed payoffs* (EDP) e_{ij} for ($\forall j \in A \setminus \{i\}$) is the statistical value for how many payoffs can be expected when i accepts the solicitation from j. It is updated by

$$e_{ij} = (1 - \alpha_e) \cdot e_{ij} + \alpha_e \cdot v_j \qquad (8)$$

after accepting the solicitation from j, where v_j is the received payoff from j and $0 < \alpha_e < 1$ is the learning rate. Note that $v_j = 0$ if the TF game failed. The parameter *expected acceptance rate* (EAR), h_{ij}, expresses the degree of acceptance of the solicitation by j; after leader i sends the solicitation message to j, h_{ij} is updated by

$$h_{ij} = (1 - \alpha_h) \cdot h_{ij} + \alpha_h \cdot \delta, \qquad (9)$$

where $\delta = 1$ if j accepted the solicitation and $\delta = 0$ otherwise. Parameter EDP is used when self-interested agents select one solicitation to pursue more payoffs. Parameter EAR is used to select more probable agents as members of TF games.

Self-interested agent i as a leader selects members in accordance with the descending order of EAR, h_{ij} ($j \in A$). When i plays a member, it selects one solicitation message based on the EDP values. In both situations, i selects a member agent and a solicitation message randomly with probability ε. Self-interested agents also have parameter greediness. As for greediness, these agents use the same formula (Formula (7)).

AS agents additionally have CD values and try to build associations similar to reciprocal agents. The leader AS agents select the members from their associations, but the member AS agents select the solicitation messages according to the EDP instead of the CD values. Furthermore, because they are interested in which agent will directly provide more payoffs and which have no dissatisfaction related to unfair payoff distributions, the CD values are updated only in Cases 1 and 2 in Sect. 4.2. We also define random agents to compare with their agents. Random agents always select members and solicitation messages randomly.

5 Experiments

5.1 Experimental Set-Up

We investigated how the game performance, which is the success rate of TF games, improved over time in the society of reciprocal agents and compared the results with those in the society of self-interested, AS, or random agents. We also compared the number of generated associations, their structures, and how learning parameters converged. The number of agents was 300 ($|A| = 300$). Twenty N-person TF games with game durations d of 3 were initiated with 20 inactive agents selected randomly every tick ($v_o = 20$). We set the game size, N, between three and seven randomly and set the game rewards as $P = N$ because agents can divide rewards equally between leader and members. The upper bound of greediness, g_{max}, was set to three, since this was the actual limit when $N = 3$. The initial values of greediness were randomly selected between 0.5 and 3. The value of β_i^{Trd} for agent $\forall i$ was randomly selected between 0.0 and 0.1 when i was created and it was fixed during each experimental trial. The initial values of CD, EDP, and EAR were set to 0.5, 1.0, and 0.5, respectively. The threshold values were defined as $F_c = 0.7$ and $F_{exp} = 0.2$. All learning rates, α_c, α_e, α_h, and α_g, were set to 0.05 and $\varepsilon = 0.01$. The data indicated below are average values from 20 independent trials.

5.2 Experimental Results: Game Performance and Association Structure

The number of successful TF games per 10 ticks is plotted in Fig. 1. This figure indicates that reciprocal agents could perform TF games much more effectively than other agents. We can also see that the performance of self-interested agents was relatively low: the self-interested agents pursue their own benefits, so conflicts are likely to occur in busy environments because they learned similar results and therefore, selected a few agents simultaneously. The game performances of AS agents slowly improved, but reciprocal agents have higher game performances than AS agents through all the ticks. This suggests that associations could contribute to the game performance in AS agents but that their learning is ineffective and slow. Because they also selected leaders who would distribute more rewards regardless of past interaction, they have few opportunities to cultivate dependability relationships; hence, AS agents could not build associations within a reasonable time.

Figure 2 plots the number of associations in the agent societies of reciprocal and AS agents. Initially, the number of associations was 300 because all agents

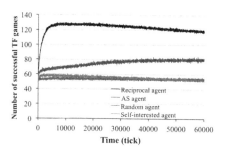

Fig. 1. Performance improvement over time.

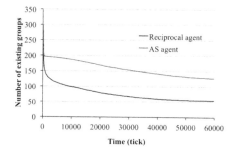

Fig. 2. Number of existing associations.

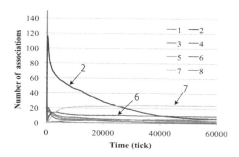

Fig. 3. Sizes of associations of reciprocal agents.

belong to their own singleton association. As each agent repeats team formation games, it can find dependable agents and invite them to it's associations. Then, agents gradually combined and formed larger associations. Thus, Fig. 2 indicates that the number of associations of reciprocal agents gradually decreased and eventually was approximately 50. However, the number of associations of AS agents was much higher. We could also observe that after 10,000 ticks, performances of reciprocal agents decreased gradually from 125 to 120 as the ticks went on.

5.3 Structural Analysis

To understand what happened in these situations, we plotted the number of associations structures of reciprocal agents in Fig. 3. As shown, seven-size associations, i.e., associations whose members were seven, gradually increased. Conversely, two-size associations rapidly decreased. We illustrate example agent associations at 1,000 ticks, 10,000 ticks, 40,000 ticks and 60,000 ticks in Fig. 4(a), (b), (c) and (d), respectively. Note that these figures were created on the basis of a certain experimental trial. The nodes in these figures express associations and the edges between associations indicate they have the shared agents. Thus, the shared agents belonged to multiple associations.

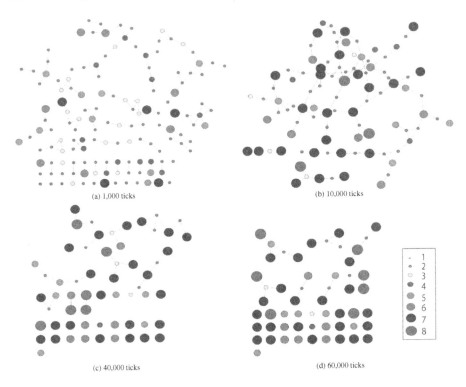

(a) 1,000 ticks

(b) 10,000 ticks

(c) 40,000 ticks

(d) 60,000 ticks

Fig. 4. Sizes of associations of reciprocal agents.

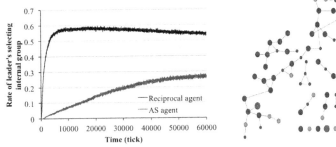

Fig. 5. Rate of selecting team members from the same associations.

Fig. 6. Structure of AS agent associations at 60,000 ticks.

Figure 4(a) and (b) indicates that many two-size associations existed and were connected with edges (shared agents). In particular, Fig. 4(b) shows that agents who belong to six- or seven-size associations also belong to other associations whose sizes were two. Then the associations were gradually combined and became large, thus reducing the number of two-size associations. Finally, almost none of the associations had edges with other associations.

We believe this is also the reason the number of successful TF games gradually decreased. In agent associations like the ones in Fig. 4(c) and (d), their members were almost completely fixed and if multiple tasks were assigned to an association, one of them was likely to fail. Of course, leaders sent solicitations to agents outside their associations, but they usually belonged to other associations and/or were already active in busy environments. We plot the number of agents that leaders selected from their local associations in Fig. 5. These curves are quite similar to those in Fig. 1 and suggest that they gradually tended to solicit agents in other associations.

Figure 6 indicates the example structure of the association of AS agents in a certain experimental trial. This figure shows that their associations also had many edges but their sizes of association were relatively small: mostly four or less. Therefore, they sent more solicitations to other agents.

These experimental results reveal an important finding: the combination of large associations and quite small associations improves the overall performance. Furthermore, reciprocal agents can take advantage of such structures of associations. Thus, we want to maintain the structures appearing around 10,000 ticks, but the current behavior of reciprocal agents is to form independent associations. We discuss this issue in Sect. 5.5.

5.4 Payoff Distribution

Figure 7 shows the average values of greediness that determine the amount of payoff distribution and the minimum acceptable payoff without declaring dissatisfaction. Note that greediness is defined for all types of agents except random agents. We can see from Fig. 7 that the greediness value at 60,000 ticks for AS agents was 1.2 and that for self-interested and reciprocal agents was 0.8. A fair distribution is when $g_i = 1.0$, so the rewards for themselves in reciprocal agents seemed slightly small. Because they formed associations, we can say that their payoff distribution is fair in the sense that they have similar greediness values. Although the average greediness in AS agents was slightly higher than 1.0, that in self-interested agents converged to relatively small values. We assume that their greediness values were tied to the poor game performance.

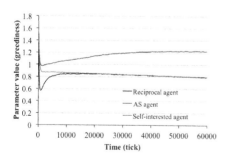

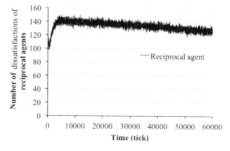

Fig. 7. Transition of average greediness value.

Fig. 8. Number of expressed dissatisfactions.

The greediness in reciprocal agents also converged to a small value (0.8), but the reason for this seems different from that in self-interested agents. To understand this phenomenon, we plot the number of agents expressing dissatisfaction in Fig. 8. This figure indicates that dissatisfaction continued to be expressed over time, and the slightly smaller value of greediness is the result of payoff distribution without dissatisfaction.

We conclude that a message of dissatisfaction to leaders is very important to maintain stable associations. From Fig. 8, the number of dissatisfactions decreased gradually after 5,000 ticks. Agents tended to belong to multiple associations at the beginning of the experiment and then gradually tended to belong to only one after that. Thus, we can see that dissatisfaction could make the greediness values stable by avoiding leaders that increased them locally.

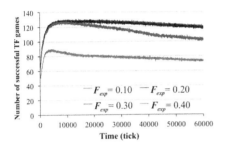 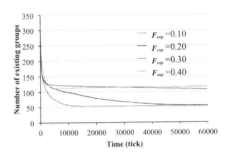

Fig. 9. Game performance with different F_{exp}.

Fig. 10. Number of associations F_{exp}.

5.5   Influence of threshold of dependability F_{exp}

The experimental results in Sect. 5.3 suggest that the edges between associations and the existence of small-size associations seemed to affect the overall performance. To understand this effect more clearly, we performed additional experiments with F_{exp} values between 0.0 and 0.4. Note that we have omitted the results for $F_{exp} = 0$ since they are the same as those for $F_{exp} = 0.1$. The number of successful TF games is plotted in Fig. 9. It indicates that reciprocal agents who have $F_{exp} = 0.4$ could perform TF games much less successfully than other reciprocal agents with other values. When $F_{exp} = 0.3$, agents could perform TF games as well as in other cases up to 10,000 ticks, but after that, the performance decreased. We cannot observe any difference between the curves of $F_{exp} = 0.2$ and 0.1. These curves also slightly decreased, as shown in Fig. 1.

Figure 10 plots the numbers of associations. It shows that the numbers of associations converged to around 50 when $F_{exp} = 0.2$ and 0.3, although their convergence speeds were different. Furthermore, the performance for $F_{exp} = 0.3$ was significantly worse than that for $F_{exp} = 0.2$ (Fig. 9). On the other hand, the numbers of associations when $F_{exp} = 0.1$ and 0.4 converged to similar values (around 120), but their performances also differed considerably as shown in Fig. 9. We would

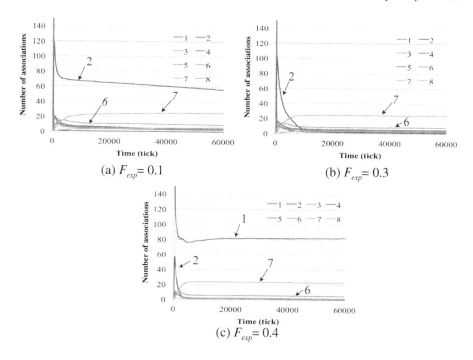

Fig. 11. Number of associations.

like to understand the reasons for these differences by referring to their association structures.

Figure 11(a), (b) and (c) plots the number of associations by breaking them down by size when $F_{exp} = 0.1$, 0.3, and 0.4, respectively. We also illustrate the structures of associations at 60,000 ticks in Fig. 12(a), (b) and (c). The graphs for $F_{exp} = 0.2$ are already shown in Figs. 3 and 4(d). By comparing Fig. 3 and 11(a), (b) and (c), we can see that when $F_{exp} = 0.1$, the number of two-size associations slowly decreased, but were still the largest in number at 60,000 ticks. In contract, two-size associations quickly decreased in other cases. Another observation is that when $F_{exp} = 0.4$, the number of single (one-size) associations was the largest but single associations almost disappeared in other cases. Meanwhile, the numbers of seven-size associations were the second-largest when $F_{exp} = 0.1$ and 0.4 and were the largest in other cases.

These observations can also be recognized from their association structures. When $F_{exp} = 0.1$, we can see the characteristics of the association structure: each large (mostly seven-size) association was connected with a number of small (mostly two-size) associations and were connected alternatively. This structure was also similar to that for $F_{exp} = 0.2$ at 10,000 ticks. This is why their game performance was quite good when $F_{exp} = 0.1$. Agents usually worked with members in the same associations. However, if some of them were already active (this may occur when some members are active for a small-size TF game), they could not join a team for

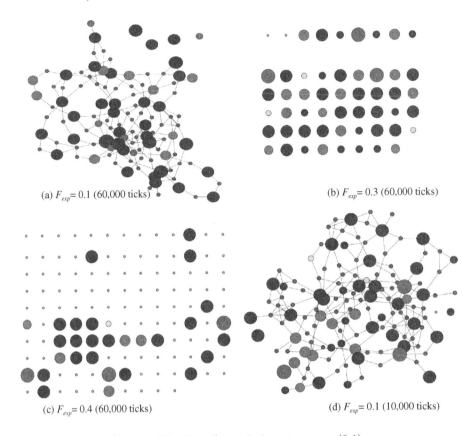

(a) F_{exp}= 0.1 (60,000 ticks)

(b) F_{exp}= 0.3 (60,000 ticks)

(c) F_{exp}= 0.4 (60,000 ticks)

(d) F_{exp}= 0.1 (10,000 ticks)

Fig. 12. Number of association structures (0.1).

a new game. Thus, leader agents solicited agents in the connected two-size associations to fill up the deficiency. Two-size associations worked as backup.

The game performance was also quite good when $F_{exp} = 0.2$ (Fig. 9), but their structure was slightly different. Figure 4(d) indicates that some large associations have edges with the two-, three- and four-size associations, but most large associations are isolated, and some of them consist of eight agents. They coped with the lack of members by enlarging associations.

We can find that, like the case of $F_{exp} = 0.2$, the game performance when $F_{exp} = 0.1$ slightly decreased over time (as shown in Fig. 9) and also seemed caused by the disappearance of edges between large and small associations when $F_{exp} = 0.1$. Actually, the number of edges at 60,000 (which was 150.2) was smaller than that at 10,000 ticks (which was 171.8; see also Fig. 12)(d), but its decreasing speed was slower than that when $F_{exp} = 0.2$.

When $F_{exp} = 0.3$, all associations were relatively large and isolated, but this association structure was ineffective; for example, when small tasks are allocated to the larger associations, many other members remain inactive. Furthermore, when $F_{exp} = 0.4$, we can observe many single associations (this also means that they cannot form associations due to the strict condition) due to frequent punishment by other agents. Note that single associations also appeared in associations of AS agents (Fig. 6).

6   Discussion

We previously conducted research to allocate subtasks to appropriate agents in a busy and large-scale distributed environment and found that allocation conflicts were a major cause of reduced overall efficiency [15]. We also found that building associations within the tasks to be done is an efficient and effective solution to this problem [15]. Teams within an association may not be the best from the viewpoint of the optimality, but if they can complete tasks with the required quality, an association-based team formation is acceptable, probably efficient, and practical in a large-scale system. We previously proposed reciprocal agents and learning for organizing associations for N-agent TF games [19], but the learning assumed that N was a constant. Thus, we have extended it here for organizing associations in TF games with a variable number of agents.

One objective of this study was to clarify the basic mechanism to build associations in a bottom-up manner and to investigate what structure of associations achieves efficient assignment of tasks by using an abstract and simplified model called a TF game. Our experiments show that one-size associations obviously worsened the game performance, while two-size associations that were connected with larger associations improved the performance. Unfortunately, the current method could not make the association structures stable: edges between associations were gradually eliminated, and the average size of associations gradually became larger to cover the deficiency of agents.

We also investigated the relationship between the values of dependability, F_{exp}, and the association structures and found that suitable structures of agent associations improved game performance. The value of F_{exp} affected the association structures as well as the speed of forming the structures. Control and learning to stably maintain suitable structures of agent associations will be the focus of our future work.

Our experiments revealed that two key pieces of information are needed to facilitate building associations from the viewpoint of individual agents. First, the agent should memorize who it worked with and share the information with other team members because the success of a TF game depends on all members in the team. Conversely, the failure of a game is caused by an unacceptance of at least one agent, for one of two reasons: the leader's selection was not appropriate and/or one or more of the members was betrayed. These correspond to the learning of CD values in Case 3 (Sect. 4.2). This is quite different from the behavior of self-interested and rational agents that act on the basis of which agents are likely to provide more payoffs directly.

Second, punishments and dissatisfaction contributed to building associations. The punishments, which represented refusals of the solicitation messages from agents whose confidence degree was low or expulsion of low-confidence agents from associations in our context, affected the speed of building associations; actually, it could make the convergence faster, but it slightly reduced actual game performance. Dissatisfaction, which can be seen as advance notice of punishment, was necessary to make established associations stable, as mentioned previously.

7   Conclusion

We described reciprocal agents that build associations for team-based tasks to avoid possible conflicts in a large-scale, busy MAS. Our objective was to perform task allocation problems efficiently. Thus, we first introduced an abstract form of this problem, called the team formation game, to identify what information and mechanisms can facilitate building associations. We experimentally showed that team formation based on the associations the reciprocal agents belong to helped the agents perform the games more efficiently than other types of agents, namely, self-interested agents and associating self-interested agents. We attempted to identify what information and mechanisms can facilitate building associations and which virtual association structure improves game performances. Our future work is to find a method to stabilize association structures.

References

1. Bardhan, R., Ghose, D.: Resource allocation and coalition formation for UAVs: a cooperative game approach. In: Proceedings of the 2013 IEEE International Conference on Control Applications, pp. 1200–1205 (2013)
2. Boloni, L., Khan, M., Turgut, D.: Agent-based coalition formation in disaster response applications. In: IEEE Workshop on Distributed Intelligent Systems: Collective Intelligence and Its Applications, pp. 259–264 (2006)
3. Bornstein, G., Yaniv, I.: Individual and group behavior in the ultimatum game: are groups more "rational" players? Exp. Econ. 1(1), 101–108 (1998)
4. Bowles, S., Choi, J.K., Hopfensitz, A.: The co-evolution of individual behaviors and social institutions. J. Theor. Biol. 223(2), 135–147 (2003)
5. Bowles, S., Fehr, E., Gintis, H.: Strong procity may evolve with or without group selection. Theor. Primatol. Proj. Newsl. 1(12), 1–25 (2003)
6. Chalkiadakis, G., Boutilier, C.: Sequentially optimal repeated coalition formation under uncertainty. Auton. Agent. Multi-Agent Syst. 24(3), 441–484 (2012)
7. Dunin-Keplicz, B.M., Verbrugge, R.: Teamwork in Multi-Agent Systems: A Formal Approach, 1st edn. Wiley Publishing, Hoboken (2010)
8. Faye, P., Aknine, S., Sene, M., Sheory, O.: Stabilizing agent's interactions in dynamic contexts. In: Proceedings of the IEEE 28th International Conference on Advanced Information Networking and Applications, AINA 2014, pp. 925–932 (2014)
9. Fehr, E., Fischbacher, U.: Why social preferences matter - the impact of non-selfish motives on competition. Econ. J. 112(478), C1–C33 (2002)
10. Fehr, E., Fischbacher, U.: Third-party punishment and social norms. Evol. Hum. Behav. 25(2), 63–87 (2004)
11. Fehr, E., Fischbacher, U., Gächter, S.: Strong reciprocity, human cooperation, and the enforcement of social norms. Hum. Nat. 13(1), 1–25 (2002)

12. Gintis, H.: Strong reciprocity and human sociality. J. Theor. Biol. **206**(2), 169–179 (2000)
13. Glinton, R., Scerri, P., Sycara, K.: Agent-based sensor coalition formation. In: 2008 11th International Conference on Information Fusion, pp. 1–7 (2008)
14. Güth, W., Schmittberger, R., Schwarze, B.: An experimental analysis of ultimatum bargaining. J. Econ. Behav. Organ. **3**(4), 367–388 (1982)
15. Hayano, M., Hamada, D., Sugawara, T.: Role and member selection in team formation using resource estimation for large-scale multi-agent systems. Neurocomput. **146**, 164–172 (2014)
16. Jones, C.L.D., Barber, K.S.: Combining job and team selection heuristics. In: Hübner, J.F., Matson, E., Boissier, O., Dignum, V. (eds.) COIN@AAMAS 2008. LNCS, vol. 5428, pp. 33–47. Springer, Heidelberg (2009)
17. Kahneman, D., Knetsch, J.L., Thaler, R.H.: Fairness and the assumptions of economics. J. Bus. **59**(4), S285–300 (1986)
18. Klusch, M., Gerber, A.: Dynamic coalition formation among rational agents. Intell. Syst. IEEE **17**(3), 42–47 (2002)
19. Miyashita, Y., Hayano, M., Sugawara, T.: Association formation based on reciprocity for conflict avoidance in allocation problems. In: Proceedings of the 19th International Workshop on Coordination, Organizations, Institutions, and Norms in Multiagent Systems (COIN@AAMAS), pp. 143–157 (2015)
20. Miyashita, Y., Hayano, M., Sugawara, T.: Self-organizational reciprocal agents for conflict avoidance in allocation problems. In: 2015 IEEE 9th International Conference on Self-Adaptive and Self-Organizing Systems (SASO), pp. 150–155 (2015)
21. Panchanathan, K., Boyd, R.: Indirect reciprocity can stabilize cooperation without the second-order free rider problem. Nature **432**(7016), 499–502 (2004)
22. Ray, D.: A Game-Theoretic Perspective on Coalition Formation. The Lipsey lectures. Oxford University Press, Oxford (2007)
23. Sheholy, O., Kraus, S.: Methods for task allocation via agent coalition formation. J. Artif. Intell. **101**, 165–200 (1998)
24. Shiba, Y., Sugawara, T.: Fair assessment of group work by mutual evaluation based on trust network. In: Proceedings of 2014 IEEE Frontiers in Education Conference, IEEE FIE 2014, pp. 821–827 (2014)
25. Shoham, Y., Leyton-Brown, K.: Multiagent Systems: Algorithmic, Game-Theoretic, and Logical Foundations. Cambridge University Press, Cambridge (2008)
26. Sims, M., Goldman, C.V., Lesser, V.: Self-organization through bottom-up coalition formation. In: Proceedings of the Second International Joint Conference on Autonomous Agents and Multiagent Systems, pp. 867–874. ACM (2003)
27. Sless, L., Hazon, N., Kraus, S., Wooldridge, M.: Forming coalitions and facilitating relationships for completing tasks in social networks. In: Proceedings of the 2014 International Conference on Autonomous Agents and Multi-Agent Systems, AAMAS 2014, pp. 261–268. International Foundation for Autonomous Agents and Multiagent Systems, Richland, SC (2014)
28. Smith, J.M.: Group selection. Q. Rev. Biol. **51**(2), 277–283 (1976)
29. Wessner, M., Pfister, H.R.: Group formation in computer-supported collaborative learning. In: Proceedings of the 2001 International ACM SIGGROUP Conference on Supporting Group Work, GROUP 2001, pp. 24–31. ACM, New York (2001)
30. Ye, D., Zhang, M., Sutanto, D.: Self-adaptation-based dynamic coalition formation in a distributed agent network: a mechanism and a brief survey. IEEE Trans. Parallel Distrib. Syst. **24**(5), 1042–1051 (2013)

Towards Team Formation
via Automated Planning

Christian Muise[1]($\boxtimes$), Frank Dignum[2], Paolo Felli[1], Tim Miller[1],
Adrian R. Pearce[1], and Liz Sonenberg[1]

[1] Department of Computing and Information Systems,
University of Melbourne, Melbourne, Australia
cjmuise@mit.edu, paolo.felli@nottingham.ac.uk,
{tmiller,adrianrp,l.sonenberg}@unimelb.edu.au
[2] Department of Information and Computing Sciences,
Universiteit Utrecht, Utrecht, The Netherlands
f.p.m.dignum@uu.nl

Abstract. Cooperative problem solving involves four key phases:
(1) finding potential members to form a team, (2) forming the team,
(3) formulating a plan for the team, and (4) executing the plan. We
extend recent work on multi-agent epistemic planning and apply it to
the problem of team formation in a blocksworld scenario. We provide an
encoding of the first three phases of team formation from the perspective
of an initiator, and show how automated planning efficiently yields conditional plans that guarantee certain collective intentions will be achieved.
The expressiveness of the epistemic planning formalism, which supports
modelling with the nested beliefs of agents, opens the prospect of broad
applicability to the operationalisation of collective intention.

1 Introduction

It is both a challenging and important problem to form a cohesive team that
can achieve a task. Wooldridge et al. [30] propose four key phases to cooperative
problem solving: (1) *potential recognition* where the team "initiator" must identify the capabilities of the agents; (2) *team formation* where the potential team
members are persuaded to join for the collective intention; (3) *plan formation*
where a plan is constructed; and (4) *plan action* where the joint plan is executed.
Dignum et al. [6] propose a framework for these four stages that relies on structured dialogue between the initiator and the agents in the domain. In this work
we introduce a novel approach for building principled and scalable mechanisms
for team formation that exploits recent advances in multi-agent epistemic planning, and we illustrate the approach by working with a model of team formation
inspired by the Dignum et al. framework (referred to as DDV in the remainder
of the paper).

We focus on the *initiator* role in team formation, which involves assessing the
potential for team formation and persuading possible members to join. While
all four phases of team formation are important, currently we address the first

© Springer International Publishing Switzerland 2016
V. Dignum et al. (Eds.): COIN 2015, LNAI 9628, pp. 282–299, 2016.
DOI: 10.1007/978-3-319-42691-4_16

three phases only: i.e., the phases that involve the initiator's deliberation prior to the execution of a plan. We take the view that the initiator will deliberate about what questions to ask, what promises to make, the composition of the team, and the potential of achieving the overall objective as a team, *all prior to the execution of any action or dialogue.* While the initiator is not strictly required to form a plan before the actual dialogue occurs, doing so can save the initiator from asking irrelevant questions and performing actions that ultimately will never lead to a solution. This is vital particularly when part of the dialogue may involve making promises to the agents that make up a team as part of the persuasion. Thus, the initiator not only plans for the required dialogue, but also for the eventual plans contingent on the possible dialogue outcomes.

The four phases of teamwork formation are general concepts. Here, we consider a specific realization of the four phases where the initiator can: (1) ask agents about their "capabilities" (e.g., can agent 4 lift blue blocks?); (2) ask and convince agents about their "intentions" to assist in a task given a particular promise (e.g., will agent 3 lift red blocks if we promise to put block 4 in room 2?); and (3) orchestrate the actions of the agents that agree to assist. The reasoning task for the initiator is to come up with a conditional plan (conditioned on the responses of the agents) such that a cohesive team can be formed to achieve the overall objective. This cannot always be guaranteed (e.g., if every agent refuses to help), but the initiator's deliberation process should at least discover the ways in which a successful team can be formed.

We model the problem from the perspective of the team initiator using an extension of the recently introduced multi-agent epistemic planning (MEP) formalism [20], which uses syntactic belief bases restricted to non-disjunctive clauses to represent nested agent beliefs [18]. MEP extends classical planning by allowing the nested belief of agents in a multi-agent environment as action preconditions and effects, and nested beliefs as goals that can be posed. Using MEP allows us to model the critical notion of an agent's belief that their own objectives have been satisfied. We extend MEP by allowing for non-deterministic action outcomes – providing a natural way to express yes/no questions for dialogue – and by using a generic fragment for the action theory that allows for team formation to take place. All of the existing MEP domain descriptions, which describe the actions that agents can take in the domain and the effect that they have on the belief of agents, can easily be plugged into the augmented system.

The realization of our approach using automated planning is both powerful and flexible. Unlike other approaches, such as BDI [25] or hierarchical plan representations [10], the plans for the agents need not be specified in advance. Rather, we can use the powerful automated planning techniques that have been developed over the recent decades to synthesize the viable plans for us [11]. This approach shifts our focus from one of creating a new solving technique to one of creating a novel encoding for existing solvers. We choose one solver in particular, but in general any viable planner can be used as a blackbox component to solve the encoded problem. As such, we do not go into detail on how the plans are generated, but rather focus on how we encode the problem of teamwork formation.

For our running example, we adapt the Blocks World for Teams (BW4T) domain [13] to include agents with varied capabilities and tasks that can require multiple agents, a natural extension given our focus on modelling team formation. In BW4T, agents carry different-coloured blocks around various rooms. In our adaptation, agents have capabilities to carry only certain colours (e.g., blocks with the blue colour can only be lifted by "blue lifters"), blocks may take on multiple colours, and agents may have multiple colour capabilities.

In the next section we provide the necessary background and notation for our approach. Following this, we describe how we have modelled the problem of teamwork formation in Sect. 3 and encoded it for automated planning in Sect. 4. We then discuss a preliminary evaluation using the BW4T domain in Sect. 5 and conclude with a discussion of related and future work in Sect. 6.

2   Background

2.1   Team Formation

Team formation based on various approaches to 'matching' potential participant skills with the requirements of a task have long been studied. Some approaches involve heuristics guided by logical analysis, e.g. [15,29], others involve formal mechanisms based on multimodal logics, e.g. [7,8], and others draw on game theoretic and optimisation techniques, e.g. [1,2,5,17,23,26]. Varying assumptions are made in the team formation stage about the knowledge that agents have about others, from complete, e.g. [29], to very limited, e.g. [3].

Although all this work is about team formation different approaches tend to focus on different parts of the issue of forming a team to accomplish a task. In the optimisation work the focus is generally on finding the best team given that it is clear which plan (or set of tasks) is to be executed [5,23]. Thus the question is how to allocate tasks to agents in an optimal way. In work related to coalition formation, e.g. [24,27], the emphasis is typically on the negotiation process between the agents in order to join and stay within a team. This can be done using game theoretic notions, in which division of possible rewards over a group play an important role. It can also be done using argumentation in which the emphasis shifts to the reasons for joining a team and persuading potential team members about the justification or importance of the team goal and or a particular plan to reach the goal, e.g. [2]. In the logic based approaches the emphasis is on the exchange of information about goals, intentions and beliefs such that the logical pre-conditions for working as a team according to the SharedPlans framework [9] are fulfilled.

In DDV the emphasis is on what is needed for a set of agents to start working as a team to achieve a joint goal. It involves at least that all the agents agree upon their role in the plan to achieve that goal (or in other words the tasks that they are willing to perform within the plan) and that they have enough information to execute their task at the right moment in time. As mentioned, we consider team formation from the perspective of the *initiator*. The first task of the initiator is to form a partial (abstract) plan for the achievement of the (team) goal. On the basis of the (type of) subgoals that it recognizes, it will determine which agents might be most suited to form the team. In order to determine this match, the initiator seeks to find out the properties of the agents, with the DDV framework focusing specifically on three aspects: their *abilities*, *opportunities*, and *willingness* to participate in team formation. Ability does not depend on the situation, but is taken as an inherent property of the agent. The aspect of opportunity takes into account the possibilities of task performance in the particular situation, involving resources and possibly other properties. The aspect of willingness considers the agents' mental attitudes towards participating in the proposed team goal. The outcome of the potential recognition stage is that the initiator knows whether or not it is possible to form a team, but has yet to engage in *team persuasion*, i.e. persuading potential team members to take on the intention to achieve the overall goal.

As our focus is on the initiator's reasoning process, we adopt a slightly altered view of the notions "goal" and "collective intention". For our work, the initiator's *original goal* is the specification of what the initiator would like to achieve as a result of forming and directing a team. The *collective intention* of this team will include both the team initiator's original goal and any subgoal arising from the team formation process.

In the rest of this paper we will show how multi-agent epistemic planning can be used to operationalize this approach, and provide a practical way to generate possible plans for the team to achieve a goal.

2.2 Multi-agent Epistemic Planning

We adopt a formalism of planning where the planning agent can reason in a limited fashion about the nested belief of other agents in the domain [20]. The state of the world in this setting is a collection of *Restricted Modal Literals* (RMLs) which are taken from the set $\mathcal{L}_{\mathcal{F}}^{Ag,d}$ defined by the following grammar:

$$\phi :: = p \mid B_i\phi \mid \neg\phi$$

where p is from a set of primitive fluents $\mathcal{F}$ and i is from a set of agents Ag. The modal proposition $B_i\phi$ states that agent i *believes* proposition ϕ, in which ϕ can be other possibly-nested beliefs. The maximum depth of nesting is limited by d. If $\mathcal{F}$, Ag, and d are all finite, then so is the set of RMLs $\mathcal{L}_{\mathcal{F}}^{Ag,d}$.

A query on the knowledge base is a simple database query [18], and this query assumes an open world. An open-world assumption allows representation of uncertainty. For example, we can express that we are certain that proposition p is true by adding p to the knowledge base, we can express we are certain that p is not true by adding $\neg p$ to the knowledge base, and we can express that we are unsure (or have no information about) the belief of p by having neither p nor $\neg p$ in the knowledge base. We can express similar uncertainty about other agents; e.g. $\neg B_i p$, $\neg B_i \neg p$ expresses our belief that agent i is uncertain of the truth of p.

Following earlier work [20], we define a *Multi-agent Epistemic Planning*
(MEP) problem as the tuple $\langle \mathcal{F}, \mathcal{A}, \mathcal{I}, \mathcal{G}, Ag, d \rangle$, where:

- $\mathcal{F}$ is a set of atomic fluents.
- $\mathcal{A}$ is a set of actions (described below).
- $\mathcal{I}$ is a subset of $\mathcal{L}_{\mathcal{F}}^{Ag,d}$ describing the initial state.
- $\mathcal{G}$ is a subset of $\mathcal{L}_{\mathcal{F}}^{Ag,d}$ describing the goal condition.
- Ag is the set of agents in the domain.
- d is the maximum depth of nesting allowed.

For every action a in $\mathcal{A}$, we will use NAME(a) to indicate the action's name.
PRECOND(a) is the subset of $\mathcal{L}_{\mathcal{F}}^{Ag,d}$ that must hold in order for a to be executable,
and EFFECTS(a) is a *set of* outcomes, of which exactly one will occur after a is
executed: i.e., the action outcomes may be *non-deterministic* [4]. The possible
outcomes of an action are known in advance, but the precise outcome is known
only after the action has been executed. Thus, we are assuming fully-observable,
non-deterministic (FOND) planning, in which actions are non-deterministic, but
their effects are fully observable after execution. This is in contrast with the
original MEP formalism where every action was necessarily deterministic.

This generalization of deterministic actions is an appealing way to model dialogue. The modifications we made to accommodate for non-deterministic actions
did not change the theoretical framework introduced by Muise et al. [20], as the
non-determinism in the domain is fully observable (i.e., the agent will know
which outcome occurs immediately after the action is executed). While this
requires the planner to handle various contingencies depending on the action
outcome, it does not alter the way beliefs are encoded using the standard MEP
formalism. The only change made was to replace the classical sub-planner with a
non-deterministic one. Using a non-deterministic planner allows us to plan for all
contingencies offline, which can be extremely helpful in avoiding bad sequences
of dialogue and bargaining actions.

Every outcome in EFFECTS(a) is a set of conditional effects that change the
state of the "world", in which the "world" includes beliefs of agents. We use
$cond \rightarrow f$ to signify the conditional effect that updates the state of the world
for f to hold in the following state when $cond$ holds in the current state. If the
condition $cond$ is empty, we will just omit the $\rightarrow$. If every action is deterministic,
then a solution to a MEP problem is a sequence of actions that, when executed
from the initial state, achieves the goal. As we allow for non-deterministic effects,
a solution is generalized to be a policy mapping reachable states (including the
initial state) to the action that the agent should execute next in that state.

The choice in modelling language we use throughout the paper reflects the
encoding that automated planners require. In practice, we have a more general
input specification, which can be found at the project's source[1].

Using a variation of MEP planning in lieu of classical planning provides
valuable modelling properties in the context of multi-agent environments. We

---

[1] http://www.haz.ca/research/tw-as-ap.

will point out some of these advantages throughout the paper in the context of our target domain, and refer the interested reader to [20] for a deeper discussion on how belief is maintained during the planning process.

2.3   Blocks World for Teams

As a testbed, we consider a version of the Blocks World For Teams (BW4T) domain [13] designed to support the study of interactions in heterogeneous teams - i.e. teams composed of both humans and agents. In BW4T, participants must navigate a series of rooms to relocate blocks in a target goal configuration. The platform has been used in several studies of moderately complex interactions involving humans and agents, e.g. [14,16], and recently extended to a richer modelling environment to allow more experimentation with human participants in more realistic settings [12]. We extend the general setting to include fluents indicating block types (each block can have one or more "colour" associated with it), as well as the capabilities for participants to lift blocks of a particular colour. The extension allows us to model the interactions of heterogeneous agents, as is typical with many team formation problems. The goal of the initiator will be to form a team that can collectively achieve the goal configuration of blocks. The task that we solve in this work is to synthesize a plan of dialogue steps that will yield such a team formation.

While not strictly required, we will associate an agent with every action that signifies the agent performing the action. For example, instead of the action *lift_blue_b1_room1* we will have actions *lift_i_blue_b1_room1* for every agent *i* in *Ag* (note that if block *b1* was also of the *red* type, we would have a separate *lift_i_red_b1_room1* action for every agent). For simplicity we include the agent and objects in the action name, but in practice these are parameterized. To ensure only the appropriate agent lifts a block, preconditions will include the agent's capability: e.g., the *lift_ag1_blue_b1_room1* action will include *can_lift_ag1_blue* as a precondition (we discuss capabilities further in Sect. 3). Other preconditions and effects include the standard ones for the BW4T domain, as well as extra effects to update the belief of agents. The following is the full description for *lift_ag1_blue_b1_room1* (we have replaced repeated effects for each agent with a single effect for agent *i*):[2]

$$\text{NAME}(a) = \textit{lift\_ag1\_blue\_b1\_room1}$$
$$\text{PRECOND}(a) = \{\textit{at\_ag1\_room1}, \textit{block\_colour\_b1\_blue},$$
$$\textit{in\_b1\_room1}, \textit{can\_lift\_ag1\_blue}\}$$
$$\text{EFFECTS}(a) = [\{\textit{holding\_ag1\_b1}, \neg \textit{in\_b1\_room1},$$
$$\textit{at\_i\_room1} \rightarrow B_i \textit{holding\_ag1\_b1},$$
$$\textit{at\_i\_room1} \rightarrow B_i \neg \textit{in\_b1\_room1}\}]$$

---

[2] Note that, as with most blocksworld encodings, the fluent *in_b1_room* is false whenever an agent is holding block *b1*.

As a result of using the MEP framework [20] in an off-the-shelf manner, additional effects will be created to maintain certain properties. For example, the effect $at\_i\_room1 \rightarrow \neg B_i \neg holding\_ag1\_b1$ would be added to maintain consistency of belief; that is, if agent i believes that agent 1 is holding $b1$, then it cannot believe agent 1 is not holding $b1$. There are similar effects on the move actions; e.g. an agent will believe the contents of a room when they enter it. Using MEP gives us a much richer environment in which to pose our teamwork formation problem. The types of inferences that are made in the MEP framework could in theory be embedded within a planning system. However, by using it in a blackbox fashion (which has the inferences compiled away into the domain description) we were able to seamlessly switch out the deterministic planner for a non-deterministic one given our setting.

3   Model of Team Formation

The initiator must assess the capabilities of the agents, and bargain with them in order to convince them to join the team. As a side-effect of bargaining, the collective intention of the eventual team may change – every promise made during the bargaining phase will become a subgoal for the team to achieve in the final state of the plan in addition to the original goal.

As discussed earlier, we adopt a model of team formation inspired by Dignum et al. [6]. Because we wish to consider team formation from the perspective of the initiator, many of the details are abstracted away from the DDV model (e.g., the precise reasoning capabilities of the other agents). Further, from the perspective of an initiator that is considering the viability of forming a team, every agent is assumed to be "blindly committed": if they have agreed to join the team, they will perform the actions prescribed to them by the initiator as expected. Thus, where the DDV model concentrates on the formation of a joint intention for a team, this paper instead concentrates on the planning and willingness of other agents to participate in the plan. Note that we are not assuming that the agents are purely cooperative – the team initiator must *convince* them that it is worthwhile to join the team through a process of negotiation. In this section, we describe our model of team formation, and contrast it with that of DDV.

The objective of the initiator is to form a team that can achieve the initiator's original goal. As part of the team formation process, the initiator must ensure that the capabilities of the agents on the team will allow the goal to be achieved, and may also need to promise certain things for potential members to join the team. The problem that we address is how the initiator can reason about which questions to ask and bargains to make. Rather than isolating dialogue planning from reasoning about goal achievement, we model both concurrently. The advantage is that we can rule out certain bargaining options that provably will never result in a viable team.

The initiator agent takes the following steps to form a team that can execute a joint plan for the initiator's original goal:

(a) assess capabilities of the agents (Sect. 4.2);

(b) bargain with the agents about promises (Sect. 4.3);
(c) given the commitments made to the agents, plan for the collective intention
of the team (Sect. 4.4).

Note again, that the initiator reasons about these steps before the communication actually takes place. Thus the plan is a conditional plan, based on the answers and commitments of the agents.

Our teamwork formation model describes only the set of potential capabilities and bargains that the initiator should consider in the reasoning process – a process that takes place before the communication is initiated. Together with an action theory describing what the agents can do, an initial state of the world, and a goal configuration, the initiator synthesizes a conditional plan for forming a team to achieve the team's collective intention.

Thus the structure of a plan can be viewed as a tree of dialogue actions (branching occurring based on the agents' response to capability assessment or bargaining), where the leaves represent either a successful team's plan or a configuration of agent responses that lead to no viable team formation (e.g., if too many agents are unwilling). If there is a chance that making further bargains will allow a team to be formed, the planning phase will detect this. Naturally, the solutions produced will use only those agents necessary, and this is detected automatically from our encoding. Figure 1 shows a high-level structure of one such plan: the stage marked 1 is where the dialogue occurs, and the nodes marked 'x' are the situations when the dialogue fails (e.g., an essential agent refuses to help). We describe the other components in more detail below.

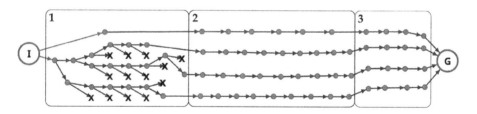

Fig. 1. Example plan for team formation. Stage 1: Capability assessment and bargaining. Stage 2: Planning steps to achieve the collective intention. Stage 3: Meta actions to ensure every promise was fulfilled.

The key components of our team formation model are: (1) the potential capabilities of the agents; and (2) the range of bargains that can be offered to an agent. Formally, given the set of agents Ag and fluents describing the world $\mathcal{F}$, a teamwork formation model $\langle Cap, \mathcal{C}, \mathcal{B} \rangle$ is a tuple where,

- $Cap \subseteq \mathcal{F}$ is a set of fluents representing the agents' capabilities;
- $\mathcal{C} : Ag \rightarrow 2^{Cap}$ maps agents to the set of their potential capabilities; and
- $\mathcal{B} : Ag \rightarrow 2^{\mathcal{F}}$ maps agents to the set of the possible bargains they will consider.

Note that for agent $ag1$, $\mathcal{C}(ag1)$ does *not* describe all of their capabilities. Rather, it describes a superset of the actual capabilities that agent $ag1$ might have. It is the responsibility of the initiator to surmise from agent $ag1$, which capabilities in the set $\mathcal{C}(ag1)$ it actually has. Our notion of capability corresponds to the DDV notion of *ability*, and the initiator is able to ask the agents if they have particular capabilities as part of the information seeking dialogue.

After the initiator knows an agent is capable of what is required of them, the initiator must "persuade" the agent to join the team. The initiator achieves this through the use of *bargaining*. The initiator can offer any fluent in the set $\mathcal{B}(ag1)$ to agent $ag1$ as a promised subgoal that will hold at the *end* of the execution (i.e., in the final state of the system). $\mathcal{B}(ag1)$ may contain fluents involving other agents, so for example we may have a pair of agents that will only join the team if the other is promised a block: $\mathcal{B}(ag1) = \{holding\_ag2\_b1\}$ and $\mathcal{B}(ag2) = \{holding\_ag1\_b2\}$. This possibility of mutual support can lead to added restrictions on team formation, making the need even greater for the initiator to plan in advance.

After a bargain is proposed, the agent can agree or disagree, and the initiator plans for both eventualities. If the agent agrees, it becomes part of the formed team and achieving the promise must be satisfied by the plan. If the agent does not agree, then the initiator can try to persuade the agent in a different way, or try to find another agent to assist.

The plan must allow the promises to be satisfied in the following sense: if agent $ag1$ joined the team on the premise that $f \in \mathcal{F}$ is achieved, the goal of the initiator must now include $B_{ag1}f$. That is, a promise made to an agent must be believed by that agent when the plan's execution is complete. This allows for behaviour whereby the initiator can form a team where the members have inconsistent intentions, as long as the individual agents believe that their promises will be fulfilled in the end. We could keep the initiator "fully honest" by placing both f and $B_{ag1}f$ in the set of goals when a promise of f is made to agent $ag1$. If the set of goals is inconsistent (e.g., an agent must have inconsistent beliefs), then no plan exists and no team can be formed.

The set of promises that an initiator commits to, along with the original goal, then constitutes what we term the collective intention of the team. While the collective intention is not explicitly represented, as is the case with DDV, the plan produced by the initiator serves as an essential basis for the team to have collective intention. In a sense, the plan produced by our encoding is a certificate that the initiator can use in order to achieve DDV's form of collective intention during the actual dialogue phase.

The concepts of *willingness* and *team persuasion* from DDV are both covered by the initiator's ability to bargain. A key aspect of our approach is that the dialogue can occur in any order. The initiator can consider inquiring about capabilities, then bargaining with some agents, then inquiring about capabilities depending on the outcome of previous dialogue. This allows the initiator to condition their dialogue strategy based on the responses they have received so far.

The DDV notion of *opportunity* assumes that the initiator thinks they are both able and have the resources in the situation to achieve something. Instead of ascribing this notion to the agents, we task the initiator with assessing whether or not agents have the opportunity to achieve a subgoal. This is a natural consequence of our assumption that the initiator is reasoning about both the dialogue and planning phases simultaneously. This shifts the complexity of gauging an agent's opportunity to achieve a subgoal to the initiator's planning phase. The advantage of this is that the initiator does not need to reason apriori about which subgoals the agent has the opportunity to achieve (which can be a complex notion given the other agents that may be on the team). When the initiator considers a formed team, they can try to synthesize a plan with the team while *implicitly* computing the opportunities of every agent.

4   Encoding Team Formation

Our general approach to team formation is to model the cognitive process of a team initiator who must make various decisions about how best to form a quality team. The mental exercise of the team initiator involves not only the enumeration of team member configurations, but also the evaluation of a given team configuration's potential to achieve the goal. By considering everything from bargaining to physical actions in the world, the initiator can rule out bad team configurations and avoid unnecessary bargaining *before* launching the initial dialogue to form a team.

We begin by describing the general encoding we use, and then elaborate on the details particular to teamwork formation. Following the general encoding, we focus on our model of capability assessment and bargaining. These are the methods the initiator uses to make an informed judgement about who to include on the team. Next, we describe the three internal stages of the initiator's reasoning. These do not correspond directly to the phases of solving a joint task, but we do point out the relation between the two.

4.1   General FOND MEP Encoding

There are two sources of input for the generated FOND encoding: (1) the original MEP problem specification; and (2) the description of bargaining and capability properties for the agents that can form a team. Both will inform the fluents, initial state, goal configuration, and actions in the domain.

Fluents. The MEP problem comes with a set of fluents $\mathcal{F}$ and agents Ag for the domain. These are combined, along with the maximum depth d, to generate fluents for the encoding that represent both what is true in the world and what the belief of each agent consists of. For example, the fluents in the BW4T domain FOND encoding will include $holding\_ag1\_b2$ and $Bag3\_in\_b1\_room4$.

Initial State. The initial state will come directly from the MEP problem as well. By adopting the MEP framework, the initial state represents the belief of the initiator. It can either be fully specified (i.e., for every fluent f, either f or $\neg f$ holds in the initial state) or partially specified (i.e., the initiator is uncertain about certain facts). The option to use a partially specified initial state opens the door to a wider class of problems that include situations where the team initiator is *not* omniscient; a realistic assumption that often is overlooked.

Goal Configuration. As with the initial state, we adopt the goal from the MEP problem for the FOND encoding. It will consist of a set of fluents that describe a partial state that must be achieved (e.g., having particular blocks placed in a specific location).

Actions. The actions for the FOND encoding will correspond to those in the MEP action theory, with the precondition and effect RMLs replaced by their compiled fluent equivalent. We assume that every action from the MEP problem has an associated agent. For example, the action for picking up block $b1$ has a copy for every agent ($pickup\_ag1\_b1$, $pickup\_ag2\_b1$, etc.). Similarly, the fluents that are required by an agent to conduct an action will have an agent associated with it (e.g., $hand\_free\_ag1 \in \textsc{Precond}(pickup\_ag1\_b1)$).

4.2   Capability Assessment

To achieve the overall goal of the team, the initiator must assess the capabilities of potential members. Some capabilities may be known in advance, but in general we assume that the initiator must consider "asking" the agents if they are capable of certain tasks. For example, the initiator may ask agent 1 if he or she can lift blue blocks. Because the initiator deliberates offline, she must consider all of the possible outcomes of a question. For the time being, we limit the form of the question to simple yes/no inquiries such as the example above. After asking the question, the initiator will continue the deliberation process in two ways: once assuming a positive response, and again assuming a negative response. Thus, we can model the question using a non-deterministic action:

$$\textsc{Name}(a) = ask\_if\_ag1\_can\_lift\_blue\_blocks$$
$$\textsc{Precond}(a) = \{\neg can\_lift\_ag1\_blue, \neg cannot\_lift\_ag1\_blue\}$$
$$\textsc{Effects}(a) = [\{can\_lift\_ag1\_blue\}, \{cannot\_lift\_ag1\_blue\}]$$

There are two important aspects of this encoding. First, one outcome will allow the initiator to orchestrate standard actions for lifting blue blocks using agent 1 (recall that a precondition of $lift\_ag1\_blue\_b2\_room1$ is that $can\_lift\_ag1\_blue$). Second, both outcomes make it impossible to ask this question a second time. This second aspect is important because we do not want to assume that repeating a question will eventually lead to a different response.

4.3   Bargaining

Once the initiator is confident that an agent has the right capability for the task, she must ensure that the agent is willing to help. This notion corresponds directly to the idea of persuasion in DDV. Rather than convincing the agent that the collective intention is achievable through dialogue, the initiator will consider making "promises" about the collective intention of the team. For example, she might tell agent 2 that if they decide to join the team, they can have block 3 at the end of the sequence.

The combination of the original goal with the set of promises made to the agents constitutes the collective intention for the team. Every agent on the team is either willing to join for free, or is willing to join for a particular price. We model this aspect of the dialogue in a fashion similar to capability assessment using the following non-deterministic action:

$$\text{NAME}(a) = bargain\_with\_ag1\_for\_holding\_ag1\_b2$$
$$\text{PRECOND}(a) = \{\neg ag1\_willing, \neg ag1\_unwilling\_holding\_ag1\_b2\}$$
$$\text{EFFECTS}(a) = [\{promised\_ag1\_holding\_ag1\_b2, ag1\_willing\},$$
$$\{ag1\_unwilling\_holding\_ag1\_b2\}]$$

Similar to the capability assessment, the initiator cannot try continually to bargain using the same offer. However, different actions may correspond to different promises that the initiator can propose in order to convince the agent to join the team. As mentioned previously, an agent can only perform an action if they are willing to be a part of the team (i.e., $ag_i\_willing$ holds). The additional fluent $promised\_ag1\_holding\_ag1\_b2$ maintains this aspect of the collective intention, and we will see next how the reasoning for the initiator ensures that the team achieves this subgoal.

4.4   Three Stages for Initiator Reasoning

The initiator's deliberation process is encoded as a FOND MEP problem, and will go through three distinct stages: (1) forming the team based on capability assessment and bargaining; (2) constructing the plan for the team; and (3) ensuring that the goal is satisfied and the promises fulfilled. In relation to the four phases of a team jointly achieving a task, stage (1) corresponds both to team assessment and team formation (phases 1 and 2 in cooperative problem solving [30]) – the initiator has the option to consider interleaving the assessment of capabilities and persuasion. Stages (2) and (3) correspond directly to plan formation (phase 3). Finally, as mentioned earlier, we do not consider the fourth phase from Wooldridge and Jennings that covers plan execution. We have marked the actions belonging to the three stages in an example plan shown in Fig. 1.

To restrict the reasoning to each of the stages, we include the following components in the encoding:

(a) We introduce the auxillary fluents *stage_formation, stage_planning*, and *stage_final*, with *stage_formation* set to true in the initial state.

(b) We introduce two actions, *start_planning* and *finish_planning*, that simply change the value of the auxillary fluents appropriately (i.e., removing the current stage and adding the next).

(c) Every capability assessment and bargaining action has the extra precondition of *stage_formation*.

(d) Every standard action has the extra precondition of *stage_planning*.

(e) We introduce new "satisfy" actions for each agent, as described below.

The above changes force all of the capability assessment and bargaining to occur before the standard planning actions are considered. Doing so forces the initiator to consider forming the team prior to considering if they can achieve the goal. However, note that the initiator reasons about all three stages *before* they physically start any dialogue.

For the final phase (i.e., stage (3)), the initiator uses the plan from stage (2) to determine if the team has achieved the collective intention. The initiator must achieve both the original goal and the presumed satisfaction of every agent. The initiator will presume an agent satisfied if either the agent was not part of the team to begin with, or by acknowledging that the agent believes any promise made to them was kept. The first of the two actions, which covers the case of an agent not part of the team, is as follows:

$$\text{NAME}(a) = satisfy\_ag1\_unwilling$$
$$\text{PRECOND}(a) = \{\neg ag1\_willing, stage\_final\}$$
$$\text{EFFECTS}(a) = [\{ag1\_satisfied\}]$$

Note that we use *ag1_willing* here additionally to indicate that the agent was a part of the team, while ¬*ag1_willing* indicates that they were not. The other action capable of "satisfying" an agent is to reaffirm that they explicitly believe the promise that was presented to them during team formation:

$$\text{NAME}(a) = satisfy\_ag1\_for\_holding\_ag1\_b2$$
$$\text{PRECOND}(a) = \{stage\_final, Bag2\_holding\_ag1\_b2,$$
$$promised\_ag1\_holding\_ag1\_b2\}$$
$$\text{EFFECTS}(a) = [\{ag1\_satisfied\}]$$

The distinction of achieving an agent's bargained promise, as opposed to having that agent believe the promise is fulfilled, is an important one. On one hand, it is not enough for the team to achieve something that was promised to an agent while the agent remains unaware of this fact. On the other hand, this provides potential for deceitful behaviour – depending on how the agent updates their belief, they may *believe* that their objective holds when in fact it does not (e.g., they see a block placed in a room they desire, and then leave the room believing that it will remain there). This level of expressiveness is an intended consequence of using MEP planning as our underlying framework instead of generic automated planning techniques. Once all of the agents have been "satisfied", the reasoning process is complete. Note that because of the stage fluents, agents can be considered satisfied only in the final stage; during which the state of the world and the beliefs of the agents cannot be altered further.

It is worth emphasizing that the 3 stages are *all solved as a single planning problem*. The conceptual separation between the actions in each of the stages is implicit in any valid solution that the planner generates. Further, the planner is equipped with an efficient means of relevance analysis and policy reuse (see [22] for a discussion), which means that partial plans found for a subset of the agents can be reused in different configurations of the team. This reasoning essentially is "free" when we use a state-of-the-art FOND planner to solve the encoded problem. We would not get this benefit without significant overhead if we were to implement the three stages individually.

Another key benefit is the embedded heuristics in the planners we use. As a natural consequence of the relevance analysis done inside of a planner when considering the best course of action, teams will typically be formed to contain no irrelevant member. This advantage is not guaranteed (i.e., our approach is *not optimal*), but is nonetheless the norm. Indeed, every team computed in our preliminary evaluation was minimal in the sense that removing one agent would render the team ineffective.

While perhaps counter-intuitive, the bundling of all stages into a single encoded problem allows us to fully leverage the planning technology at the core of our approach. Aside from the reuse of plan fragments mentioned earlier, the planner will also recognize when making a particularly bad decision early in stage (1) will prevent stages (2) or (3) to be successful. Further, we can use the produced conditional plan as a certificate for future negotiations by the team initiator (a phase out of scope for this work).

5   Preliminary Evaluation

We report on a preliminary evaluation to demonstrate the potential for solving teamwork formation problems with automated planning technology. We used the available implementation of the MEP framework [19], and wrote a compiler for team formation problems (cf. Sect. 3) that produces an encoded FOND MEP problem (cf. Sect. 4). To solve the encoded problems, we used an off-the-shelf FOND planner, PRP [22], which generates a policy for the initiator to follow. As we are using PRP in a black-box manner, we do not go into the details of how it computes a plan for the resulting encoding. The computed solutions may be suboptimal, but in general they do not contain superfluous dialogue or planning actions. By using modern planning technology, our approach is scalable to far larger problems; existing planners can solve problems with trillions of states in fractions of a second [11]. Where scalability suffers, as pointed out by Muise et al. [20], is when the depth of nesting and number of agents grows too large.

We modelled various settings for the BlocksWorld for Teams (BW4T) domain [13] with five agents, five rooms, four blocks, and three possible block colours, running four different scenarios. Each of the four scenarios tested a unique setting for the team formation (described further below), and details of the base encoding can be found in Sect. 2.3. Table 1 shows the time that it takes to synthesize a plan, including both the encoding and solving phases, as well as the final policy size measured as the number of possible states that it takes to encode the initiator's controller. All problems were run on a Linux Desktop with a 3.4 GHz processor. Valid solutions were generated for all problems.

Table 1. Plan size, encoding time, and solve time

Problem	1	2	3	4
Plan size	20	83	109	45
Solving time (s)	4.8	12.0	34.8	35.4
Encoding time (s)	16.2	16.1	16.3	15.9

Problem 1: No Bargaining. The initiator is free to consider dialogue with the potential members, but there is one agent in particular that can achieve the goal and asks nothing in return. As expected, the final plan uses this one-agent team to achieve the goal without bargaining.

Problem 2: Birds of a Feather. Problem 2 is a scenario where the goal can be achieved by any of three combinations (and their supersets) of team: 1, 2-3, and 4-5. Agent 1 is capable of achieving the original goal, but if they decline, then either team 2-3 or 4-5 must be sought after. In these cases, a further restriction in the scenario is that the agents can be persuaded to join the team only if the other agent in the pair will possess a particular block in the final state (e.g., $\mathcal{B}(ag2) = \{holding\_ag3\_b1\}$ and $\mathcal{B}(ag3) = \{holding\_ag2\_b2\}$), and (e.g., $\mathcal{B}(ag4) = \{holding\_ag5\_b1\}$ and $\mathcal{B}(ag5) = \{holding\_ag4\_b2\}$). This leads the initiator to devise a plan that forms a team with one of the pairs exclusively. Note that a superset of the teams would also work, but these inefficient teams naturally are not considered by the planner: if enough of the agents have agreed to join, then a team is formed immediately. See Fig. 1 for the full solution to problem 2 with the labels removed.

Problem 3: Bait and Switch. If the initiator acted with full honesty, only the team 1-2-5 can achieve the task in this problem. However, the initiator can find a second team that includes agent 4 instead of 5. The issue with team 1-2-4 is that agent 2 can only be persuaded if block 3 ends in room 3, while agent 4 can only be persuaded if block 3 ends in room 4. This is impossible, but the initiator's reasoning recognizes that agents 2 and 4 can both believe (one of them incorrectly) that their promise is fulfilled: in the resulting plan, agent 2 witnesses block 3 being dropped in room 3, and then the initiator directs agent 2 to walk away while agent 4 brings the block to room 4. This demonstrates the expressiveness that comes when planning with multi-agent epistemic states in lieu of the standard classical planning formalism.

Problem 4: Satisfying Suspicions. In problem 3, the agents continue to believe that the location of a block is unchanged even when they are in a different location. In problem 4, we change the action description so that an agent no longer believes that the location of blocks in a room remain constant when they exit (i.e., they only maintain beliefs about blocks in the room they currently inhabit). With this modification, the initiator correctly identifies just one possible team: 1-2-5. Problems 3 and 4 each take the planner approximately 35 s to solve, and this time largely is spent attempting to find a different configuration for dialogue acts that will result in a new team.

6   Discussion

We presented an approach for team formation from the perspective of a team initiator, whose task is to synthesize a strategy to form an effective team through capability assessment and bargaining. The team's success hinges on the members' ability to achieve a collective intention that includes the original goal plus any promises made during the bargaining process. We have made the described framework and test suite for team formation available to the wider research community at the following website:

http://www.haz.ca/research/tw-as-ap/

Demonstrating and evaluating this approach on a commonly used blocksworld-style problem set, we have shown that this planning technology can handle the encoded problems readily. The relevance analysis that comes with existing planners makes our approach well suited to tackling both the dialogue and planning phases simultaneously: often the infeasibility of a team to achieve the collective intention is recognized early in the planning phase, and a new team is considered. Additionally, including the MEP formalism reveals interesting new considerations for modelling the teamwork formation problem, as evidenced by the distinction between problems 3 and 4.

Note, however, that the only agents acting in the environment are those that are part of the formed team. We hope to relax this assumption by incorporating our research with a framework that allows us to plan in the presence of other agents [21]. The resulting system would construct a team that could adequately handle the uncertainty posed by the possible actions of agents not on our team.

As the objective in this paper was not to introduce a particular mechanism for team formation, a detailed comparison with other team formation models is not relevant here. Rather, our contribution is the introduction of a novel approach that is suitable for efficiently operationalising the requirements of multiple models. Hence, we point to the generic benefits of our planning-based approach, and posit that because the underlying representation supports complex encoding, including modelling the nested beliefs of agents, many team formation models will be amenable to implementation via planning. This also includes models in other settings where collective intention is a central concept. Of course, further work, both conceptually and empirically, is needed to put a precise scope around this claim. In particular, it would be interesting to use the work of Johnson [28] to assess the performance of a team created using our approach.

The preliminary results give a good indication that automated planning techniques can solve these types of problems. Moving forward, we will expand the encoding to include richer forms of dialogue within the team formation process. In doing so, we aim to extend this work to the domain of narrative planning, where properly sequenced speech acts play a central role.

Acknowledgements. This research is partially funded by Australian Research Council Discovery Grant DP130102825, *Foundations of Human-Agent Collaboration: Situation-Relevant Information Sharing.*

References

1. Agmon, N., Stone, P.: Leading ad hoc agents in joint action settings with multiple teammates. In: Proceedings of the 11th International Conference on Autonomous Agents and Multiagent Systems, vol. 1, pp. 341–348. IFAAMAS (2012)
2. Amgoud, L.: An argumentation-based model for reasoning about coalition structures. In: Parsons, S., Maudet, N., Moraitis, P., Rahwan, I. (eds.) ArgMAS 2005. LNCS (LNAI), vol. 4049, pp. 217–228. Springer, Heidelberg (2006)
3. Barrett, S., Agmon, N., Hazon, N., Kraus, S., Stone, P.: Communicating with unknown teammates. In: Proceedings of the Twenty-First European Conference on Artificial Intelligence, August 2014. http://www.cs.utexas.edu/users/ai-lab/? barrett:ecai14
4. Cimatti, A., Pistore, M., Roveri, M., Traverso, P.: Weak, strong, and strong cyclic planning via symbolic model checking. Artif. Intell. **147**(1), 35–84 (2003)
5. Decker, K.S., Lesser, V.R.: Designing a family of coordination algorithms. In: Proceedings of the First International Conference on Multi-Agent Systems, pp. 73–80. AAAI Press (1995)
6. Dignum, F., Dunin-Keplicz, B., Verbrugge, R.: Creating collective intention through dialogue. Log. J. IGPL **9**(2), 289–304 (2001)
7. Dunin-Kęplicz, B., Verbrugge, R.: Teamwork in Multi-Agent Systems: A Formal Approach. Wiley, Ltd (2010)
8. Grant, J., Kraus, S., Perlis, D.: Formal approaches to teamwork. In: Artëmov, S.N., et al. (ed.) We Will Show Them! Essays in Honour of Dov Gabbay, vol. 2, pp. 39–68. College Publications (2005)
9. Grosz, B., Kraus, S.: Collaborative plans for complex group actions. Artif. Intell. **86**, 269–358 (1996)
10. Hoang, H., Lee-Urban, S., Muñoz-Avila, H.: Hierarchical plan representations for encoding strategic game AI. In: Proceedings of the First Artificial Intelligence and Interactive Digital Entertainment Conference, pp. 63–68, Marina del Rey, California, USA, 1–5 June 2005 (2005)
11. Hoffmann, J.: Everything you always wanted to know about *planning*. In: Bach, J., Edelkamp, S. (eds.) KI 2011. LNCS, vol. 7006, pp. 1–13. Springer, Heidelberg (2011)
12. Johnson, M., Bradshaw, J., Duran, D., Vignati, M., Feltovich, P., Jonker, C., van Riemsdijk, M.B.: RT4T: a reconfigurable testbed for joint human-agent-robot teamwork. In: Workshop on Human-Robot Teaming, Proceedings of the Tenth Annual ACM/IEEE International Conference on Human-Robot Interaction (2015)

13. Johnson, M., Jonker, C., van Riemsdijk, B., Feltovich, P.J., Bradshaw, J.M.: Joint activity testbed: blocks world for teams (BW4T). In: Aldewereld, H., Dignum, V., Picard, G. (eds.) ESAW 2009. LNCS, vol. 5881, pp. 254–256. Springer, Heidelberg (2009)

14. Jonker, C.M., van Riemsdijk, M.B., van de Kieft, I.C., Gini, M.: Compositionality of team mental models in relation to sharedness and team performance. In: Jiang, H., Ding, W., Ali, M., Wu, X. (eds.) IEA/AIE 2012. LNCS, vol. 7345, pp. 242–251. Springer, Heidelberg (2012)

15. Kinny, D., Sonenberg, E., Ljungberg, M., Tidhar, G., Rao, A., Werner, E.: Planned team activity. In: Castelfranchi, C., Werner, E. (eds.) MAAMAW 1992. LNCS, vol. 830, pp. 227–256. Springer, Heidelberg (1994)

16. Li, S., Sun, W., Miller, T.: Communication in human-agent teams for tasks with joint action. In: COIN 2015: The XIX International Workshop on Coordination, Organizations, Institutions and Norms in Multiagent Systems, pp. 111–126 (2015)

17. Marcolino, L.S., Zhang, C., Jiang, A.X., Tambe, M.: A detailed analysis of a multi-agent diverse team. In: Balke, T., Dignum, F., van Riemsdijk, M.B., Chopra, A.K. (eds.) COIN 2013. LNCS, vol. 8386, pp. 3–24. Springer, Heidelberg (2014)

18. Muise, C., Miller, T., Felli, P., Pearce, A., Sonenberg, L.: Efficient reasoning with consistent proper epistemic knowledge bases. In: Proceedings of the 14th International Conference on Autonomous Agents and Multi-Agent Systems (2015)

19. Muise, C.: Planner for Relevant Policies: Bitbucket repository. https://bitbucket.org/haz/pdkb-planning/. Accessed 26 Jan 2015 (2015)

20. Muise, C., Belle, V., Felli, P., McIlraith, S., Miller, T., Pearce, A., Sonenberg, L.: Planning over multi-agent epistemic states: A classical planning approach. In: The 29th AAAI Conference on Artificial Intelligence (2015)

21. Muise, C., Felli, P., Miller, T., Pearce, A.R., Sonenberg, L.: Leveraging FOND planning technology to solve multi-agent planning problems. In: Workshop on Distributed and Multi-Agent Planning, DMAP 2015 (2015)

22. Muise, C., McIlraith, S.A., Beck, J.C.: Improved non-deterministic planning by exploiting state relevance. In: The 22nd International Conference on Automated Planning and Scheduling (2012)

23. Nair, R., Tambe, M.: Hybrid BDI-POMDP framework for multiagent teaming. J. Artif. Intell. Res. (JAIR) 23, 367–420 (2005)

24. Rahwan, T., Michalak, T.P., Elkind, E., Faliszewski, P., Sroka, J., Wooldridge, M., Jennings, N.R.: Constrained coalition formation. In: AAAI, vol. 11, pp. 719–725 (2011)

25. Rao, A.S., Georgeff, M.P.: BDI agents: from theory to practice. In: Proceedings of the First International Conference on Multi-Agent Systems, ICMAS 1995, pp. 312–319 (1995)

26. Sandholm, T., Lesser, V.: Coalitions among computationally bounded agents. Artif. Intell. Spec. Issue Econ. Principles Multi-Agent Syst. 94(1), 99–137 (1997)

27. Shehory, O., Kraus, S.: Methods for task allocation via agent coalition formation. Artif. Intell. 10(12), 165–200 (1998)

28. Sierhuis, M., Jonker, C., van Riemsdijk, B., Feltovich, P.J., Bradshaw, J.M., Johnson, M.: Autonomy and interdependence in human-agent-robot teams. IEEE Intell. Syst. 27(2), 43–51 (2012)

29. Tidhar, G., Rao, A.S., Sonenberg, E.A.: Guided team selection. In: Proceedings of the Second International Conference on Multi-Agent Systems, pp. 369–376. AAAI Press (1996)

30. Wooldridge, M., Jennings, N.R.: The cooperative problem-solving process. J. Log. Comput. 9(4), 563–592 (1999)

Interest-Based Negotiation for Policy-Regulated Asset Sharing

Christos Parizas[1]([⊠]), Geeth De Mel[2], Alun D. Preece[1], Murat Sensoy[3],
Seraphin B. Calo[2], and Tien Pham[4]

[1] School of Computer Science and Informatics, Cardiff University, Cardiff, UK
{C.Parizas,A.D.Preece}@cs.cardiff.ac.uk
[2] IBM T.J. Watson Research Center, Yorktown Heights, NY, USA
{grdemel,scalo}@us.ibm.com
[3] Department of Computer Science, Ozyegin University, Istanbul, Turkey
murat.sensoy@ozyegin.edu.tr
[4] US Army Research Lab, Sensors and Electron Devices Directorate,
Adelphi, MD, USA
tien.pham1.civ@mail.mil

Abstract. Resources sharing is an important but complex problem to be solved. The problem is exacerbated in a coalition context due to policy constraints, that reflect concerns regarding security, privacy and performance to name a few, placed on the resources. Thus, to effectively share resources, members of a coalition need to negotiate on policies and at times refine them to meet the needs of the operating environment. Towards achieving this goal, in this work we propose and evaluate a novel policy negotiation mechanism based on the interest-based negotiation paradigm. Interest-based negotiation, promotes collaboration when compared with the traditional, position-based negotiation approaches.

1 Introduction

Negotiation is a form of interaction usually expressed as a dialogue between two or more parties with conflicting interests that try to achieve mutual agreement about the exchange of scarce resources, resolve points of difference and craft outcomes that satisfy various interests. Chasing mutual agreements, the involved parties make proposals, trade options and offer concessions. The automation of the negotiation process and its integration with autonomic, multi-agent environments has been well-researched over the last few decades [1,2].

The theoretical approaches for automated negotiation can be classified into three major categories: (1) game theoretic (2) heuristic, and (3) argumentation based [1]. The first two represent traditional, bilateral negotiation mechanisms wherein each negotiation party exchanges offers aiming to usually satisfy their own interests. Both approaches fall under the broader spectrum of position-based negotiations (PBN), where participants attack the opposing parties' offers, trying to convince them for the suitability of their own ones. Typically, those

© Springer International Publishing Switzerland 2016
V. Dignum et al. (Eds.): COIN 2015, LNAI 9628, pp. 300–319, 2016.
DOI: 10.1007/978-3-319-42691-4_17

approaches are formalized as search problems in the space of possible deals by focusing on negotiation objectives.

Argumentation-based negotiation (ABN) has been introduced as a means to enhance automated negotiation by exchanging richer information between negotiators. Interest-based negotiation (IBN) is a type of ABN based on a mechanism, where negotiating agents exchange information about the goals that motivate the negotiation action [3,4]. IBN unlike PBN approaches, tackles the problem of negotiation, focusing on "why to negotiate for" rather than on "what to negotiate for", aiming to lead negotiating parties to win-win solutions.

Multi-party teams are often formed to support collective endeavors, which otherwise would be difficult, if not impossible, to achieve by a single party. In order to support such activities, resources belonging to collaborative partners are shared among the team members. Mechanisms, for effective resource sharing between institutions and/or individuals are actively and broadly explored in research community. This is due to the impact that different resource sharing setups and modifications (what to share, with who, when and under what conditions) can bring into the collaboration, with respect to domains such as security, privacy and performance to name only a few.

Consider for instance the following scenarios: (a) the resource sharing in corporate environments such as the recent *MobileFirst* partnership between IBM and Apple where cloud and other services are shared in a daily basis; or (b) a short-lived, mobile, opportunistic network comprised of few peer members, established for message routing or data sharing. In both cases, an access control mechanism that governs resource sharing, needs to be implemented for establishing smooth collaboration. A suitable mechanism for managing access control on resources of such systems is a policy-based management system (PBMS). A PBMS provides systems administrators with a programable, abstract layer that describes the system to be managed, enabling them to express high-level, management goals and objectives through high-level policy rules.

The more complex and heterogeneous a multi-party, collaborative formations is, the more complex the mechanism that establishes trust between collaborators is as well; this has a negative impact on developing stricter resource sharing policy rules, which raises the barriers towards smooth and effective collaboration. In such scenarios, the need for a tool for enabling authorization policy negotiation is imperative, in order for strict policy rules to be refined accordingly, so that to promote collaboration.

The work herein presents a novel, interest-based policy negotiation mechanism for enabling authorization policy negotiation in multi-party, collaborative and dynamic environments. It focuses on policy makers who are not necessarily experts in either IT or negotiation techniques. To the best of our knowledge there is no mature work done on policy negotiation in general. The vast majority of automated negotiation work: (a) deals with autonomous, multi-agent environments, (b) utilizes PBN approaches and (c) invariably ignores the special characteristics of multi-party, collaborative environments.

It is our belief that by understanding the interests behind collaborative parties' policies and by crafting options that can meet their asset sharing requirements, IBN could provide a negotiation mechanism, that promotes good collaboration unlike PBN, which inadvertently creates adversarial negotiation atmosphere. Moreover, the PBN paradigm with its fixed, opposing positions is a cumbersome negotiation method, to cope with more dynamic environments [1]. From an architectural point of view, the proposed negotiation mechanism can operate in parallel to a PBMS. Briefly, the proposed, policy IBN mechanism considers an approach that refines strict policies, in order to increase overall usability of collaborators' assets while remaining faithful to existing authorization policies. The main contributions of this of work are as follows:

1. Definition of an interest-based authorization policy negotiation model.
2. Specification of an architecture for its integration with PBMS.
3. Evaluation of policy IBN behavior through simulation experiments.

The remainder of the paper is organized as follows: in Sect. 2 we discuss previous literature on policy negotiation approaches. Section 3 presents an illustrative walkthrough of the policy negotiation mechanism. Section 4 describes the policy negotiation framework, the policy language, and its interface to PBMS by means of an architectural overview. Section 5 presents the algorithmic steps for IBN achievement through policy refinement and in Sect. 6 we evaluate IBN through simulation of multi-party, collaborative environments. We conclude this document in Sect. 7 by summarizing our contribution and outlining future research directions.

2 Background and Related Work

The first computer applications for supporting bilateral negotiations were developed in late 1960s [5]. The reason for their emergence was to assist human negotiators to overcome weaknesses related to negotiation process such as cognitive biases, emotional risks, and their inability to manage complex negotiation environments. Although there is rich literature on negotiation protocols in autonomous, Multi-agent Systems (MAS), there is very limited and no mature work done on policy negotiation.

Briefly, an agent in the context of MAS, is perceived as a software computational entity, capable of possessing the properties of autonomy, social ability, reactivity and pro-activeness [6]. In order for MAS agents to cooperatively solve problems, a comprehensive interaction is needed. Negotiation is an effective agent interaction mechanism, enabling autonomous bidirectional deliberation in both situations of competition and cooperation. For the development of sophisticated, negotiation models there are three areas that need to be considered: (a) the negotiation protocols that define the rules of interaction amongst agents, (b) the negotiation objects that contain the range of issues on which agreements must be achieved and (c) the negotiation decision making models that guide agents' concession stance [7].

Initially, automated negotiation has received considerable attention in the field of economics, utilizing the analytical methods of game theory [8], aiming to calculate the equilibrium outcome before the negotiation game is played. While interesting conceptually, the game theoretic approaches have been criticized for assuming: (a) complete and common information and (b) perfect and correct information. However, most real world problems are cases of imperfect, erroneous and incomplete information where revelation is not realistic [4].

Heuristic negotiation approaches, started to being studied to cope with the computationally expensive game theoretic ones, which unrealistically considered the agents as entities of unlimited computational resources and time. Thus, they focused on producing good, but efficient negotiation decisions, as opposed to the optimal and inefficient decisions provided by predecessors [9]. The two basic limitations of heuristic approaches were: (a) the underused agent communication and cognitive capabilities (e.g., agents' rejection as a feedback when a negotiation agreement is not achieved) and (b) the statically defined agents positions (i.e., each agent has a clearly defined and static position) [4].

The intuition behind ABN is that the negotiating parties can improve the way they negotiate by exchanging explicit information about their intentions. This information exchange reveals unknown, non-shared, incomplete, and imprecise information about the underlying attitudes of the parties involved in the nego- tiation [10]. Think for instance, a negotiation case where two negotiators after exchanging offers are very close to achieve an agreement, but lacking this extra information they give up moments before achieving it.

We see the role of PBMS in managing large, complex and dynamic systems as of a high importance and the existence of sophisticated ways to do so imper- ative. We believe that the integration of an effective negotiation mechanism on a PBMS, works towards this direction.

To the best of our knowledge, no work had previously attempted to bring the IBN paradigm into policy negotiation. The authors in [11] focus on the requirements of policy languages, which deal with trust negotiation and pay attention on the technical aspects and properties of trust models to effectively negotiate with access requests. They do not research any of the aspects of policy negotiation and the scenarios they deal with are less dynamic compared to our problem domain.

The work in [12] proposes an architecture that combines a policy-based man- agement mechanism for evaluating privacy policy rules with a policy negotiation roadmap. It is very generic and does not provide clear evidence of any effective- ness of the proposed approach, while lacking any evaluation. [13] is the first work that looks into policy negotiation and covers the area in depth. It also looks into collaborative environments and introduces the notion of ABN in policy negotia- tion. However, it focuses on a very specific application domain in which it deals with writing insurance policies. The whole process is based on a static approach maintaining a common and collaborative knowledge base.

The work discussed in [14] has many similarities to our work; it deals with cooperative environments where a PBMS is employed for managing the service composition in a distributed setting, while a negotiation framework is used to effectively compose services. The main difference with the work proposed herein is that the objective of the negotiation in [14] is the services that are managed by policies, not the policies themselves. We believe that in order to decrease the management overhead, the objective of the negotiation should be the policies. This is because policies, are the core of a PBMS and the logical component where the system's management resides.

Finally, [15] proposes a policy negotiation approach and presents its architecture. It lacks of any effectiveness evaluation while it does not consider either multi-partner or dynamic environments, following the PBN paradigm.

3   IBN and Asset Sharing Policies: Setting the Scene

Below, we provide illustrative scenarios to explain and motivate the use of IBN on policies, in charge of regulating asset sharing in collaborative environments. In Subsect. 3.1 we revisit the classic orange–chefs scenario discussed in best-selling book *Getting to YES* [3] and then we transfer the same IBN principles into an opportunistic, mobile asset sharing scenario in Subsect. 3.2.

3.1   The Chefs-Orange Scenario

Two chefs that work in the same kitchen, both want to use orange for their recipes. Unfortunately, there is only one orange left. Instead of negotiating on who is going to get the orange or some portion of it, as in a zero-sum, PBN approach, the two chefs opt to follow an IBN inspired approach. So, they ask each other why they need the orange for. In other words, they try to better understand their underlying goals of using the orange. Answering the "why" question, it turns out that one chef needs only the orange flesh (to execute a sauce recipe) while the other needs only its peel (for executing a dessert recipe) leading them to share the orange accordingly, achieving a win-win negotiation outcome.

3.2   Asset Sharing Policy Negotiation

An individual P2 wants to access a smartphone device SMD, owned by the individual P1. However, P1 has a set of restrictions which are captured by policy set R on how to share SMD with other people. These restrictions may reflect privacy concerns (e.g., by accessing their smartphone, one could have access to their photos). For the sake of clarity, in this example, we assume that the set R contains the following policy constraint R1: *do not share the device SMD with anyone else but its owner*. When P2 asks for permission to use the physical device SMD, R1 prohibits this action. Ostensibly there is little room for negotiation here with the current set of policies, if one follows a PBN approach.

However, by applying the IBN and trying to understand the underlying interests of the involving parties, we believe the situation could be handled in a satisfactory manner for both parties. For example, asking the "why" question it turns out that P2 needs a data service (as opposed to the physical device), in order to execute the task of *Email submission* and P1 does not mind sharing a data connection as a hotspot with a trusted party; if P1 could get to know why P2 needs the device for, the situation could be solved to the satisfaction of both parties. All an IBN mechanism needs to do in this case is to introduce another policy – actually a refinement of the existing policy – to R1 to say that data service can be shared among trusted parties. We argue that in such cases, by understanding the situation and broadening the space of possible negotiation deals, one can reach a win-win solution.

As stated earlier, IBN is a type of ABN where the negotiating parties exchange information about their negotiation goals, which then guide the negotiation process. Thus, the why party of the intention is of major importance when compared with the what part. We would say, that the IBN is more of a negotiation shortcut method rather than a typical negotiation process. By attacking the problem of negotiation, IBN could potentially skip the proposals making, the options trading and the need for negotiating parties to offer concession as in PBN cases. Instead of trying to negotiate on a fixed pie, it tries to find alternatives so that to expand it. In the next section, we shall introduce our IBN-based policy mechanism and provide our intuition behind the approach.

4   Interest-Based Policy Negotiation Mechanism

The designing and development of intelligent tools and protocols for enhancing the negotiation process amongst human negotiators, needs to achieve some desirable outcomes that are secured by meeting a set of systematic properties such as: guaranteed negotiation success (i.e., negotiation mechanism that guarantees agreement), simplicity (i.e., eases negotiation decision for the participants), maximization of social welfare (i.e., maximization of the sum of payoffs or utilities of participants) to name a few. A complete list of desirable negotiation outcomes and evaluation criteria as described throughout the literature can be found in [16]. The main objective of the negotiation mechanism proposed herein, is to increase of social welfare.

In scenarios that often suffer from resource scarcity (i.e., environments where resource demand exceeds supply), and many user tasks may be competing for the same resource in order to be served, like those described in introduction, the formation of coalitions offers alleviation by bringing more resources on the table. The relationships between collaborative parties in those scenarios are mostly peer-to-peer (P2P), without assuming fully cooperative relationships. Coalition partners often pursue cooperation but they deny to share sensitive intelligence that can deliver greater value to the collaborators [17]. In literature this kind of relationship model, where parties have cooperative and competitive attitudes from time to time, is called coopetition [18]. The PBMS is in charge here, playing a regulative role in order to keep balance between asset sharing and asset "protection".

The mechanism presented herein allows negotiation on policies with minimal human intervention. In traditional system management, policies associated with

PBMS are static (or rarely change); these systems, however, fail miserably in dynamic environments where policies need to adopt according to situational changes. We note, that it is not prudent to assume human operators in these environments that can effectively be on top of every change to manage PBMS(s) effectively; they require automated assistance.

Summarizing the intention behind applying IBN principles, on policy regulated asset sharing, it considers a cooperative negotiation approach, for strict policies refinement, that aims to: (a) increase social welfare by increasing the overall usability of collaborative assets while (b) remaining faithful to existing authorization policies, maintaining their core trends. Utilizing such a tool, a multilateral policy transformation can be achieved establishing a more effective PBMS, considering input and criteria from multi-party formations, for the benefit of the coalition.

The product of IBN execution is a new, refined, authorization policy rule. The IBN mechanism when refining the strict policy, considers the interest of both: asset owner and asset requestor. As far as the negotiation protocol is concerned, each negotiation session considers sets of two negotiators, so we deal with a bilateral negotiation mechanism. The issue that needs to be settled through the negotiation process, is the granting (or not) of access to non-sharable assets through policy refinement, thus, the protocol deals with single-attribute negotiations.

4.1 Policies Under Negotiation

The proposed policy negotiation framework is applied on authorization policies expressed in the Controlled English (CE) policy language [19]. CE policy language is an ontological approach that uses a Controlled Natural Language (CNL) for defining a policy representation that is both human-friendly (CNL representation) and unambiguous for computers (using a CE reasoner) [20]. CE is used to define domain models that describe the system to be managed. The domain models take the form of concept definitions and comprise objects, their properties, and the relationships amongst them. Those domain model components are the building blocks of the attribute-based CE policy language.

Each policy rule follows the if-condition(s)-then-action form and consists of four basic grammatical blocks as shown below:

- **Subject:** specifies the entities (human/machine) which interpret obligation policies or can access assets in authorization policies
- **Action:** what must be performed for obligations and what is permitted for authorization
- **Target:** objects on which actions are to be performed
- **Constraints:** boolean conditions

The utilization of CE here is two-folde. It is not only the user friendly formal representation of (a) the system to be managed and (b) its policy-based management, but it also helps decision makers who lack technical expertise to

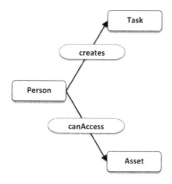

Fig. 1. Authorization policy negotiation scenario: domain model.

cope in a more transparent way with the complexities associated with policy negotiation. It does so by easing the comparison between the original and the refined policy proposed by IBN, using a user friendly representation. Figure 1 provides a graphical depiction of the CE-based domain model, which describes the smartphone access scenario of Sect. 3.2, while the CE representation of policy R1 is shown below.

```
Policy R1
If
( there is an Asset A named SMD ) and
( there is a Person P named P1 )
then
( the Person P canAccess the Asset A )
.
```

4.2   IBN Integration into Policy Regulated Asset Sharing

The role of policies in managing a system, is to guide its actions towards behaviors that would secure optimal system's outcomes. Different users have different rights, relationships and interests in regards to deployed coalition assets. Non-owner users want to gain access to assets in order to increase the probability of serving their tasks' needs, while owners want to protect their assets from unauthorized users. There is therefore a monopolistic resource usage case. The proposed negotiation approach considers both concerns in a single mechanism providing a mechanism that pursues a win-win negotiation outcome for any sets of negotiators. In other words, it tries through negotiation to redefine what is a suboptimal system outcome given: (a) the currently-deployed assets, (b) the user created tasks' needs and (c) the policies themselves.

The finite state diagram of Fig. 2 depicts the role the policy negotiation mechanism plays on tasks' implementation in collective endeavors. The human, task creator, in order to serve their appetite for information, creates tasks with

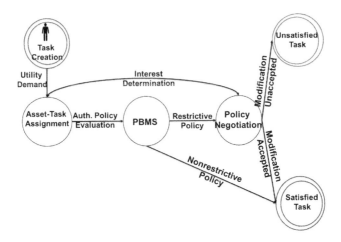

Fig. 2. Interest-based policy negotiation and task implementation.

a utility demand. The Asset-Task Assignment (ATA) component is in charge for optimizing the task utility by allocating the appropriate assets (information-providing assets) to each task. The PBMS component is responsible then, for evaluating and enforcing authorization policies made by multi-party collabora-tors. In the case of a non-restrictive authorization policy the task creator gets their task served. If the policy rule is restrictive, the policy negotiation compo-nent takes over. It first takes input from ATA, so that to define the creator's interest behind accessing the asset, and then modifies the policy rule accordingly passing it to the asset owner for confirmation. Given the asset owner's decision the task is then either satisfied or unsatisfied.

4.3   IBN Enabled PBMS

The policy negotiation framework can be integrated into a PBMS as a plug-in, enabling negotiation in policy enforcement process. A PBMS, as defined by stan-dards organizations such as IETF and DMTF consists of four basic components as shown in Fig. 3: (a) the policy management tool, (b) the policy repository, (c) the policy enforcement point, and (d) the policy decision point [21]. The pol-icy management tool is the entry point through which policy makers interface (write, update and delete) with policies to be enforced on the system. The policy repository is a specific data store where the policies generated by the manage-ment tool are held (step A1). The PEP is the logical component that can take actions on enforcing the policies' decisions, while the PDP is the logical entity that makes policy decisions for itself or for other system elements that request such decisions. Triggered by an event that needs policy's evaluation the PEP contacts PDP (step A2), which is responsible for fetching the necessary policy from policy repository (step A3, A4), evaluates it and decides the actions that need to be enforced on PEP (step A5).

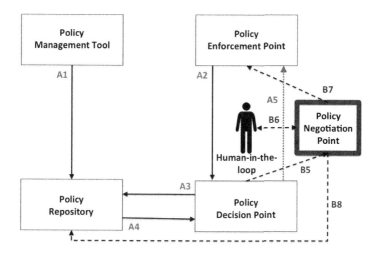

Fig. 3. IBN extended PBMS (Color figure online)

In addition to the four basic PBMS elements, Fig. 3 also includes a human-in-the-loop element, representing the roles played by the asset requestor and owner in the negotiation process. The additional component where the IBN framework resides is called Policy Negotiation Point (PNP) and lies between the PEP and PDP, interfacing also with the human-in-the-loop element. As mentioned before, the PNP is triggered to attempt to refine authorization policies when a user creates a task that cannot be served due to restrictive policies. The dashed lines show optional communication between the PBMS components, which is only established when a policy negotiation incident occurs. The red numbered part of the figure (flow paths which are prefixed by A's) describe the typical PBMS operational flow, while the green part (flow paths which are prefixed by B's) replace step A5 (red, dotted line) with the policy negotiation extension. Note that the separation between the components can be only logical when they reside in the same physical device. When PNP detects a restrictive policy (step B5) it refines it following the steps described in the following section and passes it to the asset owner for confirmation (step B6). If the asset owner accepts the refined policy rule, it is then pushed to PEP for enforcement (step B7) and either is stored in Policy Repository permanently (step B8) or can be only enforced once and then be discarded. This is on asset owner's jurisdiction. Otherwise step A5 is executed as before.

5   Achieving IBN Through Policy Refinement

The negotiators in our scenario are essentially decision makers who generally lack negotiation expertise. Thus, the IBN mechanism tries to take, as much as possible, the negotiation weight off their shoulders rather than providing them the means for making proposals and trade options themselves. However, it does not exclude them completely from the negotiation process as in fully automated models. To achieve such behavior it simply applies the IBN principles described in Chefs-Orange scenario of Sect. 3.1, exploiting the domain model's semantics, the semantics of the polices and the seamless relation between them as they both share the same CE representation.

The objective of the negotiation is the restrictive policies. Asking the why question as in Chefs-Orange scenario, to the asset requestor side, the PNP gets as a reply the reason why they need the asset for (i.e., to get their task served). Asking the why question to the asset owners/policy authors side, it gets the reasons why they do not want to grant access to their assets respectively. The prerequisite for the PNP operation here, is to have full and accurate knowledge of the managed system. This is achieved by having unlimited and unconditional access to both domain model and policy rules of Policy Repository. Unlike the majority of the proposed PBN approaches, the human-in-the-loop negotiators in our case are ignorant of the preferences of their opponents, while their knowledge in terms of the domain model reaches only the ground of their own expertise and ownership.

Utilizing CE as the formal representation for describing the system to be managed, and the representation for expressing authorization policies, eases the human-machine communication (i.e., communication between PNP and non-IT expert negotiators) for exchanging information regarding the negotiation process in a transparent way. The human-machine communication through CE conversational agents has been described in [22] where a human-machine, machine-machine and machine-human communication protocol was presented for providing intelligence to decision makers through fusing human input, unstructured with structured information. However, trying to automate as much as possible the negotiation process, the why question is rather rhetorical here (i.e., PNP does not require input from user). In the asset requestor's case, the answer to the why question is quite simple and straightforward and the PNP is aware of it just by taking input from the Asset-Task Assignment component of Fig. 2. The asset requestor clearly wants to access the asset in order to get their task served. Hence, a desired negotiation outcome as far as the asset requestor is concerned, is the derivation of a refined policy that has them included in the set of *Subject* policy block, with a positive access (i.e., canAccess) *Action*, to a *Target* set that includes the prohibited asset capable of serving their task's needs.

Inferring the answer to the why question from the asset owner's side, for understanding their interests and broadening the negotiation space, is a more challenging task. In general any application of authorization systems, aims to specify access rights to resources. A simple answer would be including the reasons why asset owners want to decline access rights to their resources in a negative authorization policy, or alternatively the reasons for granting access to their resources in a positive one. Thus, the why question from the asset owner/policy maker side can be extracted as the rationale of a policy rule. Combining the definitions from [23,24] the rationale is the reasoning pathway from contextual facts, assumptions and decisions, through the reasoning steps, which describes the development of an artifact including details of why it was designed.

Looking carefully at a policy rule, its rationale is basically described from the policy's *Condition(s)* block. The policy R1 of Sect. 4.1 is rather a simple one referring deliberately to a simple scenario and this might not be easily inferred. Considering other more complex policy rules with several conditions describing for instance constraints such as the age of the requestor or their expertise this is easier inferred.

However, this is not exactly the answer to the why question we are looking for here. Considering the policies as the means for guiding systems' actions towards behaviors to achieve optimal outcomes, the *Condition(s)* policy block refers to the actions level of the policy. Our focus here is on the higher level, this of the system's behavior. Focusing on a higher level, gives us the agility to find different policies as far as the actions are concerned, that provides the same functionality in terms of behavior; and the different policies we are looking for are those which serve the needs of the asset requestors as well. Achieving this goal, leads the negotiation to a win-win outcome like the one described in Chefs-Orange scenario. The next steps describe the process for reaching such an outcome.

In the event of a restricting authorization policy, that prohibits a task creator/asset requestor to access desired resources, in order to get their task served, the PNP, is activated taking input from ATA component as shown in input step of Fig. 4 (upper left hand side). The input refers to both: (a) the task's needs and (b) the very specific resources needed for its implementation. In a policy-based, access control system, the resources required for a task's implementation are represented by the *Target* policy rule block. If the *Target* block of the currently applied/restricting policy rule refers to a superset of the resources passed as input to PNP from ATA then the policy refinement mechanism develops as follows:

Step 1: The simplistic domain model of Fig. 1 presents only the concepts involved in the smartphone scenario of Sect. 3.2 and their relationships. It hides however their properties. Assume that the concept Asset has a property named *Provided capability* and that the Asset instance named SMD has the Provided capability property named *Tethering*. Thus, the policy R1 by denying access to SMD, it denies access to any of SMD's provided capability or in other words denies access to any of SMD's subsets capable of serving a desired task. Thus, the IBN mechanism, trying to broaden the negotiation space, separates the SMD from its Provided capability property as shown in Step1 of Fig. 4 allowing SMD's capabilities to be subject of a policy rule *Target* block.

Step 2: The concept Task has a property named *Required capability* and the Task instance *Email submission* has a number of required capabilities including that of *Tethering*. The second step of IBN process, considering input from ATA regarding task's needs, it separates it from its Required capability property as shown in Step2 of Fig. 4.

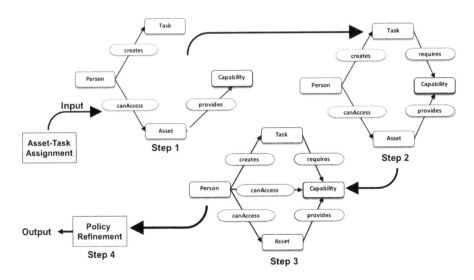

Fig. 4. IBN through Policy Refinement: Graphical representation.

Step 3: In Step 3, as shown in Fig. 4, now that required/provided Capability exists as standalone concept in the conceptual model, the IBN mechanism allows for a relationship and thus for an *Action* policy rule block to emerge between asset requestor (presented as Person concept) and asset's capabilities (presented as Capability concept). In other words the asset requestor (i.e., P2) now can access a subset/subsystem of the asset that provides required capabilities (i.e., *Tethering*), for their task's to be served and this can be expressed in CE policy rule and reasoned on CE conceptual model.

Step 4: This step performs the *policy refinement*[1]. The asset requestor (i.e., P2) is represented by the *Subject* block of the refined policy rule, which has as *Action* block a positive authorization action (i.e., canAccess) and its *Target* block refers to the provided by the prohibited Asset and required by the desired Task Capability (i.e., Tethering). The CE refined policy *R1-Refined* below is passed then to the asset owner for approval.

```
Policy R1-Refined
if
   ( there is an asset A named SMD ) and
   ( there is a Capability C named Tethering ) and
   ( there is a Person P named P2 )
then
   ( the Person P canAccess the Capability C ).
```

---

[1] Note that the term policy refinement herein refers to a different process than the policy refinement in [25], which describes the process of interpreting more general, business layer policies to more specific, system layer ones.

The asset owner P1 is in charge of approving or not the replacement of policy rule R1 from the proposed by IBN policy rule R1-Refined. In the case of approval the refined rule R1-Refined is enforced over R1 providing access to SMD's *Tethering* capability. It is then either stored in Policy Repository or can be only enforced once and then be discarded. This is on asset owner's jurisdiction.

6   Policy IBN Evaluation

Ideally, the evaluation of the behavior and effectiveness of IBN as a negotiation mechanism for policy-regulated asset sharing, should had human participants involved, operating in a collaborative environment, such as an opportunistic network scenario. Considering their own sharing constraints, they would be responsible for the approval or rejection of the refined policies proposed by IBN mechanism.

6.1   Simulation Setup

We conduct an experiment by simulating this environment, to test the policy IBN mechanism's behavior prior to carrying out a more resource-costly human participant experiment. The simulation describes an asset sharing scenario of a small, short lived opportunistic network. In the scenario, there are three basic concepts: (a) the human users, (b) their assets and (c) the tasks they create. The users are the asset owners and in charge of sharing them with others through a PBMS. Being eager for consuming information, users create tasks that require specific resources provided by the deployed assets in order to be served. Often, task creators cannot serve their tasks just by utilizing their own resources and ask for support by their peers in the opportunistic network.

The simulated, opportunistic network scenario assumes 8 users, each one of them owns one asset. There are three types of assets, as many as the types of the tasks the users can create. Each asset type has the capability to serve a particular task type meeting its information requirements. As far as the asset sharing is concerned, it is managed through policies written by asset owners. Each user opts whether to exclusively use their assets (following concerns regarding security, privacy, performance and other) or sharing them with the others. This intention is expressed through authorization policies. We do not assume any spatial constraints in the simulated network, which implies that all the users, operate in distance where their devices have enough transmission/reception capacity to communicate with each other. Moreover, one out of three asset types has a monolithic architectural design making it capable of serving only one particular task, unlike the other two, more capable devices that can operate as platforms that provide several capabilities, able to serve more than one task types.

To better visualize the simulated scenario, think of the following vignette. Eight individuals (i.e., opportunistic network's users) go hiking across a mountain. The three types of assets are: (a) a smartphone device such as the SMD described in previous sections, (b) a music player equipped with transmitter/receiver and communication protocol capabilities able to communicate with other assets of the same type and (c) a monolithic wearable pedometer device. The three possible tasks created by users are: (a) the submission of an email, which requires internet connection provided by a smartphone device, (b) a music sharing task, which is served by portable music players capable of exchanging songs and playlists with other devices of the same type and (c) a step counting task, served by the monolithic pedometer device.

The IBN mechanism, following the steps described in the previous section is only capable to be applied on polylithic assets (i.e., SMD and music player device) when strict authorization policies are applied. For the implementation of the step counting task, the user needs to physically access a pedometer device. Hence, if the user that creates and need to serve a step counting task, either does not own a pedometer device or any of the pedometer devices of the network are not shareable due to strict authorization policies, the IBN mechanism is unable to provide any policy refinement.

The total number of created tasks is 100. They are created randomly by the eight users, which implies uneven number of tasks for each user. Task types are also randomly picked as do the types of the user owned assets. As it was mentioned before, the main objective of the IBN mechanism is to increase the social welfare. To measure the effect of IBN on social welfare in our scenario we use as metrics the proportion of served and dropped tasks. A task is considered dropped (i.e., unsupported by opportunistic network's deployed assets), if there are no available resources to satisfy the task utility demand.

To have a better picture of IBN effect on social welfare, we experiment with three different asset sharing models. The first and strictest one deals with very conservative (in terms of sharing policies) users where they do not share any of their devices with their peers. In this case the asset sharing is set to 0 % and the user created tasks can only be served, if and only if their creators' devices are capable to do so. In the second experiment we set the asset sharing to 25 % namely 25 % of the total devices are shareable and finally the last and most liberal case deals with 50 % asset sharing. In all three experiments we measure the proportion of served and dropped tasks when: (a) the IBN mechanism is deactivated **IBN OFF** and (b) the IBN mechanism is activated **IBN ON**. For all six experimental cases

– *Asset sharing 0 %:* (1) IBN OFF, (2) IBN ON
– *Asset sharing 25 %:* (1) IBN OFF, (2) IBN ON
– *Asset sharing 50 %:* (1) IBN OFF, (2) IBN ON

we execute each simulation instance 100 times, averaging the measurements (i.e., the percentage of served and dropped tasks).

6.2   Simulation RedLines

For simulating the approval or rejection of the refined policies (i.e., the relaxed policies provided by IBN) we utilize a mechanism called *RedLine*. We borrowed

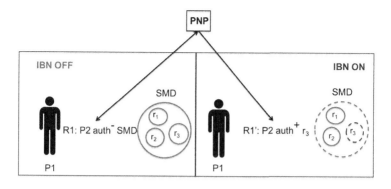

Fig. 5. PNP: IBN OFF vs IBN ON

the term RedLine from the worldwide used phrase "Red line", or "cross the red line", which means a figurative point of no return or a limit past which safety can no longer be guaranteed. Each user at the beginning of the simulation, randomly gets their RedLines settled, which defines their intention to approve or reject the refined policies. Given the complexity, in terms of assets capabilities and tasks requirements, we assume, it is difficult for opportunistic network's users to write fine-grained policies to define access control on every possible combination of them. In SMD case for instance, the asset owner P1, being unable to cope with the complexity of matching SMD's capabilities and Email submission task's requirements he opts not to share any of SMD's capabilities with P2 following personal concerns. Hence, he simply expresses his constraints at higher level, setting access control policies at the assets level only. The RedLine mechanism, defines the distance between the asset owners' high-level authorization policies and their "real" willingness to share their assets or subsets of them with their peers.

This assumption is depicted in Fig. 5. On the left hand side where IBN is inactive, user P1 expresses his strict constraints, in terms of SMD sharing with P2 through high-level policy rule R1, according to which the requestor user P2 is not allowed to access it and as a consequence he forbids access to any of SMD's subsystems (namely resources r_1, r_2 & r_3 and their provided capabilities). The PNP, activating IBN mechanism as shown on the right hand side of Fig. 5 proposes a finer-grained rule R1' according to which the requestor user R2 can access (as the dotted line circles indicate) the necessary SMD subsystem (namely resource r_3 and its provided capability) in order to get his task served. The intention of P1 in terms of approving or rejecting the refined R1' is simulated by users' RedLines mechanism.

IBN mechanism, as mentioned before, attempts to lower barriers, through policy refinement, in order to establish better collaboration through asset sharing (i.e., increase the overall number of served tasks and thus increase the social welfare) while maintaining the level of compromise from the asset owners point of view. Those users whose RedLines are more relaxed compared to their policies,

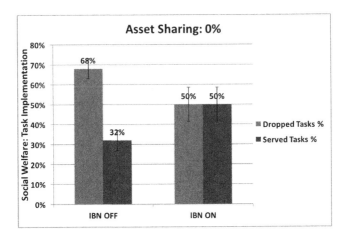

Fig. 6. IBN effect on social welfare: Asset Sharing 0 % (Color figure online)

represent those who believe that they do not compromise any of their concerns expressed through their initial, strict sharing policies and proceed with accepting the refined ones.

6.3   Simulation Results

The experimental results are presented through Figs. 6, 7 and 8 and the error bars on clustered column charts represent (+ / -) 1 Standard Deviation. In all three sets of experiments, when the IBN mechanism is activated the social welfare in terms of task implementation is higher as expected. As it is shown the effectiveness of IBN is higher in strict environments and decreases as moving to more liberal ones. In Fig. 6, for 0 % asset sharing model, the IBN OFF columns indicate that only 32 % of the total tasks are served meaning that given the users' information need only the one third of it can be served by their own resources. For the same sharing model, when IBN is activated the proportion of served tasks increases to 50 %.

In first and most strict case Fig. 6, the margin between dropped and served tasks when IBN is inactive is 36 % units. In IBN ON case the proportion of dropped and served tasks is even. In the second experiment and 25 % asset sharing model, as shown in Fig. 7, the served tasks proportion outperforms the dropped tasks' whether the IBN is active or not. With IBN ON however, the proportion of served tasks is 8 % units more compared to when IBN is OFF.

Same trend in the last and most liberal case where half of the assets in the opportunistic network are shared with the network's users. The margin here between IBN ON and IBN OFF cases almost disappears with IBN ON case performing slightly better with 2 % units. Finally, as shown in Fig. 8 in the simulated opportunistic network environment, if the asset sharing ratio is higher than 50 % the IBN mechanism has not much to offer, while it is a useful tool

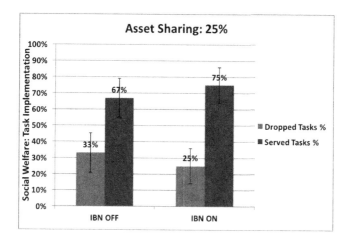

Fig. 7. IBN effect on social welfare: Asset Sharing 25 % (Color figure online)

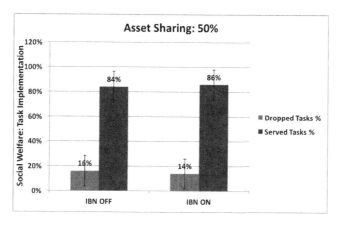

Fig. 8. IBN effect on social welfare: Asset Sharing 50 % (Color figure online)

in promoting collaboration through asset sharing, for stricter (in terms of asset sharing) environments.

7   Conclusion and Future Work

In summary the proposed IBN mechanism provides a policy refinement tool for revising asset sharing policies in dynamic, multi-party environments. The IBN paradigm is a good fit in multi-party environments, where collaboration is promoted, to achieve mutually satisfactory negotiation outcomes. The proposed mechanism is seamlessly interfaced with standardized PBMS and provides the means to directly negotiate with policies. Finally, the experimental evaluation indicates that when the IBN mechanism is activated the social welfare, in terms of task implementation, increases, while the effectiveness of IBN is higher in stricter environments and decreases as moving to more liberal ones.

As for the future research, there are plans for (a) extending the IBN steps with regards to broadening the negotiation space considering heuristics related to users and their characteristics, such as, their team affiliation that can improve IBN's effectiveness through sharing assets and provided service horizontally (e.g. inner-team) unlike the current vertical (i.e., user-to-user) approach and (b) conduct experiments involving human participants.

Acknowledgment. This research was sponsored by the US Army Research Laboratory and the UK Ministry of Defense and was accomplished under Agreement Number W911NF-06-3-0001. The views and conclusions contained in this document are those of the authors and should not be interpreted as representing the official policies, either expressed or implied, of the US Army Research Laboratory, the US Government, the UK Ministry of Defense or the UK Government. The US and UK Governments are authorized to reproduce and distribute reprints for Government purposes notwithstanding any copyright notation hereon.

References

1. Jennings, N., et al.: Automated negotiation: Prospects, methods and challenges. Group Decis. Negot. **10**(2), 199–215 (2001)
2. Walton, D., Krabbe, E.: Commitment in Dialogue: Basic Concepts of Interpersonal Reasoning. SUNY Press, Albany, New York (1995)
3. Fisher, R., et al.: Getting to Yes Negotiating an Agreement Without Giving In, 2nd edn. Random House Business Books, London (1999). Reprint
4. Pasquier, P., et al.: An empirical study of interest-based negotiation. Auton. Agent. Multi-Agent Syst. **22**(2), 249–288 (2011)
5. Delaney, M., Foroughi, A., Perkins, W.: An empirical study of the efficacy of a computerized negotiation support system (NSS). Decis. Support Syst. **20**(3), 185–197 (1997)
6. Wooldridge, M., Jennings, N.R.: Intelligent agents: theory and practice. Knowl. Eng. Rev. **10**, 115–152 (1995)
7. Faratin, P., Sierra, C., Jennings, N.R.: Negotiation decision functions for autonomous agents. Robot. Auton. Syst. **24**(3–4), 159–182 (1998). Multi-Agent Rationality
8. Martin, O., Ariel, R.: A Course in Game Theory. The MIT Press, Cambridge (1994)
9. Kraus, S.: Strategic Negotiation in Multiagent Environments. MIT Press, Cambridge (2001)
10. Rahwan, I., et al.: Argumentation-based negotiation. Knowl. Eng. Rev. **18**(4), 343–375 (2003)
11. Seamons, K., et al.: Requirements for policy languages for trust negotiation. In: 3rd International Workshop on Policies for Distributed Systems and Networks, POLICY 2002, pp. 68–79 (2002)
12. Jang, I., Shi, W., Yoo, H.: Policy negotiation system architecture for privacy protection. In: Proceedings - 4th International Conference on Networked Computing and Advanced Information Management, NCM 2008, vol. 2, pp. 592–597 (2008)

13. Comuzzi, M., Francalanci, C.: Agent-based negotiation in cooperative processes: Automatic support to underwriting insurance policies. In: ACM International Conference Proceeding Series, vol. 60, pp. 121–129 (2004)
14. Tang, J.-F., Xu, X.-L.: An adaptive model of service composition based on policy driven and multi-agent negotiation. In: Proceedings of the 2006 International Conference on Machine Learning and Cybernetics, vol. 2006, pp. 113–118 (2006)
15. Cheng, V., Hung, P., Chiu, D.: Enabling web services policy negotiation with privacy preserved using XACML. In: Proceedings of the Annual Hawaii International Conference on System Sciences (2007)
16. Sandholm, T.: Distributed rational decision making. In: Weiss, G. (ed.) Multiagent Systems, pp. 201–258. MIT Press (1999)
17. Loebecke, C., Van Fenema, P.C., Powell, P.: Co-opetition and knowledge transfer. SIGMIS Database **30**(2), 14–25 (1999)
18. Brandenburger, A., Nalebuff, A.: Co-Opetition. Doubleday, New York (1997)
19. Parizas, C., Pizzocaro, D., Preece, A., Zerfos, P.: Managing ISR sharing policies at the network edge using controlled english. In: Proceedings of Ground/Air Multisensor Interoperability, Integration, and Networking for Persistent ISR IV (2013)
20. Mott, D.: Summary of controlled english. ITACS (2010)
21. Yavatkar, R., Pendarakis, K., Guerin, R.: A framework for policy-based admission control (2000). http://www.ietf.org/rfc/rfc2753.txt. Accessed 29 Sep 2015
22. Preece, A., Braines, D., Pizzocaro, D., Parizas, C.: Human-machine conversations to support mission-oriented information provision. In: Proceedings of the Annual International Conference on Mobile Computing and Networking, MOBICOM, pp. 43–49 (2013)
23. Moran, T.P., Carroll, J.M.: Design Rationale: Concepts, Techniques, and Use. Erlbaum Associates Inc., Hillsdale (1996)
24. Dave, M., et al.: Hybrid rationale and controlled natural language for shared understanding. In: The 6th Annual Conference of Knowledge Systems for Coalition Operations (2010)
25. Bandara, A., Lupu, E., Moffett, J., Russo, A.: A goal-based approach to policy refinement. In: Proceedings - Fifth IEEE International Workshop on Policies for Distributed Systems and Networks, POLICY 2004, pp. 229–239 (2004)

An Empirical Evaluation of the Huginn Constrained Norm-Aware BDI Reasoner

Tiago Luiz Schmitz$^{(\boxtimes)}$ and Jomi Fred Hübner

Federal University of Santa Catarina, CP 476, Florianópolis, SC 88040-900, Brazil
tiagolschmitz@gmail.com, jomi.hubner@ufsc.br

Abstract. A multi-agent system can be helped by a normative system that guides its (autonomous) agents towards an expected behavior. These agents on their side have to reason about the impact of those norms in their personal desires. Considering that agents have limited resources, it is necessary to reason also about available resources and whether they are enough to reach goals generated by norms and desires. The Huggin proposes and implements a deliberation process that uses the concept of mood to reason about norms, desires and resources. The proposed deliberation process is conceived as an optimization problem known as multidimensional knapsack problem with multiple-choice. The computational complexity of this process is NP-complete and thus it can likely be a bottleneck in the agent reasoning cycle. The main goal of this paper is to identify how the desires, norms and resources (input variables) impact in the reasoning cycle execution. Considering the input variables, we empirically measure their impact on the usage percentage of Huginn in the agent overall process time. We conclude in this work that, despite of the process complexity, the impact on the reasoning is acceptable for the usual number of norms, desires and resources of current MAS applications.

1 Introduction

MAS is a suitable approach to develop open systems, where unknown agents can flow through freely. To protect these systems against malicious agents, a normative system can be used to control their behavior [1]. From the agent side, the ability to understand and interpret the normative system is a desirable feature. Normative agents shall solve conflicts between desires and norms, since they may have a desire to reach a specific goal, but a norm prohibits them to reach this goal. These agents need thus to balance what is good for them and the system and therefore decide whether to commit to a goal or not.

In the specific case where normative agents have limited resources they need to reason also about available resources. Sometimes, an agent can agree with the norm, but it does not have sufficient resources to reach the goal generated by the norm. Or, the norm's reward does not justify the required resource.

The authors are grateful for the support given by CNPq, 156992/2011-6, and 448462/2014-1 and 306301/2012-1.

© Springer International Publishing Switzerland 2016
V. Dignum et al. (Eds.): COIN 2015, LNAI 9628, pp. 320–334, 2016.
DOI: 10.1007/978-3-319-42691-4_18

An agent that is capable of reasoning about norms and managing resources can get better results for the system and for itself within its contexts. Mobile robots are an example of this kind of application, because they work with limited resources and in some cases they need to choose among norms and desires. For example, a robot on Mars has accepted a norm that obliges it to gather rocks and it also has the desire to stay in the safety zone. The rocks however are out of the safety zone. The agent also has only 5 units of fuel. Therefore the agent needs to solve the conflict between the norm and the desire (to gather rocks or to stay in the safety zone) and do not spend more fuel than it has got.

The Huginn model [2] proposes a reasoning model inspired in the mood concept [3] capable to deliberate about desires and norms, considering available resources. The proposed model is a BDI architecture extension where the main features are the following:

– The deliberation process is translated into an optimization problem (multiple-choice multidimensional knapsack);
– The model deals with conflicts between norms and desires;
– The model manages the resources to reach the best gain.

To develop these features, Huginn implementation has a process that can insert some bottlenecks in the agent reasoning cycle. Therefore the goal of this paper is the identification of **how the quantity of desires, norms, conflicts, available resources and resources types impact in the reasoning cycle execution**. To accomplish this goal, we conducted an empirical evaluation (Sect. 4) of Huginn implementation (shortly presented in Sect. 3.3).

2 Preliminaries

In this section is briefly presented the main concepts used in this paper.

2.1 Norms

Norms are representations of expected behaviors in a certain group population. Many studies [4–6] in the sociology field describe different norm types in the same normative system. This paper deals with deontic norms. These norms usually define obligations, prohibitions, and permissions for the agents. Obligations can be used to define states of the world that agents have to achieve. Prohibitions can be used to define states of the world that agents have to not achieve. Permissions are not explicitly considered in this paper, but can be seen as the negation of a prohibition.

Normally norms are not applied all the time. Their specification has thus activation and expiration conditions. The activation condition defines when the norm is active. The agent knows that when the activation condition is true, it needs to accomplish the norm. The expiration condition defines when the norm is inactive. The sanction is the negative reinforcement for an agent who does not accomplish a norm. The reward is the positive reinforcement for an agent that accomplish a norm. The Huginn adopts the norm as represented by the tuple 1:

$$\langle D, \Phi, T, A, E, S, \gamma \rangle \tag{1}$$

where $D \in \{Obl, Pro\}$ is the deontic norm's type, obligation (Obl) or prohibition (Pro); Φ is the state of the world related to the norm; T is the agent target; A is the activation condition; E is the expiration condition; S is the sanction and γ is the reward. The sanction and reward values are numbers between 0 and 1. For the norm "the driver is prohibited to run faster than 40 Km/h in urban area", the target is the driver; the norm is activated when the driver enters an urban area; is inactive when it leaves the urban area. The driver receives a sanction if he disobeys this norm and a reward if he obeys. This norm is represented by the tuple (2).

$$\langle Pro, run\_fast\_than\_40Kmh, driver, urban\_area, \neg urban\_area, 1.0, 0.1 \rangle \tag{2}$$

2.2 Desires

The Huginn proposes that a desire is composed of: a state that the agent wants to reach (Φ), a expiration condition (E), a necessity (N) and an intensity (I). Necessity and intensity are scalar values between 0 and 1. The necessity represents how much it is essential to satisfy the desire. If the agent does not satisfy the desire, it will suffer by the necessity to satisfy it. The intensity represents how much it is desirable to reach a goal. This work considers a desire as a tuple as in (3).

$$\langle \Phi, E, N, I \rangle \tag{3}$$

For example, a glutton agent has a desire with intensity 1 to be fed. However the agent has a high fat percentage, thus, in this moment, the agent has a necessity 0.2 of being fed. This desire is represented by a tuple like (4). The desire is expired when the agent has been fed.

$$\langle fed, fed, 0.2, 1 \rangle \tag{4}$$

2.3 Mood Concept

This paper uses a mood psychological concept [3] as the main inspiration for a deliberation process that considers norms, desires and resources. Thayer considers that the mood is a relation between *energy* and *tension* to gain *benefits* [7]. A person can be energetic or tired while also being tense or calm. The energy is the state of being (tired or energetic) and the tension is the psychic state of being (tense or calm). According to Thayer, people feel better when they are in a calm-energy mood. They feel worse when in a tense-tired state.

Different elements can regulate the mood. These elements can change the mood because they provide a gain of *benefit*. This gain provides a satisfaction, relaxing the being's tension. For example, people often use food to regulate mood. Thayer identifies a fundamental food-mood connection, and advises against the reliance on food as a mood regulator. Another element that can regulate the mood is the physical activity. For example, great quantities of hormones are produced during a walk. On the other hand, the walk consumes energy and generates tension during the process. However, the hormones it produces can counteract the tension, as experienced in a bad mood.

The "being" needs to find the middle term among regulatory elements (food, physical activity, and others) to reach the best mood state. Therefore, *the "being" needs to choose things that avoid tension and give more benefit, counterattacking the bad mood.*

3   Huginn

The normative reasoning based on mood enables the agent to reasoning about norms and desires considering the available resources. The Fig. 1 represents this context. The agent recognizes his desires and obtains the environmental resources and norms. Hereafter, the agent deliberates about the desires, norms and resources and, by committing to some goals, it changes its behavior to reach a better mood. The mood concept [3] allows us to conceive a deliberation process to choose the best set of desires and norms (decreasing the tensions and increasing the benefit).

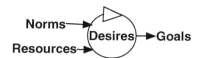

Fig. 1. Model overview

In the proposed model, the energy of the agents is the amount of resources they need to have to satisfy the norm or desire. The agent's tension represents how much it costs to do not satisfy the norm or desire. The agent's benefit represents how much it receives to satisfy the norm or desire.

The agent's energy state is a n-dimensional space, whose each dimension represents one limited resource. For example, an agent has two resources, tires and fuel. Thus the mood space is two-dimensional and it uses these resources to minimize the tension and maximize the benefit (best mood).

Considering that in deontic logic a prohibition can be expressed as an obligation to not reach a state of the world [8] and that Huginn considers that states as goals (from the agent perspective), all norms are related to goals, as well as all desires. In Huggin thus the element D of norms (1) is always *Obl* and the element St is a goal. Similarly, the element St of desires (3) is also a goal. The Huginn model proposed to model the energies, tension and benefit as an optimization problem for the agent to find the best mood (less tension and more

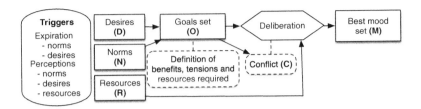

Fig. 2. Deliberation process flowchart

benefit). Therefore it is possible to use an optimization solver to find the best set of goals from norms and desires with the available resources.

In this paper the deliberation process has as inputs the desires, norms and resources and it has as output the best set of goals. The deliberation process is triggered when some event in that input data occurs. Examples of such event are norm or desire expiration, a new norm, desire, or resource. The Fig. 2 illustrates the proposed deliberation process. The hexagon represents the process of desire and norm selection, the rectangles represent sets, and the dashed box represents the definition of benefits, tensions and resources required. In the Fig. 2, the set D is the set of all desires, N is composed of all active norms and R is composed of all available resources. The set O is composed of goals included in desires and norms with definitions of benefits, tensions and resources required for each set element, C is composed of all conflicts among goals generated by norms and desires, M is the set of goals that maximizes the agent gains.

3.1   Definition of Energies, Tension and Benefit

For each goal in O it is defined: how much *tension* would be generated by not satisfying the desire or norm, how much *benefit* would be generated if that is satisfied and how much *resources* would be consumed to satisfy the desire or norm.

In this paper the tension is represented by the *loss* that the agent suffers by not fulfilling a desire or norm. The tension is represented by a function which returns a value between 0 and 1 as defined in (5).

$$tension : O \rightarrow [0..1] \tag{5}$$

The tension is based on the norm's sanction for goal originated from norms. The tension is based on the desires's necessity for goals from desires. The tension is the sum of sanction and necessity when the goal appears both in a norm and a desire. The tension is defined in (6), where $sanction(o)$ returns the norm's sanction value (the S value represented in (1)) and $necessity(o)$ returns the desire necessity value (the N value represented in (3)).

$$tension(o) = \begin{cases} sanction(o) & \text{if } o \text{ is generated by a norm} \\ necessity(o) & \text{if } o \text{ is generated by a desire} \\ sanction(o) + necessity(o) & \text{if } o \text{ is generated by both} \end{cases} \tag{6}$$

The *benefit* is the reward for the agent to satisfy a desire or norm. This benefit is a function that returns a value between 0 and 1 corresponding to the agent's gain. This function type is defined in (7).

$$benefit : O \rightarrow [0..1] \tag{7}$$

The benefit is based on the norm's reward for goal originated from norms, the desire's intensity for goal from desires and a sum of reward and intensity when it comes from both. A generic form of the benefit is defined in (8), where $reward(o)$ returns the norm reward value (the γ value represented in (1)) and $intensity(o)$ returns the desire intensity value (the I value represented in (3)).

$$benefit(o) = \begin{cases} reward(o) & \text{if } o \text{ is generated by a norm} \\ intensity(o) & \text{if } o \text{ is generated by a desire} \\ reward(o) + intensity(o) & \text{if } o \text{ is generated by both} \end{cases} \tag{8}$$

As previously presented, the available resources are the agent's energies. These represents a $|R|$-dimensional space where each dimension corresponds to a resource type r, where $r \in R$. In this way the function rr returns a real value corresponding to the required resource quantity to satisfy a goal. This function is defined in (9) and $rr(o, r)$ returns how much of resource r is necessary to satisfy the goal o.

$$rr : O \times R \rightarrow \mathbb{R}^+ \tag{9}$$

For example, one goal g originated from both a norm (with sanction 0.3 and reward 0.5) and a desire (with necessity 0.6 and intensity 0.3), has $benefit(g) = 0.8$ and $tension(g) = 0.9$.

The Huginn considers that conflicts between goals are informed by the developer as in the predicate (10). Where is possible to declare the conflict between two huginn goals ($o1$ and $o2$).

$$huginn\_conflict(o1, o2) \tag{10}$$

3.2 Deliberation

In the Huginn, the agent deliberates about which goal from the set O will be adopted to reach the best mood (set M). To do this, it needs to treat O element's conflicts and resource's conflicts that may happen.

The majority of the related work [9–11] treats the conflicts using preference systems. Therefore, a norm or desire with high-priority will be fulfilled even if it underutilized the agent's capacity. For example, an obligation with high-priority consumes 5 liters of fuel to grant a benefit. On the other hand, the agent has other two obligations with low-priority that together consume the same 5 liters of fuel, and they grant a better benefit. Therefore to fulfill the high-priority obligation the agent's capacity will be underutilized. To avoid this, the Huginn model proposes to maximize the agent's benefit, choosing non-conflicting goals that compose the best benefit using the available resources.

The Huginn models the choice of a set of non-conflicting goals as a multiple-choice knapsack problem [12]. This problem has an additional constraint in relation to the traditional knapsack problem. The items are divided into classes. To solve the problem, at most one item can be chosen per class. For example the items torch, lantern, candle, penknife, and tent are divided in three classes: light (torch, lantern, candle), cut (penknife), and shelter (tent). Therefore, a feasible solution of this problem does not contain in the knapsack a torch, a lantern or a candle simultaneously.

In the Huginn case, each class c is a set of conflicting goals and every goal belongs to one class. A goal does not have conflict if it belongs a class with just itself. With these classes and the constraint (11) it is granted that at most one element of each class will be chosen. In the constraint (11), m_o is the binary decision variable of goal o. When the m_o value is 1 the goal o is selected and when m_o is 0 it is not selected. C is a subset of the power set of O (12) that contains all classes (C) mutually exclusive (13) and collective exhaustive (14).

$$\sum_{o \in c} m_o \leq 1, c \in C \tag{11}$$

$$C \subseteq 2^O \tag{12}$$

$$c_i \cap c_j = \emptyset, i \neq j, 0 < i < |C|, 0 < j < |C| \tag{13}$$

$$\bigcup_{c \in C} c = O \tag{14}$$

For example, the goal $\neg p$, p, and q are divided in two classes, represented in (15). $\neg p$ and p are in the same class because they are obviously in conflict.

$$C = \{\{\neg p, p\}, \{q\}\} \tag{15}$$

The Huginn models the choice of set of goal respecting the available resources as a multidimensional knapsack problem [12]. To solve the resource conflict problem, each resource $r \in R$ is a constraint in the problem. Thus, a solution for the problem shall not pass the available resources limit. The inequality (16) is the optimization problem constraint that represents this condition. Where $ar(r)$ returns how much resource r the agent has.

$$\sum_{c \in C} \sum_{o \in c} (m_o rr(o, r)) \leq ar(r), \quad r \in R \tag{16}$$

The problem definition is thus presented in (17). In this problem formulation it is possible to see that the maximization function proposed to choose the desires and norms considers their benefits and tensions. This function shows mood generated by the *benefit* plus the *tension*. If the agent satisfies a desire or norm it receives the benefit and avoids the tension. For example, when some goal o is fulfilled the agent benefit is 0.5 and when the goal o is not fulfilled it loses (tension) 0.4. Therefore when the agent fulfills the goal o, it gains 0.5 and *does not lose* 0.4. Thus mood generated by the goal o is 0.9.

$$Maximize \sum_{c \in C} \sum_{o \in c} (m_o(benefit(o) + tension(o))) \qquad (17)$$

Subject to

$$\sum_{c \in C} \sum_{o \in c} (m_o rr(o, r)) \leq ar(r), r \in R$$

$$\sum_{o \in c} m_o \leq 1, c \in C$$

The solution for the optimization problem, based on the decision variable m, defines the set M as

$$M = \{o | m_o = 1\} \qquad (18)$$

3.3 Huginn for Jason - Implementation

The Huginn for Jason [13] is an implementation of the Huginn model [2]. The Jason reasoning cycle was customized including the normative deliberation as defined by Huginn. This new step identifies the goals from desires and norms and triggers the solver to select, drop, suspend or resume them. In Jason, all relevant mind change generates an event. For example, added beliefs, removed beliefs, added desires, etc. The Huginn monitors these events to identify the changes of resources and the goals from norms and desires.

The Algorithm 1 is the Huginn implementation for Jason and it has three steps. The first step (lines 2 to 7 of Algorithm 1) is a search in Events queue (F_i) for new goals from norms and desires. When a new one is found, it is added in the set (O). The second step (lines 8 to 12) of this algorithm is a search in the O set for expired elements. When an expired element is found, it is removed from the set. In the third step (line 13 to 18), the optimization is executed ($deliberation(O, C, R)$) and it produces a new set M (the set of goals that produces the best mood for the agent). Each selected goal ($m \in M$) will be resumed and each goal not selected ($o \in \{O - M\}$) will be suspended.

4   Empirical Evaluation

This section presents the design of experiments, the infrastructure and the analytical methods used to evaluate the Huginn. The Subsect. 4.1 presents the design of the experiments where we define the agents code, the input variables and the sample set size. The Subsect. 4.2 presents the infrastructure used in the experiments and the analytical methods used to extract the data of output variable, the usage percentage. The usage percentage is how much CPU time was used to execute the Huginn in relation to the other processes of the agent.

4.1   Design of Experiments

The aim of this evaluation is to answer the question: **what is the impact of each input variables in the performance of Huginn agent reasoning?**

Algorithm 1. Huginn for Jason algorithm

Inputs: Events queue (F_i); Goals set (O); Conflict set (C); Resources set (R)

1 newDeliberation←false;
2 **for** *each* $f \in F_i$ **do**
3   **if** *f means the agent has the goal o from a norm or desire* **then**
4        $O \leftarrow O \cup \{o\}$;
5   newDeliberation←true;
6   **if** *f means the agent has more resource* **then**
7   newDeliberation←true;
8 **for** *each* $o \in O$ **do**
9   **if** *expiration condition of o is true* **then**
10       $O \leftarrow O \backslash \{o\}$;
11   drop(o);
12   newDeliberation←true;
13 **if** *newDeliberation* **then**
14    $M \leftarrow deliberation(O, C, R)$;
15   **for** *each* $o \in O - M$ **do**
16   suspend(o);
17   **for** *each* $m \in M$ **do**
18   resume (m);

We choose a simple scenario to evaluate the impact of the Huginn on the reasoning cycle, because this is the main goal of this paper. In this scenario, the agent has different norms and desires, but the plan that reaches the goal generated from them is the same for all. The plan calculates the fifteenth element of the Fibonacci series. The plan is the same for all because his role in the experiment is just to simulate time consumption. Also in the designed scenario, the agent adds one new desire or norm by cycle to stress the deliberation process where the set O is continuously changed.

These experiments has four independent input variables: number of goals from desires and norms (O), conflicts between desires and norms (C), resources available (Q) and resources types (R). These variables can impact the results of the tests. In order to evaluate Huggin under these variables, their values are varied in three classes (low, medium and high) as shown in Table 1. The conflict variable (C) is a percentage of the maximal quantity of conflict. For example, 100 norms taken two by two produces and arrangement of 10000 different combinations. However, conflicts between desires and norms are symmetric, and therefore it is possible to represent 5000 combinations of conflicts. If C is 50 %, it will be randomly generated 2500 conflicts.

The sample set is composed of agent instances created using the values of the Table 1. To obtain a good sample set we observed two items: the randomness and the coverage of the sample set. To ensure the randomness, the benefits, sanctions and resources required are generated randomly, minimizing the effects of

Table 1. Variables X Values

Variable	Low	Medium	High
O	10	50	100
C	10 %	50 %	90 %
Q	30	70	100
R	1	2	3

unexpected variability in the observed responses [14]. The benefits and sanctions range is from 0 to 1. The resources required range from 0 to 10. The conflicts between pairs of goals are also randomly generated. To ensure the coverage, we combined the input variables and their values (described in the Table 1) to generate one sample for all possibles combinations. In this case, we produced 81 samples ($values^{variables} = 3^4 = 81$). To improve results accuracy, we doubled the sample set size, generating 2 samples for each possible combination. Therefore, it was randomly generated 162 samples[1].

4.2   Infrastructure and Analytical Methods

The Huginn for Jason was developed in Java with JNI to call the GLPK[2] [15] to solve the deliberation problem. We customize the reasoning cycle of the Jason agent in its version 1.4.1. The GLPK version used was 4.32. The machine employed to run the tests is an iMac with a processor 3.06 GHz (Intel Core 2 Duo), 4 GB memory (DDR3). The Operating system was OS X Yosemite. The Java version was 1.8. The profiler used was the Java HProf [16]. The GNU time was used to capture the execution elapse time.

Tests samples were executed once each to discover the CPU usage percentage of the Huginn compared to all the agent use. In the experiment, we used a profiler to discover the CPU usage of the deliberation process. To collect this information, the profiler injects code into every method entry and exit, keeping track of exact method call counts and the time spent in each method.

5   Results and Discussion

To discover the agent behavior for the obtained data we fit them into a quadratic function and observed its adherence of the data (input variables). The following sections present:

– the quadratic generic model [14] that is based on the obtained data will be fitted to reveal the relation among the input and output variables;
– the quality evaluation of the model fitted for each output variable.

---

[1] To obtain the sample set send an e-mail to: tiagolschmitz@gmail.com.
[2] http://www.gnu.org/software/glpk/.

5.1 Model Fitting

A quadratic polynomial equation produces a function of independent variables and their interaction to predict the response. In general, the response for the quadratic polynomials is described like in (19).

$$Y = \beta_0 + \sum \beta_i x_i + \sum \beta_{ii} x_i^2 + \sum \sum \beta_{ij} x_{ij} x_j \tag{19}$$

where Y is the response (in this paper the usage percentage and the execution time); β_i is the intercept coefficient, β_{ii} is the squared terms and β_{ij} is the interaction terms, and x_i and x_j are the independent variables (In our case: O, C, Q and R variables). Evaluation of variance (ANOVA)[3] was applied to estimate the effects of main variables and their potential interaction effects on the Huginn. We conducted two experiments. The relation among the usage percentage with the parameters and the relation among the execution time with the parameters. The statistical evaluation of these experiments are described in the Subsect. 5.2.

5.2 Statistical evaluation

Results obtained from the **CPU usage percentage experimentation** has a behavior described by a second order polynomial equation described in (20) that could relate the usage percentage (U) with the input variables (O, R, C, Q).

$$
\begin{aligned}
U = &- 0.2164 + 1.905O + 2.326R + 0.4186C \\
&+ 0.003221Q - 0.009929O^2 - 0.06296R^2 \\
&- 0.002555C^2 + 0.00005617Q^2 - 0.00624OR \\
&+ 0.001489OC - 0.01542RC - 0.000274OQ \\
&- 0.002835RQ + 0.00000398CQ - 0.0000272 9ORC \\
&+ 0.00009597ORQ + 0.000001758OCQ \\
&- 0.000003013RCQ - 0.0000009042ORCQ
\end{aligned}
\tag{20}
$$

R-square is a statistical measure of how close the data are to the fitted regression line. It is also known as the coefficient of determination, or the coefficient of multiple determination for multiple regression. For the experiment, the model fitted has an ANOVA R-squared equals to 0.9852. The closer the R-squared value is to 1, better the empirical model fit the actual data. On the other hand, the smaller the value of R-squared, the lesser will be the relevance of the dependent variables of the model in explaining the behavior. Therefore the predicted values match the observed values reasonably.

If the p value for models is less than 0.05, the model is significant which is desirable because it indicates that the terms in the model have a significant effect on the response. In our experiment the p-value is $< 2.2 \times 10^{-16}$. Therefore the model has a significant effect on the response. The statistical evaluation obtained from the analysis of variance (ANOVA) is a quadratic model shown in Table 2. In this case the terms related to the O and C input variables are significant.

---

[3] Using R Statistical Software.

Table 2. Anova Table: Percentual Usage

M. Terms	p value	M. Terms	p value
O	$< 2.2 \times 10^{-16}$	RC	0.1181
R	0.7021	OQ	0.7957
C	$< 2.2 \times 10^{-16}$	RQ	0.9849
Q	0.9292	CQ	0.9898
O^2	$< 2.2 \times 10^{-16}$	ORC	0.8031
R^2	0.9314	ORQ	0.8990
C^2	1.077×10^{-7}	OCQ	0.9960
Q^2	0.9268	RCQ	0.9095
OR	0.7130	$ORCQ$	0.9412
OC	1.685×10^{-6}		

The influence of O and C (variables more relevant) are observable in the graph of Fig. 3. It is possible to see the quadratic behavior of CPU usage percentage. The conflict influences directly the CPU usage percentage. For example, the point (10,10) corresponds a smaller percentage usage than the point (10,90). The same way the goals from desires and norms quantity influences in the usage percentage.

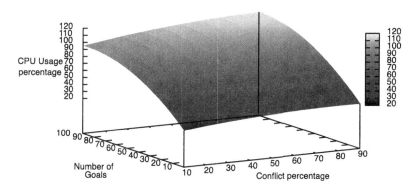

Fig. 3. CPU Usage percentage graph (Color figure online)

The mathematical model used in this evaluation could predict the behavior of Huginn for CPU use. The evaluation conducted in this paper concludes that the usage grows quickly when the numbers of desires and norms (O) and the conflicts (C) increase. Therefore, the Huginn deliberation process is recommended to agents with low quantity of norms and desires.

6   Related Works

There have been several works dealing with normative programming frameworks and middleware to support the development of normative multi-agent organizations, and such frameworks are often designed to inter-operate with existing agent's languages programs. Some of agent's architectures allow the agent to deliberate about whether to comply with norms.

For example, the BOID model proposes a BDI extension with the explicit obligation notion. Agents of type BOID [11] are composed of four components: beliefs, obligations, intentions and desires. This is one of the first models that works with obligations. This model uses static preferences to rank the components. The agent uses the ranking to deliberate about norms.

In contrast, the Carabelea's model [17] works before the agent joins the organization. This model proposes to use the social power theory [18,19] for the agent to deliberate about joining a group. The Carabelea's objective is to use this theory for the agent understands its powers and the powers of the other agents to deliberate about the entrance in the organization. Carabelea's model enables the agent to reason about dependencies among agents. On the other hand, after the agent has joined the organization, it will obey all the norms.

Kollingbaum model [9] is another model where the agent tries to fulfill all norms. But, if there are conflicts between norms the agent detects and solves them. Kollingbaum defines algorithms to detect and to solve the norms conflict. They use seven strategies: arbitrary decision, recency, seniority, cautions, bold, renegotiate and social power.

Criado model presents an architecture called n-BDI (normative BDI). The deliberation process about norms uses utility functions. Thus, the agent uses the rewards and sanctions to define which norms will be accepted [20]. Other relevant model is the N-2APL [21]. This model allows the creation of agents capable to deliberate about norms. The N-2APL adds to 2APL language [22] the support to normative concepts as obligations, prohibitions, sanctions and deadlines. The deliberation process considers deadlines and priority criteria to choose the norms.

The deliberation process proposed in Huginn has some similarities with related studies like the use of N-BDI architecture. The Huginn model has however a different deliberation process. It does not use a preference systems to select norms and desires. The deliberation process has a singular feature when compared with the related studies: it worked with limited resources to deliberate about norms and desires. In addition, the process uses another elements like rewards, sanctions, intensities and necessities to deliberate.

While most of the related works are extensions of the BDI architecture, we did not find empirical evaluations of the deliberation impact on the reasoning cycle of the agents.

7 Conclusion

This paper presents an empirical evaluation of the Huginn, constrained norm-aware BDI reasoner. In this paper, we conclude that the proposed mathematical model could predict the behavior of Huginn for CPU usage percentage. We conclude, also, that the usage grows quickly when the numbers of desires and norms (O) and the conflicts (C) increase. Therefore, the Huginn deliberation process is recommended for agents with low quantity of norms and desires. For instance, in our experiment, agents with more than 50 norms or desires spend more than 40 % of the time doing the Huginn deliberation.

The next step is to implement a real case to evaluate how the model behaves. The proposed scenario is a route planning for an Unmanned Aerial Vehicle using the Huginn.

The first future work is to handle conflicts considering more than two Huginn goals. For example, if an agent has 3 norms: (n1) ride a bicycle, (n2) arrive at point X, 5 miles away within 1 h and (n3) take a 40 mile detour then there is no conflict in pairs of norms. However, it is not feasible to fulfil all the three norms.

The second future work is to compare with others norms reasoners. To accomplish that, it this is necessary to maturate the test scenario and find a way to include the profiling tools in the other models.

The third future work is to consider the relation with others agents. In this branch we will consider the relation of power among the agents to define how this can be modelled in the Huginn.

References

1. Boella, G., Torre, L., Verhagen, H.: Introduction to normative multiagent systems. Comput. Math. Organ. Theor. **12**(2–3), 71–79 (2006)
2. Schmitz, T.L., Hübner, J.F.: Huginn: Normative reasoning based on mood. In: Bazzan, A.L.C., Pichara, K. (eds.) IBERAMIA 2014. LNCS, vol. 8864, pp. 572–584. Springer, Heidelberg (2014)
3. Thayer, R.E.: The Biopsychology of Mood and Arousal, 1st edn. Oxford University Press, Oxford (1989)
4. Rawls, J.: Two Concepts of Rules. Bobbs-Merrill reprint series in philosophy. Ardent Media, Incorporated (1955)
5. Searle, J.: Speech Acts: An Essay in the Philosophy of Language. Cambridge University Press, Cambridge (1969). Cam: [Verschiedene Aufl.]
6. Searle, J.R.: The Construction of Social Reality. Free Press, New York (1997)
7. Thayer, R.E.: The Origin of Everyday Moods: Managing Energy, Tension and Stress, 1st edn. Oxford University Press, Oxford (1996)
8. Hansson, B.: An analysis of some deontic logics. In: Hilpinen, R. (ed.) Deontic Logic: Introductory and Systematic Readings. Synthese Library, vol. 33, pp. 121–147. Springer, Netherlands (1971)
9. Kollingbaum, M.J., Norman, T.J.: Informed deliberation during norm-governed practical reasoning. In: Boissier, O., Padget, J., Dignum, V., Lindemann, G., Matson, E., Ossowski, S., Sichman, J.S., Vázquez-Salceda, J. (eds.) ANIREM 2005 and OOOP 2005. LNCS (LNAI), vol. 3913, pp. 183–197. Springer, Heidelberg (2006)

10. Pacheco, N.C.: Using Norms to Control Open Multi-Agent Systems. Tesis doctoral en informática, Departamento de Sistemas Informáticos y Computación, Universidad Politécnica de Valencia (2012)
11. Broersen, J., Dastani, M., Hulstijn, J., Huang, Z., van der Torre, L.: The BOID architecture: conflicts between beliefs, obligations, intentions and desires. In: Proceedings of the Fifth International Conference on Autonomous Agents, AGENTS 2001, pp. 9–16. ACM, New York (2001)
12. Kellerer, H., Pferschy, U., Pisinger, D.: Knapsack Problems. Springer, Heidelberg (2004)
13. Bordini, R.H., Hübner, J.F., Wooldridge, M.: Programming Multi-Agent Systems in AgentSpeak using Jason (Wiley Series in Agent Technology). Wiley-Interscience, Chichester (2007)
14. Montgomery, D.C.: Design and Analysis of Experiments. Wiley, New York (2006)
15. Makhorin, A.: Gnu Linear Programming Kit, vol. 38. Moscow Aviation Institute, Moscow (2001)
16. Liang, S., Viswanathan, D.: Comprehensive profiling support in the java virtual machine. In: USENIX Conference on Object-Oriented Technologies and Systems - COOTS, pp. 229–242 (1999)
17. Carabelea, C., Boissier, O., Castelfranchi, C.: Using social power to enable agents to reason about being part of a group. In: Gleizes, M.-P., Omicini, A., Zambonelli, F. (eds.) ESAW 2004. LNCS (LNAI), vol. 3451, pp. 166–177. Springer, Heidelberg (2005)
18. Castelfranchi, C.: A micro and macro definition of power. ProtoSociology - Int. J. Interdisc. Res. **18**, 208–268 (2002)
19. Jones, A., Sergot, M.: A formal characterisation of institutionalised power (1996)
20. Criado, N., Argente, E., Botti, V.: Rational strategies for norm compliance in the n-BDI proposal. In: De Vos, M., Fornara, N., Pitt, J.V., Vouros, G. (eds.) COIN 2010. LNCS, vol. 6541, pp. 1–20. Springer, Heidelberg (2011)
21. Alechina, N., Dastani, M., Logan, B.: Programming norm-aware agents. In: Conitzer, V., Winikoff, M., Padgham, L., van der Hoek, W. (eds.) Proceedings of the 11th International Conference on Autonomous Agents and Multiagent Systems (AAMAS 2012), Valencia, Spain, June 2012
22. Dastani, M.: 2APL: A practical agent programming language. Auton. Agent. Multiagent Syst. **16**(3), 214–248 (2008)

Implementation of Normative Practical Reasoning with Durative Actions

Zohreh Shams[1]([✉]), Marina De Vos[1], Julian Padget[1],
and Wamberto Vasconcelos[2]

[1] Department of Computer Science, University of Bath, Bath, UK
{z.shams,m.d.vos,j.a.padget}@bath.ac.uk
[2] Department of Computing Science, University of Aberdeen, Aberdeen, UK
wvasconcelos@acm.org

Abstract. Autonomous agents operating in a dynamic environment need constantly to reason about actions in pursuit of their goals, while taking into consideration possible norms imposed on those actions. Normative practical reasoning supports agents decision making about what is best for an agent to do in a given situation. What makes practical reasoning challenging is the conflict between goals that the agent is pursuing and the norms that the agent is trying to uphold. We offer a formal model that allows the agents to plan for conflicting goals and norms in presence of *durative* actions that can be executed *concurrently*. We compare plans based on decision-theoretic notions (i.e. utility) such that the utility gain of goals and utility loss of norm violations are the basis of this comparison. The set of *optimal* plans consists of plans that maximise the overall utility, each of which can be chosen by the agent to execute. The formal model is implemented computationally using answer set programming, which in turns permits the statement of the problem in terms of a logic program that can be queried for solutions with specific properties. We demonstrate how a normative practical reasoning problem can be mapped into an answer set program such that the optimal plans of the former can be obtained as the answer sets of the latter.

1 Introduction

Norms define an ideal behaviour for an autonomous agent in an open environment. However, having individual goals to pursue, self-interested agents might not want or be able always to adhere to the norms imposed on them. Depending on the way they are given a computational interpretation, norms can be regarded as *soft* or *hard constraints*. When modelled as hard constrains, norms are regarded as *regimented*, in which case the agent has no choice but blindly to follow the norms [12]. Although regimentation guarantees norm compliance, it greatly restricts agent autonomy. Conversely, *enforcement* approaches in which norms are modelled as soft constraints, leave the choice of obeying or disobeying the norms to the agent. However, in order to encourage norm compliance, there are consequences introduced in terms of punishment in case the agent violates the norm [25,29]. Moreover, in some enforcement approaches [1] the agent

© Springer International Publishing Switzerland 2016
V. Dignum et al. (Eds.): COIN 2015, LNAI 9628, pp. 335–353, 2016.
DOI: 10.1007/978-3-319-42691-4_19

is rewarded for complying with a norm. The enforcement approaches can be broadly divided in two categories. In the utility-based approaches [1,2,26] there is a utility gain/loss associated with respecting norm or not, whereas in the *pressured norm compliance* approaches [25], violating a norm or not is determined by the interference of the norm in satisfying or hindering the agent goals. Gaining better utility or not losing utility is the basis of normative reasoning in the former category, while in the latter it is the potential conflicts between norms and agent goals. If there is no such conflict, the agent only complies with a norm if there are goals that are hindered by punishment of violation, and violates the norms otherwise. On the other hand, if there is a conflict, the agent does not comply unless the goals hindered by punishment are more important than goals facilitated by compliance.

Existing work on normative practical reasoning using enforcement have considered different phases of the practical reasoning process, such as plan generation and plan selection. In [27] norms are taken into account in the agent's plan generation phase, whereas [26] takes norms into consideration when deciding how to execute a pre-generated plan with respect to the norms triggered by that plan. There is also a substantial body of work on integration of norms into the BDI architecture [30]. The BOID architecture [7] extends BDI with the concept of obligation and uses agent types such as social, selfish, etc. to handle the conflicts between beliefs, desires, intentions and obligations. Another extended BDI architecture is proposed in [9], which focusses on norm recognition and considering them in agent decision making processes. More recently, [2] proposed a novel way of utilising permission norms in a BDI agent when the agent does not have complete information about the environment it operates in.

In this paper we define an approach for practical reasoning that considers norms in both plan generation and plan selection. We extend the current work on normative plan generation such that the agent attempts to satisfy a set of potentially conflicting goals in the presence of norms, as opposed to conventional planning problems that generate plans for a single goal [26,27]. Additionally, since in reality the actions are often non-atomic, the model allows for planning with durative actions that can be executed concurrently. Durative actions reflects the real time that a machine takes to execute certain actions, which is also known as "real-time duration" of actions [6]. More importantly, another contribution of this paper is introducing an enforcement approach that is a combination of utility-based and pressure-based compliance methods mentioned earlier. In order to do so, we first extend the notion of conflict defined in [25] by allowing conflict between norms as well as between norms and goals. We then define a penalty cost for norm violation, regardless of the existence of conflict. Whenever a norm is triggered, both outcomes of norm compliance and violation and their impacts on hindering or facilitating other goals and norms, are generated and compared according to their utility. Moreover, in those cases that there are no conflicts and no goals or norms hindered by the punishment of violation: loss of utility drives the agent toward compliance. Regarding plan selection, generated plans are compared based on the utility of the goals satisfied and cost of norms violated in the entire plan. Both plan generation and plan selection mechanisms proposed here are implemented using Answer Set Programming (ASP) [15].

ASP is a declarative programming paradigm using logic programs under the answer set semantics. In this paradigm the user provides a description of a problem and ASP works out how to solve the problem by returning answer sets corresponding to problem solutions. The existence of efficient solvers to generate the answers to the provided problems has increased the application of ASP in different domains of autonomous agents and multi-agent systems such as planning [24] and normative reasoning [8,28]. Several action languages (e.g. event calculus [21], $\mathcal{A}$ [14] and its descendants (e.g. $\mathcal{B}, \mathcal{C}$ [14]), Temporal Action Logics (TAL) [11]) have been implemented in ASP [22,23], which indicates that ASP is an appropriate tool for reasoning about actions. We therefore, propose an implementation of STRIPS [13] as an action language in ASP.

This paper is organised as follows. The formal model and its semantics are proposed in Sect. 2, followed by the computational implementation of the model in Sect. 3. Section 4 provides an example that illustrates the main features of the model in action. Finally, after the discussion of related work in Sect. 5, we conclude in Sect. 6.

2   A Model for Normative Practical Reasoning

This section introduces a formal model and its semantics for normative practical reasoning in the presence of durative actions. The foundation of this model is classical planning in which an agent is presented with a set of actions and a goal. Any sequence of actions that satisfies the goal is a solution to the planning problem. In Sect. 2.1 we extend the classical planning problem by substituting a single goal with a set of potentially inconsistent goals G and a set of norms N. A solution for such a problem is any sequence of actions that satisfies at least one goal. The agent has the choice of violating or complying with triggered norms, while satisfying its goals.

2.1   Syntax

A normative planning system is a tuple $P = (FL, \Delta, A, G, N)$ where FL is a set of fluents, Δ is the initial state, A is a set of durative STRIPS-like [13] actions, G denotes the set of agent goals and N denotes a set of norms imposed on the agent that define what an agent is obliged or forbidden to do under certain conditions. We now describe each of these in more details.

Fluents: FL is a set of domain fluents that accounts for the description of the domain the agent operates in. A literal l is a fluent or its negation i.e. $l = fl$ or $l = \neg fl$ for some $fl \in FL$. For a set of literals L, we define $L^+ = \{fl | fl \in L\}$ and $L^- = \{fl | \neg fl \in L\}$ to denote the set of positive and negative fluents in L respectively. L is well-defined if there exists no fluent $fl \in FL$ such that $fl \in L$ and $\neg fl \in L$, i.e. if $L^+ \cap L^- = \emptyset$.

The semantics of the model are defined over a set of states Σ. A state $s \subseteq FL$ is determined by set of fluents that hold *true* at a given time, while the other

338   Z. Shams et al.

fluents (those that are not present) are considered to be false. A state $s \in \Sigma$ satisfies fluent $fl \in FL$, denoted $s \models fl$, if $fl \in s$. It satisfies its negation $\neg fl$ if $fl \notin s$. This notation can be extended to a set of literals as follows, set X is satisfied in state s, $s \models X$, when $\forall x \in X \cdot s \models x$.

Initial State: The set of fluents that hold at the initial state is denoted by $\Delta \subseteq FL$.

Actions: A is a set of durative STRIPS-like actions, that is actions with pre-conditions and postconditions that take a non-zero duration of time to have their effects in terms of their postconditions. A durative action $a = \langle pr, ps, d \rangle$ is composed of well-defined sets of literals $pr(a), ps(a) \subseteq FL$ to represents a's pre-conditions and postconditions and a positive number $d(a) \in \mathbb{N}$ for its duration. Postconditions are further divided into a set of add postconditions $ps(a)^+$ and a set of delete postconditions $ps(a)^-$. An action a can be executed in a state s if its preconditions hold in s (i.e. $s \models pr(a)$. The postconditions of a durative action are applied in the state s at which the action ends (i.e. $s \models ps(a)^+$ and $s \not\models ps(a)^-$).

The model does not allow parallel actions, since it is not realistic to assume that a single agent initiates several actions at the exact same point in time. Concurrency however, is allowed unless there is a concurrency conflict between actions, which prevents them from being executed in an overlapping period of time. The definition of concurrency conflict is adopted from [4] as follows: two actions a_1 and a_2 are in a concurrency conflict, if the preconditions or postconditions of a_1 contradict the preconditions or postconditions of a_2.

Goals: G denotes a set of (possibly inconsistent) goals. Goals identify the state of affairs that an agent wants to satisfy. Each goal $g = \langle r, v \rangle$ is defined as a set of well-defined literals r, that are requirements that should hold in order to satisfy the goal and a positive integer $v \in \mathbb{N}$ that shows the value or utility gain of the agent upon satisfying this goal. Goal g's requirements and value are denoted $r(g)$ and $v(g)$, respectively. Goal g is satisfied in the state s when $s \models r(g)$.

Norms: N denotes a set of event-based norms to which the agent is subject. Each norm is a tuple of the form $n = \langle d\_o, a_1, a_2, dl, c \rangle$, where

- $d\_o \in \{o, f\}$ is the deontic operator determining the type of norm, which can be an obligation or a prohibition. The agent is assumed to be operating in a permissible society, hence what is not prohibited is permitted.
- $a_1 \in A$ is the action that counts as the norm activation condition.
- $a_2 \in A$ is the action that is the subject of the obligation or prohibition.
- $dl \in \mathbb{N}$ is the norm deadline relative to the activation condition, which is the completion of execution of a_1.
- $c \in \mathbb{N}$ is the penalty cost that will be applied if the norm is violated.

An obligation expresses that taking action a_1 obliges the agent to take action a_2 within dl time units of the end of execution of a_1. Such an obligation is complied with if the agent starts executing a_2 before the deadline and is violated otherwise. A prohibition expresses that taking action a_1 prohibits the agent from taking action a_2 within dl time units of the end of execution of a_1. Such a prohibition is complied with if the agent does not start executing a_2 before the deadline and is violated otherwise.

2.2   Semantics

Let $P = (FL, \Delta, A, G, N)$ be a normative planning problem. A plan is represented by a sequence of actions taken at certain times, denoted as: $\pi = \langle (a_0, t_0), \cdots, (a_n, t_n) \rangle$. (a_i, t_i) means that action a_i is executed at time $t_i \in \mathbb{Z}^+$ s.t. $\forall i < j$ we have $t_i < t_j$. The total duration of a plan, $Makespan(\pi)$, is calculated by the relation: $Makespan(\pi) = max(t_i + d(a_i))$. The evolution of a sequence of actions for a given starting state $s_0 = \Delta$ is a sequence of states $\langle s_0, \cdots s_m \rangle$ for every discrete time interval from t_0 to m, where $m = Makespan(\pi)$. The transition relation between two states is defined by Eq. 1 below. If an action a_j ends at time t_i, state s_i results from removing all delete postconditions and adding all add postconditions of action a_j to state s_{i-1}. If there is no action ending at s_i, it remains the same as s_{i-1}.

$$\forall i > 0 : s_i = \begin{cases} (s_{i-1} \setminus ps(a_j)^-) \cup ps(a_j)^+ & i = t_j + d(a_j) \\ s_{i-1} & \text{otherwise} \end{cases} \tag{1}$$

A sequence of actions π satisfies a goal, $\pi \models g$, if there is at least one state s_i in the sequence of states caused by the sequence of actions such that $s_i \models g$. An obligation $n_1 = \langle o, a_i, a_j, dl, c \rangle$ is complied with in plan π (i.e. $\pi \models n_1$), if the action that is the norm activation condition has occurred $((a_i, t_i) \in \pi)$, and the action that is the subject of the obligation occurs $((a_j, t_j) \in \pi)$ between when the condition holds and when the deadline expires $(t_j \in [t_i + d(a_i), dl + t_i) + d(a_i))$. If a_i has occurred but a_j does not occur at all or occurs in a period other than the one specified, the obligation is violated (i.e. $\pi \not\models n_1$). In the case of prohibition $n_2 = \langle f, a_i, a_j, dl, c \rangle$, compliance happens if the action that is the norm activation condition has occurred $((a_i, t_i) \in \pi)$ and the action that is the subject of the prohibition does not occur in the period between when the condition holds and when the deadline expires $(\nexists (a_j, t_j) \in \pi \text{ s.t. } t_j \in [t_i + d(a_i), dl + t_i + d(a_i))$. If a_i has occurred and a_j occurs in the specified period, the prohibition is violated (i.e. $\pi \not\models n_2$). The set of satisfied goals, norms complied with and norms violated in plan π are denoted as G_π, $N_{cmp(\pi)}$ and $N_{vol(\pi)}$, respectively.

In classical planning, any sequence of actions that satisfies the goal is a solution to the planning problem. Extending a planning problem to cater for conflicting goals and norms requires considering different types of conflicts as follows:

Conflicting Actions. Actions a_i and a_j have a concurrency conflict iff the preconditions or postconditions of a_i contradict the preconditions or postconditions of a_j.

$$cf_{action} = \{(a_i, a_j) \text{ s.t. } \exists r \in pr(a_i) \cup ps(a_i), \neg r \in pr(a_j) \cup ps(a_j)\} \quad (2)$$

Conflicting Goals. Goal g_i and g_j are in conflict iff satisfying one requires bringing about a state of affairs that is in conflict with the state of affairs required for satisfying the other.

$$cf_{goal} = \{(g_i, g_j) \text{ s.t. } \exists r \in g_i, \neg r \in g_j\} \quad (3)$$

Conflicting Norms. Obligations $n_1 = \langle o, a_1, a_2, dl, c \rangle$ and $n_2 = \langle o, b_1, b_2, dl', c' \rangle$ are in conflict in the context of plan π iff: (i) their activation conditions hold, (ii) the obliged actions a_2 and b_2 have a concurrency conflict and (iii) a_2 is in progress during the entire period over which the agent is obliged to take action b_2. The set of conflicting obligations is formulated as:

$$cf_{oblobl}^{\pi} = \{(n_1, n_2) \text{ s.t. } (a_1, t_{a_1}), (b_1, t_{b_1}) \in \pi; (a_2, b_2) \in cf_{action};$$
$$t_{a_2} \in [t_{a_1} + d(a_1), t_{a_1} + d(a_1) + dl);$$
$$[t_{b_1} + d(b_1), t_{b_1} + d(b_1) + dl') \subseteq [t_{a_2}, t_{a_2} + d(a_2))\} \quad (4)$$

On the other hand, an obligation $n_1 = \langle o, a_1, a_2, dl, c \rangle$ and a prohibition $n_2 = \langle f, b_1, a_2, dl', c' \rangle$ are in conflict in the context of plan π iff: (i) their activation conditions hold and (ii) n_2 forbids the agent to take action a_2 during the entire period over which n_1 obliges the agent to take a_2. The set cf_{oblpro}^{π} denotes the set of conflicting obligations and prohibitions as below:

$$cf_{oblpro}^{\pi} = \{(n_1, n_2) \text{ s.t. } (a_1, t_{a_1}), (b_2, t_{b_2}) \in \pi;$$
$$[t_{a_1} + d(a_1), t_{a_1} + d(a_1) + dl) \subseteq$$
$$[t_{b_2} + d(b_2), t_{b_2} + d(b_2) + dl')\} \quad (5)$$

The entire set of conflicting goals and norms is defined as:

$$cf_{norm}^{\pi} = cf_{oblobl}^{\pi} \cup cf_{oblpro}^{\pi} \quad (6)$$

Conflicting Goals and Norms. An obligation $n = \langle o, a_1, a_2, dl, c \rangle$ and a goal g are in conflict, if taking action a_2 that is the subject of the obligation, brings about postconditions that are in conflict with the requirements of goal g. The set of conflicting goals and obligations is formulated as:

$$cf_{goalobl} = \{(g, n) \text{ s.t. } \exists r \in r(g), \neg r \in ps(a_2)\} \quad (7)$$

In addition, a prohibition $n = \langle f, a_1, a_2, dl, c' \rangle$ and a goal g are in conflict, if the postconditions of a_2 contribute to satisfying g, but taking action a_2 is prohibited by norm n.

$$cf_{goalpro} = \{(g, n) \text{ s.t. } \exists r \in r(g), r \in ps(a_2)\} \quad (8)$$

The entire set of conflicting goals and norms is defined as:

$$cf_{goalnorm} = cf_{goalobl} \cup cf_{goalpro} \quad (9)$$

A sequence of actions π is a plan for P, if all the fluents in Δ hold at time t_0 and for each i, the preconditions of action a_i hold at time t_i, as well as through the execution of a_i, and a non-empty subset of goals is satisfied in the path from initial state s_0 to the state holding at time t_m, where $m = Makespan(\pi)$. Furthermore, extending the conventional planning problem by multiple potentially conflicting goals and norms requires defining extra conditions that makes a plan a valid plan and a solution for P. Plan π is a valid plan for P iff:

1. all the fluents and only those fluents in Δ hold in the initial state: $s_0 = \Delta$
2. the preconditions of action a_1 holds at time t_{a_1} and throughout the execution of a_1:
$$\forall k \in [t_{a_1}, t_{a_1} + d(a_1)), s_k \models pr(a_1)$$
3. the set of goals satisfied by plan π is a non-empty consistent subset of goals:
$$G_\pi \subseteq G \text{ and } G_\pi \neq \emptyset \text{ and } \quad \nexists g_i, g_j \in G_\pi \text{ s.t. } (g_i, g_j) \in cf_{goal}$$
4. there is no concurrency conflict between actions that are executed concurrently:
$$\nexists (a_i, t_{a_i}), (a_j, t_{a_j}) \in \pi \text{ s.t. } t_{a_i} \leq t_{a_j} < t_{a_i} + d(a_i), (a_i, a_j) \in cf_{action}$$
5. there is no conflict between norms complied with.
$$\nexists n_i, n_j \in N_{cmp(\pi)} \text{ s.t. } (n_i, n_j) \in cf_{norm}^\pi$$
6. there is no conflict between goals satisfied and norms complied with:
$$\nexists g \in G_\pi \text{ and } n \in N_{cmp(\pi)} \text{ s.t. } (g, n) \in cf_{goalnorm}$$

Let $satisfied(\pi)$ and $violated(\pi)$ be the set of satisfied goals and violated norms in plan π. The utility of a plan π is defined by Eq. 10 where $Value$ is a function that returns the value of goals being satisfied and $Cost$ returns the penalty cost of norms being violated in that plan. The set of optimal plans, Opt, are those plans that maximise the utility.

$$Utility(\pi) = \sum_{g_i \in satisfied(\pi)} Value(g_i) - \sum_{n_j \in violated(\pi)} Cost(n_j) \qquad (10)$$

3   An Answer Set Programming Implementation

Encoding a practical reasoning problem as a declarative specification makes it possible to reason computationally about agent actions, goals and norms. This enables an agent to keep track of actions taken, goals satisfied and norms complied with or violated at each state of its evolution. More importantly, it provides the possibility of querying traces that fulfil certain requirements such as satisfying some specific goals. Consequently, instead of generating all possible traces and looking for those ones that satisfy at least one goal, only those ones that *do* satisfy at least one goal are generated.

ASP programs consist of a finite set of rules formed from atoms. Atoms are the basic components of the language that can be assigned a truth value (*true* or *false*). Literals are atoms or negated atoms. Atoms are negated using classical negation ($\neg$) or *negation as failure* (*not*). The former states that something is false, whereas the latter states something is assumed false since it cannot be proven true. The general rule syntax in ASP is: $l_0 \leftarrow l_1, \cdots, l_m, not\ l_{m+1}, \cdots, not\ l_n.$, in which l_i is an atom (e.g. a) or its negation (e.g. $\neg a$). l_0 is the rule head and $l_1, \cdots, l_m, not\ l_{m+1}, \cdots, not\ l_n$ are the body of the rule. The above rule is read as: l_0 is known/true, if $l_1, \cdots, l_m$ are known/true and none of l_{m+1}, l_n are known. If a rule body is empty, that rule is called a fact and if the head is empty, it is called a constraint indicating that none of the answers should satisfy the body.

3.1 Translating the Model into ASP

In this section, we demonstrate how a planning problem $P = (FL, \Delta, A, G, N)$ can be mapped into an answer set program such that there is a one to one correspondence between solutions for the planning problem and the answers of the program. The mapping uses the following atoms: $\texttt{state}(s)$ for denoting the states; $\texttt{time}(t, s)$ to indicate the time at state s; $\texttt{holdsat}(x, s)$ to express fluent x is true in state s; $\texttt{occurred(a,s)}$ to encode action a occurs at state s. There are additional atoms used in Figs. 2, 3, 4, 5 and 6, that will be discussed in their respective sections. Please note that the variables begin with capital letters in ASP.

Time and Initial State (Fig. 1). The facts produced by Line 1 provide the program with all available states, while Line 2 defines the order of states. The maximum number of states, q, results from sum of duration of all actions: $q = \sum_{i=1}^n d(a_i)$. The final state is therefore stated as sq in Line 3. Line 4 illustrates the initial time that increases by one unit from one state to the state next to it (Line 5). Finally, Line 6 encodes the fluents that hold at initial state $s0$.

Actions (Fig. 2). Each durative action is encoded as $\texttt{action}(a, d)$ (Line 7), where a is the name of the action and d is its duration. Recalling from Sect. 2, the preconditions $pr(a)$ of action a hold in state s if $s \models pr(a)$. This is expressed in Line 8, where $pr(a)^+$ and $pr(a)^-$ are positive and negative literals in $pr(a)$. In order to make the coding more readable we introduce the shorthand $\texttt{EX(X,S)}$ where X is a set of fluents that should hold at state S. For all $x \in X$, $\texttt{EX(X,S)}$ is translated into $\texttt{holdsat(x,S)}$ and for all $\neg x \in X$, $\texttt{EX(\neg X,S)}$ is translated into $\texttt{not EX(x,S)}$ using negation as failure. The agent has the choice to take any of its actions in any state (Line 9), however, the preconditions of a durative action should be preserved when it is in progress. A durative action is in progress, $\texttt{inprog}(A, S)$, from the state in which it begins to the state in which it ends at (Lines 10 to 11). Then, Line 12 rules out the execution of an action, when

$\forall\, k \in [0, q]$

1 | `state(sk).`

$\forall\, k \in [0, q-1]$

2 | `next(sk,s(k+1)).`

3 | `final(sq).`

4 | `time(t,s0).`
5 | `time(T+1,S2) :- time(T,S1), next(S1,S2), state(S1;S2).`

$\forall\, x \in \Delta$

6 | `holdsat(x,s0).`

Fig. 1. Rules for time component (Lines 1–5) and initial state (Line 6)

the preconditions of the action do not hold during its execution. In addition there should not be any action in progress in the final state (Line 13). Another assumption made in Sect. 2, is the prevention of parallel actions, which prevents the agent from starting two actions at the same time (Lines 14 to 15). Once an action starts in one state, the result of its execution is reflected in the state where the action ends. This is expressed through (i) Lines 16 to 17 that allow the add postconditions of the action to hold when the action ends, and (ii) Lines 18 to 19 that allow the termination of the delete postconditions. The termination happens in the state before the end state of the action. The reason for this is that all the fluents that hold in a state, hold in the next state unless they are terminated (Lines 20 to 21). Since the delete postconditions of an action are terminated in the state before the end state of the action, they will not hold in the following state, in which the action ends (i.e. they are deleted from the state).

Goals (Fig. 3). Line 22 encodes goal g with value of v. From Sect. 2, we have goal g is satisfied in state s if $s \models r(g)$. This is expressed in Line 23, where $r(g)^+$ and $r(g)^-$ are the positive and negative literals in $r(g)$.

Norms (Fig. 4). The conditional event-based norms that are the focus of this research are discussed in the previous section. Line 24 encodes norm n with penalty cost of c upon violation. Lines 25–39 deal with obligations and prohibitions of form: $n = \langle d\_o, a_1, a_2, dl, c \rangle$. In order to implement the concepts of norm compliance and violation described in Sect. 2.2, we introduce normative fluents $o(n, a_2, dl')$ and $f(n, a_2, dl')$ that first hold in the state in which action a_1's execution ends. An obligation fluent $o(n, a_2, dl')$ denotes that action a_2 should be brought about before deadline dl'or be subject to violation, whereas prohibition fluent $f(n, a_2, dl')$ denotes that action a_2 should not be brought about before deadline dl' or be subject to violation. If a_1 with duration $d1$ occurs at state S, where time is T, the agent has dl units time starting from end of action

$\forall a \in A$ s.t. $d(a)$

```
7   action(a,d).
8   pre(a,S) :- EX(pr(a)⁺,S), not EX(pr(a)⁻,S), state(S).
```

```
9    {occurred(A,S)} :- action(A,D), state(S).
10   inprog(A,S2) :- occurred(A,S1), action(A,D), time(T1,S1),
11                   time(T2,S2), state(S1;S2), T1<=T2, T2<T1+D.
12   :- inprog(Act,S), action(Act,D), state(S), not pre(Act,S).
13   :- inprog(Act,S), action(Act,D), state(S), final(S).
14   :- occurred(A1,S), occurred(A2,S), A1!=A2,
15      action(A1,D1), action(A2,D2), state(S).
```

$ps(a)^{+} = X \Leftrightarrow \forall x \in X.$

```
16   holdsat(x,S2) :- occurred(a,S1), action(a,d), state(S1;S2),
17                    time(T1,S1), time(T2,S2), T2=T1+d.
```

$ps(a)^{-} = X \Leftrightarrow \forall x \in X.$

```
18   terminated(x,S2) :- occurred(a,S1), action(a,d), state(S1;S2),
19                       time(T1,S1), time(T2,S2), T2=T1+d-1.
```

```
20   holdsat(X,S2) :- holdsat(X,S1), not terminated(X,S1),
21                    next(S1,S2), state(S1;S2).
```

Fig. 2. Rules for translating actions

$\forall g \in G$

```
22   goal(g,v).
23   satisfied(g,S) :- EX(r(g)⁺,S), not EX(r(g)⁻,S), state(S).
```

Fig. 3. Rules for translating goals

a_1 (T2=T1+$d1$) to comply with the norm imposed on it. Lines 25–26 and 32–33 indicate the establishment of obligation and prohibition fluents.

In terms of compliance and violation, the occurrence of an obliged action before the deadline expires, counts as compliance (Lines 27 to 28) and the absence of such an occurrence before the deadline is regarded as violation (Line 30). Atoms cmp(o|f(n, a, DL), S) and vol(o|f(n, a, DL), S) are used to indicate compliance or violation of norm n in state S. In both cases of compliance and violation, the norm is terminated (Lines 29 and 31). On the other hand, a prohibition is complied with if the forbidden action does not happen before the deadline (Lines 34 to 35) and is violated if it does happen before the deadline (Lines 37 to 38). As with obligations, after being complied with or violated, the prohibitions are terminated (rules 36 and 39).

3.2   Mapping of Answer Sets to Plans

In Sect. 2.2 we defined the criteria for a sequence of actions to be identified as a valid plan and solution for $P = \langle FL, \Delta, A, G, N \rangle$. Figure 5 provides the coding for the criteria. The rule in Line 41 is responsible for constraining answer sets to those that fulfil at least one goal by excluding answers that do not satisfy any goals. The input for this rule is provided in Line 40. Line 42 prevents satisfying two conflicting goals, hence guaranteeing the consistency of satisfied goals in a plan. Preventing the concurrency of conflicting actions, is implemented using Lines 43–44, by expressing that such two actions cannot be in progress together. Lines 45 and 46 provides the input for Lines 47 and 48, which exclude the possibility of satisfying a goal and complying with a norm that are conflicting. Note that the implementation prevents complying with conflicting norms automatically: (i) since it is not possible to execute two conflicting actions concurrently, if two obligations would require that, one of them has to be violated, while (ii) regarding conflicting obligation and prohibition, by definition, taking the obliged action by the agent and hence complying with the obligation causes the violation of the other norm that enforces the prohibition of taking the very same action, and vice versa.

Theorem 1. *Let program Π_{base} consist of Lines 7 – 48. Given a planning problem $P = (FL, \Delta, A, G, N)$, for every answer set Ans of Π_{base} the set of atoms of the form* occurred(a, s)[1] *in Ans encodes a solution to the planning problem P. Conversely, each solution to the problem P corresponds to a single answer set of Π_{base}.*

$\forall n = \langle o|f, a_1, a_2, dl, c \rangle \in N$

```
24   norm (n, c).

25   holdsat (o (n, a2, dl+T2), S2)  :- occurred (a1, S1), action (a1, d1),
26                    time (T1, S1),  T2=T1+d1, time (T2, S2), state (S1; S2).
27   cmp (o (n, a, DL), S)  :- holdsat (o (n, a, DL), S), occurred (a, S), action (a, d)
28                    state (S), time (T, S),  T!=DL.
29   terminated (o (n, a, DL), S)  :- cmp (o (n, a, DL), S),  state (S).
30   vol (o (n, a, DL), S)  :- holdsat (o (n, a, DL), S), time (DL, S),  state (S).
31   terminated (o (n, a, DL), S)  :- vol (o (n, a, DL), S),  state (S).
32   holdsat (f (n, a2, dl+T2), S2)  :- occurred (a1, S1), action (a1, d1),
33                    time (T1, S1),  T2=T1+d1, time (T2, S2), state (S1; S2).
34   cmp (f (n, a, DL), S)  :- holdsat (f (n, a, DL), S), action (a, d),
35                    time (DL, S), state (S).
36   terminated (f (n, a, DL), S)  :- cmp (f (n, a, DL), S), state (S).
37   vol (f (n, a, DL), S)  :- holdsat (f (n, a, DL), S), occurred (a, S),
38                    state (S), time (T, S),  T!=DL.
39   terminated (f (n, a, DL), S)  :- vol (f (n, a, DL), S), state (S).
```

Fig. 4. Rules for translating norms

---

[1] In the formal model a plan/solution π for problem P is defined as a set of action, time pairs (e.g. (a_i, t_i)), whereas in the answer sets a plan is expressed by action, state pairs (e.g. occurred(a, s)). Action, state pairs can easily be mapped to action, time pairs by replacing the state with the time that holds in that state.

346   Z. Shams et al.

```
40  satisfied(g) :- satisfied(g,S), state(S).
41  :- not satisfied(g1), ... , not satisfied(gm).
```

$\forall\,(g_1, g_2) \in cf_{goal}$

```
42  :- satisfied(g1),satisfied(g2).
```

$\forall\,(a_1, a_2) \in cf_{action}$

```
43  :- inprog(a1,S), inprog(a2,S), action(a1,d1),
44     action(a2,d2), state(S).
```

```
45  complied(n) :- cmp(o(n,a,DL),S), state(S).
46  complied(n) :- cmp(f(n,a,DL),S), state(S).
```

$\forall(g, n_1) \in cf_{goalobl}$

```
47  :- satisfied(g), complied(n1).
```

$\forall(g, n_2) \in cf_{goalpro}$

```
48  :- satisfied(g), complied(n2).
```

Fig. 5. Solutions for problem P

Proof (sketch). The proof can be obtained through structural induction. Line 9 generates all sequences of actions. Line 6 ensures that all fluents in Δ hold at t_0. Line 12 guarantees that the precondition of an action hold all through its execution. Line 41 indicates that a non-empty subset of goals has to be satisfied in a plan, while Line 42 ensures the consistency of the goals satisfied. Preventing the concurrency conflict is provided in Lines 43–44. Finally, Lines 47–48 eliminate the possibility of conflict between goals satisfied and norms complied with. This implies that the sequence of actions that is part of the answer set satisfies the conditions to be a solution to the encoded planning program. Conversely, each solution satisfies all the program's rules in a minimal fashion.

3.3 Optimised Plans

In order to find optimal plans, in Fig. 6 we show how to encode the utility function defined by Eq. 10. The sum of values of goals satisfied in a plan is calculated in Line 49. The sum of costs of norms violated in a plan is calculated in Line 49, by first providing the input for this line in Lines 50 and 51. Having calculated value(TV) and cost(TC), the utility of a plan is denoted in Line 53, which is subject to the optimisation statement in the final line.

Theorem 2. *Let program $\Pi = \Pi_{base} \cup \Pi^*$, where Π^* consists of Lines 49 – 54. Given a planning problem $P = (FL, \Delta, A, G, N)$, for every answer set Ans of Π the set of atoms of the form* occurred(a,s) *in Ans encodes an optimal solution to the planning problem P. Conversely, each optimal solution for the problem P corresponds to a single answer set of Π.*

```
49   value(TV)  :- TV = #sum [satisfied(G)  : goal(G,V) = V].
50   violated(n)  :- vol(o(n,a,DL), state(S).
51   violated(n)  :- vol(f(n,a,DL),S), state(S).
52   cost(TC)  :- TC = #sum [violated(N)  : norm(N,C) = C].
53   utility(TV-TC)  :- value(TV), cost(TC).
54   #maximize [Utility(U)=U].
```

Fig. 6. Optimised solutions for P

Proof (Sketch). Theorem 1 ensures that all solutions are represented by answer sets and vice versa. The optimality of solutions is guaranteed in this program. Line 54 ensures optimal solutions that maximise utility, which is in turn defined in Line 53 as the difference between the cost of violation (Line 52) and goal values (Line 49).

4   Illustrative Example

In this section, we provide a brief example that highlights the most important features of the proposed model. Let us consider an agent with the durative actions presented in Table 1. The agent has three goals presented with their requirements and two different set of values in Table 2. The first goal is to get some *certificate* that requires the agent to take some test, but in order to be able to attend the test, the agent first needs to pay the fee for the test. The second goal is to make a *submission* of some marking that needs to be done in the *office* and the last goal is to go on *strike*, for which the agent needs to be a member of union, not to go to *office* nor to attend any meeting on behalf of the company. In addition, one of the agent's action, *comp_funding*, has a normative consequence captured in a norm that states that if company funds are used to pay the fee for the test, the agent is obliged to attend a meeting on behalf of the company within 1 time unit of end of action *comp_funding*, which results in the payment of the fee for the test. If the agent uses the funding, but does not attend the meeting before the deadline, it is entitled to the penalty cost of 4 units.

$$n = \langle o, comp\_funding, attend\_meeting, 1, 4 \rangle$$

Table 3 shows the corresponding ASP code for this example based on the code in Sect. 3. For spacial reasons, only those rules that need instantiation are provided. For ease of reference, rules instantiated in each part of the code are titled by their corresponding figures in Sect. 3. Moreover, only one action, *drive*, and one goal, *certificate*, are encoded. The rest of the actions and goals can be coded in the same way.

Following Theorem 2, we obtain a one-to-one correspondence between the answer sets of the program in Table 3 and optimal plans for the agent to execute such that the agent utility is maximised. Table 4 illustrates the optimal plans (as translations of the answer sets) based on two different set of values in

Table 2. Plan π_1 satisfies goals *certificate* and *strike*, however due to the conflict between *strike* and norm n, the norm is inevitably violated. Additionally, the conflict between goal *strike* and *submission*, makes it impossible for the agent to satisfy *submission*. Since the sum of utility loss of violating n and not satisfying *submission*, is still less that the utility gain of satisfying *strike*, the agent prefers the former to the latter. On the other hand, in plan π_2 satisfying *submission* is preferred over satisfying *strike*, although they have the same utility gain. However, satisfying *strike* would have implied violating n, and thus incurring the penalty cost of 4. Therefore, in pursuit of maximising the utility, the agent prefers satisfying *submission* and complying with n to satisfying *strike* and violating n, which was the case in plan π_1.

5   Related Work

The interaction between an agent's individual goals and social norms has been discussed in a number of works. Some such as [26,27] use utility measurement to enforce norm compliance. In contrast, in [25] norm compliance relies on the explicit interaction between goals and norms, but if the norm compliance or violation does not hinder any goals there is no connection and hence no computational mechanism in place that enforces the norms. From a planning perspective, norms are taken into account in plan generation [27] and in plan selection [20,26]. In [27] the normative state of the agent is checked by a planner after each individual action is taken, which depending on the number of actions, imposes a high computational cost on the step-by-step generation of plans. It is the utility of individual actions here that determines norm compliance. On the other hand, [20,26] consider norms as part of plan selection, starting from the assumption

Table 1. Agent Actions

Preconditions	(Action, Duration)	Postconditions
$\neg office$	$(drive, 1)$	$office$
$\neg marking\_done, office$	$(marking, 2)$	$marking\_done$
$\neg test\_done, fee\_paid$	$(attend\_test, 1)$	$test\_done$
$\neg fee\_paid$	$(comp\_funding, 1)$	fee_paid
$\neg meeting\_attended, fee\_paid$	$(attend\_meeting, 2)$	$meeting\_attended$
$\neg union\_member$	$(join\_union, 1)$	$union\_member$

Table 2. Agent Goals

Goals	Requirements	$Value_1$	$Value_2$
$certificate$	$fee\_paid, test\_done$	8	5
$submission$	$office, marking\_done$	3	7
$strike$	$union\_member, \neg office, \neg meeting$	9	7

Table 3. Instantiated ASP code

Fig. 1.

```
state(s0;s1;s2;s3;s4;s5;s6;s7;s8).
next(s0,s1). next(s1,s2). next(s2,s3). next(s3,s4).
next(s4,s5). next(s5,s6). next(s6,s7). next(s7,s8).
final(s8).
time(0,s0).
```

Fig. 2.

```
action(drive,1).
pre(drive,S) :- not holdsat(office,S), state(S).
holdsat(office,S2) :- occurred(drive,S1),action(drive,1),time(T1,S1),
                      time(T2,S2), state(S1;S2), T2=T1+1.
```

Fig. 3.

```
goal(certificate,8).
satisfied(certificate,S) :- holdsat(fee_paid,S), holdsat(test_done,S),
                            state(S).
```

Fig. 4.

```
norm(n,4).
holdsat(o(n,attend_meeting,1+T2),S2) :- occurred(comp_funding,S1),
                  time(T1,S1),action(comp_funding,1),T2=T1+1,
                                   time(T2,S2),state(S1;S2).
cmp(o(n,attend_meeting,DL),S) :- holdsat(o(n,attend_meeting,DL),S),
            occurred(attend_meeting,S),action(attend_meeting,2),
                                   state(S),time(T,S), T != DL.
terminated(o(n,attend_meeting,DL),S) :- cmp(o(n,attend_meeting,DL),S),
                                   state(S).
vol(o(n,attend_meeting,DL),S) :- holdsat(o(n,attend_meeting,DL),S),
                   time(DL,S),action(attend_meeting,2), state(S).
terminated(o(n,attend_meeting,DL),S) :- vol(o(n,attend_meeting,DL),S),
                                   state(S).
```

Fig. 5.

```
satisfied(certificate) :- satisfied(certificate,S), state(S).
:- not satisfied(submission), not satisfied(certificate),
   not satisfied(strike).
:- satisfied(strike), satisfied(submission).
:- inprog(comp_funding,S), inprog(attend_test,S), state(S)
   action(comp_funding,1), action(attend_test,1).
:- inprog(comp_funding,S), inprog(attend_meeting,S), state(S),
   action(comp_funding,1), action(attend_meeting,2).
complied(n) :- cmp(o(n,attend_meeting,DL),S), state(S).
:- satisfied(strike),complied(n).
```

Fig. 6.

```
violated(n) :- vol(o(n,attend_meeting,DL),S), state(S).
```

that the agent has access to a library of pre-generated plans. In contrast to all of [20, 26, 27], our work deals with both plan generation and plan selection while taking account of norms, and like [26] we focus on the utility of the entire plan, unlike [27] which only considers the constituent actions in sequence.

Table 4. Optimal plans

Goal Values	Plans	Goals	Norms	*Utility*
Value₁	$\pi_1 =$ $\langle(comp\_funding, 0),$ $(union, 1),$ $(attend\_test, 2)\rangle$	$certificate, strike$	$violated(n)$	13
Value₂	$\pi_2 = \langle(drive, 0),$ $(marking, 1),$ $(comp\_funding, 2),$ $(attend\_meeting, 3),$ $(attend\_test, 4)\rangle$	$submission, certificate$	$complied(n)$	12

Some works [19,32] focus on interaction between an agent's goal and its commitments, where commitments are made by agents to one another in order to support the realisation of their goals. Our approach is different from these approaches for two main reasons: (i) commitments are deliberately made by the agent, whereas norms are externally imposed to the agent; and (ii) commitments are made to support satisfying goals, while imposed norms might be in conflict with the agent's goals and consequently, hinder some of them.

The Event Calculus (EC) [21] forms the basis for the implementation of some normative reasoning frameworks, such as [2,3]. Our proposed formal model is independent of language and could be translated to EC and hence to a computational model, but the one-step translation to ASP is preferred because the formulation of the problem is very similar to the computational model, thus there are no conceptual gaps to bridge. Furthermore, the EC implementation language is Prolog, which although syntactically similar to ASP, suffers from non-declarative functionality in the form of the cut operator, which results in a loss of completeness. Furthermore, its query-based nature that focusses on one issue at a time, makes it cumbersome to reason about all plans.

A final point is that the norm representation and implementation proposed here is expressive and realistic in respect of time and duration: specifically, since the formal model and ASP implementation handle time explicitly, it is straightforward to represent the norm deadline as a future time instant, rather than a state to be brought about.

6 Conclusions, Discussion and Future Work

An agent performing practical reasoning in an environment regulated by norms, needs constantly to weigh up the importance of goals satisfied and norms complied with against goals not satisfied and norms broken. This comparison is possible when the agent has access to all possible plans, such that the decision of which goals to pursue and which norms to respect is made based on their impact on the entire plan. We show how this impact can be captured in a utility function that permits the agent to execute a plan that maximises the utility.

The focus of plan selection in this paper is on maximising the agent utility by considering the value of goals and penalties for norm violation. While these are sensible criteria, there are others that can be taken into account. Given that actions modelled in this approach are durative, one such criterion is the duration of the entire plan. Since durative actions that do not have concurrency conflicts can be executed concurrently, there might exist some plans with the exact the same utility while one takes longer than another. We intend to extend the plan selection mechanism with additional criteria by using the existing multi-criteria optimisation mechanisms in ASP.

Just like norms, in real scenarios, goals often have a deadline before which they should be satisfied [18]). Temporally extended goals [17] are discussed in detail in agent programming languages such as GOAL [5], however they are not commonly used in practical reasoning frameworks. Substituting achievement goals with temporally extended goals increases the expressiveness of the model. It also allows defining conflict within goals and between goals and norms temporally and which results in enriching the concept of conflict in the model.

Incorporation plan revision is also an avenue for future work. As presented here, a plan once selected is acted out until its conclusion, but it is of course necessary to incorporate plan revision in order to handle the inevitable dynamic environment.

Another area of improvement is to extend the normative reasoning capability of the model by extending it for state based norms in addition to event-based norms. Such an extension would allow the expression of obligations and prohibitions to achieve or avoid some state before some deadline. A combination of event and state based norms [10] enriches the norm representation as well as normative reasoning.

Lastly, we intend to build on the current ASP implementation to provide justification for why a certain plan maximises the utility considering the goals and norms it satisfies against those it does not. A potential starting point is [31], where it is possible to explain why certain literals are part of an answer set of a program and why others are not.

References

1. Aldewereld, H., Dignum, F., García-Camino, A., Noriega, P., Rodríguez-Aguilar, J.A., Sierra, C.: Operationalisation of norms for usagein electronic institutions. In: Nakashima, H., Wellman, M.P., Weiss, G., Stone, P. (eds.) 5th International Joint Conference on Autonomous Agents and Multiagent Systems (AAMAS 2006), Hakodate, Japan, May 8–12, pp. 223–225. ACM (2006)
2. Alrawagfeh, W., Meneguzzi, F.: Utilizing permission norms in BDI practical normative reasoning. In: Ghose, A., et al. (eds.) COIN 2014. LNCS, vol. 9372, pp. 1–18. Springer, Heidelberg (2015). doi:10.1007/978-3-319-25420-3_1
3. Artikis, A., Sergot, M.J., Pitt, J.V.: Specifying norm-governed computational societies. ACM Trans. Comput. Log. 10(1), 1–42 (2009)
4. Blum, A.L., Furst, M.L.: Fast planning through planning graph analysis. Artif. Intell. 90(1), 281–300 (1997)

5. de Boer, F.S., Hindriks, K.V., van der Hoek, W., Meyer, J.-J.C.: A verification framework for agent programming with declarative goals. J. Appl. Logic **5**(2), 277–302 (2007)

6. Börger, E., Stärk, R.: Asynchronous multi-agent ASMs. In: Börger, E., Stärk, R. (eds.) Abstract State Machines, pp. 207–282. Springer, Heidelberg (2003)

7. Broersen, J., Dastani, M., Hulstijn, J., Huang, Z., van der Torre, L.: The BOID architecture: conflicts between beliefs, obligations, intentions and desires. In: Proceedings of the Fifth International Conference on Autonomous Agents. AGENTS 2001, pp. 9–16. ACM, Montreal (2001)

8. Cliffe, O., De Vos, M., Padget, J.: Answer set programming for representing and reasoning about virtual institutions. In: Inoue, K., Satoh, K., Toni, F. (eds.) CLIMA 2006. LNCS (LNAI), vol. 4371, pp. 60–79. Springer, Heidelberg (2007)

9. Criado, N., Argente, E., Botti, V.J.: A BDI architecture for normative decision making. In: van der Hoek, W., Kaminka, G.A., Lespérance, Y., Luck, M., Sen, S. (eds.) 9th International Conference on Autonomous Agents and Multiagent Systems (AAMAS 2010), Toronto, Canada, May 10–14, vol. 1–3. IFAAMAS, pp. 1383–1384 (2010)

10. De Vos, M., Balke, T., Satoh, K.: Combining event-and state-based norms. In: Gini, M.L. Shehory, O., Ito, T., Jonker, C.M. (eds.) International conference on Autonomous Agents and Multi-Agent Systems, AAMAS 2013, Saint Paul, MN, USA, May 6–10, IFAAMAS, pp. 1157–1158 (2013)

11. Doherty, P., Gustafsson, J., Karlsson, L., Kvarnström, J.: TAL: temporal action logics language specification and tutorial. Electron. Trans. Artif. Intell. **2**, 273–306 (1998)

12. Esteva, M., Rodríguez-Aguilar, J.-A., Sierra, C., Garcia, P., Arcos, J.-L.: On the formal specification of electronic institutions. In: Sierra, C., Dignum, F.P.M. (eds.) AgentLink 2000. LNCS (LNAI), vol. 1991, pp. 126–147. Springer, Heidelberg (2001)

13. Fikes, R.E., Nilsson, N.J.: STRIPS: a new approach to the application of theorem proving to problem solving. In: Proceedings of the 2Nd International Joint Conference on Artificial Intelligence. IJCAI 1971, pp. 608–620. Morgan Kaufmann Publishers Inc., San Francisco (1971)

14. Gelfond, M., Lifschitz, V.: Action languages. Electron. Trans. AI **3**, 281–300 (1998)

15. Gelfond, M., Lifschitz, V.: The stable model semantics for logic programming. In: Kowalski, R.A., Bowen, K.A. (eds.) ICLP, SLP, pp. 1070–1080. MIT Press (1988)

16. Gini, M.L., Shehory, O., Ito, T., Jonker, C.M. (eds.): International conference on Autonomous Agents and Multi-Agent Systems, AAMAS 2013, Saint Paul, MN, USA, May 6–10, 2013. IFAAMAS (2013)

17. Hindriks, K.V., van der Hoek, W., van Riemsdijk, M.B.: Agent programming with temporally extended goals. In: Sierra, C., Castelfranchi, C., Decker, K.S., Sichman, J.S. (eds.) 8th International Joint Conference on Autonomous Agents and Multiagent Systems (AAMAS 2009), Budapest, Hungary, May 10–15, 2009, vol. 1. IFAAMAS, pp. 137–144 (2009)

18. Hindriks, K.V., van Riemsdijk, M.B.: Satisfying maintenance goals. In: Baldoni, M., Son, T.C., Riemsdijk, M.B., Winikoff, M. (eds.) DALT 2007. LNCS (LNAI), vol. 4897, pp. 86–103. Springer, Heidelberg (2008)

19. Kafali, Ö., Günay, A., Yolum, P.: GOSU: computing Goal Support with commitments in multiagent systems. In: Schaub, T., Friedrich, G., O'Sullivan, B. (eds.) Frontiers in Artificial Intelligence and Applications ECAI 2014–21st European Conference on Artificial Intelligence, 18–22 , Prague, Czech Republic - Including Prestigious Applications of Intelligent Systems (PAIS 2014), vol. 263, pp. 477–482. IOS Press (2014)

20. Kollingbaum, M.: Norm-governed Practical Reasonig Agents. Ph.D. thesis. University of Aberdeen (2005)
21. Kowalski, R., Sergot, M.: A logic-based calculus of events. New Gen. Comput. **4**(1), 67–95 (1986)
22. Lee, J., Palla, R.: Reformulating temporal action logicsin answer set programming. In: Hoffmann, J., Selman, B. (eds.) Proceedings of the Twenty-SixthAAAI Conference on Artificial Intelligence, July 22-26, 2012, Toronto, Ontario, Canada. AAAI Press (2012)
23. Lee, J., Palla, R.: Reformulating the situation calculus and theevent calculus in the general theory of stable models and in answer set programming. CoRR abs/1401.4607 (2014)
24. Lifschitz, V.: Answer set programming and plan generation. Artif. Intell. **138**(1–2), 39–54 (2002)
25. y López, F.L., Luck, M., d'Inverno, M.: A normative framework for agent-based systems. In: Normative Multi-Agent Systems (NORMAS), pp. 24–35 (2005)
26. Oren, N., Vasconcelos, W., Meneguzzi, F., Luck, M.: Acting on norm constrained plans. In: Leite, J., Torroni, P., Ågotnes, T., Boella, G., van der Torre, L. (eds.) CLIMA XII 2011. LNCS, vol. 6814, pp. 347–363. Springer, Heidelberg (2011)
27. Panagiotidi, S., Vázquez-Salceda, J., Dignum, F.: Reasoning over norm compliance via planning. In: Aldewereld, H., Sichman, J.S. (eds.) COIN 2012. LNCS, vol. 7756, pp. 35–52. Springer, Heidelberg (2013)
28. Panagiotidi, S., Vázquez-Salceda, J., Vasconcelos, W.: Contextual norm-based plan evaluation via answer set programming. In: BajoPérez, J., et al. (eds.) Highlights on Practical Applications of Agentsand Multi-Agent Systems. AISC, vol. 156, pp. 197–206. Springer, Heidelberg (2012)
29. Pitt, J., Busquets, D., Riveret, R.: Formal models of social processes: the pursuit of computational justice in self-organising multi-agent systems. In: 2013 IEEE 7th International Conference on Self-Adaptive and Self-Organizing Systems (SASO), pp. 269–270 (2013)
30. Rao, A.S., Georgeff, M.P.: BDI agents: from theory to practice. In: Proceedings of The First International Conference on Multi-Agent Systems (ICMAS 1995), pp. 312–319 (1995)
31. Schulz, C., Toni, F.: Justifying Answer Sets using Argumentation. CoRR abs/1411.5635 (2014)
32. Telang, P.R., Meneguzzi, F., Singh, M.P.: Hierarchical planning about goals and commitments. In: Gini, M.L., Shehory, O., Ito, T., Jonker, C.M. (eds.) International Conference on Autonomous Agents and Multi-Agent Systems, AAMAS 2013, Saint Paul, MN, USA, May 6–10, 2013. IFAAMAS, pp. 877–884 (2013)

Multi-agent Team Formation
for Design Problems

Leandro Soriano Marcolino[1]([✉]), Haifeng Xu[1], David Gerber[3,4], Boian Kolev[2], Samori Price[2], Evangelos Pantazis[3,4], and Milind Tambe[1]

[1] Computer Science Department, University of Southern California,
Los Angeles, CA, USA
{sorianom,haifengx,tambe}@usc.edu
[2] Computer Science Department, California State University,
Dominguez Hills, Carson, USA
{bkolev1,sprice25}@toromail.csudh.edu
[3] School of Architecture, University of Southern California, Los Angeles, CA, USA
{dgerber,epantazi}@usc.edu
[4] Department of Civil Engineering, University of Southern California,
Los Angeles, CA, USA

Abstract. Design imposes a novel social choice problem: using a team of voting agents, maximize the number of optimal solutions; allowing a user to then take an aesthetical choice. In an open system of design agents, team formation is fundamental. We present the first model of agent teams for design. For maximum applicability, we envision agents that are queried for a single opinion, and multiple solutions are obtained by multiple iterations. We show that diverse teams composed of agents with different preferences maximize the number of optimal solutions, while uniform teams composed of multiple copies of the best agent are in general suboptimal. Our experiments study the model in bounded time; and we also study a real system, where agents vote to design buildings.

Keywords: Collaboration · Distributed AI · Team formation · Design and computation · Design optimization · Design automation

1 Introduction

Teams of voting agents are a powerful tool for finding the optimal solution in many applications [16,17,19]. Voting is a popular approach since it is easily parallelizable, it allows the re-use of existing agents, and there are theoretical guarantees for finding one optimal choice [2]. For design problems, however, finding one optimal solution is not enough. For example, it could be mathematically optimal under measurable metrics but lack aesthetic qualities or social acceptance by the target public. Besides, the solution could have a poor performance in some key objective of a multi-objective optimization problem. Essentially, designers need to explore a large set of optimal alternatives, to pick one solution

© Springer International Publishing Switzerland 2016
V. Dignum et al. (Eds.): COIN 2015, LNAI 9628, pp. 354–375, 2016.
DOI: 10.1007/978-3-319-42691-4_20

not only according to her aesthetic taste (and/or the one of the target public), but also according to preferences that may be unknown or not formalized [7,25].

Hence, we actually need systems that find as many optimal solutions as possible, allowing a human to explore such optimal alternatives to make a choice. Even if a user does not want to consider too many solutions, they can be filtered and clustered [5], and be presented in manageable ways [21], allowing her to easily make an informed choice. Therefore, a system of voting agents that produces a unique optimal solution is insufficient, and we propose the novel social choice problem of maximizing the number of optimal alternatives found by a voting system. As ranked voting may suffer from noisy rankings when using existing agents [11], we study multiple plurality voting iterations, allowing great applicability and re-use of existing agents.

Traditionally, social choice studies the optimality of voting rules, assuming a certain noise models for the agents, and rankings composed of a linear order over alternatives [1,2]. Hence, there is a single optimal choice, and a system is successful if it can return that optimal choice with high probability. More recently, several works have been considering cases where there is a partial order over alternatives [20,26], or where the agents output pairwise comparisons instead of rankings [4]. However, these works still focus on finding an optimal alternative, or a fixed-sized set of optimal alternatives (where the size is known beforehand). Therefore, they still provide no help in finding the maximum set of optimal solutions. Moreover, they assume agents that are able to output comparisons among all actions with fairly good precision, and the use of multiple voting iterations has never been studied. When considering agents with different preferences, the field is focused on verifying if voting rules satisfy a set of axioms that are considered to be important to achieve fairness [18]. Meanwhile, the computational design literature has not yet found the potential of teams of voting agents. They study traditional optimization techniques [28], or swarms of agents that interact on the geometric space to emerge aesthetically complex shapes [22,23].

In this work we bring together the social choice and computational design fields. We present a theoretical study of which kinds of teams are desirable for design problems, and how their size may effect optimality. In doing so, we show many novel results for the study of multi-agent systems. Instead of studying agents with different preferences in order to verify fairness axioms, we show here that agents with different preferences are actually fundamental when voting to find a "truth" (i.e., optimal decisions). On the other hand, agents with the same set of preferences significantly harm the performance, and in general the number of optimal solutions *decreases* as the size of the team grows. Such results were never seen before in the social choice literature. Our theoretical development draws a novel connection between social choice and *number theory*, instead of the traditional connections with *bayesian probability theory*. This novel connection allows us to show that the optimal diverse team size is constant with high probability, and a prime number of optimal actions may impose problems. We also show that we can maximize the number of optimal solutions with agents with different preferences as the team size grows, as long as the team size grows *carefully*. Moreover, we simulate design agents in synthetic experiments to further study our model, confirming the predictions of our theory and providing realistic insights into what happens when systems run with bounded computational time. Finally, we present experiments in a highly relevant domain: architectural design, where we show teams of real design agents that vote to choose the best qualifying and energy-efficient design solutions for buildings.

2 Related Work

Voting systems have been extensively used for many different applications [16,17,19]. Mostly because, under some assumptions, they provide optimality guarantees for finding an optimal choice [2]. For many real problems, however, finding one optimal solution is not enough, and we actually want to find the maximum number of optimal solutions. However, most of the social choice literature is about finding a correct ranking in domains where there is a linear order over the alternatives, and hence a unique optimal decision [1,2]. Recent works, however, are considering more complex domains. Xia and Conitzer [26] study the problem of finding k optimal solutions, where k is known beforehand, by aggregating rankings from each agent. However, not only do they need strong assumptions about the quality of the rankings of such agents, but they also show that calculating the *maximum likelihood estimation* (MLE) from the rankings is an NP-hard problem. Procaccia *et al.* [20] study a similar perspective, where the objective is to find the top k options given rankings from each agent, where, again, k is known in advance. However, in their case, they assume there still exists one unique truly optimal choice, hidden among these top k alternatives. Elkind and Shah [4], motivated by the crowdsourcing domain, study the case where instead of rankings, the voters output pairwise comparisons among all actions, which may not follow transitivity. However, their final objective is still to pick a single winner, not to maximize the set of optimal solutions found by a voting system. Finally, outputting a full comparison among all actions can be a burden for an agent [12]. Jiang *et al.* [11] show that actual agents can have very noisy rankings, and therefore do not follow the assumptions of previous works in social choice. Hence, as any agent is able to output at least one action (i.e., a single vote), we study here systems where agents vote across multiple iterations.

Concerning distributed optimization, our work is related to the study of distributed genetic algorithms [13]. Our experimental section relates to the "island model", where populations evolve concurrently. Normally, however, the populations interact by transferring offsprings, not by voting, and a theoretical study of voting teams which must maximize the number of optimal solutions was never performed. Additionally, the use of multiple classifiers has been a very successful technique in machine learning, in the study of ensemble systems [19]. None of these works, however, explore the potential of multiple agents in maximizing the set of optimal solutions for design problems.

In computational design, automated methods that can provide a high number of optimal alternatives are highly desirable, as it is hard for the human designers to manually find optimal solutions, and they need a large solution pool in order to pick one that fits their aesthetic/subjective evaluation and/or to make a complex trade-off among different objectives that cannot be formalized into a single function [6,24]. One common method for generating alternatives is to use genetic algorithms [27]. Other optimization methods have also been explored [28]. Another line of work in computational design uses a swarm of agents that move and interact in the geometric space, while depositing material, and hence emerging complex geometrical shapes [22,23]. Although such works are able to design and create intricate geometries, they are not yet using these agent teams to optimize the designs, let alone finding a maximum number of optimal solutions.

3   Design Domains

We consider in this work domains where the objective is to find the highest number of optimal solutions. We show that design is one of such domains. One of the most common computational design approaches is to use *parametric designs* [5,8], where a human designer creates an initial design of a product using *computer-aided design* tools. However, instead of manually deciding all aspects of the product, she leaves *free parameters*, whose values can be modified to change the design of the product. It is up to the designer to decide which parameters are going to be available, their valid types and their valid range.

This approach is used because design is an inherently complex problem. Although a human is able to test and evaluate a few solutions looking for optimality, the number of different possibilities that she can manually create is highly limited, especially under the (common) hard time-constraints. In Fig. 1, we show a simple example in the context of architectural design,

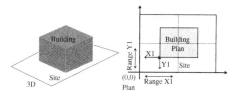

Fig. 1. A parametric design of a building, showing two parameters: $X1$ and $Y1$.

where the parameters $X1$ and $Y1$ are being used to specify the position of the lower left corner of the building relative to the site boundary.

The design of a product normally occurs over multiple phases, where increasing levels of details are decided and optimized. Our work is focused on the initial design phase, when multiple possible design alternatives are analyzed in order to choose one for further study and optimization. This initial design phase is, however, very important to the final performance of a product [21]. For example, in the context of architectural design (as how we explore later in our experiments), it has been acknowledged that it has a high impact on the overall building performance [3]. Design problems are in general multi-objective, since a product normally must be optimized across different objectives. For example, a product should have a low cost, but at the same time high quality. Hence, there are a large number of optimal solutions, all tied in a *Pareto frontier*. For the computational system, these optimal solutions are all equivalent. However, a human may have unknown preferences, may dynamically decide to value some objective over another when handling intricate trade-offs, and/or may choose the option that most pleases her own aesthetic taste or the one of the target public/client.

Note that choosing a design according to aesthetics is an undefined problem, since there are no formal definitions to compare among different options. Hence, the best that a system can do is to provide a human with a large number of optimal solutions (according to other measurable factors), allowing her to freely decide among equally optimal solutions — but most probably with different aesthetic qualities. Therefore, it is natural that in design problems we are going to have many possible solutions, and we want to find as many optimal ones as possible. In fact, the exploration of a large space of possible alternatives is essential in design, as recently shown by other researchers [7,14,25]. There are many benefits in discovering a large number of optimal solutions:

Knowledge "Does not Hurt": We argue that having more optimal solutions to choose from is not worse than having less. Although some works in psychology show that humans may get frustrated in the face of too many options, especially under time pressure [9,10], we argue that if a designer has enough time or motivation to analyze only x solutions, she can do so with a system that provides more than x optimal solutions by sampling the exact amount that she desires. However, she will never be able to do so with a system that provides less than x optimal solutions. Note also that the works in psychology [9,10] were taken in the context of consumers deciding among products to purchase, not in the context of design exploration. As mentioned before, in design the necessity of large exploration spaces is recognized [7,14,25]. Moreover, as we discuss in detail later, voting systems could be combined with another system that identify and eliminate solutions that are similar by applying clustering and analysis techniques, and that presents the optimal alternatives to a human in a manageable way [5,21].

Knowledge Increases Confidence in Optimality: In general design problems, the true Pareto frontier is unknown. Genetic algorithms are widely used in order to *estimate* it. The only knowledge available for the system to evaluate the optimality is in comparison with the other solutions that are also being evaluated during the optimization process [6]. Many apparently "optimal" solutions are actually discovered to be sub-optimal as we find more solutions. Hence, finding a higher number of optimal solutions decreases the risk of a designer picking a wrong choice that was initially outputted as "optimal" by a system (for example, the single agents, as we will show later).

Knowledge Increases Aesthetic Qualities: If a human has a larger set of optimal solutions to choose from, there is a greater likelihood that at least one of these solutions is going to be of high aesthetic quality according to her preferences, or the ones of the target public [7].

Knowledge Increases Diversity of Options: In general, when a system x has more optimal solutions available than a system y, it does not necessarily imply that the solutions in the system x are more similar, while the optimal solutions in y are more different/diverse. In fact, all things equal (i.e., the algorithms are equally able to find unique solutions), the greater the amount of optimal solutions, the higher the likelihood that we have more diverse solutions available. Of course we could have some algorithm x that produces many optimal solutions by creating small variations of one unique solution, but here we do not consider these potentially misleading systems. Again, we assume that such solutions could be identified and filtered by another system [5,21].

4   Agent Teams for Design Problems

We consider here a team of agents that vote together at each decision point of the design of a product. For the sake of clarity and precision, we present in this section an idealized model. In Sect. 4.1 we generalize our model to more complex situations, and in Sect. 5 we generalize further by performing synthetic experiments. Let $\boldsymbol{\Phi}$ be a set of agents ϕ, and $\boldsymbol{\Omega}$ a set of world states ω. Each ω has an associated set of possible actions $\boldsymbol{A_\omega}$. For example, each world state may represent a parameter of a parametric design problem, and each action may represent a possible value for such parameter. At each world state, each agent ϕ outputs an action a, an optimal action according to the agent's imperfect evaluation – which may or may not be a truly optimal action. Hence, there is a probability p_j that the agent outputs a certain action a_j. The teams take the action decided by *plurality voting* (i.e., the team takes the decision voted by the largest number of agents – we consider ties are broken uniformly at random).

We assume first that the world states are independent, and by taking an optimal action at all world states we find an optimal solution for the entire problem. That is, we assume first that by taking locally optimal decisions at each design decision point, a globally optimal solution is obtained. We generalize this assumption later, in Proposition 8 (in Sect. 4.1), where we consider design problems with correlated parameters.

In this paper our objective goes beyond finding one optimal solution, we want to maximize the number of optimal solutions that we can find. For greater applicability, we consider here agents that output a single action. Hence, we generate multiple solutions by re-applying the voting procedure across all world states multiple times (which are called *voting iterations* – one *iteration* goes across all world states, forming one solution). Formally, let $\boldsymbol{S}$ be the set of (unique) optimal solutions that we find by re-applying the voting procedure through z iterations. Our objective is to maximize $|\boldsymbol{S}|$. We will show that, under some conditions, we can achieve that when $z \to \infty$.

We consider that at each world state ω there is a subset $\boldsymbol{Good_\omega} \subset \boldsymbol{A_\omega}$ of optimal actions in ω. An optimal solution is going to be composed by assigning any $a \in \boldsymbol{Good_\omega}$ in world state ω – for all world states. Conversely, we consider the complementary subset $\boldsymbol{Bad_\omega} \subset \boldsymbol{A_\omega}$, such that $\boldsymbol{Good_\omega} \cup \boldsymbol{Bad_\omega} = \boldsymbol{A_\omega}, \boldsymbol{Good_\omega} \cap \boldsymbol{Bad_\omega} = \emptyset$. We drop the subscripts ω when it is clear that we are referring to a certain world state.

One fundamental problem is selecting which agents should form a team. By the classical voting theories, one would expect the best teams to be uniform teams composed of multiple copies of the best agent [2,15]. Here we show, however, that for design problems uniform teams need very strong assumptions to be optimal, and in most cases they actually converge to always outputting a single solution – an undesirable outcome. However, diverse teams are optimal as long as the team size grows *carefully*, as we explain later in Theorem 1.

We call a team *optimal* when: (i) $|S| \rightarrow \prod_\omega |Good_\omega|$ as $z \rightarrow \infty$, and (ii) all optimal solutions are chosen by the team with the same probability $1/\prod_\omega |Good_\omega|$. Otherwise, even though the team still produces all optimal solutions, it would tend to repeat already generated solutions whose probability is higher. Since in practice there are time bounds, such condition is fundamental to have as many optimal solutions as possible in limited time. Also note that condition (ii) subsumes condition (i), but we keep both for clarity.

We first consider agents whose pdfs are independent and identically distributed. Let p_j^{Good} be the probability of voting for $a_j \in \mathbf{Good}$, and p_k^{Bad} be the probability of voting for $a_k \in \mathbf{Bad}$. Let $n := |\Phi|$ be the size of the team, and N_l be the number of agents that vote for a_l in a certain voting iteration. If $\forall a_j \in \mathbf{Good}, a_k \in \mathbf{Bad}, p_j^{Good} > p_k^{Bad}$, the team is going to find one optimal solution with probability 1 as $n \rightarrow \infty$:

Observation 1. The probability of a team outputting one optimal solution goes to 1 as $n \rightarrow \infty$, if $p_j^{Good} > p_k^{Bad}, \forall a_j \in \mathbf{Good}, a_k \in \mathbf{Bad}$.

Note that as the agents are independent and identically distributed, we can model the process of pooling the opinions of n agents as a multinomial distribution with n trials (and the probability of any class k of the multinomial corresponds to the probability p_k of voting for an action a_k). Hence, for each action a_l, the expected number of votes is given by $E[N_l] = n \times p_l$. Therefore, by the *law of large numbers*, if $p_j^{Good} > p_k^{Bad} \ \forall a_j \in \mathbf{Good}, a_k \in \mathbf{Bad}$, we have that $N_j > N_k$. Hence, the team will pick an action $a_j \in \mathbf{Good}$, in all world states, if n is large enough (i.e., $n \rightarrow \infty$).

However, with a team made of copies of the same agent, the system is likely to lose the ability to generate new solutions as n increases. If, for each ω, we have an action a_m^ω such that $p_m^{Good} > p_j^{Good} \ \forall a_m^\omega \neq a_j^\omega$, the team converges to picking only action a_m^ω. Hence, $|S| = 1$, which is a very negative result for design problems. Therefore, contrary to traditional social choice, here it is not the case that increasing the team size always improves performance. We formalize this notion in Proposition 1 below, where we also show the conditions for a uniform team to be optimal. Let $p_{Good} := \sum_j p_j^{Good}$ be the probability of picking any action in $\mathbf{Good}$. We re-write the probability of an action a_j^{Good} as: $p_j^{Good} := \frac{p_{Good}}{|Good|} + \lambda_j$, where $\sum_j \lambda_j := 0$. Hence, some λ_j are positive, and some are negative (unless they are all equal to 0). Let $\boldsymbol{\lambda}^+$ be the set of $\lambda_j > 0$. Let λ^{High} be the maximum possible value for $\lambda_j \in \boldsymbol{\lambda}^+$, such that the relation $p_j^{Good} > p_k^{Bad}$, $\forall a_j \in \mathbf{Good}, a_k \in \mathbf{Bad}$ is preserved. We show that when $z \rightarrow \infty$, $|S|$ is the highest as $\max \boldsymbol{\lambda}^+ \rightarrow 0$, and the lowest (i.e., one) as $\min \boldsymbol{\lambda}^+ \rightarrow \lambda^{High}$. Note that $\max \boldsymbol{\lambda}^+ \rightarrow 0$ represents the situation where the probability is equally divided among all optimal actions, and $\min \boldsymbol{\lambda}^+ \rightarrow \lambda^{High}$ represents the case where one optimal action receives a high probability in comparison with the other optimal actions.

Proposition 1. *The maximum value for $|\boldsymbol{S}|$ is $\prod_{\omega} |\boldsymbol{Good}_{\omega}|$. When $z, n \to \infty$, as $\max \boldsymbol{\lambda}^+ \to 0$, $|\boldsymbol{S}| \to \prod_{\omega} |\boldsymbol{Good}_{\omega}|$. Conversely, as $\min \boldsymbol{\lambda}^+ \to \lambda^{High}$, $|\boldsymbol{S}| \to 1$.*

Proof. As $\max \boldsymbol{\lambda}^+ \to 0$, $\lambda_j \to 0$, $\forall a_j$. Hence, $E[N_j] \to n \times \frac{p_{Good}}{|Good|}$, $\forall a_j \in \boldsymbol{Good}$. Because ties are broken randomly, at each world state ω, each $a_j \in \boldsymbol{Good}_{\omega}$ is selected by the team with equal probability $\frac{1}{|\boldsymbol{Good}_{\omega}|}$. As $E[N_j] = E[N_k]$ $\forall a_j, a_k \in \boldsymbol{Good}$, we have that at each ω it is possible to choose $|\boldsymbol{Good}_{\omega}|$ different actions. Hence, there are $\prod_{\omega} |\boldsymbol{Good}_{\omega}|$ possible combinations of solutions. At each voting iteration, ties are broken at each ω randomly, and one possible combination is generated. As $z \to \infty$, eventually we cover all possible combinations, and $|\boldsymbol{S}| \to \prod_{\omega} |\boldsymbol{Good}_{\omega}|$.

Conversely, as $\min \boldsymbol{\lambda}^+ \to \lambda^{High}$, $E[N_j] \to n \times p_j^{Good}$ for one fixed a_j such that $p_j^{Good} > p_k^{Good}$, $\forall a_j \neq a_k \in \boldsymbol{Good}$. Consequently, $E[N_j] > E[N_k]$, at each ω. Hence, there is no tie in any world state, and the team picks a fixed a_j^{ω} at each world state. Therefore, even if $z \to \infty$, $|\boldsymbol{S}| \to 1$. Note that we do not say here that the same action is picked across world states (as a_j^{ω} may differ for each ω), but that the same optimal solution is picked for all voting iterations. ∎

Therefore, uniform teams need a very strong assumption to satisfy condition (i): the probability of voting for optimal actions must be uniformly distributed over all optimal actions (i.e., $\max \boldsymbol{\lambda}^+ \to 0$). If $\max \boldsymbol{\lambda}^+ \to 0$, condition (ii) is also satisfied as n grows, because of Observation 1 (i.e., the probability of outputting a suboptimal solution goes to 0) and because of the fact that all actions are equally likely to be chosen; hence each solution is chosen with equal probability $1/ \prod_{\omega} |\boldsymbol{Good}_{\omega}|$.

We show that, alternatively, we can use agents with different "preferences" (i.e., "diverse" agents), to maximize $|\boldsymbol{S}|$. We consider here agents that have about the same ability in problem-solving, but they prefer different optimal actions. As the agents have similar ability, we consider here the probabilities to be the same across agents, except for the actions in $\boldsymbol{Good}$, as each agent ϕ_i has a subset $\boldsymbol{Good}^i \subset \boldsymbol{Good}$ consisting of its preferred actions (which are more likely to be chosen than other actions). We denote by p_{ij} the probability of agent ϕ_i voting for action a_j. Hence, we define the pdf of the diverse agents as: $\forall a_j \in \boldsymbol{Good}^i$, let $p_{Good^i} := \sum_j p_{ij}$, $p_{ij} := \frac{p_{Good^i}}{|\boldsymbol{Good}^i|}$; $\forall a_j \in \boldsymbol{Good} \setminus \boldsymbol{Good}^i$, $p_{ij} := \frac{p_{Good} - p_{Good^i}}{|\boldsymbol{Good} \setminus \boldsymbol{Good}^i|}$; and $\forall a_k \notin \boldsymbol{Good}^i$, $a_j \in \boldsymbol{Good}^i$, $p_{ij} > p_{ik}$. $\boldsymbol{Good}^i \cap \boldsymbol{Good}^l$ (of agents ϕ_i and ϕ_l) is not necessarily $\emptyset$. The pdfs are strictly defined in this section for the sake of clarity and precision, but in the next section and in our synthetic experiments we generalize further. In Fig. 2 we show an illustrative example.

Let's consider we can draw diverse agents from a distribution $\mathcal{F}$. Each agent ϕ_i has $r < |\boldsymbol{Good}|$ actions in its $\boldsymbol{Good}^i$, and we assume that all actions in $\boldsymbol{Good}$ are equally likely to be selected to form $\boldsymbol{Good}^i$ (since they are all equally optimal). Note that r is the same for all agents (as, again, we assume they have

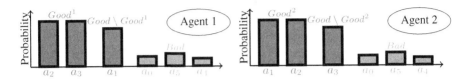

Fig. 2. Illustrative example of the probability distribution functions of two diverse agents.

the same pdfs, but different preferences), and that we also cover the case where each agent prefers a single action (which would be $r := 1$). We show that by drawing n agents from $\mathcal{F}$, the team is optimal for large n with probability 1, as long as n is a multiple of a divisor (> 1) of each $|\textbf{\textit{Good}}_\omega|$. We also show that the minimum necessary optimal team size is constant with high probability as the number of world states grow. We start with the following:

Proposition 2. *If a team of size n is optimal at a world state, then $gcd(n, |\textbf{\textit{Good}}|) > 1$. That is, n and $|\textbf{\textit{Good}}|$ are not co-prime.*

Proof (by contradiction). By the optimality requirement (ii), each action must be in the $\textbf{\textit{Good}}^i$ set of the same number of agents. Otherwise, if an action a_i is preferred by a larger number of agents than another action a_j, the team would pick a_i with a larger probability than a_j. Hence, we must have that:

$$n \times r = k \times |\textbf{\textit{Good}}|, \tag{1}$$

where k is a constant $\in \mathbb{N}_{>0}$. k represents the number of agents that have a given action a_j in its $\textbf{\textit{Good}}^i$. Note that it must be the same for all optimal actions, and therefore we have a single constant. If n and $|\textbf{\textit{Good}}|$ are co-prime, then it must be the case that r is divisible by $|\textbf{\textit{Good}}|$. However, this yields $r \geq |\textbf{\textit{Good}}|$, which contradicts our assumption. Therefore, n and $|\textbf{\textit{Good}}|$ are not co-prime. ∎

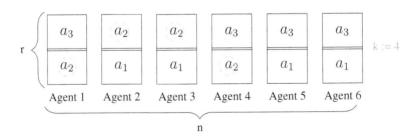

Fig. 3. Illustrative example of Eq. 1. Each action is in the list of preferences of 4 agents ($k := 4$). As an example, we mark with a dashed circle one of the actions, a_2.

We illustrate Eq. 1 with an example in Fig. 3. In the figure we show 6 agents ($n := 6$), with 2 preferred actions each ($r := 2$). Note that each action is preferred by 4 agents, and hence we show a case where $k := 4$. As an example, we mark with a dashed circle one of the actions, a_2. In such case, the team will have an equal probability of picking all optimal actions, and optimality condition (ii) would be satisfied if the probability of picking suboptimal actions is 0. If, for example, we now change agent 5 to prefer actions a_2 and a_3 (replacing action a_1 by a_2), then the team would be more likely to pick action a_2 by plurality voting than any other action, and it would be less likely to pick action a_1 than any other action. As the number of voting iterations is limited in actual applications, this situation is not desirable.

Note that we could also have a case where one agent prefers a larger number of actions than others. For example, we could change agent 5 to prefer actions a_1, a_2 and a_3. However, as the agent has a limited amount of probability distributed over the actions in the $\boldsymbol{Good}^i$ set (i.e., p_{Good^i}), we have that necessarily the probability of the agent voting for a_1 and a_3 would drop; hence, the team would pick a_2 more often than the other actions, and a_1 and a_3 less often than the other actions. This does not mean, however, that there is a single optimal configuration for each number of optimal actions $|\boldsymbol{Good}|$. There are multiple possible solutions for Eq. 1, but in any possible solution we will find that the size of the team n and $|\boldsymbol{Good}|$ are not co-prime.

Proposition 2 is a necessary but not sufficient condition for optimality. If Eq. 1 is satisfied, all optimal actions will be selected with the same probability, but it is still necessary for the probability of picking suboptimal actions to go to 0 to fully satisfy condition (ii). That will be the case if $p_{Good^i} = 1$, or if $n \to \infty$, since $p_j^{Good} > p_k^{Bad}$, $\forall a_j \in \boldsymbol{Good}, a_k \in \boldsymbol{Bad}$. Note that Proposition 2 implies hard restrictions for world states where $|\boldsymbol{Good}|$ is prime, or for teams with prime size n: if n is prime, $|\boldsymbol{Good}|$ must be a multiple of n; and if $|\boldsymbol{Good}|$ is prime, n must be a multiple of $|\boldsymbol{Good}|$.

Let's analyze across a set of world states $\boldsymbol{\Omega}$. For a team of fixed size n, Proposition 2 applies across all world states. Hence, the team size must be a multiple of a divisor (> 1) of each $|\boldsymbol{Good}_\omega|$. Note that the pdfs of the agents (and also r) may change according to ω. Let $\boldsymbol{D}$ be a set containing one divisor of each world state (if two or more world states have a common divisor x, it will be representable by only one $x \in \boldsymbol{D}$). Hence, $\forall \omega, \exists d \in \boldsymbol{D}$, such that $d \mid |\boldsymbol{Good}_\omega|$; and $\forall d \in \boldsymbol{D}, \exists \boldsymbol{Good}_\omega$, such that $d \mid |\boldsymbol{Good}_\omega|$. There are multiple possible $\boldsymbol{D}$ sets, from the superset of all possibilities $\mathscr{D}$. Therefore, we can now study the minimum size necessary for an optimal team. Applying Proposition 2 at each world state ω, we have that the minimum size necessary for an optimal team is $n = \min_{D \in \mathscr{D}} \prod_{d \in D} d$. Hence, our worst case is when each $|\boldsymbol{Good}_\omega|$ is a unique prime, as the team will have to be a product of all (unique) optimal action space sizes:

Proposition 3. *In the worst case, the minimum team size is exponential in the size of the world states $|\boldsymbol{\Omega}|$. In the best case, the minimum necessary team size is a constant with $|\boldsymbol{\Omega}|$.*

Proof. In the worst case, each added world state ω has a unique prime optimal action space size. Hence, the minimum team size is at least the product of the first $|\Omega|$ primes, which, by the *prime number theorem*, has growth rate $\exp((1+o(1))|\Omega|\log|\Omega|)$. In the best case, each added $\boldsymbol{Good}_\omega$ has a common divisor with previous ones, and the minimum necessary team size does not change. ∎

However, we show that the worst case happens with low probability, and the best case with high probability. Let G be the maximum possible $|\boldsymbol{Good}|$, and $M := |\Omega|$. Assume that each world state ω_j will have a uniformly randomly drawn number of optimal actions, denoted as m_j, for all $j = 1,\ldots,M$ (i.e., $\forall\omega \in \Omega$). We assume that G is large enough, so that the probability that a given m_j has factor p is $1/p$.

Proposition 4. *The probability that the minimum necessary team size grows exponentially tends to 0, and the probability that it is constant tends to 1, as $M \to \infty$.*

Proof. It is sufficient to show that the probability that $m_1,\ldots,m_{M-1}$ are all co-prime with m_M tends to 0 as $M \to \infty$. That is, we show that when adding a new world state ω_M, its $|\boldsymbol{Good}_\omega|$ will have a common factor with the size of the $\boldsymbol{Good}$ set of some of the other world states with high probability. Given any prime p, the probability that at least one of any independently randomly generated $M-1$ numbers $m_1,...,m_{M-1}$ has factor p is $1 - (1 - \frac{1}{p})^{M-1}$, while the probability that one independently randomly generated number m_M has factor p is $\frac{1}{p}$ (for large enough G). Therefore, the probability m_M shares common factor p with at least one of $m_1,\ldots,m_{M-1}$ is $\frac{1-(1-\frac{1}{p})^{M-1}}{p}$. The probability that m_M is co-prime with all $m_1,\ldots,m_{M-1}$ is:

$$\prod_{\text{all primes } p} [1 - \frac{1 - (1 - \frac{1}{p})^{M-1}}{p}],$$

which, as $M \to \infty$, tends to:

$$\prod_{\text{all primes } p} (1 - \frac{1}{p}) = \frac{1}{\zeta(1)} = 0,$$

where $\zeta(s)$ is the Riemann zeta function. The last equality holds true since:

$$\zeta(1) = \prod_{\text{all primes } p} \frac{1}{1-p^{-1}} = \sum_{i=1}^{\infty} \frac{1}{i} \to \infty$$

(as shown by Euler). Hence, with high probability, when adding a new world state ω, $|\boldsymbol{Good}_\omega|$ will share a common factor with a world state already in Ω. ∎

Finally, in the next theorem we show that a diverse team of agents is always optimal as the team grows, as long as it grows *carefully*. That is, we show that for large diverse teams we will be able to satisfy the optimality conditions (i) and (ii), as long as the team size is a multiple of a divisor of $|\boldsymbol{Good}_\omega|$, $\forall\omega \in \Omega$. Again, we assume that G is large enough, so that the probability that a given m_j has factor p is $1/p$.

Theorem 1. *Let $D \in \mathscr{D}$ be a set containing one factor from each $\textbf{Good}_\omega$. For arbitrary n, the probability that we generate (by drawing from a distribution $\mathcal{F}$) an optimal team of size n converges to 0 as $|\mathbf{\Omega}| \to \infty$. However, if $n = c \prod_{d \in D} d$, then the probability that the team is optimal tends to 1 as $c \to \infty$.*

Proof. For an arbitrary team size n, let $\textbf{P}$ be the set of its prime factors. Given one $p \in \textbf{P}$, the probability that p is not a factor of $|\textbf{Good}_\omega|$ is $1 - 1/p$. The probability that all $p \in \textbf{P}$ are not factors is: $\prod_p (1 - 1/p)$. As $0 < \prod_p (1 - 1/p) < 1$, the probability that at least one $p \in \textbf{P}$ is a factor of $|\textbf{Good}_\omega|$ is $1 - \prod_p (1 - 1/p) < 1$. For $|\mathbf{\Omega}|$ tests, the probability that at least one p is a factor in all of them is:

$$\left(1 - \prod_p (1 - 1/p) \right)^{|\mathbf{\Omega}|},$$

which tends to 0, as $|\mathbf{\Omega}| \to \infty$. Hence, the probability that $\gcd(n, |\textbf{Good}_\omega|) = 1$ for at least one ω tends to 1, and the probability that the team can be optimal tends to 0.

However, if:

$$n = c \prod_{d \in D} d,$$

then $\gcd(n, |\textbf{Good}_\omega|) \neq 1 \; \forall \omega \in \mathbf{\Omega}$, satisfying the necessary condition in Proposition 2 at all world states. Let n_j be the number of agents ϕ_i that have a_j in its $\textbf{Good}^i$, and $P(n_j = n_k)$ be the probability that $n_j = n_k$ (that is, the probability that the same number of agents have a_j and a_k in their $\textbf{Good}^i$). As each a_j has equal probability of being in a $\textbf{Good}^i$, for a large number of drawings from $\mathcal{F}$ (i.e., $c \to \infty$), we have that $P(n_j = n_k) \to 1, \forall a_j, a_k \in \textbf{Good}_\omega, \forall \omega$, by the *law of large numbers*. Hence, each optimal solution will be selected with the same probability. Moreover, as $p_j^{Good} > p_k^{Bad}, \forall a_j \in \textbf{Good}, a_k \in \textbf{Bad}$, the probability of picking a suboptimal solution converges to 0 (as $n \to \infty$ with $c \to \infty$), and hence the probability of picking each of the optimal solutions converges to $1/\prod_\omega |\textbf{Good}_\omega|$ (satisfying optimality condition (ii)). ∎

If it is expensive to test values for n such that Theorem 1 is satisfied, we can choose $n = c \prod_\omega |\textbf{Good}_\omega|$, as it immediately implies the conditions of the theorem. Moreover, if we know the size of all $|\textbf{Good}_\omega|$, we can check if n and $|\textbf{Good}_\omega|$ are co-prime in $O(h)$ time (where h is the number of digits in the smaller number), using the *Euclidean algorithm*. Hence, we can test all world states in $O(|\mathbf{\Omega}|h)$ time.

4.1 Generalizations

In this section we present several generalizations from our initial idealized model, in order to cover more realistic situations. We start by generalizing our theory to cases where the agents do not have only a probability of $p_{ij} := \frac{p_{Good^i}}{|Good^i|}$ or $p_{ij} := \frac{p_{Good} - p_{Good^i}}{|Good \backslash Good^i|}$ to vote for actions in $\textbf{Good}$ (depending if the action is in

Good^i or not), but now can have different probabilities distributed over the actions in **Good**. Hence, we now model each agent as having a set of **Good^i** sets, each with its own probability distributed over the actions in the set. For this generalization, we still consider that the agents have the same pdf, but different preferences. That is, the agents may have different actions at each **Good^i** set, but their size and the number of sets is the same across agents.

Hence, we denote each **Good^i** set j as $_j$**Good^i**. Each also has its own $p_{j\,Good^i}$ total probability, that will be equally distributed among all actions in $_j$**Good^i**, in a similar fashion as before. As mentioned, the content of each $_j$**Good^i** set may differ across agents, but we consider the $p_{j\,Good^i}$ to be the same across agents. Note that the case where each action has a different probability is defined as the situation where each $|_j$**Good$^i|$** $:= 1$. Similarly as before, we consider that each agent ϕ_i has $_jr < |$**Good**$|$ actions at each $_j$**Good^i**, and all actions in **Good** are equally likely to be selected to form each $_j$**Good^i**. In Fig. 4 we show an illustrative example of the pdf of two agents with multiple $_j$**Good^i** sets.

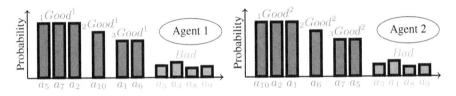

Fig. 4. Illustrative example of the probability distribution functions of two agents with multiple $_j$**Good^i** sets.

Proposition 5. *Theorem 1 still applies under the more general model stated above. That is, if $n = c\prod_{d \in D} d$, then the probability that the team is optimal tends to 1 as $c \to \infty$.*

Proof. Similarly as before, for each $_j$**Good^i** we must have that:

$$n \times {}_jr = {}_jk \times |\textbf{Good}|, \tag{2}$$

so that for each $_j$**Good^i** we have that $_jk$ agents have a given action a in its $_j$**Good^i**. As the total probability $p_{j\,Good^i}$ of each set is the same across agents, we have that each optimal action will be selected by the team with the same probability when Eq. 2 is satisfied for all $_j$**Good^i**. Hence, across world states, each optimal solution will also have the same probability of being selected. Similarly as in Proposition 2, for Eq. 2 to be satisfied, we must have that n and $|$**Good**$|$ are not co-prime, and that will be true when $n = c\prod_{d \in D} d$.

Let $_jn_l$ be the number of agents ϕ_i that have a_l in its $_j$**Good^i**, and $P(_jn_l = {}_jn_m)$ be the probability that $_jn_l = {}_jn_m$. Like before, as each a_l has equal probability of being in a $_j$**Good^i**, for a large number of drawings from $\mathcal{F}$

(i.e., $c \to \infty$), we have that $P(_j n_l = {}_j n_m) \to 1, \forall a_l, a_m \in \boldsymbol{Good}_\omega, \forall \omega$, by the *law of large numbers*.

Notice that this happens for all $_j \boldsymbol{Good}^i$ sets. Hence, all optimal actions will be selected with the same probability by the team. Like before, as $p_l^{Good} > p_m^{Bad}$, $\forall a_l \in \boldsymbol{Good}, a_m \in \boldsymbol{Bad}$, the probability of picking a suboptimal action converges to 0 (as $n \to \infty$ with $c \to \infty$), and hence the probability of picking each of the optimal solutions converges to $1/\prod_\omega |\boldsymbol{Good}_\omega|$ (satisfying optimality condition (ii)). ∎

Now we present our second generalization. We show that Theorem 1 still applies for agents ϕ_i with different probabilities over optimal actions p_{Good^i}. We consider here a more general definition of *optimal* team: the difference between the probabilities of picking each optimal solution and $1/\prod_\omega |\boldsymbol{Good}_\omega|$ must be as small as possible.

Hence, let $p_j^{\boldsymbol{\Phi}}$ be the probability of team $\boldsymbol{\Phi}$ picking optimal action a_j, the optimal team is such that $\vartheta := \sum_{a_j} |p_j^{\boldsymbol{\Phi}} - 1/|\boldsymbol{Good}_\omega||, \forall a_j \in \boldsymbol{Good}_\omega$ is minimized ($\forall \omega \in \boldsymbol{\Omega}$). We focus here in a single world state ω, as by minimizing ϑ in each world state we are also making the difference between the probability of picking each optimal solution and $1/\prod_\omega |\boldsymbol{Good}_\omega|$ as small as possible. Hence, the original definition in the previous section is the case where $\vartheta := 0$.

Proposition 6. *Theorem 1 still applies when $|p_{Good^i} - p_{Good^j}| \leq \epsilon, \forall \phi_i, \phi_j$, for small enough $\epsilon > 0$.*

Proof. Let $\boldsymbol{\Phi}$ be an optimal team, where p_{Good^i} is the same for all agents ϕ_i. Hence, the probability of all actions in $\boldsymbol{Good}$ being selected by the team is the same. I.e., $p_k^{\boldsymbol{\Phi}} = p_l^{\boldsymbol{\Phi}}, \forall a_k, a_l \in \boldsymbol{Good}$, and $\vartheta := 0$. Let $\Delta := \sum_{a_k \in \boldsymbol{Good}} \sum_{a_l \in \boldsymbol{Good}} |p_k^{\boldsymbol{\Phi}} - p_l^{\boldsymbol{\Phi}}|$ be the difference between the probabilities of the team taking each optimal action. In the rest of the proof we will disturb the probabilities p_{Good^i} of sets of agents, which will change Δ. We focus in studying the variation in Δ, as minimizing the variation in Δ also minimizes the variation in ϑ.

We prove by mathematical induction. Assume we change the p_{Good^i} of x agents ϕ_i, and Δ is as small as possible. Now we will change $x + 1$ agents. Let's pick one agent ϕ_i and increase its p_{Good^i} by $\delta \leq \epsilon$. It follows that $p_k^{\boldsymbol{\Phi}} > p_l^{\boldsymbol{\Phi}}, \forall a_k \in \boldsymbol{Good}^i, a_l \notin \boldsymbol{Good}^i$, and the new $\Delta' := \sum_{a_k \in \boldsymbol{Good}} \sum_{a_l \in \boldsymbol{Good}} |p_k^{\boldsymbol{\Phi}} - p_l^{\boldsymbol{\Phi}}| > \Delta$.

If we add one more agent ϕ_j, such that $\boldsymbol{Good}^j \cap \boldsymbol{Good}^i = \emptyset$, the probability of voting for actions $a_m \in \boldsymbol{Good}^j$ increases. For small enough ϵ, p_{Good^j} will be too large to precisely equalize the probabilities, and it follows that $p_m^{\boldsymbol{\Phi}} > p_k^{\boldsymbol{\Phi}} > p_l^{\boldsymbol{\Phi}}, \forall a_m \in \boldsymbol{Good}^j, a_k \in \boldsymbol{Good}^i, a_l \notin \boldsymbol{Good}^i \cup \boldsymbol{Good}^j$, and $\Delta'' := \sum_{a_k \in \boldsymbol{Good}} \sum_{a_l \in \boldsymbol{Good}} |p_k^{\boldsymbol{\Phi}} - p_l^{\boldsymbol{\Phi}}| > \Delta'$. The same applies for each newly added agent, until we have a new team such that $n = c \prod_{d \in \boldsymbol{D}} d$ (again, satisfying the conditions of the theorem).

The base case follows trivially. If we did not change the probability of any agent (i.e., $x := 0$), and we now increase p_{Good^i} of a single agent ϕ_i, $p_k^{\boldsymbol{\Phi}} > p_l^{\boldsymbol{\Phi}}, \forall a_k \in \boldsymbol{Good}^i, a_l \notin \boldsymbol{Good}^i$, and $\Delta' > \Delta$. By the same argument as before, adding more agents will only increase Δ', until $n = c \prod_{d \in \boldsymbol{D}} d$. ∎

Thirdly, we also generalize to the case where the number of preferred actions r changes for each agent. We consider that the number of actions in the $\boldsymbol{Good^i}$ of each agent ϕ_i (r^i) is decided according to a uniform distribution on the interval $[1, r']$.

Proposition 7. *If $n = r' \times c \prod_{d \in \boldsymbol{D}} d$, the probability that the team is optimal $\rightarrow 1$ as $c \rightarrow \infty$.*

Proof. For large n, the number of agents with $r^i = 1, \ldots, r'$ is the same. Therefore, if for each subset $\boldsymbol{\Phi^i} \subset \boldsymbol{\Phi}$, such that $r^\phi = i, \forall \phi \in \boldsymbol{\Phi^i}$, we have that $p_k^{\boldsymbol{\Phi^i}} = p_l^{\boldsymbol{\Phi^i}}$, $\forall a_k, a_l \in \boldsymbol{Good}$, we will have that $p_k^{\boldsymbol{\Phi}} = p_l^{\boldsymbol{\Phi}}, \forall a_k, a_l \in \boldsymbol{Good}$. Given an optimal team of size n, we have r' subsets $\boldsymbol{\Phi^i}$ of size n/r' each. It follows by Theorem 1 that $n/r' = c \prod_{d \in \boldsymbol{D}} d$, and:

$$n = r' \times n/r' = r' \times c \prod_{d \in \boldsymbol{D}} d,$$

hence n also follows the necessary conditions in Proposition 2. Similarly as in Theorem 1, as $n \rightarrow \infty$ with $c \rightarrow \infty$, the probability of picking a suboptimal solution converges to 0, and the probability of picking each of the optimal solutions converges to $1/\prod_\omega |\boldsymbol{Good_\omega}|$ (satisfying optimality condition (ii)). ∎

Lastly, we discuss the assumption that world states are independent. In design problems they could actually be correlated. We present below a constructive proof showing that we can use our model to study design problems with correlated parameters.

Proposition 8. *The previous results apply for problems with correlated parameters.*

Proof. Let's consider a design problem with a set $\boldsymbol{\Upsilon}$ of parameters υ. We can divide $\boldsymbol{\Upsilon}$ in $\boldsymbol{\Upsilon_k}$ sets, where all $\upsilon \in \boldsymbol{\Upsilon_k}$ are correlated, but υ_i and υ_j are independent, $\forall \upsilon_i \in \boldsymbol{\Upsilon_i}, \upsilon_j \in \boldsymbol{\Upsilon_j}, i \neq j$. That is, all parameters υ in a $\boldsymbol{\Upsilon_k}$ set are correlated, but the parameters between two different $\boldsymbol{\Upsilon_k}$ sets are independent. This can always be performed, as in the worst case where all parameters are correlated, we can have a single $\boldsymbol{\Upsilon_k} := \boldsymbol{\Upsilon}$.

Now, instead of modeling each design parameter υ as a world state ω (as in our original model), we can model each set $\boldsymbol{\Upsilon_k}$ as a world state ω. Hence, instead of an action a being one value assigned to a parameter υ, an action a now represents one full combination of values to each υ_k in a set $\boldsymbol{\Upsilon_k}$. Therefore, instead of voting at each parameter υ, each agent ϕ_i now votes for one combination of value assignments (of correlated parameters) at each set $\boldsymbol{\Upsilon_k}$. As all sets $\boldsymbol{\Upsilon_k}$ are independent, we still have agents voting for independent world states ω and the previous results still apply. In the worst case, where all parameters of the problem are correlated, we would have agents voting for entire solutions, and the model would be considered as having a single world state. ∎

5   Synthetic Experiments

We run synthetic experiments, where we simulate design agents and evaluate diverse and uniform teams (henceforth *diverse* and *uniform*). We randomly create pdfs for the agents, and simulate voting iterations across a series of world states. We repeat all our experiments 100 times, and in the graphs we plot the average and the confidence interval of our results (according to a *t-test* with $p := 0.01$). We run 1000 voting iterations (z), and measure how many

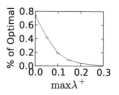

Fig. 5. Percentage as max $\boldsymbol{\lambda}^+$ grows.

optimal solutions the team is able to find. We study a scenario where the number of actions $(|\boldsymbol{A}|) := 100$, and the number of optimal actions per world state $(|\boldsymbol{Good}_\omega|)$ is, respectively: $< 2, 3, 5, 5, 5 >$, in a total of 750 optimal solutions.

At each repetition of our experiment, we randomly create a pdf for the agents. We start by studying the impact of max $\boldsymbol{\lambda}^+$ in *uniform*. When creating the *uniform* team, the total probability of playing any of the optimal actions (i.e., p_{Good}) is randomly assigned (uniform distribution) between 0.6 and 0.8. We fix the size of the team (25) and evaluate different max $\boldsymbol{\lambda}^+$ in Fig. 5. As expected from Proposition 1, for max $\boldsymbol{\lambda}^+ := 0$ the system finds the highest number of optimal solutions; and as max $\boldsymbol{\lambda}^+$ increases, it quickly drops.

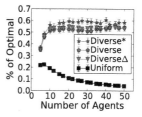

Fig. 6. Percentage of optimal solutions as # agents grows.

We then study the impact of increasing the number of agents, for *uniform* and *diverse*. To generate a *diverse* team, we draw randomly a r_ω in an interval U for each world state, that will be the size of $|\boldsymbol{Good}^i|$. We study three variants: *diverse**, where $U := (0, |\boldsymbol{Good}_\omega|]$; *diverse*, where $U := (0, |\boldsymbol{Good}_\omega|)$, and *diverse*$\Delta$, where we allow agents to have different r_ω^i, also drawn from $(0, |\boldsymbol{Good}_\omega|)$. We independently create pdfs randomly for each agent ϕ_i. For each agent we draw a number between 0.6 and 0.8 to distribute over the set of optimal actions, and randomly decide r_ω actions to compose its $\boldsymbol{Good}^i$ set. We distribute equally 80 % of the probability of voting over optimal actions on the actions of that set.

As we can see, in Fig. 6, the number of solutions *decreases* for *uniform* as the number of agents grows. Normally, in social choice, we expect the performance to improve as teams get larger, so this is a novel result. It is, however, expected from our Proposition 1. *Diverse*, on the other hand, improves in performance for all 3 versions, as predicted by our theory. However, the system seems to converge for a fixed z, as the performance does not increase much after around 20 agents. Hence, in Fig. 7 we study larger *diverse*

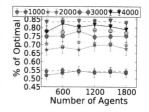

Fig. 7.   Percentage   for larger teams.

(continuous line) and *diverse*Δ teams (dashed line), going all the However, with

a team made of copies of theway up to 1800 agents. We also study four different number of voting iterations (z, shown in the figure by different lines): 1000, 2000, 3000, 4000. As we can see, although adding more agents was not really improving the performance in the experimental scenario under study, there is clearly a statistically significant improvement ($p < 0.01$) by increasing the number of voting iterations, with the system improving from finding around 53 % of the optimal solutions, all the way up to finding more than 80 % of them. However, there is a *diminishing returns* effect, as the impact of adding more iterations decreases as the actual number of iterations grow larger. We also note that *diverseΔ* is better than *diverse*, and the difference increases as z grows.

As we can see, although theoretically possible, it is still a challenge to have a system that can find all the possible optimal solutions. Moreover, it would be expensive to pool the votes of agents through a large number of voting iterations. However, as we show next, we can actually approximate this process in a real system, by pooling only a small number of solutions from each agent, and executing many voting iterations by aggregating different combinations of these solutions.

6 Experiments in Architectural Design

6.1 Architectural Design Domain

We study a real system for architectural building design. This is a fundamental domain, since the design of a building impacts its energy usage during its whole life-span [3,6]. We use Beagle [6], a multi-objective design optimization software that assists users in the early stage design of buildings. First, the designer creates a parametric design, containing (as discussed in Sect. 3) a set of parameters that can be modified within a specified range, allowing the creation of many variations. The ranges are defined according to the legislation (i.e., setback, maximum height, etc.), or the intention of the designer (for example, the general shape of the building). We use designs from Gerber and Lin [6], shown in Fig. 8: *base*, a simple building type with uniform program (i.e., tenant type); *office park*, a multi-tenant grouping of towers; and *contemporary*, a double "twisted" tower that includes multiple occupancy types, relevant to contemporary architectural practices.

Base

Office Park

Contemporary

Fig. 8. Parametric designs.

Beagle uses a genetic algorithm (GA) to optimize the building design based on three objectives: energy efficiency, financial performance and area requirements. In detail, the objective functions are: S_{obj} : max $SPCS$; E_{obj} : min EUI; F_{obj} : max NPV. SPCS is the Spatial Programming Compliance Score, EUI is the Energy Use Intensity and NPV is the Net Present Value, defined as follows.

SPCS defines how well a building conforms to the project requirements (by measuring how close the area dedicated to different activities is to a given specification). Let L be a list of activities (in our designs, L=<Office, Hotel, Retail, Parking>), $area(l)$ be the total area in a building dedicated to activity l and $requirement(l)$ be the area for activity l given in a project specification. SPCS is defined as: $SPCS := 100 \times \left(1 - \frac{\sum_{l \in L} |area(l) - requirement(l)|}{|L|}\right)$.

EUI regulates the overall energy performance of the building. This is an estimated overall building energy consumption in relation to the overall building floor area. The process to obtain the energy analysis result is automated in Beagle through Autodesk Green Building Studio (GBS) web service.

Finally, **NPV** is a commonly used financial evaluation. It measures the financial performance for the whole building life cycle, given by: $NPV := \left(\sum_{t=1}^{T} \frac{c_t}{(1+r)^t}\right) - c_0$, where T is the Cash Flow Time Span, r is the Annual Rate of Return, c_0 is the construction cost, and $c_t := $ Revenue $-$ Operation Cost.

Many options affect the execution of the GA, including: initial population size, size of the population, selection size, crossover ratio, mutation ratio, maximum iteration. Further details about Beagle are at Gerber and Lin [6]. In the end of the optimization process, the GA outputs a set of solutions. These are considered "optimal", according to the internal evaluation of the GA, but are not necessarily so. As in our theory, for each parameter the assigned value is going to be one of the optimal ones with a certain probability. In fact, most of the solutions outputted by the GAs are later identified as sub-optimal and eliminated in comparison with better ones found by the teams.

We model each run of the GA as an agent ϕ. Each parameter of the parametric design is a world state ω, where the agents decide among different actions $\mathbf{A}$ (i.e., possible values for the current parameter). Our model assumes independent multiple voting iterations across all world states. However, in general it could be expensive to pool agents for votes in a large number of iterations. Therefore, in order to test the applicability of the predictions of our model in more realistic scenarios, in our experiments we pool only 3 solutions per agent, but run multiple voting iterations by aggregating over all possible combinations of them. That is, at each combination we pick one solution per agent, and vote across all the parameters, in a total of 81 voting iterations with 4 agents.

6.2 Empirical Results

We run experiments across the different parametric designs shown in Fig. 8. These are designs with increasing complexity. More details about the designs and the meanings of each parameter are available in Gerber and Lin [6]. We create 4 different agents, using different options for the GA, as shown in Table 1 (Initial Population and Maximum Iteration were

Table 1. GA parameters.

Agent	PZ	SZ	CR	MR
Agent 1	12	10	0.8	0.1
Agent 2	18	8	0.6	0.2
Agent 3	24	16	0.55	0.15
Agent 4	30	20	0.4	0.25

kept as constants: 10 and 5. PZ = Population Size, SZ = Selection Size, CR = Crossover Ratio, MR = Mutation Ratio). We are dealing here with real (and consequently complex) design problems, where the true set of optimal solutions is unknown. We approach the problem in a comparative fashion: when evaluating different systems, we consider the union of the set of solutions of all of them. That is, let $\boldsymbol{H}_x$ be the set of solutions of system x; we consider the set $\mathcal{H} := \bigcup_x \boldsymbol{H}_x$. We compare all solutions in $\mathcal{H}$, and consider as optimal the best solutions in $\mathcal{H}$, forming the set of optimal solutions $\mathcal{O}$. We use the concept of Pareto dominance: the best solutions in $\mathcal{H}$ are the ones that *dominate* all other solutions (i.e., they are better in all 3 objectives). As we know which system generated each solution $o \in \mathcal{O}$, we estimate the set of optimal solutions $\boldsymbol{S}_x$ of each system.

Although our theory focuses on *plurality voting*, we also present results using the *mean* and the *median* of the opinions of the agents. That is, given one combination (a set of one solution from each agent), we also generate a new solution by calculating the *mean* or the *median* of the values from each agent across all parameters. Also, when performing the voting aggregation (*vote*), we consider values that are the same up to 3 decimal places as equal. Concerning *uniform*, we evaluate a team composed of copies of the "best" agent. By "best", we mean the agent that finds the highest number of optimal solutions. According to Proposition 1, such an agent should be the one with the lowest $\max \boldsymbol{\lambda}^+$, and we can predict that voting among copies of that agent generates a large number of optimal solutions. Hence, for each design, we first compare all solutions of all agents, to estimate which one has the largest set of optimal solutions $\boldsymbol{S}$. We, then, run that agent multiple times, creating *uniform*. For *diverse*, we consider one copy of each agent in Table 1. We aggregate the solutions of *diverse* and *uniform*. We run 81 aggregation iterations, by selecting 3 solutions from each agent ϕ_i, in its set of solutions $\boldsymbol{H}_i$, and aggregating all possible combinations of these solutions. We evaluate together the solutions of all agents and all teams (i.e., we construct $\mathcal{H}$ with the solutions of all systems), in order to estimate the size of $\boldsymbol{S}_x$ of each system.

Since the true optimal solutions set is unknown, we first plot the percentage of unique solutions found by each system in relation to the total number of unique optimal solutions in $\mathcal{H}$. Hence, in Fig. 9(a), we show the percentage of optimal solutions for all systems, in relation to $|\mathcal{O}|$. For clarity, we represent the result of the individual agents by the one that had the highest percentage. As we can see, in all parametric designs the teams find a significantly larger percentage of optimal solutions than the individual agents. The agents find less than 1 % of the solutions, while the teams are in general always close to or above 15 %. In total (considering all aggregation methods and all agents), for all three parametric designs the agents find only about 1 % of the optimal solutions, while *uniform* finds around 51 % and *diverse* 47 %. Looking at *vote*, in *base diverse* finds a larger percentage of optimal solutions than *uniform* (around 9.4 % for *uniform*, while 11.6 % for *diverse*). In *office park* and *contemporary*, however, *uniform* finds more solutions than *diverse*. Based on Proposition 1, we expect that this is caused by the best agent having a lower $\max \boldsymbol{\lambda}^+$ in *office park* and *contemporary* than in *base*.

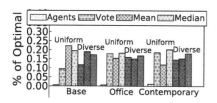

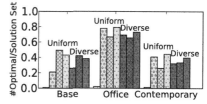

(a) Percentage in relation to all solutions found by all systems.

(b) Percentage in relation to the number of solutions of each system.

Fig. 9. Percentage of optimal solutions of each system.

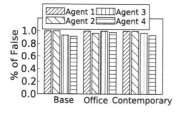

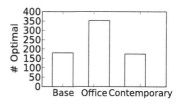

(a) False optimal solutions that are eliminated.

(b) Number of unique optimal solutions.

Fig. 10. Additional analysis.

Figure 9(b) shows the percentage of optimal solutions found, in relation to the size of the set of evaluated solutions of each system. That is, let O_x be the set of optimal solutions of system x, in $\mathcal{O}$. We show $\frac{|O_x|}{|H_x|}$. Concerning *vote*, the teams are able to find a new optimal solution around 20 % of the time for *base*, around 73 % of the time for *office park* and around 36 % of the time for *contemporary*. Meanwhile, for the individual agents it is close to 0 %. We can see that teams have great potential for generating new optimal solutions, as expected from our theory. However, as studied in our synthetic experiments, we can expect some *diminishing returns* when increasing the number of voting iterations. It is interesting to note that the performance of the teams is much higher for *office park* than for the other two parametric designs. In *base* and *contemporary*, the building mass is parametrized into a single volume, while in *office park* the building mass has multiple volumes. Hence, a possible explanation is that the division in multiple volumes facilitated the generation of multiple optimal solutions, since these can be combined in many different ways. We also plot in Fig. 10(a) the percentage of solutions that were reported to be optimal by each agent, but were later discovered to be suboptimal by evaluating $\mathcal{H}$. A large amount of solutions are eliminated, close to 100 %, helping the designer to avoid making a poor decision, and increasing her confidence that the set of optimal solutions found represent well the "true" Pareto frontier. Moreover, we test for duplicated solutions across different aggregation methods, different teams and different agents. The number is small: only 4 in *contemporary*, and none in *base* and *office park*. Hence, we are providing a high coverage of the Pareto frontier for the designer. We show the total number of optimal solutions in Fig. 10(b).

7 Conclusion

Design imposes a novel problem to social choice: maximize the number of optimal solutions. We present a new model for agent teams, that shows the potential of voting agents to be *creative*, by generating a large number of optimal solutions to the designer. Our analysis, which builds a new connection with *number theory*, shows that: (i) uniform teams are in general suboptimal, and converge to a unique solution; (ii) diverse teams are optimal as long as the team's size grows *carefully*; (iii) the minimum optimal team size is constant with high probability; (iv) the worst case for teams is a prime number of optimal actions. Experiments considered bounded time and relaxed assumptions. We also show results in architecture, where teams find a large number of solutions.

Acknowledgments. This research is supported by MURI grant W911NF-11-1-0332, and the National Science Foundation under grant 1231001.

References

1. Caragiannis, I., Procaccia, A.D., Shah, N.: When do noisy votes reveal the truth?. In: EC, pp. 143–160. ACM, New York (2013)
2. Conitzer, V., Sandholm, T.: Common voting rules as maximum likelihood estimators. In: UAI, pp. 145–152 (2005)
3. Echenagucia, T.M., Capozzoli, A., Cascone, Y., Sassone, M.: The early design stage of a building envelope. Appl. Energy **154**, 577–591 (2015)
4. Elkind, E., Shah, N.: Electing the most probable without eliminating the irrational: Voting over intransitive domains. In: UAI (2014)
5. Erhan, H., Wang, I., Shireen, N.: Interacting with thousands: A parametric-space exploration method in generative design. In: ACADIA (2014)
6. Gerber, D.J., Lin, S.H.E.: Designing in complexity: Simulation, integration, and multidisciplinary design optimization for architecture. Simulation **90**(8), 936–959 (2014)
7. Gero, J., Sosa, R.: Complexity measures as a basis for mass customization of novel designs. Environ. Plan. B: Plan. Des. **35**(1), 3–15 (2008)
8. Globa, A., Donn, M., Moloney, J.: Abstraction versus cased-based: A comparative study of two approaches to support parametric design. In: ACADIA (2014)
9. Haynes, G.A.: Testing the boundaries of the choice overload phenomenon. Psychol. Mark. **26**(3), 204–212 (2009)
10. Iyengar, S., Lepper, M.: When choice is demotivating: Can one desire too much of a good thing? J. Pers. Soc. Psychol. **79**, 995–1006 (2000)
11. Jiang, A.X., Marcolino, L.S., Procaccia, A.D., Sandholm, T., Shah, N., Tambe, M.: Diverse randomized agents vote to win. In: NIPS (2014)
12. Kalech, M., Kraus, S., Kaminka, G.A., Goldman, C.V.: Practical voting rules with partial information. JAAMAS **22**, 151–182 (2011)

13. Knysh, D.S., Kureichik, V.M.: Parallel genetic algorithms: A survey and problem state of the art. J. Comput. Syst. Sci. Int. **49**(4), 579–589 (2010)
14. van Langen, P., Brazier, F.: Design space exploration revisited. Artif. Intell. Eng. Des. Anal. Manuf. **20**, 113–119 (2006)
15. List, C., Goodin, R.E.: Epistemic democracy: generalizing the condorcet jury theorem. J. Polit. Philos. **9**, 277–306 (2001)
16. Mao, A., Procaccia, A.D., Chen, Y.: Better human computation through principled voting. In: AAAI (2013)
17. Marcolino, L.S., Xu, H., Jiang, A.X., Tambe, M., Bowring, E.: Give a hard problem to a diverse team: Exploring large action spaces. In: AAAI (2014)
18. Nurmi, H.: Comparing Voting Systems. Springer, Heidelberg (1987)
19. Polikar, R.: Ensemble learning. In: Zhang, C., Ma, Y. (eds.) Ensemble Machine Learning: Methods and Applications, pp. 1–34. Springer, Heidelberg (2012)
20. Procaccia, A.D., Reddi, S.J., Shah, N.: A maximum likelihood approach for selecting sets of alternatives. In: UAI (2012)
21. Smith, B.N., Xu, A., Bailey, B.P.: Improving interaction models for generating and managing alternative ideas during early design work. In: Graphics Interface Conference (2010)
22. Snooks, R.: Encoding behavioral matter. In: Proceedings of the International Symposium on Algorithmic Design for Architecture and Urban Design. ALGODE (2011)
23. Vehlken, S.: Computational swarming: A cultural technique for generative architecture. Footprint - Delft Archit. Theor. J. 15 (2014)
24. Welch, C., Moloney, J., Moleta, T.: Selective interference: Emergent complexity informed by programmatic, social and performative criteria. In: ACADIA (2014)
25. Woodbury, R.F., Burrow, A.L.: Whither design space? Artif. Intell. Eng. Des. Anal. Manuf. **20**, 63–82 (2006)
26. Xia, L., Conitzer, V.: A maximum likelihood approach towards aggregating partial orders. In: IJCAI (2011)
27. Zavala, G.R., Nebro, A.J., Luna, F., Coello, C.A.C.: A survey of multi-objective metaheuristics applied to structural optimization. Struct. Multi. Optim. **49**, 537–558 (2014)
28. Zhao, F., Li, G., Yang, C., Abraham, A., Liu, H.: A human-computer cooperative particle swarm optimization based immune algorithm for layout design. Neurocomputing **132**, 68–78 (2014)

Security and Robustness for Collaborative Monitors

Bas Testerink[1]($\boxtimes$), Nils Bulling[2], and Mehdi Dastani[1]

[1] Utrecht University, Utrecht, Netherlands
{B.J.G.Testerink,M.M.Dastani}@uu.nl
[2] Delft University of Technology, Delft, Netherlands
n.bulling@tudelft.nl

Abstract. Decentralized monitors can be subject to robustness and security risks. Robustness risks include attacks on the monitor's infrastructure in order to disable parts of its functionality. Security risks include attacks that try to extract information from the monitor and thereby possibly leak sensitive information. Formal methods to analyze the design of a monitor with respect to these issues can help to create more secure designs and/or identify critical parts. In this paper we specify a model for analyzing robustness and security risks for collaborative monitors constructed from a network of local monitors.

Keywords: Monitoring · Runtime verification · Security

1 Introduction

Normative systems help to make sure that agents behave according to preset guidelines/norms in multi-agent systems [5]. One approach is provided by exogenous normative systems where norms are explicit. The normative aspect of the multi-agent system is captured by an exogenous—to the agents—organization or institution. With this approach it must be verified whether any norm violation occurs in the multi-agent system's execution. Monitoring large distributed multi-agent systems such as traffic, smart grids and economic markets requires decentralized approaches. Monolithic centralized monitors can impose a bottleneck due to the distributed nature of multi-agent systems and a single point of failure in case of break downs.

A major concern of many decentralized verification applications is their robustness and security. The data that is gathered from a multi-agent system can severely compromise the agents' privacy if leaked. Adversaries can also try to take down parts of the network to impede its functioning. Formal models of decentralized monitors allow for the analysis of critical parts in monitors in terms of robustness and security. Such an analysis allows the developers of decentralized monitors to invest more resources in critical parts. In this paper we present a formal model for decentralized monitors that supports their formal analysis to face the aspects of robustness and security when designing a monitor. As an

© Springer International Publishing Switzerland 2016
V. Dignum et al. (Eds.): COIN 2015, LNAI 9628, pp. 376–395, 2016.
DOI: 10.1007/978-3-319-42691-4_21

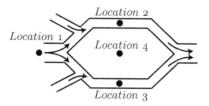

Fig. 1. Example scenario. Black dots indicate locations, arrows indicate traffic flow and double lines indicate roads.

example we shall use an abstract traffic monitoring scenario (Example 1). Traffic monitoring faces many challenges, including physical attacks on the monitor infrastructure and the privacy of individuals (cf. [7]).

In our approach we assume that monitors observe the execution trace of a system in order to detect specific properties of its behavior. These properties are expressed in linear-time temporal logic (LTL) [14]. Temporal logics have been used in the past to analyze normative systems (e.g. [1,2]). For the structure of decentralized monitors we draw inspiration from existing popular decentralized monitoring techniques such as wireless sensor networks (WSNs). The structure of a WSN is that a collection of information gathering nodes route sensor data towards a sink, which acts as the central data gathering point. Intermediate data aggregation is often used to increase security and save energy. In our decentralized framework a network of local monitors collaborates to verify properties. We call such a network a collaborative monitor. Each local monitor is assumed to make observations on its own and can in addition to that query other local monitors with respect to their (aggregated) observations. This allows to enhance privacy as monitors only obtain an aggregated value. This is similar to the frameworks proposed in [3,17]. However, different from those two frameworks we assume that information flows through the network without temporal delay. Also, instead of sharing observations as in [17] or progressed formulas as in [3], local monitors in our framework combine their input into a single evaluation (true, false, or 'yet unknown') and share that with other neighboring local monitors.

The contribution of this paper is a formal framework for specifying collaborative monitors. The model allows to analyze how critical specific local monitors are with respect to the security and robustness of the collaborative monitor. We believe that the presented design methodology is not only beneficial for the design and development of decentralized monitors using LTL, but can also provide insights into design-time and/or runtime analysis of robustness and security risks for other decentralized verification technologies. We leave a study of technical properties for future work.

Example 1 (Smart Infrastructure Scenario). Throughout this paper we give examples using a simple smart infrastructure scenario. We assume that there are various traffic streams that at some point merge together, as shown in Fig. 1. The aim of the smart infrastructure is to maximize throughput by minimizing traffic jams at locations 2 and 3. To this end there is a road side unit (RSU) at location 1 which informs passing vehicles whether location 2 or location 3 is jammed. Which, if this is the case, will hopefully cause vehicles to choose the non-jammed route. A local monitor at location 1 monitors whether vehicles that pass location 1 will end up in a traffic jam at either location 2 or 3. Each location has a local monitor with-short range communication capabilities that observes the vehicles which pass by, except for the monitor at location 4 which observes nothing, but can relay long distance messages. The monitors at locations 2 and 3 can, in addition to observing individual vehicles, also determine whether their location is jammed. The local monitor at location 1 should be able to verify whether a vehicle that passes location 1 does not end up in a traffic jam.

The rest of the paper is structured as follows. In Sect. 2 we summarize related work and background literature that influenced this paper. In Sect. 3 we present the model for collaborative monitors that we use to describe robustness in Sect. 4 and security in Sect. 5. In Sect. 6 we discuss possible changes in the framework's assumptions and future work.

2   Related Work and Background

The field of wireless sensor networks (WSNs) contains a vast amount of identified robustness and security risks as well as countermeasures (cf. [11,12]). Example risks include the malfunctioning of hardware and software and attempts by an adversary to eavesdrop on communication. Countermeasures include various techniques such as routing protocols and encryption. The aim of countermeasures is to keep the monitoring service online if local monitors malfunction and prevent sensitive information from being obtained by an adversary. The requirements of WSNs are commonly organized by: (1) data confidentiality (only intended receivers can see sensitive data), (2) data integrity and freshness (data is correct and new), (3) protection against Sybil attacks (the imitation of monitors) and (4) availability (continued operation of monitors).

Protection against confidentiality and availability attacks will be the main focus of this paper. Data integrity and freshness is assumed. I.e., we assume that monitors either work correctly or they are unavailable, but cannot for instance send false information. Different kinds of attacks can be categorized between attacks that change the network topology (e.g. physically compromising a node or communication line, or a wormhole attack that connects two nodes) and those that extract information from the network (capture and/or imitation of nodes). We shall address the case that a local monitor can malfunction. This encapsulates both aggressive and non-aggressive failures of local monitors. We shall also discuss the case that an attacker can query a local monitor without proper authorization. This encapsulates Sybil attacks.

WSNs also suffer from hardware constraints. Sensors tend to have limited power and communication capabilities. A common practice to limit energy usage is to use intermediate aggregation of data between the source of data and the sink. Data aggregation also helps to optimize any other monitoring system by reducing the amount of required communication. There are many works dedicated to security in data aggregation systems [10]. We note that the concept of privacy in data aggregation literature is generally interpreted as privacy of sensors. For instance, if a sensor computes the average velocity of all vehicles, then it may receive from other sensors the average velocities of partitions of the set of vehicles. Privacy in related literature would mean that it is not known which sensors provided what data to compute the total average velocity. In this paper we consider only privacy in the form of the privacy of agents. For instance, in our example scenario the location of a specific vehicle can be seen as privacy sensitive information. Therefore, instead of a monitor sharing separately the velocity of the vehicle and whether location 2 is jammed, it may share the evaluation of the conjunction of these two facts. If a receiver obtains this evaluation and it is false, then the receiver cannot derive whether the vehicle was not at location 2 or whether there was a traffic jam. Note that if the evaluation is true, then it is known that the vehicle was at location 2.

Security related papers on wireless networks for monitoring tend to focus on how to prevent security risks by using cryptography (e.g. [13]) and/or special routing protocols (e.g. [8]). Our approach is complementary to this. We do not look at runtime implementation techniques for preventing risks, but address design time questions and analysis to see where potential robustness and security risks lie. We believe design based analysis can help in further improving decentralized monitors. Depending on the practical limitations of an application it might not be possible to always make a perfect design. But our work can help in determining which parts of a network require more advanced/expensive hardware to increase safety.

WSNs usually concern sensor readings of continuous parameters. However, we take a logical approach with discrete values as this fits better with the declarative nature of normative systems theory. Many normative systems express norms as conditional obligations/prohibitions with deadlines (cf. [2]). Such constructions can often be expressed as properties about a system's behavior over time. This has led us to opting for linear temporal logic. Monitors that perform runtime verification of properties that are expressed in LTL can be modeled with automata [4] or progression systems [6]. For our framework it is not important which one is used. As for decentralized LTL verification there are the proposals from [3,17]. However the framework in [3] is built on assumptions that do not support our intended scenarios. For one, in their framework all monitors are connected to each other whereas we want to investigate specific topologies. The framework from [17] does allow different topologies but data is not aggregated by local monitors. Also we have no notion of information delay, which both frameworks have.

As in [3,17] we assume that the monitors work synchronously. This means that at any moment all monitors are (partially) observing the same behavior of the multi-agent system. In various decentralized monitoring communication protocols synchronization is introduced in order to have data freshness (e.g. SNEP [13]). We assume that the monitors are connected in an acyclic manner and that the aggregation operation of local monitors is taking a combination of the input, as explained in the next section.

3   Monitor Model

The task of a monitor is to verify whether the monitored system's behavior satisfies a property. The behavior of the system is a trace of states, and properties are expressed as LTL formulas. We first introduce preliminaries. Then, we explain the architecture of collaborative monitors and how views of local monitors and their in-between connections give rise to their locally verifiable properties. The basic idea of our verification model has been published as an extended abstract in [16].

3.1   Formal Setting

Let Π be a set of propositional symbols. A transition system (over Π) is given by a tuple $T = (S, R, V)$ where S is a state space, $R \subseteq S^2$ a serial transition relation, and $V : S \to 2^{\Pi}$ an evaluation function which returns the propositions that hold at a given state. We assume that Π, S, V a are fixed throughout this article if not said otherwise.

An *infinite trace* is defined as an infinite sequence $\sigma = s_0 s_1 \ldots$ of states interconnected by R, i.e. $(s_i, s_{i+1}) \in R$ for all $i \in \mathbb{N}_0$. Similarly, a *finite trace* is given by $s_0 \ldots s_k$. The set of infinite and finite traces over T is denoted by Tr_T^i and Tr_T^f, respectively. The set of all traces is denoted by $\mathsf{Tr}_T = \mathsf{Tr}_T^i \cup \mathsf{Tr}_T^f$. The *length* of a trace, i.e. the number of states on it, is denoted by $|\sigma|$; in particular, if $\sigma \in \mathsf{Tr}_T^i$ then $|\sigma| = \infty$. We use $\sigma[i]$ to refer to state i on σ where $0 \leq i < |\sigma|$. We shall often take traces as first-class citizen if it is not important to highlight the transition system which generated them; in that case, we omit mentioning T as subscript and whenever it is clear from context. Given a finite trace σ we write $\sigma \mathsf{Tr}^i$ to refer to all infinite traces in Tr^i that extend σ, i.e. which have σ as initial prefix. Similarly, we assume that Tr refers to a set of traces (over T) in the remainder of this paper.

We use linear-time temporal logic LTL [14] for specifying properties. Formulas of LTL are defined by the following grammar:

$$\varphi := p \mid \neg\varphi \mid \varphi \vee \psi \mid \bigcirc\varphi \mid \varphi\,\mathcal{U}\,\psi$$

where $p \in \Pi$ is a propositional symbol. As usual, we use $\Diamond\varphi$ as macro for $\top\mathcal{U}\varphi$ (sometime in the future φ holds) and $\Box\varphi$ (always φ) for $\neg\Diamond\neg\varphi$.

Definition 1 (Infinite LTL Semantics). *Let* $T = (S, R, V)$ *be a transition system,* $\sigma \in \mathsf{Tr}^i$ *be an infinite trace and* $i \in \mathbb{N}_0$ *an index. The infinite trace semantics for LTL is defined by relation* $\models$ *as follows:*

$$
\begin{aligned}
T, \sigma, i &\models p && \Leftrightarrow p \in V(\sigma[i]) \\
T, \sigma, i &\models \neg\varphi && \Leftrightarrow T, \sigma, i \not\models \varphi \\
T, \sigma, i &\models \varphi \vee \psi && \Leftrightarrow T, \sigma, i \models \varphi \text{ or } T, \sigma, i \models \psi \\
T, \sigma, i &\models \bigcirc\varphi && \Leftrightarrow T, \sigma, i+1 \models \varphi \\
T, \sigma, i &\models \varphi \mathcal{U}\psi && \Leftrightarrow \exists j \in [i, \infty] : T, \sigma, j \models \psi \text{ and} \\
& && \quad\quad \forall k \in [i, j-1] : T, \sigma, k \models \varphi
\end{aligned}
$$

The finite trace semantics for LTL of [4] evaluates a formula to t (true), f (false) or ? (unknown). The intuitive reading for t is that the property holds for a given finite trace, therefore also for all finite and infinite extensions of that trace. Analogously, f means that the property does not hold independent of the future behavior of the system. Finally, ? means that the current finite trace can be extended such that the property holds or does not hold; the satisfaction of the formula is still open.

Definition 2 (Finite LTL Semantics). *Let $T = (S, R, V)$ be a transition system, $\sigma \in \mathsf{Tr}^f$ be a finite trace and $j \in [0, |\sigma| - 1]$ an index. The finite trace semantics for LTL is defined by relation $[\cdot]_{\sigma,j}^T$ as follows:*

$$
[\varphi]_{\sigma,j}^T = \begin{cases} t \text{ if } \forall \sigma' \in \sigma\mathsf{Tr}^i : T, \sigma', j \models \varphi \\ f \text{ if } \forall \sigma' \in \sigma\mathsf{Tr}^i : T, \sigma', j \not\models \varphi \\ ? \text{ otherwise} \end{cases}
$$

We write $[\varphi]_{\sigma}^T$ for $[\varphi]_{\sigma,0}^T$. Moreover, we use $T, \sigma, j \models^3 \varphi$ to refer to $[\varphi]_{\sigma,j}^T = t$, and $\mathsf{Tr}^f \models^3 \varphi$ if for all finite traces $\sigma \in \mathsf{Tr}^f$ we have that $T, \sigma, 0 \models^3 \varphi$.

3.2 Local and Collaborative Monitors

Before we define local monitors, we first discuss their capability of aggregating (ternary) evaluations of formulae into a single evaluation. Ultimately, we will use this aggregation to obtain the evaluation of an LTL property on a finite trace. A monitor aggregates evaluations using propositional formula α which we evaluate using Kleene's ternary semantics [9].

Definition 3 (Aggregation Formula). *An aggregation formula with k variables is a propositional formula α with k propositional symbols $x_1, \ldots, x_k$ which can take on the values in $\{t, f, ?\}$. Aggregation formulae are evaluated using Kleene's ternary semantics shown in Fig. 2. Given truth values $v_1, \ldots, v_k \in \{t, f, ?\}$ we write $\alpha(v_1, \ldots v_k)$ to refer to the evaluation of α if truth value v_i is assigned to variable x_i.*

Each local monitor has its own sensing capabilities which allow the local monitor to verify an LTL formula on any finite execution trace. The basic idea of an observation formula φ is that the monitor can distinguish all infinite traces where φ holds from those where φ does not hold. This is from a specification perspective. However, we are especially interested how the monitor makes a

a	$\neg a$
f	t
$?$	$?$
t	f

$a \wedge b$	b		
	f	$?$	t
f	f	f	f
a $?$	f	$?$	$?$
t	f	$?$	t

$a \vee b$	b		
	f	$?$	t
f	f	$?$	t
a $?$	$?$	$?$	t
t	t	t	t

Fig. 2. Truth definition of Kleene logic.

decision at run-time. For example, if the monitor is assumed to be able to observe $\Diamond p$, it does not mean that at run-time the monitor can always decide after a finite number of steps whether the current trace is a $\Diamond p$ trace or not. In addition to the monitor's observation formula we allow it to use inputs of other monitors according to a given aggregation formula.

Definition 4 (Local Monitor). *A local monitor is a tuple* $m = (\alpha, \varphi)$, *where* α *is an aggregation formula over* $k + 1$ *variables for some* $k \geq 0$, *and* φ *is an LTL formula, called* m's *observation formula.*

For any aggregation formula α with $k + 1$ variables we assume that the variables are named $o, x_1, \ldots, x_k$ and are ordered. Moreover, we shall also write $\alpha(o, x_1, \ldots, x_k)$ if we want to make the variable names explicit. Note the difference to $\alpha(v_0, \ldots, v_k)$ for truth values v_i, $i = 0, \ldots, k$. The intuition of $\alpha(o, x_1, \ldots, x_k)$ is that the monitor aggregates its current observation, encoded in o, with the input evaluations $x_1, \ldots, x_k$ of its neighboring local monitors according to α. By convention we reserve the first variable for the evaluation of the monitor's observation formula.

Example 2 (Local Monitor). For simplicity we talk about a specific vehicle in our examples. Local monitors m_1, m_2 and m_3 can observe the location of the vehicle (l_i stands for "the vehicle is at location i"). m_2 and m_3 can also observe traffic jams at their location (j_i means "location i is jammed"). We assume a transition system $T = (S, R, V)$ as a model of our scenario. The state space is $S = \{s_0, \ldots, s_5\}$. The transition relation consists of all pairs (s_0, s_i) and (s_i, s_5) with $i \in \{1, \ldots, 4\}$ and (s_5, s_5). The valuation function is given by $V(s_0) = \{l_1\}, V(s_1) = \{l_2\}, V(s_2) = \{l_2, j_2\}, V(s_3) = \{l_3\}, V(s_4) = \{l_3, j_3\}$ and finally $V(s_5) = \emptyset$. Hence, for each infinite trace in Tr that starts at s_0 there is a moment where either l_2 or l_3 is visited by the vehicle, and in that state either the vehicle is in a jam or not. As an example monitor we consider the monitor $m_1 = (\alpha_1, \varphi_1)$, where $\alpha_1 = o \wedge x_1$ is a formula with two variables. For instance given that o is the valuation of φ_1 and x_1 is an input valuation then if o's valuation is true (t) and $x_1 = ?$ then $\alpha(t, ?)$ is evaluated to $?$ by Kleene's semantics. Monitor 1 can observe whether l_1 holds for a given state. This allows m_1 to monitor a formula $\varphi_1 = \Diamond l_1$ (the vehicle is at location 1 at some moment).

A collaborative monitor is modeled by a directed acyclic graph of local monitors. The main reason for acyclicity is to avoid unnecessary complexities for the formulation of collaborative LTL verification. The connections between local monitors is referred to as the query relation. This relation is given by a function that given a local monitor m returns the connected local monitors in the order of their input for the aggregation formula of m. In the following definition we use M^k for the set of monitor tuples of length k.

Definition 5 (Collaborative Monitor Specification). *A collaborative monitor C is specified by (M, qry), where M is a non-empty set of local monitors, $\mathsf{qry} : M \to \{\epsilon\} \cup \bigcup_{k=1}^{|M|} M^k$ is a query relation with $\mathsf{qry}(m) = (m_1, \ldots, m_j)$ for $j = 1, \ldots, |M|$ iff $m = (\alpha, \varphi)$ where α is an aggregation formula over $j + 1$ variables. Moreover, qry is assumed to be acyclic[1]. The empty sequence is denoted by ϵ.*

In the case that $\mathsf{qry}(m) = \epsilon$ (the empty sequence) the monitor cannot query other monitors.

Example 3 (Collaborative Monitor Specification). Figure 3 shows a representation of the example collaborative monitor. Monitors m_2 and m_3 are assumed to be able to see whether the vehicle is at their location, and whether there is a jam at their location. This allows monitor m_2 to distinguish traces where $\Box(\neg j_2 \lor \neg l_2)$ either holds or not. The formula is read as "The vehicle is never at location 2 whilst there is a jam at location 2". We use this formula as the observation formula of m_2. m_3 has the same observation formula, but with respect to location 3. Both m_2 and m_3 do not receive any input. m_4 has no observation capabilities. We set its observation formula to $\top$[2]. The monitor aggregates inputs from m_2 and m_3 which will represent the statement "the vehicle has been in a traffic jam". Finally, as discussed in the previous example, m_1 can observe $\Diamond l_1$ and aggregates, using input from m_4, whether the vehicle at some point has passed through location 1 and whether the vehicle has been in a traffic jam. Formally the collaborative monitor from the example scenario is specified by (M, qry) where:

- $M = \{m_1, m_2, m_3, m_4\}$.
- $\mathsf{qry}(m_1) = (m_4)$, $\mathsf{qry}(m_2) = \mathsf{qry}(m_3) = \varepsilon$ (no input), $\mathsf{qry}(m_4) = (m_2, m_3)$.

For a local monitor, let o be the observation formula's evaluation variable, and x and y be input evaluations variables. The local monitors are given by:

- $m_1 = (\alpha_1, \varphi_1)$, $\alpha_1(o, x) = o \land x$, $\varphi_1 = \Diamond l_1$.
- $m_2 = (\alpha_2, \varphi_2)$, $\alpha_2(o) = o$, $\varphi_2 = \Box(\neg j_2 \lor \neg l_2)$.
- $m_3 = (\alpha_3, \varphi_3)$, $\alpha_3(o) = o$, $\varphi_3 = \Box(\neg j_3 \lor \neg l_3)$.
- $m_4 = (\alpha_4, \varphi_4)$, $\alpha_4(o, x, y) = o \land x \land y$, $\varphi_4 = \top$.

---

[1] Firstly, let *reachable* be inductively defined as: m' is reachable from m if m' is among $\mathsf{qry}(m) = (m_1, \ldots, m_k)$. Furthermore by transitivity if m'' is reachable by m' and m' is reachable from m, then m'' is reachable by m. Acyclicity means that there is no $m \in M$ such that m is reachable from m.

[2] We note that the choice of $\top$ for "no observation" only makes sense because of m_4's aggregation formula $o \land x \land y$ as defined below.

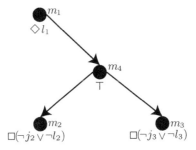

Fig. 3. Example collaborative monitor. Nodes are local monitors with at the right their name, arrows indicate the query relation, below monitors are the observation formulas.

For example, monitor m_4 is assumed to be able to distinguish all traces satisfying $\varphi = \Box(\neg j_2 \vee \neg l_2) \wedge \Box(\neg j_3 \vee \neg l_3) \equiv \Box((\neg j_2 \vee \neg l_2) \wedge (\neg j_3 \vee \neg l_3))$. This formula is evaluated to false (f) if and only if at some point the vehicle is at a jammed location. Monitor m_1 is assumed to be able to distinguish all traces satisfying $\varphi' \equiv \Diamond l_1 \wedge \varphi$. This formula is evaluated to false if and only if at some point the vehicle passes location 1 and if at some point the vehicle is at a jammed location. (Note that this follows from the way the model is constructed.)

Local monitors are models of runtime monitoring applications. In a runtime system the monitor does not have access to the infinite trace that a monitored system produces. Instead, the behavior of the system is revealed incrementally as it develops at runtime. Therefore, it is up to a monitor to determine whether some property is true, false or unknown given a finite trace. We shall therefore analyze local and collaborative monitors by using finite traces of the monitored system. Consider the local monitor $m_2 = (\alpha_2, \varphi_2)$ from our example scenario and an arbitrary trace $\sigma \in \mathsf{Tr}^f$ for an example model T of our scenario. The input that m_2 provides to m_4 given σ is given by the application of α_2 on the valuation $[\varphi_2]_\sigma^T$. This also holds for $m_3 = (\alpha_3, \varphi_3)$. The input that $m_4 = (\alpha_4, \varphi_4)$ provides to m_1 given σ is hence $\alpha_4([\varphi_4]_\sigma^T, \alpha_2([\varphi_2]_\sigma^T), \alpha_3([\varphi_3]_\sigma^T))$. The inputs of an aggregation formula are ultimately the evaluation of LTL formulas on a given trace. Hence, the input that for instance m_4 provides to m_1 given a trace σ is equivalent to the evaluation of some Boolean combination φ of the formulas φ_4, φ_2 and φ_3. We call this Boolean combination the m_4-aggregate. If a local monitor m can query m', then it means that m can query the evaluation of the m'-aggregate. It is important to note, however, that only the evaluation of the aggregate is communicated and not the truth values of its composed parts. This is an important feature of our model to ensure privacy and security properties. Because for each local monitor the aggregation formula is fixed, it means that given a collaborative monitor all the aggregates can be determined at design-time. Also note that due to acyclicity there are local monitors $m = (\alpha, \varphi)$ without neighbors and hence for such local monitors their m-aggregate is equivalent to a Boolean combination of the monitor's observation formula φ, providing four alternatives: φ, $\neg\varphi$, $\varphi \wedge \neg\varphi$ or $\varphi \vee \neg\varphi$. To see this, observe that any 3-valued function α on a single input necessarily maps ? to ? and any $x \neq$? to $\alpha(x) \neq$?. Hence only four possible different functions are possible given a single variable aggregation formula.

Definition 6 (Aggregate, Agg_m). *Let T be a transition system and $C = (M, \mathsf{qry})$ be a collaborative monitor. A mapping $\mathsf{Agg} : M \to \mathsf{LTL}$ is called an M-aggregation iff for all $m = (\alpha, \varphi) \in M$ and all $\sigma \in \mathsf{Tr}^f$ we have that*

$$[\mathsf{Agg}(m)]_\sigma^T \equiv \alpha([\varphi]_\sigma^T, [\mathsf{Agg}(m_1)]_\sigma^T, \ldots, [\mathsf{Agg}(m_k)]_\sigma^T).$$

where $\mathsf{qry}(m) = (m_1, \ldots, m_k)$. We simply call $\mathsf{Agg}(m)$ the m-aggregate (wrt. Agg) and denote it by Agg_m.

The following proposition shows that an M-aggregation always exists and also how it can be constructed. We also note that the result makes use of the acyclicity of a collaborative monitor.

Proposition 1. *Let T be a transition system and $C = (M, \mathsf{qry})$ be a collaborative monitor. Then, an M-aggregation exists. Moreover, an M-aggregation can be effectively constructed such that for each $m = (\alpha, \varphi) \in M$ with $\mathsf{qry}(m) = (m_1, \ldots, m_k)$ the m-aggregate Agg_m is given by $\mathsf{Agg}_m = \alpha[\varphi/o, \mathsf{Agg}_{m_1}/x_1, \ldots, \mathsf{Agg}_{m_k}/x_k]$ where $\alpha[\psi/x]$ denotes that variable x is replaced by formula ψ in α.*

Proof (Sketch). Due to acyclicity there are local monitors $m = (\alpha, \varphi) \in M$ such that $\mathsf{qry}(m) = \epsilon$ returns no local monitors. For these local monitors α is an aggregation formula with one variable o. We can construct the m-aggregate of such a local monitor $m = (\alpha, \varphi)$ by syntactically replacing the variable o in α by φ and maintaining the Boolean connectives. Now we can proceed inductively. Let $m' = (\alpha'(o', x_1, ..., x_k), \varphi') \in M$ be a monitor where $\mathsf{qry}(m') = (m_1, \ldots, m_k)$ and the aggregates or Agg_{m_i} for $i = 1, \ldots, k$ are already constructed. We can construct the m'-aggregate by syntactically replacing in α' the first variable o' by φ', and each variable x_i by the m_i-aggregate for $i \in 1, ..., k$. Hence, proceeding bottom-up, we can construct the M-aggregation Agg. □

Example 4 (Aggregate). The m_1-aggregate Agg_{m_1} is equal to $\Diamond l_1 \wedge \mathsf{Agg}_{m_4} = \Diamond l_1 \wedge \mathsf{Agg}_{m_2} \wedge \mathsf{Agg}_{m_3} = \Diamond l_1 \wedge \Box(\neg j_2 \vee \neg l_2) \wedge \Box(\neg j_3 \vee \neg l_3)$. This corresponds with the assumption from Example 3 that m_1 should be able to distinguish between traces where the vehicle passes through location one and a traffic jam, and those where this does not happen.

3.3   Monitorability and Expressivity

For various robustness and security issues, and from a design perspective, it is useful to determine what kind of formulas can be collaboratively verified by local monitors. We first recall the notion of (non)monitorability, which is an adaptation of the one from [4,15]. The difference is that we assume an underlying transition system. A formula φ is nonmonitorable after a finite trace σ if φ can never be evaluated to a conclusive true or false after σ given the finite LTL semantics. For φ to be monitorable it means that there is no finite trace such that φ is nonmonitorable after that trace. We highlight that monitorable does not mean that it will be possible to evaluate the truth of the formula, but only that the possibility is not excluded. Consider for example the formula $\Diamond p$ and a transition system with two states q_1 and q_2 with $R = \{(q_1, q_1), (q_1, q_2), (q_2, q_2)\}$ and only q_2 is labeled with a proposition p. Then, after each finite trace $\Diamond p$ is monitorable as each finite trace can be extended to evaluate the formula true or false. However, after each finite trace q_1^* no definite evaluation can be given.

Definition 7 ((Non)monitorable [4]). *Let T be a transition system, $\sigma \in \mathsf{Tr}^f$ be a finite trace, and φ be an arbitrary LTL-formula. We say that φ is Tr-nonmonitorable after σ iff for all finite traces $\sigma' \in \sigma\mathsf{Tr}^f$ it holds that $[\varphi]_{\sigma'}^T =?$. We say that φ is Tr-monitorable iff there is no finite trace $\sigma \in \mathsf{Tr}^f$ such that φ is Tr-nonmonitorable after σ.*

Note that a formula is defined to be nonmonitorable *after a specific* finite trace, and monitorable if no such trace exists. Hence nonmonitorable is a different concept than "not monitorable". For a formula to be "not monitorable" it means that there is a trace such that the formula becomes nonmonitorable after that trace.

Remark 1 (Monitorability). The definition of (non)-monitorability requires a transition system/set of traces. As a consequence, a formula can be not monitorable for one transition system, but monitorable for another. Consider for example the formula $\Box \Diamond p$. Let $T = (S, R, V)$ be a transition system with $S = \{s_0, s_1\}, R = S \times S$ and $V(s_0) = \{p\}$ and $V(s_1) = \emptyset$. For all finite traces $\sigma \in \mathsf{Tr}^f$ of T it holds that $[\Box \Diamond p]_\sigma^T =?$, hence $\Box \Diamond p$ is not Tr-monitorable. Let $T' = (\{s_0\}, \{(s_0, s_0)\}, V')$, such that $V'(s_0) = \emptyset$. The set of traces Tr' contains only traces in which p never holds. Hence, $[\Box \Diamond p]_\sigma^{T'} = f$ for each $\sigma \in \mathsf{Tr}^{f'}$, which makes the formula Tr'-monitorable.

The next proposition captures the observation that monitorability is invariant regarding equivalent formulae.

Proposition 2. *Let T be a transition system and φ and ψ LTL-formulae. If $\mathsf{Tr}^f \models^3 \varphi \leftrightarrow \psi$, then φ is Tr-monitorable iff ψ is Tr-monitorable.*

Proof (Sketch). Because $\mathsf{Tr}^f \models^3 \varphi \leftrightarrow \psi$ it means that $\forall \sigma \in \mathsf{Tr}^f : [\varphi]_\sigma^T = [\psi]_\sigma^T$. Hence, if φ is monitorable then for each trace $\sigma \in \mathsf{Tr}^f$ it holds that there must be a $\sigma' \in \sigma\mathsf{Tr}^f$ such that $[\varphi]_{\sigma'}^T \neq?$ and by extension $[\psi]_{\sigma'}^T \neq?$, hence ψ is then also monitorable. The other way around is exactly the same if we switch φ and ψ. □

We are interested in whether a local monitor m can verify a specific LTL formula φ for any trace. The m-aggregate is syntactically defined. If φ and Agg_m

give the same result on all traces of a transition system and φ is monitorable, or alternatively if Agg_m is monitorable (cf. Proposition 2) then the monitor can detect all definite evaluations of φ.

Example 5 (Monitorability). The formula $\psi = \lozenge l_1 \wedge \square((\neg j_2 \vee \neg l_2) \wedge (\neg j_3 \vee \neg l_3))$ is equivalent to Agg_{m_1} from Example 4. As we assumed that the vehicle will pass maximally once through a location, and it will at some point go through either location 2 or 3, we have that for any trace where the vehicle has not passed location 2 or 3, there is an extension in which the vehicle passes these locations. Then, when it passes a location, there is either a traffic jam or not. After the vehicle passes location 2 or 3, all extensions of the trace will not contain another state where the vehicle passes location 2 or 3. Therefore, any trace in which either location is passed will evaluate ψ to t or f, which makes ψ Tr-monitorable.

We assume that each collaborative monitor has the purpose that one or more local monitors can observe a specific formula. We call the specification of this purpose the expressiveness constraint of the collaborative monitor which is a set of local monitor/formula pairs (m, φ) where the local monitor m must be able to observe formula φ.

Definition 8 (Expressiveness Constraint). *An expressiveness constraint for a collaborative monitor $C = (M, \mathsf{qry})$ is a relation $E \subseteq M \times \mathsf{LTL}$ consisting of pairs of local monitors and formulae. The collaborative monitor C Tr-satisfies the expressiveness constraint E iff for each $(m, \varphi) \in E$ it holds that $\mathsf{Tr} \models^3 \varphi \leftrightarrow \mathsf{Agg}_m$.*

Example 6 (Expressiveness Constraint). An expressiveness constraint for the example scenario is $E = \{(m_1, \varphi)\}$ where $\varphi = \lozenge l_1 \wedge \square(\neg j_2 \vee \neg l_2) \wedge \square(\neg j_3 \vee \neg l_3)$ is from Example 4. Because φ is equivalent to Agg_{m_1}, it means that the example collaborative monitor Tr-satisfies the expressiveness constraint E.

4   Robustness

Suppose we are given a collaborative monitor which satisfies some expressiveness constraint. For various reasons, such as physical sabotaging attacks, local monitors and/or communication links between them can malfunction. From a system designer's perspective it can make sense to construct a monitor with some redundancy such that the expressiveness constraint is still satisfied when some components malfunction. In this section we analyze the robustness of monitors; that is, to which degree local monitor failures affect the functioning of the collaborative monitor.

4.1   Monitor Malfunctioning

Conceptually, one may imagine that a failing local monitor is removed from the collaborative monitor. For another local monitor the malfunction may cause a situation where one of its inputs no longer exists, hence its aggregation formula has to be updated. We update the aggregation formula by removing the occurrences of the variable that corresponds to the failing monitor.

Definition 9 (Local Monitor Malfunctioning). *Let $C = (M, \mathsf{qry})$ be a collaborative monitor, and $F \subseteq M$ be a set of malfunctioning monitors. We define the collaborative monitor $C|_F = (M', \mathsf{qry}')$ as follows:*

- *$M' = M \setminus F$.*
- *for each $m \in M$ it holds that $\mathsf{qry}'(m)$ equals $\mathsf{qry}(m)$ but with each local monitors in F being removed from the tuple.*
- *M contains all $m = (\alpha, \varphi) \in M \setminus F$ where $\mathsf{qry}(m) = (m_1, \ldots, m_k)$ but each $\alpha(o, x_1, \ldots, x_k)$ is replaced by α' which is obtained by the following procedure that is repeated until no variable x_i for $m_i \in F$ remains:*
    1. *If $l_i \in \{x_i, \neg x_i, \neg\neg x_i, \ldots\}$ occurs in a disjunctive subformula $l_i \vee \varphi$ or conjunctive subformula $l_i \wedge \varphi$ of α then this subformula is rewritten to φ.*
    2. *If α equals l_i with $l_i \in \{x_i, \neg x_i, \neg\neg x_i, \ldots\}$, then $\alpha' = \top$.*

Intuitively, the definition expresses that input from malfunction monitors are ignored in a sense that they can no longer help to classify traces.

Example 7 (Local Monitor Malfunctioning). If $F = \{m_4\}$ then monitor 4 is removed. The resulting collaborative monitor is $C|_F = (M', \mathsf{qry}')$ where $M' = \{m_1, m_2, m_3\}$ and $\mathsf{qry}'(m_i) = \mathsf{qry}(m_i)$ for $i = 2$ and $i = 3$, and $\mathsf{qry}'(m_1) = \varepsilon$ is the empty sequence. The malfunction causes $\alpha_1 = o \wedge x$ to be updated to $\alpha_1' = o$, which means that Agg_{m_1} becomes equivalent to $\Diamond l_1$.

We limit ourselves to local monitor malfunctioning, but communication malfunctioning can be straightforwardly defined as well. Instead of removing local monitors, only the query relation is updated. For example, if communication from m_1 to m_4 malfunctions then the new query relation removes m_4 from m_1's input sequence of local monitors. The aggregation formula is updated following the same procedure proposed for local monitor malfunctioning. An extension of malfunctioning where monitors send false information is also interesting and left for future research.

4.2   Monitor Robustness

In a hostile environment local monitors can be damaged, but they can also malfunction for other reasons (e.g. running out of energy). We aim at quantifying robustness in terms of how much damage a collaborative monitor can take before its expressiveness constraint is not satisfied any more. This damage can be expressed as a set of potentially malfunctioning local monitors or a number specifying the number of malfunctioning local monitors. We consider monitors that do not occur in an expressiveness constraint to be supporting monitors. k-robustness is a measurement of how many of such monitors may fail before the expressiveness constraint is not satisfied.

Definition 10 (Collaborative Monitor Robustness). *Let* $C = (M, \mathsf{qry})$ *be a collaborative monitor* Tr*-satisfying the expressiveness constraint* E, $M' = \{m \mid m \in M, (m, \varphi) \notin E\}$ *and* $F \subseteq M$ *be a subset of local monitors. We say that* C *is* F*-robust for* E *and* Tr *if* $C|_F$ Tr*-satisfies* E. *We say that* C *is* k*-robust for* E *and* Tr, $k \in \mathbb{N}_0$, *if* C *is* F'*-robust for* E *and* Tr *for any* $F' \subseteq M'$ *with* $|F'| \leq k$.

We note that given a collaborative monitor C, 0-robustness is equivalent to $\emptyset$-robustness for some E and Tr which simply means that C Tr-satisfies E. If every local monitor occurs in E with some φ then only 0-robustness can be obtained.

Example 8 (Collaborative Monitor Robustness). Let $F = \{m_4\}$ and E be as in Example 6. The collaborative monitor is not F-robust for E. However, assume we allow that m_2 and m_3 can potentially switch to more energy costly but long range communication. This can be modeled by including m_2 and m_3 in $\mathsf{qry}(m_1)$. Also assume that in that case Agg_{m_1} is equivalent to $\varphi_1 \wedge (\mathsf{Agg}_{m_4} \vee (\mathsf{Agg}_{m_2} \wedge (\mathsf{Agg}_{m_3})))$. In this scenario, if m_4 fails then the new m_1-aggregate becomes $\varphi_1 \wedge (\mathsf{Agg}_{m_2} \wedge \mathsf{Agg}_{m_3})$. Hence, the monitor would be F-robust. Also, given E the example collaborative monitor can only be 0-robust.

Aside from a specific attack we might wonder how much damage a monitor can take in general before it fails. This is especially useful in scenarios with many homogeneous local monitors such as botnets where attacks can be widespread and targeting any point in the network. This notion is captured by k-robustness. To determine the k of k-robustness, one has to consider the potential set of monitors which might fail and then check for each set of monitors of size k whether the collaborative monitor is robust with respect to those subsets and its expressiveness constraints. We leave a detailed investigation for future studies.

4.3 Fail Tolerance

Recall from Sect. 2 that we aimed at providing basic metrics to determine critical parts of a collaborative monitor, and that data availability is one of the topics that we address. In wireless sensor networks data availability is a concept that describes that data is available to monitor some property because enough sensors are working properly. Hence, robustness is related to data availability as it deals with scenarios where monitors fail. Intuitively we want to capture for a local monitor how critical its functioning is for the collaborative monitor. We shall use a fairly simple qualification called fail tolerance for determining how critical a local monitor is. This can be used as a basis for more sophisticated metrics. Recall that the presented analysis is for design purposes. In an implementation one has to deploy a mechanism for detecting whether a monitor has failed.

For a collaborative monitor C, a local monitor m in C, and an expressiveness constraint E, we call monitor m k-fail tolerant if alongside m at least $k - 1$ other monitors must fail before C cannot satisfy E, and without m's failure the expressiveness constraint would be satisfied. In particular, m being 1-fail tolerant means that m's correct functioning is absolutely critical for the collaborative monitor, because alongside m zero other monitors must fail before the expressiveness constraint is not satisfied. Similarly, m being k-fail tolerant and $k > 1$ indicates that there is some redundancy wrt. m. For instance if m is 2-fail tolerant then the expressiveness constraint is not violated if only m fails. Therefore, there must be some other monitor that has some redundancy with m. Being ∞-fail tolerant would indicate that the collaborative monitor does not depend on m's functioning for satisfying its expressiveness constraints. That is, if the collaborative monitor does not satisfy an expressiveness constraint E due to any set of failing monitors, then it would still not satisfy E if m did not fail.

Definition 11 (Fail Tolerant). *Let T be a transition system, $C = (M, \mathsf{qry})$ be a collaborative monitor and E be an expressiveness constraint. For a monitor $m \in M$ we say m is k-fail tolerant wrt. E and Tr, $k < \infty$ iff there is a $F \subseteq M$ of size k such that:*

- *(1) $m \in F$, C is not F-robust for E and Tr, and for each subset $F' \subseteq F \setminus \{m\}$ C is F'-robust for E and Tr, and*
- *(2) there is no $F' \subseteq M$ such that (1) holds for F' and $|F'| < |F|$.*

If there does not exist a $k < \infty$ such that m is k-fail tolerant, then we say that m is ∞-fail tolerant.

Example 9 (Fail Tolerance). All monitors in our example scenario are 1-fail tolerant, as each of them observes vital information for the goal aggregate in m_1. However, see Fig. 4 for an illustration of more robust collaborative monitors. In the left monitor we assume only one expressiveness constraint such that m_7 must be able to aggregate $p \wedge q \wedge r$, hence m_7 is 1-fail tolerant. m_1 is 1-fail tolerant as its failure will immediately let the whole monitor fail. m_2 is 2-fail tolerant as its failure together with m_3 will let the whole monitor fail. Note that m_1 together with m_2 is not considered for m_2's fail tolerance as m_1 was already 1-fail tolerant. Monitors m_4 to m_6 are 3-fail tolerant.

In the right collaborative monitor of Fig. 4 we assume that m_5 must be able to aggregate $p \wedge q$ and hence it is 1-fail tolerant. All the other monitors are 2-fail tolerant, and the collaborative monitor as a whole is 1-robust.

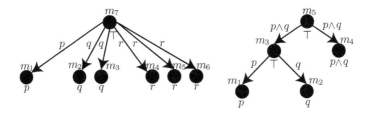

Fig. 4. Example collaborative monitors. Nodes are local monitors with on the top their name, arrows indicate the query relation, below monitors are the observation formulas. An arrow from a monitor m_i to m_j is labeled with the m_j-aggregate.

We note that if a monitor is k-robust, then the lowest i-fail tolerance that a local monitor can have aside from 1 is $(k + 1)$.

Given a monitor design we can now see how critical a local monitor is in terms of its functioning. A straightforward expansion of this fail tolerance analysis is to not only check for F-robustness, but also look at which expressiveness pairs (m, φ) are not satisfied anymore in case the monitor is not F-robust. If not all expressiveness constraints are equally important, then for tolerance analysis this can be taken into account. Also looking at how many pairs are not satisfied is an important ingredient should one want to specify graceful degradation for collaborative monitors. At runtime the collaborative monitor can benefit from fail tolerance analysis by assigning higher reparation priorities to critical monitors, if possible.

5   Security

When it comes to the security of a collaborative monitor, we focus on the possible information an attacker can extract from the monitor. We say an attacker extracts an LTL property φ if the attacker can extract from the collaborative monitor the evaluation of φ given an arbitrary finite trace.

5.1   Information Extraction

In practice there are various ways in which an attacker can extract information. The attacker can intercept and interpret messages, query other monitors by pretending to be authorized and capture a monitor. To analyze intercepted messages it is required to know what messages are exactly exchanged, something which is not covered in our model. Also our model is not suited for analyzing how a monitor can be reprogrammed, given that we only have semantical representations and no program specifications of monitors. Therefore we focus on the situation where the attacker can ask a query by pretending to be authorized. This can in practice occur, for example, if the attacker pretends to be a local monitor from the network.

We assume that like monitors the attacker can aggregate extracted information by using some aggregation formula. However, for the attacker this is not a fixed formula. Hence, given the aggregates that it obtains from the collaborative monitor it can combine them by standard Boolean connectives. In the following $\mathsf{PL}(X)$ denotes all possible formulae that can obtained by applying Boolean connectives to elements in X.

Definition 12 (Monitor Attack). *Let $C = (M, \mathsf{qry})$ be a collaborative monitor. An attack $\mathsf{att} \subseteq M$ is a set of local monitors. The set of extracted properties $\mathcal{L}_{\mathsf{att}}^C$ is $\mathsf{PL}(\{\mathsf{Agg}_m | m \in \mathsf{att}\})$.*

If the framework is extended and other forms of attacks, such as eavesdropping on communication, can also be analyzed then these will contribute to the set of extracted properties. Note that if some φ is extracted from the monitor,

392   B. Testerink et al.

then the attacker may still not know whether the system's behavior satisfies this property given a finite trace, because the evaluation may be inconclusive.

Example 10 (Monitor Attack). If an attacker can imitate m_4 then it will be able to query m_2 and m_3. In that case $\mathsf{att} = \{m_2, m_3\}$ and the extracted properties are $\mathsf{PL}(\{\mathsf{Agg}_{m_2}, \mathsf{Agg}_{m_3}\})$. For instance the attacker can determine given an arbitrary trace what the evaluation is of $\neg\Box(\neg j_2 \vee \neg l_2) \vee \neg\Box(\neg j_3 \vee \neg l_3)$ (somewhere in the future there was a jam at either location and/or the vehicle was at either location).

5.2   Safety

For monitor safety we look at whether a specific attack can be used to observe some given property from the collaborative monitor. We assume the attacker knows what an aggregate represents. That is, if it obtains information on the evaluation of the m-aggregate for a monitor m, then it knows that the m-aggregate is Agg_m.

Definition 13 (Monitor Safety). *Let T be transition system, C be a collaborative monitor, att be an attack and φ be an* LTL *formula. We say that C is Tr-safe for φ and att iff there is no $\psi \in \mathcal{L}_{\mathsf{att}}^C$ such that $\mathsf{Tr}^f \models^3 \varphi \leftrightarrow \psi$.*

Example 11 (Monitor Safety). Given $\mathsf{att} = \{m_1, m_2, m_3, m_4\}$ the example collaborative monitor is Tr-safe for $\varphi = \Diamond(l_1 \wedge \Diamond l_2)$ and att. It is also Tr-safe for $\psi = \Diamond(l_1 \wedge \Diamond l_3)$ and att. This means that even if the attacker can obtain all available aggregates, it still cannot determine for a trace whether the vehicle used or may use in the future the route through locations 1 and 2 or through locations 1 and 3, respectively.

The space of potential attacks is heavily restricted by practical details that are not covered by our model. For instance if in a network some local monitor only has wired connections to other local monitors in a safe environment, then it might be impossible that local monitor is targeted for an attack. Therefore we focus on analyzing security risks wrt. potentially attacked local monitors and with the assumption that the attack is practically feasible. The security constraint of a monitor consist of a set of monitors that can potentially be attacked and a set of properties that represent sensitive information. The analysis of what properties count as sensitive should be part of the system's design methodology. These will differ per practical real-world scenario. A monitor satisfies its security constraint if none of the considered attacks allows the attacker to monitor a sensitive property.

Definition 14 (Security Constraints). *Let T be a transition system and $C = (M, \mathsf{qry})$ be a collaborative monitor. A security constraint for C is defined as (A, P) where $A \subseteq M$ is a set of local monitors and $P \subseteq$ LTL *is a set of sensitive properties. C Tr-satisfies its security constraint iff for each and $\varphi \in P$, C is Tr-safe for φ and A.*

It should be noted that for some constraint (A, P) a not monitorable property $\varphi \in P$ might still be reasonable to consider as sensitive information. There is the possibility that given the behavior of the monitored system at runtime such a formula will always be evaluated to '?', but this is not guaranteed to be the case, unless φ is nonmonitorable after the empty trace.

Example 12 (Security Constraint). Let $M = \{m_1, m_2, m_3, m_4\}$, φ and ψ be as in Example 11 and $(A, P) = (M, \{\varphi, \psi\})$ be the scenario's security constraint. The example collaborative monitor Tr-satisfies its security constraint (A, P). This means that no matter which local monitors are attacked, the route of the vehicle remains private.

5.3   Attack Tolerance

For security we also want to know how critical an attack on a monitor can be. That is, if a certain monitor's aggregate can be obtained, how bad is that? In contrast to robustness, this is only interesting if the collaborative monitor *does not* satisfy its security constraint. Because that would indicate that there are combinations of monitors such that the attack on those monitors would reveal sensitive information. The attack tolerance of a local monitor m indicates how many other monitors need to be attacked in addition to m before sensitive information is leaked. A local monitor is maximally attack tolerant if it cannot contribute to any security leakage at all.

Definition 15 (Attack Tolerant). *Let $C = (M, \mathsf{qry})$ be a collaborative monitor and (A, P) be its security constraint. For an attack $\mathsf{att} \subseteq A$ and a local monitor $m \in \mathsf{att}$ we say that m is contributing to att iff $P \cap \mathcal{L}_{\mathsf{att}}^C \neq \emptyset$ and $P \cap \mathcal{L}_{\mathsf{att}'}^C \subset P \cap \mathcal{L}_{\mathsf{att}}^C$, where and $\mathsf{att}' = \mathsf{att} \setminus \{m\}$. For a monitor $m \in M$ we define:*

- *m is k-attack tolerant iff $\mathsf{att} \subseteq A$ is the smallest attack such that m is contributing to att and $k = |\mathsf{att}|$.*
- *m is ∞-attack tolerant iff there is no $\mathsf{att} \subseteq A$ such that $m \in \mathsf{att}$ and m is contributing to att.*

If $C = (M, \mathsf{qry})$ Tr-satisfies a security constraint then all local monitors are ∞-attack tolerant. If a local monitor m is 1-attack tolerant then the m-aggregate is equivalent to a sensitive property, or the aggregate's negation is. The maximal attack tolerance value for a local monitor aside from ∞ is $|M|$.

Example 13 (Attack Tolerant). In our example scenario the monitor Tr-satisfies the example security constraint and hence all monitors are ∞-attack tolerant. If in the right monitor of Fig. 4 the security constraint is $(\{m_1, \ldots, m_7\}, \{p \wedge q\})$ then m_1 and m_2 are 2-attack tolerant and the other local monitors are 1-attack tolerant.

Now we can determine how attack tolerant a local monitor is, which is an indicator for how critical the local monitor is for the security of the collaborative monitor. Based on this basic framework several extensions are possible. For instance if a monitor is easier to attack than another (i.e. a simple sensor in a WSN versus a sophisticated sink), then the tolerance of the easier target should be decreased relatively to the harder target. In a runtime environment if attacks are detected then new attack tolerance values can be computed with the knowledge that some local monitors are already attacked. This could for instance be countered with low attack tolerance local monitors switching to more secure, albeit energy and/or more overhead cost expensive, communication protocols.

6   Discussion and Conclusion

In this paper we presented a formal framework for collaborative monitors, which are networks of local monitors. We have drawn inspiration from the wireless sensor network literature to specify the interaction between local monitors. The local monitors in a collaborative monitor are models of monitors that aggregate local and distributed observations. The model for monitoring is suitable for scenarios where it is unfeasible to have a centralized monitor that can observe the entire state of the system that is monitored. Also, aggregation is useful in scenarios where communication is expensive, as it can reduce the cost of communication. Aggregation may also improve the security of a monitor. We discussed how aspects related to robustness and safety can be investigated in the framework. The model for robustness and safety allows a designer to detect the importance of the correct functioning and safety of a local monitor. In an application that implements the model this may help the designer to decide upon what counter measures to take against potentially failing or attacked monitors.

The contribution of this paper is just a first step towards a formal framework for modeling and analyzing collaborative monitor applications. At several points we explained how the framework could be extended. The runtime analysis of communication failures and the effects of different communication protocols from related literature provide interesting directions for future research. Also, the concepts of robustness and safety can be extended to model, e.g., graceful degradation of a collaborative monitor's functioning and safety. We also left the investigation of formal properties of the framework, e.g. complexity and synthesis results, for future work.

References

1. Agotnes, T., Van Der Hoek, W., Rodriguez-Aguilar, J., Sierra, C., Wooldridge, M.: On the logic of normative systems. In: Proceedings of the Twentieth International Joint Conference on Artificial Intelligence (IJCAI 2007), pp. 1181–1186 (2007)
2. Alechina, N., Dastani, M., Logan, B.: Reasoning about normative update. In: Proceedings of the Twenty-Third International Joint Conference on Artificial Intelligence, IJCAI 2013, pp. 20–26. AAAI Press (2013)

3. Bauer, A., Falcone, Y.: Decentralised LTL monitoring. In: Giannakopoulou, D., Méry, D. (eds.) FM 2012. LNCS, vol. 7436, pp. 85–100. Springer, Heidelberg (2012)
4. Bauer, A., Leucker, M., Schallhart, C.: Runtime verification for LTL and TLTL. ACM Trans. Softw. Eng. Methodol. **20**(4), 14:1–14:64 (2011)
5. Boella, G., Torre, L.V.D.: Introduction to normative multiagent systems. Comput. Math. Organ. Theory **12**, 71–79 (2006)
6. Havelund, K., Rosu, G.: Monitoring programs using rewriting. In: Proceedings of the 16th Annual International Conference on Automated Software Engineering (ASE 2001), pp. 135–143. IEEE (2001)
7. Hoh, B., Gruteser, M., Xiong, H., Alrabady, A.: Enhancing security and privacy in traffic-monitoring systems. IEEE Pervasive Comput. **5**(4), 38–46 (2006)
8. Karlof, C., Wagner, D.: Secure routing in wireless sensor networks: attacks and countermeasures. Elsevier's AdHoc Netw. J. Spec. Issue Sens. Netw. Appl. Protoc. **1**(2–3), 293–315 (2003)
9. Kleene, S.C.: Introduction to Metamathematics. North-Holland Publisher Company, The Netherlands (1952)
10. Ozdemir, S., Xiao, Y.: Secure data aggregation in wireless sensor networks: a comprehensive overview. Comput. Netw. **53**(12), 2022–2037 (2009)
11. Pathan, A., Lee, H.-W., Hong, C.S.: Security in wireless sensor networks: issues and challenges. In: The 8th International Conference on Advanced Communication Technology, ICACT 2006, vol. 2, pages 6 pp. -1048, February 2006
12. Perrig, A., Stankovic, J., Wagner, D.: Security in wireless sensor networks. Commun. ACM **47**(6), 53–57 (2004)
13. Perrig, A., Szewczyk, R., Tygar, J.D., Wen, V., Culler, D.E.: SPINS: security protocols for sensor networks. Wirel. Netw. **8**(5), 521–534 (2002)
14. Pnueli, A.: The temporal logic of programs. In: 18th Annual Symposium onFoundations of Computer Science, pp. 46–57, October 1977
15. Pnueli, A., Zaks, A.: PSL model checking and run-time verification via testers. In: Misra, J., Nipkow, T., Sekerinski, E. (eds.) FM 2006. LNCS, vol. 4085, pp. 573–586. Springer, Heidelberg (2006)
16. Testerink, B., Bulling, N., Dastani, M.: A model for collaborative runtime verification. In: Proceedings of the 2015 International Conference on Autonomous Agents and Multiagent Systems, pp. 1781–1782 (2015)
17. Testerink, B., Dastani, M., Meyer, J.-J.: Norm monitoring through observation sharing. In: Herzig, A., Lorini, E. (eds.) Proceedings of the European Conference on Social Intelligence, pp. 291–304 (2014)

An Interactive, Generative Punch and Judy Show Using Institutions, ASP and Emotional Agents

Matt Thompson[1(✉)], Julian Padget[1], and Steve Battle[2]

[1] Department of Computer Science, University of Bath, Bath, UK
{m.r.thompson,j.a.padget}@bath.ac.uk
[2] Department of Computer Science and Creative Technologies,
University of the West of England, Bristol, UK
steve.battle@uwe.ac.uk

Abstract. Using Punch and Judy as a story domain, we describe an interactive puppet show, where the flow and content of the story can be influenced by the actions of the audience. As the puppet show is acted out, the audience reacts to events by cheering or booing the characters. This affects the agents' emotional state, potentially causing them to change their actions, altering the course of the narrative. An institutional normative model is used to constrain the narrative so that it remains consistent with the Punch and Judy canon. Through this vignette of a socio-technical system (STS), comprising human and software actors, an institutional model – derived from narrative theory – and (simplistic) technological interaction artifacts, we begin to be able to explore some of the issues that can arise in STS through the prism of the World-Institution-Technology (WIT) model.

1 Introduction

Agent-based approaches for interactive narrative generation use intelligent agents to model the characters in a story. The agents respond to the interactions of a player with dialogue or actions fitting the shape of a story. However, these agents have little autonomy in their actions, bound as they are to the strict requirements of their role in the narrative.

Other approaches to balancing authorial control with player or character agency include the use of director agents [15], reincorporation of player actions back into the narrative [29] and mediation to prevent narrative-breaking actions [26].

An institutional model can be used as a normative framework for governing the actions of agents in a story. By describing the rules of a narrative in terms

An earlier version of this work was presented at the AI & Games symposium, held as part of AISB 2015, Canterbury, UK.

M. Thompson—Supported by an Engineering Doctorate studentship through the EPSRC Centre for Doctoral Training in Digital Entertainment at the University of Bath.

V. Dignum et al. (Eds.): COIN 2015, LNAI 9628, pp. 396–417, 2016.
DOI: 10.1007/978-3-319-42691-4_22

of social expectations, the agents are encouraged to perform certain types of actions while still retaining the option to break free of these expectations. As in society in the real world, breaking agreed norms comes with consequences, and only generally happens in exceptional circumstances. One situation where this may reasonably occur is when agents experience emotions. An agent experiencing an extreme emotion – in respect of some emotional model – such as rage or depression, may be allowed to act unusually or uncharacteristically. Allowing characters to break with the norms of the narrative enables them to be 'pushed too far' by circumstances, with results that can add an extra dimension of richness to the telling.

There are two novel aspects to the approach we describe here: (i) the use of an institutional model to describe a narrative 'world' or domain, and (ii) how emotional models can give intelligent agents an alternative form of autonomy – from being limited by knowledge, reasoning capacity and time (bounded-rationality) and self-interest – both to act in idiosyncratic ways and to react emotionally to input from the audience.

Here we present an implementation in the form of an interactive Punch and Judy puppet show, in which the course of the story changes in accordance with the responses that come from the audience.

The structure of the system takes cues from the WIT model [22] which offers a pattern for analysing socio-technical systems through the interaction of three views of a system: (i) the world view (W), as human and software agents see it: in this case, the audience (human) and the actors (BDI agents) playing roles in Punch and Judy, (ii) the institutional view (I) that sets out the regulation of the system: in this case the narrative structure corresponding to Punch and Judy, captured in terms of Propp's [23] story moves and roles, and (iii) the technological view (T) that identifies the components (software and hardware) that enable the realization of the system, in this case, the means to capture audience input and the visualisation of the performance. More importantly, WIT emphasises the role of the institution both as regulator and monitor of behaviour, which is exactly what we see in our system, since through permission and obligation it directs the actors towards the conclusion of the narrative, while also observing their actions for adherence to the narrative structure.

The puppets in the show are each realised by belief-desire-intention (BDI) agents augmented with a valence, arousal, dominance (VAD) emotional model, which we describe in Sect. 4. The story is modelled by a set of institutional norms (Sect. 6) that describe the Punch and Judy story domain in terms of Propp's 'story moves' [23] (Sect. 2). In Sect. 6, we discuss the architecture and the means for the audience to interact with the system. The focus here is on the more technical aspects of the system and how the various components fit together, while more detail on the narrative side appears in [28].

2   Propp's Story Moves and Roles

To express story events as an institution, we need some sort of formalisation for the analysis of the story – rather than an arbitrary selection of features – and so we look to narrative theory for inspiration. Instead of describing parts of the Punch and Judy story explicitly (such as 'Punch is expected to hit the policeman in this scene'), it is desirable to describe scenes in a more abstract way using roles ('The villain fights the victim in this scene'). The use of more general story fragments allows us to reuse them in multiple scenes, or even in other stories.

Narratology, and structuralism in particular, supply such generalised building blocks for stories. Russian formalism is an early movement in narrative theory that sought to formalise the elements of narrative, and Vladimir Propp was a prominent figure in this school. One outcome of this movement was Propp's 1928 formalism derived from the study of Russian folktales, *The Morphology of the Folktale* [23], which is what we use to build a model to direct the course of the narrative. Propp is widely used – and criticised – in the domains of computational models of narrative and digital story telling [8], but retains appeal through it's simple but relatively effective modelling capacity. In his formalism, Propp identifies recurring characters, which become roles and motifs, which become action fragments, in Russian folklore, distilling them down to a concise syntax with which to describe stories. Propp's event-driven style translates comfortably to an institutional framework for event-based norms. However, while these action fragments fit the Punch and Judy story adequately, we note that the role labels can sound rather awkward because of the apparent semantic import of the textual label.

In Propp's formalism, characters have *roles*, such as *hero, villain, dispatcher, false hero*, and more. Characters performing a certain role are able to perform a subset of *story moves*, which are actions that make the narrative progress. For example, the *dispatcher* might send the *hero* on a quest, or the *victim* may issue an *interdiction* to the *villain*, which is then *violated*.

Propp defines a total of 31 distinct story functions. Each such function is denoted by a number and symbol in order to provide a succinct way of describing entire stories by reference to the constituent story functions. Examples of such functions are:

– One of the members of a family absents himself from home: *absentation*.
– An interdiction is addressed to the hero: *interdiction*.
– The victim submits to deception and thereby unwittingly helps his enemy: *complicity*.
– The villain causes harm or injury to a member of the family: *villainy*.

Each of these functions can vary in subtle ways. For example, the *villainy* function can be realised as one of 19 distinct forms of villainous deed, including *the villain abducts a person, the villain seizes the daylight*, and *the villain makes a threat of cannibalism*. These functions are enacted by characters following certain roles. Each role (or *dramatis persona* in Propp's definition) has a *sphere of action* consisting of the functions that they are able to perform at a particular point in the story. Propp defines seven roles each of which has distinct spheres of action: *villain*, *donor*, *helper*, *princess*, *dispatcher*, *hero*, and *false hero*. In a typical story, one story function will follow another as the tale progresses in a sequence of cause and effect. Propp's formalism does however also allow for simultaneous story functions.

2.1   Propp Example: Sausages and Crocodile Scene

To provide some context for Punch and Judy, since it is a peculiarly British phenomenon, although with Italian origins, we quote from Wikipedia:

> Punch and Judy is a traditional, popular, and usually very violent puppet show featuring Mr Punch and his wife, Judy. The performance consists of a sequence of short scenes, each depicting an interaction between two characters, most typically Mr. Punch and one other character (who usually falls victim to Mr. Punch's club). It is often associated with traditional British seaside culture. The Punch and Judy show has roots in the 16th-century Italian commedia dell'arte.
> http://en.wikipedia.org/wiki/Punch_and_Judy, retrieved 2015-05-06.

The common elements of Punch and Judy are easily described in terms of Propp's story functions. Here we pick one scene to use as an example: the scene where Punch battles a crocodile in order to safeguard some sausages. In this scene, Joey the clown (our narrator) asks Punch to guard the sausages. Once Joey has left the stage, a crocodile appears and eats the sausages. Punch fights with the crocodile, but it escapes. Joey then returns to find that his sausages are gone. The corresponding story functions are:

1. Joey tells Punch to look after the sausages (*interdiction*).
2. Joey has some reservations, but decides to trust Punch (*complicity*).
3. Joey gives the sausages to Punch (*provision or receipt of a magical agent*).
4. Joey leaves the stage (*absentation*).
5. A crocodile enters the stage and eats the sausages (*violation*).
6. Punch fights with the crocodile (*struggle*).
7. Joey returns to find that the sausages are gone (*return*).

Some features of Punch and Judy map to story functions better than others (for example, it is debatable as to whether or not the sausages can be considered a "magical agent"), but for the most part Propp's formalism seems well suited to Punch and Judy. The advantage of using Propp to model the Punch and Judy story domain is that the story function concept captures the notion of actual story (brute) events counting as [11] story function (institutional) events and hence leading to the construction and evolution of institutional models.

3   Institutional Model

An institution describes a set of 'social' norms describing the permitted and obliged behaviour of interacting agents. Noriega's 'Fish Market' thesis [3] describe how an institutional model can be used to regiment the actions of agents in a fish market auction. Several [2,5,9] extend this idea to build systems where institutions actively regulate the actions of agents, while still allowing them to decide what to do. We build on the work of Cliffe et al. [7] and Lee et al. [14] to adapt it for the world of narrative, using an institutional model to describe the story world of Punch and Judy in terms of Propp's story moves and character roles, through which the actors acquire powers and permissions appropriate to the character and the story function in which they are participating.

Institutional models use concepts from deontic logic to provide obligations and permissions that act on interacting agents in an environment. By combining this approach with Propp's concepts of *roles* and *story moves*, we describe a Propp-style formalism of Punch and Judy in terms of what agents are *obliged* and *permitted* to do at certain points in the story.

For example, in one Punch and Judy scene, a policeman enters the stage and attempts to apprehend Punch. According to the rules of the Punch and Judy world, Punch has an obligation to kill the policeman by the end of the scene (as this is what the audience expects to happen, having seen other Punch and Judy shows). The policeman has an obligation to try his best to catch Punch. Both agents have permission to be on the stage during the scene. The policeman only has permission to chase Punch if he can see him (Punch is obliged to hide from him at the start of the scene).

The permissions an agent has, on the one hand, constrain the choices of actions available to them at any given moment. Obligations, on the other hand, affect the goals of an agent. Whether or not an agent actively tries to fulfil an obligation depends on their emotional state.

3.1   Institution Example

To illustrate the application of institutional modelling, we here continue the 'sausages and crocodile' scene example from Sect. 2.1, taking the Propp story functions and describing them in an institutional model. We define our institution in terms of *fluents*, *events*, *powers*, *permissions* and *obligations*, following [7], to which the interested reader is referred for the full details of the formal model, including the generate ($\mathcal{G}$) and consequence ($\mathcal{C}$) relations, which are only described here in sufficient depth for the model being presented.

Fluents. These are properties that may or may not hold true at some instant in time, and that change over the course of time. *Institutional events* are able to *initiate* or *terminate* fluents at points in time. A fluent could describe whether a character is currently on stage, the scene of the story that is currently being acted out, or whether or not the character is happy at that moment in time. Domain fluents ($\mathcal{D}$) describe domain-specific properties that can hold at a certain point in time. In the Punch and Judy domain, these can be whether or not an agent is on stage, or their role in the narrative:

$$\mathcal{D} = \{\texttt{onstage}, \texttt{hero}, \texttt{villain}, \texttt{victim}, \texttt{donor}, \texttt{item}\}$$

Institutional fluents consist of (institutional) *powers*, *permissions* and *obligations*. An **institutional power** ($\mathcal{W}$) describes whether or not an external event has the authority to generate a meaningful institutional event. Taking an example from Propp's formalism, an *absentation* event can only be generated by an external event brought about by a *donor* character (such as their leaving the stage). Therefore, any characters other than the donor character would not have the institutional power to generate an *absentation* institutional event when they leave the stage. The possible empowerments (institutional events) from Propp used in Punch and Judy are:

$$\mathcal{W} = \{\texttt{pow(introduction)}, \texttt{pow(interdiction)}, \texttt{pow(give)},$$
$$\texttt{pow(absentation)}, \texttt{pow(violation)}, \texttt{pow(return)}\}$$

Permissions. ($\mathcal{P}$) are associated with external actions that agents are permitted to do at a certain instant in time. These can be thought of as the set of *socially permitted* actions available to an agent. While it is possible for an agent to perform other actions, societal norms usually discourage them from doing so. For example, it would not make sense in the world of Punch and Judy if Punch were to give the sausages to the Policeman. It is always Joey who gives the sausages to Punch. Also, it would be strange if Joey were to do this in the middle of a scene where Punch and Judy are arguing. We make sure agents' actions are governed so as to allow them only a certain subset of permitted actions at any one time. The set of permission fluents is:

$$\mathcal{P} = \{\texttt{perm(leavestage)}, \texttt{perm(enterstage)}, \texttt{perm(die)}, \texttt{perm(kill)},$$
$$\texttt{perm(hit)}, \texttt{perm(give)}, \texttt{perm(fight)}\}$$

Obligations. ($\mathcal{O}$) are institutional facts that contain actions agents *should* do before a certain deadline. If the action is not performed in time, a *violation event* is triggered, which may result in a penalty being incurred. While an agent may be obliged to perform an action, it is entirely their choice whether or not they actually do so. They must weigh up whether or not pursuing other courses of action is worth accepting the penalty that an unfulfilled obligation brings.

Anybody who has seen a Punch and Judy show knows that at some point Joey tells Punch to guard some sausages, before disappearing offstage. Joey's departure is modelled in the institution as the *absentation* event. It could also be said that Joey has an obligation to leave the stage as part of the *absentation* event, otherwise the story function is violated. This can be described in the institution as:

$$\begin{aligned}
\mathcal{E}_{obs} = \{&\mathtt{startshow, leavestage, enterstage, die, give,}\\
&\mathtt{harmed, hit, fight, kill, escape}\}
\end{aligned} \tag{1}$$

$$\begin{aligned}
\mathcal{E}_{instevent} = \{&\mathtt{introduction, interdiction, receipt, absentation,}\\
&\mathtt{violation, return, struggle, defeat, complicity,}\\
&\mathtt{victory, escape}\}
\end{aligned} \tag{2}$$

$$\begin{aligned}
\mathcal{E}_{viol} = \{&\mathtt{viol(introduction), viol(interdiction), viol(receipt),}\\
&\mathtt{viol(absentation), viol(violation), viol(return),}\\
&\mathtt{viol(struggle), viol(defeat), viol(complicity)}\\
&\mathtt{viol(victory), viol(escape)}\}
\end{aligned} \tag{3}$$

Fig. 1. External, institutional and violation events for Punch and Judy

$$\mathcal{O} = \{\mathrm{obl}(\mathtt{leavestage, absentation, viol(absentation))}\}$$

The first argument is the external event that must be triggered according to the obligation, the second argument is the institutional deadline event, and the third argument is the violation event which is triggered if the obligation is not fulfilled before the deadline.

Events. Cliffe's model specifies three types of **event**: *external events* (or 'observed events', $\mathcal{E}_{obs}$), *institutional events* ($\mathcal{E}_{instevent}$) and *violation events* ($\mathcal{E}_{viol}$). Examples of each are given in Fig. 1. *External events* are observed to happen in the agents' environment, which can *generate institutional events* which occur only within the institional model, leading to the *initiation* or *termination* of (domain) fluents, permissions, obligations or institutional powers. An external event could be an agent leaving the stage, an agent hitting another, or an agent dying. Internal events include narrative events such as scene changes, or the triggering of Propp story functions such as *absentation* or *interdiction* (described in Sect. 2). *Violation* is the name of a Propp story function, and is included as an internal event, although it has no relation to the violation events of an institution. Violation events occur when an agent has failed to fulfil an obligation before the specified deadline. These can be implemented in the form of a penalty, by decreasing an agent's health, for example.

Event Generation and Consequences. An **event generation** function, $\mathcal{G}$, describes how events ($\mathcal{E}$, usually external, but can also be internal) can generate other (usually institutional) events, conditional upon the current institutional state ($\mathcal{X}$). This is the counts-as relation. For example, if an agent leaves the stage while the *interdiction* event holds, they trigger the *leavestage* event. This combination generates the *absentation* institutional event (rule 7). Further examples appear in Fig. 2.

$$\mathcal{G}(\mathcal{X},\mathcal{E}): \begin{cases} \langle \emptyset, tellprotect(\texttt{donor},\texttt{villain},\texttt{item}) \rangle \rightarrow \{interdiction\} & (4) \\ \langle \{interdiction\}, agree(\texttt{villain}) \rangle \rangle \rightarrow \{complicity\} & (5) \\ \langle \emptyset, give(\texttt{donor},\texttt{villain},\texttt{item}) \rangle \rangle \rightarrow \{receipt\} & (6) \\ \langle \{interdiction\}, leavestage(\texttt{donor}) \rangle \rightarrow \{absentation\} & (7) \\ \langle \{interdiction\}, harmed(\texttt{item}) \rangle \rightarrow \{violation\} & (8) \\ \langle \{interdiction, absentation\}, enterstage(\texttt{donor}) \rangle \rightarrow \{return\} & (9) \\ \langle \emptyset, hit(\texttt{donor},\texttt{villain}) \rangle \rightarrow \{struggle\} & (10) \end{cases}$$

Fig. 2. Event generation in the sausage scene

$$\mathcal{C}^{\uparrow}(\mathcal{X},\mathcal{E}): \begin{cases} \langle \emptyset, \texttt{interdiction} \rangle \rightarrow \{active(\texttt{interdiction}), \\ \qquad\qquad\qquad perm(give(\texttt{donor},\texttt{villain},\texttt{item}))\} & (11) \\ \langle \emptyset, \texttt{receipt} \rangle \rightarrow \{perm(leavestage(\texttt{donor}))\} & (12) \\ \langle \{active(absentation)\}, \\ \texttt{enterstage(villain)} \rangle \rightarrow \{obl(eat(\texttt{villain},\texttt{sausages}), \\ \qquad\qquad\qquad return, viol(violation))\} & (13) \\ \langle \{active(interdiction)\}, \\ \texttt{leavestage(donor)} \rangle \rightarrow \{obl(\texttt{enterstage(donor)}, \\ \qquad\qquad\qquad eat(\texttt{villain},\texttt{sausages}), \\ \qquad\qquad\qquad viol(return))\} & (14) \\ \{active(interdiction)\}, \\ \qquad\qquad \texttt{violation} \rangle \rightarrow \{perm(\texttt{enterstage(dispatcher)})\} & (15) \\ \langle \{active(absentation), \\ \quad active(violation)\}, \\ \qquad\qquad \texttt{return} \rangle \rightarrow \{perm(hit(\texttt{donor},\texttt{villain}))\} & (16) \end{cases}$$

Fig. 3. Fluent initiation in the sausage scene

$$\mathcal{C}^{\downarrow}(\mathcal{X},\mathcal{E}): \begin{cases} \langle \emptyset, \texttt{interdiction} \rangle \rightarrow \{perm(give(\texttt{donor},\texttt{villain},\texttt{item}))\} & (17) \\ \langle \{active(interdiction)\}, \\ \qquad\qquad \texttt{absentation} \rangle \rightarrow \{perm(leavestage(\texttt{donor}))\} & (18) \\ \langle \{active(interdiction)\}, \\ \qquad\qquad \texttt{violation} \rangle \rightarrow \{active(interdiction)\} & (19) \\ \langle \{active(absentation), \\ \quad active(violation)\}, \\ \qquad\qquad \texttt{return} \rangle \rightarrow \{active(absentation)\} & (20) \end{cases}$$

Fig. 4. Fluent termination in the sausage scene

Event generation functions follow a $\langle$preconditions$\rangle \rightarrow \{$postconditions$\}$ format. The preconditions consist of a set of fluents that hold at that time, along with an event to have occurred. The postconditions are the events that are generated. The generation functions are used to generate internal, institutional events from external events.

Consider the Punch and Judy scenario described in Sect. 2.1. There are seven institutional events (story functions) that occur during this scene: *interdiction, complicity, receipt* (from Propp's *receipt of a magical agent*) *absentation, violation, struggle, return*. These institutional events are all generated by external events. The *interdiction* is generated when Joey tells Punch to protect the sausages. Punch agreeing amounts to *complicity*. Joey *gives* punch the sausages (*receipt*), then leaves the stage (*absentation*). The crocodile eating the sausages is a *violation* of Punch's oath, the agents fight (*struggle*), then Joey enters the stage again (*return*).

It is desirable that these story functions occur in this sequence in order for a satisfying narrative to emerge. Agents may decide to perform actions that diverge from this set of events, but the institution is guiding them towards the most fitting outcome for a *Punch and Judy* world. For this reason, a currently active story function can be the precondition for event generation. For example, the *receipt* event may only be triggered if an agent externally performs a *give* action **and** if the *complicity* event currently holds (rule 6). Examples of event generation function for this scenario, complete with preconditions, are listed in rules 4–10 (Fig. 2).

Consequences consist of fluents, permissions and obligations that are *initiated* ($\mathcal{C}^{\uparrow}$) or *terminated* ($\mathcal{C}^{\downarrow}$) by institutional events. For example, the institutional event *receipt* initiates the donor agent's permission to leave the stage, triggering the *absentation* event (rule 12). When the *interdiction* event is currently active and a *violation* event occurs, the interdiction event is terminated (19). Rules 11–20 in Figs. 3 and 4 describe the initiation and termination of fluents in the Punch and Judy sausages scene detailed in Sect. 2.1.

4   VAD Emotional Model

In order to make the agents acting out the Punch and Judy show more believable, we apply an emotional model to affect their actions and decisions. For this, we use the valence-arousal (circumplex) model first described by Russell [27]. To give each character its own distinct personality, we extend this model with an extra dimension: dominance, as used by Ahn et al. [1] in their model for conversational virtual humans. This dominance level is affected by the reactions of the audience to the agents' actions. For example, Judy may become more dominant as her suggestions to hit Punch with a stick are cheered on by the audience, emboldening her into acting out her impulses. A detailed description appears in the text in Fig. 5.

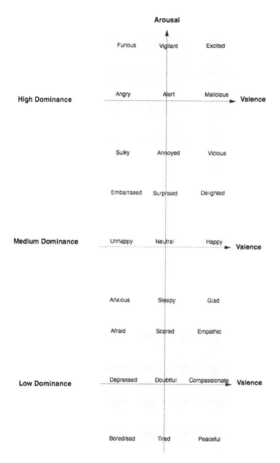

Fig. 5. VAD emotional values (figure adapted from Ahn et al.) [1]

The VAD model illustrates how valence, arousal and dominance values map to identifiable emotions. Valence, arousal and dominance can each have a value of low, medium or high. This allows the agents to have a total of 27 distinct emotional states. The valence and arousal levels of each agent are affected by the actions of other agents. For example, a character being chased around the stage by Punch will see their valence level drop while their arousal increases. According to Russell's circumplex model of emotion [27], this would result in them becoming *afraid* (if their dominance level is low).

An agent's emotional state affects its ability to fulfil its institutional obligations. An agent that is *furious* might have no problem carrying out an obligation that requires them to kill another agent. If that same agent is *happy* or *depressed*, however, they might not have the appropriate motivation to perform such a violent action.

It is important to note that the emotional model is part of the agent belief state, and not held in the institution. We want to explore how the characters of the story might be able to choose actions based on their emotional state. While the institution could theoretically calculate the emotional state for each agent in turn and dictate this to them along with the norms of the narrative, it makes sense to decouple this feature from the narrative institution in order to separate the characters from the events of the story.

Agents' emotional states change according to their interactions with the audience. This is unrelated to what is happening in the narrative, and so this underscores the decision not to include any emotional modelling in the institution. Also, we want the agents to have some degree of freedom within the narrative world. They should be allowed to determine their emotions themselves, so that in extreme emotional states they can perform 'irrational' or 'extreme' actions that may not necessarily fit into the narrative.

Listing 1.1. Emotional rules for a character with medium dominance

```
1   emotion(sleepy)     :- valence(0)  & arousal(-1) & dominance(0).
2   emotion(neutral)    :- valence(0)  & arousal(0)  & dominance(0).
3   emotion(surprised)  :- valence(0)  & arousal(1)  & dominance(0).
4   emotion(anxious)    :- valence(-1) & arousal(-1) & dominance(0).
5   emotion(unhappy)    :- valence(-1) & arousal(0)  & dominance(0).
6   emotion(embarrassed) :- valence(-1) & arousal(1)  & dominance(0).
7   emotion(glad)       :- valence(1)  & arousal(-1) & dominance(0).
8   emotion(happy)      :- valence(1)  & arousal(0)  & dominance(0).
9   emotion(delighted)  :- valence(1)  & arousal(1)  & dominance(0).
```

4.1   VAD Emotions in Jason

Emotions are implemented as beliefs inside an agent. An agent believes it has a certain level of valence, arousal and dominance, and it works out its emotional state based on a combination of these three factors. When the audience cheers or boos them, this changes the belief holding the relevant emotional variable, and their emotional state as a whole is recalculated.

Valence, arousal and dominance values can take values of -1 (low), 0 (medium) or 1 (high). Listing 1.1 shows the emotional belief rules for an agent with medium dominance (a dominance level of 0). Note that an agent maintains beliefs about both its current emotion label (such as sleepy or happy) and the separate valence, arousal and dominance values at the same time. Similar sets of rules handle the belief emotion for the other dominance levels.

Every time an emotional variable (valence, arousal, or dominance) changes, an agent's emotion is changed according to the rules in Listing 1.1. While an agent's valence, arousal and dominance belief values affect the way it makes decisions internally, the results of combinations of these values (sleepy, happy, etc.) are broadcast as external actions. The reason for this is that an agent's emotional state may affect the way in which the character is animated: changing the speed at which they move or turning their smile into a frown, for example. For this reason, whenever an emotional change takes place, the new emotion is published as an external action of the agent so that observing entities may perceive it. The Bath sensor framework described in Sect. 6 provides the means for this evidence of the agent's internal state change to be received by the animation system and reflected accordingly in the display.

Listing 1.2 shows the AgentSpeak rules describing how an agent's valence and dominance levels are changed by the audience cheering or booing their actions. These AgentSpeak plans describe what the agent should do in response to a goal addition (denoted by a +! at the start of the plan name) or a belief addition (prefixed by a simple +). In the case of Listing 1.2, the +!changeMood plan updates the agent's emotional state based on its valence-arousal-dominance values and broadcasts the result as an external action. The +response plans raise or lower an agent's valence and dominance levels depending on whether the agent perceives a "boo" or "cheer" response from the audience.

An agent announces what they intend to do, then waits three seconds. During this time, they have the belief that they are 'asking' the audience, and listen for

Listing 1.2. AgentSpeak rules for changing an agent's emotional values from audience responses

```
1    +!changeMood
2        <- ?emotion(Z);
3            emotion(Z).
4    +response(_, boo) : asking
5        <- -+valence(-1);
6            -+dominance(-1);
7            !changeMood.
8    +response(_, cheer) : asking
9        <- -+valence(1);
10           -+dominance(1);
11           !changeMood.
```

a response. A boo reduces an agent's valence and dominance, while a cheer raises them. For each response, the **changeMood** goal is triggered, which looks up and broadcasts the agent's emotional state to the other agents and environment.

5   Agent Decision Making

The agents choose which goals to pursue according to three factors: their permitted actions, their obliged actions and their emotional state. Though obliged actions are given priority, and while agents' decisions are generally constrained by their permitted actions, an agent's emotional state has the final say in its decisions. In this way, an agent will follow the social norms of the narrative, but only according to their own mood.

Agent Goals and Plans. The agents are implemented using a belief-desire-intention (BDI) psychological model using the Jason platform [4]. An agent's knowledge about the state of their world and themselves are stored as *beliefs*, with new information coming in from the environment getting added to their belief base as *percepts*, which are ephemeral and only last for one reasoning cycle of an agent.

Agents are created with goals and plan libraries. Any goal that an agent is set on carrying out at any point is an *intention*, whereas a goal that an agent has but is not yet pursuing is a *desire*. Plan libraries describe the steps agents need to take in order to achieve goals, as well as how to react to changes in agents' environments.

Norms as Percepts. When an event occurs, it is added to the event timeline, which is used to query the ASP (Answer Set Programming) solver to obtain the set of norms that hold after the new event has occurred. The new permissions and obligations are then added to each agent as *percepts*. Each time this happens, the set of permitted and obliged actions that an agent sees is changed to be only those that apply at that instant in time, with the previous norms being discarded.

Agents choose between permitted and obliged actions based on their emotional state at the point of decision making. Obliged actions are given a higher priority over permitted ones for most of the emotional states that an agent can be in, though not always. If an agent is in a sulky mood, for example, they may decide to ignore what they are obliged to do by the narrative, even though they know there will be consequences.

For example, in the scene where Joey gives the sausages to Punch, Punch may see that he has permission to eat the sausages, drop them, fight the crocodile, run away (leave the stage) or shout for help at the crocodile or audience. His obligation for the scene, in accordance with the Punch and Judy narrative world, is to either eat the sausages himself, or let the crocodile have them. This ends Propp's *interdiction* story function with a *violation* function. Note that his obligation in this case is not to guard the sausages as asked to by Joey. While Joey's entrusting of the sausages is certainly an obligation in itself, Punch's main obligations are to the narrative. Lesser obligations towards characters in the story can be implemented as having a lower priority than those of the story itself.

Similarly, at times of extreme emotion, an agent may decide to disregard their set of permitted actions entirely, instead acting out their innermost desires. For example, an angry Punch might decide to just attack Joey instead of agreeing to look after the sausages, or he might just decide to give up and leave if he is depressed. The key point is that the norms act as the will of the *narrative*, guiding the story forward, rather than a strict set of rules that the agents must follow at all costs.

Violation events add percepts to the agents telling them that they are in violation of the narrative norms. Once an agent receives such a percept, an emotional variable is changed. Typically, their dominance will decrease. The reasoning behind this is that if agents are unwilling to participate in the story, they should have less influence in its course of events.

6   Architecture

Multi-agent System. We use the JASON framework for belief-desire-intention (BDI) agents [4], programming our agents in the AgentSpeak language. The VAD emotional model is represented inside each agent as a set of beliefs. Each agent has beliefs for its *valence, arousal* and *dominance* levels, each of which can take the value of low, medium or high, as discussed in Sect. 4. This combination of VAD values creates one of the 27 emotional states shown in Fig. 5, affecting whether or not an agent breaks from its permitted or obliged behaviour.

Institutional Framework. To describe our institutional model, we use InstAL [7], a domain-specific (action) language for describing institutions that compiles to AnsProlog, a declarative programming language for Answer Set Programming (ASP). InstAL's semantics are inspired by the Situation Calculus [24] and the Event Calculus [13]. InstAL describes how external events generate institutional events, which then initiate or terminate fluents that hold at certain points in time.

These fluents can include the permissions and obligations that describe what an agent is permitted or obliged to do when, as described in Sect. 3. For example, if an agent with the role of *dispatcher* leaves the stage, it generates the Propp *absentation* move in the institution, but only if the *interdiction* function is active (i.e., the *activeFunction(interdiction)* fluent holds):

```
1   leaveStage(X) generates intAbsentation(X)
2       if role(X, dispatcher), activeFunction(interdiction);
```

Listing 1.3. Encoding of Propp's *absentation* function

```
1   intAbsentation(X) initiates activeFunction(
        absentation);
2   intAbsentation(X) initiates perm(harm(Y, Z)) if
        role(Y, villain), objStage(Z), onStage(Y),
        activeFunction(interdiction);
3   intAbsentation(X) initiates perm(harm(Y, Z)) if
        role(Y, ambusher), objStage(Z), onStage(Y),
        activeFunction(interdiction);
4   intAbsentation(X) initiates perm(enterStage(X)),
        activeFunction(absentation);
5   intAbsentation(X) initiates perm(enterStage(croc)
        ) if objStage(sausages);
6   intAbsentation(X) terminates onStage(X), perm(
        leaveStage(X));
```

> The *activeFunction(absentation)* function holds after any *intAbsentation* institutional event, indicating that that Propp function is currently underway

> The *absentation* function gives the villain permission to harm an object, if both are on stage and the *interdiction* function is active

> Same as above, but for *ambusher* role

> The absented character has permission to re-enter the stage at any point during the *absentation* function

> The crocodile has permission to enter the stage if the sausages are on stage

> The *absentation* function means that the absented character is no longer on stage, and cannot leave the stage (as they have already done so)

which generates the following AnsProlog code:

```
1   occurred(intAbsentation(X),pj,I) :-
2       occurred(leaveStage(X),pj,I),
3       holdsat(pow(pj,intAbsentation(X)),pj,I),
4       holdsat(role(X,donor),pj,I),
5       holdsat(activeFunction(interdiction),pj,I),
6       agent(X), inst(pj), instant(I).
```

> The internal *absentation* event occurs if the following conditions are met:
> - X leaves the stage
> - X has the power to leave the stage
> - X has the role of donor
> - the *interdiction* function is active
> - X is an agent, pj is an institution, I is an instant

The *absentation* institutional event gives the crocodile permission to enter the stage if there are any sausages on the stage. It also terminates the permission of the absented agent to leave the stage, as they have already done so:

```
1   intAbsentation(X) initiates perm(enterStage(croc)
        ) if objStage(sausages);
2   intAbsentation(X) terminates onStage(X), perm(
        leaveStage(X));
```

> The *absentation* function gives the crocodile permission to enter the stage if the sausages are on stage

> The *absentation* function means that once X leaves the stage, they are no longer on stage

which generates the following:

```
1    initiated(perm(enterStage(croc)),pj,I) :-
2        occurred(intAbsentation(X),pj,I),
3        holdsat(live(pj),pj,I), inst(pj),
4        holdsat(objStage(sausages),pj,I),
5        agent(X), inst(pj), instant(I).
```

The crocodile gets permission to enter the stage if the following conditions are met:

- the *absentation* function event has occured

- the pj institution is running

- the sausages are on stage

The show has started

The sausages scene has started

Punch has entered the stage

Joey has entered the stage

Listing 1.4. Possible full trace for sausages scene

```
1    observed(startShow,pj,0).
2    observed(startScene(sausages),pj,1).
3    observed(enterStage(punch),pj,2).
4    observed(enterStage(joey),pj,3).
5    observed(say(joey,  give),pj,4).
6    observed(say(joey,  protect),pj,5).
7    observed(give(joey,punch,sausages),pj,6).
8    observed(leaveStage(joey),pj,7).
9    observed(say(punch, harm),pj,8).
10   observed(enterStage(croc),pj,9).
11   observed(take(croc,  sausages),pj,10).
12   observed(eat(croc,  sausages),pj,11).
13   observed(leaveStage(croc),pj,12).
14   observed(enterStage(joey),pj,13).
15   observed(hit(joey,  punch),pj,14).
16   observed(leaveStage(joey),pj,15).
17   observed(leaveStage(punch),pj,16).
18   observed(startScene(end),pj,17).
```

Joey says he will give Punch the sausages

Joey tells Punch to protect the sausages

Joey gives the sausages to Punch

Joey leaves the stage

Punch says he will eat the sausages

The crocodile enters the stage

The crocodile takes the sausages

The crocodile eats the sausages

The crocodile leaves the stage

Joey enters the stage

Joey hits Punch

Joey leaves the stage

Punch leaves the stage

The scene ends

By combining statements such as the above, we can build a complete description of the sausages scene in terms of agent norms, such as the Propp *absentation* function, shown in Listing 1.3. InstAL rules like those shown above and in Listing 1.3 are compiled into AnsProlog, then we use the *clingo* answer set solver [10] to ground the program, and 'solve' queries by finding all permissions and obligations that apply to any agents, given a sequence of events as the query input. The agents' percepts are then updated with their permitted and obliged actions from that time instant onwards. Thus, the institutional model acts as a social narrative sensor, interpreting actors' actions in the context of the combination of the concrete narrative and the abstract story moves which detach (instantiate) the norms that guide the actors in the direction of the conclusion of the story arc.

A query is simply a list of external events in chronological order, also called a *trace*. A possible trace describing the actions of agents acting out the *sausages* is described in Listing 1.4. The 'pj' in the trace is the name of the institution that observes the events, while the number is the enumeration of events in the sequence.

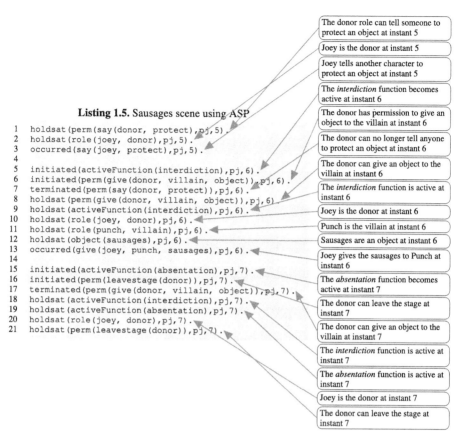

Listing 1.5. Sausages scene using ASP

```
1   holdsat(perm(say(donor, protect),pj,5).
2   holdsat(role(joey, donor),pj,5).
3   occurred(say(joey, protect),pj,5).
4
5   initiated(activeFunction(interdiction),pj,6).
6   initiated(perm(give(donor, villain, object)),pj,6).
7   terminated(perm(say(donor, protect)),pj,6).
8   holdsat(perm(give(donor, villain, object)),pj,6).
9   holdsat(activeFunction(interdiction),pj,6).
10  holdsat(role(joey, donor),pj,6).
11  holdsat(role(punch, villain),pj,6).
12  holdsat(object(sausages),pj,6).
13  occurred(give(joey, punch, sausages),pj,6).
14
15  initiated(activeFunction(absentation),pj,7).
16  initiated(perm(leavestage(donor)),pj,7).
17  terminated(perm(give(donor, villain, object)),pj,7).
18  holdsat(activeFunction(interdiction),pj,7).
19  holdsat(activeFunction(absentation),pj,7).
20  holdsat(role(joey, donor),pj,7).
21  holdsat(perm(leavestage(donor)),pj,7).
```

The callout boxes read:

- The donor role can tell someone to protect an object at instant 5
- Joey is the donor at instant 5
- Joey tells another character to protect an object at instant 5
- The *interdiction* function becomes active at instant 6
- The donor has permission to give an object to the villain at instant 6
- The donor can no longer tell anyone to protect an object at instant 6
- The donor can give an object to the villain at instant 6
- The *interdiction* function is active at instant 6
- Joey is the donor at instant 6
- Punch is the villain at instant 6
- Sausages are an object at instant 6
- Joey gives the sausages to Punch at instant 6
- The *absentation* function becomes active at instant 7
- The donor can leave the stage at instant 7
- The donor can give an object to the villain at instant 7
- The *interdiction* function is active at instant 7
- The *absentation* function is active at instant 7
- Joey is the donor at instant 7
- The donor can leave the stage at instant 7

Each *observed* event triggers a corresponding *occurs* event inside the institution, as determined by the generates relation. Listing 1.5 shows an extract from an answer set output for the trace queried against the ASP description of the sausages scenario, for events 5 to 7 of the scene. Starting with an initial set of fluents that hold at instant 5, only fluents that have been initiated and not terminated hold at the next instant. For ease of reading, the listing only shows roles that hold at certain instants when they have some effect on the scene, although in practice, all role fluents hold throughout the scene. Figure 6 shows a visualisation of the answer set for the trace in Listing 1.4.

Bath Sensor Framework. The components communicate using the Bath Sensor Framework (BSF) [14], through publish/subscribe-style communication between distributed software components, in this case connecting intelligent agents with their virtual environments. It currently uses the XMPP publish/subscribe protocol for communication between agents, environment and other software components. Each agent subscribes to receive notifications of environment changes via the appropriate topic node in the XMPP server, which relays messages between publishers and subscribers. If any environment change occurs, all subscribed agents are informed of the changes.

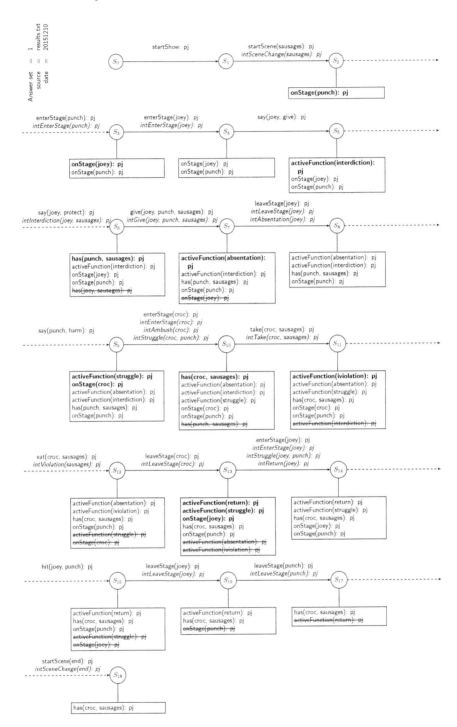

Fig. 6. Trace visualisation

Audience Interaction. The puppet show is designed to be run in front of either a single user's computer, or on a large display in front of an audience. The user/audience is instructed to cheer or boo the actions of the characters of the show, which will be picked up by a microphone and 'heard' by the agents. This will then affect the emotional state of the agents and change the actions they make in the show. Their actions are constrained by the set of 'Punch and Judy' world norms as described in the institutional model.

There are many different ways in which the audience's responses can affect the outcomes of the show. If the audience craves a more 'traditional' Punch and Judy experience, then they can cheer Punch into beating and killing all of his adversaries (including his wife, Judy). Alternatively, a more mischievous audience could goad Judy into killing Punch and then taking over his role as sadist and killer for the rest of the show. The narrative outcomes are dependent on how the audience responds to the action, yet still conform to the rules of the Punch and Judy story world.

Fig. 7. A screenshot of the Punch and Judy show

The animation engine that shows the visual output of the agents actions is written in Javascript and the Phaser game framework. It runs entirely in a browser, and communicates with BSF using the Strophe XMPP library.

If the user allows the program access to their microphone, they can cheer or boo the actions of the agents by shouting into the microphone. Otherwise, they can simulate these actions by clicking on 'cheer' or 'boo' buttons at the bottom of the screen (Fig. 7).

7   Related Work

Many approaches exist for creating interactive drama using agents as characters. Carnegie Mellon's OZ project [20] is one of the first major research efforts to use agents for interactive narrative. A dramatic structure is given to the narrative by means of a *drama manager*, which is able to see all of the actions occurring in the story world and can change anything in order to create a better experience for the user. While a drama manager rigidly enforces agents to conform to the expectations of a story, our approach differs in that it regulates the agents, allowing them some degree of agency. This allows the agents to break from the set of actions suggested by a story function. If multiple institutions present alternative sets of story functions to the agents as norms, then this means that the agents would have some freedom to change the course of the story, while the institutions ensure a coherent narrative.

Ideas from the OZ project were later developed into what became Mateas's and Stern's *Façade*, where players interact with the characters of the story through natural language. In this game, the player attends the party of a young couple (Grace and Trip) celebrating their wedding anniversary. As the course of events unfold however, the player learns that all is not as happy as it seems.

In Façade, the smallest unit of narrative action is called a *story beat*, taken from McKee's book on authorial style for screenwriters [21]. The simulation constantly monitors what the user is doing and how it may lead from the current story beat to another. Story beats have preconditions and effects on the state of the narrative, so it is the drama manager's job to work out when it makes sense to initiate a certain beat. They can be thought as analogous to Propp's story functions, but in contrast to the work presented here, operate at a lower level of abstraction, describing specific agent goals and the steps needed to achieve them. Our use of norms allows abstract story components to be written without the need to write agent goals for story events. Instead, their existing plans are governed by institutions, and guided towards taking actions to fulfil the story components.

Riedl and Young make much use of agents and planners in their work on interactive narrative. Addressing the problem of balancing character believability with plot coherence, they present a planner-based solution for story generation [25]. Their planner is described as an 'intent-driven partial order causal link' planner, planning actions for agents in a multi-agent system based on causality and intention. In this case, *intention* refers to a component of agents based on the Belief Desire Intention (BDI) framework. Their planner observes the actions of the agents in the system and infers their intentions. While their planners have the flexibility to revise their plans based on user interactions, they still rely on an author creating all possible alternative plans that allow the agents to act out a story. Again, our use of institutions allows for story authoring on a higher level, where an author need not be concerned with writing plans.

8   Conclusions and Future Work

With our approach to interactive narrative generation, we regulate the rules of the story domain using an institutional model. This model describes what each agent is permitted and obliged to do at any point in the story. This approach alone would be too rigid, however. The audience's interactions (cheering or booing) may alter the course of the narrative, but the agents would still have blindly to follow a pre-determined set of paths. By giving our agents emotional models that change their willingness to follow the narrative, a degree of unpredictability enters each performance, giving the impression that the agents are indeed characters capable of free will. The VAD emotional model is essentially reactive and quite simplistic. A more deeply-rooted emotional response, perhaps better aligned with BDI, could be achieved, based on the appraisal theory of emotion.

We also note that Propp's formalism is very specific to Russian folktales and could be replaced with something more general, such as Lehnert's story functions [16]. Cavazza et al. [6] suggest the use of Linear Logic as a promising possibility for narrative formalisation, with Martens et al. [19] exploring its use further.

In our current approach, we describe the use of institutions for the modelling of narrative. There are two major unconsidered aspects in the current implementation, namely how to manage multiple scenes and how to preserve information between scenes.

The current Propp-based method is only suitable for modelling either one scene per institution or the complete narrative as a fixed sequence of scenes as one institution. Either way, the order of scenes is not governed in any way, but is pre-determined, whereas to create a truly non-linear narrative, the sequence must be changeable as the simulation or game is running. A solution would be a mechanism to coordinate multiple institutions dynamically, but still according to some higher level narrative. [12] describe the use of *metanorms* or *higher-order norms* to enable institutions to govern other institutions, which could be applied in InstAL to create a multi-tier institution for narrative.

A second issue is how to retain information between scenes: if a set of narrative events have occurred in one scene, their consequences often need to be carried over to other scenes, which implies the transfer of fluents between institutions. [17] describe a mechanism to bridge institutions, which could be used to control the flow of events and facts between institution instances.

In meeting both these requirements, a *hierarchy* of institutions is needed to govern the narrative world: a kind of 'scene director' institution to manage the flow between scene institutions, and a means to share information in order to achieve narrative consistency and persistence. Such a combination of multi-tiered and co-operating institutions offers the potential for the generation of a much richer way of regulating narrative events in a multi-agent system. The simple proof-of-concept set out in this paper provides a first step towards developing an institutional model for narrative as well as a preliminary validation of the WIT model.

References

1. Ahn, J., Gobron, S., Garcia, D., Silvestre, Q., Thalmann, D., Boulic, R.: An NVC emotional model for conversational virtual humans in a 3D chatting environment. In: Perales, F.J., Fisher, R.B., Moeslund, T.B. (eds.) AMDO 2012. LNCS, vol. 7378, pp. 47–57. Springer, Heidelberg (2012)
2. Artikis, A., Sergot, M., Pitt, J.: Specifying norm-governed computational societies. ACM Trans. Comput. Logic (TOCL) **10**(1), 1 (2009)
3. Blanco-Vigil, P.C.N.: Agent mediated auctions: the fishmarket metaphor. Ph.D. thesis, Universitat Autònoma de Barcelona (1998)
4. Bordini, R.H., Hübner, J.F., Wooldridge, M.: Programming Multi-Agent Systems in AgentSpeak Using Jason. Wiley, New York (2007)
5. Cardoso, H.L., Oliveira, E.: Institutional reality and norms: specifying and monitoring agent organizations. Int. J. Coop. Inf. Syst. **16**(01), 67–95 (2007)

6. Cavazza, M., Champagnat, R., Leonardi, R.: The IRIS network of excellence: future directions in interactive storytelling. In: Iurgel, I.A., Zagalo, N., Petta, P. (eds.) ICIDS 2009. LNCS, vol. 5915, pp. 8–13. Springer, Heidelberg (2009)

7. Cliffe, O., De Vos, M., Padget, J.: Specifying and reasoning about multiple institutions. In: Noriega, P., Vázquez-Salceda, J., Boella, G., Boissier, O., Dignum, V., Fornara, N., Matson, E. (eds.) COIN 2006. LNCS (LNAI), vol. 4386, pp. 67–85. Springer, Heidelberg (2007). ISBN: 978-3-540-74457-3. http://dx.doi.org/10.1007/978-3-540-74459-7_5

8. Crawford, C.: Chris Crawford on Interactive Storytelling. New Riders, Indianapolis (2012)

9. Fornara, N., Viganò, F., Colombetti, M.: Agent communication and artificial institutions. Auton. Agent. Multi-Agent Syst. **14**(2), 121–142 (2007)

10. Gebser, M., Kaufmann, B., Kaminski, R., Ostrowski, M., Schaub, T., Schneider, M.: Potassco: the potsdam answer set solving collection. AI Commun. **24**(2), 107–124 (2011)

11. Jones, A.J., Sergot, M.: A formal characterisation of institutionalised power. Logic J. IGPL **4**(3), 427–443 (1996)

12. King, T.C., Li, T., Vos, M.D., Dignum, V., Jonker, C.M., Padget, J., van Riemsdijk, M.B.: A framework for institutions governing institutions. In: Weiss, G., Yolum, P., Bordini, R. H., Elkind, E. (eds.) Proceedings of the 2015 International Conference on Autonomous Agents and Multiagent Systems, AAMAS 2015, 4–8 May, 2015, Istanbul, Turkey, pp. 473–481. ACM (2015)

13. Kowalski, R., Sergot, M.: A logic-based calculus of events. In: Kowalski, R., Sergot, M. (eds.) Foundations of Knowledge Base Management. Topics in Information Systems. Springer, Heidelberg (1989)

14. Lee, J., Baines, V., Padget, J.: Decoupling cognitive agents and virtual environments. In: Dignum, F., Brom, C., Hindriks, K., Beer, M., Richards, D. (eds.) CAVE 2012. LNCS, vol. 7764, pp. 17–36. Springer, Heidelberg (2013)

15. Lee, S., Mott, B., Lester, J.: Learning director agent strategies: an inductive framework for modeling director agents. In: AAAI Conference on Artificial Intelligence and Interactive Digital Entertainment (2011). http://aaai.org/ocs/index.php/AIIDE/AIIDE11WS/paper/view/4107. Accessed June 2015

16. Lehnert, W.G.: Plot units and narrative summarization. Cognitive Sci. **5**(4), 293–331 (1981)

17. Li, T.: Normative conflict detection and resolution in cooperating institutions. In: 23rd International Joint Conference on Artificial Intelligence (IJCAI 2013), pp. 3231–3232 (2013). See also [18]

18. Li, T.: Normative Conflict Detection and Resolution in Cooperating Institutions. Ph.D. thesis, University of Bath, July 2014

19. Martens, C., Bosser, A.-G., Ferreira, J.F., Cavazza, M.: Linear logic programming for narrative generation. In: Cabalar, P., Son, T.C. (eds.) LPNMR 2013. LNCS, vol. 8148, pp. 427–432. Springer, Heidelberg (2013)

20. Mateas, M.: An Oz-centric review of interactive drama and believable agents. In: Veloso, M.M., Wooldridge, M.J. (eds.) Artificial Intelligence Today. LNCS (LNAI), vol. 1600, pp. 297–328. Springer, Heidelberg (1999)

21. McKee, R.: Substance, Structure, Style, and the Principles of Screenwriting. HarperCollins, New York (1997)

22. Noriega, P., Padget, J., Verhagen, H., d'Inverno, M.: Towards a framework for socio-cognitive technical systems. In: Ghose, A., Oren, N., Telang, P., Thangarajah, J. (eds.) Coordination, Organizations, Institutions, and Norms in Agent Systems X. LNCS, vol. 9372, pp. 164–181. Springer, Switzerland (2015)

23. Propp, V.: Morphology of the Folktale, 2nd edn. University of Texas Press, Austin (1968). 1928, Trans. Svatava Pirkova-Jakobson
24. Reiter, R.: The frame problem in the situation calculus: a simple solution (sometimes) and a completeness result for goal regression. Artif. Intell. Math. Theor. Comput. Papers Honor John McCarthy **27**, 359–380 (1991)
25. Riedl, M.O., Young, R.M.: An intent-driven planner for multi-agent story generation. In: Proceedings of the Third International Joint Conference on Autonomous Agents and Multiagent Systems, vol. 1, pp. 186–193. IEEE Computer Society (2004)
26. Robertson, J., Young, R.: Modelling character knowledge in plan-based interactive narrative to extend accomodative mediation. In: Paper Presented at AIIDE Workshop (2013)
27. Russell, J.A.: A circumplex model of affect. J. Pers. Soc. Psychol. **39**(6), 1161 (1980)
28. Thompson, M., Padget, J., Battle, S.: Governing narrative events with institutional norms. In: Finlayson, M. A., Miller, B., Lieto, A., Ronfard, R., (eds.) 6th Workshop on Computational Models of Narrative (CMN 2015), vol. 45 of OpenAccess Series in Informatics (OASIcs), pp. 142–151, Dagstuhl, Germany. Schloss Dagstuhl-Leibniz-Zentrum fuer Informatik (2015)
29. Tomaszewski, Z.: On the use of reincorporation in interactive drama. In: Proceedings AAAI Conference on Artificial Intelligence and Interactive Digital Entertainment. http://aaai.org/ocs/index.php/AIIDE/AIIDE11WS/paper/view/4106. Accessed 9 June 2015

Quantified Degrees of Group Responsibility

Vahid Yazdanpanah$^{(\boxtimes)}$ and Mehdi Dastani

Utrecht University, Utrecht, The Netherlands
v.yazdanpanah@students.uu.nl, m.m.dastani@uu.nl

Abstract. This paper builds on an existing notion of group responsibility and proposes two ways to define the degree of group responsibility: *structural* and *functional* degrees of responsibility. These notions measure potential responsibilities of agent groups for avoiding a state of affairs. According to these notions, a degree of responsibility for a state of affairs can be assigned to a group of agents if, and to the extent that, the group of the agents have potential to preclude the state of affairs. These notions will be formally specified and their properties will be analyzed.

1 Introduction

The concept of responsibility has been extensively investigated in philosophy and computer science. Each proposal focuses on specific aspects of responsibility. For example, [1] focuses on the causal aspect of responsibility and defines a notion of graded responsibility, [2] focuses on the organizational aspect of responsibility, [3] argues that group responsibility should be distributed to individual responsibility, [4] focuses on the interaction aspect of responsibility and defines an agent's responsibility in terms of the agent's causal contribution, and [5] focuses on the strategic aspect of group responsibility and defines various notions of group responsibility. In some of these proposals, the concept of responsibility is defined with respect to a realized event "in past" while in other approaches it is defined as the responsibility for the realization of some event "in future". This introduces a major dimension of responsibility, namely backward-looking and forward-looking responsibility [6]. Backward-looking approaches reason about level of causality or contribution of agents in the occurrence of an already realized outcome while forward-looking notions are focused on the capacities of agents towards a state of affairs.

Although some of the existing approaches are designed to measure the degree of responsibility, they either constitute a backward-looking (instead of forward-looking) notion of responsibility [1], provide qualitative (instead of quantitative) levels of responsibility [7,8], or focus on individual (instead of group) responsibility [4]. To our knowledge, there is no forward-looking approach that could measure the degree of group responsibility quantitatively. Such notion would enable reasoning on the potential responsibility of an agent group towards a state of affairs in strategic settings, e.g., collective decision making scenarios. In this paper, we build on a forward-looking approach to group responsibility and

© Springer International Publishing Switzerland 2016
V. Dignum et al. (Eds.): COIN 2015, LNAI 9628, pp. 418–436, 2016.
DOI: 10.1007/978-3-319-42691-4_23

define two notions of responsibility degrees. The first concept is based on the partial or complete power of an agent group to preclude a state of affairs while the second concept is based on the potentiality of an agent group to reach a state where the agent group possesses the complete power to preclude the state of affairs. This results in a distinction between what we will call the "structural responsibility" versus the "functional responsibility" of an agent group. In our proposal, an agent group has the full responsibility, if it has an action profile to preclude the state of affairs. All other agent groups that do not have full responsibility, but may have contribution to responsible agent groups, will be assigned a partial degree of responsibility.

The paper is structured as follows. In Sect. 2 we provide a brief analysis of the concept of group responsibility from a power-based point of view. Section 3 presents the framework in which our proposed notions will be formally characterized. In Sects. 4 and 5 we introduce the notions that capture our conception of *degree of group responsibility* with respect to a given state of affairs and analyze their properties. Finally, concluding remarks and future work directions will be presented in Sect. 7.

2   Group Responsibility: A Power-Based Analysis

In order to illustrate our conception of group responsibility and the nuances in degrees of responsibility, we follow [1] and use a voting scenario to explain the degree of responsibility of agents' groups for voting outcomes. The voting scenario considers a small congress with ten members consisting of five Democrats (D), three Republicans (R), and two Greens (G). We assume that there is a voting in progress on a specific bill (B). Without losing generality and to reduce the combinatorial complexity of the setting, we assume that all members of a party vote either in favour of or against the bill B. Table 1 illustrates the eight possible voting outcomes. Note that in this scenario, six positive votes are sufficient for the approval of B. For example, row 4 shows the case where R and D vote against B and the bill is disapproved. For this case we say that the group RD votes against B. It should also be noted that our assumption reduces parties to individual agents with specific weights such that the question raises as why we use this party setting instead of a simple voting of three agents whose votes have different weights. The motivation is that this setting is realistic and makes the weighted votes of each agent (party) more intuitive.

Following [5] we believe that it is reasonable to assign the responsibility for a specific state of affairs to a group of agents if they jointly have the power to avoid the state of affairs[1]. According to [9], the preclusive power is the ability of a group to preclude a given state of affairs which entails that a group with preclusive power, has the potential but might not practice the preclusion of a given state of affairs. For our voting scenario, this suggests to assign responsibility to the group GR consisting of parties G and R since they can jointly

---

[1] See [5] for a detailed discussion on why to focus on avoiding instead of enforcing a state of affairs.

Table 1. Voting results

	G(2)	R(3)	D(5)	Result
0	−	−	−	✗
1	−	−	+.	✗
2	−	+	−	✗
3	−	+	+	✓
4	+	−	−	✗
5	+	−	+	✓
6	+	+	−	✗
7	+	+	+	✓

Table 2. War incidence

	Congress	President	War
0	−	−	✗
1	−	+	✗
2	+	−	✗
3	+	+	✓

disapprove B. Note that the state of affair to be avoided can also be the state of affairs where B is disapproved. In this case, the group can be assigned the responsibility to avoid disproving B. Similarly, groups D, GD, RD, and GRD have preclusive power with respect to the approval of B as they have sufficient members (weights) to avoid the approval of B. Note that none of the other two groups, i.e., G and R, could preclude the approval of B independently. However, based on [5], the agent groups that consist of a smaller sub-group with preclusive power, must be excluded from the set of responsible groups. Hence, we consider GR and D as being responsible groups for the approval of B. The intuition for this concept of responsibility is supported by the fact that the lobby groups are willing (i.e., it is economically rational) to invest resources in parties that have the power to avoid a specific state of affairs.

We build on the ideas in [5] and propose two orthogonal approaches to capture our conception of *degree* of group responsibility towards a state of affairs. Our intuition suggests that the *degree* of responsibility of a group of agents towards a state of affairs should reflect the extent they structurally or functionally can contribute to the groups that have preclusive power with respect to the state of affairs. In the sequel, we will explain the conception of *degree of responsibility* according to the structural and functional approaches, and illustrate both approaches by means of our voting scenario example.

Our conception of *structural responsibility degree* is based on the following observation in the voting scenario. We deem that regarding the approval of B, although the groups G and R have no preclusive power independently, they nevertheless have a share in the composition of GR with preclusive power regarding the approval of B. Hence, we say that any group that shares members with responsible groups, should be assigned a degree of responsibility that reflects its proportional contribution to the groups with preclusive power. For example, group R with three members, has larger share in GR than the group G has. Therefore, we believe that the relative size of a group and its share in the groups with the preclusive power are substantial parameters in formulation of the notion of responsibility degree. In this case, the larger share of R in GR in comparison with the share of G in GR will be positively reflected in R's responsibility degree. These parameters will be explained in details later. We would like to emphasize that this concept of responsibility degree is supported by the fact that lobby groups do proportionally support political parties that can play a role in some key decisions. In a sense, the lobby groups consider political parties responsible for some decision and therefore they are willing to support the parties.

The second approach in capturing the notion of *functional responsibility degree* addresses the dynamics of preclusive power of a specific group. Suppose that the bill B was about declaration of the congress to the President (P) which enables P to start a war (Table 2). Roughly speaking, P will be in charge only after the approval of the congress. When we are reasoning at the moment when the voting is in progress in the congress, it is reasonable to assume that groups GR and D are responsible as they have preclusive power to avoid the war. Moreover, after the approval of B, the President P is the only group with preclusive power to avoid the war. Hence, we believe that although P alone would not have the preclusive power before the approval of B in the congress, it is rationally justifiable for an anti-war campaign to invest resources on P, even before the approval voting of the congress, simply because there exists possibilities where P will have the preclusive power to avoid the war. Accordingly, a reasonable differentiation could be made between the groups which do have the chance of acquiring the preclusive power and those they do not have any chance of power acquisition. This functional notion of responsibility degree addresses the eventuality of a state in which an agent group possesses the preclusive power regarding a given state of affairs.

Note that following [5], our notions of group responsibility are locally bounded as they will be defined with respect to some source state. Hence, a group might be responsible in a specific state and not responsible in the other states regarding a given state of affairs. Additionally, our proposed notions for responsibility degree have dependency to the global setting. In the voting scenario, the global setting that ten voters are situated in three parties of G (2 members), R (3 members) and D (5 members), is crucial for the responsibility degrees that are assigned to various groups. Any change in the global setting may alter the responsibility degree of various groups. For example, when two members of the Republican party secede from R and form a new Tea Party T, we face a different global setting, which in turn causes the responsibility degrees assigned to various groups to change. This is due to the fact that the new setting introduces new groups such as RGT with preclusive power regarding the approval of B. Our analysis is not limited to the voting scenarios, but can be applied to other situations as shown later in this paper.

3   Models and Preliminary Notions

The behaviour of a multi-agent system is often modelled by concurrent game structures (CGS) [10]. Such structures specify possible state of the system, agents' abilities at each state, and the outcome of concurrent actions at each state.

Definition 1 (Concurrent game structures [10]). *A concurrent game structure is a tuple $M = (N, Q, Act, d, o)$, where $N = \{1, ..., k\}$ is a nonempty finite set of agents, Q is a nonempty set of system states, Act is a nonempty and finite set of atomic actions, $d : N \times Q \to \mathcal{P}(Act)$ is a function that identifies the set of available actions for each agent $i \in N$ at each state $q \in Q$, and o is a deterministic and partial transition function that assigns a state $q' = o(q, \alpha_1, ..., \alpha_k)$ to a state q and an action profile $(\alpha_1, ..., \alpha_k)$ such that all k agents in N choose actions in the action profile respectively. An action profile $\bar{\alpha} = (\alpha_1, ..., \alpha_k)$ is a sequence that consists of actions $\alpha_i \in d(i, q)$ for all players in N. In case $o(q, \alpha_1, ..., \alpha_k)$ is undefined then $o(q, \alpha'_1, ..., \alpha'_k)$ is undefined for each action profile $(\alpha'_1, ..., \alpha'_k)$. For the sake of notation simplicity, $d(i, q)$ will be written as $d_i(q)$ and $d_C(q) := \prod_{i \in C} d_i(q)$.*

A *state of affairs* refers to a set $S \subseteq Q$, $\bar{S}$ denotes the set $Q \backslash S$, and $(\alpha_C, \alpha_{N \backslash C})$ denotes the action profile, where α_C is the actions of the agents in group C and $\alpha_{N \backslash C}$ denotes the actions of the rest of the agents. Following the setting of [5], we recall the definitions of *q-enforce*, *q-avoid*, *q-responsible* and *weakly q-responsible* (See [5] for details and properties of these notions).

Definition 2 (Agent groups: strategic abilities and responsibility [5]). *Let $M = (N, Q, Act, d, o)$ be a CGS, $q \in Q$ be a specific state, and S a state of affairs. We have the following concepts.*

1. *$C \subseteq N$ can q-enforce S in M iff there is a joint action $\alpha_C \in d_C(q)$ such that for all joint actions $\alpha_{N \backslash C} \in d_{N \backslash C}(q)$, $o(q, (\alpha_C, \alpha_{N \backslash C})) \in S$.*
2. *$C \subseteq N$ can q-avoid S in M iff for all $\alpha_{N \backslash C} \in d_{N \backslash C}(q)$ there is $\alpha_C \in d_C(q)$ such that $o(q, (\alpha_C, \alpha_{N \backslash C})) \in \bar{S}$.*
3. *$C \subseteq N$ is q-responsible for S in M iff C can q-enforce $\bar{S}$ and for all other $C' \subseteq N$ that can q-enforce $\bar{S}$, we have that $C \subseteq C'$.*
4. *$C \subseteq N$ is weakly q-responsible for S in M^2 iff C is a minimal group that can q-enforce $\bar{S}$.*

Considering the voting scenario from Sect. 2, groups GD, RD and GRD can q_s-enforce the approval of B while groups D, GR, GD, RD, and GRD can q_s-avoid the approval of B. In this scenario, q_s denotes the starting moment of the voting progress. Note that the notions of q-enforce and q-avoid correlate with the notions of, respectively, α-effectivity and β-effectivity in [11]. In this scenario, we have no q_s-responsible group for approval of B and two groups D and GR are weakly q_s-responsible for the approval of B. Note that the groups GD, RD, and GRD are not weakly q_s-responsible for the approval of B as they are not minimal.

The concept of (weakly) q-responsibility merely assigns responsibility to groups with preclusive power and considers all other groups as not being responsible. As we have argued in Sect. 2, we believe that responsibility can be assigned to all groups, even those without preclusive power, though to a certain degree

---

^{2} In further references, "in M" might be omitted wherever it is clear from the context.

including zero degree. In order to define our notions of responsibility degree, we first introduce two notions of *structural power difference* and *power acquisition sequence*. Given an arbitrary group C, a state q, and a state of affair S, the first notion concerns the number of missing elements in C that when added to C makes it a (weakly) q-responsible groups for a S, and the second notion concerns a sequence of action profiles from given state q that leads to a state q' where C is (weakly) q'-responsible for S. According to the first notion, group C can gain preclusive power for S if supported by some additional members, and according to the second notion C can gain preclusive power for S in some potentially reachable state.

Let M be a multi-agent system, S a state of affairs in M, C an arbitrary group, and $\hat{C}$ be a (weakly) q-responsible group for S in M.

Definition 3 (Power measures). *We say that the structural power difference of C and $\hat{C}$ in $q \in Q$ with respect to S, denoted by $\Theta_q^{S,M}(\hat{C}, C)$, is equal to cardinality of $\hat{C} \backslash C$. Moreover, we say that C has a power acquisition sequence $\langle \bar{\alpha}_1, ..., \bar{\alpha}_n \rangle$ in $q' \in Q$ for S in M iff for $q_i \in Q$, $o(q_i, \bar{\alpha}_i) = q_{i+1}$ for $1 \leq i \leq n$ such that $q' = q_1$ and $q_{n+1} = q''$ and C is (weakly) q''-responsible for S in M.*

Consider the war approval declaration of the congress to the president (P) in Sect. 2. Here, we can see that the structural power difference of the group G and the weakly q_s-responsible group GR is equal to 3. Moreover, the singleton group P that is not responsible in q_s has the opportunity of being responsible for the war in states other than q_s. Note that power acquisition sequence does not necessarily need to be unique. If the group C is not (weakly) responsible in a state q, the existence of any power acquisition sequence with a length higher than zero implies that the group could potentially reach a state q' (from the current state of q) where C is (weakly) q'-responsible for S. This notion also covers the cases where C is already in a (weakly) responsible state where the minimum length of power acquisition sequence is taken to be zero. In this case, the group is already (weakly) q-responsible for S. For example, in the voting scenario, group D is weakly responsible for the state of affairs and therefore, the minimum length of a power acquisition sequence is zero. When we are reasoning in a source state q, the notion of *power acquisition sequence*, enables us to differentiate between the non (weakly) q-responsible groups that do have the opportunity of becoming (weakly) q'-responsible for a given state of affairs ($q \neq q'$) and those they do not. Moreover, we emphasize that the availability of a *power acquisition sequence* for an arbitrary group C from a source state q to a state q' in which C is (weakly) q-responsible for the state of affairs, does not necessitate the existence of an independent strategy for C to reach q' from q.

4   Structural Degree of Responsibility

Structural degree of responsibility addresses the preclusive power of a group for a given state of affairs by means of the *maximum* contribution that the group has in a (weakly) responsible group for the state of affairs. To illustrate the intuition behind this notion, consider again the voting scenario in the Sect. 2. If an anti-war campaign wants to invest its limited resources to prevent the bill start a war, we deem that it is reasonable to invest more on R than G, if the resources admit such a choice. Although neither R nor G could prevent the war individually, larger contribution of R in groups with preclusive power, i.e. GR and D, entitles R to be assigned with larger degree of responsibility than G. This intuition will be reflected in the formulation of *structural degree of responsibility*.

Definition 4 (Structural degree of responsibility). *Let $\mathbb{W}_q^{S,M}$ denote the set of all (weakly) q-responsible groups for state of affairs S in multi-agent system M, and $C \subseteq N$ be an arbitrary group. In case $\mathbb{W}_q^{S,M} = \varnothing$, the structural degree of q-responsibility of any C for S in M is undefined; otherwise, the structural degree of q-responsibility of C for S in M denoted $\mathcal{SDR}_q^{S,M}(C)$, is defined as follows:*

$$\mathcal{SDR}_q^{S,M}(C) = \max_{\hat{C} \in \mathbb{W}_q^{S,M}} (\{i \mid i = 1 - \frac{\Theta_q^{S,M}(\hat{C},C)}{|\hat{C}|}\})$$

Intuitively, $\mathcal{SDR}_q^{S,M}(C)$ measures the highest contribution of a group C in a (weakly) q-responsible $\hat{C}$ for S. Hence, structural degree of responsibility is in range of $[0,1]$. In sequel, we write $\mathcal{SDR}_q^S(C)$ and $\mathbb{W}_q^S$ instead of $\mathcal{SDR}_q^{S,M}(C)$ and $\mathbb{W}_q^{S,M}$, respectively.

Proposition 1 (Full structural responsibility). *The structural degree of q-responsibility of group C for S is equal to 1 iff C is either a (weakly) q-responsible group for S or $C \supseteq \hat{C}$ such that $\hat{C}$ is (weakly) q-responsible for S.*

Proof. Follows directly from Definition 4 and definition of (weak) responsibility in [5]. ☐

Example 1. Consider again the voting scenario from Sect. 2 (Fig. 1). In this scenario, we have an initial state q_s in which all voters can use their votes in favour or against the approval of the bill B (no abstention or null vote is allowed). The majority of six votes (or more) in favour of B will be considered as the state of affairs consisting of states q_7, q_5 and q_3. This multi-agent system can be modelled as CGS $M = (N, Q, Act, d, o)$, where $N = \{1, ..., 10\}$, $Q = \{q_s, q_0, ..., q_7\}$, $Act = \{0, 1, wait\}$, $d_i(q_s) = \{0, 1\}$ and $d_i(q) = \{wait\}$ for all $i \in N$ and $q \in Q \backslash \{q_s\}$. Voters are situated in three parties such that $G = \{1, 2\}$, $R = \{3, 4, 5\}$ and $D = \{6, 7, 8, 9, 10\}$. For notation convenience, actions of party members will be written collectively in the action profiles, e.g., we write $(0, 1, 0)$ to denote the action profile $(0, 0, 1, 1, 1, 0, 0, 0, 0, 0)$. The outcome function is as illustrated in Fig. 1 (e.g., $o(q_s, (0, 0, 1)) = q_1$ is illustrated by the arrow from q_s to q_1). Moreover, the simplifying assumption that all party members vote collectively is implemented by $o(q_s, \bar{\alpha}') = q_s$ for all possible action profiles $\bar{\alpha}'$ in which party members act differently. We observe that the set of weakly q_s-responsible groups in this example is $\{GR, D\}$. Using Definition 4, the structural degree of q_s-responsibility of G will be equal to $max(\{2/5, 0/5\}) = 2/5$ and $\mathcal{SDR}_{q_s}^S(R) = 3/5$.

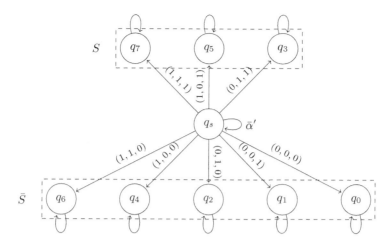

Fig. 1. Voting scenario

A similar calculation leads to the conclusion that the structural degree of q_s-responsibility for all (weakly) q_s-responsible groups, i.e., GR and D, and their super-sets is equal to 1. The structural degree of q_s-responsibility of empty group ($\varnothing$) is equal to 0 as the structural power difference of the empty group with all (weakly) q_s-responsible groups $\hat{C}$ is equal to the cardinality of $\hat{C}$.

A group C might share members with various (weakly) q-responsible groups, therefore the largest structural share of C in (weakly) q-responsible groups for S, will be considered to form the $\mathcal{SDR}_q^S(C)$. We would like to stress that our notions for responsibility degrees are formulated based on the maximum expected power of a group to preclude a state of affairs. While we believe that in legal theory, and with respect to its backward-looking approach, the minimum preclusive power of a group need be taken into account for assessing culpability, our focus as a forward-looking approach will be on maximum expected preclusive power of a group regarding a given state of affairs.

The following lemma introduces a responsibility paradox case in which our presented notion of *structural degree of responsibility* is not applicable as a notion for reasoning about responsibility of groups of agents.

Lemma 1 (Applicability constraint: responsibility paradox). *The empty group is (unique) q-responsible for S iff the structural degree of q-responsibility of all possible groups C for S is equal to 1.*

Proof. "⇒": Based on Proposition 1, if the empty group ($\varnothing$) is q-responsible for S, the structural degree of q-responsibility of the empty group and all its super-groups, i.e., all the possible groups, is equal to 1.

"⇐": According to Proposition 1, and because the empty group is only a super-group of itself, the premise entails that the empty group must be either a weakly q-responsible group for S or the unique q-responsible group for S.

Based on [5], if the empty group is weakly q-responsible for S, then it is the q-responsible group for S. □

The common avoidability of S implies that the occurrence of S is impossible by means of any action profile in q. In other words, given the specification of a CGS model M, a state of affairs S and a source state q in M, no action profile $\bar{\alpha}$ leads to a state $q_s \in S$. Common avoidability of a state of affairs, correlates with the impossibility notion $\neg\Diamond S$ in modal logic [12]. An impossible state of affairs S in q, entitles all the possible groups to be "fully responsible". The impossibility of S neutralizes the space of groups with respect to their structural degree of q-responsibility for S. Therefore, we believe that in cases where the empty group is responsible for a given state of affairs, as S is impossible, full degree of structural responsibility of a group is not an apt measure, does not imply the preclusive power of any group, and hence, not an applicable reasoning notion for one who is willing to invest resources in the groups of agents that have the preclusive power over S. Note that in case the empty set is not responsible for S, its structural degree of responsibility is equal to 0 because its structural power difference with all (weakly) responsible groups $\hat{C}$ is equal to the cardinality of $\hat{C}$.

The next theorem illustrates a case in which a singleton group possesses the preclusive power over a state of affairs. The existence of such a *dictator* agent in a state q, polarizes the space of all possible groups with respect to their structural degree of q-responsibility for the state of affairs.

Theorem 1 (Polarizing dictatorship). *Let $\hat{C}$ be a singleton group, q an arbitrary state and S a possible state of affairs (in sense of Lemma 1). Then, $\hat{C}$ is a (unique) q-responsible group for S iff for any arbitrary group C, $\mathcal{SDR}_q^S(C) \in \{0,1\}$, where $\mathcal{SDR}_q^S(C \in I) = 1$ and $\mathcal{SDR}_q^S(C \in O) = 0$ for $I = \{C|C \supseteq \hat{C}\}$ and $O = \{C|C \not\supseteq \hat{C}\}$.*

Proof. "⇒": Based on Proposition 1, the structural degree of q-responsibility of any group $C \supseteq \hat{C}$ is equal to 1. In other cases, the structural degree of q-responsibility of $C \not\supseteq \hat{C}$ is equal to 0 because C shares no element with $\hat{C}$, which is the singleton (unique) q-responsible group for S.

"⇐": Here we have a partition $W = \{I,O\}$ of all possible groups. As S is not an impossible state of affair in sense of Lemma 1, the empty group is not q-responsible for S but has the structural degree of q-responsibility equal to 0; and therefore a member of O. I as a set of all groups with structural degree of responsibility equal to 1, is a non-empty set either; because there exists at least one group in I which is $\hat{C}$. Hence, $\mathcal{SDR}_q^S(\hat{C} \in I) = 1$ and necessarily there exists at least one non-empty weakly q-responsible group for S, i.e., $\mathbb{W}_q^S \neq \varnothing$. Accordingly, based on Proposition 1, and as $\hat{C}$ is a singleton, $\hat{C} \in \mathbb{W}_q^S$. Moreover, based on Proposition 1, we have that $\mathbb{W}_q^S \subseteq I$. As $\hat{C}$ is a subset of all groups in I, we conclude that $\hat{C} \subseteq \mathbb{W}_q^S$. Thus, $\hat{C}$ is a weakly q-responsible group and is a subset of all possible weakly q-responsible groups for S. Therefore, $\hat{C}$ is the unique singleton q-responsible group or the q-*dictator* for S. □

Example 2 (Operating room scenario). Consider a surgery operation room where a patient is going to be operated. In this surgery operation a surgeon D, a surgeon assistant A and an anesthesiologist N are involved. In this scenario, each agent, i.e., D, A and N, can decide to perform her role in healthcare delivery or to refuse. If the anesthesiologist chooses to refuse or if both the surgeon and the assistant decide to refuse, the patient will die. When all three agents choose to perform their tasks, the patient will recover in the state of *good health*. Finally, an exclusive refusal of the assistant or the surgeon, results in *medium health* or *infirm health*, respectively. This multi-agent scenario can be modelled as a CGS M, as shown in Fig. 2. This CGS is specified as $M = (\{D, A, N\}, \{q_s, q_1, q_2, q_3, q_4\}, \{perform, refuse, wait\}, d, o)$ where $d_i(q_s) = \{perform, refuse\}$ and $d_i(q) = \{wait\}$ for all $i \in \{D, A, N\}$ and $q \in \{q_1, q_2, q_3, q_4\}$. The outcome function o is shown in the Fig. 2, e.g. $o(q_s, (perform, refuse, perform)) = q_2$. The star $\star$ represents any available action, i.e. $\star \in \{perform, refuse\}$. In this example the weakly q_s-responsible groups for death of the patient (at state q_4) are DN and AN. Hence, the structural degree of q_s-responsibility of all possible groups, i.e., D, A, N, DA, DN, AN, and DAN, for q_4, could be measured based on their maximum contribution in DN and AN. Accordingly, the structural degree of q_s-responsibility of groups D, A, N and DA will be $1/2$. All groups of DN, AN and DAN have the structural degree of q_s-responsibility equal to 1 which reflects their preclusive power to avoid the death of P.

As our concept of group responsibility is based on the preclusive power of a group over a given state of affairs, the following monotonicity property shows that increasing the size of a group by adding new elements, does not have a negative effect on the preclusive power. This property, as formulated below, correlates with the monotonicity of power and power indices [13,14].

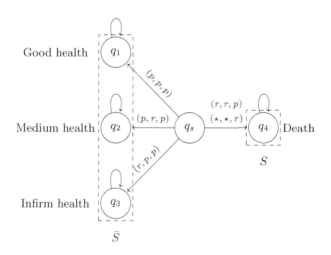

Fig. 2. Operating room scenario

Proposition 2 (Structural monotonicity). *Let C and C' be two arbitrary groups such that $C \subseteq C'$. If $\mathbb{W}_q^{S,M} \neq \varnothing$ then $\mathcal{SDR}_q^S(C) \leq \mathcal{SDR}_q^S(C')$.*

Proof. By definition, the structural degree of q-responsibility of C for S, in case it is not undefined in general, reflects the maximum share of C in all possible weakly q-responsible groups for S. Hence, as the structural degree of q-responsibility has a value in range $[0, 1]$, the elements in $C' \backslash C$ could have no negative effect on this degree. □

Note that the other way does not hold in general; because the structural degree of q-responsibility of the groups C and C', might be formulated based on their maximum contribution in two distinct weakly q-responsible groups. Consider the operating room scenario in Example 2. As presented, $\mathcal{SDR}_{q_s}^S(A) = 1/2 leq \mathcal{SDR}_{q_s}^S(DN) = 1$ but $A \nsubseteq DN$.

The following theorem shows that in case of existence of a unique nonempty q-responsible group for a state of affairs, the structural degree of q-responsibility of any group could be calculated cumulatively based on the degrees of disjoint subsets. In this case, for any two arbitrary groups C_1 and C_2, the summation of their structural degree of q-responsibility will be equal to the degree of the unified group.

Theorem 2 (Conditional cumulativity). *If there exists a nonempty (unique) q-responsible group for S, then for any arbitrary group C and partition $P = \{C_1, ..., C_n\}$ of C, we have $\sum_{i=1}^n \mathcal{SDR}_q^S(C_i) = \mathcal{SDR}_q^S(C)$.*

Proof. Suppose $\hat{C}$ is the q-responsible group for S. Then, as $\hat{C}$ is unique (See [5]), the structural degree of q-responsibility of any group $C_i \in P$, could be reformulated based on its contribution to $\hat{C}$. Thus, $\sum_{i=1}^n \mathcal{SDR}_q^S(C_i)$ is equal to $\sum_{i=1}^n \frac{|\hat{C} \cap C_i|}{|\hat{C}|}$. The whole equation is equal to $\frac{1}{|\hat{C}|} \sum_{i=1}^n |\hat{C} \cap C_i|$. Hence, as P is a partition of C, we have $\frac{|\hat{C} \cap C|}{|\hat{C}|}$ which is equal to $\mathcal{SDR}_q^S(C)$. □

5   Functional Degree of Responsibility

Functional degree of responsibility addresses the dynamics of preclusive power of a specific group with respect to a given state of affairs. We remind the example from Sect. 2 where the president will be in charge, regarding the war decision, only after the approval of the congress. It is our understanding that the existence of a sequence of action profiles that leads to a state where the president becomes responsible for the war decision rationalizes the investment of an anti-war campaign on the president, even before the approval of the congress.

The functional degree of responsibility of a group C in a state q will be calculated based on the notion of *power acquisition sequence* by tracing the number of necessary state transitions from q, in order to reach a state q' in which the group C is (weakly) q'-responsible for S. The length of a shortest power acquisition sequence form q to q', illustrates the *potentiality* of preclusive power of the group C. If two groups have the capacity of reaching a state in which they have the preclusive power over the state of affairs S, we say that the group which has the shorter path has a higher potential preclusive power and thus gets the larger functional degree of responsibility. Accordingly, a group which is already in a responsible state, has full potential to avoid a state of affairs. Hence, it will be assigned with maximum functional degree of responsibility equal to one.

Definition 5 (Functional degree of responsibility). *Let $\mathbb{P}_q^{S,M}(C)$ denote the set of all power acquisition sequences of group $C \subseteq N$ in q for S in M. Let also $\ell = \min\limits_{k \in \mathbb{P}_q^{S,M}(C)} (\{i \mid i = length(k)\})$ be the length of a shortest power acquisition sequence. The functional degree of q-responsibility of C for S in M, denoted by $\mathcal{FDR}_q^{S,M}(C)$, is defined as follows:*

$$\mathcal{FDR}_q^{S,M}(C) = \begin{cases} 0 & \text{if } \mathbb{P}_q^{S,M}(C) = \varnothing \\ \frac{1}{(\ell+1)} & \text{otherwise} \end{cases}$$

The notion of $\mathcal{FDR}_q^{S,M}(C)$ is formulated based on the minimum length of power acquisition sequences, which taken to be 0 if C is a (weakly) q-responsible group for S. In such a case, C has already an action profile to avoid S in q. Hence, the functional degree of q-responsibility of C for S will be equal to 1. If no power acquisition sequence k does exist for C (i.e., $\mathbb{P}_q^{S,M}(C) = \varnothing$), then the minimum length of power acquisition sequences is taken to be ∞ such that the functional degree of q-responsibility of C for S becomes 0. In other cases $\mathcal{FDR}_q^{S,M}(C)$ will be strictly between zero and one. In sequel, we write $\mathcal{FDR}_q^S(C)$ and $\mathbb{P}_q^S(C)$ instead of $\mathcal{FDR}_q^{S,M}(C)$ and $\mathbb{P}_q^{S,M}(C)$, respectively.

Proposition 3 (Full functionality implies full responsibility). *Let $\hat{C}$ be a group, q an arbitrary state and S a given state of affairs. If $\mathcal{FDR}_q^S(\hat{C}) = 1$, then the structural degree of q-responsibility of $\hat{C}$ for S is equal to 1.*

Proof. According to Definition 5, only for (weakly) q-responsible groups C, $\mathcal{FDR}_q^S(C) = 1$. Hence, based on Proposition 1, for the group $\hat{C}$ with functional degree of q-responsibility equal to 1, we have that $\mathcal{SDR}_q^S(\hat{C}) = 1$. □

Note that the other side does not hold in general because $\mathcal{SDR}_q^S(C) = 1$ also includes the cases in which C is a proper super-set of a responsible group. For instance, consider the operating room scenario in Example 2. As presented, $\mathcal{SDR}_{q_s}^S(ADN) = 1$ but as it is not minimal, it is not weakly q_s-responsible for S. Hence, the functional degree of q_s-responsibility of ADN for S is not equal to one. In fact, $\mathcal{FDR}_{q_s}^S(ADN) = 0$ as there is no eventual state q' in which the group ADN is weakly q'-responsible for S.

Example 3 (War powers resolution). Consider again the voting scenario in the congress, as explained in Sect. 2; but now extended with a new *president* agent P. The decision of starting a war W should first be approved by a majority of the congress members (six votes or more in favour of W) after which the president makes the final decision. Hence, P has the preclusive power which is conditioned on the approval of the congress members. Moreover, we have a simplifying assumption that no party member acts independently and thus assume that all members of a party vote either in favor of or against the W. In this scenario, which is illustrated in Fig. 3, we have an initial state q_s in which all the congress members could use their votes in favour or against the approval of W (no abstention or null vote is allowed). In this example, W will be considered as the state of affairs consisting of states q_{11}, q_{12}, and q_{13}. This multi-agent scenario can be modelled by the CGS $M = (N, Q, Act, d, o)$, where $N = \{1, ..., 11\}$ (the first ten agents are the voters in the congress followed by the president), $Q = \{q_s, q_0, ..., q_{13}\}$, $Act = \{0, 1, wait\}$, $d_i(q_s) = \{0, 1\}$ for all $i \in \{1, ..., 10\}$, $d_{11}(q_s) = \{wait\}$, $d_i(q) = \{wait\}$ for all $i \in \{1, ..., 10\}$ and $q \in \{q_0, ..., q_{13}\}$, $d_{11}(r) = \{wait\}$ for $r \in (\{q_0, q_1, q_2, q_4, q_6\} \cup \{q_8, ..., q_{13}\})$, and $d_{11}(t) = \{0, 1\}$ for $t \in \{q_3, q_5, q_7\}$. The outcome function o is illustrated in Fig. 3 where for example $o(q_s, (1, 0, 0, \star)) = q_4$ in which the war W will not take place because of the disapproval of the congress ($\star$ represents any available action). For notation convenience, actions of party members will be written collectively in the action profiles, e.g., we write $(0, 1, 0, \star)$ to denote the action profile $(0, 0, 1, 1, 1, 0, 0, 0, 0, \star)$. Moreover, the simplifying assumption that all party members vote collectively is implemented by $o(q_s, \bar{a}') = q_s$ for all possible action profiles $\bar{a}'$ in which at least one party member acts independently.

The set of all weakly q_s-responsible groups $\mathbb{W}_{q_s}^W$ consists of two groups of GR and D. These two are the minimal groups with the preclusive power over W in q_s. If an anti-war campaign wants to negotiate and invest its limited resources in order to avoid the war W, convincing any of groups in $\mathbb{W}_{q_s}^W$, can avoid the war. However, it is observable that convincing the president is also adequate. Although the president has no preclusive power in q_s over W, there exist some accessible states from q_s (i.e., q_3, q_5, and q_7), in which P is responsible for the state of affairs. This potential capacity of P, will be addressed by means of the introduced notion of *functional degree of responsibility*. Two weakly q_s-responsible groups GR and D, have the functional degree of q_s-responsibility of 1 for W because they already have sufficient power to avoid W in source state q_s. Groups $\varnothing$, G, R, D, GD, RD, and GRD are not (weakly) q_s-responsible for W and no power acquisition sequence exists for these groups. Accordingly, their functional degree of q_s-responsibility for W is 0. Groups PG, PR, PD, PGR, PGD, PRD and $PGRD$, have the potentiality of possessing the preclusive power in other states, i.e., q_3, q_5, and q_7, but none of them will be minimal group with preclusive power over W. Note that minimality is a requirement for being a (weakly) responsible group [5]. Hence, the functional degree of q_s-responsibility for all these groups will be 0. The group which has a chance of becoming a (weakly) responsible group in states other than q_s (i.e., q_3, q_5, and q_7) is P. In fact, the President is the (unique) responsible group for W in states q_3, q_5, and q_7. As the minimum length of power acquisition sequence for P is 1, the functional degree of q_s-responsibility of P for W is $1/2$. Although, P has no

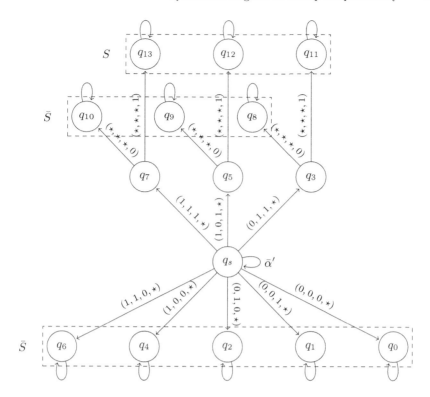

Fig. 3. War powers resolution

independent action profile to avoid W in q_s, there exists a *power acquisition sequence* for P through which P acquires the preclusive power over W.

The next proposition illustrates that through a shortest power acquisition sequence, the potentiality that the group is responsible for the state of affairs, increases strictly. This potential reaches its highest possible value where the group "really" has the preclusive power over the state of affairs as a (weakly) responsible group. Note that there is a one-to-one correspondence between any power acquisition sequence $P = \langle \bar{\alpha}_1, ..., \bar{\alpha}_n \rangle$ in q for a group C for S and the sequence of states $\langle q_1 = q, ..., q_{n+1} \rangle$ due to the deterministic nature of the action profiles $\bar{\alpha}_i$ for $1 \leq i \leq n$, i.e., $o(q_i, \bar{\alpha}_i) = q_{i+1}$ and $q = q_1$ and $q' = q_{n+1}$ and C is (weakly) q'-responsible for S. Hence, in the following, we write $P = \langle q_1, ..., q_{n+1} \rangle$ and interchangeably use it instead of $P = \langle \bar{\alpha}_1, ..., \bar{\alpha}_n \rangle$. Therefore, we simply refer to any state q_i as a state "in" the power acquisition sequence P.

Proposition 4 (Strictly increasing functionality). *Let $P = \langle q_1, ..., q_{n+1} \rangle$ ($n \geq 1$) be a power acquisition sequence in $q = q_1$ for a group C for S. Then, for any tuple of states (q_i, q_{i+1}), $1 \leq i \leq n$, $\mathcal{FDR}^S_{q_i}(C) < \mathcal{FDR}^S_{q_{i+1}}(C)$ iff P is a shortest power acquisition sequence in q for C for S.*

Proof. "⇒": Suppose the claim is false. Then, although the functional degree of responsibility of C for S is strictly increasing from q_1 to q_{n+1} in P, there exists a shorter power acquisition sequence $P' = \langle q'_1, ..., q'_{m+1} \rangle$ ($n > m \geq 0$) in $q = q'_1$ for C for S. Note that as degrees are strictly increasing, for any states q_a and q_b in P ($q_a \neq q_b$) we have that $\mathcal{FDR}^S_{q_a}(C) \neq \mathcal{FDR}^S_{q_b}(C)$. Both P and P' end in a state in which C is (weakly) responsible for S. Thus, for states q_{n+1} and q'_{m+1} we have that $\mathcal{FDR}^S_{q_{n+1} \in P}(C) = \mathcal{FDR}^S_{q'_{m+1} \in P'}(C) = 1$. If we trace back step by step through both sequences, the functional degree of responsibility of C for S is equal in corresponding states in P and P'. For example, for the states q_n and q'_m, we have that $\mathcal{FDR}^S_{q_n}(C) = \mathcal{FDR}^S_{q'_m}(C) = 1/2$ ($m \geq 1$). By continuing the stepwise process of matching all states in P' with corresponding states in P, as number of states in P' is strictly less than P and both sequences start in same state of $q = q_1 = q'_1$, we reach the corresponding states q_{n+1-k} and q'_{m+1-k} for $0 \leq k \leq m$ where $\mathcal{FDR}^S_{q_{n+1-k}}(C) = \mathcal{FDR}^S_{q'_{m+1-k}}(C)$ and $q_{n+1-k} \neq q'_{m+1-k}$ and both states of q_{n+1-k} and q'_{m+1-k} are in P. This contradicts with the assumption that for any states q_a and q_b in P, if $q_a \neq q_b$, we have that $\mathcal{FDR}^S_{q_a}(C) \neq \mathcal{FDR}^S_{q_b}(C)$.

"⇐": Suppose the sequence P is a shortest power acquisition sequence in q for C for S. According to Definitions 3 and 5, the functional degree of q_i-responsibility of C for S must be formulated based on the sequence $P_i = \langle \bar{\alpha}_i, ..., \bar{\alpha}_n \rangle$ as a sub-sequence of P. Accordingly, length of P_i is equal to $\ell_i = n - i + 1$. Hence, in each state q_{i+1}, the length of a shortest power acquisition sequence for C for S, ℓ_{i+1}, will be one unit shorter than ℓ_i. Finally, as $\ell \geq 0$, the functional degree of responsibility of C for S in each state q_{i+1} in P is strictly larger than in the state q_i in P.   □

The following propositions focus on the cases in which a group has partial degrees of functional and structural responsibility in a specific state. In former, we can reason about the degree of responsibility of the group in some states other than the current sate while in the latter, we can reason about the degree of responsibility of some other groups in the current state.

Proposition 5 (Global signalling of partial functional degree). *Let C be a group with functional degree of q-responsibility $1/k$ for S where k is a natural number. Then, it is guaranteed that there exists at least $k - 1$ states $\hat{q}$ such that $\mathcal{FDR}^S_{\hat{q}}(C) > \mathcal{FDR}^S_q(C)$ and at least one state q' such that $\mathcal{FDR}^S_{q'}(C) = \mathcal{SDR}^S_{q'}(C) = 1$.*

Proof. According to Proposition 4, the functional degree of responsibility of C for S is strictly increasing during a shortest power acquisition sequence in q for C for S. This sequence passes $k - 2$ states and reaches a state q'. Hence, the existence of at least $k-1$ states in which C has functional degree of responsibility larger than $1/k$ for S, and one state in which the functional and structural degree of responsibility of C is equal to 1 for S is guaranteed.   □

Note that based on Definition 5, the functional degree of responsibility could always be written in form of $1/k$ ($k \in \mathbb{N}$) unless it is equal to 0.

Proposition 6 (Local signalling of partial structural degree). *Let C be a group with structural degree of q-responsibility of k for S such that $0 < k < 1$. Then, there exists at least a group $\hat{C}$ with structural and functional degree of q-responsibility of 1 for S.*

Proof. Based on Definition 4, k is assigned to C based on its contribution in a (weakly) q-responsible group which has the structural and functional degree of q-responsibility of 1 for S. □

In general, the existence of a group $\hat{C}$ with the structural and the functional degree of q-responsibility of 1, could not guarantee the existence of a group with structural degree of q-responsibility of k such that $0 < k < 1$. As explained in Theorem 1, cases in which we have a singleton q-responsible group for S are counterexamples for such a claim.

6   Related Work

Presented notions for degree of group responsibility follow the responsibility notions in [5] and are in coherence with the concept of preclusive power in [9]. Our notion of *functional degree of responsibility* of an agent group is based on the minimum length of a sequence from a source state towards a state in which the agent group has power over a given state of affairs. This step-wise formulation was put forward by [1] in a quantified degree of responsibility as a backward-looking approach. However, [1] traces the steps in a causal network and studies the degree of causality, whereas we define our notions in strategic settings by means of a similar formulation. The other connection is to the [4] in which the notion of *avoidance potential* is central. There are two main differences between our approach and [4]. First, our notion of preclusion of a state of affairs is a property of a group, whereas in [4] the avoidance potential for a state of affairs is a property of a strategy of an individual agent. Second, the notion of preclusion in our case considers the power of a group while avoidance potential in [4] considers the probability of other agents to choose a strategy such that the strategy of the agent in question has no contribution to the establishment of the state of affairs.

As our degrees of group responsibility are based on quantifying the structural and functional potentials of agent groups in multi-agent systems, we would like to provide a brief comparison between our approach and the two well-known power indices, the Banzhaf index (with its related measure) [15], and the Shpley-Shubik index [16]. A main distinction is that both indices measure the power or contribution of individual agents in possible coalitions, rather than measuring the power of agent groups. The methodological difference between Banzhaf measure and our measure is that we formulate the degree of group responsibility based on the maximum contribution of an agent group to groups with preclusive power (structural degree) or minimum number of transitions that is necessary for a group to gain preclusive power (functional degree). This is different than the Banzhaf measure, where the main parameter is the probability that an agent would be the so called *swing player* with the ability to transform a "looser" group (of agents) to a "winner" group. Moreover, we focus on the ability of groups to preclude a state of affairs and base our notions on the potential of groups to *q-enforce* the complement of state of affairs (See Definition 2). This is different than "winner" groups in both the Banzhaf measure and the Shpley-Shubik index as they are the agent groups with the ability to determine the outcome which may be more related to the ability of agent groups to *q-enforce* a state of affairs (See *q-control* in [5]). Finally, in the Shpley-Shubik index, the order in which agents join a group plays an important role, which we believe is more relevant for the group/coalition formation process [17,18]. We stand before the group formation process, reason about all the possible agent groups, and assign them forward-looking degrees of group responsibility with respect to their potentials to avoid the materialization of a given state of affairs.

7   Conclusion and Future Work

In this paper, we proposed a forward-looking approach to measure the degree of group responsibility. The proposed notions can be used as a tool for analyzing the potential responsibility of agent groups towards a state of affairs. In our approach, full structural and functional degrees of responsibility towards a state of affairs are assigned to agent groups, if they can preclude the state of affairs. All other groups that may contribute to such responsible groups receive a partial structural degree of responsibility. Also, all other groups for which there exists a path to a state in which they possess the preclusive power receive a partial functional degree of responsibility. The structural degree of responsibility captures the responsibility of a group based on accumulated preclusive power of included agents while the functional degree of responsibility captures the responsibility of a group due to the potentiality of reaching a state in which it has the preclusive power.

We plan to apply our presented methodology for analyzing forward-looking responsibility to backward-looking responsibility. We believe that integrating the responsibility notions as proposed in [1,4] with our methodology could lead to a graded notion for backward-looking responsibility in strategic settings. In such extension, one could reason from a realized outcome state and assign a degree of blameworthiness to agent groups in liability determination principles from legal domain such as *contributory negligence*. In this paper we used concurrent game structure in its original form as we had a logical approach to formalize our two notions for degree of group responsibility. In an extended version, we plan to use probabilistic concurrent game structures to make our notions also applicable in probabilistic settings (See [19,20]). Finally, we aim at extending our framework with logical characterizations of the proposed notions based on the coalitional logic with quantification [5,21,22].

References

1. Chockler, H., Halpern, J.Y.: Responsibility and blame: a structural-model approach. J. Artif. Intell. Res. (JAIR) **22**, 93–115 (2004)
2. Grossi, D., Royakkers, L.M.M., Dignum, F.: Organizational structure and responsibility. Artif. Intell. Law **15**(3), 223–249 (2007)
3. Miller, S.: Collective moral responsibility: An individualist account. Midwest Stud. Philos. **30**(1), 176–193 (2006)
4. Braham, M., Van Hees, M.: An anatomy of moral responsibility. Mind **121**(483), 601–634 (2012)
5. Bulling, N., Dastani, M.: Coalitional responsibility in strategic settings. In: Leite, J., Son, T.C., Torroni, P., van der Torre, L., Woltran, S. (eds.) CLIMA XIV 2013. LNCS, vol. 8143, pp. 172–189. Springer, Heidelberg (2013)
6. van de Poel, I.: The relation between forward-looking and backward-looking responsibility. In: Vincent, N.A., van de Poel, I., van den Hoven, J. (eds.) Moral Responsibility. Library of Ethics and Applied Philosophy, vol. 27, pp. 37–52. Springer, Dordrecht (2011)
7. Sulzer, J.L.: Attribution of responsibility as a function of the structure, quality, and intensity of the event. Ph.D. thesis, University of Florida (1965)
8. Shaver, K.: The Attribution of Blame: Causality, Responsibility, and Blameworthiness. Springer, New York (2012)
9. Miller, N.R.: Power in game forms. In: Holler, M.J. (ed.) Power, Voting, and Voting Power, pp. 33–51. Springer, Würzburg (1982)
10. Alur, R., Henzinger, T.A., Kupferman, O.: Alternating-time temporal logic. J. ACM **49**(5), 672–713 (2002)
11. Pauly, M.: Logic for social software. Universiteit van Amsterdam (2001)
12. Kripke, S.A.: Semantical analysis of modal logic i normal modal propositional calculi. Math. Logic Q. **9**(5–6), 67–96 (1963)
13. Turnovec, F.: Monotonicity of power indices. In: Stewart, T., van den Honert, R. (eds.) Trends in Multicriteria Decision Making. Lecture Notes in Economics and Mathematical Systems, vol. 465, pp. 199–214. Springer, Heidelberg (1998)
14. Holler, M.J., Napel, S.: Monotonicity of power and power measures. Theor. Decis. **56**(1–2), 93–111 (2004)
15. Banzhaf III, J.F.: Weighted voting doesn't work: A mathematical analysis. Rutgers L. Rev. **19**, 317 (1964)
16. Shapley, L.S., Shubik, M.: A method for evaluating the distribution of power in a committee system. Am. Polit. Sci. Rev. **48**(03), 787–792 (1954)
17. Rahwan, T., Michalak, T.P., Elkind, E., Faliszewski, P., Sroka, J., Wooldridge, M., Jennings, N.R.: Constrained coalition formation. In: Burgard, W., Roth, D. (eds.) Proceedings of the Twenty-Fifth AAAI Conference on Artificial Intelligence, AAAI 2011, San Francisco, California, USA, 7–11 August 2011. AAAI Press (2011)
18. Griffiths, N., Luck, M.: Coalition formation through motivation and trust. In: Proceedings of the Second International Joint Conference on Autonomous Agents and Multiagent Systems, AAMAS, 14–18 July 2003, Melbourne, Victoria, Australia, pp. 17–24. ACM (2003)
19. Chen, T., Lu, J.: Probabilistic alternating-time temporal logic and model checking algorithm. In: Lei, J. (ed.) Proceedings of the Fourth International Conference on Fuzzy Systems and Knowledge Discovery, FSKD 2007, 24–27 August 2007, Haikou, Hainan, China, vol. 2, pp. 35–39. IEEE Computer Society (2007)

20. Huang, X., Su, K., Zhang, C.: Probabilistic alternating-time temporal logic of incomplete information and synchronous perfect recall. In: Hoffmann, J., Selman, B. (eds.) Proceedings of the Twenty-Sixth AAAI Conference on Artificial Intelligence, 22–26 July 2012, Toronto, Ontario, Canada. AAAI Press (2012)
21. Ågotnes, T., van der Hoek, W., Wooldridge, M.: Quantified coalition logic. Synthese **165**(2), 269–294 (2008)
22. Pauly, M.: A modal logic for coalitional power in games. J. Log. Comput. **12**(1), 149–166 (2002)

Author Index

Printed in the United States
By Bookmasters